ALCOHOL 13% BY VOL.

GOLD SEAL
Pinot Chardonnay
NEW YORK STATE WINE
1964
Produced & Bottled by GOLD SEAL VINEYARDS, INC., Hammondsport, New York

1971
Mirassou
Monterey-San...
White B...
Produced and Bottled by M...
San Jose, Calif.
Alcohol 12%   By Volume

Novitiate
CALIFORNIA
BLACK MUSCAT
Jesuit Wines
PRODUCED AND BOTTLED BY
Novitiate of Los Gatos
LOS GATOS, CALIFORNIA
ALCOHOL 20%
BY VOLUME

ALCOHOL 14% BY VOLUME

BRONTE
SISTER LAKES DISTRICT
PREMIUM MICHIGAN
BACO NOIR
Alcohol 12% By Volume
MADE AND BOTTLED BY
Bronte Champagne & Wine Co., Inc.
AT THE BRONTE VINEYARDS, HARTFORD, MICHIGAN

Mother Vineyard
Southern
SCUPPERNONG
WINE
MADE FROM
NORTH CAROLINA SCUPPERNONG GRAPES
Produced and Bottled by
MOTHER VINEYARD WINE CO.
Petersburg, Vir...

MEIER'S
ISLE St. GEORGE
OHIO STATE
HAUT
SAUTERNES
ALCOHOL 12% BY VOLUME
PRODUCED AND BOTTLED BY
Meier's Wine Cellars Inc.
SILVERTON, OHIO, B.W. 45
OWNERS OF THE WORLD FAMOUS
ISLE ST. GEORGE VINEYARDS IN LAKE ERIE

KOSHER
FOR PASSOVER
MANISCHEWITZ
CONCORD GRAPE
SPECIALLY SWEETENED
ALCOHOL 12.5% BY VOLUME
MADE AND BOTTLED BY
MANISCHEWITZ WINE CO., NEW YORK, N.Y.   B.W. 23
THE TRADITIONAL KOSHER WINE

GUILD · VINO DA
TAVOLA
RED
CALIFORNIA TABLE WINE
MADE AND BOTTLED BY GUILD WINE CO., LODI, CALIF. ALC. 12½% BY VOL.

EXTRA QUALITY
PINOT
Canadian Champagne
Bright's
ESTD 1874
CONTENTS
26 FLUID OZ.

E & J
GALLO
HEARTY BURGUNDY
OF CALIFORNIA
We are often told by knowledgeable people that they are
delighted in having discovered a great wine in Hearty
Burgundy. Its rich, full-bodied flavor—from extremely
fine varietal grapes—will surprise you. Made and bottled
at the Gallo Vineyards in Modesto, Calif. Alc. 14% by vol.

Paul Masson.

California Brut Champagne
PRODUCED AND BOTTLED BY PAUL MASSON VINEYARDS · SARATOGA, CALIFORNIA

Beaulieu
Vineyard
BV
ESTATE BOTTLED
GEORGES DE LATOUR
PRIVATE RESERVE
NAPA VALLEY CABERNET SAUVIGNON
PRODUCED & BOTTLED BY BEAULIEU VINEYARD
AT RUTHERFORD, NAPA COUNTY, CALIFORNIA
ALCOHOL 12% BY VOLUME

Canepa
Select Estate Bottled

Lakes Region
Foch
ROBUST NEW HAMPSHIRE BURGUNDY
NATURAL FERMENTED WINE
Produced by

Old Wine
Cellar
Bonded Winery No. 25
AMANA, IOWA
PIESTENGEL
Rhubarb Wine
Alcoholic Content 16-18% by Volume
Naturally fermented, other than standard wine. Fermented
with excess sugar and water. This wine is carefully produced
...Iowa Only.

FETZER
1970
ESTATE BOTTLED · MENDOCINO
DRY SAUVIGNON BLANC
PRODUCED AND BOTTLED BY
FETZER VINEYARDS
REDWOOD VALLEY CALIFORNIA
ALCOHOL 12% BY VOLUME

Inglenook

PRODUCED AND BOTTLED BY
Boordy Vineyard
CHILLED
SERVE THIS
Boordyblümchen
A Light White Table Wine Recalling
The Muskateller Of Austria And Germany
Alcoholic Contents
12% By Volume   1965   J. & P. Wagner, Props.
Riderwood, Maryland

MAISON FONDEL EN 1880
Hanns Wiederkehr
ARKANSAS
CHAMPAGNE
EXTRA DRY
NATURALLY FERMENTED IN THE BOTTLE

Stone Hill Wine Cellars

OLD MISSOURI
Sweet Catawba
GRAPE WINE

NAPA VALLEY
CHARBONO
1968

W9-BKB-352

The Wines of America

Also by LEON D. ADAMS

The Wine Study Course
The Commonsense Book of Wine
The Commonsense Book of Drinking
Striped Bass Fishing in California and Oregon

LEON D. ADAMS

THE WINES OF AMERICA

SECOND EDITION, REVISED

Illustrated with Photographs and Maps

McGraw-Hill Book Company • 1978
New York   St. Louis   San Francisco   Mexico   Toronto   Düsseldorf

Book design and principal maps by Anita Walker Scott.

Copyright © 1973, 1978 by Leon D. Adams.

All rights reserved.

Printed in the United States of America.

No part of this book may be reproduced, stored in a retrieval system, or transmitted, in any form or by any means, electronic, mechanical, photocopying, recording, or otherwise, without the prior written permission of the publisher.

Library of Congress Cataloging in Publication Data

Adams, Leon David, 1905–
The wines of America.
Includes bibliographical references and index. 1. Wine and wine making—United States. 2. Wine and wine making—Canada. 3. Wine and wine making—Mexico. I. Title.
TP557.A3 1978   663′.22′0973   78–57527 ISBN 0–07–000317–3

Published in association with SAN FRANCISCO BOOK COMPANY.

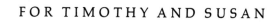

FOR TIMOTHY AND SUSAN

Contents

MAPS

Preface to the Second Edition

THE FAVORABLE RECEPTION this book has received since its publication in 1973 is most gratifying to the author, but it also imposes a responsibility. As the one book that attempts to tell the whole story of winegrowing in America, it should be kept up to date. Hence the second edition, for which I have retraced my travels along the wine trails that crisscross this continent, tasting the current vintages and updating the stories of the people behind the wines.

A great deal is new. The wine revolution, which began in the late 1960s, has spread and grown dramatically since the first edition of *The Wines of America* appeared. More than 200 new wineries have begun production. There now are more than 700 in the nation. New ones have opened in twenty-three states: California, both Carolinas, Hawaii, Idaho, Indiana, Kentucky, Maryland, Michigan, Minnesota, Mississippi, Missouri, New Jersey, New Mexico, New York, Ohio, Oregon, Pennsylvania, Rhode Island, Texas, Virginia, Washington, and Wisconsin. Eleven new wineries are in states that had produced little or no wine in this century. Still more were being planned at press time.

Since the first edition, seventeen states have changed their laws to encourage the establishment of farm wineries, which are essential to the prosperity of vineyards. States where wine sale has been restricted to liquor stores have also begun changing their laws to make table wines available in grocery stores, where they are convenient for the public to buy together with the other ingredients of the evening meal.

The quarter-million acres of fine wine grapes planted during the 1970s have now come into full bearing, supplying wines greatly improved over those described in the first edition, and supplying Americans with wines superior to those available in any other country in the world. New advances in vinicultural research and in wine technology have enabled this country's winegrowers to produce table wines that are always appealingly palatable—the first time anywhere that such reliability has been achieved. This improvement in taste is the chief cause of the continuing meteoric rise in table wine consumption in the United States.

New kinds of wine have appeared, not previously grown in the New World. Botrytized, semi-dry, German-style white table wines are contributing to the unprecedented boom in white wine consumption, which during the past five years has begun to replace the cocktail as the national pre-meal beverage. Other new types include the weeks-old, fresh-tasting *nouveau* or *primeur* reds, which until now came only from the Beaujolais region of France. The white-wine boom is spreading to the chief mealtime wines, the reds.

Annual per-capita consumption of wine from all sources in the United States has almost doubled in eleven years, approaching 1.9 gallons in 1977. This is more than three times the .568-gallon record in 1914, the highest pre-Prohibition year. Even more spectacular has been the growth in table-wine consumption, which has more than trebled, from .448 to 1.45 gallon per capita per year. Literally millions of American families have adopted the light, dry and semi-dry types as part of their meals. Meanwhile, the consumption of dessert wines and of the light, sweet, usually carbonated "pop" wines has declined and seems to be leveling off. I see evidence that the "pop" types that appeal to youth have served as a bridge, that the young soon turn from these sweet wines to the drier, traditional mealtime kinds. *Fortune*, reporting in 1976 on the national trend among consumers switching from strong drinks to wines, noted one result of potent cultural significance: that "the younger of them, in particular, appear to find drunkenness unseemly." Perhaps, by developing among the nation's youth a social intolerance of drunken bahavior, the wine revolution can civilize drinking in America.

Barring catastrophes, table-wine use in the United States should reach five gallons per capita during the 1980s. There are not yet enough vineyards planted in this country to supply the grapes that will then be required. The wine revolution still has only begun.

Since the first edition, hundreds of new classes in wine

appreciation and tasting have opened on college campuses and in cities across the nation. I perceive a trend away from label-drinking wine snobbery toward daily use of the young, appealingly palatable, healthful wines sold in convenient jugs and now also in plastic bags. I call these the *everyday* wines. They are the most important wines in any country. They cost less than milk to produce and are priced to fit within the family budget for everyday meals. Costlier vintages, priced like works of art (which many are), are bought only for special occasions; I call them *Sunday* wines. Importer Peter M. F. Sichel expresses the importance of everyday wines when he says: "Wine belongs on the table, not on a pedestal."

When the wine revolution began a little over a decade ago, many considered it merely a fad because it resembled in many ways the fads of the past that swept across the nation and soon faded away. Today wine is being recognized as an integral, wholesome new part of the national diet. After four centuries during which Americans dined without wine, it is finally here to stay.

LEON D. ADAMS

Sausalito, California
May 1978

Preface to the First Edition

THAT A comprehensive book about American wines is long overdue is obvious from the statistic that nine out of ten bottles of the wines Americans drink are American-grown.

Other writers, who for decades have kept adding to the hundreds of volumes that extol the vintages of Europe, have recently discovered that California wines compare favorably with the Old World kinds and have begun giving them moderate praise. Yet hundreds of other excellent wines produced in California and in the more than a dozen other winegrowing states are still ignored, and the real story of wine in this country has not yet been told.

Meanwhile, a nationwide upsurge in winegrowing is in progress because at long last the civilized custom of dining with wine is spreading across America. An unprecedented boom in grape-planting is opening new vineyard areas and reviving the long-dormant wine industries of states whose wines were famous a century ago, but whose vineyards withered and died before World War I in the path of Prohibition. New champagne cellars are now operating in Michigan, Illinois, and the Ozark grape district of Arkansas, and old wineries have been reopened in Missouri. Vineyards lately planted with unfamiliar grape varieties are yielding wines, as yet unknown outside their localities, in Indiana, Maryland, New Hampshire, Oregon, Pennsylvania, South Carolina, Washington, and other states whose climates long were thought inhospitable to any vines except the native kinds. New fragrances found in grapes are beginning to broaden the taste horizons and expand the wine cellars of a generation thus far acquainted only with traditional wine tastes.

Exploring the wine trails that now crisscross America is a Bacchic voyage of discovery. Wines still unknown to connoisseurs are waiting to be tasted, not only in the showplace wineries of California and New York, which already are visited by hundreds of thousands of tourists each year, but in scores of other hospitable cellars across the continent. Canada and Mexico are important on the borders of the American winescape, and I have included chapters on their wines, which until now have been only sketchily described in English-language publications.

This book is therefore intended for those who would like to know the full range of America's grapes and wines—the new as well as the old, the costly rare vintages and the ones that come in economical jugs—where you can see them produced, the origins of the colorful people who produce them, and the facts behind their romantic stories.

Each of the regions has its own vinous history, rich in human, dramatic quality. In some it is the struggle for survival against local and national dry politics. In others it is a story of victory achieved, after centuries of failure, over vine pests that defeated all past attempts to grow wine grapes. Many fabulous characters, past and present, play leading roles in these dramas. I tell some of their individual stories, because, although the quality of a wine depends first on the grape, it depends no less on the aims and character, than on the talent, of the vintner.

And woven in the strange, stormy history of the wine industry there is another of deeper cultural significance that merits pondering: the evolution of a nation's mores and attitudes toward drinking. In particular, Americans are revising their concept of wine. They once regarded it as merely another intoxicant, one of the trio that connote revelry, "wine, women, and song." Today millions of average families have adopted the light, dry table wines as part of their daily meals, while a younger generation is sampling the new, still lighter kinds that "pop" and compete with beer. Wine use in this country has more than trebled since the Second World War—a change of tremendous social and dietary importance—and yet the trend to wine as an American beverage has just begun.

My forty-plus years of traveling and tasting through America's vineyards have covered most, though not all, of the wineries which both grow grapes and make wines. During the seven years of compiling and writing this book, the meteoric rise in table wine consumption was causing revolutionary changes in the vineyards and wineries. To describe these changes and to include the new vineyards that are springing up across the continent, I have had repeatedly to revise each chapter after it was finished, and only as of press time is the book "complete."

While it might go without saying, I should emphasize that nearly all of the wines I describe were tasted at the wineries, where they had been stored in dark, cool cellars—not at restaurants or after purchase in stores, where too often the light table and sparkling wines are injured by heat, light, and other improper storage conditions. Such partial spoilage seems to occur most often in the Midwest and South, where the perishable nature of these types apparently is not yet understood, and especially in Mexico, where, except at the wineries, I found few table wines that were not at least partially oxidized.

For that matter, you are unlikely ever to taste the identical wine that any writer describes. For wines, unlike most other alcoholic beverages, are constantly changing—not only from vintage to vintage as the weather in the vineyard changes, but also while they age in their bottles. A taster's description of a wine is merely a personal memoir; the next cask, blend, or even the next bottle may be a different product, for this is a characteristic of wine. No writer can promise, when a wine has given him a great taste experience, that another bottle under the same label will deliver the same thrill for you.

Before my wine-snob friends denounce me for tolerating the foxy, Concord-grape-juice taste which they find objectionable in many native wines, let me point out that we are far outnumbered by the millions of Americans and Canadians who prefer that "real grape taste" in their drinks and even in their grape chewing gum. I have been exposed all my life to European and California wines, which are made of Vinifera grapes, and I therefore prefer them. But I do not find the flavor of the Labrusca grapes objectionable, and I rate the Labrusca wines impartially.

Anyone who presumes to pass judgment on the qualities of wines ought to define his standards and his terminology. Most of our leading connoisseurs, if challenged to do so, would have to confess that they pronounce an American wine "fine," "good," or "ordinary" according to how closely it may or may not resemble a counterpart among the most publicized and costliest of French or German wines. They are therefore unable to appreciate the new taste experiences offered by many American wines. Idolizing the wines of Europe as classic, they seldom recognize any wine of this country as "great." Fame, scarcity, and high prices usually explain their choices of the European wines they cite as models of perfection; and with these they stock their cellars, usually to incite the envy of fellow collectors. This kind of snobbery would be harmless if it were not for the annoying habit most such collectors have of referring to the costly rarities as "the good wines," thereby inevitably classing all other wines under the antonym "bad." Equally unfortunate is their custom of calling good wines "ordinary," a more derogatory term in English than in the French *ordinaire,* which means "regular" or "standard."

Since there has never been a truly international wine jury, consisting of both American and European experts, to taste wines solely on their individual merits (and with the labels hidden), I have had to invent one. My imaginary jury consists of the several hundred connoisseurs of my acquaintance, representing all of the different Old and New World tastes. My ratings of individual wines are what I believe would be the impartial verdicts of this jury if it existed.

And, in my lexicon, a wine that is sound and palatable is "good"; a spoiled, partially spoiled, or otherwise unpalatable wine is "bad"; a wine true to its type and markedly superior in taste, nose, and balance to the "good" ones of that type is "fine"; and a "fine" wine which gives the connoisseur of that wine type such pure delight to his senses as to be unforgettable, deserves to be called "great."

These distinctions are important to the purposes of this book. For among its purposes is to help gain recognition and provide encouragement for the new pioneers of winegrowing in many old and new localities throughout America where I have watched vines being planted lately. For I am one of those who believe that wine finally will become the national mealtime beverage when its production is no longer concentrated in only a few states—when winegrowing becomes truly a nationwide industry.

Sausalito, California   Leon D. Adams
January 1973

1

America's Surprising Wines

I N THE quantity of wine it produces annually, the United States ranks sixth among the winegrowing nations.* In the average quality of its wines, it ranks first.

The standard wines of America, available everywhere in thrifty jugs, are superior to any that householders in other lands get to drink with their daily meals. The best American wines, produced by the several dozen vineyards which aim for highest quality and premium prices, have equaled many of the Old World's finest. The latter fact, often demonstrated in "blind" comparative tastings with the classic wines of Europe, is all the more surprising when it is remembered that Europe, with its two thousand years of experience, has thousands of vineyards whose vintages are sought after and treasured by connoisseurs, while the United States has had only these relatively few.

This country has two advantages over the Old World in wine growing. One is in climates more hospitable to grapes—a subject about which a good deal follows, because climate is the key to the fascinating lore of wine. The other advantage is that of having started anew. The American wine industry, reborn when National Prohibition ended in 1933, chose the scientific approach to quality. Rejecting the traditions, cobwebbed cellars, and primitive methods that hinder wine progress in much of Europe, it utilized the new research in viticulture and enology, in which the United States now leads the world—research that has removed most of the guesswork from winemaking.

*Commercial wine production in the U.S. averages 350 million gallons yearly, compared to 1.8 billion gallons in Italy, 1.7 billion in France, 900 million in Spain, 800 million in the U.S.S.R., 600 million in Argentina, 234 million in Portugal, 230 million in Germany, and 200 million in Romania.

Exported now to other countries, where they compete on even terms with the world-famous wines of France and Germany, American wines are still improving. As yet they have only approached the great quality they can achieve in the future. Already they are a serious challenge to Old World wines sold in this country, to such an extent that European vintners have begun imitating American wine names. (Nor is merely equaling European wines as great an achievement as it might seem because, as is well known in the wine trade, the wines under many famous French and German labels have changed greatly, not necessarily for the better, since the Second World War.) But just as artists in other fields give their best performances for appreciative audiences, this country's winegrowers have continued improving their products to the extent that the wine-buying public has shown its willingness to appreciate and pay for them.

There is much to appreciate, not only in the fine wines of California, New York, and Ohio, but also in the vastly improved table wines of Arkansas, Michigan, Oregon, and Washington,

The Cabernet Sauvignon grape variety, the *cépage noble* of Bordeaux in France, also makes the finest red wines produced in California.

The Wine Institute

which as yet are seldom found outside their borders. Connoisseurs in Maryland, Pennsylvania, Indiana, Illinois, Missouri, and Virginia who seek rare and good wines can find them at small vineyards in their own states, and thereby can promote the agricultural economy of their regions. The southern states, the last citadels of the Prohibition movement, can help both their faltering agriculture and the cause of temperance by speeding the revival of their once important winegrowing industry, originally based on the Scuppernong grape. New York and Ohio, whose distinctive wines long have been made of native grapes, merit recognition for their superior new wine types made from exotic grape varieties planted since the 1950s. As for California, that state's premium wineries in recent years could not plant new vineyards fast enough to keep up with the soaring demand for their finest "varietal" table wines. Some of their Chardonnays, Cabernet Sauvignons, and Pinot Noirs are even being rationed, a case or two per month to each of the best stores and restaurants, which reserve single bottles for their favorite patrons.

How little known are some states' wines is evident from the now-famous Department of State wine list, issued in 1966, of American wines which our embassies and consulates were urged to serve "with pride and confidence" to their guests in foreign countries under Former President Lyndon B. Johnson's "drink American" policy. I was one of the six so-called experts whom the Department summoned to Washington to compare our tasting notes and to prepare the list.* From all of our cumulative knowledge, the six of us were able to agree on recommending only eighty-nine wines—seventy from California, sixteen from New York, two from Ohio, and one from Maryland—just four of the thirty states in which wine is now produced commercially. From my notes on the many excellent wines I have tasted since, it would be easy now to quintuple both the number of wines and the number of states the list represents.

America produces good wines of every type made elsewhere on the globe. It also makes many types that are entirely its own. In fact, this country offers the widest spectrum of wine flavors that can be found anywhere in the world. This results principally from its wide variety of climates. It is climate that principally determines which grape varieties can produce the best wine

---

*The others were Dr. Maynard Amerine, Creighton Churchill, Robert J. Misch, and the late Harold Grossman and Tom Marvel.

quality where. The right soil is essential, of course, but good soils for grape growing can be found almost anywhere, while ideal climatic conditions cannot. Each climatic district and each vineyard with its own microclimate will produce, from the same grape variety, a distinctly different wine. The Riesling grown in the warmer parts of the Napa Valley differs appreciably from Riesling grown on the cooler hillsides a few miles to the west, from Riesling grown at Piesport on the Moselle, and from Riesling grown in western Oregon or at Hammondsport, New York. And the Catawba grape makes a different wine when grown on Isle St. George in the middle of Lake Erie from Catawba grown in the Ozark region of Missouri and Arkansas. Differences in the exposure of vines to sunlight even in the same vineyard influence wine flavors, too. (Yes, differences in soil account in part for differences in wines—especially between the wines of single vineyards—but European producers are inconsistent in claiming that soils are the chief reason the wines of their best vineyard districts are unique. Well-drained, warm soils capable of adequately nourishing the vines are essential for quality and yield. It is not true, as they would have us believe, that a special soil component climbs up through the vine, enters into the grape and its juice, and gives the wine a distinctive taste.)

America is one vast Vineland, so named by the Norse explorer Leif Ericson when he landed on Newfoundland *circa* A.D. 1000. Whether the berries he found growing wild there were really grapes as the saga says, or squashberries as some botanists now contend, Ericson was right. For in the expanse of North America between 50° north latitude in Canada and 20° north latitude in Central Mexico are the greatest natural grape-growing areas on earth. More species of the genus Vitis, the grapevine, grow wild here than in all the rest of the world combined. The borders of the United States, which extend from 49° latitude in the State of Washington to 25° latitude in Texas and Florida, encompass vast regions superior, in terms of growing season temperatures, to Germany's Rhineland at 50° latitude and to Champagne and Burgundy at 49° and 47° latitude in France. This country has hundreds of such areas, with enough total acreage to accommodate the Rhineland, Moselle, Champagne, Burgundy, and Bordeaux regions several times over.

In California's equable climate, with its long rainless growing seasons and its mild winters, grapes transplanted from Europe thrive as well as, and often better than, in their Old World homelands. This is why California wines resemble those of Europe; they are made from the same grape varieties—the species called *Vitis vinifera*. These Old World grapes also have long made some of the wines of eastern Washington, western Oregon, and southern New Mexico. But in the East and Midwest, the rigorous winters, false springs, and humid summers make it difficult to grow the delicate Vinifera, and here the hardier native "slip-skin" grapes, which are mostly domesticated hybrids of *Vitis Labrusca*, are mainly grown. This is why most eastern wines have, in varying degrees, the fragrant, grapy or foxy flavor you taste in Concord grape juice, jelly, and jam. Only since the 1950s have Vinifera been grown successfully in the East, yielding wines that lately have amazed connoisseurs. In recent decades the climates of many eastern and midwestern states have been found hospitable to still another group of hardy grape varieties, the French-American hybrids. These are crosses of native American grapes with Vinifera, developed by grape breeders in France. Increasingly planted east of the Rockies now, these hybrids are making wines different in taste from both of their parents, but definitely of European, not Labrusca character. The southeastern states, with their humid climates which are inhospitable to most bunch grapes, are the natural home for still another American grape species, the Muscadines, *Vitis rotundifolia*. The Muscadines are more like cherries than like grapes, and the best-known variety is the Scuppernong. Nor are these the complete assortment, as will be seen in the chapters which describe individual wines and the districts where they are grown.

Actually, grapes grow in all fifty states, and any grape can make wine. Grapes are the most widely grown fruit in America, having passed apples in recent years. This country has almost 800,000 acres of vineyards, about one fortieth of the total in the world. Commercial winegrowing is impractical, however, in areas with growing seasons of less than 120 days between the killing spring and autumn frosts. This rules out only western Montana, Wyoming, much of Colorado, the northern portions of Maine, of Minnesota, of North Dakota, and of Wisconsin, and eastern Nevada, southeastern Oregon, and Alaska. Before 1900, wines were grown successfully in such unlikely-seeming states as Idaho, Indiana, Kansas, Kentucky, Mississippi, Nebraska, Oklahoma, Tennessee, and West Virginia. As evidence, the skeletons of old wineries still can be seen in many of the rural areas which once supported their vineyards. Wineries are springing up in some of these states now. The rest will produce

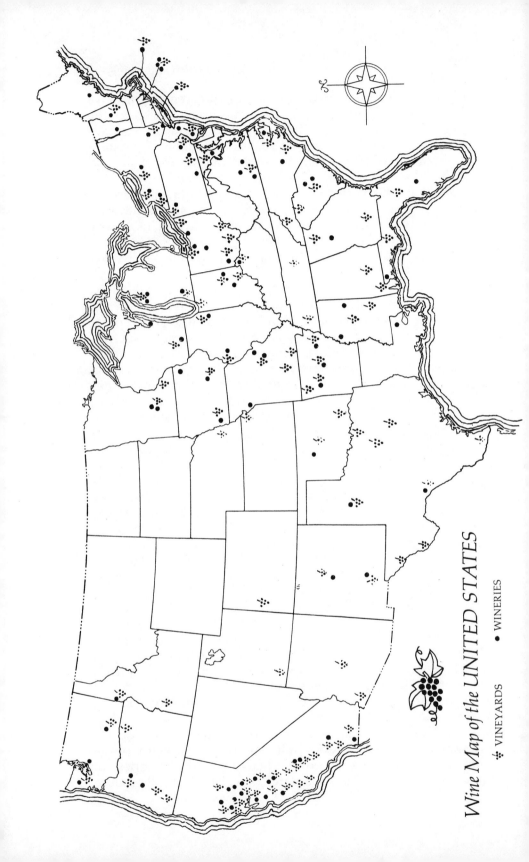

Wine Map of the UNITED STATES

⚜ VINEYARDS   ● WINERIES

wines again, when their legislators, departments of agriculture, and their horticultural scientists awake to the exploding new demand for table wine in this country, to the progress being made elsewhere, and to the fact that now, for the first time in three quarters of a century, Federal research money can be obtained to assist them.

California, with 646,000 acres of vineyards, more than three times the grape acreage of all the other states combined, produces almost four million tons of grapes annually and supplies nearly three fourths of the wine consumed in this country. New York, with 43,000 acres, Washington, with 22,500, Michigan, 17,000, Pennsylvania, 9,000, Ohio, 4,000, and other states with smaller vineyard acreages, produce altogether about a sixth of the wine consumed. The remainder, about one seventh of the total, consists of foreign wines, imported mainly from Italy, France, Spain, Portugal, and Germany. California also supplies some other states' vintners each year with well over a million gallons of neutral bulk wines, wine spirits, and condensed juice (called grape concentrate) for blending with their own production.

The dominance of California prompts some people in other states to question whether wine can be grown profitably anywhere else, since California can produce the common types more cheaply and until recent years has had a chronic grape surplus of a quarter-million tons per year. The best answer is the example of other states' thriving wineries, especially those of New York, a state which has steadily increased its share of the wine market. The eastern states compete by making the kinds of wine California cannot grow. Again it is a matter of climate, for the chief California wine districts do not grow the Labrusca-type grapes which make the highly flavored eastern wines, such as Catawba, Delaware, Niagara, and Concord. These grapes fail to ripen properly in the mild California weather. In fact, the Concord grape juice which my children drank at breakfast in our California home had to come from grapes grown in eastern Washington. Actually, the grape surpluses that long plagued California consisted of leftover raisin and table grapes—not of the fragile, shy-bearing, finest wine-grape varieties of which until now there has been a shortage throughout the world, because they are expensive to grow.

The flavor difference between the principal wines of western and eastern America has seldom been better expressed than in these two conversations: A few years ago, as I was leaving

Dozens of wine storage caves like this one were dug at Nauvoo, Illinois, by the Icarians when they established vineyards there about 1850.

home on an eastern tasting trip, a leading California vintner said to me, "You're wasting your time. Eastern wines have no future. Their grapes have that foxy taste that real wine drinkers can't stand." A month later, when I was tasting Labrusca and Scuppernong wines in a Virginia winery, the proprietor, Mack Sands, explained to me why he was expanding his production in three eastern states. "Those California wines have no future," he said, "because their Vinifera grapes lack flavor. Americans want real grape flavor in wine. Our grapes here in the East are the only ones that have got it."

To most Americans, "grape flavor" *means* that foxy taste. It comes chiefly from an ester, methyl anthranilate, which occurs in Labrusca grapes, and which can also be made synthetically. Completely dry wines made of Labrusca varieties are too harsh for the average palate, but millions of Americans like this flavor in sweet and semisweet wines. Some of the best eastern champagnes and sauternes owe their appeal, I think, to the hint of Labrusca fragrance in their taste, delicately balanced, however, by judicious blending with California wine or with the nonfoxy juice of the French hybrids. These were the kinds of wine the late Captain Paul Garrett had in mind when he tried unsuccessfully in 1934 to convince the California winegrowers that someday blends of Labrusca from the East and Vinifera from the West would help to make this a wine-drinking nation.

Thirty-six years later, the biggest California vintners began doing as Garrett advised, bringing Labrusca juices and concentrate from other states to add flavor to their Cold Duck, kosher-type, and other wines.

The fact that there are plenty of buyers for both California and other states' wines is obvious from the rate at which the consumption of both has grown. Wine use has more than trebled since the Second World War, and is certain to multiply in the coming decades. In recent years wineries of both West and East have not only expanded their vineyards, but have searched for new lands with suitable climates in which to plant premium grapes for the vastly greater markets they foresee in the future. Moreover, population growth in California threatens that state's chief fine-wine districts. Real estate subdivisions and rising taxes on farmland in these favored areas already have crowded many of their oldest vineyards out of existence. As a result, new vineyards have been planted in many localities that had not produced wine for a century, and in others that have never grown wine grapes before.

Yet America still is far from becoming a wine-drinking country. The chief obstacles that still prevent regular wine use from becoming nationwide are outmoded state laws, relics of Prohibition, that hamper the production and sale of wine. In most states, exorbitant license fees and burdensome red-tape requirements prevent farmers from opening small wineries and selling their grapes to the public in the form of wine. And although wine is now sold in all fifty states, more than half make it difficult to buy. Twenty-six states impose taxes or markups on light table wines at rates ranging from fifty cents to $1.50 per gallon. When added to the seventeen-cent Federal tax, these result in pricing light wines as a luxury or as a sinful indulgence, instead of as an article of food. Twenty-three states forbid the sale of table wines in groceries, restricting it to liquor outlets. This necessitates an inconvenient extra stop for the housewife when she goes shopping for food, and, furthermore, many liquor stores are not the kind of places where she is willing to be seen. One of the reasons per capita wine use in California is more than double that of the nation as a whole is that virtually all food stores in California sell wine. (When supermarkets in England began stocking wine during the 1960s, table wine consumption in that country jumped 15 percent in a single year.) At this writing, thirty-two states still have many legally dry localities, counties, cities, or towns, and forty-three of the fifty states still have local or state blue laws forbidding the

sale of any alcoholic beverage on Sundays. These are some of
the reasons why the civilized custom of drinking wine with
meals has not yet spread to such states as Iowa, Kentucky, West
Virginia, Tennessee, Kansas, Arkansas, and Mississippi. Yearly wine consumption in these states still is less than six pints per
inhabitant, as compared to one and three fourths gallons per
year average for the nation. Oklahoma still prohibits its restaurants from serving their patrons so much as a glass of table wine
with a meal. It is remarkable that in spite of the obstacles to
wine-drinking that exist in most of this country, consumption
of this beverage has increased as it has. The obstacles will be
removed only when enough Americans and enough of their
legislators come to realize that wine belongs with food. For
table wine is used principally at mealtimes; it is the only true
mealtime beverage. This cannot be said of water, coffee, tea,
soft drinks, beer, or of milk. Dry table wine, the principal kind
of wine used in the world, and cheaper than milk to produce, is
the only beverage that has few other uses except to accompany
the main course of a meal.

Another impediment to wine use, though a lesser one, is
snobbery, which is defined as drinking the label, not the wine.
The average American householder still seldom serves any
wine and only thinks of doing so for some special occasion,
such as the entertainment of important guests. Although more
or less content in his daily life with his modest home and
moderately-priced automobile, he feels that if he serves a wine
he must impress the guests with his affluence. For this purpose
a reasonably-priced American wine will not do. Instead, he
buys one of the high-priced imports or one of the rarest of
California vintages the wine snobs recommend, and the rest of
the time lives by bread alone.

No matter how fine an average American wine may be, the
American snob dares not praise it highly, for fear of being
thought naive, or even chauvinistic, which to him would be
worse. Credit this to the fantastically successful propaganda
campaign the European vintners have waged throughout the
world for more than a century, to the effect that only their
climates and soils can produce truly fine wines. They have made
it unfashionable in this country to describe any wine as "great"
unless it comes from a French chateau or a German castle.

Most British and American writers of wine books (some of
whom are active in the sale of imports) have long helped to
spread this attitude as gospel. When they occasionally praise a
table wine from Spain, Portugal, or Italy, they are careful first to

deny that it possibly can be equal or superior to the classic wines of France or Germany. For many years they sneered at all American wines, comparing them to French *ordinaires*. Lately, however, their tone has abruptly changed. These writers now compete with one another in cautiously worded praise of California wines, with such statements as that "the New World vintages have come of age." British author Hugh Johnson currently leads the competition, declaring that "the best of California's wines today are among the world's best."

The fact is that of the 1.7 billion gallons of wine France produces annually, less than 5 percent is better than ordinary. By artful publicity the French have succeeded in clothing the rest of their output with the glamour of the rare 5 percent. With American wines the reverse has occurred. About 10 percent of this country's wines are of premium quality, but many of the finest vintages are little known and hard to find. Consequently, the nine tenths of American wines that are only of standard quality and are readily available are what most people think of as typifying American wines.

There are two ways to cope with wine snobbery. One is to compare wines with their labels hidden, a method I highly recommend. A California vintner friend of mine secretly switches the contents of bottles and then enjoys hearing his label-drinker friends praise his own wines over imports. The other way is to send American wines to Europe and challenge the imports on their home grounds. Several American vineyards now export their wines to England, Switzerland, Belgium, and to scores of other countries around the world. But not to France, which annually imports millions of gallons from many other countries, but stubbornly refuses to admit regular commercial shipments from the United States.

Now comes the question most often asked about American wines: how *do* they compare with the wines of Europe? The reply usually given evades the question by pointing out that wines, being farm products, are necessarily individuals, that no two natural wines can ever be identical in taste, and therefore that they should never be compared. This of course is nonsense; part of the fun in wines is in comparing them. What the inquirer wants to know is whether there are any basic differences in flavor or aroma between American wines and imports in general, that he himself can distinguish by taste. The answer is that there is no marked difference between American and European wines of the same types and ages when both are made of the identical grape varieties, grown in similar climates, aged in casks made of the same variety of oak, and when both are given the same treatment and care in the vineyard and winery. Even experienced tasters cannot distinguish between a fine American Chardonnay and a fine French White Burgundy, or between the best Napa Gamay Noir and the best French Beaujolais. This was confirmed by French experts in a "blind" tasting at Paris in 1976, when a California Chardonnay outscored four leading White Burgundies (and a California Cabernet outscored four French *grand cru* clarets).

But note, please, that I have qualified my answer, and note in particular the reference to the same variety of oak. For if only the grape varieties, the vineyard climates, and the care given the grapes and wines are identical, there still is one difference that even a neophyte taster can distinguish. It is the peculiar, complex bouquet of European wines that are aged in small wooden casks—a bouquet heretofore seldom found in barrel-aged American wines. For more than a century, nobody ever guessed why this difference existed. In recent years, its cause has been learned. It results from the different species of oak trees that grow on the European and American continents, the kinds of oak from which wine barrels are made. The complex bouquet comes from the wood, not from the grapes. How this was discovered accidentally, through the stubbornness of an amateur California winegrower in the late 1950s, will be related in Chapter 13. Now that many American vintners have imported European oak casks and have aged some of their wines in them, woody bouquet is no longer an Old World exclusive.

This is not to say that America as yet has any wines closely resembling French sauternes or Italian chiantis, but neither have France and Italy any wines like our Catawba, Sauvignon Blanc, or Cabernet Sauvignon. Each country, because of differences in climate or in the grape varieties it alone grows, still has some wines that are exclusively its own. Nor does America yet offer any vintages to compete with seventy-five-dollar-a-bottle Romanée Conti 1953 or with a Rheingau Trockenbeerenauslese 1934 at one hundred dollars. One of the drawbacks of American fine wines, besides the fact that they are little known, is that they still generally lack the great bouquet from long bottle-aging that connoisseurs exclaim over. Too few years have yet elapsed since Repeal to provide many venerable rarities, and the American system of collecting annual inventory taxes on producers' aging stocks has prevented the wineries from holding back their wines for many years after bottling. The consumer who wants really old American wines must buy them young and age them himself in his cellar. On the other hand, among white wines, which require less age than reds, there are a few California and New York Chardonnays for which true wine lovers are gladly paying higher prices per bottle in preference to well-known imports.

Nomenclature is another reason most American wines compete at a disadvantage with imports in the snob trade. For the bulk of this country's wine is sold as burgundy, sauterne, chablis, rhine wine, champagne, port, and sherry—names which refer to old winegrowing districts in Europe. It is fashionable among Europe-minded connoisseurs to denounce all such wines as "imitations." Behind this charge is the French government, which for many years has been trying to persuade all other wine countries to stop using wine-type names of French origin. Several nations, including Spain and Mexico, have yielded to this pressure officially, though they, too, continue selling many of their wines at home under the French-type names. Spain conducts a campaign abroad similar to that of the French, hoping to acquire a world monopoly on sherry (named by the British, who have trouble pronouncing Latin names, for the Andalusian sherry-producing district around Xéres or Jerez de la Frontera). Germany surrendered to the French on this issue long ago, and calls its sparkling wines *Sekt* (derived from *sec,* the French word for "dry") instead of "champagne," and Italian vintners call their champagnes *spumante.* Russia, however, goes on making vast quantities of its "shampanskoe," "portvein," "madera," and "koniak." The United States regulation defines fourteen* wine-type names of European geographic origin as "semi-generic" and requires them to be prominently qualified on labels with the true place of origin, as "American Burgundy," "California Sherry," "Ohio Champagne," "Napa Valley Chablis," etc. If the United States ever could be persuaded to give up the generic names, France, in particular, would reap overnight a monopoly on the vast markets which American vintners have built in this country for champagne, burgundy, sauterne, and chablis by spending countless millions in advertising and promotion during the past century. These wine names have been anchored in the American language for generations, along with French bread, French rolls, French dressing, French fried potatoes, French toast, Danish pastry, English muffins, Russian rye, Swiss cheese,

---

*The fourteen: burgundy, claret, chablis, champagne, chianti, malaga, madeira, moselle, port, rhine wine, hock, sauterne, sherry, tokay.

Irish stew, English toffee, hamburger steak, Dutch ovens, Dutch doors, Venetian blinds, India ink, and chinaware. The generic names are the only ones the average wine buyer understands. What else, the American vintners ask, could you possibly call champagne?

A puzzling consequence of such labeling is that American vintners, being individuals, have never agreed on just what the semi-generic European names mean. Sauternes are always white and burgundies are always red (unless labeled white), but these wines can range in taste all the way from bone-dry to semisweet, depending upon which American winery makes them. I wonder how the citizens of the small Burgundian town of Chablis, world-famed solely for its dry white wine, must have felt when they first learned in 1965 that Gallo of California had begun labeling one of its two rosé wines as "pink chablis," and more recently when the Italian Swiss Colony introduced a red wine labeled "ruby chablis." Anyone accustomed to drinking California burgundy experiences a shock when he first samples one of the foxy-tasting New York and Ohio burgundies, while the regular buyers of those New York and Ohio burgundies are equally shocked when they taste the California version. (But rather than try to unravel here the mysteries of American wine nomenclature and labeling regulations, I attempt to do so in Chapter 26, where vintage labels, "produced," "made," and "estate-bottled" are also explained.)

As a defense against the criticism of their generic wine-type labels, American vintners are making increased use of grape-variety names for their wines. They find this profitable, because varietal names suggest rarity and quality, intangible elements for which buyers are willing to pay extra. Burgundy brings a higher price when it is labeled Pinot Noir, sauterne when it is sold as Sémillon, and chablis when the label calls it Chardonnay. In consequence, as might be expected, the "varietal wine" list has grown considerably in recent years. It once consisted mainly of Riesling, Cabernet, Zinfandel, and muscatel from California, and Catawba and Scuppernong from the East. But now, there are almost one hundred varietal names on American wines, including three different Rieslings, six different Pinots, and numerous varietally labeled wines of the French-American hybrid grapes with such names as Baco Noir, Seibel 10878, and Seyval Blanc (formerly Seyve-Villard 5276). The result is delicious confusion—partly because the average grape variety can be called by any of several names—and especially in spelling and pronunciation. The latter is why many restaurants find it necessary to print a number opposite each tongue-twisting item on their wine lists.

And now the European vintners have begun imitating the American varietal labels, renaming Bordeaux, Burgundy, and Spanish wines for "varietal grapes"—the Old World's ultimate recognition of American success.

Varietally-named wines are not necessarily better than those with generic labels. Some premium wineries that sell both "varietal" and "generic" wines produce burgundies that are among the best red wine buys on the market. They must, because wines labeled "burgundy" and bearing their premium brands must be markedly better than popular-priced burgundies, many of which are very good.

The quality of varietally-labeled wines depends partly on how much of the expensive "varietal" grape the wine contains. Federal regulations have only required that a wine derive at least 51 percent of its volume from the grape variety named on the label. Consequently some vintners have stretched the quantity with 49 percent of less expensive, ordinary grapes. But at press time, the Government was considering a proposed amendment, supported by most vintners, that would raise the 51 percent minimum to 75 percent. When that change in the regulations becomes effective, the stretching of varietally-named wines will decline and their average quality will improve.

Why aren't American wines named for the vineyard districts, as most European wines are? Picture the quandary in which this would place the vintners in such centers as St. Helena, Saratoga, Healdsburg, Hammondsport, and Cincinnati. For each of them makes several, and in some cases thirty or more, different wine types—including some from grapes grown outside their home districts—in order to sell "a complete line" under their brand names. But place-name labeling presents no problem to European vintners, because they sell wines produced by others. European vintners are primarily shippers (*négociants*); they buy their wines from producers in many districts. They, too, sell "complete lines" of geographically-labeled wines under their companies' brand names, whereas the American vintners produce most or all of their own.

A third kind of American wine nomenclature, that usually combines some generic, varietal, and district meaning, has emerged in recent years and deserves mention. It is the proprietary name, which identifies both the wine and the brand. Current examples include the Beaumont and Beauclair of Beaulieu Vineyard; the Rubion, Baroque, Emerald Dry, and

Rhine Castle of Paul Masson; the Chateau La Salle of The Christian Brothers; and the Lake Country Red, White, and Pink from Taylor of New York. Perhaps such proprietary names, as their numbers grow in years to come, eventually will silence the Europe-minded critics and end the nomenclature wrangle.

In contrast to Europe, with its scores of thousands of small wineries, all of the American wines we are discussing come from fewer than eight hundred bonded wineries. These range in size from the few dozen barrels in Winfield Tucker's and Donald Seibert's tiny South County Vineyard cellar at Slocum, Rhode Island, to the mammoth 93-million-gallon Gallo Winery at Livingston, California, which is by far the world's largest. There were more than a thousand bonded wineries in this country as recently as the 1930s. The number has shrunk because large wineries, with the advantages of mechanization, automation, and efficient mass marketing, have grown larger, while many smaller ones who could not afford these things have gone out of business.

But now we have scores of entirely new winegrowers, who are reversing this trend. Some have opened wineries and acquired vineyards because they see the wine business expanding and becoming profitable for others. The majority, however, are primarily hobbyists—I call them the oenothusiasts—who are motivated less by hope of profits than by love of fine wines. After the Second World War, home winemaking became widely popular as a hobby in the United States, to such an extent that a new industry was created to supply the hobbyists with materials and equipment. Many of these hobbyists began to grow their own grapes, first planting vines in backyards, and in some cases buying additional land and establishing small vineyards. Then, some of the oenothusiasts, finding their grape crops produced more wine than the two hundred gallons per year the United States Government permits a householder to make and process, decided to bond their cellars and sell their wines. The result was that while many medium-sized commercial vintners, no longer able to compete with the giants, were closing their wineries during the postwar years, fully as many nonprofessionals were opening new wineries to pursue their avocation. Fascinated by the romance and greatness of wine, many of these new small growers are now striving to produce the world's finest bottles of wine.

In another industry, such a development might seem unimportant. But as later chapters will show, from Nicholas Longworth, a lawyer, to Philip Wagner, a journalist, avocational vintners have led the way to much of the progress of winegrowing in America. It is the new oenothusiasts who are now pioneering by planting vines and opening little wineries in new districts and in localities that supported wineries a century ago. It is they who are making winegrowing again a nationwide industry.

At hand is a ten-year-old issue of *Fortune* magazine with a lavish spread of pictures of wealthy Americans' great wine cellars—all but one filled entirely with famous-label European wines. As rarities, some of the single bottles named are worth large sums of money. (Philatelists, too, pay fortunes for single postage stamps with which they cannot even mail a letter.) This country now has an increasing number of wines that deserve a place beside Europe's finest. Those collectors who stock great cellars have now begun to explore American vineyards and to choose wines for their worth in drinking delight. Such collections as those pictured in that *Fortune* article are beginning to include many American wines.

2

Four Centuries of History

AMERICAN WINES have entered world competition as youngsters, for most of the present wine industry dates from the repeal of Prohibition in 1933, and most of its best vineyards were not planted until a full generation later. Yet, as Samuel Johnson said, "the present state of things is the consequence of the past," and the wines of today reflect in their flavors many long-forgotten events of the past four centuries.

Single dramatic episodes in American wine history have been portrayed in romantic pageants enacted at local vintage festivals and in several epic novels and motion pictures. But a complete story of winegrowing in this country would require volumes, because it would cover some four hundred years, at least thirty-three states, and a thousand historic vineyards. Its cast of characters would include European despots, American Presidents, senators, and governors, Spanish padres, grape breeders, temperance crusaders, wine-minded journalists, college professors, and a whole procession of eminent vintners, both past and present.

Although winegrowing has influenced the economy and culture of many states, you are unlikely to find wine even mentioned in their histories, because the Prohibitionists erased it. Like the dictators who rewrite nations' histories to blot out other ideologies than their own, the fanatical forces responsible for Prohibition spent years of zealous effort obliterating all of the favorable references to wine they could find in printed texts, failing only to remove them from the Bible.* As a result, few

---

*They did succeed, however, in getting references to "wine" changed to "cakes of raisins" in *The Short Bible* published by Scribner's in 1924.

Americans now associate winegrowing with such historic figures as Lord Delaware, William Penn, Thomas Jefferson, the elder Nicholas Longworth, Padre Junípero Serra, General Vallejo, Captain John Sutter, or Leland Stanford. And scarcely anyone now living in Cincinnati, St. Louis, Pittsburgh, or Los Angeles realizes that these cities were winemaking centers a century ago. Even California, whose oldest industry is winegrowing, has begun only in recent years to designate its most famous old wineries as state historical landmarks because of their growing value as tourist attractions. The official textbook from which school children are taught California's history discusses virtually every product of the state's farms and factories, but never once mentions wine.

Each vineyard region in America has its own romantic story, the highlights of which I include in the later chapters devoted to the wines of the various states. Here I only touch on some of the major developments. Of particular interest are the stormy, tragic happenings during the Prohibition period and the striking changes which since Repeal have revolutionized winegrowing and wine-drinking throughout the nation. And because the events influencing wine in this country have occurred at widely separated places and times and might otherwise seem unconnected, I have also prepared a brief Chronology of Wine in North America, which appears as Chapter 27.

• 2 •

The first American wines were made of wild grapes. Between 1562 and 1564, the first French Huguenots to reach North America made wine of the Scuppernong grapes they found growing near the present site of Jacksonville in Florida. Other early arrivals fermented the native grapes, too: the Jamestown colonists in Virginia in 1609 and the Mayflower Pilgrims at Plymouth to help celebrate the first Thanksgiving in 1623.

Then began more than three centuries of attempts to grow the fragile Old World wine grape, the Vinifera, in the East, all of them failing miserably. In 1619, Lord Delaware brought vines to Virginia from France and also French *vignerons* to tend them and to make the wine. The Virginia colonial assembly passed a law in 1623 requiring that every householder plant ten vines, and from 1651 to 1693 offered the colonists prizes for wine production, with no winners. In 1632, Governor John Winthrop of Massachusetts was granted Governor's Island in Boston Harbor on which to plant wine grapes. In 1643, Queen Christina of Sweden ordered John Printz, the governor of New Sweden, to encourage grape planting, and in 1662 Lord Baltimore tried unsuccessfully to grow them in Maryland. William Penn brought French and Spanish vines to plant near Philadelphia in 1683. Later plantings in Florida, Georgia, South Carolina, Rhode Island, and New York, and those of Jefferson at Monticello after 1773, also failed. The European vines took root and sometimes yielded small quantities of wine, but soon lost their leaves and died. The cold eastern winters were blamed, but what chiefly did the killing were plant diseases and insect pests, to which the wild vines that grow in these areas are immune. Had the colonists possessed the resistant varieties and modern chemical sprays which now enable Vinifera and its relatives to grow in many eastern states, wine in this country would have had a very different history. Indeed, if the early attempts to grow wine grapes had succeeded, America probably never would have come to Prohibition. Without good wine as a moderate daily beverage, the colonists and their descendants drank hard apple cider, then applejack and rum, and finally adopted whiskey as the national drink.

Wild grapes were still the principal source of American wines when in 1769*, six years before the American Revolution, Padre Serra is said to have brought Vinifera cuttings to California from Mexico when he founded Mission San Diego. If he actually planted them on his arrival, the date of the first California vintage could have been 1773. For the next sixty years, the only wine made in California was that fermented by the Franciscan friars at their chain of missions, mostly for the Mass, and for their own use on the table and as medicine.

• 3 •

The beginning of commerical winegrowing in this country dates from before the Revolution, when the first domesticated native wine grape was introduced in the East and came under regular cultivation. It was the red Alexander, later miscalled the Cape grape, a foxy Labrusca seedling (probably an accidental cross with Vinifera). James Alexander, the gardener to Thomas Penn, a son of William Penn, had found it growing near the

---

*But the Mission grape, a Vinifera variety, was grown earlier for winemaking at the Franciscan missions in New Mexico; see Chapter 20. And the date when the grape was introduced to California is still a subject of dispute. Some say it was planted first at Mission San Juan Capistrano in 1779.

Schuylkill River in the vicinity of Philadelphia, and planted it in Penn's garden. The hardy Alexander withstood the cold winters and the vine pests that had killed the delicate European plants. Of the ten Alexander vines that grew in his Virginia garden, President Jefferson wrote prophetically in 1809 that

it will be well to push the culture of this grape without losing time and efforts in the search of foreign vines which it will take centuries to adapt to our soil and climate.

Jefferson's advice was heeded: The first extensive vineyards in Pennsylvania, Ohio, and Indiana were planted with the Alexander in the early 1800s. (To answer the perennial question of "which was first," Pennsylvania can claim this country's earliest commercial venture in winegrowing—at Spring Mill on the Susquehanna River northwest of Philadelphia, where the Pennsylvania Vine Company, formed in 1793, made wine in underground vaults from the Alexander grapes grown in its adjoining vineyard.) During the next half-century, scores of native varieties better than the Alexander were found or bred by nurserymen and grape breeders. The pink Catawba was introduced in 1823 by Major John Adlum of Washington, D.C.; the blue Isabella of South Carolina by William Prince of Flushing, New York, about 1816; the purple Concord in 1854 by Ephraim Wales Bull of Massachusetts, and the green Elvira by Jacob Rommel of Missouri in 1870, to mention only a few.

Planting of the domesticated native grapes spread through much of the East and Midwest, encouraged by the Federal and state governments. By 1840, winegrowing ventures had begun in Alabama, Missouri, Maryland, New York, and North Carolina, in addition to the states already named. Some, especially that of Nicholas Longworth at Cincinnati, prospered greatly. Others, such as those of the Kentucky Vineyard Society in that state, ended in failure. Ohio, the leading wine-producing state of the Union in the 1850s, was surpassed in the 1860s by Missouri. By 1880, when the Department of Agriculture published a special report on the progress of grape culture and wine production in the nation, winegrowing enterprises were also shown to be flourishing in Georgia, Illinois, Iowa, Kansas, Michigan, Mississippi, New Jersey, New Mexico, New York, Tennessee, Virginia, and West Virginia.

• 4 •

In the meantime, California had come into the picture. When the Franciscan missions were secularized in the 1830s, a few

Oldest winery in California is this little adobe building at Mission San Gabriel, founded near Los Angeles in 1771. On its stone floor Indians trod the grapes which Franciscan padres fermented into wine for the Mass and for sale.

commercial vineyards were planted at Los Angeles. After the Gold Rush, of 1849, many of the newcomers turned from digging for precious metal to pressing liquid gold from grapes. News of their profits made from wine quickly spread, and an epidemic of vine fever swept the state. The California legislature, to stimulate the new industry, offered a four-year exemption from taxes for all new vineyards planted. Vines soon dotted hills and valleys through much of the 700-mile-long state.

California was boomed abroad as a new paradise discovered for the vine, a land of sunshine where grapes easily reached full ripeness every year. Experts came from France to investigate. In 1862, they reported in the French viticultural journal *Revue Viticole*, that, indeed, California was one American region "capable of entering competition with the wines of Europe . . . in the distant future."

Better Vinifera grapes than the Mission variety, which Padre Serra had brought from Mexico, were imported early from France and Germany. By 1856, one California vintner was already shipping his wines to England, Germany, Russia, Australia, and China, and the state's wines soon began winning medals for quality at international exhibitions.

But the vine-planting boom in California soon created a surplus. In 1867, grapes were sold there for as little as two dollars a ton and wine for ten cents a gallon. Then, in 1869, the first transcontinental railroad was completed. It opened a quick route for wine shipments to the cities of the East and Midwest. California, already producing more wine than any of the eastern states, invaded their markets across the continent.

• 5 •

The eastern markets in the late 1860s and 1870s were controlled by the Ohio, Missouri, and New York producers, and they bitterly opposed the imports from California. Vincent Carosso, in his scholarly history of *The California Wine Industry*, records that the eastern vintners accused the California shippers of selling their wines under counterfeit French and German labels (which was often true) and of putting California labels on eastern wines. Later, Carosso states, the easterners' tactics changed, and merchants in New York and Boston put California labels on the worst adulterated European and blended wines, while selling the best lots from California as European. Spoiled, doctored, and falsely labeled wines were widely sold.

A national pure wine law was urgently needed, and that intensified the East-West struggle. California wanted such a law to prohibit the addition of sugar in winemaking. This the easterners opposed, because in vineyard regions with short, rainy growing seasons—such as Germany, northern France, and the eastern and midwestern states of this country—grapes often fail to develop enough sugar of their own to make wines with the necessary minimum alcoholic content, and also their juice is excessively tart. Such wines need to have sugar added during fermentation and to have their acidity lowered. But California, with its long, dry, sunny growing season, has more than enough sugar in its grapes and often not enough acidity; and since 1887 the state has prohibited any sweetening of its standard wine types except with fresh or condensed grape juice.

When the easterners protested that a Federal law against sugar in winemaking would put them out of business, a California vintner infuriated them with an invitation "to move their wineries to California's sunny clime, where pure wine can be made from the juice of grapes alone." The battle raged from the 1800s until the limited use of sugar was recognized by an act of Congress in 1894. Meanwhile, some of the eastern wineries had begun their present practice of buying neutral California wines in bulk to blend with their own and to soften their pronounced Labrusca and Scuppernong flavors. The East-West schism over sugar recurred following the repeal of Prohibition, but was healed after the Second World War, when both sides agreed on rules, since applied by the Federal Government, on the use of sugar by the vintners outside California. The leading eastern vintners have always supported legal restrictions to prevent the few unscrupulous operators from using excessive quantities of sugar and water to stretch the number of gallons obtainable from each ton of grapes.

Before 1900, winegrowing was a full-grown, proud American industry. The brands of leading California, New York, Ohio, Missouri, and New Jersey wineries were competing with European vintages on many of the best restaurant wine lists. California wines in barrels were being exported regularly to England, Germany, Canada, Mexico, Central America, Australia, and the Orient, in direct competition with the wines of Europe. (It has been claimed but never substantiated that some went to France and returned to this country under French labels.) From the three dozen medals and four honorable mentions which American wines received at the Paris Exposition of 1900*, it is evident that their quality was excellent by international standards. I have tasted pre-Prohibition American wines that I would describe as great.

• 6 •

But while the industry was reaching maturity during the nineteenth century, the cancer which was to destroy it was already eating away at its vitals. Actually, it took the Drys a hundred years to terrorize and lobby Americans into accepting

---

*The award winners were, from California: C. A. Baldwin, Cupertino; Ben Lomond Wine Co., Santa Cruz; Beringer Brothers, St. Helena; California Wine Association, San Francisco; California Winery, Sacramento; Chaix & Bernard, Oakville; Cuesta Francisco, no address given; Germain Wine Co., Los Angeles; Theodore Gier Co., Oakland; Grierson, Oldham & Co., San Francisco; Gundlach-Bundschu Wine Co., Sonoma; Secondo Guasti, Los Angeles; J. O'B. Gunn, Windsor; Charles Hammond, Upper Lake; Hastings Estate, Angwin; Richard Heney, Jr., Cupertino; Italian Swiss Agricultural Colony, Asti; W. S. Keyes, Liparita Vineyard, Angwin; Pierre Klein, Mountain View; Paul Masson, Saratoga; William Palmtag, Hollister; Repsold Company, Napa; Sierra Madre Vintage Co., Lamanda; Julius Paul Smith, Livermore; Southern California Wine Co., Los Angeles; Leland Stanford's Vineyard, Vina; To Kalon Wine Co., Oakville; H. J. Woolacutt, Los Angeles. From Florida: San Luis Vineyard, Tallahassee. From New Jersey: H. T. Dewey & Sons, Egg Harbor. From New York: Brotherhood Wine Co., Washingtonville; Empire State Wine Co., Penn Yan; Germania Wine Cellars, Hammondsport; Pleasant Valley Wine Co., Rheims; Urbana Wine Co., Urbana. From North Carolina: Garrett & Co., Weldon. From Ohio: Engels & Krudwig Wine Co. and M. Hommel, both of Sandusky. From Virginia: Monticello Wine Co., Charlottesville. From Washington, D.C.: Christian Zander.

National Prohibition in 1920. Although the early temperance advocates aimed only at hard liquor and favored "light wine, beer, and happiness," even the first American dry law, Indiana's 1816 prohibition against Sunday sale, made no exception for wine. As early as the 1830s, thousands of children were signing the pledge to abstain forever from all forms of alcohol, "the subtle poison of the devil." By the 1840s, the wineries' markets began drying up, as scores of towns and counties voted themselves dry in New York, Michigan, Indiana, Georgia, Ohio, New Hampshire, and Iowa. But even while thousands of pulpits thundered that to drink anything alcoholic meant eternal damnation, the wine men could not believe that their business was threatened. For they, too, opposed the drinking of whiskey. Professor George Husmann, the pioneer of scientific winegrowing in Missouri, innocently predicted in 1866 that soon

wine, the most wholesome and purest of all stimulating drinks, will be within the reach of the common laborer and take the place of the noxious and poisonous liquors which are now the curse of so many of our laboring men and have blighted the happiness of so many homes.

Then whole states began going dry—Kansas in 1880, Iowa two years later, followed by Georgia, Oklahoma, Mississippi, North Carolina, Tennessee, West Virginia, and Virginia. Some of these states allowed the making of wine to continue for sale elsewhere, but this did not help their vintners. Barred from selling their wines locally, and unable to compete elsewhere with the wines from California, many of them closed their doors. The ruins of their great stone cellars still can be seen in many parts of the Bible Belt. Most of their vineyards were allowed to die.

The vintners in the "wet" states still could not see their approaching doom, because occasional shortages of wine made their business seem good. What caused the shortages was the phylloxera vine pest, which between 1860 and 1900 destroyed vast portions of the vineyards of Europe and California in the most destructive plant-disease epidemic of all time. And meanwhile the Drys were at work, busily brainwashing the nation against alcohol in any form. They demanded that mention of wine be removed from school and college texts, even including the Greek and Roman classics. At their insistence medicinal wines were dropped from the United States Pharmacopeia. They published books attempting to prove that the wine praised in the Bible was really unfermented grape juice. The Kansas

State Horticultural Society printed the praises of fresh grapes as food, proclaiming that

To the glory of Kansas, 99½ percent of this luscious fruit which grows freely throughout the state, too good to be made a chief source of the degradation of the race, is used without fermentation.

By 1914, when the First World War broke out in Europe, thirty-three American states had gone dry. Then, having instilled in the nation the mass guilt feeling about alcohol that now seems incredible to most people born since the 1930s, the Drys put over Wartime Prohibition in 1919, followed by the Eighteenth Amendment and the Volstead National Prohibition Act in 1920.

• 7 •

What happened next was totally unexpected. At first, the gloomy winegrowers began ripping out their vineyards, but soon they were wishing they hadn't. For the Drys had overlooked, or else failed to understand, an obscure provision of the Volstead Act—Section 29, which dealt with the home production of fruit juices. Originally placed in the law to placate the Virginia apple farmers, Section 29 permitted a householder to make "nonintoxicating cider and fruit juices exclusively for use in his home" to the extent of 200 gallons yearly. In 1920 began the peddling of "juice grapes"* to home winemakers and bootleggers from pushcarts in New York and from trucks in Boston and other cities. Suddenly, grape prices at the vineyards leaped from ten dollars a ton to the unheard-of-figure of one hundred dollars, and this started a feverish new rush of vine-planting across the nation. Soon more "nonintoxicating" wine was being made in America's basements each year than the commercial wineries had ever made before. Prohibition had brought the growers a bonanza.

The California grape growers, grown wealthy overnight, had only one gripe—a shortage of refrigerator cars—which they bitterly blamed on the railroads. Prosperity in the vineyard areas lasted exactly five years. Then, in 1925, the beleaguered railroads obliged by abruptly ending the car shortage. With plenty of refrigerator cars, too much fruit was shipped, and when it rotted at the eastern terminals waiting for buyers who already had enough, the bottom dropped out of the grape

---

*To blot out memory of the Bacchic role of vineyards, the Department of Agriculture changed "wine grapes" in its statistical crop reports to the euphemism "juice grapes."

market. From the collapse in 1925, except during the Second World War, California suffered from a chronic surplus of grapes until 1971.

More than a hundred wineries in California and New Jersey, Ohio, and Missouri survived the dry laws. Throughout Prohibition, they legally made sacramental wines and champagnes for the clergy, medicinal wines for sale by druggists on doctors' prescriptions, medicated wine tonics which required no prescription, salted wines for cooking (salted to make them undrinkable), and grape juice both fresh and condensed as a concentrate. Medicinal wine tonic became a popular tipple, because buyers soon learned its secret; when refrigerated, the horrible-tasting medicaments settled to the bottom of the bottle, leaving a drinkable wine. Of the sacramental wines, the greatest volume was sold through rabbis, because the Jewish faith requires the religious use of wine in the home. Anybody could call himself a rabbi and get a permit to buy wine legally, merely by presenting a list of his congregation. Millions of all faiths and of no faith became members of fake synagogues, some without their knowledge when the lists were copied from telephone directories. (My next-door neighbor in San Francisco

Oldest active winery in the United States is the Brotherhood Corporation, established in 1839 at Washingtonville in the Hudson River Valley of New York. It kept open through Prohibition, producing sacramental wines.

bought port and sherry at four dollars a gallon from a rabbi whose synagogue was a hall bedroom, which he called "Congregation L'Chayim.")

• 8 •

Some of the wineries profited richly from their sales of tonics and sacramental wines, but after the grape market collapse, the vineyardists remained in a desperate state of depression. California vineyard land that had jumped in price from $200 to $2,500 an acre in 1923 sold for $250 an acre in 1926, when some farmers offered their bankers deeds to their land to pay their debts. For a time, the grape industry looked to grape concentrate for salvation. Grape juice in kegs and also packages of pressed grapes called "wine bricks" were being sold to some home winemakers. With each keg or package came a yeast pill to start fermentation and a printed warning not to use it "because if you do, this will turn into wine, which would be illegal."

A "wine brick" (package of pressed grapes) sold during Prohibition to make wine in American homes. With it came a yeast pill to start fermentation.

Brookside Museum

Captain Paul Garrett, of Virginia Dare fame, had a brilliant new idea. Why not sell concentrated grape juice in cans, together with complete winemaking and bottling "service" right in the buyer's home, and thus make wine available to everyone? And still more brilliant, why not let President Herbert Hoover's new farm relief program finance the scheme, since nobody needed relief more than the bankrupt grape industry? In 1929, Garrett led the largest surviving wineries of California into a giant combine with his New York wineries, called Fruit Industries, Inc. Mrs. Mabel Walker Willebrandt, the star of the attorney general's enforcement staff in Washington, D.C., was hired by the combine to avert any clashes with the Prohibition law. Fruit Industries got millions in loans from Hoover's Federal Farm Board to "salvage the grape surplus" by making it into grape concentrate. In 1931, the concentrate, called "Vine-Glo" (in a naming contest among grape growers, this name won over "Merri-Cal"), was advertised for sale throughout the nation. Full-page newspaper ads announced "Home delivery—guaranteed consumer satisfaction—Port, Virginia Dare, Muscatel, Tokay, Sauterne, Riesling, Claret, Burgundy—It's Legal!" Some of the wines expertly made from the Vine-Glo syrup were of surprisingly good quality. But when the Drys got a glimpse of the Vine-Glo ads and learned that "home delivery" meant winemaking service in the home, they were furious. They stormed Washington with protests. Soon the telephone rang at the Fruit Industries office in San Francisco. An official voice from Washington ordered: "Quit! Now, today, as of this minute!" The California Vineyardists Association pleaded for reversal, but to no avail. The Association denounced the Hoover administration for "betraying the grape industry," and Vine-Glo died on the vine.

In 1932, as the dry era neared its close, a bill introduced in Congress brought new hope to the growers. It aimed to legalize light wine and beer without waiting for Repeal. Eleven percent by volume was proposed as the permissible alcoholic content for wine, and 3.2 percent alcohol by weight for beer, on the ground that beverages of these strengths would be "nonintoxicating." Hoping to speed the bill's passage—but without consulting the winegrowers—Senator William Gibbs McAdoo of California proposed a compromise: make 3.2 percent the figure for both wine and beer. To the wine people's disgust, the bill as thus amended was promptly passed. A few vintners actually diluted some wine to 3.2 percent and sold it—a watery, unappealing fluid which they scornfully christened "McAdoo wine."

· 9 ·

The end of Prohibition on December 5, 1933, found the
remnants of the wine industry mostly in ruins after thirteen dry
years. Almost the only fine, aged wines available were held by
the few altar-wine producers for the Catholic clergy, who have
always demanded quality in the wines they use to celebrate the
Mass. Speculators, expecting quick profits, reopened many old
cellars, some with casks moldy from long disuse. Wines hastily
made in October and already half-spoiled flooded the country
during that frenzied December. Their contents still fermenting,
bottles blew up on thousands of store shelves and in windows,
creating an odorous reputation for all products of the grape. In
California, several million gallons of wine were condemned by
the State Department of Public Health as unfit to drink and
were either distilled into alcohol, turned into vinegar, or destroyed. Sound wines, too, spoiled after leaving the wineries,
because restaurateurs and storekeepers, unaware that table and
sparkling wines are perishable, stored the bottles standing up,
allowing the corks to dry out and the wines to become acetic or
oxidized.

Although the Eighteenth Amendment was dead, vast areas of
the nation remained legally dry under state and local Prohibition laws.* Dry-minded state legislatures imposed high taxes
on wine, treating it as merely another form of liquor. In most of
the states, exorbitant license fees and burdensome regulations
prevented farmers from starting wineries to sell their grapes in
the form of wine. Seventeen states established state or municipal monopoly liquor stores, the forbidding kinds of outlets
which discourage housewives from venturing inside to shop for
wine. These stores usually offer only skimpy assortments, and
consumers cannot order wines mailed to them from other
states, because the postal laws still prohibit the shipment of any
alcoholic beverage by parcel post.

· 10 ·

A whole generation of maturing Americans, grown accustomed to bathtub gin and moonshine, were ignorant of wine, a

---

*State prohibition was not repealed by Kansas until 1948; Oklahoma remained dry until
1959, and Mississippi until 1966. Even as recently as 1970, local Prohibition laws in 32
states still barred the sale of wine in 589 of the nation's 3078 counties and in hundreds
more towns and school districts, representing 10 percent of the nation's area and 6
percent of the population.

foreign-seeming beverage which to them tasted sour—as many of the early shipments were. Most of the table wines made shortly after Repeal were poor in quality, and many were undrinkable. Some of their defects could have been corrected, but the main trouble was a lack of grapes suitable to make good dry table wines. Prohibition had left the nation with a vast acreage of vineyards growing the wrong grapes. During the "juice grape" boom of the 1920s, many California growers had grafted over their fine Riesling, Pinot, and Cabernet vines, whose tiny, thin-skinned grapes brought them only $50 a ton, to such coarse, thick-skinned varieties as the Alicante Bouschet, which brought $100 a ton at the vineyards because it shipped and sold well. (The Alicante also had red juice, and bootleggers could make 700 gallons of "dago red" from a single ton by adding sugar and water.) In the eastern states, too, the best native wine-grape varieties had been largely replaced by the hardy Concord, which is good for fresh grape juice but when fermented dry makes harsh, foxy-tasting table wines. The foreign-born, who had continued drinking wine with their meals throughout Prohibition, rejected the new commercial wines, preferring to go on buying grapes and making their own.

And to make matters worse, a flood of awesome books and articles, written by dilettantes strutting their knowledge, warned Americans that rigid rules must be observed in serving wines—only certain types with certain foods, in certain glasses, and at certain specific temperatures. Rather than risk committing social blunders, millions avoided serving wine in their homes at all. Except for sometimes sampling the cheap red wines served with spaghetti in Italian restaurants, and buying occasional bottles of sherry or port, most native-born buyers of alcoholic beverages stuck to beer and hard liquor.

As a result, there was little demand at Repeal for the dry, light (usually 12 percent) table wines, which are the principal wine types of the world because they are used almost entirely with food. One group of wines sold well—the dessert wines—port, sherry, tokay, and muscatel. At that time, these dessert wines were classed legally as "fortified" because they were strengthened with brandy to 20 percent alcoholic content. Because the federal tax on wine is only a fraction of the tax on liquor, "fortified wine" was the cheapest intoxicant available, and much of it was drunk by the derelicts called "winos" on the skid rows of the nation. This situation created grave trouble for the wineries, as will be seen presently. Before Prohibition, table wines had outsold dessert wines in the United States by as much as three to one. But in 1935, the California wineries were shipping three gallons of dessert wines to one of table wines, and the wineries of Arkansas, Michigan, and Washington made the dessert or "fortified" types almost exclusively.

Such were the appalling legacies that Prohibition left in its wake. The once-proud American wine industry, which before 1900 had exported its wines around the world and won prizes at international competitions, was reborn in ruins. It was making the wrong kinds of wine from the wrong kinds of grapes for the wrong kind of consumers in a whiskey-drinking nation with guilt feelings about imbibing in general and a confused attitude toward wine in particular. Some of the vintners doubted that winegrowing would ever recover as a respected, economically sound industry. When a ruinous glut of the grape and wine markets developed after the 1935 vintage, many a grape grower, mourning the bonanza of the early "juice grape" shipping days, openly regretted the repeal of the dry law.

• 11 •

Would the Government, which had destroyed the industry, help to restore it? Some members of President Franklin D. Roosevelt's administration thought it should. There was ample precedent for Federal assistance; the Department of Agriculture had encouraged winegrowing for more than a century, operating experimental vineyards and breeding wine grapes until Prohibition intervened. As late as 1880, the only Federal census statistics of state-by-state grape production were given in gallons of wine made, because the chief purpose of planting vineyards was to grow wine. This was always the case in other countries; nine tenths of the world's grapes are grown for wine. Shipping of fresh grapes as a dessert fruit was unimportant until refrigerated freight cars were adapted for fruit shipments about 1887, and the raisin industry remained small until the 1890s.

Promptly at Repeal, Eleanor Roosevelt began serving American wines in the White House, restoring the custom that had prevailed until "Lemonade Lucy," the wife of President Rutherford B. Hayes, stopped in 1877.

Dr. Rexford Guy Tugwell, a member of Roosevelt's famed "Brain Trust," made elaborate plans to restore winegrowing as a nationwide industry. Tugwell, who then was the assistant secretary of agriculture, even favored exempting wine and beer from taxation in order to hold down the consumption of hard liquor. In 1933 he sent the Agriculture Department's Dr.

Charles A. Magoon to Europe to collect the newest wine yeast cultures. At Tugwell's direction, two complete model wineries were built, one at the Government's giant agricultural research center in Beltsville, Maryland, and the other at the Meridian, Mississippi, research station which served the southeastern states. Both wineries were fully equipped with crushers, presses, underground vats, and there was a brandy still at Beltsville.

But neither model winery ever crushed a grape. Congressman Clarence Cannon of Missouri, the perennial chairman of the House Appropriations Committee, was a lifelong Prohibitionist, and when word reached him of what Tugwell was doing, the project was doomed. "No Federal money shall go to any fermentation industry!" Cannon thundered, and he threatened to block the entire Department of Agriculture appropriation unless the wine work was suppressed forthwith. Cannon prevailed. The model wineries were stripped of their equipment, which was sold as government surplus.* During the next thirty years, "wine" was a word the Department's scientists feared to utter, and they would look around furtively before even mentioning "juice." It therefore deserves mention that when Representative Cannon died in May 1964, two Federal wine-quality research projects were promptly approved in Washington, D.C., and the work quickly got under way in the Agriculture Department's regional research laboratory at Albany, California, and at the Geneva Experiment Station in New York State.

• 12 •

A shortage of trained winemakers plagued the wineries at Repeal. Old-timers with better jobs elsewhere were reluctant to return to the cellars. Partially spoiled wines were doctored by chemists, who only made them worse. But back in 1880, by an act of the Legislature, the University of California had established a special department to conduct wine research and to teach winemaking at its Berkeley campus. And fortunately, this fifty-three-year-old wine school was still intact. It had continued through Prohibition under the innocent title of "the fruit products laboratory," concocting nonalcoholic grape drinks and

*The Beltsville winery now houses a seed and nut laboratory and is called the West Building. How it came to be built is a legend still told and retold there. The winery at Meridian stood empty, its original purpose a whispered secret, until the station there was closed in 1965. On a visit several years ago to the Hallcrest Vineyard near Felton, California, I watched a shiny little crusher-stemmer receiving Cabernet Sauvignon grapes and learned that it came from the Government's model winery at Beltsville, the winery that never crushed a grape.

grape jellies and teaching students the scientific processing of other fruits. Professors Frederic T. Bioletti and William Vere Cruess quickly switched their courses back to winemaking, and soon were graduating classes of enologists to man the wineries. The University launched new programs of wine research and grape breeding, took over the Federal Government's neglected vineyard in Napa County, established an experimental winery and brandy distillery at its Davis campus, and developed intensive new instruction in vineyard and winery operation.

Except in New York, where Professors Ulysses Prentiss Hedrick and his colleagues resumed their wine-grape-breeding work at the Geneva Station in 1934, the other grape states did little or nothing at Repeal to help their winegrowers or to improve their vineyards.

In Maryland, however, an amateur winemaker and newspaperman named Philip Wagner began about 1935 to plant a different kind of wine grape which was destined to change the taste of many American wines during the next few decades. Until then, virtually all of the wine grown outside of California had been made of native American grape varieties with their distinctive, usually foxy flavors. Wagner imported and planted the French hybrids, the nonfoxy crosses of Vinifera with indigenous American grapes, and proved that with the hardiness inherited from their native parents, they could thrive where the delicate Old World grapes had failed. These new grape varieties spread during the 1940s to vineyards in New York and Ohio; and by the 1970s, wines without the slightest trace of foxiness were being made from the hybrids in no less than twenty states. Wagner, the amateur, had spread the hybrids almost as far as the legendary Johnny Appleseed once spread the apple tree.

• 13 •

About this time, another journalist, wine writer Frank Musselman Schoonmaker, started still another trend that has influenced viniana profoundly in this country. Having entered the importing business in New York City following Repeal, Schoonmaker in 1939 added to his import line an assortment of the best California, Ohio, and New York State wines he could find, having them bottled by the wineries as Schoonmaker Selections. As an importer, he refused to call his American wines sauterne, rhine wine, chablis, or burgundy, the European type names they generally had borne before Prohibition. Instead Schoonmaker gave them varietal labels, naming each wine for the grape variety from which it was principally made. Varietal labels were not new, because wines called Cabernet, Riesling, Zinfandel, Catawba, Delaware, and Scuppernong had been on the market before the turn of the century. But Schoonmaker introduced additional grape names the wine-buying public had never heard of: Chardonnay, Pinot Blanc, Grey Riesling, Sémillon, Gamay, Pinot Noir, Grenache Rosé, Niagara, Elvira, Moore's Diamond. His wine selections were excellent; their strange names suggested rare quality and provided topics for conversation. These were extra values for which connoisseurs, until then the buyers of imports almost exclusively, were ready to pay. When other vintners saw Schoonmaker's American "varietals" begin to sell at premium prices in the best stores and restaurants, they lost little time in following suit. Varietal labels soon became the mark of the costliest American wines. Then, of course, more grape names began appearing on labels, and the "varietal" wine list grew during the next two decades to include Barbera, Chenin Blanc, Folle Blanche, Gewürztraminer, Green Hungarian, Petite Sirah, Pinot Saint George, Sylvaner, and dozens more.

An ironic twist developed when European vintners, recognizing a good thing, began in the 1960s to imitate the new American labels. Until then, only a few European wines—the Alsatian, some Italian, and the muscatels—had used any varietal names. But now, for the first time, there began appearing, on American store shelves, wines from France and Spain newly christened "Pinot Noir," "Chardonnay," and "Cabernet Sauvignon," mostly at low prices and of doubtful authenticity in most cases.

Amidst the chaos at Prohibition's end, a group of old-line California winegrowers organized the Wine Institute and set out to rehabilitate their industry. In 1934, they obtained reissuance of the state's minimum wine quality standards. They worked with the eastern producers toward national standards, which were issued by the Federal Government two years later.

The Wine Institute's founders believed that by producing sound, inexpensive table wine and by educating the public to drink it daily with food, they could wean America from whiskey and gin and make this a wine-drinking country. Their models were France and Italy, whose yearly wine consumption approximates thirty gallons per capita and consists almost entirely of table wine. This had always been the goal of such historic figures as Jefferson, Longworth, and Husmann, and of

California's winegrowing senators, Leland Stanford and George Hearst.

In 1938, the Wine Institute persuaded the state's wineries to tax themselves for a nationwide educational campaign to spread the gospel of wine as the beverage of temperate, civilized dining. To administer the program, they created the Wine Advisory Board under supervision of the State Department of Agriculture. Advertisements, articles, booklets, and leaflets by the millions urged Americans to glamorize their dinners with wine and to use it in cooking.

Wine use grew. Consumption of commercial wine in the United States rose from 33 million gallons in 1934 to almost 90 million in 1940, nearly all of it American-grown. The 1940 volume amounted to eight tenths of a gallon per capita, compared to a mere half gallon in the highest pre-Prohibition year. But while the advertisements preached the use of light table wine with food, more than two thirds of the total consumed—almost all of the increase—was of the port-sherry-muscatel group, the 20 percent dessert or "fortified" wines. Table wine, on which the industry's future depended, was still its stepchild. Many of the growers became convinced that the Advisory Board's efforts to promote table wine were a waste of their money, that Americans could never be taught to drink wine with meals. If this country would ever consume as much table wine as dessert wine, they said, it would represent the millennium.

The misuse of dessert wine by the "winos" endangered the legal and social status of wine following Repeal. What made it worse was the word "fortified," invented by the British to describe sweet wines preserved by the 200-year-old process of adding brandy to arrest fermentation. Unfortunately, the American wine regulations in 1936 had copied those of England, and included this frightening nine-letter word as the legal designation for dessert wines. As a result, "fortified wine" began to be blamed for the miseries of the depraved alcoholics who drank it because it was cheap. Many people, to avoid associating themselves with "winos," even banned the 20 percent wines from their homes. Soon laws to tax "fortified wine" out of existence or to prohibit its sale entirely were proposed in several state legislatures. The legislators had no objection to port, sherry, tokay, or muscatel, overlooking the fact that they contained brandy, but they imagined that any wine called "fortified" must pack some mysterious power. In 1938, the vintners decided to get rid of the word, and they

persuaded the Government to ban it from all labels and advertisements. But the thought of dessert wine as "fortified" stuck
in the public mind. In 1951, Treasury officials recommended to
the House Ways and Means Committee that the Federal tax
rates on wines be tripled on the ground that such wine was
competing unfairly with high-taxed whiskey. A bill containing
the new rates was promptly voted by the Committee. It was a
body blow to the wine industry. At stake were the keys to its
very existence: the historic tax advantage of wine over liquor
and beer; the classification of wine as an article of food, and the
treatment of winegrowing as an agricultural pursuit separate
from the distilling and brewing industries. Alarm spread
through the vineyard areas, and growers from all the grape
states besieged Washington with protests. Amendments to the
tax bill in the Senate Finance Committee provided for smaller
increases, resulting in the present rates of 17 cents per gallon on
table wines and 67 cents on dessert wines. But to get the last
mention of "fortified" erased from Federal regulations required
an act of Congress, the wine law of 1954.

· 14 ·

The gains in wine consumption were interrupted during the
Second World War, because almost three fourths of the raisin
grapes previously used by the California wineries were diverted
for use as food, and wine was in short supply. Also during the
war, the whiskey distillers invaded the wine industry. What
caused the invasion was the Government's order converting
liquor distilleries to the production of alcohol for war uses (an
order which included the wineries' brandy stills). The distillers'
only purpose in buying wineries was to provide their sales
forces with something besides scarce liquor to sell during the
war. But wine benefited from the distiller invasion, because the
liquor firms supplied sorely needed capital for winery improvements, and they taught this country's winegrowers valuable
lessons about packaging their products attractively. Only a
dozen of the many hundreds of wine companies were actually
acquired by the big whiskey firms; and when the war ended,
most of the wineries were sold back to the growers.

At the conflict's end, wineries were rebuilt and re-equipped,
and the planting of better grapes was accelerated. The number
of wineries shrank, however, as many small growers gave up or
were absorbed by the large firms. Of some 1,300 bonded
wineries operating in 16 states in 1936, only 271 were left—but
in 20 states—by 1960.

Frank Schoonmaker, the wine writer and importer who popularized the naming of American wines for the grape varieties from which they are made.

In 1946, the University of California released the first new varieties created in its grape-breeding program at Davis. Two of these, Ruby Cabernet and Emerald Riesling, made such good table wines that their planting since has spread throughout California and to several other countries. Meanwhile, too, Philip Wagner's French hybrid grapes had begun appearing in the New York and Ohio vineyards.

Winemaking, regarded for centuries as an art rather than a science, then began to benefit from modern research. Knowledge of the chemistry of grapes and wine advanced more in the decades following the Second World War than in the preceding two thousand years. The American vintners, in the process of rebuilding, with a new breed of technically trained winemakers, took advantage of the new knowledge, while most producers in the Old World were satisfied to continue making wine by rule of thumb as in the past. During the 1950s, the University of California at Davis became the world's leading center of viticultural and enological research. Winegrowers in other countries started sending their sons to Davis to be trained, and their governments invited experts of the Davis faculty to come and advise them on ways to improve their wines. The American Society of Enologists was founded in California in 1950. With its annual technical conferences and its quarterly *American Journal of Enology and Viticulture*, the Society attracted an international membership and became the leading organization of the winemaking profession in the world.

• 15 •

The quality of American wines improved after the war. Some of the wineries had replaced the coarse shipping-grape varieties in their vineyards with superior wine grapes. By 1956, the twenty-third year after Repeal, the California producers of premium wines felt they were ready to challenge the wines of Europe. They set up comparative tastings in cities across the country, pitting the best California vintages against their most famous Old World rivals. Bottles from France, Germany, Italy, Spain, Portugal, and California were bought at random from store shelves, the prices of the imports averaging double those of their native counterparts. Dealers and consumers were invited to come and taste the wines "blind," i.e., from numbered glasses; the bottle labels were hidden. Nearly 1,500 tasters came to sixty-eight such tastings in three years. They sampled the wines and wrote their preferences on secret ballots. When the votes were counted, the results astonished even the Californians: California outscored Europe on champagnes, red table wines, and sherries, while the European white table wines, rosés, and ports were preferred over California's; and in the total point scores, California came out slightly ahead.

Only California wines could be thus compared directly with those from Europe, because both are made of the same Vinifera grape varieties. Eastern wines, being made of the foxy native grapes and as yet to a limited extent from French hybrids, could not. But California's monopoly of fine Vinifera wines was about to end. For while the "blind" tastings were going on, a new chapter in American wine history was opening near the town of Hammondsport in the Finger Lakes district of New York State. There, after three centuries during which repeated attempts to grow Vinifera grapes in the East had failed miserably, a Russian-born German emigré named Dr. Konstantin Frank had planted a vineyard of such Old World grapes as Riesling and Chardonnay, and his vines were thriving in the New York climate. In 1957, their first crop was made into wine, and with each successive vintage these vines have confounded the viticultural experts who had predicted they soon must die in the frigid winters.

• 16 •

By the mid-1950s, average yearly wine use in the United States had risen to 145 million gallons, and per capita consumption was approaching nine tenths of a gallon. Of this total, California supplied 119 million gallons, 22 other states produced about 19 million, and 7 million were imports from Europe. New kinds of wine were beginning to court the beer-and-cola palates of Americans: the sweet, Concord-flavored kosher type; the soft red "vinos," successors to the old, astringent "dago red"; new semi-sweet versions of rosé; white and red table wines with slight carbonation; and the flood of 20 percent "special natural" flavored wines with such coined names as Thunderbird and Silver Satin. But two thirds of the total still was high-alcohol dessert wine, the same proportion as before the war.

Despite the crazy quilt of different state laws, wine distribution improved. The leading California and New York premium producers began teaching restaurant, hotel, and club staffs, wherever the laws permitted, how to store table wines properly and how to sell them with meals. People who had never bought wine before sampled it in these establishments and began serving it to guests in their homes. But of all the developments during this decade, none did more to advance the use of wine in America than the vast improvement of the mass-produced, inexpensive California table wines, made possible by the enormous recent advances in grape-growing and winemaking technology. In the past most of these low-priced wines had been shipped across the country in tank cars to more than a thousand local bottlers, who sold them, not always in sound condition, under a multitude of local brands. But now, the largest California mass producers switched to bottling their own wines, and launched multimillion-dollar advertising campaigns on television to make their brands known. This, for the first time, brought reliably palatable, branded table wines in convenient jugs within the reach of millions of households at prices low enough for everyday use. By 1960, fewer than 200 local bottlers remained in business. These were mostly old-time vintners who had maintained the quality of the wines sold under their names.

• 17 •

The war had brought changes in popular tastes for food and drink. Millions of young Americans of both sexes, after military sojourns in the wine countries overseas, came home with a liking for continental cuisine and its liquid accompaniment, table wine. Postwar touring, spurred by bargain air fares, lured still more Americans to Europe, and they, too, returned with a new appreciation of wine. At home, people with new affluence and leisure took up gourmet cookery, and publishers noted the steady sales growth of books on wines and international cuisine. Wine tastings became popular as a new kind of social event in homes and at club and charity functions. Millions discovered wine as a symbol of status and culture. When college extension courses in wine appreciation were first offered for a fee, the classes were quickly oversubscribed by people thirsty for vinous knowledge.

Attitudes toward drinking were changing. As population shifted from rural areas to the cities, the old Bible Belt view of all imbibing as sinful began to fade. Dry counties in the "local option" states voted wet in increasing numbers, sending the WCTU forces down to ignominious defeat, and new movements were organized to repeal the remaining "blue laws" against the sale of liquor on Sundays. Women's magazines for half a century had refused to print advertisements for alcoholic beverages, but now solicited ads for wine and beer. Housewives, who had always left liquor purchasing to their husbands as an exclusive prerogative of males, began buying the wine to serve with the family dinner.

• 18 •

What the grape growers a generation earlier had called "the millennium"—when the nation would drink as much table wine as dessert wine—came in 1968. Table wine, the industry's stepchild, had doubled in consumption volume, and champagnes, which are table wines with bubbles, had more than trebled in only ten years. Millions of Americans were adding dry table wines to their daily meals, while dessert wine consumption remained virtually unchanged. A few of the states with government-monopoly liquor stores began amending their laws to let table wines be sold in grocery stores. By 1972, total U.S. wine consumption had soared to nearly 340 million gallons, over a gallon and a half per capita, three times the rate before Prohibition, and these figures appeared certain to double again in ten more years. There were forecasts that wine might reach three, five, even ten gallons per capita, that the country eventually could consume a billion gallons per year.

These developments set off the wine revolution with reverberations across the continent and to wine countries around the world. Abruptly the whole national pattern of grape growing was reversed. To supply the better grapes required to make table wines, new vineyards were needed; California's surplus raisin and table grapes and the East's leftover Concords would no longer do. Several state legislatures, despite Prohibitionist opposition, voted appropriations for wine-grape research. A wave of vine-planting unparalleled in world history spread across the United States. Entirely new winegrowing districts were discovered and were planted with thousands of acres in California and in the Yakima Valley of Washington. Winegrowing returned to the Sacramento Valley and to the old Sierra foothill gold-mining regions; to Pennsylvania, Indiana, and to the area around Hermann in Missouri; to the Willamette Valley of Oregon, and to the Ohio River Valley near Cincinnati, where Nicholas Longworth had made a famous Sparkling Catawba more than a century ago. The planting of Scuppernong grapes for wine was revived in the Carolinas and Georgia. New York and Michigan expanded their acreage of Labrusca-type grapes and of Philip Wagner's French hybrids. New plantings of Dr. Frank's unexpectedly successful Vinifera appeared in Maryland, Ohio, and several other eastern states. The vintners of Arkansas switched their attention from dessert wines to table wines and champagnes. New wineries opened for business in Oregon, Washington, Maryland, Missouri, Michigan, Indiana, Idaho, New York, and for the first time in memory, in New Hampshire, Massachusetts, Oklahoma, Texas, Kentucky, and Rhode Island.

Entirely new kinds of American wine made their appearance: the low-alcohol, flavored "pop" types, *nouveau* reds and German-style semi-dry whites. Light wines made of apples, pears, and strawberries became competitors of beer for the favor of American youth. Ultramodern wineries were built, with research laboratories, mechanical grape harvesters, field-crushers, temperature-controlled stainless steel tanks, new European oak casks, micropore filters, and computerized processing equipment to turn out increasing volumes of the best standardized wines in the world.

Wine suddenly became Big Business in America. Giant corporations in other fields, led by the returning whiskey distillers, snapped up control of famous old family wineries. Food-processing, brewing, tobacco, and oil companies, some of them multinational conglomerates, invested millions in the booming United States table wine industry. French and Swiss wine interests planted vineyards and built wineries in California. In 1977, the giant Coca-Cola Company of Atlanta invested in the wine industry, buying the Taylor and Great Western wineries in New York State as its first step, then acquiring two California wineries, Sterling in the Napa Valley, and the Monterey Vineyard.

Connoisseurs who long had sneered at all American wines began to discover that some California vintages were equaling and even surpassing many of the classic wines of Europe. Viewing wine as an art form, they began to pay astronomical per-bottle prices for the rarest California table wines. Meanwhile, the less expensive table wines in jugs and in the new "bag-in-the-box" plastic pouches became stocked by restaurants, and for the first time in this country's history, table wines by the glass and carafe became an accepted part of the ordinary restaurant meal. Everyday quality California Central Valley white table wines, made fresh and appealingly palatable by technological advances in viniculture, became so popular, served cold as temperate substitutes for pre-meal cocktails, that the mid-1970s witnessed a nationwide boom in white-wine sales. (Some of the Valley wineries had not yet learned to make appealingly palatable reds.)

Thousands of investors and speculators scrambled during the early 1970s to buy shares of winery stock issues. Seemingly unaware of the past boom-and-bust history of winegrowing described earlier in this chapter, many of them organized tax-shelter partnerships and financed the planting of a quarter-million acres of new vineyards in California. Conglomerates even bought up vineyards and wineries in Europe, South America, and Australia to help supply this country's growing thirst.

As in the grape-planting booms of the past, too many vineyards were planted too fast. Grape prices nose-dived in 1974 and 1975. Soon newspaper headlines were proclaiming that the wine boom had fizzled, that a huge grape surplus faced the nation, that there were "rivers of surplus wine," and that new wineries already were changing hands.

But unnoticed by the headline writers, table wine consumption in the United States was continuing to grow at a steady pace. The overplanting was a lucky mistake, because California's new surplus vineyards saved the wine industry from a supply shortage during the disastrous drought years of 1976 and 1977. Moreover, there still were far from enough vineyards planted in the United States to meet the wine demand conservatively expected to develop by the 1980s.

Yet in another direction at the same time, American wine was becoming increasingly a romantic little business, as adventurous new pioneers of winegrowing started tiny new vineyards and built mini-wineries to produce handmade wines for the future in localities where this was done a century ago and in many others where wine was never grown before.

But most important, because a nation's wines inevitably are judged by the very best it produces, was the fact that American premium wines had surpassed in quality those produced in the pre-Prohibition past. They again were challenging, both at home and in export markets abroad, the finest wines produced in the rest of the world.

In the fifth decade since the rebirth of winegrowing in America, the nation was at last becoming the "Vineland" which Leif Ericson had named it a thousand years earlier. An entirely new chapter in the remarkable four-century history of wine in America had begun.

3

Scuppernong Country—
The Original American Wine

IN THE southeastern states, and nowhere else in the world, there grows a grape so fragrant that the early navigators, approaching the coast in September, detected its rich scent long before they made landfall. It is the Scuppernong, from which southerners have been making wine for almost four centuries to drink with their corn pone, fish muddle, and cake. This was the first, the original American wine.

The greenish-bronze Scuppernong and its many-hued relatives of the *Vitis rotundifolia* or Muscadine family are unlike any other grapes. They grow not in bunches but in clusters, each berry as large and rotund as a cherry or a marble. They are seldom picked; instead, men walk beneath the vines, beating the canes with tobacco sticks, causing the ripe grapes to drop onto sheets or hammocks laid on the ground. As you drive through Scuppernong country, almost every farm you see has its single vine, a dense, tangled mass behind the house, as much a part of the scene as the tobacco barn. A single Scuppernong vine may cover a whole acre and produce, even without cultivation, a ton of fruit yielding five barrels of wine.

The juice of Scuppernong, if fermented dry, makes an amber, strong-tasting, intriguing though usually somewhat harsh wine. But when the wine is sweetened, as winemakers in Scuppernong country have always done, it becomes an exotic nectar reminiscent of fresh plums, with a musky aroma and taste entirely its own. The flavor of Scuppernong is so pronounced that if its wine is blended with Concord, the Scuppernong character will overwhelm and hide the foxy Concord taste. It was to such a blend of Scuppernong and Concord, with California wine added, that the late Captain Paul Garrett gave

Scuppernongs (Muscadines) are unlike any other grapes. They grow not in bunches but in clusters, each berry as large and rotund as a cherry or a marble. These grapes, bred by horticulturist Byard O. Fry at the University of Georgia Experiment Station near Griffin, are an inch in diameter.

the name Virginia Dare, and it was the best-selling wine in the United States during the two decades before Prohibition.

• 2 •

If you travel the Atlantic Coast Line Highway in North Carolina and wish to visit a modern Scuppernong vineyard, look up Raymond Hartsfield, whose place is eight miles northeast of Holly Ridge in Onslow County. When I was last there, he had twenty-five acres of Muscadine vines neatly trained on overhead arbors, with one perfectly flowered (male) vine for each nine vines with pistillate (female) blossoms. Hartsfield gets eight tons to the acre, but he has lost two entire crops in recent years to the hurricanes that roar in at harvest season from the Atlantic; this part of the coast is known as Hurricane Alley.

Hartsfield once operated the only winery in North Carolina, the Onslow Wine Cellar. He closed it in 1968 to devote his full time to raising grapes, which he ships to a winery in Virginia. North Carolina had thirteen wineries back in 1947, when Hartsfield and his father first planted vines on their former tobacco fields. In the following year, Burke and Catawba Counties voted dry, putting several of the wineries out of business, and the rest, fearing that the entire state might follow, closed their cellars one by one. The grape growers began destroying their vineyards, but the Hartsfields started enlarging theirs, for they had heard that the demand for Scuppernong wine was rising—not in the Prohibitionist-dominated South, but in the northern wet states.

In 1961, Richards Wine Cellars in Virginia, the principal producer of Scuppernong wine, offered Carolina farmers five-year contracts to grow Muscadines at two hundred dollars a ton and also offered to provide them with vines to plant. A vineyard-planting boom started in North Carolina, where farmers' income from flue-cured tobacco was declining. Members of the New River Grape Growers Association set out many vineyards in Onslow, Moore, Jones, Robeson, and Lenoir counties.

Although Muscadine grapes can be eaten fresh or made into juice, jam, or jelly, the purpose of the plantings was to produce grapes for wine. In 1965, the North Carolina Legislature, convinced that the state's winegrowing industry was about to be reborn, voted a $166,000 appropriation for Muscadine grape and

Scuppernong Country

🍇 MUSCADINES 🍇 BUNCH GRAPES

wine research and for grower education. At the State University in Raleigh, Dr. William Nesbitt started breeding new Muscadine varieties especially suited for winemaking, soon adding tests of bunch grapes suited for North Carolina climates. Dr. Dan Carroll set up an experimental winery in the Food Science Department to develop new types of Muscadine table wine. James A. Graham, the state director of agriculture, predicted that "North Carolina Scuppernong will someday win a place among the distinctive wines of the world."

Grape acreage in the state jumped from less than 400 acres in 1966 to more than 3,000 acres in 1977. New varieties of Muscadines, self-fertile and more vigorous than Scuppernong, were introduced. They now come in all colors, jet black, red, freckled, and in pearl hues as well as in the traditional bronze. (This presents a problem in wine labeling, for the Muscadines have such names as Mish, Hunt, Creek, Thomas, Higgins, Tarheel, Magnolia, Noble, and Carlos, while the only name northern consumers know for Muscadine wine is Scuppernong. The recent trend, which makes sense, has been to label any wine made predominantly from Muscadines as Scuppernong.)

• 3 •

Although Muscadines thrive in the humid Coastal Plain and Piedmont Plateau areas of all the southeastern states, North Carolina claims Scuppernong as its own. The first account of these grapes occurs in the logbook of Giovanni da Verrazano, the Florentine navigator who in 1524 explored the Cape Fear River Valley for France. He reported "many vines growing naturally there" and that "without all doubt they would yield excellent wines." Amadas and Barlow, sent by Sir Walter Raleigh to explore the Carolina coast from Roanoke Island in 1584, described a land "so full of grapes as the very beating and surge of the sea overflowed them . . . In all the world, the like abundance is not to be found."

Legend credits Raleigh with discovering the Scuppernong grape on Roanoke Island and introducing it elsewhere. This accounts for the fame of the so-called "Mother vine," once called the Walter Raleigh vine, which is one of the tourist attractions at Manteo on the historic island near the site of Raleigh's Lost Colony. The vine has a trunk almost two feet thick, is said to be at least three hundred years old, and still produces grapes. With a few neighboring vines, it supplied the Mother Vineyard Winery, which operated at Manteo until 1954.

The Scuppernong "Mother Vine" on Roanoke Island, North Carolina, covers half an acre. Pictured with the vine is Raymond Hartsfield, who grows twenty-five acres of Scuppernongs in his vineyard at Holly Ridge, N.C.

Scuppernong was named for a town, which was named for a river, which was named for a tree. "Ascopo" was the Algonquin Indian name for the sweet bay tree. "Ascuponung," meaning place of the Ascopo, appeared on old maps of North Carolina as the name of the river in Washington County, near Albemarle Sound. Later maps spelled it Cuscoponung, then Cusponung, next Scuponung and Scupuning, until by 1800 the spelling of the river had become Scuppernong. The grape, however, was merely called the White Grape until James Blount of the town of Scuppernong took the census of Washington County in 1810 and reported 1,368 gallons of wine made there in "this small but very interesting branch of our infant manufactures." An article in the Raleigh (North Carolina) *Star* for January 11, 1811, commenting on Blount's report, was the first to call it "The Scuppernong Grape." Eight years later, Nathaniel Macon, a member of Congress, sent samples of Scuppernong, through Governor Barbour of North Carolina as an intermediary, to Thomas Jefferson, who complained because brandy had been added to the wine. The *American Farmer* for October 1, 1819, related that

Many farmers near Fayetteville in North Carolina have for years past drank excellent wine of their own making from the native grape . . .

Wine is made along the Cape Fear River from Fayetteville to the Sea, a distance of near seventy miles, and the farmers use it as freely as cider is used in New England. It is common for a farmer to make eight or ten barrels of wine annually for his own use, and many sell considerable quantities.

How widespread early winegrowing was in North Carolina is evidenced by the place names that remain on its road maps and railroad stations, such as Tokay, Medoc, Cognac, Niagara, Vina Vista, and Catawba. The late Professor Carlos Williams, the Raleigh horticulturist, told me that the Pettigrew State Park in Washington County was originally the Pettigrew Vineyard and the site of a winery. The *American Wine Press* for March 1, 1897, mentions the 1,200-acre Niagara Vineyard sixty miles south of Raleigh, and contains an advertisement of Colonel Wharton Green's Tokay Vineyard, three miles north of Fayetteville, and of his 100,000-gallon winery. Other North Carolina wineries, before and since Prohibition, had such addresses as Conover, Eagle Springs, Gibson, Louisburg, Murphy, Peachland, Samarcand, Tryon, Warrenton, Willard, and Wilmington.

· 4 ·

The fabulous Captain Paul Garrett, who became a multimillionaire selling wine with the Scuppernong flavor, was a North Carolinian. He was the dean of American vintners when I knew him in the early '30s, a tall, portly, forceful man with a deep voice and a soft southern accent. His title of "captain" was not military, but was bestowed by his employees, who also called him "the boss."

He was born in 1863, the third year of the Civil War, on the Edgecombe County farm of his father, country doctor Francis Marion Garrett. In 1865, his father and his wealthy uncle, Charles Garrett, purchased North Carolina's first commercial winery, the Medoc Vineyard, established in 1835 by Sidney Weller near Enfield in neighboring Halifax County. Weller, a northerner, had made a fortune growing mulberries, had lost it in the silk business, then planted vines among his mulberry trees, and, although an ardent Prohibitionist, had become wealthy again by making and selling wine.

At the age of fourteen, Paul quit military prep school and went to live with his uncle, who ran the winery, to learn the wine business. He worked in the vineyard, bought grapes from growers in neighboring counties, made the wine, loaded barrels on wagons, and taught Sunday school in the village of Ringwood. At twenty-one, when his uncle died, he became a salesman for the Garrett winery. He traveled through Arkansas, Tennessee, and Texas with a vial of Scuppernong wine in his pocket, inviting saloonkeepers to taste and to buy it for sale in competition with whiskey. In 1900, when he was thirty-seven, he contracted to sell the winery's entire output, but when his commissions mounted, the winery's new proprietor refused to deliver. Paul then established his own winery, first at Littleton, then at Chockoyotte, near Weldon, calling it Garrett & Company.

In the next nineteen years, Paul Garrett built a nationwide wine empire. He started by outbidding other wineries for Scuppernong grapes, buying all he could find. He began blending the juice with New York and California wines, but kept the Scuppernong flavor predominant. He called Scuppernong "the finest wine in the world," but saw drawbacks in its name: other vintners could use it on spurious wines; it was well known in the South, but the name meant nothing to northerners. Garrett also knew it was garbled from an Indian word, and he tried spelling it "Escapernong." He objected, too, to labeling American wines after European types as "sauternes" or "burgundy." Seeking a name that no one else could copy, he tried calling his white wine "Minnehaha" and his red "Pocahontas." Then he had a better idea: Because Scuppernong was the first American wine, he named it for the first child born of English parents in America—Virginia Dare—and Virginia Dare white and red became known to almost everybody in the nation.

By 1903 Garrett had five wineries in North Carolina, the largest one at Aberdeen, and vineyards on Dare Island and at Plymouth. But mounting Prohibitionist strength in the state threatened his wineries, so he established a larger plant at Norfolk in neighboring Virginia. When North Carolina went dry in 1908, he had to rush the juice from his Aberdeen cellar to Norfolk before fermentation could set in and make it illegal. Nine years later, Virginia, too, had gone dry, and Garrett moved permanently to New York State. By 1913, he had established vineyards and wineries at Penn Yan, Canandaigua, and Hammondsport in the Finger Lakes District and also the Mission Vineyard and Winery at Cucamonga in Southern California. When Wartime Prohibition began in 1919, he had seventeen plants processing grape juice or wine in North Carolina, Virginia, Ohio, Missouri, New York, and California, with a total capacity of ten million gallons.

Garrett could have retired with his millions, but refusing to

Captain Paul Garrett, the North
Carolinian whose Scuppernong-
flavored "Virginia Dare" was the
best-known American wine before
and after National Prohibition.

believe that Prohibition could last, he sought ways to hold his
empire together until Repeal. He first sold dealcoholized Virginia Dare wine, which buyers spiked with alcohol, but its popularity soon waned. Then he lost a million dollars promoting a
cola-flavored grape drink called Satenet, and another million on
a venture in the flavoring extract business. He recouped with his
Virginia Dare wine tonic, and then with grape concentrate for
home winemaking. Then there was his ill-fated "Vine-Glo"
venture, described in Chapter 2. Meanwhile he crusaded for
modification of the Volstead Act to permit the sale of light wine,
which he called "the antitoxin of alcoholism." If table wine
could be sold as food, free of taxes like other farm products, he
said, the winegrowing industry could furnish employment to
eight million Americans.

When Repeal arrived in 1933, Garrett was the only vintner
ready again to sell his wine in every wet state. Virginia Dare
white and red were displayed in every wine store, and millions
hummed the first* singing commercial ever broadcast for wine,
"Say it again . . . Virginia Dare."

The enthusiastic Captain ranged through the South in the
early 1930s, urging more planting of Scuppernong vineyards.
He enlisted the help of Harry L. Hopkins and the Federal Rural
Resettlement Administration. It was arranged that Scuppernong vines, five acres per family, would provide the chief cash
crop for resettled farmers in Georgia and South Carolina, the

*But not the first advertisement ever sung for wine, because French champagne firms
during the nineteenth century regularly paid performers in the music halls of England to
sing such songs as "Champagne Charlie," which advertised Moët et Chandon, and
"Clicquot, the Wine for Me."

cash crop second to tung oil trees in Florida, and the crop second to strawberries in Louisiana. In North Carolina, sufficient vines were propagated to set out four thousand acres. At Garrett's prompting, a grape growers' co-operative was organized to start a winery in Virginia.

But few new vineyards were planted. Dry congressmen forbade Harry Hopkins to make grapes the basis for the economy of any Rural Resettlement projects. Besides, Garrett's campaign was forty years too early. Not enough markets were open for wine as yet; much of the nation and most of the South, in particular, were still legally dry.

Scuppernong grapes continued to be scarce, and Virginia Dare gradually lost its unique flavor. As Garrett was compelled to rely more on his California vineyards for grapes, Virginia Dare became more and more a bland-tasting California wine.

In his sixty-second year as a vintner, still preaching "American wines for Americans," Captain Garrett fell ill of pneumonia in New York City, and on March 18, 1940, he died at the age of seventy-six. His family life had been tragic, three of his four sons dying as infants. When his fourth son, Charles, died in 1930 at the age of sixteen, the Captain built in his memory a great chapel on Bluff Point overlooking Keuka Lake in New York State, an architectural gem in the woods, which he deeded to the Rochester Diocese of the Episcopal Church. There the Captain and his wife are buried with their sons. Garrett's wine empire went out of existence, but his Scuppernong blend called Virginia Dare and his idea of building an American wine industry have survived.

• 5 •

Scuppernong and its Muscadine relatives are the principal grapes grown on the humid Coastal Plain of North Carolina and the other southeastern states. Bunch grapes, the kinds that grow elsewhere, are attacked here by Pierce's Disease, an insect-borne bacterium to which the Muscadines are resistant. Bunch grapes, such as Catawba and Concord, do grow at higher elevations on the Piedmont Plateau. Catawba, incidentally, gets its name from the Catawba River in Buncombe County, where it is said to have been discovered in 1802.

North Carolina had no wineries after Raymond Hartsfield, mentioned earlier, closed his Onslow Cellar at Holly Ridge in 1968. Five years later, to attract new wineries, the state legislature reduced the minimum annual winery license fee from $1,000 to $100 and cut the state tax on native table wine to five cents a gallon, leaving it at sixty cents on out-of-state wines. Now North Carolina has three new wineries and expects soon to have more.

On Route 32 four miles east of Edenton on Albemarle Sound, the 13,000-gallon Deerfield Vineyards Wine Cellars was opened in 1974. It uses the Muscadine grapes grown on the Wood family's eighty acres of vineyards ten miles to the east. Deerfield makes pleasant demi-sec and sweet white and red native grape wines and the best dry Scuppernong I have tasted anywhere in the South. Key to the dry wine's pleasing flavor is its 30 percent blend with Delaware grapes from New York State. The winery, a converted farm building, is open weekdays for tasting and tours. George and Benbury Wood and their stepbrother Frank Williams are members of one of Edenton's oldest families, descendants of the colonists who settled there in the 1600s.

The Tarheel State's second new winery is the 40,000-gallon Duplin Wine Cellar, opened in 1976 in the legally dry Duplin County farming community of Rose Hill. It is owned by eleven farmers who have seventy-five acres of young Muscadine vineyards in five southeastern Carolina counties. The winemakers are former high school principal David Fussell and his brother Dan, whose twelve acres outside the town were planted in 1972. In modern stainless steel cooperage, with the State University's Dr. Dan Carroll as their advisor, they make vintage-dated dry, semi-dry, and sweet table wines named Carlos, Noble, Scuppernong, and Carolina Country wine and sell them in cities that are legally wet.

The famous Biltmore Estate of the late philanthropist George Washington Vanderbilt in the foothills of the Blue Ridge Mountains near Asheville has the state's third new winery, bonded in 1977. It is a 5,000-gallon experiment by the founder's grandson, William A. Vanderbilt Cecil, in growing fine table wines, not of Muscadines but mainly of French-American hybrid grapes. The first Château Biltmore wines are tentatively scheduled for introduction by 1979. Wines named for the fabulous four-acre French Renaissance mansion on this 11,000-acre estate can bring new prestige and glamor to winegrowing in the South. Although the three-acre Biltmore vineyard is still experimental, the quality of the 1977 vintage was reported satisfactory, and the vineyard, planted since 1971, was about to be doubled in size. Outcome of the test depends on how well the vines, which include some Vinifera varieties, withstand damage at the 2,300 to 2,600-foot altitude from late spring frosts.

In the mountains southeast of Asheville, a thermal (frost-free) belt extends northeastward from Tryon, a Polk County community of estates and summer homes. There were vineyards and wineries around Tryon before Prohibition. A wine press and casks that once were part of the Vollmer winery are still preserved at the Charles Briggs residence on Vineyard Road. Tryon's wine tradition has been revived by retired General Electric executive Bryan H. Doble, who has grown French hybrids and Vinifera on his Oak Knoll vineyard since 1965. He makes extraordinarily good Cabernet Sauvignon, Foch, Chelois, White Riesling, Aurora, and Verdelet in his modern home wine cellar. Two more Vinifera vineyards have been planted nearby with cuttings from Oak Knoll. One is on the estate of Harry Evans, a retired Air Force general. The other belongs to Chicago allergist Clifford Kalb.

A permit for a fourth North Carolina winery was issued in 1977 to John C. Dockery, who has forty acres of Muscadines near Rockingham in the southwestern part of the state.

• 6 •

The southern Bible Belt was described by the late Will Rogers as those states where citizens "stagger to the polls to vote dry." These are the last tottering strongholds of the professional Prohibitionists and their political allies, the moonshiners of the Blue Ridge and Great Smoky Mountains. As late as 1975, more than a third of the counties in the South still were legally dry (about half in Alabama, Georgia, and Mississippi, two thirds in Tennessee). Wine, where available, was burdened with exorbitant taxes or variously restricted in sale. This, and the drinking customs—Coca-Cola in the morning, as traditional as the Englishman's afternoon tea, and corn liquor with branch water as the beverage of hospitality—help to explain why little table wine heretofore has been drunk in the South. It is changing gradually now, however, because with the influx of industry thousands of families have moved in from the northern states where the use of dry table wines is becoming customary. Per capita wine consumption in the South has more than doubled in ten years, and more dry counties are voting wet. Winegrowing is reviving in those southern states where the political strength of the Drys is waning, but it lags in those states where they are still strong.

• 7 •

South Carolina, although legally wet, is a case in point. It has two thousand acres of vineyards and led the southern states in grape growing until North Carolina experienced its recent Muscadine-planting boom. But much of South Carolina's 6,000-ton grape crop is shipped fresh or as unfermented juice to wineries in New York, Virginia, and Georgia, and the state's promotional literature makes no mention of wine.

Among the scrub pines in the Sand Hills country near Patrick in Chesterfield County is the largest single vineyard in the South, three hundred acres neatly planted with Muscadine and Labrusca grape varieties and with dewberries for blackberry wine. Adjoining the vineyard is the oldest winery in South Carolina, Tenner Brothers. It is an unprepossessing concrete structure, recently increased in capacity to a million gallons by a battery of outdoor wine tanks of stainless steel, and is not open to visitors; it is absentee-owned. Sal, Al, and Lukie Tenner, former Charleston tire dealers, entered the wine and restaurant business at Charlotte, North Carolina, in 1935, then established the winery at Patrick in 1953 when South Carolina granted them a preferential tax on wine made from South Carolina grapes and berries. The tax on their wine was 45 cents* a gallon compared to $1.08 on wines from outside the state. Several years later the Tenner Brothers had financial difficulties, and in 1966 they sold out to Mack Sands's companies, which operate the Richards winery in Virginia, the Canandaigua winery in New York State, and the Bisceglia winery in California.

South Carolina has two new wineries. At Woodruff in Spartanburg County, Richard Leizear in 1976 organized a group of grape growers headed by Dr. Guy Blakely, a Woodruff physician, to convert Leizear's Oakview Farm grape-juice plant into the half-million-gallon Oakview Plantations winery. Leizear, who lectures teetotaling Baptists about wine in the Bible, has had the winery painted with vertical maroon and gold stripes. The main products are Golden Muscadine, Scuppernong, Paladin table wines, a rose pink of Catawba, and appetizer, dessert, apple, and peach wines. They can be bought by the case at the winery, but there are no tours.

At Lake City on the Coastal Plain in Florence County, wine buff dentist Dr. James Truluck and his wife Kay planted twenty acres of French hybrid grapes in 1971 and two years later began making table wines in their home. They next built a three-story 35,000-gallon winery with an underground aging cellar, modeled after those Dr. Truluck admired while he was with the Air Force Dental Corps in southern France in 1959. By 1977,

*Now 57.6 cents a gallon

Truluck white, rosé, and red table wines were being sold in Lake City and Charleston stores. Thus far, the vineyard and winery have been supported by Dr. Truluck's dental practice, but now that he has converted his family's pre-Civil War house into a retail store and tasting room, he thinks his investment may begin to pay.

A South Carolina Grape Festival is celebrated each August at York, sponsored by the York County Grape Growers Association and the York Junior Chamber of Commerce. The festival features include grape judging, a grape stomping, a beauty pageant, a queen contest, and a parade. For the first nine years the program contained nothing about wine, but since 1974 the growers' wives have been distributing their recipes for home-made wine to the celebrants. Concord was the county's main grape variety when the festival was founded, but because of its low sugar content, many of the vineyards have been replanted lately with Muscadines. York County grape growers own two new mechanical harvesters, which work especially well in Scuppernong vineyards. The growers have also talked of building a winery, but when Virginia vintner Mack Sands increased the price he had been paying them for Scuppernongs, the winery proposal died.

The South Carolina Agricultural Experiment Station at Clemson University has a three-acre experimental vineyard, but the University has no wine research program. However, Horticulture Professor Harold J. Sefick, who has bred grapes at Clemson for twenty years, happens to have a hobby interest in winemaking. Of necessity, he conducts his wine experiments at home.

South Carolina's best wines, says Professor Sefick, are made by an amateur named Eugene Charles. Since 1948, at his home near the little city of Seneca in the Piedmont, Mr. Charles has been growing French hybrid and Labrusca grapes and has made wine scientifically, reporting his results regularly to other oenothusiasts throughout the South. On the summer afternoon when I visited him, however, all of his recent vintages had been consumed.

Although the Drys have kept South Carolina's winegrowing history a secret, they have neglected to change the state map. It still shows the town of Bordeaux (originally New Bordeaux), named for the most famous wine city of France. New Bordeaux was founded by French Huguenot emigrés, who in 1764 were granted 30,000 acres by the British government to found a grape and wine industry along the upper Savannah River.

In ampelographies you will find that three of the most successful native American wine grapes originated in South Carolina; the Isabella about 1816, the Lenoir in 1829, and the Herbemont, grown by Nicholas Herbemont of Columbia in the 1820s.

Old-time residents of Abbeville, in the South Carolina Piedmont, still remember Dr. Joseph Togno's Montevino vineyard and winery; the physician's rock house, built in 1859, is a landmark of the town. The City of Aiken, near the Savannah River nuclear bomb plant, was famous in the 1860s for a claret made there by Benson and Merrier's Winery from Isabella grapes. The Aiken Vinegrowing Society published in 1858 an essay on winegrowing in the South in which the author, A. de Caradeuc, advised farmers to grow grapes in addition to their cotton, sugar, and rice:

A few leisure days in the winter, of which there are so many, and a few hours in the grassy season, devoted to one or two acres of his hitherto poorest and most worthless land, will insure him a handsome income, and a pleasant beverage more wholesome and agreeable than Peach Mobby or Persimmon Beer, and more conducive to his and his children's morals than Whiskey, that bane of our country, which it will finally drive out of use.

• 8 •

General James E. Oglethorpe, the founder of Georgia in 1733, required the first settlers to plant grapes as well as other farm products for shipment to England. Although Oglethorpe prohibited drinking in the colony, there is evidence that wine was made during the General's time. The first commercial winegrower in Georgia probably was Thomas McCall, whose vineyard was planted in Laurens County on the Oconee River before 1823. The *Southern Cultivator* in December 1858 referred to Charles Axt of Crawfordsville in Taliaferro County as "one of the most successful vintners of the South." By 1880, when the United States Department of Agriculture made its study of grape and wine production, Georgia was the sixth largest winegrowing state in the nation, producing 903,244 gallons from 2,991 acres of vineyards, almost double the gallonage made in New York State in that year. The leading Georgia winegrowing counties were Bibb, Chatham, Fulton, Houston, Pulaski, and Randolph. Wild Scuppernong was the chief grape used, but the Norton, a red bunch grape, was reported making the best Georgia wine. In the 1890s, the Georgia Vineyard Company at

Tallapoosa in Haralson County was making fifty thousand gallons of wine and juice annually, and forty families in a Hungarian settlement nearby were making wines that sold at fancy prices in New York. All of this ended, however, when the state went dry in 1907.

Concord grapes grow in Georgia's upper Piedmont, especially around Gainesville, but only Scuppernong and other Muscadines survive long in most other parts of the state. There are prolific Scuppernong vineyards in Sumter County, which is the home county of former peanut farmer President Jimmy Carter (Plains). A large Muscadine vineyard thrives among the lakes at marvelous Callaway Gardens near Pine Mountain in Harris County. The Gardens use the crop to make Muscadine preserves, jelly, and sauce, which are featured in its country gift and food stores. There is also a delectable Muscadine ice cream.

Georgia, unlike South Carolina, encourages wine research. Dr. Moustapha Hamdy makes Muscadine wines in the University's Food Science Department at Athens, and new Muscadine varieties have been developed at the Horticultural Research Station at Experiment, south of Atlanta. Its Fry grape, named for retired Georgia grape breeder Byard O. Fry, is almost as large as a golf ball. Planting of Muscadines by Georgia farmers has quintupled from two hundred acres in 1969 to more than a thousand acres in 1977. Easy to cultivate and to harvest mechanically, they yield almost ten tons to the acre. Most Muscadines are grown to make wine, but not for Georgians to drink. Much of the crop is shipped to Virginia and New York to be made into Scuppernong wine for consumption in the North.

Georgia has only one winery, the million-gallon Monarch Wine Company of Georgia at Atlanta, the largest maker of peach wine in the world. The state sets a minimum $1,000 per year winery license fee, which discourages farmers from opening any more. A preferential tax favors Georgia wines, but prohibits blending with out-of-state grapes, necessary to make dry Muscadine table wines. The Monarch winery began in 1936, when Georgia repealed its prohibition law, and when Governor Eugene Talmadge was looking for a way to dispose of the state's peach surplus. Word of the Governor's search reached Charles Gilsten, who happened to be in Atlanta on a selling trip for Leo Star's Monarch Winery of New York. Gilsten, a native Atlantan and former newsboy, went to see Talmadge and made him a proposition: if the state would let Georgia table and dessert wines be taxed at twenty and fifty cents a gallon respectively, compared to a dollar and two dollars a gallon on out-of-state wines, Monarch would open a winery. The Governor accepted, the tax legislation was passed, and Gilsten, independent of the New York firm, opened the largest winery in the South.* Besides wines from peaches and berries, he made grape wines from Muscadines, Concord, and other varieties grown in Georgia, adding grape concentrate and high-proof brandy from California. When Georgia farmers objected to the use of California brandy, Monarch built its own distillery at Roberta in Crawford County and now makes its high-proof brandy from Georgia fruits.

· 9 ·

When the British admiral, Sir John Hawkins, relieved the starving French Huguenots at Fort Caroline in Florida in 1565, he found they had "twenty hogshead of wine made from the native grapes." Since the grapes almost certainly were Muscadines, that Florida Scuppernong, made four centuries ago, was the original American wine.

In Florida, as in the other colonies, there were attempts to grow Vinifera grapes brought from Europe, with the same disappointing results. After the Civil War, immigrants to Florida from the North brought their favorite Labrusca grapes, such as Concord, Niagara, Worden, and Ives. Extensive plantings were made around Orlando, and by 1894 there were five hundred acres in Orange County alone, but by 1900 most of these vineyards had died. Then came the Prohibition-era grape boom of the 1920s. Nearly five thousand acres of new vineyards were planted in Lake, Orange, and Putnam Counties, this time mainly of the Munson hybrid varieties from Texas. A decade later, most of these vines, too, had succumbed to "the grape decline" (Pierce's Disease), which attacks most bunch grapes in Florida. After each of these debacles, there remained only the native Muscadines.

Florida Scuppernong wine has been made for two decades at Ralph Weaver's Bartels Winery in Pensacola, the only one of the state's few small wineries that has produced wine from grapes. (Others in recent years have made orange, berry, and honey wines.) But the Bartels Winery, in the cellar of Bartels Restaurant, may not continue, says Weaver, because the state legislature has increased the annual license fee from $100 to $1,000 and also has raised the tax on Florida wine.

*The tax rates have since risen to 40¢, $1, $1.50, and $2.50 a gallon respectively.

Weaver and the 400-member Florida Grape Growers Association want the state to cut back the license fee and the tax rate so that small farmer wineries can start and survive. Many small vineyards have been planted in Florida with Muscadines and new bunch grape varieties, resistant to Pierce's Disease, bred by Professors Loren H. Stover and John A. Mortensen of the state's Agricultural Research Center at Leesburg. Association past president Esmond Grosz and his wife Malinda hope to build a winery on their Malinda's Vineyard, between Ocala and Gainesville. Foster Burgess of Freeport also plans a winery when his eleven acres of young Muscadines in the Florida Panhandle begin yielding grapes.

"We believe there are possibilities for wine production in Florida, perhaps eventually on a large scale," say Professors Stover and Mortensen, whose disease-resistant bunch grapes are named Stover, Norris, Blue Lake, Lake Emerald, and Liberty. Stover is neutral in flavor, but Blue Lake and Lake Emerald have strong Labrusca tastes. Dr. Robert P. Bates of the University of Florida Food Science Laboratory at Gainesville, using both the new Florida bunch grapes and Muscadines, has made some better than drinkable experimental wines.

• 10 •

America's new interest in winegrowing has spread to Alabama, the very heart of Dixie. Like the other southern states, Alabama had vineyards and wineries a century ago. The 1880 Federal wine production census reported 422,670 gallons of wine produced from grapes grown in thirteen counties.

The Cotton State now has a prospering commercial vineyard at Perdido in Baldwin County, fifty miles northeast of Mobile. At the Rabun-Perdido exit from Interstate 65, civil engineer Jim Eddins and his biologist wife Marianne planted some fifty acres of Scuppernongs and other Muscadines in 1972. Within three years they were selling their grapes to "U-pick" home winemakers and to the Bartels Winery in Florida, besides making table wine for their own use in their house-trailer home among the vines. They also teach a night class in wine appreciation at Faulkner Junior College in nearby Bay Minette. Marianne raises annual flocks of white Chinese geese, which weed the Perdido Vineyard efficiently during the summer and then are sold on the poultry market for the holidays.

When the Perdido Vineyard in southern Alabama was a year old, the Tennessee Valley Authority (which has major operations in Alabama) planted an experimental acre of bunch grapes on reclaimed strip-mined coal land on Sand Mountain near Fabius in De Kalb County, near the northern edge of the state. TVA soil expert Dr. David A. Mays of Muscle Shoals reports the vines doing well, especially the French hybrid wine grapes. Mine operator Rex Mitchell also has planted wine grapes on reclaimed mining land on the Warrior River in Chilton County, owned by Sara Mayfield of Tuscaloosa.

The most enthusiastic proponent of winegrowing in Alabama is Dr. Booker T. Whatley, professor of plant and soil science at Tuskegee Institute, the black college where the great Dr. George Washington Carver developed hundreds of new uses for peanuts and sweet potatoes. Dr. Whatley predicts that Muscadine grapes "will form the basis for a grape and wine industry in southern Alabama" and backs his prediction with new Muscadine grapes he has bred in the Institute's vineyard. Experimental wines are being made from the Tuskegee grapes at Mississippi State University until the Institute gets a wine laboratory of its own.

What few Alabamans know is that their state had two commercial vineyards and wineries as recently as forty years ago. Fred Hagendorfer had the first post-Repeal Alabama winery near Elberta in Baldwin County. The Bartels Winery started near Elberta in 1937, but was moved to Pensacola, Florida, when Alabama failed to grant it a license. Hagendorfer's old wine press recently was sold to a home winemaker, and remnants of the Bartels Alabama vineyard were uprooted in 1976.

• 11 •

Mississippi, which repealed its state Prohibition law in 1966, has produced wine in the past and is starting to do so again.

The *Southern Cultivator*, in March 1875, described the Scuppernong wine made by J. M. Taylor of Rienzi, Alcorn County, Mississippi, as "nonpareil, a great gift of the gods to the Sunny South." Dr. Dunbar Rowland's *History of Mississippi* records that wines from twenty Mississippi counties were exhibited in 1885 at the World Industrial and Cotton Exposition in New Orleans. There were thirty-one wineries in Holly Springs, Enterprise, Forest, Meridian, Waynesboro, Carthage, Oxford, and Pontotoc until the state went dry in 1908.

It is therefore not surprising that with Mississippians drinking a million gallons of newly legalized wine from elsewhere in 1967, a Committee to Promote Winery Legislation was formed with the object of getting wineries started in the state. Leaders in the effort were William G. Bodker of Jackson, an amateur winemaker who grows Muscadines and bunch (non-Muscadine) grapes in the foothills of the Yazoo Delta; Hamilton Allen, who grows Muscadines and makes wine at home near Port Gibson in Claiborne County, and John Bagwell, who teaches school in Tennessee and has a vineyard at Bruce in Calhoun County.

A survey by the State Research and Development Board confirmed that the Magnolia State could grow grapes profitably.

Mississippi State University at Starkville promptly launched a wine research project. New test vineyards of dozens of wine grape varieties were planted in four corners of the state, supervised by MSU horticulturist Jean P. Overcash. To house wine research, a Swiss-type chalet was built on a hill overlooking the campus; it is the handsomest enology laboratory in the nation. Microbiologist Boris Stojanovic, whose parents were winegrowers in Yugoslavia, was put in charge and began making experimental dry table wines of Muscadines.

The obstacle to starting Mississippi wineries was a state law that set $1,800 per year as the minimum winery license fee. In 1976 Senator William G. Burgin, who has a five-year-old vineyard of two acres near his home at Columbus, got the legislature to enact a Mississippi Native Wine Law. It set a $10 minimum winery license and cut the Mississippi thirty-five-cent per gallon wine tax to five cents on wine made principally from Mississippi fruit.

Within months there were three applications to start Mississippi wineries.

Ottis Rushing and his agronomist son Sam converted their dairy barn east of Merigold in Bolivar County into the 35,000-gallon "Winery Rushing." They equipped it with modern tanks, refrigeration, and a centrifuge. In 1977, with Dr. Stojanovic's help, Sam Rushing and his wife Diana, using Muscadine grapes purchased in North Carolina, made the first wines produced legally in Mississippi in eighty years. The state allows them to use grapes from other states until their thirty-acre Muscadine vineyard begins to bear grapes in 1980.

Senator Burgin meanwhile prepared to build a winery on his Thousand Oaks Vineyard, on Highway 82 east of Columbus, in time to crush the first post-Repeal vintage of Mississippi-grown grapes in 1978.

A third Mississippi winery was being planned by Dr. Alex

Mathers, the former director of scientific services for the Federal bureau in Washington that supervises the nation's wine industry. Dr. Mathers, a past president of the American Institute of Chemists, has made wine for many years on his family estate at Matherville in Wayne County. He has begun expanding his Almarla Vineyard to twenty-five acres. Dr. Scott Galbreath of Natchez, with a ten-year-old vineyard in Adams County, was also thinking of starting a winery.

With the Magnolia State's wine industry being reborn at an accelerating pace, the University at Starkville in 1977 employed a second enologist to help Dr. Stojanovic. He is the appropriately named Richard P. Vine, whose seventeen years' experience includes winemaking at the Pleasant Valley winery in the Finger Lakes of New York, then at the now defunct Niagara Falls Wine Cellar at Lewiston, New York, and four years as chief enologist of the Warner Vineyards in Paw Paw, Michigan. He is also the co-author, with Walter S. Taylor, of *Home Winemaker's Handbook*, published in 1968.

• 12 •

Tennessee, too, was once a winegrowing state and is likely to become one again. A Catawba wine from the Willowbeck Vineyard, near Wartrace in New Bedford County, won first prize at the 1857 State Fair in Nashville and at the 1875 Louisville National Fair in competition with wines from northern states. The Chattanooga *Times* in 1880 reported there were "150 acres around Chattanooga within a radius of five miles entirely devoted to grape culture" and that "nearly every cultivated field between Rossville and the railroad tunnel has a vineyard of some size."

The Volunteer State, like neighboring Mississippi, has taken steps to revive its wine industry. In 1977, the Tennessee Legislature passed a Grape and Wine Law setting a $50 annual winery license fee. It also reduced the state's exorbitant $1.18 per gallon wine tax to five cents on wine made from farm products grown in Tennessee. Wineries may be expected to start when enough vineyards are planted; the state had fewer than seventy-five acres of grapes when the law was passed.

This results from the work of the Tennessee Viticultural and Oenological Society, organized by hobbyist winegrowers throughout the state in 1973. Judge William O. Beach, president of the Society, grows White Riesling, Chardonnay, Pinot Noir, and French hybrids near his home at Clarksville and makes fine table wines and champagne when he isn't presiding over the Montgomery County Court. His wines have won prizes in home winemakers' competitions at Nashville and Atlanta.

Tennessee has many different climates between the Great Smoky Mountains on the east and the Mississippi River on the west. There are many small vineyards—of bunch grapes on the central plateau, where there are traces of pre-Prohibition wineries, and of Scuppernongs at lower elevations. At the urging of the TVOS, a test vineyard was planted at Crossville on the Cumberland Plateau by University of Tennessee pomologist Charles Mullins, and it already has produced grapes suitable for table wines. The Tennessee Valley Authority and the University have also planted experimental vineyards on reclaimed strip-mined coal land in four Tennessee counties. Grape growing is of special interest as a way to supplement the declining income of Tennessee tobacco growers.

• 13 •

In Louisiana, Jesuit priests made wine for altar use as early as 1750, before wine grapes were brought to California. Most of the wine made since in the Bayou State, however, has come from fruits other than grapes. There were many wineries in Louisiana before Prohibition, and several were started after Repeal in 1933, fermenting the oranges of Plaquemines Parish. Only one winery is left, at Port Sulphur in southeastern Louisiana, and its main product is orange wine.

If the progress thus far made in reviving southeastern viniculture continues, the flavor spectrum of good American wines is likely soon to include many from the southeastern states.

4

The Middle Atlantic States

WINE TOURING in eastern America can be both a fascinating and a puzzling experience. Why is it, you may wonder, that Virginia, with centuries of winegrowing history, has become dotted with scores of little wine estates during just the past few years, while four big Virginia wineries, using mainly fruit grown elsewhere, have been turning out millions of gallons of wine yearly for decades? How does one explain why Pennsylvania, with more than nine thousand acres planted to grapes, had not even one producing winery until 1963, but now has fifteen? What has enabled little New Jersey, with only several hundred acres of vines, to make as much as 800,000 gallons of wine per year? And how does it happen that vines from a seven-acre vineyard in Maryland have revolutionized the planting of wine grapes in hundreds of localities in the United States and Canada? To unravel these paradoxes, one needs to know some of the wine history of these states, their wet-dry politics, and the widely different taste preferences for wine that are emerging in America.

• 2 •

Virginia, as we have seen, was the first of the colonies to cultivate grapes for wine. The attempts to grow Vinifera, which began in 1619 under Lord Delaware, continued in Virginia for almost two centuries. Some of the vineyards succeeded in producing quantities of wine before plant diseases and insect pests killed the European vines. About 1716, historian Robert Beverley won a wager of seven hundred guineas from his neighbors by producing seven hundred gallons in a single vintage from his three-acre vineyard at Beverley Park in King and Queen County. But Beverley apparently made the wine from native wild grapes, which he cultivated together with his few French vines. The only Virginia wines of any note in the eighteenth century were the red and white Rapidan, made by a colony of Germans who settled on the Rapidan River, in Spotsylvania County after 1770. George Washington planted a garden vineyard at Mount Vernon, but there is no record of his having made any wine, although he made cider and distilled considerable quantities of applejack. In 1773, Dr. Filippo Mazzei of Tuscany brought Italian winegrowers with ten thousand European vine cuttings in a chartered ship to establish wine-growing in Virginia. Most of Mazzei's cuttings were planted at Monticello, the estate of Thomas Jefferson, in what is now Albermarle County. For thirty years Jefferson continued trying to grow Vinifera, even importing some of his vines directly from Château d'Yquem, and he is said once to have even imported some French soil. An advocate of wine as a temperate beverage, he hoped to establish winegrowing as an American industry, and while minister to France from 1785 to 1789, he made his own scientific studies of viticulture and winemaking. Jefferson finally admitted his failure with Vinifera when he recommended in 1809 that native vines, such as the Alexander, be planted instead.

In 1835, Dr. D. N. Norton of Richmond produced a domesticated non-foxy native blue grape that made Virginia claret wine famous during the latter half of the nineteenth century. The Norton was virtually a Virginia monopoly, because this grape variety is difficult to ripen in regions north of the Potomac. Following the Civil War, winegrowing based on the Norton and other native grapes spread through the Piedmont and Blue Ridge regions. The Virginia Winegrowers Association had branches in Albemarle, Norfolk, Warren, and Fairfax, the leading grape-growing counties. The Monticello Wine Company at Charlottesville became so noted for its Norton Claret, which won a gold medal at Vienna in 1873 and a silver medal at Paris in 1878, that the city was called "the capital of the Virginia wine belt." The company's Delaware, Catawba, Hock, Norton Port, Virginia Sherry, and grape brandy, as well as the Claret, were sold throughout the East.

Virginia's wine production totaled 232,479 gallons by 1880, making it the eleventh largest wine-producing state in the Union. But during the next few decades, cities, counties, and whole states were going dry. Competition from California wine was increasing. The markets for Virginia wines began to

shrink. Grape prices declined, growers neglected their vineyards, and the vines soon died. When Virginia passed its state
prohibition law in 1914, few vineyards of any size remained in
the state.

A move to revive the Virginia wine industry was started by
Captain Paul Garrett when National Prohibition ended in 1933.
Garrett praised "the noble Virginia Claret," and Professor
Ulysses P. Hedrick, the great New York viticulturist, described
the Norton as "the best red wine grape grown in the Eastern
states . . . best when grown in the soil and climate of central
Virginia." A few of the old wineries reopened, and in 1934 the
Monticello Grape Growers Co-operative Association was
formed at Charlottesville with Bernard Peyton Chamberlain, an
amateur winegrower and author of a wine book, as its president. Extensive plantings of grapes in the Piedmont counties
were planned, but they never materialized; only a few thousand
gallons of claret were made by the association. Again, some
new vineyards were planted after the Second World War, but
lacking a market for their grapes, they were soon abandoned.
When Professor George D. Oberle, who had organized the new
wine-grape testing program at New York's Geneva Experiment
Station, joined the Virginia Polytechnic Institute College of
Agriculture at Blacksburg in 1948, he found nine wineries still
bonded to operate in the state. But three were just then going
out of business, and most of the others seemed likely to follow.

One Virginia winery was making and selling wine of its own
grapes. It was unknown to most Virginians. On an arm of the
Roanoke River at Clarksville in Mecklenburg County, John
June Lewis, a black veteran of the First World War, had planted
eight acres of vines when Prohibition was repealed in 1933 and
had been making table wines for sale to his neighbors.

To historic Petersburg in Virginia after Repeal came Mordecai
E. (Mack) Sands, retracing the footsteps of Captain Paul
Garrett. Sands had decided to produce sweet Scuppernong
wines in Virginia, as Garrett did, from grapes grown in the
southeastern states. Since he opened Richard's Wine Cellar on
Pocahontas Street in Petersburg in 1951, the winery has grown
to more than two million gallons. Also like Garrett, Sands and
his son Marvin persuaded farmers throughout the South to
plant thousands of acres with Scuppernongs. But why make
Scuppernong wine in Virginia when the grapes are grown in
states farther south? The Sandses have not explained, but it
may be remembered that Garrett, too, established a winery in
Virginia to avoid the hazards of Prohibition elections in the then
Dry-dominated South.

Born in Brooklyn in 1898, Mack Sands entered the wine business in 1932 as a partner of Joey Applebaum in Geffen Industries, a small Long Island City winery which turned out millions of gallons during the early years following Repeal. Many of today's Federal wine regulations are said to have been aimed at reducing Geffen Industries' copious output from relatively few tons of fresh grapes. After Applebaum retired wealthy in 1945, Sands established a winery at Canandaigua, New York, where Garrett had had one of his many plants. Then, leaving his son Marvin in charge at Canandaigua, Mack Sands moved to Virginia to open the Richard's winery, which he named for his infant grandson. In 1956, the Sandses bought the Mother Vineyard Winery at Manteo, North Carolina, moved it to Petersburg, and adopted the Mother Vineyard name for their Scuppernong wine. Later they added the Tenner Brothers vineyard and winery at Patrick, South Carolina. Now, with their wineries in three eastern states and the Bisceglia winery in California acquired in 1976, the Sandses have become the biggest vintners in the East. Their sweet pink Labrusca-flavored (20 percent) Richard's Wild Irish Rose, made at Canandaigua, is the largest-selling wine of its kind.

But for Mack Sands to become the successor to Garrett, one thing remained: to recover the Virginia Dare name. Following the Captain's death in 1940, Garrett & Company had moved to Cucamonga in California, then twice had been merged with California wineries. Ownership of the Virginia Dare brand meanwhile had passed to the Guild Wine Company of Lodi, California. The Sandses finally contracted with the Guild Company for a franchise to use the name. In 1967, Virginia Dare wines came back on the market. But only the white Virginia Dare has the Scuppernong flavor. The Sandses use the same Virginia Dare brand name on a "complete line" of generic, Labrusca, and blackberry wine types, all bottled at Canandaigua.

The three other large Virginia wineries have made mainly fruit and berry wines, but Laird & Company's Virginia Wine Cellar at North Garden, which traces its founding back to 1780, also makes a "Sly Fox" brand of Labrusca grape wine.

• 3 •

In the early 1970s the wine revolution reached old Virginia. Scores of new vineyards were planted by oenothusiasts who planned their own château wineries, encouraged by a Virginia law that favors small winegrowers who sell their wines at their wineries. Landowners in the rolling hills of the Piedmont envisioned wine grapes as profitable new farm crop that could save their estates from the wave of urbanization approaching from Washington, an hour's drive away.

The first new Virginia plantings were of the French-American hybrid grapes popularized by Philip Wagner across the Potomac in Maryland. Then came Dr. Konstantin Frank from New York State, who damns the hybrids and advocates planting the Old World's Vinifera grapes instead. At Dr. Frank's urging, retired State Department press attaché Robert de Treville Lawrence in 1971 planted three fourths of an acre with Vinifera on his Highbury estate near The Plains in Fauquier County. Three years later, with his first thirty-five-gallon vintage of Vinifera wines, Lawrence founded the Vinifera Wine Growers Association and with its journal launched an ardent campaign to develop a commercial Vinifera wine industry in Virginia. The campaign is succeeding, except that most of the new Virginia wineries prefer to grow the French hybrids rather than the Vinifera types.

Guided by Dr. Frank, the Mellon family of Pittsburgh added an experimental Vinifera vineyard to their 1,800-acre Kinloch Farm northeast of The Plains. Elizabeth Furness planted fifteen acres with Vinifera on her 500-acre livestock farm south of Middleburg, bought winemaking equipment from France, and converted her fifty-cow dairy barn into the future Piedmont Vineyard Winery for her grandson, William Worrall. Ignoring Lawrence's Vinifera campaign, patent lawyer W. Brown Morton commissioned his daughter Lucie to plant a French-hybrid vineyard on Morland, his Potomac shore estate south of Washington. Lucie, who holds a degree in viticulture from Montpellier in France, has become a viticultural consultant and also teaches home winemaking to those who buy her father's grapes.

The first three château wineries built in Virginia in generations opened for business in 1976. First to offer its French-hybrid wines for sale was airline pilot Charles Raney's Farfelu Vineyard, which overlooks the Rappahannock River near Flint Hill in Rappahannock County. Second, by a month, was Archie M. and Josephine Smith's Meredyth Vineyard on Route 628 five miles south of Middleburg on the west side of the Bull Run Mountains. The Smiths began planting their twenty-seven acres of hybrids in 1972 and with Richard Vine as their consultant, turned an ancient stable into a modern ten-thousand-gallon winery. In 1977, their son Dr. Archie III, a philosophy instructor at Oxford University, returned from

England with his bride Suzanne to help his parents carry it on. He gave up philosophy for winegrowing, he says, because of the favorable public reception for Meredyth wines. The third new Virginia winery is on investment banker Albert C. Weed's La Abra (The Cove) Farm in the Blue Ridge foothills of Nelson County, three miles northeast of Lovingston. Weed's first vintage in 1976 was of apple wine.

At Barboursville in Orange County, twenty miles north of Charlottesville, is the most ambitious winegrowing project in Virginia, based on Vinifera. On a seven-hundred-acre Jefferson-era estate, vineyardist Gabrielle Rausse from the Zonin winery near Vicenza in northern Italy planted in 1976 the first five acres of what London financier Jonathan Todhunter and Gianni Zonin say will become a 250-acre Vinifera vineyard with a future winery. The initial planting was of Chardonnay, Riesling, Cabernet Sauvignon, and Merlot. In 1978, on Island View Farm near Culpeper in northern Virginia, viticulturist Joachim Hollerith began planting Riesling and Chardonnay for Dr. Gerhard W.R. Guth, a wealthy physician of Hamburg, Germany, who planned to build a winery there.

At a "blind" tasting reported by *Washington Post* writer William Rice, Farfelu and Meredyth Vineyards' estate-bottled 1975 Seyval Blanc, Meredyth's Villard Blanc and Rougeon Rosé, and Farfelu Dry Red were matched against five young wines from California, Maryland, and New York. A wine-wise group of tasters awarded the highest scores to the Maryland and California samples, the second highest to three of the Virginia wines, and the lowest score to a Labrusca-flavored wine from New York State.

The Norton grape, which first made Virginia wines famous, is not used by any of the new Virginia wineries.

• 4 •

West Virginia, too, once had its own wine industry, and since the Second World War there have been proposals to resurrect it as a means of relieving unemployment in chronically depressed Appalachia. Wine was made in the Kanawha River Valley near Charleston as early as 1826, when Nicholas Longworth was just beginning to plant Catawba along the Ohio River at Cincinnati. In that year, the Charleston *Western Courier* told of a dinner in the city at which toasts were drunk in a local wine of "excellent quality." Still to be seen in the hills behind Dunbar, near Charleston, are the vaulted stone cellars of the Friend Brothers' Winery, built into a hillside that was lined with hundreds of acres of vines long before the Civil War. Scarcity of labor during the war forced the Dunbar winery to close about 1864. The report of the commissioner of agriculture to President Lincoln for the year 1863 described vineyards and wineries extending along the river as far north as Wheeling. It mentions one vineyard on Zane's Island that produced 500 gallons to the acre. The West Virginia wine industry staged a comeback after the Civil War, and eleven counties were still reporting wine production as late as 1880.

In 1966 there was a proposal to plant wine grapes again in the Kanawha River Valley. It was to be part of an Office of Economic Opportunity program, similar to Captain Garrett's Rural Resettlement project in the South thirty years earlier. West Virginia agricultural economists vetoed the proposal because there appeared to be little demand for wine in the state. Perhaps it will be revived now, because wine consumption in West Virginia has since increased by 45 percent. Also, recent tests show that vineyards can be planted successfully on the state's extensive areas of strip-mined coal land. But the idea of winegrowing in West Virginia remains unattractive because the sale of wine is still restricted to stores owned by the state monopoly system. A bill to allow table wine sale in food stores passed the legislature in 1972 but was killed by a governor's veto.

• 5 •

In Maryland, the seventeenth-century attempts to grow Old World wine grapes differed little from those in Virginia. Lord Baltimore, who is credited in many books with planting a three-hundred acre vineyard on St. Mary's River in 1662, did establish "The Vineyard" land grant, but no vines were ever planted there. Recent research by Dr. John R. McGrew in Maryland discloses that Lord Baltimore's vines were brought from Europe but that they died before they reached the site. All of the early Maryland wines were made from wild grapes, says Dr. McGrew, until about 1756 when Colonel Benjamin Tasker, Jr., planted two acres with the Alexander grape at his estate, Belair (now a Levittown), in Prince George's County, and made his first "burgundy" three years later.

Winegrowing evidently then became popular, for the state legislature in 1828 incorporated a Maryland Society for Promoting the Culture of the Vine, empowering it to establish vineyards and to produce wine "for the purpose of introducing into the State of Maryland, and into our country generally, the extensive cultivation of the vine."

A Maryland resident of this period, Major John Adlum, gave America the Catawba grape. Adlum, a soldier of the Revolution, a judge, and a surveyor, settled after the war on Pierce's Mill Road, near Georgetown, and for many years experimented in winegrowing and other horticultural research. His estate of 200 acres, which he named "The Vineyard," is now a part of Rock Creek Park in Washington, D.C. In 1823, Adlum wrote *A Memoir on the Cultivation of the Vine in America and the Best Mode of Making Wine,* the first book on winegrowing to be published in this country. In it he relates his unsuccessful attempts to grow foreign vines and his subsequent success in making acceptable wines from indigenous grapes.

Adlum found the Catawba growing beside an inn operated by a Mrs. Scholl at Clarksburg in Montgomery County, Maryland. Mrs. Scholl's father appears to have acquired the grape directly from North Carolina, where it is said to have been found growing wild in 1802. One version credits a Senator Davy with bringing the vines to his friends in Maryland as gifts for their gardens. Adlum took cuttings from Mrs. Scholl's vines and planted them in his vineyard. The wine he made from their grapes was better than any he had made before. He first named the wine "Tokay" and sent samples to all the members of Congress. He also sent Thomas Jefferson a sample with one of his red wines. A letter from Jefferson to Adlum on April 11, 1823, reads:

I received the two bottles of wine you were so kind as to send me. The first, called Tokay, is a truly fine wine, of high flavor, and, as you assure me, there was not a drop of brandy in it; I may say it is a wine of good body of its own. The second bottle, a red wine, I tried when I had good judges at the table. We agreed it was a wine one might always drink with satisfaction, but of no particular excellence.

Adlum renamed the grape Catawba, which is evidence that he was aware of its origin on that river in North Carolina. He supplied cuttings to Nicholas Longworth, who planted them at Cincinnati and made the grape and its wine world famous. Longworth later offered a reward of five hundred dollars to anyone who could find a better native variety than the Catawba. A quarter-century later he wrote that "its equal has not yet been found." Adlum said, in a letter to Longworth, that

In bringing this grape into public notice, I have rendered my country a greater service than I would have done, had I paid off the National Debt.

• 6 •

Because in the mid-1930s a home winemaker in Baltimore disliked the Labrusca flavor of a wine he made from native grapes, the course of winegrowing in much of North America has been altered significantly during the past few decades. Failing to grow in Maryland the Vinifera grapes he preferred, this amateur introduced to this country the French-American hybrid varieties that are now planted extensively for winemaking in most states east of the Rockies and in both eastern and western Canada.

The amateur was Philip Marshall Wagner, an editorial writer for the Baltimore *Evening Sun*. Born in 1904 at New Haven, he grew up in Ann Arbor, Michigan, where his father was a professor of Romance languages at the university. His parents drank wine with their meals at home, and Philip developed the taste of a connoisseur. When he joined the *Sun* in 1930, the eleventh year of Prohibition, his liking for wine led him to make it at home in partnership with a next-door neighbor. Finding it easier to make bad wine than good, he began reading French texts on viniculture. Soon he had written a text in English, *American Wines and How to Make Them*, as a service to fellow amateurs.

Wagner had begun by buying grapes from California to make his wine, but when Prohibition was ending in 1933, his favorite varieties, Zinfandel and Carignane, were not being shipped to the East; the reopened wineries were using them in California. He then made a vintage out of the eastern Delaware grape, but being accustomed only to Vinifera wines, he had no liking for its Labrusca taste. Wondering what else he could use to make his wine, he happened to read about the hybrid vines that were being grown in France. He ordered a supply from Bordeaux, found others already in some American collections, and planted at Baltimore all he could get. By 1936, Wagner had made some wines from the hybrids that convinced him it was possible to grow, east of the Rocky Mountains, "wines that taste like wine."

He began writing articles and revised his book to tell others about the French hybrids. Then, people came asking to buy vines from him, and he soon found himself in the nursery business.

Philip and Jocelyn Wagner at their little Boordy Vineyard winery at Riderwood, a suburb of Baltimore.

More vines planted meant more grapes harvested from his vineyard—more than enough grapes to make the two hundred gallons per year the Government permits a householder to produce free of tax. So the Wagners, Philip and his wife Jocelyn, built a winery. Then, when the winery, bonded in 1945, was full, the quantity of wine was more than they could drink, and the excess had to be sold. Wagner made his first sales to Baltimore restaurants, delivering the wines himself on the way to his office each morning. When he was too busy, having by then become editor of both the *Sun* papers, Jocelyn made the deliveries; and both Wagners came to know the tradesmen's entrances of most hotels, restaurants, and clubs in Baltimore.

It was not long before connoisseurs in New York and Washington learned that entirely new kinds of American wines were being made in Maryland. More orders for wine than the Wagners could fill came from stores and hotels throughout the East. Making only eight thousand gallons per year, they could have sold twenty times as much. But they decided not to try, and they turned over their wine sales to a Washington wholesaler.

"Boordy Vineyard, J. & P. Wagner, Props." consists of a little wood-and-stucco, French-type winery and seven hillside acres beside the Wagners' colonial farmhouse in Riderwood, one of Baltimore's more exclusive northern suburbs. Boordy Vineyard is difficult for a stranger to find, which is just as well, because visitors are received by appointment only. What does "Boordy" mean? "Nothing," reply the Wagners, "except a small Maryland vineyard and its delightful products."

The Wagners' wines are four, each vintage-labeled: the

regular white, which is fresh and delicate; another white named Boordyblümchen, made from some of the newer French hybrids; the rosé, soft and fruity; and the red, in which Philip finds a resemblance to some of the Loire Valley reds of France. He does not regard any of the Boordy Vineyard wines as great, because they usually are best when drunk young. However, I have tasted at the winery some vintages that had developed an appreciable bouquet after several years of age in the bottle.

Tall and lanky, with a mop of wavy graying hair, Philip Wagner looks more like an editor or a New England college professor than a grape farmer and winemaker. He is noted as a taster, has made many trips to Europe, and has served twice on wine juries in California. In tasting Boordy wines, however, Philip defers to *la vigneronne*, Jocelyn, who, he says, has a palate "as accurate as a barometer." In 1964 he retired from the *Sun* to devote most of his time to the vineyard, but has continued to write a syndicated twice-a-week newspaper column on public affairs. He also keeps updating his books; in 1976 he completely rewrote his forty-year-old classic, then in its fifth edition, and gave it a new title, *Grapes into Wine*. The output of the Boordy nursery, enlarged by planting on neighbors' lands, is completely sold out a year before the vines are ready. The Wagners have supplied vines to all of the principal eastern and midwestern wineries, to the multiplying numbers of amateur growers in every state except Hawaii, and to research stations in several states and in Guatemala, Venezuela, and the Congo.

In 1968, the Wagners and little Boordy Vineyard suddenly became part of the grape and wine industries of two much more important winegrowing states—New York and Washington—through a "pooling of resources" with the big Seneca Foods Corporation of Dundee, Westfield, and Williamson, New York, and of Prosser, Washington. But at Riderwood, Boordy Vineyard and its wines remain unchanged, and—between their flights in the Seneca plane to supervise its wine operations in other states—the colonial farmhouse beside the cellar is still the Wagners' home.

• 7 •

Wagner and his hybrids have made possible most of the small winegrowing ventures that have started up in several eastern states since the Second World War. Several of these are in Maryland. It was also Wagner who convinced officials of his state to set its $50-per-year license fee for farmers who produce wine from Maryland-grown grapes. The figure is reasonable, compared to the exorbitant license fees charged in other states, but the Maryland law has a grievous flaw. It doesn't allow the Maryland winery to sell its wine except to licensed distributors and retailers. Few small wineries can operate profitably unless they can sell their output directly to consumers at the vineyards. Bills to allow wine to be sold at Maryland wineries, strongly opposed by liquor retailers, were defeated three times in five years. Because an amendment now allows the sale of a single bottle, some of the wineries have permitted tasting and cellar tours.

Maryland's next winegrowing venture after the Wagners' was the Cároli Vineyard, started in the 1950s by Dr. Charles Southward Singleton, professor of humanistic studies at Johns Hopkins University. At New Windsor in Carroll County, Dr. Singleton planted French hybrid grapes to make wine for his own consumption, but thinking its quality would improve if made in larger lots, he planted more vines and bonded his barn as a winery. Then he decided to replant his vineyard with Vinifera, closed his winery, and returned to being a home winemaker.

Another Johns Hopkins savant started the state's third winery, the Montbray Wine Cellars, in 1966. It is near Westminster in Silver Run Valley, a quiet, idyllic depression in the undulating hills ten miles north of Westminster, only two miles from the Pennsylvania border. Dr. G. Hamilton Mowbray, a researcher in psychology, discovered the fascination of wine while studying for his doctorate at Cambridge University in England. Returning to Maryland to do research in the sensory processes at the University's world-famed Applied Physics Laboratory, he began growing hybrids in collaboration with Dr. Singleton. But a visit to Hammondsport, New York, in 1958 convinced Dr. Mowbray that Konstantin Frank is right about Vinifera for the East and that the Old World grapes, if given the proper rootstocks and spray-protection from vine pests, should grow as well in Maryland as Wagner's French hybrids do. As soon as he could get vines, he planted Chardonnay, White Riesling, Pinot Noir, and Muscat Ottonel. They survived a series of winter freezes and thrived so well that he sold his home, because there was not enough land, bought a hundred-acre tract at Silver Run, moved his vines there, and planted additional Chardonnay and Riesling, to which he since has added Cabernet Sauvignon. His 7,000-gallon winery (named for a Norman ancestor) is in an old German-style barn, which he has insulated, and on which he has painted a Pennsylvania

Dutch hex sign to keep away hailstorms and floods ("It works," says Mowbray; "we've had neither").

His first wines, introduced in 1968, were of hybrids (Seyve-Villard White and Ravat Red), but Mowbray made history three years later by bottling Maryland's first-ever, commercially-grown Vinifera wines, a White Riesling and a Chardonnay. Although hybrid vines still occupy two thirds of his twenty-acre vineyard and require only half as much care as his Vinifera, Mowbray says: "If I were starting anew here I'd plant mostly Vinifera, plus enough Seyval Blanc and Maréchal Foch to supply the good but more reasonably-priced table wines that those hybrid varieties provide."

Montbray is a family operation. Dr. Mowbray is the wine-maker, but his wife Phyllis does the labeling, keeps the books and helps in the vineyard, and son John comes from New York to help with the vintage. Two nights a week Dr. Mowbray teaches classes in winemaking and wine appreciation, one night at the University of Maryland, the next at a community college in Washington. Montbray wines, all aged in oak, are distinctive and flavorful. The Maryland sample that outscored nine wines from California, Virginia, and New York in the Washington "blind" tasting mentioned on an earlier page was the Montbray 1974 Seyve-Villard.

A record October freeze in 1974 enabled Dr. Mowbray to make America's first counterpart of Germany's rare *Eisweins*. Grapes left unpicked in Rhineland vineyards freeze on the vines in some winters and are pressed while frozen to make these fragrant sweet nectars. But the Mowbrays' hundred bottles of Maryland Ice Wine were still unsold when I last inquired, because the Government bureau which approves wine labels could not yet decide on what such an American wine could be labeled.

Maryland now has a total of seven wineries. Near Triadelphia Lake in Montgomery County, twenty miles from Washington, orthodontist Dr. Thomas Provenza and his wife Barbara bonded their attractive Provenza Vineyard winery in 1974 and crushed the French hybrid grapes from their hillside vineyard nearby. The Provenzas, long-time home winemakers, got the idea of going commercial from discussions with fellow members of the American Wine Society's Maryland chapter after planting their first patch of vines in 1970. Now they have fifteen producing acres, tended by university horticulture students Lee and John Paul. The main Provenza wines are Batojolo red and white, an acronym from Barbara and their old home-winemaking friends Joe and Lois Price.

In eastern Frederick County, energy research analyst John (Jack) Aellen (cq), his wife Lucille, and their six children in 1973 began planting two acres of French hybrid grapes on their Berrywine Plantation Livestock farm. Four years later they bonded part of their cow barn and made their first wine from Maryland, Virginia, and Pennsylvania grapes. Aellen decided on winegrowing as an avocation because he says grapes are a good crop for a blind man. He was virtually blinded by a chemical explosion in 1957, but he can distinguish between light and dark. The Aellens' winery is six miles northwest of Mount Airy on Glisans Mill Road.

Some twenty miles west of the Aellens, on Church Hill Road near Myersville, pharmacist W. Bret Byrd and his school teacher wife Sharon began planting their fifteen-acre vineyard of Vinifera vines in 1972. They next built a 10,000-gallon concrete block winery into a hillside, with a tennis court on the roof. Their wines are sold under two names—Byrd for varietally labeled types such as Chardonnay, and the name of their estate, Church Hill Manor, for those labeled simply "table wine." Besides their winery venture, they are in the nursery business, selling vines that Byrd grafts to rootstocks in their garage.

On Stone Road near Westminster is the Bon Spuronza winery, bonded in 1976. A year later, Pentagon propulsion engineer Robert Ziem and his wife Ruth opened Maryland's seventh winery at the south end of Downsville, eight miles south of Hagerstown. Their two-acre vineyard of French hybrids, Dutchess, and Delaware is already being doubled in size.

Several more Maryland vineyards are noncommercial, including urban planner Robert Dickmann's Trigonne Vineyard, principally of hybrids, on the outskirts of Silver Spring. At Carrollton, southwest of Westminster, lawyer Charles Carroll has planted three acres of hybrids and Vinifera on the same hillside of pre-Revolution Doughoregan Manor where a namesake ancestor grew the Alexander grape eight generations ago. John Ripley and Peter Black have five acres of hybrids on their Cedar Point Vineyard near Maryland's eastern shore. They and Carroll sell their grapes to Philip and Jocelyn Wagner to make Boordy Vineyard wines.

After three centuries, Lord Baltimore's vision of Maryland vineyards growing wines that resemble those of Europe is at last being realized.

• 8 •

New Jersey, despite its small size, is the ninth state in the nation in volume of wine production. Although much of the wine is made from grapes grown elsewhere, the Garden State has several historic and otherwise interesting vineyards and wineries that are well worth visiting, especially those which offer tasting and cellar tours.

One is the House of Renault, with its half-million-gallon winery and hundred-plus acres of vineyard on Bremen Avenue near Egg Harbor City, a southern New Jersey town that got its name from the nests of sea birds found by early Swedish fishermen along the nearby inlets from the sea. The firm of L. N. Renault & Sons has grown grapes and made wine here for more than a century. Louis Nicholas Renault came to the United States from France before the Civil War to represent the ancient champagne house of the Duke of Montebello at Rheims. Deciding to settle and make champagne in this country, he studied locations in both East and West, and was most impressed with the vineyards already thriving around Egg Harbor in Atlantic County. In 1864, he bought land for the present Renault vineyard, and by 1870 had introduced his New Jersey Champagne.

Renault and neighboring wineries won prizes for their wines at the Centennial Exposition at Philadelphia in 1876, and Egg Harbor soon became known as "the wine city." During the seventies and eighties, leading citizens and officials of Philadelphia came each year to the wine-tasting receptions held for them by the Egg Harbor vintners.

Louis Renault died in 1913 at the age of ninety-one and was succeeded by his son Felix. In 1919, John D'Agostino bought the company and operated it under a government permit through the fourteen years of Prohibition. His chief product was Renault Wine Tonic, which had an alcoholic content of 22 percent and was sold in virtually every drugstore in the nation. After Repeal, he acquired two old California wineries, Montebello at St. Helena and St. George at Fresno, and brought their wines in tank cars to Egg Harbor City for blending and bottling. His Charmat-process champagnes, mostly blends of California with New Jersey Labrusca wine, were sold nationwide. They were advertised by giant images of Renault bottles, which for many years lined highway roadsides in Massachusetts, Florida, and California.

When D'Agostino was killed in a car crash in 1948, his sister Maria took charge of Renault. Having a talent for design, Miss D'Agostino, an auburn-haired, five-foot-tall dynamo, transformed the old winery into a showplace. She built a château-style hospitality house for visitors, hundreds of whom now come daily from the resorts and beaches of Atlantic City, which is only eighteen miles away. In 1966, she added a museum that displays only one item—wineglasses. These are not ordinary glasses. On thirty-five trips to Europe, Miss D'Agostino assembled hundreds of masterpieces of wineglass art, made for kings, queens, and merchant princes since the Middle Ages. But decoration and glass-collecting were only her avocations, for her principal interest was in the winery. It is also her home; although the ownership of Renault has changed three times since 1970, Maria still keeps her apartment upstairs in one of the winery buildings.

Joseph P. Milza, publisher of the Toms River, N.J., *Daily Observer,* now owns the vineyards and winery and has plans to capitalize in the future on Renault's record of uninterrupted winegrowing in New Jersey during the past hundred-plus years.

The early-day Egg Harbor winegrowers, such as Renault and Hiram Dewey & Sons, grew a grape named Noah, which originated at Nauvoo in Illinois but thrived best in the mild climate and sandy, chalky soils of southern New Jersey. The Noah imparted a characteristic dry, tart, faintly foxy flavor to their white wines that no other eastern wine district could match. When the phylloxera aphid was devastating the vineyards of Europe in the 1870s, Noah vines were imported from America and planted extensively in France, and Noah is one of the few American grape varieties still grown there to make wine. In 1972, the Renault winery did something it probably should have done a century ago. It introduced a semi-dry wine advertised as "new, dry and different," labeled "New Jersey State Noah White Varietal Dinner Wine."

Another New Jersey winery worth visiting for its tour and tasting is the 100,000-gallon Gross Highland cellar at Absecon, just north of Atlantic City. It makes champagnes and red and white table wines, principally of grapes from its own vineyard of eighty acres. The best Gross wine, to my taste, is its red Maréchal Foch. Most of the others, though expertly made by enologist Edward Moulton, have in varying degrees the Labrusca taste from such varieties as Noah, Dutchess, Niagara, and Ives. The late John Gross, a German winemaker from Hungary, opened this winery in 1934. It is now headed by his grandson Bernard F. (Skip) D'Arcy.

Atlantic County has three more wineries: the Tomasello Winery on White Horse Pike at Hammonton, with a seventy-acre vineyard that dates from 1888; the John Schuster &

Son cellar, founded at Egg Harbor City in 1868; and Savo Balic's winery on Route 40 at Mays Landing, which he opened in 1974. Urban sprawl has displaced the dozens of other vineyards that once flourished in this coastal part of the Garden State.

There are three small wineries in west-central New Jersey. The Jacob Lee cellar still makes old-fashioned Labrusca-type table wines from the grapes that grow across Route 130 at Bordentown, and there is Matthew Antuzzi's cellar on the Bridgeboro-Moorestown Road south of Delran. Off Route 519 at the crossroads village of Kingwood in rural Hunterdon County is the B. & B. Vineyard. The name represents John Boyd and Robert Bodine, onetime roommates at the University of Pennsylvania, who got the idea of starting a winery when Boyd's wife Dolores made him a gift of a home-winemaking kit. Boyd now makes the wine and Dolores runs a cheese shop in the cellar; Bodine has gone back to stockbrokering.

• 9 •

In Cumberland County, New Jersey, there is a town named Vineland—but for its vineyards, not for its wines. It was founded as a bone-dry community in the early 1860s by a real estate developer named Charles K. Landis. To Vineland there came in 1868 a man who fanatically hated wine, a dentist named Thomas B. Welch. It was here that Welch started the fresh grape juice industry, which led to the planting of Concord grapes across the United States—and a century later to the development of the kosher type of wine.

Dr. Welch, the Communion steward of his Methodist church, happened to read of Louis Pasteur's studies of the fermentation of wine, published in France in 1866. This suggested to Welch a way to improve the decoction of raisins steeped in water which Prohibitionist ministers of the time used for Communion in place of wine. Experimenting in his kitchen at Vineland, he succeeded in sterilizing the sweet juice of New Jersey grapes, and by 1870 had begun a small business with his son Charles, also a dentist, selling "Dr. Welch's Unfermented Wine" for church use. Later, when sales of the product spread from churches to drugstores and groceries, the name was changed to "Dr. Welch's Grape Juice."

In the '80s and '90s, grape rot attacked many New Jersey vineyards, and the Welch Company, needing more grapes, moved in 1896 to a new vineyard area at Watkins Glen in the Finger Lakes District of New York. A year later, the Doctors

Welch Foods, Inc.

Dr. Thomas Bramwell Welch, the wine-hating New Jersey dentist who founded the grape-juice industry, which led to the planting of Concord grapes across North America and a century later to the development of the kosher type of American wine.

Welch built a processing plant at Westfield in the Chautauqua Grape Belt. During the next half century, a chain of Welch plants, which are now owned by the National Grape Co-operative (also called Welch Foods), spread to Pennsylvania, Michigan, Arkansas, and to the State of Washington.

What the wine-hating Doctors Welch never knew, because they died in 1903 and 1926, was that a half-century after the father's death the Welch Grape Juice Company would start making a fermented Welch wine.

• 10 •

How can little New Jersey, with less than a thousand acres of vineyards, produce almost 800,000 gallons of wine annually? The answer is partly that some New Jersey wine is from other fruits, apples in particular. Since 1851, except during Prohibition, the oldest distiller in this country has been operating the old-fashioned Laird and Company applejack distillery at Scobeyville in Monmouth County. The firm was founded here in 1780 and has operated additional plants at North Garden, Virginia, and Lyons, New York, making apple wine and the distilled liquor that once was called "New Jersey lightning." Another answer is in the 400,000-gallon Tribuno winery at Lodi near Hackensack, where the well-known Tribuno dry, sweet, and "half-and-half" vermouths are made from neutral California wines with the addition of secret formulas of herbs, flowers, and roots.

Yet New Jersey's Director of Agriculture, Philip Alampi, says there are areas in the agricultural southern half of the state that could be profitably planted to wine grapes. Harold Applegate, who has a home vineyard of Vinifera at Cranbury, four miles east of Princeton, says rising prices of land and corresponding tax increases are driving farmers off the land in that area. But the biggest area of idle land in the entire New York metropolitan complex is located in southern New Jersey. It is the Pine Barrens, 620 desolate square miles of pine and scrub oak, inhabited principally by deer, foxes, rabbits, and quail, and as yet untouched by urbanization. Although the Pine Barren soils are considered too thin and sandy for farming, a part of the Renault vineyard is at the southern edge of the Barrens and produces healthy grape crops. Neither Rutgers, the State University, nor its Cooperative Extension Service has yet conducted any grape-growing tests in New Jersey, as their counterparts are beginning to do in many other states.

• 11 •

Pennsylvania, where commercial winegrowing began, now ranks fifth in the nation in grape production (after California, New York, Washington, and Michigan), harvesting 54,000 tons yearly from more than 11,000 acres of vineyards. But until now, only a small fraction of this tonnage has been produced for wine. Most of the grapes have been Concords, grown for grape juice. Since the repeal of Prohibition, Pennsylvania has supplied some of its grapes to wineries in neighboring states, but until 1963 produced no wine of its own.

Now, because a new Pennsylvania law encourages winegrowing, scores of small vineyards have been planted in the northwestern and southeastern parts of the state. There now are seventeen Pennsylvania wineries, and more are being planned.

The Keystone State has a strange wine history. William Penn attempted to establish a Pennsylvania wine industry, bringing French and Spanish vines to Philadelphia in 1683. "The consequence," he predicted, "will be as good as any European countries of the same latitude do yield." Penn's attempt to start a vineyard failed, but the Penn Colony's interpreter, Conrad Weiser, succeeded. Weiser's vineyard, near Womelsdorf in the Tulpehocken Valley, where his home is now a state park, regularly supplied Riesling vines to the governor of Virginia during the 1750s, according to his diaries.

As mentioned earlier, it was near Philadelphia that the first domesticated native wine grape was discovered by James Alexander before the Revolution.

In 1793, a Frenchman, Pierre Legaux, founded the Pennsylvania Vine Company to cultivate European grapes and produce wine at Spring Mill, on the north bank of the Schuylkill near the present Philadelphia suburb of Conshohocken. Alexander's was the only grape that survived. Legaux claimed it was one of the Vinifera varieties he had imported from the Cape of Good Hope, and he named it the Cape of Constantia. Others called it the Cape, Black Madeira, Schuylkill Muscadell, and eventually the Alexander. From the Spring Mill Vineyard, the Alexander spread throughout Pennsylvania, and to Ohio, Virginia, Kentucky, and Indiana during the early part of the nineteenth century. Legaux's company did not prosper, however. Its vineyard and winery were abandoned several years before his death in 1827.

Meanwhile, Thomas Eichelberger from Germany planted Alexander grapes about 1818 between York and the Susquehanna River, and York became the center of early viticulture in Pennsylvania. There also were vineyards along the Schuylkill from Reading to the Germantown section of Philadelphia, where in 1830 Edward H. Bonsall had a winery and a vineyard of Alexander, Isabella, and Catawba.

But the Pittsburgh area, west of the Alleghenies, soon outdistanced the eastern part of the state in wine production. Grape planting began there as early as 1793, when Colonel George Morgan, a friend of Benjamin Franklin, started a vineyard at Morganza, Washington County. It was "Father" George Rapp, the leader of the communistic theocracy known as the Harmonie Society, who made the Pittsburgh district known for its wines. Rapp, the son of a grape grower of Württemberg, came to Pennsylvania in 1803, seeking land on which to settle his followers. He bought 5,000 acres on Connoquenessing Creek in Butler County, brought two hundred families of Rappists in three shiploads from Germany in 1804, and built the town of Harmony. The colonists planted ten acres of Old World grapevines and also produced silk, but because the vines died, they abandoned the place in 1814 and established New Harmony in the Wabash Valley of Indiana.

In 1824, the Harmonists returned to the Pittsburgh area, and on 3,000 acres along the Ohio River, eighteen miles north of the city, they built another town and named it Economy. Here they again planted vineyards, apparently of native grapes, and established several industries, including a winery and a distillery. Economy became famous for its wines, woolens, and other products. The colony declined after Rapp's death in 1847, but its industries, including winegrowing, continued for more than fifty years.

Evidently more vineyards were planted in the vicinity, because in the Patent Office report for 1855, Victor Scriba of Pittsburgh described forty to fifty acres of vines, principally Catawba, growing on hillsides facing the Allegheny, Monongahela, and Ohio Rivers. He wrote that "the wine made from the Catawba, as well as from the Isabella grapes, is good and praiseworthy, and sells from one to two dollars a gallon."

In 1880, when the special census of United States wine production was made, Allegheny County led the state in wine production with 45,000 gallons, compared to a total of 13,000 gallons made in Adams, Bucks, Cumberland, Lancaster, and Northumberland Counties in southeastern Pennsylvania.

Winemaking around Pittsburgh continued at least until 1900. *The American Wine Press and Mineral Water News,* in its issue for November of that year, refers to the claret, Riesling, and Catawba wine still being produced by the Economy Wine Vaults.

But one of "Father" Rapp's teachings, in addition to sobriety and simple living, was celibacy; and by 1905 few of the Harmonists remained, victims to their own virtue; and the Society was dissolved. In 1912, Economy was renamed Ambridge. Two city blocks of the old Economy buildings have been preserved by the state at Ambridge, including dwellings, shops, granary, Rapp's thirty-five-room Great House, and the Music Hall, in the cellar of which are the colony's wine storage vaults. Wine is still made in the Economy vaults, but not for sale. Daniel Reibel, in charge of the cellar, picks a bushel of grapes each autumn from the arbor beside the building. He invites a few young visitors to wash their feet and to tread on the fruit, and then ferments another vintage of Economy wine.

A third Pennsylvania vineyard district was established in the middle of the last century in Erie County, along the shore of Lake Erie. At North East, a town strangely named because it is in the far northwestern corner of the state, the South Shore Wine Company began making wine in 1863 from Isabella and Catawba grapes. The winery building, with its cavernous cellars, still stands and houses the South Shore Inn restaurant. Thirty years later, Concord grapes had replaced wine varieties in the district because Americans were learning to drink bottled grape juice, which had been introduced to the public by Dr. Charles Welch at the 1893 Chicago World's Fair. In 1900 the Welch Company established at North East the world's biggest

grape juice plant. Although a few Erie County wineries continued operating until Prohibition in 1920, Concord grapes have
been the county's chief farm crop ever since.

• 13 •

When Prohibition was repealed in 1933, scores of wineries
reopened in New York, New Jersey, and Ohio, but not in
Pennsylvania. For the Keystone State had adopted a beverage
control system purposely designed to discourage the purchase
of liquor or wine. It created a gigantic state liquor monopoly,
the Pennsylvania Liquor Control Board, which operates the
some seven hundred liquor stores in the state.

Nobody but an amateur would have wanted to start a winery
under this system, for wine could only be sold through the
state-operated stores. But there was one such amateur. Philadelphia businessman Melvin S. Gordon, while vacationing in
Europe in the mid-1950s, had toured vineyards and become
interested in fine wines. On his return home he began reading
books about grapes and started making wine in his kitchen. He
then bought a farm at Birchrunville, a crossroads in Chester
County eight miles west of Valley Forge, added a tractor,
several barrels, a grape crusher, and a hand-bottling machine,
and planted some French hybrid vines he got from Philip
Wagner at Baltimore. His vines produced well, and in 1963 he
bonded the tiny Conestoga Vineyard winery, the first to be
established in Pennsylvania in this century. When his 1964
vintage was ready, he offered it to the Liquor Control Board. He
was waiting for the Board to buy it when I paid him a visit in
1966. I tasted wines from several of his barrels. A white, made
of Seibel 4986 (a variety now called Rayon d'Or), had a fresh,
fruity flavor reminiscent of Sylvaner and was the best wine
made of a French hybrid that I sampled during the entire trip.
Gordon, however, preferred his red, a full-flavored blend of
several hybrids in which the Maréchal Foch variety predominated. But Gordon couldn't serve me any of his wines at lunch. In
order to drink his own wine, he would have had to buy it at a
state store.

A year later, the Liquor Board started selling Gordon's wines.
Word that wines were actually being grown in Pennsylvania
reached the state's leading restaurateurs, and some of them
placed orders for them with the Board. Conestoga wines were
soon added to the wine lists of famed Coventry Forge Inn,
Original Bookbinders, Kimberton Country House, and a score
of other three-star establishments.

• 14 •

Meanwhile, other amateur winemakers far north in Erie County had a better idea. One was Douglas P. Moorhead, who while a soldier stationed in Germany in 1957 had visited vineyards on the Rhine and tasted wines of the White (Johannisberg) Riesling grape. A graduate in pomology from Pennsylvania State University and the son of an Erie County Concord grower, Moorhead resolved that when he returned to America, he would plant the true Riesling in his family's vineyard at Moorheadville. He obtained vines of Riesling and other Vinifera from Dr. Konstantin Frank and also some French hybrids from Philip Wagner. He began making wines in the family cellar and discussed them with other amateur winemakers who often bought grapes from his father. One of these was William Konnerth of Erie, a former newspaper reporter and a true wine enthusiast. In 1960 Moorhead and Konnerth organized the Erie County Wine Club with fifteen fellow home winemakers. Before long they had a waiting list of others wanting to join. Because winemaking equipment for amateurs was difficult to buy, the two young men made joint purchases for the club. This soon became a business, which they named Presque Isle Wine Cellars to express their hope of someday starting a winery. The firm grew rapidly and now furnishes thousands of home winemakers throughout the country with grapes, juice, winemaking equipment and supplies, including a $1.25 booklet on winemaking by Konnerth that is one of the best you can buy.

Moorhead's Vinifera and hybrid plantings thrived in the meantime. He became convinced that Erie County, with its 194-day growing season, has the best climate for high-quality white table wines and champagnes in the East, equaled only by the Lake Erie Islands. Neighboring growers became interested and made trial plantings of both groups of wine grapes. A committee of growers was formed in 1967 to consider starting wineries in the county. State Secretary of Agriculture Leland H. Bull became interested and allocated state funds to Pennsylvania State University's experiment station at North East for a study of wine-grape growing.

The growers' committee found that for wineries to operate profitably, the Pennsylvania law would have to be changed, that farmer wineries should be permitted to sell their wines to the public and to restaurants without going through the Control

Board. In 1967, a bill was introduced in the legislature, seeking to permit Pennsylvania winegrowers to sell at their winery premises table wines of their own production from Pennsylvania grapes. The Liquor Control Board opposed the bill, insisting that only the state monopoly stores should be allowed to sell wine. Its powerful opposition kept the measure dormant for a year. But on the last day of the next legislative session, in August 1968, the farmers and their supporters succeeded in bringing the bill to a vote. It passed both houses, 171 to 13 and 36 to 9.

Within weeks of their victory, Erie County grape growers began building wineries to crush the 1969 vintage. North East soon became a mecca for wine lovers and tourists. On a five-mile stretch off US 20 and Route 5, three wineries now offer cellar tours and tasting daily (but no tasting on Sundays; Pennsylvania has not yet repealed its blue laws). First to open in 1969 was the Moorheads' 10,000-gallon Presque Isle winery at Moorheadville, three miles west of North East. It produces excellent French-hybrid and Vinifera wines, including Aligoté, Chardonnay, Gamay Beaujolais, and one of the two best oak-aged Cabernet Sauvignons I have thus far found in the East. The other fine Cabernet is grown nearby by Doug Moorhead's cousin John, who hopes to have his own winery someday. At Presque Isle you now are welcomed by Doug's wife and partner Marlene; Konnerth has retired.

Three miles northwest on Route 5 is the 150,000-gallon Penn-Shore winery, owned by a group of growers headed by George Luke, Blair McCord, and George Sceiford. Its tasting room offers fourteen wines ranging from pink and white Catawba to champagne and sparkling burgundy. Also on Route 5, just beyond the state university's field research station, is the Spanish-style Mazza Vineyard winery of 50,000 gallons, opened in 1974 by Joseph Mazza and his son Robert. Their Geisenheim-trained enologist Helmut Kranich makes vintage-dated Riesling, Traminer, Chardonnay, Pinot Gris, and Cabernet as well as several French-hybrid and native American wine types. The Mazzas' Vinifera grapes come from the nearby Lakehaven Vineyard of Dr. Salvatore Sellaro, an Erie anesthesiologist and wine connoisseur.

The Pennsylvania law allows "limited wineries" to produce up to 100,000 gallons per year from Pennsylvania-grown fruit. They may sell their table wines to restaurants and to the state monopoly store system as well as to consumers. Passage of the law in 1968 started Penn State University on a program of wine research and annual wine conferences to encourage the planting of wine grapes.

Excitement about the state's new wine industry started a wave of vineyard planting in southeastern Pennsylvania, where winegrowing had begun almost two centuries before. Too many vines were planted at first, creating an excess supply of grapes before new wineries could be built. The state now allows the wineries to open branch retail premises in the cities in order to sell more Pennsylvania wines. Penn-Shore has the first branch, called the South Mountain Winery, in downtown Philadelphia. Mazza Vineyards has a branch in Pittsburgh and is planning to open more.

By 1977, eight producing vineyards and wineries were offering cellar tours and tasting in six counties west and north of Philadelphia. The oldest, a good place to start a southeast wine tour, is the Conestoga Vineyard (mentioned earlier) on Flowing Springs Road in Birchrunville. Chemical engineer David Fondots and his wife Patricia bought the vineyard and winery from Mel Gordon in 1974. They have doubled its capacity to 12,000 gallons and have added a retail branch in St. Peter's Village near Pottstown. Across the Schuylkill River in Montgomery County, on Mill Road two miles northwest of Schwenksville, is the Wilmont winery, opened in 1976 by electrical engineer Attila Salamon and farmer Frank Wilmer on Wilmer's five-acre vineyard.

Bucks County, farther west, has two wineries. On Route 413 three miles south of Buckingham, newspaper ad manager Jerry Forest and his wife Kathy planted their ten-acre vineyard of French hybrids in 1966. Jerry is the winemaker and Kathy tends the vines, which she covers with tobacco netting in autumn to protect them from grape-stealing birds. A short distance north, on US 202 in the village of Soleburg, is the Bucks County Vineyards winery and wine museum, which realizes a dream of many years by Arthur Gerold, a New York theatrical costumer and wine buff. Housed in a converted antique barn, the museum displays color transparencies of Pennsylvania grapes, a collection of seventeenth-century wineglasses, and mannequins attired in early American costumes. Gerold's son Peter manages the winery and its four-acre vineyard, with California-trained wine instructor Robert Miltner as his consulting enologist.

On Route 143 two miles north of Lenhartsville in Berks County is the Dutch Country Wine Cellar, opened in 1976 by

Philadelphia businessman Gabriel J. Tenaglia on a twelve-acre vineyard managed by his son Mark.

The busiest and third oldest Pennsylvania winery is H. Peterman Wood's Pequea Valley (pronounced Peck-way) Vineyard cellar, which attracts some 60,000 visitors per year and sells them most of Pequa's white, red, and apple wines by the bottle and by the case. Directional signs on Route 272 guide you to the winery, which is eight miles southwest of Lancaster on the bank of Pequea Creek, a tributary of the Susquehanna. Lancaster is the heart of the Pennsylvania Dutch Country. Wood's seventeen acres of vines are mainly tended by Amish men, who still wear austere Old World costumes and drive little black buggies. The Amish also still make wine in their homes as they did in Germany. But the more numerous Mennonites in the area disapprove of the Pennsylvania wineries. The Mennonites, like the Amish, also made wine in Germany, but became stern teetotalers after they came to this country.

Also in Dutch Country is the Conoy Winery on Route One north of Bainbridge on the Susquehanna River. Retired Lancaster bridge builder J. Richard Nissley and his son John began planting vines on the Nissley cattle farm in 1972. Four years later they installed stainless steel winemaking equipment in a century-old stone farm building. Their enologist is Pennsylvania's first woman winemaker. Carmen Kanner won her degree in viticulture and enology at Pennsylvania State University in time to make the first Conoy wines in 1977, a faultless red of De Chaunac and an Aurora white.

Farther west, eight miles beyond Gettysburg, is Ronald Cooper's Adams County Winery, a mile northwest of Orrtanna on Peach Tree Road. Cooper, born in England where he became a home winemaker, has planted his three-acre vineyard mostly with Vinifera varieties. He thinks Gewürztraminer may prove the best grape for this part of Pennsylvania. His other interest is in building pipe organs, and he plans to provide regular organ concerts at the winery.

In downtown Lewistown is the 5,000-gallon Lembo Vineyard winery, opened by former restaurateurs Josephine and Antoinette Lembo in 1977 to make Seyval Blanc, Chelois, and De Chaunac wines from the grapes on their nearby six-acre farm.

At New Brighton, Beaver County, thirty miles north of Pittsburgh, is the 5,000-gallon Lapic Winery, the newest in Pennsylvania, bonded in 1977. Paul and Josephine Lapic and Paul's brother Walter, with a four-acre vineyard, plan to produce six table wines.

Pennsylvania's limited-winery law has inspired similar legislation in a dozen other states. Thus far it has been copied in Indiana, which now has six farm wineries, and it has influenced the farm winery laws of New York State, Kentucky, North Carolina, Mississippi, and Tennessee. To Pennsylvania farmers belongs the credit for advancing the trend toward winegrowing as an integral part of agriculture in the East, South, and Midwest.

5

Ohio, Once the Premier Wine State

THE RISE and decline of Ohio wines could supply compelling material for a historical novel, because the Ohio wine star has risen not once, but twice, each time only to fall; and now it is rising again. Scores of new vineyards and fifteen new wineries producing new kinds of wine have sprung up since 1965 in Ohio, including nine near Cincinnati, where the state's wine industry began more than a century and a half ago.

This could also make an epic movie, with such characters as wine-millionaire Nicholas Longworth, poet and connoisseur Henry Wadsworth Longfellow, and Ohio's colorful winegrowers of today. And if filmed in such settings as the storied Ohio River, the ancient wine caves beneath Cincinnati and Sandusky, and the vine-clad islands of Lake Erie, the plot could weave war, intrigue, politics, and Prohibition-era gunplay without veering a grape's-width from actual history.

• 2 •

Nicholas Longworth*, the five-foot-one "crazy Jerseyman," came to Cincinnati from Newark in 1803 at the age of twenty-one with little more than the clothes on his back. It was the year Ohio became a state. He studied law for six months, established a lucrative practice, invested in land in the mushrooming town, and became the wealthiest man in Ohio. Winegrowing then was just beginning along the riverbanks at Cincinnati. It became Longworth's hobby. He also saw that drunkenness

---

*The great-grandfather of the Nicholas Longworth who was Speaker of the House during the Coolidge administrations, and who was the son-in-law of President Theodore Roosevelt.

93

decreased in direct proportion to the use of light table wines, and he decided that by producing such wines he could woo Americans away from hard liquor.

In 1823, Longworth planted a vineyard on Bald Hill, overlooking the Ohio River in the part of Cincinnati known as Tusculum. The site is now the city's Frederick H. Alms Memorial Park, in which some of the old vine roots still grow. He imported thousands of vines from Europe, but they died, so he made his first wine from the native Alexander and Isabella. Then he heard of a "wonder grape," the Catawba, grown by Major John Adlum of Georgetown, and in 1825 he obtained Catawba cuttings from Adlum. Three years later, when Longworth tasted the first Catawba wine pressed from his grapes, he quit his law practice and gave his full attention to winegrowing. By 1842 he was cultivating 1,200 acres of vineyards at Tusculum, in the Delhi Hills, and on the present site of Eden Park, and began making America's first champagne.

Longworth's white Catawba wine and his champagne, which he called Sparkling Catawba, were sold throughout the East and even in faraway California. They were so successful that California winegrowers began planting Catawba grapes and attempted to copy the sensational Ohio wines. Longworth once accused New York hotels of substituting French champagnes for his, which he sold them at the then fancy price of twelve dollars a case. His fame reached England. A writer for the *Illustrated London News* in 1858 described the still Catawba as "a finer wine of the hock species and flavour than any hock that comes from the Rhine," and declared that "the Sparkling Catawba, of the pure, unadulterated juice of the odoriferous Catawba grape, transcends the Champagne of France."

But a more lasting tribute was the "Ode to Catawba Wine" by Longfellow, which begins:

> Very good in its way
> Is the Verzenay,
> Or the Sillery soft and creamy;
> But Catawba wine
> Has a taste more divine,
> More dulcet, delicious, and dreamy.

Some say the gift of a few bottles from Longworth inspired Longfellow to write the poem at his Cambridge home in 1854. But it is evident to anyone who reads all eleven stanzas that the bard had actually visited Cincinnati and had learned from Longworth about the many American grape varieties named in the "Ode," including the grape that "grows by the Beautiful River."

• 3 •

Ohio was the premier wine state by 1859, producing nearly 570,000 gallons yearly, more than a third of the national total, twice as much as California. Cincinnati was "the queen of the West"; the Ohio was "the Rhine of America." There were 3,000 acres of vineyards along the river between Cincinnati and Ripley, forty miles upstream, and a large acreage under vines across the river in Kentucky.

But just as Cincinnati's wine star reached its zenith, a plague began to spread through its vineyards. The violet-hued skins of the Catawba grapes were turning black, and many of the berries were found to be hollow shells. A cobwebby growth wilted the leaves and stems, and the vines began to die. Black rot and oïdium (powdery mildew) wrought this destruction at a time when modern preventive sprays were still unknown.

Longworth had half a million bottles in the caves beneath his two Cincinnati "wine houses" in 1860, but was running short of grapes to produce more wine. His dream fading, the little man in his latter years grew absent-minded; he carried numerous papers in his hat and a memorandum sheet pinned to his coat sleeve. When he died in 1863, two years after the outbreak of the Civil War, his business was divided among his heirs, and it was abandoned a few years later, for most of the vineyards were dead. Not less than 10,000 acres of vines in southwestern Ohio were obliterated by the "vine sickness" during the late '50s and '60s, and only a few were replaced. Cincinnati wines were virtually a thing of the past.

• 4 •

In the meantime another part of Ohio, two hundred miles north of Cincinnati, was achieving prominence as a winegrowing district. Grape planting had begun as early as 1836 along the shore of Lake Erie and on the islands that extend toward the Canadian border. Here the lake-tempered breezes kept the vines free of disease. In the decade after 1860, at least 7,000 acres of vineyards were planted in northern Ohio, from Toledo to beyond Cleveland, some by growers who migrated from Cincinnati. In 1870, a half-million-gallon winery on Middle Bass Island claimed to be the largest in the nation, and the Lenk winery at Toledo turned out 400,000 gallons in that year. By

Nicholas Longworth, "the crazy Jerseyman," who founded the Ohio champagne industry, planting his first vineyard in 1823 and making the first American champagne in 1842.

One of Nicholas Longworth's Catawba vineyards on the Ohio River near Cincinnati *circa* 1850.

1900 several of the Sandusky wineries had won medals for their wines at judgings in this country and in Paris and Rome. The comeback of Ohio wines was complete.

• 5 •

Then, in 1920, came Prohibition, and the Ohio wine industry collapsed for the second time. During the dry years, several of the state's vintners continued to operate by government permit, making small quantities of sacramental and medicinal wines. Others made wines without official sanction, and when Federal food and drug officers approached some of the Lake Erie Islands to inspect the vines for spray residues, they were driven away by shotgun blasts.

Grape acreage along the lake again increased during the 1920s to supply home winemakers and bootleggers. At this time, however, most of the Ohio vineyards switched from wine grapes to Concords because of the expanding market for fresh grape juice. But the wineries around Sandusky maintained their vineyards of Catawba and other wine grapes, and at Repeal in

1933 they were ready to cash in on the boom demand they expected for wines. Richer in historic background than most of the New York wineries, with the best grape-growing climate in the East, and with wines distinctly different from those of California, they had the best opportunity to install their brands again on the best hotel and restaurant wine lists of the East and Midwest. But the Sandusky vintners let the opportunity at Repeal slip through their fingers. Instead of concentrating on selling their quality wines and champagnes, they tried to compete for volume sales with the low-priced wines shipped to local bottlers in tank cars from California. The Ohio wineries even tried unsuccessfully to get their legislature to levy a dollar-a-gallon tax on wines from outside the state. Meanwhile the vintners of New York's Finger Lakes District seized the chance that Ohio had muffed, and Finger Lakes champagnes became the chief sparkling wines sold in the United States. In 1937, there were 161 wineries in Ohio. By 1967, there were twenty-five left, only fifteen making wine from Ohio grapes.

• 6 •

Yet for today's wine tourist, no other district in America offers historic vineyards and colorful wineries in settings as uniquely spectacular as those that still operate along the shore and on the "Wine Islands" of Lake Erie.

From Sandusky eastward to the Pennsylvania border, a ten-mile-wide strip of land facing Lake Erie is dotted with vineyards, though many are now threatened by urbanization. West of Cleveland, which has several large bonded cellars, are three producing wineries. On Detroit Road in the Cleveland suburb of Westlake is the 180,000-gallon Dover Vineyard winery, established in 1934 by eighteen grape growers of Cuyahoga and Lorain Counties. Zoltan Wolovits, a winemaker who came here from Hungary following the 1956 revolution, owns it now. The winery is under the same roof as the Dover Chalet restaurant, and diners there are sometimes privileged to watch how the wines are made. Also on Detroit Road, Carl Limpert and his wife Julia still make Concord, apple, and "Golden Sunshine Grape" wines on the twenty-six acres remaining of their once much larger Limpert Fruit Farm, which dates from the 1860s. On Webber Road in adjoining Avon Lake, Allan Klingshirn runs the ten-acre vineyard his father started in 1935. Nearby on Walker Road, Alex Christ tends his father's twenty-three acres and continues making Concord and Niagara jug wines; his father has retired.

East of Cleveland, in Geauga, Lake, and Ashtabula Counties, is the main Concord area of Ohio. Most of the grapes are now harvested mechanically. The three old roadside wineries between Wickliffe and Geneva have not changed, except that the Willoughby winery has been moved to adjoining Willowick. Morris Cohodas from Lithuania still grows mostly Concords on his fifty acres on County Line Road near Geneva. His son Alvin hitchhiked to the University of California at Davis in 1950 and trained for a winegrowing career, but on returning home took a food laboratory job instead.

• 7 •

A new generation of oenothusiasts brought the wine revolution and three new wineries to northeastern Ohio's Concord grape district in the early 1970s.

The first was industrial engineer Arnulf Esterer, a home winemaker who had happened to read about Konstantin Frank, the pioneer grower of Vinifera at Hammondsport, New York. Esterer went to Hammondsport, worked without pay for Dr. Frank during the 1967 and 1968 vintages, and learned Frank's secrets of growing Vinifera in the East. The following year, in partnership with Ashtabula wine buff Tom Hubbard, Esterer planted Chardonnay and Johannisberg (White) Riesling beside Interstate 90 six miles from the Lake Erie shore, ten miles west of Conneaut, Ohio. They named the vineyard Markko for the Finnish ex-policeman who sold them the land. The little Markko Vineyard and winery were four years old when I happened by in October of 1973 and sampled its 1972 Riesling from the cask. I was amazed; its fresh Riesling fragrance was closer to a young Moselle than any dry American Riesling I have tasted yet. My notes made that afternoon read: "Is it an accident? Can he duplicate this wine?" Esterer's later vintages of Riesling have approached the 1972 in quality. His first Chardonnays, aged in American oak, could hold up their heads against most comparable California wines. When I next visited Markko Vineyard in 1976, Esterer had just picked his first crop of Cabernet Sauvignon, planted four years before. His wife Kate had quit her job as Conneaut's rural mail carrier to help in the winery and care for their home and four children. Markko Vineyard still is only ten acres and is difficult to find. Take the Route 7 (Youngstown) exit from I-90, then the second right turn onto South Ridge Road, which goes under the freeway to the vineyard and winery. Phone ahead for an appointment.

It was on that same day in 1973 that I met in the neighborhood another home winemaker named Willett Worthy. A North Madison investment banker, Worthy had just finished planting nine acres of Chardonnay, Gamay Beaujolais, Pinot Noir, and French hybrids on Route 528 six miles south of Madison. Now he has twenty acres, has built the first part of his Grand River winery, and is devoting full-time to his winegrowing career. The first Grand River (he says he may change the name) wines are Pinot Noir, Gamay Beaujolais Rosé, and two French hybrid wines he has named September and October Red.

All of Worthy's 1975 crop went to northern Ohio's newest wine producer, the Cedar Hill Wine Company. This 5,000-gallon winery is jammed incredibly into the basement of Dr. Thomas Wykoff's tiny Au Provence French provincial restaurant in the Cleveland Heights section of Cleveland. Dr. Wykoff, who heads the ear-nose-throat department of St. Luke's Hospital, began home winemaking and French cooking in 1970 when he returned to Cleveland from an assistant professorship at a medical school in New Orleans. To combine these new interests, he converted an old beauty shop into a ten-table restaurant, first installing modern winemaking equipment in the basement. He makes a dozen excellent wines including Pinot Noir, Chancellor, Chambourcin, and several blends of his own. They are only for sale in the restaurant, where a liberal supply is also used in the kitchen. The name of the doctor's wines is "Chateau Lagniappe," a New Orleans expression of "a little bit extra."

Also in the early '70s, Anthony P. Debevc of Madison, Ohio, earned his pomology degree at Ohio State University and persuaded his father Tony J. Debevc to add ten acres of French hybrid grapes to the thirty acres of Concords grandfather Antone from Slovenia had planted before Prohibition in the Grand River Valley near Madison. To decide what to do with the new grapes, the Debevcs and their wives Beth and Rosemarie first toured eastern vineyards and wineries, and decided to start a winery of their own. With lumber from an old barn, the father and son built a two-story chalet beside the vineyard on Doty Road and named it Chalet Debonné. Downstairs is the winery; wines are for sale in the tasting room upstairs. The wives and Anthony's sister Donnieella serve cheese, crackers, sausage, and homemade bread Tuesdays through Saturdays. Accordion music is provided until midnight on Wednesdays and Fridays. The winery has now been expanded to 40,000 gallons.

Anthony P. says they may soon plant some Vinifera vines and perhaps start making a champagne.

• 8 •

Sandusky, which succeeded Cincinnati as the wine capital of Ohio, is a venerable lakefront city with strange diagonal thoroughfares. When Longworth's vineyards at Cincinnati died, the Catawba found its adopted home here, as local maps with such landmarks as Catawba Point, Catawba Island, and Catawba Road testify. Sandusky, situated midway between Cleveland and Toledo, is now the center of a miles-long strip of summer resorts and beaches that is billed, with the neighboring islands, as "Lake Erie Vacationland." Near the city's straggling waterfront stand several century-old wineries, some of whose wine caves are tunneled beneath the streets. The Engels & Krudwig cellar on East Water Street, founded in 1863 and once famed for its wines called Diedesheimer and Laubenheimer, is still bonded because old wines remain in some of the casks. But in recent years builder Edward Feick and his wife Anita have converted the upper portion of the building into a series of retail shops. Nearby is the John G. Dorn winery, which began in 1872 with Longworth's original casks, but closed in 1957. On Clinton Street stood the great cellar of Michel Hommel, whose 1889 champagne won him medals at Chicago's Columbian World Exposition in 1893 and at the Paris Exposition of 1900, but it was closed in 1967 and soon afterward was destroyed by fire.

There still are two wineries at Venice, four miles west of Sandusky. One is the small cellar of the late William Steuk beside the four acres that remain of his grandfather's vineyard, which dates from 1855. Steuk produced sparkling Catawba and an assortment of table wines "for sentimental reasons," he told me some months before he died in 1975. When I was there a year later, Steuk's widow Margaret had hired a young pre-medical student named Tim Parker to work in the wine cellar.

The other Venice winery adjoins the forty-acre Mantey Vineyard and 80,000-gallon winery on Bardshar Road. Paul Mantey, whose grandfather began making wine in 1880 for the German immigrant families around Sandusky, operates the winery while his younger brother Don cares for the vineyard. For decades the principal Mantey wines were Catawba, sauterne, port, and sherry in screw-capped bottles. When dry mealtime wines began to be popular in the late 1950s and early 1960s, the Manteys started planting French hybrids in place of their old native vines and soon were also selling a Baco Noir and a Baco rosé. Now the Mantey Vineyard has come out with 1976 vintage estate-bottled Johannisberg Riesling and Seyval Blanc in traditional bottles with straight corks.

The oldest Mantey brother, Norman, has his own winery five miles away on the peninsula called Catawba Island, across Sandusky Bay. Norman, a balding veteran of World War II guerrilla fighting in the swamps of Bougainville, must be the busiest vintner in Ohio, for he performs at three jobs. First, he runs his Mon Ami Champagne Company in an ivy-covered four-story limestone cellar built about 1872, making a Chardonnay and six different Labrusca and French hybrid champagnes. Second, he sells the output of both his own and his brothers' winery by flying his single-engined plane each week to call on wine wholesalers in cities throughout Ohio. His third job is at night, when he runs the Mon Ami restaurant upstairs from the winery and serves steaks, sauerkraut balls, and Mon Ami wines by the glass and by the bottle. With its picturesque vaulted cellars, the Mon Ami winery could become a showplace for the wine industry of the Sandusky area if the proprietor didn't work at so hectic a pace. He has no time to show the vaults to visitors.

• 9 •

Jutting above the surface of Lake Erie, between Sandusky and the Canadian boundary that bisects the lake, is the cluster of little, oddly shaped islands that long grew Ohio's finest wines. The Lake Erie Islands are a viticultural curiosity: being warmed in late autumn by the surrounding waters, they enjoy the longest grape-growing season in the northeastern United States. The grapes here are harvested as much as six weeks after the vintage ends on the mainland. In the winter, the lake freezes over, so solidly that automobiles can cross to the islands, and even this benefits the vineyards, because the cold air in spring delays the buds from opening until the danger of spring frosts has passed. From Sandusky and nearby Port Clinton, ferryboats serve the islets, except when the lake freezes over, and they carry most of the grape harvest to the mainland.

In all the world there is no transportation system quite like the islands' air service. Hopping from island to island and to Port Clinton daily throughout the year are three relics of the early age of aviation, the 1928 vintage Ford tri-motors famed as the "Tin Geese." Only eleven of these lumbering, corrugated-metal planes are known still to exist. Ralph Dietrich's Island

Airlines is fortunate to own its little fleet, because modern planes of this size cannot use the island airstrips. Flipping between islets only one to eleven miles apart, they carry the islanders' children to and from high school on the mainland, and they also deliver groceries, coal, pianos, and island wines.

Kelley's Island, the largest on the United States side of the lake, was planted with grapes by 1846, and here the first winery north of Cincinnati was built five years later. By 1880 its vineyards covered 750 acres and supported five wineries. Because Kelley's is the closest of the group to the mainland, summer cottages, camps, and beach clubs have supplanted all but one of its vineyards. Winegrowing is now almost entirely confined to the three Bass Islands, so named for the fishing on the reefs along their shores.

South Bass, now more often called Put-in-Bay, is the most famous because of its War of 1812 history and the lofty Peace Monument that stands at the entrance to its bay. It was from here that Commodore Oliver Hazard Perry sailed to meet the British fleet on September 12, 1813, and here he put in after the battle to send his memorable dispatch of victory: "We have met the enemy and they are ours—two ships, two brigs, one schooner, and one sloop." In earlier days, when paddlewheel steamers brought vacationists from Cleveland and Toledo, there were palatial hotels on this island. A streetcar line once ran from the steamer dock to the sprawling Victory Hotel, since destroyed by a great fire.

There are still vineyards on both sides of quaint Put-in-Bay village, but with tourism now the principal industry, only one winery, the Heineman Cellar, remains active. Norman Heineman, born on the island, and his son Louis till the twenty-acre vineyard that Norman's father Gustav planted after coming here in 1883 from the winegrowing region of Baden in Germany. In 1897, a year after the winery was built, workmen digging a well on the property stumbled into a huge cave of green crystal stalactites. The Heinemans charge tourists a fee to visit the cave, and a tour of the winery is included. They make eight kinds of table wine, including a dry white Catawba and a blend of Catawba and Concord that they call "Sweet Belle." The wines are sold by the glass or bottle, and some of the visitors like them well enough to order shipments made by the case to their homes on the mainland.

From South Bass it is only a rowboat ride to pistol-shaped, three-mile-long Middle Bass Island and its chief landmark, the Lonz Winery, a frowning medieval-style castle on the lakeshore. To the yachting fraternity of the entire Great Lakes region, this winery with its nearby harbor became a haven for bacchanalian festivity after the repeal of Prohibition. Island-born George Lonz, a bubbling, droll, Falstaffian host, sold his Isle de Fleurs Champagne by the bottle, rented guests the glasses in which to drink it, and often played the violin to entertain them. His visitors on a summer afternoon numbered as many as two thousand, brought by planes and by a fleet of up to two hundred boats. The forty-five-acre vineyard adjoining the winery dates from 1862, when it was planted by Andrew Wehrle from Alsace. He also built the original winery, but it was replaced twice following disastrous fires. It was Lonz who in 1942 built its turrets and battlements, once aptly described as "a mason's caprice." Lonz died in 1969 and the winery continued operating for a time, but closed three years later because the weekend crowds finally became too much to manage. When the winery and wines and equipment were sold at auction in 1976, the future of the castle and vineyard was still undetermined. But George Lonz had left a lasting legacy for Ohio viniculture; a fund in his name for viticultural and enological scholarships at Ohio State University.

From the Lonz castle it is an easy walk to the remaining winery on Middle Bass. It is owned by the Bretz family. Leslie Bretz, born there on Christmas Day in 1893, inherited the little cellar from his grandfather, Joseph Miller from Baden, who built it in 1865. Florence Bretz, a coastguardsman's daughter,

George Lonz built this winery castle in 1942 on Middle Bass Island in Lake Erie to make his Isle de Fleurs Ohio champagnes.

came here from the mainland during the twenties to teach in the island grammar school, and married Leslie a year later. With one of their three sons, Walter, they make bottle-fermented champagne and sparkling burgundy, Catawba, Delaware, and claret wines, and an unfermented Concord juice, using only the grapes from their twenty-two-acre vineyard. Tourists buy their entire output. Leslie Bretz doubts whether the islands' thin layer of topsoil, gradually becoming thinner on South Bass, can continue supporting vines for many more years.

But on bell-shaped Isle St. George, which most charts show as North Bass Island, they think differently. "Of course this topsoil is thin," said the late Henry O. Sonneman, who once owned most of this island, and whose Meier's Wine Cellars of Cincinnati still is Ohio's largest wine producer. "Vines have been growing here since 1844, and they'll still be producing the best grapes in America a century from now." These islands are mounds of limestone rising from the bottom of Lake Erie, the shallowest of the Great Lakes. The soil is cultivated to a depth of only two inches, but the limestone underneath is crisscrossed by fissures and caves, through which the water circulates, and to which the roots of the vines readily penetrate. Sometimes the limestone must be blasted with dynamite in order to plant more vines.

Isle St. George is only a mile long and covers 700-odd acres. Its highest point is scarcely fourteen feet above the lake level. It is eighteen miles from the mainland, a mile and a half from the international boundary. Some of the twelve families who live on the island are descendants of the earliest winegrowers. There is a one-room grammar school, but the older children fly daily to and from Port Clinton High School, occasionally staying overnight on the mainland when their aerial school bus is grounded by fog or storm. There are no stores on the island, but a telephone call via the inter-island cable can bring an air taxi in less time than you can get a taxi in your city. TV reception is of the best, and there is year-round fishing, because when the lake freezes over, its surface becomes dotted with wooden shanties, outfitted with stoves inside, for anglers who come from far and near to fish through holes in the ice.

Sonneman bought the Isle St. George vineyards in 1941 and expanded them to cover half the island. He grew Catawba, Delaware, and French hybrids, harvested a thousand tons yearly with the new mechanical harvesting machines, and crushed the grapes at a press house near the boat dock. The fresh must (unfermented juice) then was carried in stainless steel tanks by ferry and truck to his Cincinnati winery for fermentation, aging, and bottling. Thinking the island climate might also be right for Old World vines, Sonneman also made an experimental planting of Vinifera. The new owners of Meier's now have found that Sonneman was right. In 1977, they arranged to replant more of the island vineyard with such noble Vinifera as White Riesling, Chardonnay, and Gewürztraminer. With these they plan to produce finer wines in the 1980s than were ever grown on the Lake Erie Islands before.

• 10 •

Henry Sonneman was a stocky little man with a contagious grin and a limp. He was born in 1904 on his parents' farm outside Cincinnati and learned grape growing from his father, who had a small vineyard supplying grapes to home winemakers. In 1928 Sonneman bought the seventy-year-old Meier's Grape Juice Company, where he had been employed washing bottles and cleaning tanks while attending night classes at the University of Cincinnati. Bavarian immigrant John Meier's Catawba vineyard, planted in Longworth's time, was long gone; the company's grapes came from Kelley's Island. When Sonneman became the boss, he made "Meier's Unfermented Catawba Grape Juice" popular throughout this country and Canada.

At Repeal he began making wine, but his little juice plant couldn't compete with the big Sandusky, New York, and California wineries. Sonneman felt that Ohio should produce distinctively different Ohio wines and sell them at premium prices, and decided to do it himself.

He did it by acquiring the Isle St. George vineyards and a cellar at Sandusky, but kept his main winery at Silverton, ten miles from the center of Cincinnati. He built its capacity to two million gallons and shipped Meier's wines, champagnes and Catawba juice to forty states and two foreign countries. His Meier's Catawba and sun-baked cream sherry were the only Ohio wines that were recommended on the 1966 State Department wine list.

The Meier's winery was sold after Sonneman's death in 1974 to Paramount Distillers of Cleveland. It still makes most of the wines and champagnes popularized by its founder. Situated on Plainfield Pike off US 22 at Silverton, it attracts thousands of visitors who tour the big cellars and stop in the *weinstube* to sample the Meier's wines.

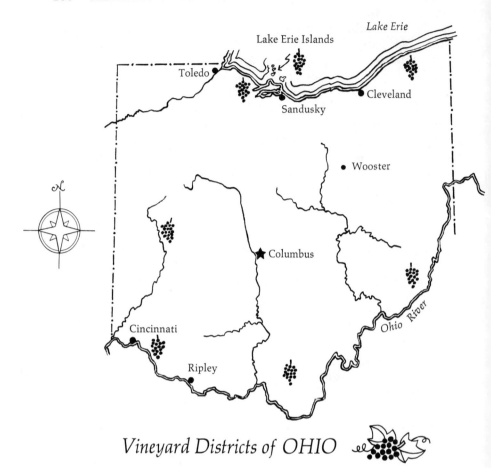

Vineyard Districts of OHIO

• 11 •

It was Sonneman who sparked the revival of the wine industry in southern Ohio. After the Second World War, he began touring the world's vineyards, visiting every winegrowing area in Europe, Australia, Africa, and the Americas. From each trip he returned more convinced that Ohio could once again regain its laurels as a premium winegrowing state. He began talking with growers, bankers, and state officials about the need to replant Ohio's Concord vineyards with wine grapes. He showed them that to supply his wineries, he was buying wine grapes and juice from Missouri, Michigan, Kentucky, and New York.

In particular, he pointed out that modern viticultural technology could make vines grow again along the Ohio River, where

Longworth's vineyards had once flourished, and where farmers were facing a tobacco surplus. Winegrowing, he said, could help solve the problems of economically depressed Appalachia.

At Sonneman's urging, state horticulturists in 1960 planted several wine-grape varieties in the new experimental substation at Ripley on the Ohio River. The vines thrived. The State Department of Development then made a study which showed a potential grape-growing belt with at least 175 frost-free days per year along a 250-mile stretch of the Ohio River. It suggested that twenty southern Ohio counties, from Cincinnati to Marietta, might grow wine grapes profitably. In 1964, at a farmers' meeting in Ripley, Ohio Governor James Rhodes heard the study report. Waving a wine bottle over his head, he declared: "We can grow as fine grapes and wines here as anywhere in the world."

Dr. Garth Cahoon, from Utah State University, was assigned in 1965 to plant demonstration vineyards of wine grapes on farms along the northern bank of the Ohio. At the state's main research center in Wooster, Dr. James Gallander from Oregon State University set up a wine laboratory. Someone questioned whether Dr. Cahoon would lead a winegrowing project, since he is a member of the ultra-dry Mormon Church. Cahoon replied that the original Mormons used wine for Communion before their successors switched to water, and that the Mormons' prophet, Joseph Smith, in the *Doctrine and Covenants,* had specified "wine, yea, pure juice of the grape," though with the proviso that "it is made new among you."

In the following spring, eleven more demonstration vineyards were planted in river counties as far east as Marietta. The state supplied the vines and the farmers furnished the land, equipment, and labor. There was great excitement; history was being made. Dr. Cahoon predicted vineyard yields of six tons per acre, and the event was recorded on television, radio, and in newspaper interviews.

Then Wistar and Ursula Marting, who had one of the state's experimental plantings on their Tarula Farm at Clarksville, planted a commercial vineyard of their own and began building a winery. By 1968 the Martings were selling their first French hybrid, Catawba, and Niagara wines at the farm and to stores and restaurants in nearby cities. Next, Sonneman's son and daughter, Jack and Janet, planted thirty-five acres of hybrids near New Richmond in Clermont County (but their Jac Jan Vineyard later was sold for a housing development).

In 1969, Kenneth and Jim Schuchter planted twenty acres of

hybrids on their truck farm on US 22 two miles west of Morrow in Warren County. A year later they opened the Valley Vineyard winery and soon were doubling its size. Dozens more vineyards since have been planted in southern Ohio and in neighboring Indiana. Seven more wineries have been opened along the Ohio River and in the western and central counties. The Tarula Vineyard winery has continued to prosper despite Wistar Marting's death in 1975.

On Bethel-New Hope Road west of Neal's Corner, Charles and Alice McIntosh added French hybrids to their vineyard of Labrusca varieties and built a hospitality room where they serve their wines with Wisconsin cheese. On the Ohio River shore three miles west of Manchester, veteran home winemaker Kenneth Moyer planted ten acres of hybrids in 1970. He then converted a former dance hall into a winery and restaurant where his wife Mary prepares gourmet-quality foods and serves Moyer's wines and bottle-fermented champagne. Many of their patrons drive the seventy miles from Cincinnati, and in summer some come by boat.

On Route 56 four miles east of Circleville in Pickaway County, nurseryman Jack Goode and his wife Judy have built the Shawnee Vineyard restaurant and basement winery beside their thirty acres of hybrids. At Springfield, on Upper Valley Pike near Wittenberg University, home winemaker Dan Hafle planted nine acres of hybrids in 1973. His wife Lee serves Hafle Vineyard wines with meat and cheese in their winery, a converted barn that dates back almost two centuries. Near Cardington, southeast of Marion, Carroll Hubbell tends the six-acre Le Boudin Vineyard while his wife Ruth makes their wines.

Four more wineries started in Ohio in 1977. Businessman Homer K. Monroe built the Vinterra Vineyard winery with a tasting room on the eight acres of French hybrids he had planted along Stoker Road two miles northeast of Houston. His wife Phyllis presides over the tasting room. Systems analyst Norman Greene and his wife Marion installed stainless steel tanks and oak barrels in a 120-year-old tobacco barn on Highway 48, six miles north of Lebanon, and named it the Colonial Vineyards winery. They have twenty acres of French hybrids and Catawba, planted since 1974. Aircraft quality control engineer Ralph Wise and his wife Laura bonded the 2,000-gallon Brush Creek Vineyards winery in a 150-year-old three-story log barn on Newkirk Lane fourteen miles northwest of Peebles, and were starting to treble the size of their young three-acre vineyard of hybrids, Concord, and Niagara grapes. Warren Sublette, who once was Tarula Vineyard's winemaker, installed winemaking equipment in the cellar of the former Bellevue Brewery on Central Parkway near downtown Cincinnati and began selling eight Sublette wines with nightly folk music and cheese.

The revival of the Ohio wine industry is now celebrated each October with a wine festival at Morrow, attended by thousands.

What more could a novelist ask for an ending? Ohio winegrowing has returned to the cradle from which it sprung. Lush vineyards again are yielding good table wines on Ohio hillsides, all the way from Longfellow's "Beautiful River" to the Lake Erie shore. More than a century after Nicholas Longworth's death, his dream of creating an American Rhineland in Ohio is coming true.

6

New York, Champion of the East

A MENTION of New York State wines usually brings, from the average consumer of California or European wines, a remark about "that foxy taste." Vintners of New York and other eastern states abhor the word "foxy," and in deference to them I normally say "Labrusca" instead. But "foxy" is in the dictionaries and ampelographies, and it is the word commonly used to describe the *Vitis labrusca* flavor of such native American grapes as Concord, Catawba, Delaware, Niagara, Dutchess, and Ives—from which most New York wines have long been made.

However, not all wines containing these grapes are percepti- bly foxy, for the Labrusca taste is readily softened, by blending with wines of neutral flavors, to a point at which only a hint of fruity fragrance remains. There is no Labrusca taste at all in the new eastern wine types that are made entirely from the French-American hybrid grapes, nor in New York sherries, from which it is removed by a heat-and-oxygen process; nor in those New York muscatels which are made from the Canada Muscat grape. And now that Dr. Konstantin Frank has shown that Vinifera grapes, too, can be grown there, New York winegrowers are beginning to challenge both California and Europe with small quantities of Old World wine types made from the true *cépages nobles,* such as White Riesling and Chardonnay.

But if the Labrusca flavor has been a handicap to the New York wineries, it certainly is not evident in the steady rate at which they have increased their share of the American market for wines. Between 1960 and 1978, vintners of the Empire State more than trebled their total wine production and almost doubled their output of champagne. In an average year, New

York now produces about thirty-six million gallons of wine and is thereby second to California, which makes nine times as much. Of the thirty-six million gallons, almost a tenth, or well over three million, is champagne—about a fourth as much of this bubbly wine as California makes. New York's best wines are its champagnes, white table, and dessert types. Its typical dry reds leave something to be desired, but are improving steadily with the increased use of lately-planted French hybrid and Vinifera grapes in their blends. Almost two thirds of New York grapes still are Concords. Four thousand acres of new hybrids accounted for most of the 16 percent increase in the state's vineyard acreage from 37,000 in 1970 to 43,000 in 1975.

New York State has four principal vineyard districts, each with distinctive wines and colorful wineries that are covered in two following chapters; and now a fifth district, which is described in this chapter, is being planted with vines. Best known, because of its scenic attractions and large wineries, is the Finger Lakes district in the west-central part of the state. But more important, because it has half of the total vineyard

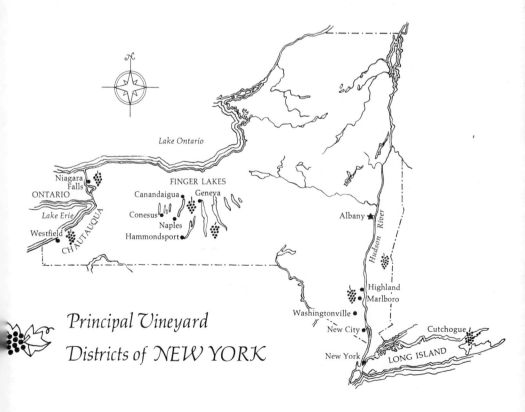

Principal Vineyard Districts of NEW YORK

acreage, is the Chautauqua district, in the far western corner, bordering Lake Erie. Third in importance is Niagara County, which extends westward from Niagara Falls. The fourth district is the Hudson Valley, only an hour or two from Manhattan. The fifth, which is both old and new, is the northeastern end of Long Island.

In this book's first edition, I counted thirty-nine New York wineries. Most of them, located in and around New York and other cities, had no vineyards but handled grapes, juices, and wines that were shipped in from the grape-growing areas and from other states. During the 1960s and 1970s, more than a million gallons of California bulk wines were shipped annually to New York wineries for blending purposes, in addition to California neutral brandy used in producing New York dessert wines.

Less than half of the state's 175,000-ton average annual grape crop was used by New York wineries. The rest was used in fresh Concord grape juice, jelly, or jam, or was eaten fresh. A partial explanation is found in the peculiar history of winegrowing in New York. Prohibitionist influence during the past century accounts for the predominance of the Concord grape and for New York's strange beverage control laws, which long discouraged the establishment of additional wineries and actually discouraged the purchase of wine.

• 2 •

New York was one of the first states to cultivate grapes, but was one of the last in the East to develop a wine industry. Vineyards were planted on Manhattan Island more than three hundred years ago, when Peter Stuyvesant was governor of New Netherland between 1647 and 1664. Stuyvesant sternly regulated the sale of liquor, but he favored the use of wine. He even authored an ordinance requiring that sailors on the high seas be provided with a daily ration of wine to protect their health. His successor, the first English governor of New York, Richard Nicolls, granted a monopoly to one Paulus Richards to plant a vineyard on Long Island. The French Protestants who settled in Ulster County on the Hudson after 1667 tried unsuccessfully to grow European grapes, but they then cultivated wild grapes to make wine for use in their homes. The healthy crops from their vines so impressed Governor Nicolls' successor that he expressed the belief, in a letter to the Lords of Trade in London, that the New York colony alone could produce enough wine to supply all the dominions of the Crown. In 1737, Robert Prince established the Linnaen Gardens at Flushing on Long Island, and from there the Isabella wine grape of South Carolina was introduced throughout the East after 1816. Vines grew in New York City as late as 1846, when the horticulturist, Alden Spooner, published a book on winemaking. Spooner described the wine he made at his own vineyard in Brooklyn, and mentioned other vineyards thriving there, on Manhattan, and at Southampton and New Utrecht on Long Island.

In 1818, a Baptist deacon, Elijah Fay, planted the first vineyard in what is now the Chautauqua Grape Belt along Lake Erie in western New York State and eastern Pennsylvania. Near the present village of Brocton in Chautauqua County, he set out wild vines which he had brought from New England. Because the wild grapes were harsh and excessively foxy, he replaced them in 1824 with Isabella and Catawba, and in 1830 Deacon Fay made ten gallons of wine. But it was not until 1859, when wineries were already operating along the lakeshore in Ohio, that the first of several "wine houses" around Brocton was built by the Deacon's son, Joseph Fay.

But the temperance movement, born in 1808 at Moreau in Saratoga County, was beginning to spread. By 1835 the state temperance society was advocating total abstinence from alcoholic beverages in any form. From New York State the temperance movement evolved into the nationwide crusade that brought about National Prohibition in 1920. In 1845, the Drys got a law passed prohibiting the public sale of liquor in New York State, but it was repealed two years later. They scored again in 1855, obtaining the passage of another state prohibition law, but it was declared unconstitutional.

Chautauqua County, where the Fays lived, was one of the centers of the dry crusade. It was also where the Concord grape variety was introduced—not for winemaking, because dry wine made from Concord is harsh—but as a table grape. The temperance crusaders, with psalm-singing fervor, exhorted farmers of the Chautauqua district to produce grapes, not wine. It was dry influence, as much as the later development of the grape juice industry by the ardent Prohibitionist Dr. Welch, that caused the Chautauqua-Erie Grape Belt to become a fresh-grape district instead of a wine center. Although wine-grape varieties have lately been introduced in this three-county district, nine tenths of the vines here still are Concords.

Winemaking began tardily in the Finger Lakes district, too. The Finger Lakes wineries credit the start of their industry to the Reverend William Bostwick, an Episcopal minister, who in 1829 brought Catawba and Isabella vine shoots from the Hudson River Valley and planted them in the rectory garden of his new church at Hammondsport on Keuka Lake. He gave cuttings to his parishioners, and soon there were vines in most gardens in the neighborhood. In 1850, at South Pulteney, four miles up the lake from Hammondsport, Andrew Reisinger, a vinedresser from Germany, planted a vineyard in which he introduced pruning and cultivation, operations unheard of before in the region. But it was not until 1860 that the commercial production of wine began in the area, with the building of the Pleasant Valley Winery near Hammondsport. This was concurrent with the death of the Cincinnati wine industry, then three decades old, from the vine disease that killed Nicholas Longworth's vineyards along the Ohio River. The Pleasant Valley Winery began by hiring champagne makers from Cincinnati. Other wineries began springing up around Hammondsport, and this created interest in wine-grape growing here at a time when the Concord variety was taking over in the Chautauqua region. Today, although the Finger Lakes district still produces only a third of the state's total grape crop, almost half of its vineyards are planted to wine varieties.

The oldest wine district in New York State is the Hudson River Valley. The first commercial winery there opened in 1839, two decades before those at Brocton and Hammondsport.

In the Niagara district, grape growing began about 1840, but as in the Finger Lakes region, there is no record of wine being made commercially there before 1860.

The foregoing explains why, in the extensive report on wine production in the United States which E.M. Erskine, secretary of the British Legation in Washington, prepared for his government in 1859, New York State's infant wine industry was not even mentioned. Erskine gave enthusiastic descriptions of winegrowing in Ohio, Missouri, Indiana, Illinois, Pennsylvania, Kentucky, Tennessee, Arkansas, the Carolinas, and California. His omission of New York could scarcely have been inadvertent.

The Finger Lakes wine industry expanded rapidly after the Civil War and this soon became the chief wine-producing region of New York State. An influx of German and Swiss immigrants, many of them from wine districts, helped to improve vineyard practices. As wineries were built along the lakes, their wines began winning medals for quality in Paris, Vienna, and Brussels, and the vintners proclaimed their district "the Rhine and Epernay of America." In 1882, the Geneva Experiment Station was founded, and it began a program of grape breeding and vineyard improvement. New York wines grew steadily better, and by the turn of the century such New York brands as Great Western were listed by restaurants and hotels across the country. I have in my files a copy of the menu of a banquet held at the Waldorf-Astoria Hotel by the American Winegrowers Association in February 1916. Of three dozen wines on the list for this dinner, eleven were from the Finger Lakes and Hudson Valley districts of New York, fifteen were from California, three from New Jersey, and one from Ohio.

When Wartime Prohibition began in 1919, most of the New York wineries were forced to close. Yet the ruin wrought in the industry was less complete than in California. Several of the New York vintners managed to survive the dry years by switching to the production of grape juice. Most of it was sold in kegs with labels that said: "Caution—Do not add yeast or admit air or the contents will ferment." This, of course, is what the buyers proceeded to do.

With their Labrusca-flavored grapes, New York vintners also developed superior bottled grape juices, jams, and jellies— products which California, because it grows the relatively bland Vinifera grape varieties, has never been able to match. A few of the New York wineries also obtained government permits to continue making wine and champagne for sacramental, tonic, and cooking uses. When Captain Paul Garrett in 1929 organized Fruit Industries, the giant grape-concentrate combine head-quartered in California, Garrett's own Finger Lakes and Brooklyn wineries were the only ones in New York State to join. The chief Finger Lakes vintners, having remained independent with their own production and sales organizations, were thus better prepared to resume full-scale wine production and sale, when Prohibition ended in 1933, than were most of their California competitors.

• 3 •

In the latter years of the dry era, when early repeal of the Prohibition Amendment was anticipated, public officials in most of the states set to work writing laws and regulations intended to control the sale of liquor within their borders as soon as it would become legal. Each state devised a different system that reflected the attitude of its legislators toward drinking. In New York, Prohibitionist influence was still strong, and it was strongest in the upstate counties that controlled the legislature at Albany. In consequence, the New York law that was written and became effective in 1933 was aimed at restricting the production and consumption of liquor—and it lumped wine with hard liquor. It discouraged the establishment of wineries by setting exorbitant annual license and filing fees. Farmers, who would have opened small wineries to sell their grapes in fermented form to their neighbors, could not afford to pay the fees. (The minimum New York winery license was $635, plus other fees and bond requirements making the total cost more than $1,000 per year. Included was $250 for the privilege of sale at the winery, without which few small winegrowers can exist.)

Worse, the law restricted to liquor stores the sale of wine for home consumption, while it allowed food stores to sell beer. The State Liquor Authority at first issued some 1,700 liquor store licenses to serve all of New York's sixty-two counties. These licenses promptly skyrocketed in value, to such a point that one retailer in New York City sold the key to his store for $60,000 more than the value of his stock. Then the store owners, to protect their monopoly on the sale of wine and liquor by the package, organized strong associations and established a well-financed lobby in Albany. For four decades, this lobby has defeated every bill introduced in the legislature to let food stores sell wine. Liquor stores in the state now number about 5,000, but housewives don't shop in liquor stores for the main ingredients of family meals. And to make the stores especially uninviting, a provision of the law prohibits them from stocking anything except sealed packages of liquor and wine— not even soda, lemon juice, cigarettes, or nuts, let alone such household merchandise as wine glassware. The buying of wine for its principal use—that of a daily mealtime beverage, the natural accompaniment of food—has thus been discouraged by the New York law, as effectively as it is discouraged by the state monopoly stores in Pennsylvania and other monopoly states.

· 4 ·

A local wine revolution exploded in New York State in the mid-1970s. It was ignited by a sharp drop in New York wineries' buying of local grapes to produce New York State wines. Some of the big wineries, finding their customers preferred wines with less Labrusca flavor than in the past, were increasing their purchases of bulk California wines for use in their blends. For decades before the 1970s, the local farmers had prospered by selling most of their grapes to the wineries and the rest to the grape-juice plants. But before the 1975 harvest, the wineries notified the growers they would buy only a fraction of the year's grape crop.

Suddenly faced by a grape glut, the farmers left hundreds of tons of that year's grapes to rot on the vines. A deepening gloom spread through the vineyards. It turned to anger in 1976 when the state's biggest winery came out with three new New York-California blends advertised as "New Taylor Wines from the State of Californewyork."

The angry farmers began to notice how the grape growers in neighboring Pennsylvania were starting new wineries on their farms to sell their wines at retail, a practice the New York law restricted to 5 percent of the quantity the winery produced. A few New York growers sought to start their own wineries, but found they could not pay the excessive license fees. They demanded that the state come to their aid. Legislators were sympathetic, but little happened until some of the farmers threatened to back the recurring bills at Albany to permit the sale of wine in grocery stores.

In 1976, in a hitherto unprecedented action, Governor Hugh Carey announced a state-sponsored program to promote the sale of New York wines in stores and restaurants. He proclaimed November of that year as "New York State Wine Month" and held an elaborate tasting in the Four Seasons Restaurant at which most of the wines wholly produced from grapes grown in the state were displayed. The Governor also sponsored a bill in the legislature to reduce the minimum license fee for small farmer wineries to $125 per year. Although the farm winery bill contained flaws that might cause small wineries to fail, it was passed by the legislature, and in a publicized ceremony was signed into law.

Immediately scores of farmers banded together to build wineries. Within a year, twelve new cellars were opened for business or were under construction, increasing the state total from thirty-nine wineries to fifty-one. Until the farm winery bill became law, New York State had just twelve wineries producing wine primarily from grapes grown on their own vineyards. That number doubled within two years following passage of the farm winery law. Most of the new farm wineries aim to produce "château" wines the way small winegrowing estates do in California and in Bordeaux. New York's local grape growers' revolution changed the face of viniculture in the Empire State.

But the revolution was not yet over. The farmers next pushed new bills in the legislature to allow the farm wineries to hold tastings, to stay open Sundays, to offer their wines freely for sale at the cellars, and to open branch outlets in the cities. The new bills were passed with Governor Carey's support and signed into law. When they were allowed to stay open on Sundays, the wineries' sales immediately soared. The seventy-eight-year-old Schapiro kosher winery on Rivington Street in New York City was one of the first opened to the public, advertising daily wine-tasting cellar tours.

Meanwhile, the perennial bill to permit the sale of wine in food stores was re-introduced and as in the past was fought tooth and nail by the liquor lobby. This time it was amended to specify that for the first five years the groceries could sell only wines grown in New York State; but although strongly backed by the state's grape growers, it was defeated, too. When a food-store wine bill eventually passes in New York, it will be followed by the other eastern states, including Pennsylvania and Connecticut, that have restricted wine sales to liquor stores since the repeal of Prohibition.

• 5 •

The Empire State's fifth winegrowing district is the breadbasket of New York City, the still largely rural north fork of Long Island between Peconic Bay and the Sound. If the 1975 Cabernet Sauvignon, Pinot Noir, and Chardonnay I tasted from the casks at the 20,000-gallon Hargrave Vineyard winery are fair examples, this district may be the future Pauillac or Côte d'Or of New York.

Alexander and Louisa Hargrave's forty-six-acre Vinifera vineyard, planted in 1973 near the farm village of Cutchogue in Southold Township, has inspired a score of other Long Islanders to plant forty additional acres in the hope that these noble wine grapes will make their land more valuable for farming than for housing developments. Cutchogue is two hours from the city via Routes 495 and 25. Urbanization now threatens some forty thousand acres in Suffolk County that grow potatoes, cabbage, cauliflower, and strawberries.

Hargrave, who stands six-feet-seven, was studying Chinese literature at Princeton in 1965 when at a Harvard party he met five-foot-six Louisa Thomas, who was studying American Government at Smith College. Hargrave, from upstate New York where his lawyer-banker father was a director of the Taylor winery, was thinking of becoming a winegrower. Louisa suggested that a good place to start would be on Long Island, where she was born.

Their research showed that northeastern Long Island has a 210-day growing season, forty-five days longer than in the Finger Lakes, and much milder winters. They also studied the history of Suffolk County and found that in the early 1700s Moses "the Frenchman" Fournier had had extensive vineyards there. This decided them to buy a sixty-six-acre former potato farm and to plant Chardonnay, White Riesling, Cabernet Sauvignon, and Pinot Noir. Two years later, with their vines growing well, they air-conditioned an old potato cellar and equipped it as their winery with stainless steel and new oak casks.

Up to this writing, the Hargraves' chief problems have been hungry birds, which require them to cover the borders of their vineyard with plastic netting each July, and Hurricane Belle, which in 1976 showered the grape leaves with salt spray.

The Hargrave Vineyard 1975 Pinot Noir that I tasted from the cask was adequate in color, light in tannin, and fresh and flavorful like a young French burgundy. The Cabernet had the grace and delicacy of a fine Médoc and sufficient tannin and body to promise a noble future. The Chardonnay tasted like a young premium California wine. The Pinot Noir went on sale in 1977 in New York City and at the winery, and every bottle soon was sold.

Earlier Long Island grape growers are John and Anne Wickham, whose Vinifera vineyard at Cutchogue dates from 1962, but it contains only table-grape varieties because John Wickham is interested only in fresh fruit. A year after the Hargraves began planting, film and television star Diahn Williams and her lawyer husband Tom McGrath started an acre of Vinifera on the island of Lloyd Neck, which is much closer to the city. They talk of someday bonding the cellar of their Norman-style Château Eastfair and offering their wines for sale.

The new Long Island winegrowers are now helping to dissolve the old public impression that all New York State wines have "that foxy taste."

7

The Finger Lakes Wineries

FIVE LARGE Finger Lakes District wineries—Pleasant Valley, Taylor, Gold Seal, Widmer's, and Canandaigua Industries—produce three fourths of the wine made in New York State. Taylor, which also owns Pleasant Valley, is the third largest producer of bottle-fermented champagnes in the world, next to Henkell in Germany and Moët et Chandon in France. This chapter describes these principal Finger Lakes wineries and some of their interesting neighbors, and probes the controversy over the kinds of grapes to be grown for eastern wines in future decades—the native Labrusca types, the French-American hybrids, or the Old World Vinifera wine-bearing family.

• 2 •

The Finger Lakes—Canandaigua, Keuka, Seneca, Cayuga, Owasco, Skaneateles, and half a dozen others—are so long, narrow, and parallel in their north-south direction that the Indians thought them the imprint of the hands of the Great Spirit. Scooped out by glacial action ages ago, these deep blue lakes make the eleven counties of the district a spectacularly scenic vacationland. Among its chief attractions are the picturesque vineyards and wineries, most of which offer cellar tours and tasting hospitality to visitors.

As in other vineyard regions that border bodies of water, the Finger Lakes temper the extremes of temperature along their shores and thereby protect the grapevines from the killing frosts of spring and fall. The growing season here, though it averages only 135 to 150 days, a third shorter than in California, is usually dry and warm enough to allow the grapes to ripen. In this respect, nearly every year in the Finger Lakes District is a vintage year—the envy of European winegrowers.

Taylor Wine Company

The gas-operated "bird-banger" fires a shotgun-like blast every 45 to 60 seconds to frighten birds away from the ripening grapes in this Finger Lakes vineyard.

The snowy winters, however, average several degrees colder than in Germany and France. Winter temperatures sometimes drop to eighteen or twenty degrees below zero*, and protracted freezes in some years have damaged the vines. There already is snow on the ground when the pruning is under way in December, following the first fall freeze.

The first vine shoots appear in May, followed by leaves and by the tiny flower clusters. When the grapes begin to ripen in late August, robins and starlings descend on the vineyards to peck at the fruit. Then the bird-bangers set up their fearful clatter to frighten the birds away. These gas-operated mechanical noise-makers let go a shotgunlike blast every 45 to 60 seconds, the times varying so that the feathered thieves don't become accustomed to regular intervals of the noise. The bird-bangers are more effective than the scarecrows, stuffed owls, and fake snakes the growers have used in the past.

By the second week of September, the early-ripening varieties are juicy and sweet, and you can smell the grapes when you approach the Finger Lakes. Now the vintage season begins, usually lasting through the fourth week of October. Hundreds of area residents and townspeople formerly did the picking, but mechanical harvesting machines, which appeared in the region for the first time in 1968, have now supplanted most of the human vintagers. Each machine harvests an acre an hour and does the work of forty pairs of human hands. Straddling a row of vines, the robot slaps the wires on which the canes are trained, shaking the grapes off their stems onto a conveyor, which discharges them into plastic-lined boxes on a trailer moving alongside.

*Nine degrees below zero was the lowest temperature recorded at Geisenheim in Germany's Rheingau during the first half of this century, while nine above zero was the minimum on the Moselle at Trier.

Vineyards border Keuka, "the Crooked Lake" near Hammondsport, N.Y.

Grapes can be grown on the rocky, steep, and rolling hillsides near any of the lakes, but at present the vineyards are concentrated along Lakes Canandaigua, Keuka, Seneca, and Cayuga in Steuben, Yates, Schuyler, Seneca, and Ontario Counties. Keuka, known as "The Crooked Lake" because of its irregular Y shape, has vines along its hillsides all the way from Hammondsport at its southern end to Branchport and Penn Yan at the northwestern and northeastern tips. Between the two forks of Keuka, lofty Bluff Point with its Captain Paul Garrett chapel extends twelve miles into the lake and is gracefully draped with vines. In early days excursion steamers plied the larger lakes, and once, during a rate war between rival steamship companies, vacationists could travel seventeen miles on Keuka from Hammondsport to Penn Yan for a ten-cent fare. Now highways border the shores, and the lakes serve for such sports as boating, swimming, and fishing, but not for skating, for the lakes seldom freeze over.

• 3 •

In the quiet, pleasant town of Hammondsport, the birthplace of pioneer aviator Glenn Curtiss, winemaking is the principal industry. Each September, the local Episcopal Church holds a public Sunday service in a vineyard overlooking Keuka Lake to bless the grape harvest. The annual district wine festival, also in September, is held forty miles southeast of Hammondsport at the community college in Corning.

Driving southwest from the town, the first big winery you see is the oldest in the district, the Pleasant Valley Wine Company, home of Great Western wines and champagnes. It is named for the narrow valley through which the inlet to Keuka Lake flows. Above a tree-shaded archway that leads into the original underground wine vault is a stone plate carved with the names of Charles Davenport Champlin and his farmer neighbors who founded the company in 1860. Today the cool vault, walled with hand-cut native stone, serves as a unique tasting room for the thousands of visitors who annually tour the six-million-gallon winery and sample its products. Here the first New York State champagne was made when the Civil War ended in 1865. Joseph Masson, trained in France and hired by Champlin from the M. Werk champagne cellars in Cincinnati, made it and called it Sparkling Catawba as Nicholas Longworth did. Two years later the wine was entered in the Paris Exposition, and though the fruity Labrusca taste was strange to the European judges, they gave it an honorable mention award. Joseph Masson was joined at Hammondsport by his brother Jules, who had been superintendent of the Longworth Wine House at Cincinnati until the grape sickness obliterated the vineyards there. In 1870, the Masson brothers served a new sparkling blend of Delaware and Catawba to a meeting of the Pleasant Valley Grape Growers Association. Presiding at the meeting was famed horticulturist Colonel Marshall Wilder of Boston, who on tasting the wine exclaimed: "Truly, this will be the great champagne of the West!" By "West," Wilder explained, he meant "our entire continent," the New World. His remark gave Great Western champagne its name, strange though it seems for a product of New York State.

In 1873 at the Vienna Exposition, Great Western became the first American champagne to win a gold medal in Europe, and it later gathered additional prizes at Brussels, Philadelphia, and Paris. For half a century before Prohibition, this champagne "from Rheims, New York" was the leading sparkling wine made in this country. "Rheims" was the name of a post office in the winery; and though the office was closed long ago, the old address still appeared on the company's letterhead until 1970. Rheims is also the name of the winery's station on the eight-mile-long, single-track Bath & Hammondsport Railroad, built by the company's owners in 1872 to haul their wine and brandy to market. The B. & H., still operating profitably today, is famous for its nickname, "The Champagne Trail," and also for its slogan, "Not as long as the others but just as wide."

When Prohibition came, Pleasant Valley was one of the few wineries to keep open because it held a Government permit to make wines for sacramental use. This permit, however, did not include the winery's principal product, champagne, because officials of the Prohibition Bureau insisted that champagne was not a wine. Pleasant Valley's chief owners, Malburn and Charles Champlin, grandsons of the founder, filed suit against the Government. Rather than fight the suit, the Bureau granted them special permission to sell champagne to the clergy. For two years the Champlins enjoyed a rich monopoly as the only winery privileged to supply bubbly to servants of the Lord. But then other vintners made a fuss, and the Government again yielded, permitting competitors' sacramental wines to sparkle, too. Pleasant Valley's business then dwindled, but the company still managed to survive, by selling grape juice to home wine-makers, until Repeal. When Charles Champlin died in 1950, Pleasant Valley stock was sold to eastern financiers.

For many years past, the owners of the neighboring Taylor Winery had had their eyes on Great Western, and in 1961 the Taylor family saw a chance to buy its stock. They acquired a controlling interest and made the production and sale of Great Western wines an independent division of Taylor.

The late Greyton Taylor and his son Walter (of whom more presently) took charge of the Pleasant Valley winery and began

Oldest of the Finger Lakes (New York) wineries is the Pleasant Valley Wine Company, Bonded Winery No. 1, founded at Hammondsport in 1860.

Taylor Wine Company Library

The cellar crew at New York State's Pleasant Valley winery in 1884.

adding "varietals" to its list of "generic" table wines. The first three "varietals" were Delaware and Diamond, named for white Labrusca grape varieties, and Isabella, which makes a Labrusca rosé. In 1964, Pleasant Valley made history by introducing the first Finger Lakes wines made entirely of the new French-American hybrid grapes. The company then began changing its generically named table wines to "varietals" named for the increasing proportions of the many-numbered French grapes in their blends. "Aurora" was added to the label of medium-sweet Great Western Sauterne. The burgundy, which is almost dry, became "Baco Noir," and the claret, which is lighter-bodied, became "Chelois"—with a back label giving an anglicized pronunciation: "Shell-oy," which later was erased in response to a storm of protest from students of French.* The plan was that when consumers eventually learn these varietal names, the old generic names would be dropped. Aurora is the new name coined for the hybrid Seibel 5279, Chelois is Seibel 10878, and Baco is the hybrid that lately has improved the flavor of many New York State burgundies. In addition to these, Pleasant Valley has introduced a series of new wines since my first edition appeared. Great Western Spumante resembles the Italian muscat-flavored champagne for which it is named, but owes its muskiness to the New York hybrid called Canada

*This is still hotly debated in the eastern grape districts. Say "shell-wah" to an anglophile and he may reply: "Tell me how you pronounce 'Illinois'!"

Muscat. Veritas, a new rosé of Niagara, Isabella, Catawba, and Concord, comes in a potbellied screwcapped bottle suitable as a decanter. Also under screwcaps are the company's inexpensive California-New York blends called Valley chablis, rosé, and burgundy. Varietally-labeled Great Western table wines come in traditional bottles with traditional straight corks.

• 4 •

Walk a scant hundred yards from the Great Western cellars and you reach the Taylor winery. By acquiring the Pleasant Valley Company in 1961, Taylor became legally, as well as in fact, New York's "Bonded Winery No. 1." With its capacity of thirty million gallons, Taylor is now the largest American winery outside of California.

When I first visited Hammondsport in the late 1930s, Taylor consisted of just four buildings, the main one a four-story mansard-roofed structure with vaults cut back into the stone hillside. This quaint pre-Prohibition edifice now serves as a visitor reception center and office building. It is now flanked by a complex of three dozen new above-ground processing and aging cellars and warehouses covering some fifty acres. Taylor is an ultramodern winery, with batteries of pneumatic presses and rows of epoxy-lined steel tanks holding 100,000 gallons each, in sharp contrast to the smaller, old-fashioned redwood and oak casks that are still required for the aging of its wines. Everything here has a gleaming look; pumps, valves, tanks are bright and spic and span. Shining miles of stainless-steel and pyrex-glass pipes carry Taylor wines through laboratory-controlled, precisely timed processes and finally to high-speed bottling machines, after which they are cased for shipment around the world. The traditional method of clarifying bottle-fermented champagnes has recently been mechanized by introduction of the transfer process, in which the champagnes are filtered instead of being disgorged by hand.

Taylor dates from 1880, when Walter Taylor, a master cooper, came to Hammondsport with his bride to make barrels for the thriving wineries. The young couple settled on a seven-acre vineyard, and two years later bought a seventy-acre farm on Bully Hill, north of town. Taylor planted half of it to Ives and Delaware, the grapes then most in demand for red and white wines. He had worked with his father, George Taylor, before his marriage, and he now brought his father and mother to the farm. They made table wines and sold them in barrels to dealers in New York City. Three sons and two daughters were born to Walter and Addie Taylor between 1883 and 1903. All five grew up in the business and helped it grow. Salesmen, selling Taylor wine in bottles and barrels, covered territories in several states before the First World War.

In 1919, when Wartime Prohibition began, most of the Hammondsport wineries closed their doors, but the Taylors decided to go into the grape juice business instead. The four-story, mansard-roofed Columbia Winery, built in 1886, was one of those for sale, and the Taylors bought it and moved there from Bully Hill. During the dry era they sold fresh and concentrated grape juice to home winemakers and food distributors in the northeastern states. When the Taylors saw the end of Prohibition was ahead, they began modernizing the winery. At Repeal their wines were among the first on the market and they began their climb to leadership in the East. On taking over the Pleasant Valley winery, the Taylor Wine Company "went public," the first major American winery to put its stock on the open market, and soon had stockholders throughout the United States.

New York grapes for Taylor and Pleasant Valley wines are purchased under contract from growers cultivating more than a thousand acres. French hybrid varieties, first planted in the 1950s, have been a steadily increasing part of the two wineries' grape supply. A few years ago I asked the late Fred Taylor, the eldest of the three Taylor brothers, whether any planting of Vinifera varieties was being planned by the Taylor growers. His reply was "No—why should we try to do in New York State what they do so easily in California? The wines we grow are different from those of California and Europe, and ours please the American taste."

Until the Taylors died—Fred in 1968, Greyton two years later, and Clarence in 1976—the management of Taylor was a family clan. George A. Lawrence, who followed Fred as president, was the husband of Flora Taylor's daughter, Mary Lucy Keeler. Seaton "Zeke" Mendall, the Taylor vineyard consultant, was married to the late Rosalie Zimmer, the daughter of Lucy Taylor Zimmer. But being a Taylor was not essential to a career with the company. The outstanding example was Russell B. Douglas, the vice president of marketing and a company director, whose sales-planning genius made Taylor the largest-selling wine brand at its price level in the United States.

"Uncomplicated wines," port, sherry, sauterne, rhine, burgundy, claret, rosé, champagnes, sparkling burgundy, and vermouths have long been the mainstays of the Taylor line. The once-strong Labrusca flavors of Taylor table wines have become gradually less pronounced as the lately planted vineyards have yielded increased supplies of French hybrid grapes. Taylor Sauterne still retains its distinct grapy flavor of Delaware and Catawba, but the champagnes and the still rosé have only a hint of Labrusca fragrance. There now are four Taylor wines with proprietary names: Lake Country Red, White, Pink, and Gold. All three are blends with the French-American grapes, but have enough Labrusca character to make them distinctly different from California wines. But in 1976, Taylor, recognizing Americans' growing preference for non-Labrusca table wines, introduced those three "Californewyork" blends mentioned on an earlier page.

In 1977, with the Taylors gone, both the Taylor and Pleasant Valley wineries were purchased by the giant Coca-Cola Company of Atlanta, Georgia, in an exchange of stock valued at $93 million. In the next few months, Coke bought two California wineries, Sterling in the Napa Valley and the Monterey Vineyard cellar. With thirty-three million gallons' total capacity, Coke of Atlanta became fifth in the nation in winery ownership, about equal to the independent Coca-Cola Bottling Company of New York. This is of particularly historic Bacchic interest because Coca-Cola has now come full circle. Few realize that in 1885, before Coca-Cola became the American temperance drink, it was French Wine Coca, a flavored wine.

• 5 •

On Bully Hill Road, a mile and a half north of Hammondsport, are the 75,000-gallon Bully Hill winery, the Greyton H. Taylor Wine Museum, and the Winemaker's Shop. These are the works of Walter Stephen Taylor, the grandson of the Taylor winery's founder and once his late father's assistant at the Pleasant Valley winery.

Fired by his uncles in 1970 for publicly attacking the Taylor companies, Walter installed his own winery in his grandfather's horse barn and converted the original wooden winery into the museum dedicated to his father. The chief museum exhibits are relics of the more than fifty wineries that once operated around the Finger Lakes—vineyard implements, coopers' tools, presses, bottles, old wine advertisements, and early books about wine. One of the prizes is an ancient brandy still, a reminder that the pre-Prohibition wineries here also made and sold brandy. The Winemaker's Shop next door sells grape juice, winemaking equipment and supplies to amateur enologists. Walter is the co-author, with one-time Pleasant Valley winemaker Richard P. Vine, of *Home Winemaker's Handbook* (New York: Harper & Row, 1968), and he illustrated the book himself.

The Bully Hill winery turns out estate-bottled table wines labeled with the names of French hybrids, plus "varietals" of the native Delaware, Diamond, and Ives, and blends of hybrids and Labrusca types called Bully Hill red, white, and rosé. Added in 1976 was a bottle-fermented brut champagne produced from Seyval Blanc. Walter is assisted by Geisenheim-trained Hermann Wiemer, who also operates his own nursery business and helps other New York growers to establish Vinifera vineyards.

To sell his wines, six-foot-three, mustachioed Walter Taylor flies and hitchhikes across the country, wearing blue jeans and hiking boots and carrying a back-pack, guitar, harmonica, and a box of grapevines. He often distributes vines to his fellow passengers when he travels by air. Walter continually denounces other New York wineries for using California wines in their blends and for ameliorating wines with sugar and water to reduce their acidity—entirely legal practices considered necessary in the East. His slogan "Wine without Water" particularly annoys his neighbors, who point out that Walter sugars his wines, too. Walter's zany sales methods obviously work, because Bully Hill wines are sold in forty states.

• 6 •

Four miles up West Lake Road (Route 54A) from Hammondsport is venerable Gold Seal, the most imposing stone winery in the East. Founded in 1865 as the Urbana Wine Company, it is the second oldest in the district and looks its age, with its many stories under nineteenth-century gabled roofs crowned by lines of dormer windows and a pair of steeples. Only the highway and a narrow line of trees separate the winery from the waters of Keuka Lake, where steamers docked in early days to bring supplies and to load champagne. On the steep slopes above the winery is the company's original vineyard, expanded to 500 acres in recent years. This is the home of nationally distributed Gold Seal, Henri Marchant, and Charles Fournier wines and champagnes.

When the surrender of General Lee at Appomattox Courthouse was ending the Civil War in the spring of 1865, a group of Hammondsport merchants and Urbana Township farmers, following the example of Charles Champlin and his neighbors at Pleasant Valley, organized the Urbana Company to build the winery, and to make champagne. Their product was first called

"Imperial," but in 1887 was renamed "Gold Seal." The firm prospered, under the successive leadership of Clark Bell, D.M. Hildreth, and Walter Hildreth, for half a century before Prohibition. During the thirteen-year dry era, when it was headed by Corning newspaper publisher and former Congressman Edwin Stewart Underhill* and his son, it made sacramental and medicinal wines as the Gold Seal Products Company. At Repeal in 1933 the firm name was changed back to Urbana. In 1957, during a two-year association with Louis Benoist of Almadén in California, the company became Gold Seal Vineyards, Inc. In 1959 control was purchased by a group of eastern investors headed by Arthur Brody and Paul Schlem, who now are respectively the president and the chairman of the board. Since 1975 the company's wines have been marketed by Seagram's Browne Vintners.

In the first full century of operation, wine production at Gold Seal Vineyards was headed by only four men, all of French heritage. The first was Charles Le Breton, hired from the Roederer champagne cellars of Rheims. Jules Crance, from Moët et Chandon at Epernay, served from 1871 to 1923, and was succeeded by his son, Eugene. In 1934, President Underhill of Urbana asked Charles Fournier, the chief winemaker of Veuve Clicquot Ponsardin at Rheims, to recommend someone who could restore Gold Seal to its pre-Prohibition greatness. Fournier took the job himself, came to Hammondsport as Urbana production manager, brought his own champagne yeast culture from Veuve Clicquot, and became an American citizen.

Educated at the University of Paris and at French and Swiss wine schools, Fournier had seen the planting of the improved French hybrid grapes spreading in those countries. In 1936, while Philip Wagner was getting started with the hybrids in Maryland, Fournier introduced the Seibel 1000 and Ravat 6 varieties to Hammondsport. He introduced his own champagne blend, Charles Fournier Brut, to the American market in 1943, and it scored an immediate success. In 1950, for the first time in the history of the California State Fair at Sacramento, eastern and foreign wines were invited to be judged in open competition with those produced in California. Charles Fournier New York State Champagne was awarded the only gold medal—an event

*Of the same Underhill family whose members pioneered commercial grape growing in the Hudson Valley. All were descendants of Captain John Underhill, who came from England in the seventeenth century.

so discomfiting to the California vintners that no out-of-state wines were invited to their State Fair again.

In 1953, Fournier hired Dr. Konstantin Frank to start a nursery of Vinifera grapes at Urbana. The story of Dr. Frank and of his association with Fournier is told in the following section, but it should be pointed out here that the first Vinifera wines produced commercially in the East came from Fournier at Gold Seal. I was one of those present at the Winter 1961 dinner of the San Francisco Wine and Food Society in historic Jack's Restaurant when Gold Seal New York State 1959 Chardonnay and Johannisberg Riesling were served for the first time in the West. To the several California vintners in attendance that memorable night, it was a shock to realize that their long-acknowledged monopoly on the production of fine Vinifera wines in North America might at last be at an end.

Tall, lean, bespectacled Charles Fournier, who in appearance and speech resembles a foreign diplomat more than a vintner, retired in 1967 at the age of sixty-five, but continues visiting the winery daily as a consultant and as the honorary lifetime president of Gold Seal. Production of the wines is now supervised by another French-trained enologist, technical director Guy Devaux from the Societé Marne et Champagne of Epernay.

Their French heritage does not cause Fournier and Devaux to undervalue the "real grape" flavor of the principal New York State grapes. Since 1972 Gold Seal has been producing a sweet, slightly bubbly red wine labeled "Labrusca" for that family of native grapes. It has become so popular, despite some confusion with the Lambrusco wines from Italy, that Gold Seal since has added a sweet "Labrusca white."

The best-selling table wine, of the seemingly endless list Gold Seal makes, is Catawba Pink, a medium-sweet Labrusca-flavored rosé. But the company's finest are its vintage-dated Chardonnays, the Fournier Brut Champagne that won the gold medal in California, and Fournier Chablis Nature. The latter is the non-sparkling cuvée for the champagne, a blend of Chardonnay and several hybrids, with a delicate fruity fragrance scarcely recognizable as Labrusca and only in the aftertaste. Since Fournier's retirement, his Riesling Spätlese has been made in occasional years when "the noble mold" (*Botrytis cinerea*, which grows naturally in the Hammondsport district) has contributed its character to the grapes. In other years, the Rieslings become part of Gold Seal's Rhine Wine blend. From the company's Valois vineyard, planted in 1969 on the east side of Seneca Lake, an estate-bottled Johannisberg Riesling was introduced in 1976.

• 7 •

On Middle Road, a short drive from the Gold Seal Vineyard brings you to the small winery, the Vinifera vineyard, and the one-story red brick house of Dr. Konstantin Frank. A sturdy, proud, assertive man, he is the Russian-born German scientist who, after countless others had failed for three centuries, has shown dramatically that the Old World grape, the Vinifera, can be grown in eastern America. He is also the most controversial figure in the eastern wine industry, because he publicly condemns the French-American hybrid grapes which others have planted in preference to Vinifera.

Konstantin Frank was born in the Ukraine on July 4, 1899, the fourth of ten children of a farmer whose crops included grapes. He fought in the White Russian army, studied agriculture at the polytechnic institute of Odessa, organized collective farms in southern Ukraine for the Communists, then completed his studies, taught viticulture and enology, and did grape research at the local agricultural institute. During the German occupation, he became the institute's director. When the Second World War ended, he went to Austria and Bavaria and managed farm properties for the American occupation forces.

In 1951, at the age of fifty-two, Dr. Frank emigrated with his wife and three children to America, arriving in New York with forty dollars, unable to speak English. He got a job washing dishes at an Automat restaurant and saved enough to buy a one-way ticket to the nearest grape research station—the New York State Experiment Station at Geneva. There he described his Russian experience and applied for work on grapes. But instead, he says bitterly, "they let me hoe blueberries," and for two years he did only menial work.

Seeing the Finger Lakes growers planting the new French hybrids, he inquired why Vinifera were not being planted instead. The winters are too cold here, he was told; the delicate European varieties were likely to die when the ground froze. Having grown Vinifera himself in Russia—"where the temperature goes to forty below, where we had to bury the entire vine in the winter, where when we spit, it froze before it hit the ground"—Dr. Frank vehemently disagreed. He argued that the Old World grapes planted in the East during past centuries could not have died from cold, that rather they were killed by

Donald J. Flanagan, Buffalo NY

Dr. Konstantin Frank, the Russian-born German scientist who proved that the Old World's Vinifera grapes can be grown in eastern America, and who opposes the French-American hybrids.

diseases and pests; and these, he pointed out, modern science now had ways to control.

His argument came to the attention of Charles Fournier. Gold Seal's then president, too, had known frigid winters in Europe, and had seen Chardonnay and Pinot Noir thriving at Rheims and Epernay, seven degrees of latitude farther north than Hammondsport, after winters when temperatures in the French Champagne district fell below zero. Fournier realized that the emigré scientist might be right, and in 1953 hired him as a consultant for Gold Seal Vineyards.

Dr. Frank told Fournier what his research in Russia had shown: that what were needed in climates where the ground froze in winter were hardy roots onto which the Vinifera vines could be grafted—roots that would ripen the wood of the vine before the first winter freeze. To search for such roots, the two men set out on a tour of the Northeast countryside. In the garden of a convent at Québec in Canada, they found Pinot vines growing and were told that they yielded wine, in that stern climate, in one year out of three. From the monk in charge of the garden, they obtained some of his roots. Back at Gold Seal, they began grafting—to the Canadian roots and some of their local ones—Riesling, Chardonnay, Gewürztraminer, and Cabernet Sauvignon vines they obtained from the University of California vineyard at Davis.

During the next five years, thousands of experimental grafts were made and planted. In February 1957 came the critical test: temperatures on the lake slopes plummeted to twenty-five degrees below zero. Some of the hardiest Labrusca vines, Dutchess and Isabella in particular, were frozen and bore no grapes that year. On some of the Concord, Delaware, and Catawba vines, a tenth to a third of the buds were killed. But on the first Riesling and Chardonnay vines that had been grafted on hardy roots, fewer than a tenth of the buds showed any damage. And when vintage time came in the fall of that year, these vines at Gold Seal produced ripe grapes at a rate that promised crops of three to four tons per acre. Fournier needed no further convincing, but began planting the noble Vinifera vines as fast as he could get enough rootstocks on which to graft them.

Dr. Frank, triumphant, bought a tract of land nearby and started planting a vineyard of his own. When the first commercial New York State Vinifera wines, made at Gold Seal, were introduced in 1961, Dr. Frank proclaimed it "the second discovery of America," his own contribution to the nation of which he had become a citizen. He built his own winery, named it Vinifera Wine Cellars, and put his own wines on the market in 1965. He since has increased the winery's capacity to 60,000 gallons and his vineyard to seventy-eight acres, and has imported from Russia and Germany cold-resistant strains of additional Vinifera grape varieties. A son-in-law, Walter Volz, now manages the vineyard, and Dr. Frank's son, Willibald, markets the wines.

Virtually everyone who has tasted the Vinifera wines of Hammondsport has praised them. Dr. Frank's Trockenbeerenauslese 1961 was served in the White House and in the executive mansion at Albany. When first introduced, it was priced in stores at forty-five dollars a bottle and outsold equivalent German wines that cost a third less. Some of his Chardonnays that I have tasted at the winery have had the full character of French white burgundies, and one of his four-year-old Pinot Noirs had the nose of a ten-year-old wine.

But none of the big Finger Lakes wineries except Gold Seal has been willing to plant any commercial acreage of Vinifera. Dr. Frank blames the Geneva Experiment Station, which has pronounced the Vinifera varieties "marginal," less hardy than the French hybrids, too risky to be cultivated by anyone except an expert, and not recommended for large-scale commercial planting in New York State.

This enrages Dr. Frank, who incidentally enjoys a fight. He insists that the Vinifera require no more care than the hybrids and claims that they ripen better at Hammondsport than in Germany or France. "The Genevians say the growers must be experts to grow these grapes here," he fumes. "The poor Italian and Russian peasants with their shovels can do it, but the American farmer with his push-button tools cannot. It is unbelievable that the hybrids, prohibited everywhere except in

France and the United States, not good enough for poor Italian or even poor Russian peasants, can be called good enough for the Americans, the most prosperous people in the world."

Answering Dr. Frank's attacks, the Geneva Station still recommends the hybrids, but concedes in its publications that his Riesling wines are "comparable to those of Germany," that his Chardonnay and Pinot Noir "stand with the finest French burgundies," and that "there is undoubtedly a place for a certain percentage of these superb connoisseurs' wines."

Charles Fournier, the man in the middle of the controversy, is a close friend of Dr. Frank, whom he calls "Kotja," but has avoided taking either side. When Fournier told me that Gold Seal would continue to grow Vinifera, he explained: "It is still a young experiment. We feel safer with the hybrids, but we love the Vinifera wines." Fournier believes the future of Vinifera in the East depends on the wine-buying public, that if we are willing to pay the prices for fine eastern wines that we pay for prestige European labels, the eastern vintners will find it profitable to plant the *cépages nobles* and to produce superlative wines of their types.

• 8 •

Returning on Middle Road toward Hammondsport from Dr. Frank's winery, you may be able to visit one of New York State's newest farmer wineries. At this writing it was being built on the Heron Hill Vineyard of Peter Johnstone and his partner, grape grower John Ingle of Naples.

Johnstone, a former copywriter for a New York City advertising agency, came here in 1970 and planted twenty acres of Chardonnay and White Riesling. By 1977 the vines were showing good growth despite some winter injury (also evident in Dr. Frank's vineyard) and Johnstone broke ground for a 20,000-gallon winery since built on two levels into the side of Bully Hill. Heron Hill is only the third Vinifera vineyard on Lake Keuka; the others are Dr. Frank's and Gold Seal's.

• 9 •

At the head of Seneca Lake are the city of Geneva and the big State Agricultural Experiment Station, where a stepped-up program of grape and wine research has been under way since 1962.

It was at the Geneva Station, founded in 1882 and associated with Cornell University, that famed horticulturist Ulysses Prentiss Hedrick and his colleagues crossbred and tamed many American wild vines and developed some of the varieties now used in making eastern wines. Dr. Hedrick, born in 1870 in a log cabin in Iowa, came to Geneva in 1905 via agricultural colleges in Michigan, Utah, and Oregon. A prolific writer, he was the great chronicler of grapes in America and is chiefly remembered for his monumental book on *Grapes of New York* (1908). Winegrowing was Hedrick's chief interest, and when Prohibition put a stop to his winemaking research, he saved the Geneva Station's best grapes for himself and had his chauffeur take them home and make them into wine for him. Hedrick espoused the homely art of fermentation and wrote two books of advice to home winemakers and amateur vineyardists. He was also the first—long before Dr. Frank—to prove that it is possible to grow Vinifera in the East. "We know now how to control the insects and fungi that attack them," he wrote in 1945 in his *Grapes and Wines from Home Vineyards.* Hedrick, however, found it necessary to cover his Vinifera vines with earth before each winter to keep them from freezing. (But, at Hammondsport, Dr. Frank contends that the Vinifera varieties Hedrick tested at Geneva did not include the cold-resistant strains of the noble grapes grown in northern Europe. Dr. Frank only hills up the earth to protect his vines at the point where they are grafted, the same winter protection given to grafted hybrid vines.)

When Repeal came in 1933, Prohibitionist influence was still strong at Albany, and a request by Cornell University for a state appropriation of $50,000 for wine research at Geneva was flatly turned down. Although wine work at the station was taboo, Professors Richard Wellington and George D. Oberle organized a grape-testing and wine quality improvement program with New York and Canadian wineries, in whose cellars their experimental wines were made. When Dr. Oberle moved to Virginia in 1948, and Dr. Hedrick died three years later, Professor John Einset and others carried on this program. During the next decade, as winegrowing grew in importance and the Drys' political strength waned, the repeated requests by Cornell for wine research funds won support and a state appropriation was finally approved in 1962. Federal purse strings, too, were unloosed two years later at the death of fanatical dry Congressman Clarence Cannon, and "wine" was no longer a word the Geneva professors feared to pronounce. Cornell went so far as to publish a bulletin on home winemaking, authored by Dr. Willard B. Robinson—the first of its kind to come from any American university.

Although New York State has no separate college department of viticulture and enology such as that at the University of California, the Department of Pomology at Cornell has been renamed "Pomology and Viticulture" since 1974. Besides undergraduate courses in viticultural subjects and food fermentation taught at Cornell, there is advanced instruction at Geneva, where graduate and post-doctoral students work on wine projects. Experimental wines made at Geneva now number six hundred per year. Annual workshops are held there for professional enologists, with extra sessions at intervals for farm wineries and amateurs. Cornell's grape-breeding program has been expanded far beyond its proportions in Hedrick's time. A new non-foxy wine grape named Cayuga White, developed by Dr. John Einset, has been widely planted since its release in 1973. Dr. Robert Pool from the University of California, who now heads the breeding program, emphasizes hybrids but believes Vinifera white wines grown in New York State can equal or excel California's. A seven-year grafting study by Dr. Keith Kimball at Geneva has shown Concord growers how to convert their vineyards in a single year to grow hybrids or Vinifera instead. The advances in research at Geneva helped lead to the formation in 1976 of an eastern section of the American Society of Enologists, headed by the Taylor winery's research director Andrew Rice.

A faculty group of Cornell amateur winemakers, who call themselves the Ithaca Oenological Union, helped Dr. Frank in 1967 to organize the American Wine Society, which had its headquarters at the home of Emeritus Professor of Chemistry Albert W. Laubengayer until it was moved seven years later to Michigan.

• 10 •

A revival of winegrowing is in progress between Seneca and Cayuga Lakes, southeast of Geneva. Some say this area has the best climate for wine grapes, especially Vinifera, in all of the Finger Lakes district. There were wineries here before Prohibition.

The first winery to start between the lakes in more than half a century was built in 1977. It is navy veteran Stanley Wagner's 50,000-gallon Wagner Farms cellar on Route 414 three miles south of Lodi near the east shore of Seneca. His family has farmed here since Revolutionary days. Wagner grows French hybrids to make his wines, but he also raises Concords. With his two mechanical harvesters he picks grapes for fourteen other growers.

South of Wagner, at the oldtime lake resort of Valois, Kenneth Barber, president of the New York State Wine Grape Growers Association, also plans a winery. Several neighboring farmers have talked of starting a cooperative winery to use the grapes of two hundred growers.

On the west shore of Cayuga near Ovid, President Robert Plane of Clarkson University, an expert home winemaker, and his wife Mary Moore Plane, a former Cornell administrator, have planted forty-five acres of Vinifera, hybrids, and Dutchess and hope someday to be making Cayuga Vineyard wines for sale. At Cobblestone Farm on the lake seven miles north of Ovid, Peter and Bonnie Hahn dream of starting a winery on the young hybrid vineyard beside their famous house, built of cobblestones by Julius Bull in 1833.

• 11 •

In earlier days ferryboats from Valois crossed Seneca Lake, but now, to visit the wineries west of the lake, you must drive around it through either Geneva or Watkins Glen.

On Route 14, nine miles north of Watkins Glen, is the 25,000-gallon Glenora Wine Cellar. It was built in 1977, a year after the passage of the farm winery law, by Eastman Beers, his son-in-law Gene Pierce, and two fellow farmers who cultivate a total of 250 acres, mostly of hybrids, around Dundee. Their winemaker is a California-trained New Yorker, John Williams, who after graduating from Cornell earned a degree in enology at UC Davis.

From there it is several miles northwest to the metal-roofed Villa d'Ingianni winery on Route 54, which skirts the east shore of Keuka Lake. Dr. Vincente d'Ingianni, who came here from New Orleans in 1960, conducts his medical practice from his home beside the small winery, which he opened in 1973. His dozen wines range from Johannisberg Riesling, Delaware, and Baco Noir to sauterne.

Another seven-mile drive takes you to Penn Yan at the head of Keuka, where a new Finger Lakes Grape Festival was inaugurated in 1976. The festival was held annually ten miles west at Naples until 1970, when unruly crowds forced that small town to give it up. Now revived on the spacious Yates County fairgrounds in Penn Yan, the celebration (on the last weekend of September) features outdoor concerts, parade, art show, bus tours of the vineyards, grape cookery contest, judging of homemade wines, grape stompings, and a festival ball. (Yes, Penn Yan sounds like an Indian name, but it stands for

Pennsylvanians and Yankees, the earliest settlers of this area.)

In Penn Yan the principal attraction until 1977 was the Boordy Vineyards winery on Liberty Street. It once was Captain Paul Garrett's Penn Yan Cellar. If the "Boordy" name reminds you of Philip and Jocelyn Wagner's vineyard at Riderwood near Baltimore, you are correct. Arthur Wolcott, the president of Seneca Foods Corporation, a big processor of applesauce and fresh grape juice, persuaded Wagner to "pool the resources" of Seneca and the Wagners to produce Boordy Vineyard wines in two more states for nationwide sale. New York State Boordy wines were made at Penn Yan beginning in 1970, and Washington State Boordy wines were made in Seneca's grape-juice plant at Prosser. But neither was successful; the Boordy Prosser plant was closed in 1976, and the one at Penn Yan in the following year.

• 12 •

Naples, at the south end of Canandaigua Lake in Ontario County, has been the home of Widmer's wines since their first vintage in 1888. Widmer's Wine Cellars, with its capacity of four million gallons, is the only winery in Naples Valley and is its chief industry and tourist attraction.

Yankees of English and Scottish origin were the first settlers in this valley. Presumably it was they who named it incongruously for Naples in Italy, for surely the German and German-Swiss immigrants who arrived in the mid-nineteenth century would have named it the Rhine Valley, which it more nearly resembles, and from which many of them came. Most local histories credit the founding of the Naples grape industry to the German vinedresser, Andrew Reisinger, who came here from the Hammondsport district in 1852, although Edward A. McKay, an attorney of Naples village, had planted a vineyard of Isabella grapes four years before. It was also a German, Hiram Maxfield, the leading banker of Naples, who built the first winery here in 1861.

Maxfield's wines and champagne were already well established when in 1882 John Jacob Widmer came to Naples with his family from the Swiss village of Scherz. Jacob wanted to go into the wine business, but there already were several wineries around Naples, and banker-vintner Maxfield, to discourage more competition, refused to lend Widmer any money. Jacob succeeded, however, in getting a thousand-dollar loan from the rival Granby bank. He bought and cleared a tract of land, and planted grapes on its western slope to get the morning sun. By

The Widmer Winery's "cellar on the roof" in which sherry ages outdoors in oak barrels for four years at Naples, New York.

day, Jacob and his wife Lisette toiled in the vineyard, and by night they built their home with a stone-walled basement, in which they made their first wine. By 1910 their business had grown to such a point that they could afford to send their youngest son, Will, to the Royal Wine School of Germany at Geisenheim. There Will was trained in Old World viniculture and wine lore, which the company and its products still reflect today.

During Prohibition, the rival Maxfield Cellars closed down, but the Widmers kept going by making grape juice, nonalcoholic wine jellies and wine sauce. At Repeal in 1933, Widmer's and Maxfield's both resumed making wine, but Widmer's was already far ahead. Then President Will Widmer bought out and absorbed the competitor whose founder, half a century earlier, had refused John Jacob Widmer a loan.

While at the Geisenheim wine school, Will Widmer had learned that when Riesling grapes are left late on the vines in autumn, they grow sweeter and richer, and that sometimes a beneficent mold grows on them, causing them to shrivel and to develop an unusual flavor and aroma. He also learned that wines made from such grapes bring premium prices when labeled "Spätlese" (late picking), still higher prices when labeled "Auslese" (selected picking), and astronomical prices when labeled "Trockenbeerenauslese" (dried-berry-selection). The kindly mold is *Botrytis cinerea,* called *Edelfäule* in Germany and *pourriture noble* in France. In the fall of 1939, Widmer went walking through his vineyard after the harvest. On some of the leftover white grapes he saw a gray mold developing, and he decided it must be the *Edelfäule*. He picked all the graying berries he could find, fermented their juice, and ended up with eleven gallons of Spätlese wine. The grape variety wasn't the true Riesling, the noble member of the Vinifera family, but the Labrusca variety known as Missouri Riesling, planted by his father many years before. Dr. Ulysses Hedrick's books state that the Missouri Riesling was bred about 1860 by Nicholas Grein of Hermann, Missouri, by crossing Taylor, a local *Vitis riparia* seedling, with a Labrusca variety. But to Will Widmer, the wine tasted like Riesling, and "Widmer's New York State Riesling" is what he called it, and what its label continued to say—in some years with "Spätlese" or "Auslese" added—until Will Widmer died in 1968. Widmer always insisted that Hedrick's books were wrong, that Missouri Riesling must have been at least a relative of the true White Riesling, or that at least its Labrusca parent must have had some Vinifera blood.

The samples of Widmer Riesling Spätlese that I tasted in those years indeed resembled good semi-dry German Rhine wines, and to my surprise, because I have tasted other wines of Missouri Rieslings, the Widmer versions had no noticeable Labrusca taste.

When in 1939 author-importer Frank Schoonmaker was looking for American "varietal" wines to sell with his line of imports, his nationwide tasting tour took him to Naples. He found Widmer's like the other eastern wineries, selling most of its wines as sauterne, burgundy, rhine, port, and sherry, but Will Widmer also had some unblended wines of Elvira and Delaware. Beginning in 1941, Schoonmaker introduced the eastern wine-buying public to Canandaigua Lake Elvira and Delaware, and with them an assortment of "varietal" wines made from Widmer's other grapes: Niagara, Salem, Dutchess, Vergennes, Moore's Diamond, and Isabella. Widmer's thus became the first New York State winery to specialize in "varietal" wines. During the next three decades Niagara became the best seller among the company's long list of wines. The samples of Widmer's Lake Niagara I have tasted have shown me why. To my taste it has been the ideal blend of the grapy Labrusca flavor in a tart, medium-sweet white wine.

Widmer's has been different in several additional ways. One is its use of vintage labeling, which the other Finger Lakes wineries formerly avoided because they preferred to blend together wines of different years. I once tasted at the winery an eleven-year-old Widmerheimer which was remarkably fresh for a white table wine of that age and which, though made of native

Tying vines to trellis wires in the Widmer Vineyard at Naples, New York.

grapes, had no perceptible Labrusca taste. This was also true of an eleven-year-old port, which, I was amazed to learn, was made entirely of Concord grapes. Eastern winemakers claim the foxiness disappears from Labrusca wines if they are stored for several years in small casks.

Widmer's chief trademark is its "cellar on the roof." The first thing you notice as you drive up the valley toward the winery is the main cellar roof covered with barrels—some twelve thousand of them in tiers four deep—enough to cover several acres. In these barrels, exposed to summer heat and winter snow, the sherries are aged for four years before blending in a solera-like system. I have seen sherries aged outdoors this way in Ohio, California, Mexico, and South America (in Uruguay, it is done in glass jugs), but never in the vast quantity exposed at Widmer.

In 1961, control of Widmer's was purchased by Rochester financiers George and Walter Todd, who brought in as president of the company a professional manager named Ernest Reveal. Nine years later, Widmer's was sold to the R. T. French Company, the Rochester producer of mustard and spices which in turn is owned by Reckitt & Colman, the London spice and food products firm which also has wine interests in Europe and Australia. Reveal started Widmer's producing its own champagne (made by the Charmat process when I was last there) and introduced three new Widmer proprietary table wines, French hybrid-Labrusca-California blends named Naples Valley Red, White, and Pink.

Then Widmer's in 1970, after testing Vinifera vines to see how they would grow at Naples, became the first New York

State vintner since Captain Paul Garrett to cross the continent and plant its own vineyard in California. In a million-dollar venture, it purchased and planted nearly 500 acres in the Alexander Valley of Sonoma County with such red wine varieties as Cabernet Sauvignon and Pinot Noir. Wines of these grapes were produced under the Widmer label by the Louis Martini winery for a few years, but much of the Widmer vineyard in California since has been sold.

Visitors to the big Finger Lakes wineries, such as Widmer's, are hospitably received. The cellar tours offered are interesting, and each ends with a glass of wine, except for youngsters, who get grape juice. But it is well to remember, in planning a trip to the lakes, to inquire first when each winery will be open. In years past, the largest ones were closed on holidays and Sundays (because of the peculiar New York hours allotted for drinking). Some were closed on Saturdays, too, and Taylor and Widmer were shut down completely during the last two full weeks of July. At the height of the tourist season, winery-visiting is so popular that people who miss the last afternoon tour of a cellar have been known to stay overnight in the district to join the first tour in the morning. Wines can now be purchased at most of the wineries, but some of them, respectful of the powerful associations of New York liquor store owners, would sell only sample packages of half a dozen bottles to visitors, advising those who wished larger quantities to make such purchases at retail stores.

• 13 •

In the city of Canandaigua, at the opposite end of the lake from Naples, is the second largest Finger Lakes District winery, Canandaigua Industries. Its sprawling 12-million-gallon plant offers no visitor tours, nor is it surrounded by vineyards. It is the main New York winery of Marvin and Mack Sands, who also own Richard's Cellars in Virginia, Tenner Brothers vineyard and winery in South Carolina, and the Bisceglia Bros. winery in the San Joaquin Valley of California.

Back in 1954, Marvin Sands was operating Canandaigua as a bulk wine plant when he and his sales manager, Robert Meenan, had a bright thought. What occurred to them was that pink wines might sell in greater volume in this country if their French name—*vin rosé*, which Americans have difficulty pronouncing—were changed to simply "rose." This gave them the idea for what since has become one of the largest selling wines in the nation—their Richard's Wild Irish Rose. Pink, sweet, Labrusca-flavored (and named for Marvin's eldest son, Richard), it comes in both 20 percent and 14 percent versions, and the latter is a grapy, quite pleasant rosé. They now bottle many of their wines, but have continued their bulk wine business, shipping kosher, other Labrusca, and fruit wines in tank cars from coast to coast. They have also purchased the old Putnam or Hammondsport winery in Hammondsport to make their own champagnes.

Meanwhile, Mack Sands pursues his dream of emulating the late Captain Garrett by making Virginia Dare wine at Canandaigua, where Garrett had one of his many wineries. Garrett's idea was to blend the wines of East and West, and this the Sandses also do, advertising their Virginia Dare as "the best of California and New York State blended in a single wine." But they have ignored one of the keys to Garrett's original success, which was to make the name mean only an individual, distinctive wine with the Scuppernong wine of the South as part of its blend. Instead, Virginia Dare now represents a "complete line" of generic types, from sauterne and burgundy to port and sherry. Only two of the "line," Virginia Dare White and Rosé, contain some Scuppernong wine. And whether the white closely resembles the wine Captain Garrett served me in 1934, I cannot, after half a lifetime, be sure.

• 14 •

Another Finger Lakes winery that is interesting to visit is at the O-Neh-Da Vineyard, hidden among the hills beside Hemlock Lake in Livingston County. O-Neh-Da is the Seneca Indian word for hemlock. The vineyard's post office address is Conesus, but it is reached by a roundabout route through Livonia Center or Hemlock, the nearest villages.

This is the only Church-owned winery outside of California, the property of a missionary order, the Society of the Divine Word. On the way there, a visit to the lovely grottoes beside St. Michael's Seminary is alone worth the trip. The old-fashioned winery, with two underground levels, is small, compared to the Catholic wineries in California, holding only 150,000 gallons.

O-Neh-Da Vineyard was founded in 1872 by Bishop Bernard McQuaid, the first Catholic bishop of Rochester, who said, "We can retire to the peaceful slopes of Hemlock Lake and in the cultivation of the grapes help priests to say Mass with wine that is wine." For half a century before Prohibition, O-Neh-Da made altar wines for the clergy. The winery was closed during the dry era, and only twenty acres of the vineyard were left when it reopened in 1936. Its rehabilitation was entrusted to German-born winemaker Leo Goering, who came in that year from the famed Geisenheim Institute. By 1968 the vines again covered more than a hundred acres, and enough wine was being produced to supply the clergy throughout the East. In that year the property was leased by the Society to the Cribari family of Fresno, California, who make and sell altar wines nationally through their Barry Wine Company, which is headed by Albert B. (Skip) Cribari.

Leo Goering has retired but still lives behind the winery. O-Neh-Da wines are still made from the Labrusca and French hybrid grapes he planted. Goering trained John J. Cicero, who was born at nearby Livonia, to succeed him as the viticulturist and winemaker. Winery manager Bob Hayward and Cicero show visitors through the cellars on weekdays and invite them to taste the wines. Most of the visitors prefer the Delaware altar wine and the haut sauterne, which is made mostly of the Elvira grape.

Cicero and his wife Janet also have their own Livonia Vineyard of French hybrids, which they began planting in 1966. Now they have opened their own small farm winery on Shelly Road a half-mile south of Livonia.

8

Chautauqua, Niagara, and the Hudson Valley

HE Chautauqua-Erie Grape Belt, the sixty-mile-long stretch of New York's Lake Erie shore which the fanatical Prohibitionists, Doctors Thomas and Charles Welch, made famous as "the grape juice capital of the world," has also become a winegrowing district.

Five wineries, two of them opened since the farm winery law was passed in 1976, and more than five hundred other growers now have wine-grape vineyards in the district, where for generations most of the grapes grown have been Concords for fresh use and for juice. The curious fact is that while the Finger Lakes were becoming the chief winemaking district of the East at the end of the nineteenth century, temperance crusaders were persuading Chautauqua Belt farmers not to plant the grapes used for wine, but to plant Concords instead. Now, with the soaring national demand for table wines, the wineries in the Finger Lakes and other parts of New York State are depending on the Chautauqua Belt vineyards to furnish a large part of their wine-grape supply.

This is the district which the late Professor Ulysses Hedrick called, because of its climate, "the second most important viticultural section in eastern America, next to the Finger Lakes." In grape production, however, it is first, because its 23,000 acres of vines, of which fully a ninth are now wine-grape varieties, produce more than half of the state's total annual harvest. Almost a hundred of the new mechanical harvesting machines now operate here, picking more than four fifths of the grape crop.

The Grape Belt is narrow, extending inland from Lake Erie only three to sixteen miles, because grapes grow only in those sections where lake breezes protect the vines from spring and fall frosts. In New York State, the Belt extends from Erie County southwestward to the Pennsylvania border. The Chautauqua County shore section, one of the most productive, is now threatened by urbanization, which worries the Chautauqua farmers because they have nowhere else to go.

• 2 •

It was near Brocton in Chautauqua County that Baptist Deacon Elijah Fay founded the grape industry of western New York and northwestern Pennsylvania, when he planted his vineyard of wild grapes in 1818. At Brocton the first winery in the area was built in 1859 by Deacon Fay's son Joseph, with two partners, Garrett Ryckman and Rufus Haywood. Additional wineries soon started up nearby: the Wine House of Thomas Quigley in 1862, the South Shore Wine Company across the Pennsylvania line a year later, the Empire Vineyards winery of Ralph D. Fuller in 1867, and the Jonas Martin cellar, on the foundation of which St. Patrick's Church in Brocton now stands.

Brocton is also where the bearded mystic, Thomas Lake Harris, built a winery in 1867 to make his "Brotherhood" wines, which he claimed were "infused with the divine aura, potentialized in the joy spirit." The strange story of Harris centers around his utopian "Brotherhood of the New Life" and his semi-communistic colonies in three states. Relics of his Brocton colony, which he named "The Use," can still be seen near the lakeshore. Harris's great house on West Lake Road is now the residence of businessman Douglas Hayes. The ground floor of the winery, on Peerless Street, serves a family as a garage and chicken coop, but the underground cellar is still intact. Mrs. Prudence Work, editor of the Brocton *Beacon,* has found the ruins of at least six more nineteenth-century wineries between Brocton and nearby Portland.

While the Chautauqua Belt wineries thrived during the 1870s, using Delaware, Catawba, and Isabella grapes, Ephraim Bull's new Concord grape variety was introduced to the district. With the Concord, a table-grape industry began to develop. At the same time, the dry crusade, which had begun in the eastern part of the state, was spreading westward. It found its strongest footholds in two Chautauqua County villages, Jamestown and Fredonia. At Fredonia, in 1873, Mrs. Esther McNeil organized the first unit of the Woman's Christian Temperance Union. Her WCTU ladies, denouncing the local wineries for the sin of allowing grapes to ferment, exhorted all God-fearing farmers to plant the Concord in place of the Delaware and Catawba, because the Concord was tolerated as a fresh eating grape, while the Delaware and Catawba were grown only to make wine.

During the 1880s, table grapes sold well in the eastern cities, and Concord planting reached boom proportions. Chautauqua County merchants, doctors, and lawyers, everyone who could shake loose a down payment, bought farms and set out more Concord vineyards. Two factories were built just to make the baskets in which the grapes were shipped for sale. Concord production swelled to such a point during the 1890s that much of the crop remained unsold. The bottom then dropped out of the market, and many who had invested their last dollars were ruined.

In 1897, attracted by the surplus of cheap Concords, there came to Chautauqua County the ardent dry dentists, the Doctors Welch, who had started the grape juice industry. Only a year earlier they had moved their juice-pressing operation from Vineland, New Jersey, to Watkins Glen in the Finger Lakes District. The Watkins Glen operation was successful, but they chose a new site at Westfield, eight miles southwest of Brocton, and built there the world's first large grape juice plant. The Welches were then launching the first advertising campaign for their product; renamed only seven years earlier, it was now "grape juice" instead of "unfermented wine." Dr. Charles Welch gave up his dental practice when he moved to Westfield, and became its most prominent citizen. Old residents still remember him for his shock of white hair, his flowing artist-style ties, the autos in which he raced between the plant and the vineyards, and the high-toned restaurant he opened at the Welch plant, where Concord grape juice was always served, but never any wine or liquor. It became a tradition in the county that Dr. Welch personally would start each grape-picking season by issuing a ten-minute blast of the Westfield plant's steam whistle. By 1913, when Secretary of State William Jennings Bryan shocked the diplomatic world by serving Welch's Grape Juice instead of wine to the British ambassador at a state dinner in Washington, an entire Welch Block had been constructed in Westfield.

Wartime Prohibition forced the local wineries to close, but the vineyardists still prospered, selling their surplus grapes to home winemakers and bootleggers in the cities. Local boosters then established an annual grape festival at Brocton. Notable for the absence of any mention of Bacchus, it celebrated instead the memory of Deacon Fay and praised only the fresh Concord grape and its pasteurized juice. By the end of the 1920s, the fact that the county had once produced wine was almost forgotten.

At Repeal, in 1933, two small wineries were opened in the district. One was at Fredonia. The other, at Brocton, was primarily a grape juice plant that began making wine as a sideline. Its proprietor was the financial wizard, Jacob Merrill (Jack) Kaplan, once known as "the Boston molasses king." In 1945, Kaplan bought control of the Welch Grape Juice Company from a Tennessee banking syndicate, which had acquired it after the death of Dr. Charles Welch in 1926. And at the Brocton plant in 1950, Kaplan put the Welch Company into the wine business—a development at which the Doctors Welch, father and son, must have revolved many times in their graves. This was when the new kosher wine type, in which extra sweetening makes the Concord flavor pleasant to taste in a wine, was setting sensational sales records in every state where wine was sold. Wineries across the country were buying Concord grapes or juice and rushing into production with their own versions of the sweet kosher wine. Kaplan's idea was that by giving his version the Welch name, which signified the Concord flavor to millions, he could outsell the kosher leaders, Manischewitz and Mogen David. But his "Welch's Refreshment Wine" failed to sell, perhaps because its label didn't say it was kosher. And in 1959 the Welch Company, which Kaplan meanwhile had sold to the National Grape Co-operative Association, abruptly discontinued making wine.

• 3 •

In 1960, a young agricultural expert named Fred Johnson came home to Westfield, his birthplace, after a ten-year stay in South America. He surveyed the seventy-year-old Concord vineyard his father had left him, studied the trends in local agriculture, and concluded that the long-range future of the Chautauqua Grape Belt lay not in producing more Welch's Grape Juice nor in supplying the kosher wineries, but in growing distinctive dry table wines.

He began ripping out his Concord vines and replanting most of his 125 acres with wine grapes—French hybrids, Delaware, and Ives. In what had been the farm's cold storage house for apples, he installed casks and a crusher, and in 1961 he started the Frederick S. Johnson Vineyards Winery, the first to open in the area in twenty-eight years, and began making the Chautauqua district's first estate-bottled wines.

Johnson, a torpedo-bomber pilot in the Pacific during the Second World War, was not a stranger to winemaking. As a boy, he had helped his father make wine at home from Delaware and Catawba grapes, and at Cornell he had been trained in horticulture and chemistry. After the war, as a specialist in tropical agriculture, he had worked on pineapples for Dole in Hawaii, then had set up Nelson Rockefeller's plantations in Venezuela and Ecuador. Exposed during his travels to the wines of many countries, he was amazed that Chautauqua had not become an important wine district long ago.

His 75,000-gallon winery uses only part of his grapes; the rest are sold fresh. His "Johnson Estate" labels, which he designed himself, picture his vineyard and the 145-year-old brick house in which he was born. His wines, which have won a consumer following in New York State, include Seyval Blanc, Chancellor Noir, Delaware, Dry White, Rosé, Dry Red, and Vin Rouge. But his best thus far is a wine Johnson had never intended to make. In 1975, he had promised to sell his Delaware crop to another winery. The buyer decided he could not use them, and the grapes remained unpicked for several weeks. They became infected with Botrytis, the "noble mold," and young winemaker William Gulvin made them into a late-harvest type. Johnson and his wife Cecily named the wine Liebestropfchen (little love drops). It created a sensation at tastings, winning a silver medal at the Wineries Unlimited judging of eastern wines at Lancaster, Pennsylvania, in 1977. Johnson sees the Chautauqua district's future in such wines as his white French hybrids, which contain enough Delaware to give them fragrance without a recognizable Labrusca taste. Vineyard and winery tours and tasting are offered visitors from June through August at the Johnson winery on West Main Road.

• 4 •

When table-wine consumption in the United States reached unprecedented levels in the mid-1960s, wineries as distant as Ohio and Illinois reached into the Chautauqua Belt to buy more grapes. In 1967, the Mogen David Wine Corporation of Chicago, which had bought most of its grapes in Michigan, Pennsylvania, and Ohio, decided to begin growing its own around Westfield and to open its own winery there. It was a case of the winery going to the vineyard.

Mogen David acquired 500 acres of Chautauqua vineyard land and a grape juice plant, which it turned into a winery, with two more plants for wine storage. It now has a total capacity of two million gallons at Westfield. And though Mogen David is the world's biggest maker of kosher Concord wine, its new plantings include French hybrids (Maréchal Foch and Seyve-Villard 5247) and experimental plots of Vinifera varieties such as Cabernet Sauvignon, Pinot Noir, White Riesling, and Chardonnay. Next to the Welch Company, Mogen David is now the biggest single user of Chautauqua grapes.

• 5 •

Fourteen miles from Westfield, on the other side of Brocton, is Fredonia, which orator Chauncey Depew once called "the most beautiful village in New York State." In Depew's time, guidebooks listed as Fredonia's chief landmark the drinking-water fountain erected in memory of WCTU pioneer Esther McNeil. The fountain still gushes forth the drink of temperance in Lafayette Park in the center of town, but guidebooks nowadays ignore the lady, and instead list as a tourist attraction the Fredonia Products Company winery on Water Street, because it offers free cellar tours and wine tasting on weekdays (and if especially arranged, on weekends as well). This is the winery that Leo Star's Manischewitz wine built from a few small tanks in the year of Repeal to its present capacity of four million gallons, not counting its additional new plant and bottling cellar at nearby Dunkirk. The Fredonia winery is operated by a galaxy of Leo Star's nephews, and makes kosher, Concord, and fruit wines under five of its own brands, which can be tasted in its Winston Treasure Room. But its principal product is fresh grape juice, which it ships in giant refrigerated tank trucks to Brooklyn to be made into Manischewitz wines.

In 1964 the Fredonia firm, which had long used local Concords and had never had to grow its own grapes, began planting 500 acres of wine grapes—Delawares, Catawbas, and French hybrids—in mostly virgin land west of the town.

• 6 •

From US Route 20, east of Fredonia, South Roberts Road leads to the Woodbury Fruit Farm near Dunkirk and to one of the finest Vinifera vineyards in the East. Dunkirk lawyer Robert Woodbury and his wife Martha, dedicated home winemakers, produced there in 1972 the first Vinifera vintage in Chautauqua

County, a Chardonnay which, had I tasted it "blind," I could have mistaken for a fine white burgundy. Credit its quality not to their cellar expertise, but to the microclimate and the care they lavish on their vineyard three miles inland from Lake Erie. I since have tasted an equally fine Chardonnay made at a winery in Rhode Island from grapes the vintner purchased from the Woodburys.

Off Route 39, between Fredonia and Forestville, is the 16,000-gallon Merritt Estate winery, the first to open in the Chautauqua Belt under the 1976 farm winery law. The cool cellar, equipped for modern production and aging, provides a home for the wine grapes grown on the Triple M Farms, which are named for the late noted horticulturist James M. Merritt and his sons William and James. Merritt Estate's winemaker is Casablanca-born, French-trained enologist Raymond Knafo, who came from Morocco to New York State in 1966 to do wine research at Cornell University and then became the Boordy Vineyards' winemaker at Penn Yan. The red wines he made there won gold and silver medals at competitions in Czechoslovakia in 1972 and 1975.

At nearby Sheridan, another farm winery was built in 1977 by the Feinen Brothers, David, Ronald, and Richard, who with their late father Rudolph had added French hybrids to the Labrusca types grown on their vineyards. Farther north along the lake, near Angola, Faustino Galante and his son Charles opened the 4,000-gallon Galante's Farm Winery on their old fifteen-acre Fredonia and Concord vineyard on Erie Road.

• 7 •

Dry influence in the Grape Belt is not yet dead. A history of the county's grape industry, published serially in a county newspaper, scrupulously avoids any mention of wine. The Chautauqua County Historical Museum in Westfield still contains no mementos of the early-day wineries. And wine is still illegal at Chautauqua, the famous century-old summer center of religion, education, music and recreation on Chautauqua Lake. This is not surprising, for Chautauqua is where the WCTU really began. There in 1873, Mrs. McNeil's fanatical females laid the detailed plans for the national organization that was formed at Cleveland a year later, the plans that ultimately brought about National Prohibition. To this day, the owners of homes at Chautauqua hold their property on a condition, fortunately not enforced, that if any "intoxicating liquor" is ever used on their premises, their land, houses, and all the contents are automatically forfeited to the Chautauqua Institution.

But by the 1970s the local view of wine had begun to change. When, for example, Silver Creek holds its annual Festival of Grapes in that Grape Belt town in September, the printed program contains advertisements for the Fredonia Winery and from local dealers in wine; and a home-winemaking contest is now one of the main festival events, ranking in public interest with the baking contest, the festival ball, the crowning of the queen, and the parade.

• 8 •

New York's third most important winegrowing district is Niagara County, with some 2,800 acres of vineyards. At this writing Niagara County had no commercial wineries, but with a third of the vineyard acreage planted to wine grapes, wines are likely to be produced there again.

Viticulturally as well as geologically, the Niagara district is unique. It consists of the Niagara Peninsula, only twenty-five to thirty miles in width, that separates Lake Erie from Lake Ontario. Through the peninsula flows the Niagara River, rushing over the falls and down its deep gorge, spilling the waters of Lakes Erie, Superior, Michigan, and Huron into Lake Ontario. The inland seas on both sides of the peninsula moderate its climate, making the plains that face Lake Ontario a land of peach and cherry orchards and vineyards. On the Canadian side of the river, which is the international border, virtually the entire grape and wine industry of eastern Canada is situated, with twelve times the vineyard acreage on the New York side. There are spots where the Canadian and New York vineyards, separated by the river, are less than two miles apart.

The winter climate is milder, with fewer days recording below-zero temperatures, than in any of the other grape districts of New York. An eighteen-year study by the Geneva Experiment Station, published in 1968, showed that Lewiston, Westfield, and Long Island are best suited for the cold-tender grape varieties such as Vinifera (of which Niagara has several acres) that make the finest wines.

Winegrowing in Niagara County began before the Civil War. County Historian Clarence O. Lewis has found records showing that a winery operated at Lockport during the 1860s and that it had vineyards on both sides of the town. It was at Lockport, in 1868, that the Niagara grape variety, sometimes called the white Concord, was created by crossing Concord with a vine called Cassady. A Niagara-growing boom followed and lasted until the 1890s, when too many grapes were produced, the market collapsed, and many vineyards were uprooted.

A new grape-planting rush in Niagara County began in the late 1960s. It continued despite the warning by Viticultural Extension Specialist Trenholm D. Jordan, who advised farmers not to plant vines until they could be certain of a market for their grapes. By the mid-1970s, the farmers had learned that Jordan was right.

A single winery operated at Lewiston from 1933 to 1970, specializing in champagnes. It was Château Gay, opened at Repeal by the Canadian firm which owned the Château Gai winery near the Canadian city of Niagara Falls. Bought in 1937 by Dr. Hector Carveth, it prospered until it was moved to an ornate new building in 1966. Four years later the wine company went bankrupt, all the winery equipment was dismantled and sold, and the building was offered for sale. Richard P. Vine, who had just quit his job at the Pleasant Valley winery to plant a vineyard in Indiana, heard about the sale. With an equally young wine-buff partner named Edward Moulton, Vine bought the empty building in 1971 and named it the Niagara Falls Wine Cellar. In less than a year they re-equipped it with casks and machinery, bought their first grapes in the Chautauqua Belt, and offered ten wines for sale. It took them two years to learn the lesson that bitter experience has taught many other small wineries, that their finances must be sufficient not only to start production, but sufficient also to establish a market for their wines. They closed the winery; Vine moved to Michigan and then to Mississippi; and Moulton to New Jersey, where he is the enologist of the Gross Highland Winery at Absecon. The opportunity still exists for a future Niagara winery to offer tours and tasting for the millions of visitors who come from everywhere to gaze at the awesome Falls.

There is one Niagara grower of fine wines, Lockport attorney Richard Lein. On his Fairmount Farm five miles west of that city, Lein grows French hybrids, the noble Vinifera varieties, and also the new Siegfried Riesling hybrid of Germany, not yet established in the United States. But Lein's three-acre vineyard and home wine cellar are only his avocation; his wines are not for sale.

• 9 •

The Hudson River Valley, with nine wineries and some 1,200 acres of vineyards, is the oldest winegrowing district in the United States. Wine has been made continuously in this historic valley for at least three centuries, since French Protestant refugees settled at New Paltz in Ulster County in 1677. When their plantings of European vines failed, the Frenchmen made wine of the native wild grapes until such domesticated varieties as the Isabella became available early in the nineteenth century.

The first large commercial vineyard in the valley was planted with the Isabella about 1827 on Croton Point, the peninsula that is now Westchester County's Croton Point Park, on the east shore of the Hudson thirty-five miles north of New York City. No marker or plaque exists to tell the thousands who now enjoy picnicking at the park that this was once their state's most famous vineyard. Campers who take shelter in the great cavern hollowed out of the hillside are unaware that it originally served as the aging vault for Croton Point wines.

Dr. Richard T. Underhill, the bachelor physician who planted vines there, was so enthusiastic about grape culture that he abandoned his medical practice in the city to give the vineyard his full time. He was also the first American advocate of the Grape Cure, the diet of fresh grapes then popular in Europe, where it was believed to prevent dyspepsia, liver ailments, and a long list of other diseases. Dr. Underhill first sold his grapes fresh, but later established a winery on the peninsula. His Croton Point wines were offered in New York City during the 1860s as "the pure product of the grape, neither drugged, liquored, nor watered, recommended by leading physicians in all cases where a stimulant of a bracing character is required." Members of the Underhill family were prominent in the New York wine industry for several more decades.

• 10 •

The oldest active winery in the United States is at Washingtonville, several miles from the river in Orange County. It is the Brotherhood Corporation winery, established in 1839. Its ancient caves, which resemble those beneath old wineries in Europe, are the largest wine storage tunnels I have found in North America. They are well worth visiting, though some of the capacious vaults are empty, and the great vineyards which once covered this part of the valley are no more. The last vines were uprooted in 1960 to enlarge the winery's parking lot, where a dollar charge is made for parking in the afternoons.

Situated only fifty-one miles from New York City, the Brotherhood winery now specializes in selling its wines at retail to visitors, of whom more than 300,000 come each year for free tours of its caves and to sample the wines (also free) from paper cups. Two dozen hosts deliver impressive one-hour lectures on the romance and the making of wine and on its uses in cooking. Merry evening parties are held in the cellars for the Brotherhood of Wine Tasters, loyal customers who sometimes use professional-type scorecards to rate the Brotherhood wines. I found their quality adequate, typical products of the Delaware, Catawba, and other Labrusca grapes the company buys in the Hudson Valley, Chautauqua, and Niagara districts. Of the twenty types the company sells, the best were the brut champagne, the sparkling burgundy, and the sauterne, in which the Labrusca taste was least pronounced.

I went to Washingtonville expecting to unravel there the early history of Brotherhood wines and their connection with the fabulous Thomas Lake Harris, whose utopian Brotherhood of the New Life gave the wines their name. My research in California had shown that Harris's religious semi-communistic Brotherhood had first made wine in the Hudson Valley before it moved to Brocton, then to the Fountain Grove Vineyard in Santa Rosa, California. I therefore assumed that it was at the Brotherhood winery that Harris's winemaking began. Imagine my disappointment when Columbia-trained Francis Llado Farrell, who had owned the Brotherhood winery since 1948, told me he had never heard of such a person as Thomas Lake Harris, nor of his Brotherhood religious cult either!

Since that visit, the mystery has been cleared up by further research, by studying the numerous books that have been written about the fantastic career of Harris, and by Farrell's wife Eloise, who has investigated the local historical sources.

The founder of this Brotherhood winery was not the English-born Harris, but Jean Jaques from France, who settled at Washingtonville in 1816. Jaques, a shoemaker, was the first to plant grapes in Orange County, soon after Dr. Underhill started his vineyard at Croton Point. In 1838, Jaques sent his first grapes to market and received for them only thirteen cents a pound, so he decided in the following year to make his crop into wine. He sold some to the First Presbyterian Church, of which he was an elder. For many years thereafter, Jaques had a prospering trade in sacramental wines, which kept the Brotherhood winery open during Prohibition. It still enjoys a lucrative clerical trade.

Harris's Brotherhood of the New Life first made wine during the 1860s, not at Washingtonville, but at his third colony, which was at Amenia in the Hudson Valley. (His first two colonies were at Mountain Cove, West Virginia, and at Wassaic, New York.) Winegrowing was the Amenia colony's industry. It kept the disciples busy while angels dictated the sermons and celestial poems that Harris claimed came to him when he was in a trance. He preached that his wines had divine and miraculous powers, "the finer electro-vinous spirit of the collective body of the grape," and that therefore they brought joy without alcoholic intoxication.

There were bizarre occult and sexual practices in his colonies, including "celibate marriage," Harris dictating where wives and husbands were to sleep, usually apart. Harris was the patriarch, wielding absolute power and holding the devout members' personal fortunes. His disciples included many wealthy people, including Laurence Oliphant, the renowned British author and former Parliament member, and Lady Maria Oliphant, his mother. It was with Lady Oliphant's jewels that Harris purchased the larger tract at Brocton, to which the colony moved from Amenia in 1867. Eight years later Harris abandoned his heaven at Brocton to found his new one at the Fountain Grove Vineyard in California; the colony at Brocton fell apart soon after he left. Harris ruled at Fountain Grove until 1892, when embroiled in lawsuits and scandals about free love, he suddenly left Fountain Grove in the charge of his samurai Japanese secretary, Baron Kanaye Nagasawa, and sailed for England. He lived there for a time, and died in New York in 1906.

Meanwhile, Brotherhood wines and Brotherhood Grand Monarque Champagne were being sold throughout the United States and even in Europe and Africa. The Brotherhood Wine Company had its own five-story building at Washington and Spring Streets in New York City and boasted of vineyards at Washingtonville and at Hammondsport in the Finger Lakes.

But how could Harris, in trouble with his disciples at Amenia, at Brocton, then in California, have possibly built this vast wine business, and what was its connection with his Brotherhood of the New Life?

The answer, it turns out, was a pair of enterprising New York wine merchants—Jesse and Edward R. Emerson, father and son. During the 1870s, the Emersons bought the wine from Harris's Brotherhood colony at Brocton, and also bought some wine from Jaques, blended them together, and sold the blend, with Harris's blessing, under his Brotherhood name. Then in 1885, Harris having left for California, and Jean Jaques and two of his sons having died, the surviving Jaques son, Charles, sold the Washingtonville winery to the Emersons. They promptly changed its name from Blooming Grove, which Jaques had called it, to Brotherhood.

• 11 •

There are no million-gallon wineries in the Hudson Valley such as those in the Finger Lakes. The Brotherhood cellars hold a quarter-million gallons; the Royal Wine Corporation at Milton and the Marlboro Industries winery at Marlboro, which specialize in kosher wines, and the Hudson Valley winery at Highland, are of comparable size.

But because of the valley's proximity to New York City, there are more hobbyist winegrowers in this locality than anywhere else in New York State. Only four have thus far bonded their cellars to sell their wines, three of them since the extortionate New York State winery license fees were reduced from $1,000 to $125 by the farm winery law in 1976.

• 12 •

Near New City, twenty-eight miles up the Hudson from Manhattan, is the High Tor Vineyard, which for a quarter of a century was the most famous small winegrowing estate in eastern America. Its winery was closed in 1976, but it may be reopened because its wines are still in demand. High Tor is the subject of a delightful book, *The Vintage Years* (New York: Harper & Row), written by its founder, playwright Everett Crosby.

From his boyhood in California, Crosby had cherished a dream of someday becoming a winegrower. When he came to New York he planted a grapevine on the terrace of his penthouse apartment in the city, and when he moved to West Nyack in Rockland County, he planted vines around his house there. In 1949 he bought an old farm atop High Tor, the craggy mountain about which Maxwell Anderson wrote his prizewinning play of that name, and finally planted his dream vineyard there. Crosby's High Tor wines, introduced in 1954, were the first in New York State to be made entirely of French hybrids. They were praised by connoisseurs and were featured on the wine lists of prestigious New York restaurants and clubs. The samples I tasted at the winery on my visits to the Hudson Valley were evidence that they deserved their fame. The four-year-old Rockland Red was rich in tannin, perfectly balanced, and had developed a bottle bouquet; his white was dry and fragrant, and the rosé was as fine as any pink wine made of Vinifera grapes.

After lavishing care on his vineyard for twenty-three years, Crosby sold High Tor in 1971 to a younger oenothusiast named Richard Voigt, who owns the Peppermill Restaurants in Connecticut. Voigt's winemaker was an Episcopalian priest named Father Thomas Lee Hayes. I have known many clerical winemakers in the Catholic Church-owned wineries, but Father Hayes is the first American enologist to wear the robes of the Episcopal faith. Voigt closed the winery when Father Hayes moved to the Finger Lakes, but has kept half of the eighty-acre vineyard, and, because people still ask for High Tor wines, says he may start to make them again.

• 13 •

The most charming small winery in New York State is Benmarl Vineyard, which is perched on a hill above Route 9W, overlooking the Hudson at Marlboro in Ulster County.

From his five-year stay in Europe following the Second World War, when he became a member of Burgundy's Confrérie des Chevaliers du Tastevin, the noted illustrator Mark Miller wanted to become a winegrower. He found the site in 1956, the original fifty-acre vineyard where in 1867 Andrew J. Caywood developed the Dutchess grape, one of the best of the white Labrusca varieties. Miller found some of the ancient vines still growing on the property and the crumbling ruin of a century-old winery nearby. Records of the town of Marlboro dating from the 1700s are decorated with its symbol, a bunch of grapes. He named the estate Benmarl; ben is early Gaelic for hill, marl describes its slaty soil.

Miller planted a dozen acres with French hybrid vines and a half-acre with Chardonnay. Before building his winery, he organized fellow wine lovers into a unique kind of co-operative. Members of the Benmarl Societé des Vignerons bought vine-rights of two vines each, which entitled each *vigneron* to the Droit du Seigneur, an invitation to help with the harvest, and the right to a dozen bottles of personally labeled wine.

After two years' operation as a society of amateurs, Miller was producing enough Benmarl wines, over what the Societé required, to offer some for sale. They soon began appearing on the wine lists of leading New York restaurants and in the better New York stores. Most of the wine still goes to the 425 Societé members, but the vineyard since has been enlarged to seventy acres and the winery to 50,000 gallons to provide more wine.

Benmarl is a family operation of Mark, whose sculptures adorn the grounds, his wife Dene, who designed the rustic buildings, and their sons Eric and Kim. Visitors are received by appointment on weekdays and Saturday afternoons. There are seven Benmarl wines: estate-bottled, vintage dated Seyval Blanc, Blanc Domaine, Rouge Domaine, Baco Noir, Rosé Domaine, Cuvée du Vigneron, and Chardonnay.

• 14 •

Between Marlboro and Milton, four miles north, there are three more wineries. After decades of winemaking in California, in Mexico, and at the Brotherhood winery, Italian-trained veteran enologist Joseph Cagnasso has settled on his own vineyard and has converted a century-old barn on Highway 9W into his own farm winery.

Downhill from Benmarl, Arnold Kneitel's Marlboro Industries winery makes kosher wines and champagnes, but as yet has no tasting room for visitors. However, the Herzog family's Royal kosher winery at nearby Milton entertains thousands of visitors each summer in two public tasting rooms, one in the winery and the other in the old New York Central railroad station on the Hudson shore. Royal charges a dollar for parking.

• 15 •

On a lofty bluff overlooking the Hudson near Highland, there is a 200-acre Italian winegrowing estate, so nearly perfect in its setting of vines on rolling hills that it might have been transplanted in one piece from the hills of Tuscany. In the middle of the vineyard, clustered around the manor house and garden, are stone winery buildings and the homes of families of vineyard workers, some of whom have lived here all their lives.

This is the Hudson Valley Wine Company, established by Alexander Bolognesi from Bologna after he retired from a Wall Street banking career in 1907. It still produces the same estate-bottled Labrusca wines and champagnes that the Bolognesi family did, though it has been owned since 1972 by former importer Herb Feinberg, one of the three brothers who have operated Monsieur Henri Wines.

When I first visited the estate, Bolognesi's widow, Valentina, maintained a firm rule against visitors to the winery. The new owner, however, saw it as the Hudson Valley's perfect tourist attraction. He has established winery tours and tasting daily from mid-February to late November, a Saturday evening champagne film festival by reservation, and a restaurant in the manor house for group luncheons and dinners. The only flaw is a two-dollar charge for parking, but the tour and tasting are more than worth the cost. Hudson Valley still has the same Italian winemaker, Sam Williams, who was born on the estate; his father was the Bolognesis' vineyard manager. The vineyard is entirely of wine-grape varieties, Catawba, Chelois, Concord, and Iona. The winery is preparing to introduce estate-bottled Chelois, Baco, and Chancellor wines. To reach the estate, take the New York Thruway to New Paltz, go west on Route 299, and turn south on Highway 9W past the mid-Hudson bridge.

• 16 •

Across the Hudson north of Poughkeepsie, three hobbyist winegrowers have started the first wineries to operate in Dutchess County since Thomas Lake Harris's Brotherhood of the New Life abandoned its vineyard colony at Amenia more than a century ago. Novelist William Wetmore has built a 6,000-gallon winery on his fifteen-acre Cascade Mountain Vineyard of French hybrids six miles north of Amenia at the intersection of Flint Hill and Cascade Mountain Roads. A few miles west of Wetmore, on Schultzville Road two miles from Clinton Corners, New York book designer Ben Feder has installed an 8,000-gallon winery in the ancient barn on his twelve-acre Clinton Vineyard. Feder grows only white grapes, mainly the Seyval Blanc hybrid, but also has four acres of White Riesling and Chardonnay. Ten miles north of Amenia, on their two-acre Northeast Vineyard near the village of Millerton, New York heart surgeon George Green and his artist wife Sheila have installed a thousand-gallon winery in the cellar of their country home on Silver Mountain Road. Winegrowing appeals especially to physicians, says Dr. Green, "because wine, like other living things, leads a precarious existence, but when it survives in good health, it lives for years and years."

These new Hudson Valley winegrowers represent one of the many contributions to New York agriculture by the enactment of the state's farm winery law. While the chief purpose of that legislation was to enable growers to sell their grapes as wine where they sell their other fruit, the law also makes it possible, for those to whom winegrowing is an avocation, to support that cultural and artistic endeavor.

9

The Vine Grows in New England

I N THEIR book on *American Wines,* published in 1941, Frank Schoonmaker and Tom Marvel speculated that if the American colonies had undertaken from the start to cultivate the hardy native grapes, instead of attempting in vain to grow the delicate Old World varieties, a winegrowing industry would have developed in the stern climates of the New England states as it did elsewhere in the East. They went on to declare that if given the right conditions, such a development eventually would be "inevitable."

The "inevitable" is coming to pass, but not with the hardy native grapes. It is happening with the delicate Old World grapes, which modern advances in viticulture have now made it possible to grow in these climates. Moreover, oenothusiasts are finding that some parts of New England are as climatically suited for grape growing as some of the present viticultural areas of other eastern states. And although winegrowing in New England still is mostly in a pioneering stage, five farm-winery owners are already growing commercial wines in New Hampshire, Massachusetts, and Rhode Island, causing excitement among farmers in these and neighboring states.

• 2 •

The history of winegrowing in New England goes back two centuries, but has been obscured by time and by dry attitudes in American agriculture, which focused attention on fresh grapes rather than on wine. That grapes grow abundantly, both wild and under cultivation, in this part of America is shown by the names given in colonial times to such places as Martha's

Vineyard,* the twenty-mile-long island off the Massachusetts coast, and to the island town called Vineyard Haven. Nantucket Island also was once noted for its grapes.

The great seal of the State of Connecticut is a picture of three grapevines bearing fruit, symbolizing one of the agricultural activities of the early settlers. During the seventeenth century a large planting of European vines was made at the mouth of the Piscataqua River near the present site of Portsmouth, New Hampshire, and presumably it failed. But an early Massachusetts vineyard, the one planted by Governor John Winthrop on Governor's Island in Boston Harbor (which is now part of Logan International Airport), apparently produced grapes for a time. The payment Governor Winthrop undertook to make for the island in 1632—a hogshead of wine per year—was actually made by him and his heirs in the form of wine (sometimes of apples), until Adam Winthrop made a cash settlement in 1683.

Grape growing in Massachusetts during the nineteenth century is described by Alden Spooner in his book about winemaking, published in 1846. "Great quantities of grapes are raised in and about Boston," Spooner wrote, "but we do not know of any large vineyards for wine. Men of wealth raise foreign varieties in hot houses, and the finest grapes I have ever seen were at horticultural exhibitions in that city."

New England's principal contribution to American viticulture was the Concord grape, named for the historic town in Massachusetts whence it came—the principal grape now grown in the eastern, midwestern, and northwestern states. Its originator, Ephraim Wales Bull, became interested in grape growing as a boy, when his father had a vineyard at Bullville in the Hudson River Valley of New York. As a young man, employed as a goldbeater in Boston, Bull raised grapes in his garden on Fayette Street in that city, and on a larger scale when he moved in 1836 to Concord, where he also made his own wine. There, in 1843, trying to find a hardier dark grape than the Isabella, he sowed the seeds of numerous whole grapes that he picked from the local wild Labrusca vines. Among the seedlings that sprouted, one of the hardiest and most prolific yielded, in 1849, the purple, foxy-flavored grape he named the Concord. Bull propagated the vine from cuttings, and in 1854 he offered the Concord to nurseries at five dollars per vine. But the nursery-

*Historians have found no trace of any "Martha" for whom the island might have been named. Current opinion is that the name is a corruption of "Martin," referring to a friend of either the discoverer, Bartholomew Gosnold, or of the first proprietor, Thomas Mayhew.

men propagated the vine themselves, and Bull earned little from the countless millions of its progeny that were planted throughout the nation. He became embittered, and died a poor man in Concord's Home for the Aged in 1895. Bull's tombstone records his resentment against commercial nurseries in these words: "He sowed, but others reaped." One of the historic shrines of Concord is Bull's Grapevine Cottage on Lexington Road, next door to the Wayside, which once was the home of his friend, Nathaniel Hawthorne. Visitors there are told that a massive grapevine beside the cottage, still bearing abundant crops each season, is Bull's original Concord vine.

I have found only one record of commercial winegrowing in New England during the nineteenth century. It is a letter published in the *American Wine Press and Mineral Water News* for August 1900. The writer, one Albert Bernard of Meriden, Connecticut, described Meriden as a wine-producing locality at that time. In particular, he mentioned a "Coe Farm" southwest of Meriden as having cultivated Concord and Worden grapes for wine between 1894 and 1897, and as having produced "a superior claret" that was sold in Hartford and in New York City.

• 3 •

Connecticut has many small vineyards, most of them planted by amateur winemakers who commute from their offices in New York. In 1963, wine merchant Ciro Buonocore of North Haven planted several acres of French hybrids there and made a Connecticut wine for several years, but he failed to interest the state administration in his idea that grapes might replace tobacco as a farm crop. I have visited only one Connecticut vineyard thus far, the acre of hybrid vines Don Singewald has cultivated since 1969 behind his father Elmer's Town Line Liquor Store on US 7 at the north edge of Norwalk. Don had hoped to plant on twenty adjoining acres and to grow wines for sale in the store, but gave up when he learned that the state's minimum winery license fee was $1,600 per year. Several grape growers in northern Connecticut then asked the legislature to enact a farm winery law like the one New York State had adopted in 1976. The legislature consented, reducing the fee to $160. When the bill became law in 1978, at least three avocational vineyardists were preparing applications for Connecticut farm wineries.

· 4 ·

The first winery in New Hampshire is the almost incredible achievement of John J. Canepa and his wife Lucille. They have launched a winegrowing industry in the center of the Granite State, where so far as is known, nobody has ever grown wine before.

The Canepas moved to Laconia, New Hampshire, from New York in 1958 because John was offered a job as pharmacist in the Laconia Clinic. They made their new home in a cottage on Governor's Island in nearby Lake Winnipesaukee, where they had spent several summer vacations. On walks on the island roads during that autumn, they noticed the profuse growth of the wild winter grapevine, which, pruned only by wintry gales, climbs sixty feet high in the pine trees. They picked some of the grapes, found them almost as sweet as the famous syrup the New Hampshire farmers obtain from the sap of their maple trees; and the Canepas' dream of becoming winegrowers was born. John had known wine since childhood, when his Italian-born father crushed grapes each autumn in the family garage and served the fermented juice, diluted with water, to his children. As a pharmacist, John knew chemistry, and he had learned some wine technology from the part-time job he had held during his senior year at Columbia University, analyzing samples for a wine importer. The Canepas decided it would be fun to try, in a region where grapes grew wild, to grow them under cultivation for wine.

They began searching for literature on viticulture. They visited the state university at Durham, learned that Belknap County had exactly twelve grapevines, and that the only variety recommended for this climate was the Beta, which makes a harsh, almost undrinkable wine. Undiscouraged, they sent for the book called *General Viticulture* by California's Professor Albert Winkler, and devoured its contents. Winkler's tabulation of summer temperatures in the world's chief winegrowing regions gave the Canepas a clue. They obtained records of weather at Laconia for twenty years and discovered that heat summation during their normal 150-day growing season measured higher than in Germany's Rhineland and was almost equal to that of the Champagne region of France. On weekends and days off from the clinic, the Canepas searched the fields and mountains and found many spots with southern exposure, sheltered from the cold northwest winds, with microclimates tempered by the nearby lakes. Next, they began visiting and studying the techniques of successful winegrowers in such other eastern states as Pennsylvania, Maryland, and New York. They meanwhile selected vines of American and French hybrid grape varieties that might mature in New Hampshire and survive the Laconia winters, which dip to fifteen and twenty degrees below zero.

In the spring of 1965, John planted 800 vines on three test sites, Lucille helping to dig the holes. When the buds sprouted green shoots, the Canepas chased the deer away. The vines showed good summer growth. University horticulturists and agricultural officials showed some interest, but stayed on the sidelines, skeptical.

The winter of 1965–66 was severe, and some of the vines died, but when most of them leafed out well in the following spring, excitement spread through the neighborhood. Blueberry farmers Marshall Hodsdon and Gordon Bean decided to plant an acre of grapes each. County Agent Horace Ballard and Horticulture Professor C.A. "Kelly" Langer came from the university to see what was going on. They found the Canepas already planting a thousand more vines. Word of what was happening reached New York City, and a wine merchant there wrote the Canepas, offering to sell any wine they might produce. That summer and autumn, there began a pilgrimage to Laconia of professional experts who wanted to see for themselves the improbable sight of wine grapes growing in New Hampshire. Tom Marvel came with his wife, and pointed out that Laconia is almost in the same latitude as New York's famous Finger Lakes. Next came professors from the Geneva, New York, research station, followed by Seaton Mendall, the chief of viticulture for the Taylor wineries of New York, and each of them offered advice. In 1967, the French hybrid vines yielded a thousand pounds of grapes, and the procession of visitors swelled, with Ernest Reveal, the president of Widmer's Wine Cellars from Naples, New York, scores of New Hampshire farmers, and more professors from the state university. Pictures of the Canepas and their visitors appeared on the front page of the Laconia *Citizen,* and the *Sunday News* at Manchester devoted a full picture page to the state's future wine industry. The Boston Sunday *Globe* photographed the Canepas' vineyard with the caption, "Soon, Yankee Wine." The Grape Growers Association of New Hampshire was organized with Canepa as chairman.

After the 1968 vintage, when their vineyard yielded three tons of grapes testing 18 to 20 percent in sugar content, the

Canepas bought a 150-acre farm on Cotton Hill near Belmont and increased their plantings to twenty-five acres. John quit his job at the clinic and began building and equipping a modern winery, the White Mountain Vineyards of New Hampshire, on Durrell Mountain Road, just off Route 107. The cellar was finished and bonded in time to ferment all six tons of the 1969 vintage. In 1970, only five years after the planting of their first vines, Canepa estate-bottled Foch* New Hampshire Burgundy and Lakes Region Dry White Dinner Wine went on sale in the state monopoly liquor stores and in a dozen New Hampshire restaurants.

The White Mountain Vineyards winery has since been enlarged to 80,000 gallons. John has added blends with California wines, as well as apple and strawberry wines which he ships to stores in nearby states. The winery has become a tourist attraction and is listed in the New Hampshire Recreation Calendar. Lucille serves the winery visitors her seedless Concord grape muffins, except when she is away singing at weddings or funerals, or is busy driving the tractor in the vineyard.

Farmers have planted nearly 200 acres of French hybrids around the New Hampshire lakes and several others have started vineyards in Vermont and in central and southern Maine. Now Canepa is working with other growers to get an amendment to the New Hampshire law, like the one in Pennsylvania, to let him sell his wine directly to consumers and restaurants instead of through the state monopoly store system. A bill has also been proposed that would have New Hampshire follow the example of Vermont, which is also a monopoly state, in allowing the sale of table wine in grocery stores.

• 5 •

The first Massachusetts winegrowers licensed in well over a century are producing Vinifera wines on the island named Martha's Vineyard, in the Atlantic Ocean ten miles from the southern tip of Cape Cod. Electronics engineer George Mathiesen and his wife Catherine, home winemakers from California who had built a summer home on the island, decided in 1971 to try growing grapes because they found the island climate, moderated by the ocean, is relatively mild.

Their first three-acre vineyard, planted that year with vines from Dr. Konstantin Frank, was enlarged to twenty acres a year

---

*"Foch" refers to the French hybrid grape variety called Maréchal Foch, which is a cross of American *Vitis riparia* grapes with Burgundy's noble Gamay and Pinot Noir.

later, when they built their 4,000-gallon winery and for practice in using its modern equipment, made their first wine from California Zinfandel grapes purchased in Boston.

When their first Massachusetts-grown Vinifera wine was bottled with the help of six of their children and was ready for sale in November 1975, the Mathiesens were surprised to find in the Edgarton *Vineyard Gazette* a full-page advertisement picturing their winery, that read "Chicama Vineyards Massachusetts 1974 Chardonnay" with this signature: "Mom & Dad, after five years, Congratulations! We're all proud to be a part of Bonded Winery Massachusetts No. 1. Love, Kris, Lynn, Paul, Robin, Chance, Michael, Tim, Sean."

The Chardonnay, excellent by any standard, and the 1974 White Riesling, also better than acceptable, went on sale in the seven island liquor stores at $7.49 a bottle the day the ad appeared and all were promptly sold. Massachusetts newspapers and no less than four television stations, one with a national hookup, covered the historic event.

Chicama Vineyard (pronounced Cha-*kay*-ma and named for the Indian path that reaches it from Stony Hill Road) now covers thirty acres and includes Gewürztraminer, Cabernet Sauvignon, Pinot Noir, Gamay Beaujolais, Pinot Gris, two Russian white varieties, Rkatsiteli and Mzvani, and two acres of Vinifera table grapes, which are sold fresh on the island and on nearby Nantucket to the east. Chicama vines are protected by sprinklers from frost, from birds by electronic bird-distress calls every thirty seconds, and from deer by fences eight feet high. Production from the first vineyard has averaged two tons per acre, but younger vines in a new patch on better soil are showing better yields. To help the Mathiesens, the Massachusetts legislature in 1977 enacted a farm winery law that reduced the state minimum winery license fee from $4,500 to $22. The law now allows wine sales at the winery as well as wholesaling to restaurants and stores.

Four island neighbors have planted additional vineyards with vines from the Chicama nursery, including twelve acres at Vineyard Haven by James Norton, a retired professor of Oriental religions, and his wife Sonya. Mathiesen says there also are some favorable microclimates for winegrowing on Cape Cod.

• 6 •

Rhode Island, the smallest and most densely populated of the fifty states, has one of the mildest climates in the East, and had vineyards and wineries until Prohibition. Although it is not an island, it benefits from the influence of Narragansett Bay and of the rivers that flow into Rhode Island Sound. With young vineyards already producing in New Hampshire, on Martha's Vineyard, and on Long Island, it was not surprising that three wineries were bonded on vineyards in different parts of Rhode Island beginning in 1974.

The state's first home-grown wines, labeled estate-bottled Rhode Island Red and America's Cup White, reached the market in 1977 from Jim and Lolly Mitchell's just-completed 15,000-gallon Sakonnet Vineyard winery on West Main Road north of Little Compton in Newport County. Helping the Mitchells to produce wine that year were Sister Anne and Sister Hannah, Dominican nuns on a year's sabbatical from a Litchfield, Connecticut, Catholic high school. I saw the Sakonnet winery under construction and the vineyard, thirty-six acres of vigorous French hybrid and Vinifera vines, when I briefly re-visited Rhode Island in 1976. Mitchell, trained as a chemical engineer, says that temperatures at Little Compton rarely fall below zero and that the average is within two degrees of the minimum at Bordeaux.

Rhode Island Winery Number One, because it was the first one to be bonded in the state, is in the former dairy barn of H. Winfield Tucker's turf and potato farm on Indian Corner Road near the tiny post office of Slocum in Washington County on the west side of Narragansett Bay. Tucker and his partner, investment analyst Don Siebert, have two acres of young Vinifera vines. I tasted an excellent wine there, a 1974 Chardonnay that Siebert made from grapes grown at the Woodbury Farms in Chautauqua County, New York.

The third of the Rhode Island vineyards, which I failed to visit because I missed the ferryboat from Bristol, is on former business consultant William Bacon's Sunset Hill Farm on seven-mile-long Prudence Island near the middle of Narragansett Bay. Bacon, his island-born wife Natalie, and their son Nathaniel cultivate ten acres of Chardonnay and Gamay Beaujolais which they planted in 1973. They made their first 800 gallons of wine three years later in a converted milk shed. Another son, William, teaches at the island's one-room school and has helped them to clear ten more acres to be planted with vines. (Rhode Island passed a farm winery law in 1978.)

Although the winegrowing industry of New England is still young, enough has already happened to bear out the Boston Sunday *Globe's* prediction, made in 1967, of "Soon, Yankee Wine!"

10

Wines of Some Mid-Continent States

A T HERMANN, MISSOURI, in 1866, the year after the Civil War, Professor George Husmann penned his first book, *The Native Grape and the Manufacture of American Wines.*

"The nation is affected with grape fever," he wrote. "I firmly believe that this continent is destined to be the greatest wine-producing country in the world. America will be, from the Atlantic to the Pacific, one smiling and happy Wineland, where each laborer shall sit under his own vine, and none will be too poor to enjoy the purest and most wholesome of all stimulants, good, cheap, native wine."

In that year Missouri surpassed Ohio as the second largest winegrowing state of the Union, and the grape-planting fever was spreading through such neighboring states as Iowa, Kansas, and Illinois.

But local prohibition laws and vine diseases were also spreading while Husmann wrote his book. Too many grapes were being planted for the wineries to absorb, and the prices paid for grapes declined. Vineyards became neglected, were attacked by plant pests, and were abandoned to die. Husmann, professor of horticulture at the University of Missouri, abandoned his home state in 1881 to become a winemaker in California's Napa Valley. He had discovered in a single visit during that summer how ideal the conditions were for winegrowing there.

National Prohibition in 1920 closed all of the mid-continent wineries except two monasteries which continued producing altar wines. A few dozen commercial wineries reopened in 1933, but much of the area was still legally dry, and there was little demand for any wine except the cheapest dessert types. Eighteen states between the Appalachians and the Rockies (not counting Michigan) have produced less than three percent of American wine since Repeal.

Yet all of these states are natural grape-growing country; Labrusca-type grapes flourish in tens of thousands of midwestern gardens, and more vine species grow wild here than anywhere else on earth. Most of the wine produced in the world today comes from vineyards grafted to, or crossed by hybridizing with, native midwestern vines.

• 2 •

More than a century since Husmann wrote his book, millions of Americans, including midwesterners, have begun buying table wines for mealtime use, and now there is grape fever in Missouri again. New vineyards have been planted and old ones are expanding in a dozen Missouri counties. Ten wineries with their own vineyards have been established within the past few years, giving the state a total of thirteen.

Professor Husmann's hometown, the picture-book Missouri River hamlet of Hermann, is one of the places where it is happening. For the first time in half a century, wine is flowing from the huge, turreted Stone Hill Winery, which Michael Poeschel from Germany began building in 1847 on the hilltop at the south edge of town. It once held more than a million gallons and was the second largest in the nation. Its wines, such as Hermannsberger, Starkenberger, and Black Pearl, won eight gold medals at world's fairs between 1873 and 1904. When Prohibition closed the winery, Ottmar Stark ordered all of its vineyards destroyed, virtually ruining the economy of the town. The great Stone Hill cellars then were used to cultivate mushrooms, producing sixty-five tons of the fungi per year.

In 1965, farmer James Held, whose ancestors came to Hermann 128 years earlier, saw that table wines were becoming popular in Missouri. He arranged to move into the second floor of the old winery with his wife Betty Ann and their four children. The Helds installed antique casks and his grandfather's wooden roller-crusher in one of the underground vaults and made a thousand gallons of Catawba wine. Their first wine sold so well that they since have cleared the mushroom beds out of the other seven vaults and now turn out 60,000 gallons per year of Missouri Riesling, Catawba, Niagara, Norton Seedling, Concord, and Gasconade Red, White, and Rosé. The Helds have quadrupled to forty acres their vineyard of Norton, Catawba, and French hybrid vines on the Gasconade River hills, and

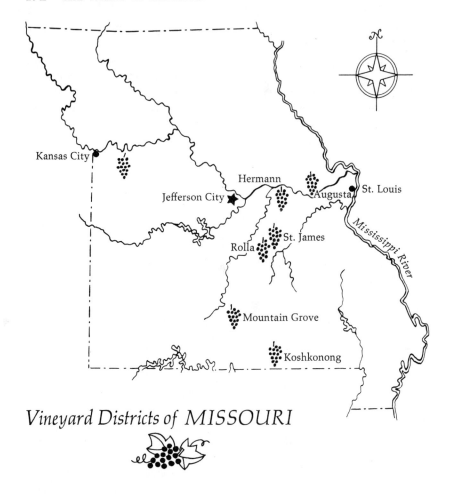

Vineyard Districts of MISSOURI

have sent their son Jonathan to study enology at Fresno State University in California. Stone Hill now offers wine tasting and a tour of its cellars for a dollar, and has opened its own wine museum.

Wine has been part of the flavor of Hermann since grapes were first planted there by Jacob Fugger in 1843. Many of its citizens, including the Helds, rear their children by "the Hermann formula: the first year wine, the second year wine and sauerkraut." The revival of Hermann's "days of wine and glory" is now celebrated on the third weekend of each May with German bands, folk dancing, knackwurst, and a house tour of "Little Germany." In autumn the Helds hold a three-week Oktoberfest at the winery.

• 3 •

Another historic Missouri winery was reopened in 1968 at Augusta, a town of German heritage on the Missouri River bluffs thirty miles west of St. Louis. The proprietor is young accountant Lucian Dressel, who became enamored of wine during his travels in Europe. On completing his studies at Harvard and Columbia, he recognized the trend to wine-drinking in America and decided to become a winegrower. Touring with his wife Eva, he found the place at Augusta where there were eleven wineries before Prohibition and six of their crumbling skeletons remained. Another old brick cellar with underground storage vaults was in better condition; it had been converted into an apartment house and was for sale. The Dressels bought it and discovered that this was originally the Mount Pleasant Vineyard of Friedrich Münch, a famous Lutheran minister and grape breeder, who once wrote a book in German, its title in English, *School for American Grape Culture.* Münch built the winery in 1881 and his prize-winning wines were known from coast to coast.

Dressel replanted two dozen acres of the original vineyard with French hybrids and Labrusca types and named his first wines of the hybrids "Emigré" Red, White, and Rosé. He since has planted and made wines of three grape varieties grown long ago by Münch. One is a non-foxy cross made by the late Texas grape breeder Thomas Volney Munson between the Herbemont of South Carolina and the Mississippi Valley post-oak wild grape; Munson named the cross for Münch. Dressel's 1975 vintage of Münch was a dry red wine I liked, somewhat like Italy's light Valpolicella but with a powerful bouquet of its own. Another, also not foxy, is the Norton grape of Virginia, which Münch called Cynthianna, a name and spelling Dressel has retained. Third was Missouri Riesling, the grape bred at Hermann about 1860. Dressel's 1975 Missouri Riesling was not detectably foxy and had an aroma of botrytis, the noble mold.

Emigré Red and these Mount Pleasant historic wines have attracted some attention from out-of-state connoisseurs. With the increased planting of new grape varieties in many more states, Dressel foresees a time when each district east of the Rockies will become known for the wine types that grow best in its various soils and climates. He predicts that while New York State thus far has been better known for its whites than for its reds, the Missouri River area will become recognized as producing the fullest-bodied red wines.

Meanwhile, Dressel has built an additional cellar and a tasting room with a patio where visitors bring their own cheeses to enjoy with his wines. Most of the local visitors seem to prefer his sweet red and white Concord and his medium-dry Mount Pleasant Rosé.

• 4 •

Three miles west of Augusta, also on the river, is a winery named Montelle (little mountain) Vineyards. Former St. Louis journalist Clayton Byers and his wife Nissel make wine in an old smokehouse from the French and New York hybrid grapes they began planting in 1970. Their son Brian, who once worked at the Tarula Vineyard in Ohio, and another son, Bruce, are also interested in the winery. The Byerses also use grapes from the nearby vineyard of Robert and Ella Knoernschild.

Handsomest winery in the river area is the Austrian chalet built by New York psychologist Albert Firestone, a distant relative of the rubber kings, on the several acres of French hybrids he began planting in 1975. Dr. Firestone's vineyard is on state road TT three miles north of the old German town of Dutzow.

Also new along the river are aircraft engineer Nicholas Lamb's 15,000-gallon Green Valley Vineyard winery fifteen miles west of Hermann at Portland, and Harold and Larry Kruger's 3,000-gallon winery and two-acre vineyard off Highway 41, two miles west of Arrow Rock, near Nelson.

• 5 •

Wine grapes are being planted again in the part of Missouri's Ozark Plateau known as Big Prairie, where the principal grapes grown are Concords for the Welch co-operative's grape juice plant at Springdale, Arkansas.

Near St. James, where the Ozark Grape Festival is held each September, Concord-grower William B. Stoltz began adding wine varieties in 1965 to his seventy-acre Concord vineyard on South Bishop Avenue three miles northeast of town. He planted mainly such Labrusca wine types as Missouri Riesling, Catawba, and Delaware, but also some French and New York State hybrids. In 1968 he opened the 5,000-gallon Stoltz Vineyard Winery and introduced several native Ozark table wines, which he named for his grapes, and also an "old-Fashioned Missouri Sweet Grape Wine." Stoltz soon found that many people in the area especially liked those of his wines with the least Labrusca flavor. With his sons William and Robert, he since has expanded his vineyard to a hundred acres, with two thirds of it now in the hybrids, has expanded his winery to 25,000 gallons, and has introduced such new wines as "Rose der Liebe" and estate-bottled Dinner White.

• 6 •

A second winery opened at St. James in 1970 and began producing the only champagne now made wholly of Missouri grapes. It is James and Patricia Hofherr's St. James Winery, on the access road beside Interstate Highway 44. Hofherr holds a degree in microbiology from the University of Texas. He had five years' experience with the Bardenheier winery at St. Louis before coming to St. James and also had made champagne for a year at the Post Winery in Altus, Arkansas. He chose the Big Prairie section as the place for his winery because most of Missouri's 2,500 acres of vineyards are there. The St. James Winery holds 45,000 gallons and is new from the ground up, with an inviting rustic tasting and sales room. Hofherr makes three bottle-fermented sparkling wines, a brut and a pink champagne and an almost-dry Cold Duck. I found the pink the best of the three. His table wines range from Catawba and Niagara to such popular hybrid types as Aurore, Chelois, and Baco Noir. To my taste his best were his Villard Blanc of that white hybrid, a red of the hybrid called Cascade, and a flavorful dry red of the rare Neva Munson grape. Hofherr talks of someday planting Vinifera varieties, which he thinks should grow well in the Ozarks.

• 7 •

Off Interstate 44 east of St. James is the village of Rosati, named by Italian immigrants at the turn of the century for their bishop who built the first Catholic cathedral west of the Mississippi. At the edge of the village is Robert and Sally Ashby's 54,000-gallon Rosati winery, popular with tourists who stop to taste wines and Catawba grape juice in its wine garden.

Growers who had planted Concords for sale to Welch built the winery during the Depression years of the late 1930s to provide a home for surplus grapes the co-op could not buy. When the Second World War broke out, Welch bought the place as a grape depot. German war prisoners were quartered in the winery and made preserves for the military until the war ended. Damaged by fire in 1969, it was bought and rebuilt by

Ashby, a veteran horticulturist who once taught agriculture at the state university branch in St. James. The Ashbys' horticulturist son Henry cares for their seventy-acre vineyard, and son-in-law Ronald E. Moreland is their winemaker. Ronald and his wife Liz also have started their own champagne cellar in the former Royal Brewery at Weston, northwest of Kansas City.

• 8 •

On the Meramec River near Steelville, a few miles southeast of St. James, is Dr. Axel Norman Arneson's Peaceful Bend Vineyard. His winery, a two-story wooden structure with a Dutch barn-style roof, is built into a hillside with earth on three of its sides.

Dr. Arneson, professor of clinical obstetrics and gynecology at Washington University School of Medicine in St. Louis, first learned about winemaking by helping his father ferment grapes for their home use in Texas during Prohibition. His travels in later years through Europe so stimulated his interest in viticulture that in 1951 he purchased some French hybrid vines from Philip Wagner and planted them on his Missouri farm. When Peaceful Bend winery was first bonded in 1972, the doctor made only two red table wines, each a blend of several hybrids. The red was named Meramec for the river and the white was called Courtois, the name of the township and of a nearby Ozark mountain stream. When I was there in 1976, he had added a pink dry wine and named it Huzzah Crawford County Rosé. The name of the winery, which is on Highway M, comes from the deep bend the river takes at the Arneson farm. The doctor is fascinated with the history of Missouri viniculture and is writing a book that traces Professor George Husmann's career.

A fifth winery in the Big Prairie area was opened in 1975 by St. Louis postal clerk Laurence Ziegler on his Concord vineyard outside the town of Cuba. A year later, a group of farmers headed by Catawba grower Hershel Gray bonded the 5,000-gallon Ozark Mountain winery in Gray's concrete milk barn near Chestnut Ridge, thirteen miles south of Ozark.

• 9 •

Another sign that winegrowing is coming back in Missouri is that the state's biggest vintner, Bardenheier's Wine Cellars of St. Louis, which mainly blends and bottles California wines for sale in thirty midwestern states, has become a Missouri winegrower, too, and is preparing to make its own local champagne.

The Bardenheier Brothers, John, Joseph, Carl, and George, whose grandfather founded the firm in 1873, noticed in the mid-1960s that Ohio and New York wineries were buying most of the Catawba grapes that grow around the Missouri Fruit Experiment Station at Mountain Grove. They decided to enlarge their St. Louis cellar and to begin making some wines of their own. "Our state's wine industry is reviving," said brother Carl, who was trained in enology at the University of California, "and we're going to be part of it."

In 1970, the Bardenheiers planted their first vineyard, fifty acres of native and French hybrid varieties, on the big Lost River Ranch of Ott Coelln at Koshkonong on US Highway 63 in southern Missouri. This is the area, six miles from the Arkansas border, where Michael Brand, the founder of nearby Brandsville, began producing Ozark Maid wines in 1887. The land reverted to cattle grazing when Brand closed his winery in 1904.

The success of the Bardenheiers' first planting was celebrated in 1972 when the vineyard was blessed in a ceremony which I think was unprecedented, for it was conducted jointly by a Methodist minister and a Catholic priest. Three years later the Bardenheiers introduced their first Missouri Valley wines, reds named Chelois, Maréchal Foch, and Baco Noir.

· 10 ·

Winegrowing has also returned to far western Missouri, near the border of Kansas. University of Missouri philosophy professor George Gale, his wife Carol, and architect Dutton Biggs have planted a five-acre vineyard of French hybrids and have built the 3,500-gallon Midi Vineyard winery on Road F in Jackson County, four miles from Lone Jack. I have tasted their first wine, an excellent red of the Leon Millot grape. Dr. Gale is teaching a course in Wine and Civilization at the University's Kansas City campus.

But vineyards and wineries are only a cherished memory in the old winegrowing district around St. Charles on the Missouri River, twenty miles northwest of St. Louis. I remember a visit during the 1960s to the last winery at St. Charles, still operating then in the basement of Emil Wepprich's home next door to his Wepprich's Wine Gardens, a bit of old Germany where waltzes filled the air on moonlit evenings. When his grandfather founded the winery in 1859 it was surrounded by hillside vineyards, but Wepprich sold the land a century later to developers who uprooted the vines. The terraced gardens are still there, however, and its new owners Bill and Chris Hallam cherish the wine tradition. They have preserved the little winery, complete with its antique presses and casks, and they offer their guests free winery tours.

• 11 •

The late Irvin Brucker, a St. Louis oenothusiast, spent half a lifetime gathering the history of Missouri winegrowing and once published some of it in a mimeographed publication he called *The Wine Press,* but he had enough unpublished material left to fill a fascinating book.

The first Missouri wine was made in 1823 from wild grapes by the French Jesuit priests who founded the St. Stanislaus Seminary at Florissant, now a St. Louis suburb. They later planted vineyards around the Seminary and sold both sacramental and commercial Florissant Valley wines in the St. Louis area for more than a century. When the winery at Florissant closed in 1960 for lack of labor, it was the oldest in this country, having produced wine continuously for 147 years. The Seminary's vineyard was uprooted, except that Brother Eilert, who had tended it for most of his life, kept the best half-acre and continued making wine as his hobby until the Seminary closed in 1973. When Lucian Dressel was buying equipment for his Mount Pleasant Vineyard winery, he found the ancient casks at Florissant being broken up for firewood, and rescued them for his winery at Augusta.

There were wineries in forty-eight Missouri counties before Prohibition. Bluffton, Boonville, Cape Girardeaux, Hannibal, Owensville, and Stanton were some of the addresses on famous Missouri wine labels. In the Kansas City area, the town of Independence, with Shaffer's Winery and Lohse's Native Wine Garden, was known for its wine long before Missourians came to know Harry Truman. A history of Newton County records that in 1867 grape breeder Hermann Jaeger of Neosho advised French viticulturists to graft their phylloxera-devastated vineyards onto wild Ozark vine roots. He shipped them seventeen carloads of rootings and later was awarded the Cross of the French Legion of Honor.

St. Louis was the nation's chief early center of wine study and research and was also the home of Missouri's most famous winery. The story of Cook's Imperial Champagne Cellar is one of the strangest in the annals of this country's wines. The cellar is still in existence, a stone-arched maze four levels deep beneath an entire city block on Cass Avenue—but it is now a vinegar plant. Built in 1832 by the Missouri Wine Company, it was purchased in 1859 by Chicago connoisseur and political leader Isaac Cook, who made its Missouri champagne famous. Reopened after Prohibition by new owners as the American Wine Company, it was headed by Alsace-born Adolf Heck, Sr., the father of the Heck brothers who later owned the Korbel vineyard in California. Heck was uncomfortably short of capital until a little-known Swiss firm invested in Cook's stock in 1939. Five years later, during the Second World War, Government investigators tracing Nazi investments in this country discovered that the secret owner of the Missouri winery was Hitler's foreign minister, ex-champagne salesman Joachim von Ribbentrop. The American Wine Company was seized by the Government and was sold several times until it became part of the Schenley liquor empire in 1946, the same year von Ribbentrop was hanged for his war crimes. Since 1954 Cook's champagnes have been made as Heck, Sr., made them—from California wines with eastern Catawba in the blend—but at the Guild winery in Lodi, California.

Missouri's greatest contribution to the wine industry was the work of Professor Husmann. Like Jaeger, he shipped millions of phylloxera-resistant vines from Missouri to re-establish the dying vineyards of Europe. He established at St. Louis *The Grape Culturist,* one of the earliest American periodicals on viticulture, and wrote two books after the one quoted from at the beginning of this chapter. On moving to California, Husmann helped to overcome the phylloxera plague there. He made prize-winning wines for the Talcoa Vineyard of Napa and the Oak Glen Vineyard of Chiles Valley until he died in 1902.

• 12 •

Winegrowing is also reviving with great excitement in Indiana, where it flourished over 150 years ago. Seven bonded wineries have opened in the Hoosier State in a period of seven years, and owners of new vineyards are preparing to start half a dozen more.

When Pennsylvania enacted its law permitting small wineries in 1968, University of Indiana law professor William Oliver saw in this a way to turn his winegrowing hobby into a business. He wrote a virtual copy of the Pennsylvania law, got it passed by the Indiana Legislature in 1971, and a year later opened the Oliver Winery on Highway 37 seven miles north of the university campus at Bloomington.

His winery is prospering. He produces estate-bottled table

wines from his French hybrids and mead from Indiana honey and has enlarged his vineyard from sixteen to forty acres and the winery to 60,000 gallons. In the tasting room where his wife Mary presides, visitors can buy wine by the glass, bottle, or case from eleven to six daily, but not on Sunday until Indiana repeals its blue laws. Cheese, bread, and sausage are also for sale and can be enjoyed in the winery's picnic ground.

Twelve miles east of Oliver's winery, Ben and Leora Sparks have planted thirty acres of hybrids on their Possum Trot Farm near Trevlac on the north shore of Lake Lemon, have outfitted their century-old barn with the latest equipment as the future Possum Trot Winery, and are adding a tasting room. Sparks, a retired navy commander, heads the Indiana Winegrowers Guild, which holds an annual grape-wine symposium in conjunction with the Purdue University Department of Agriculture.

• 13 •

The most elaborate winery in Indiana, with the largest single planting of wine grapes—seventy-two acres—is the Banholzer Wine Cellars in the far northwestern corner of the state. It is three miles east of Hesston on County Road 1000 North, a mile from the Michigan border, seven miles from Lake Michigan. The winery's billboards on I-94 call this "Indiana wine country," a name bestowed at a ceremony in 1975 attended by Governor Otis M. Bowen, who has a cellar of Indiana wines in the executive mansion.

Carl and Janet Banholzer sold their interest in Michigan's Tabor Hill Vineyard in 1971 and started their vineyard here in the following year. Most of the vines are French hybrids, but twenty-five acres grow such Vinifera varieties as Chardonnay, Gewürztraminer, Cabernet Sauvignon, and Pinot Noir. Their first Vinifera vintage was 300 gallons of Cabernet Sauvignon in 1975. A sample I tasted from the cask that winter was excellent. A few bottles released for sale in the following year brought $21 each in Chicago. As the first Cabernet grown commercially in Indiana, it inspired articles in the New York *Times* and in the Paris *Le Monde*. The remaining bottles were saved for future distribution to members of a society organized among the winery's regular patrons.

Banholzer wines have proprietary names: Vidalesque for a blend of Vidal Blanc, Seyval, Baco Noir, and Aligoté; Neumontal for a Seyval, Ravat, Chardonnay blend; Kaisertahl is Foch and Pinot Noir; Picnic Rosé is Seyval Blanc and Baco Noir.

Banholzer calls them "American wines made by a German from French grapes." Visitors are offered two wines to taste, shown a film about winegrowing, and are toured through the cellar, where murals by local artist Sylvia Obert on sixteen wine vats depict the history of wine in civilization since 6,000 B.C.

South Bend, the home of Notre Dame University, has a 6,000-gallon winery named Rauner & Sons, opened in 1977 in a former store building north of the campus on US 31. The proprietors are Reverend James Rauner, a Notre Dame alumnus who teaches theology at St. Joseph's High School, his wife Eleanor, and the four eldest of their eight children, teen-aged Peter, Paul, John, and Joe. Their enologist is Margaret Kastner, a chemistry graduate who is working for her doctorate at Notre Dame. The wines are called River City Vineyards for the three acres of French hybrids the Rauners planted in 1973 on a St. Joseph County farm.

• 14 •

In Indiana's far southwestern corner, the Wabash River Valley, is the 34,000-gallon Golden Rain Tree Winery on the St. Wendel-Blairsville Road. It is named for the Oriental tree that rains its golden blossoms in June in the vicinity of historic New Harmony, fifteen miles away.

The modern underground winery, bonded in 1975, makes seven wines from lately planted French hybrids and offers them for tasting in a Swiss chalet that is connected by a tunnel to the cellar. As at the Oliver Winery, wines can be bought by the case, bottle, or glass, and cheeses and other food items are available to be enjoyed with the wines. Winemaker Murli Dharmadhikari, a Hindu who earned his Ph.D. in viticulture and enology at Ohio State University, came to Indiana from the Shawnee Vineyard winery in Ohio. Nine Posey County farmers and businessmen, headed by Albert (Bud) Weil, Evansville furniture dealer Ed Small, and soil conservation technologist Harley Kauffman, founded the winery to revive grape growing in the area. They choose the best dry red wine from each vintage to be featured as their "Directors' Choice."

• 15 •

If you go exploring southern Indiana wineries, you should stop at Saint Meinrad Archabbey and Theological Seminary at US 460 and state Route 545. Besides its famous buildings, stained-glass windows, and art collection, the Archabbey also has the oldest winery in the state. Wine has been made there since the monastery was established in 1854. The first wines were made of wild grapes, but a ten-acre vineyard of Concords was planted there around the turn of the century. About 5,000 gallons of wine are made in the monastery basement each year, not for sale but for the Mass and to accompany the monks' evening meal. The Concord wine, which needed sweetening to be palatable, was not popular with the 160 resident priests and brothers, so in 1973 Brother David Petri was sent to Konstantin Frank's New York State vineyard to work for a year learning to make drier wine and to bring back and plant some of Dr. Frank's Vinifera vines. During the 1976–1977 winter, minus-twenty-two temperatures killed the Vinifera vines to the ground, while the Concords survived. Brother David is now thinking of planting French hybrids, which also make acceptable dry wines.

• 16 •

New vineyards have sprung up lately along Indiana's Ohio River shore. At Cape Sandy, south of Leavenworth, John J. Easley planted twenty acres of hybrids with some Vinifera in 1970. His winery, named Easley Enterprises, is at Indianapolis, in an old creamery building on North College Avenue. His first red wines, Cape Sandy Baco Noir and De Chaunac, were introduced in 1977.

Cincinnati photographer-sculptor Michael Amadeo Mancuso, grandson of an Italian winemaker, surveyed Ohio in the late 1960s for a place to start a winery, decided that the Buckeye State already had enough, and chose the old Indiana river town of Madison, once called "the typical American town." His wife Elizabeth searched the vicinity and found a secluded former dairy farm with picturesque buildings on Dugan Hollow Road in the hills, that might have been planned for a winegrowing estate. They planted hybrids on two sites, moved in with winemaking equipment they had bought, and named the place Villa Medeo for Mancuso's middle name. Elizabeth made their first wine from purchased grapes in 1974 with Michael doing the heavy work. Three of the wines served in their homey tasting room bear Italian names, Robusto Red, Bella Fiamme, and Bianca alla Bianca. The others are Vidal, Seyval, Baco, Niagara, and Concord Rosé.

Other Cincinnatians have explored the Indiana shore of the river, where grapes were grown in the 1860s for Nicholas

Longworth's Ohio wineries, and have begun planting Vinifera and hybrid vineyards in Dearborn County. Notable among them are Dr. Donald A. Shumrick, chairman of otolaryngology at the University of Cincinnati Medical Center, and his neighbor Dr. Charles Amann. Dr. Shumrick and his wife Nora are planning to build the Château Pomije (her Bohemian family name) winery on their twenty-acre mostly Vinifera vineyard in New Alsace. Their son Terry has studied viticulture at Ohio State University and has worked in a California vineyard.

• 16 •

Vineyards and winemaking have come back to Vevay, Switzerland County, where winegrowing began in 1804, twelve years before Indiana became a state. Cincinnati machinist Alvin Meyer and his wife Margaret, home winemakers, came to this river town to camp with their eleven children in 1968. They attended the town's first Swiss Wine Festival, which celebrated Vevay's vinous history with Swiss bands, a carnival, quilting bees, and *steintossen* (stone-tossing) and grape-stomping contests. The stomping contestants jumped barefoot on grapes (brought at first from California) in wooden tubs fitted with spigots. The winners were those who pressed the most juice through the spigots into jars. The festival was discontinued six years later because the crowds it attracted were too large.

The Meyers planted three acres of hybrids on a bluff above the town and in 1974 opened their 2,000-gallon Swiss Valley Vineyards winery and tasting room. It is in the former Ferry Street home of "Captain Jack," the first skipper of the side-wheel paddleboat *Martha Graham,* which still ferries visitors across the river from Kentucky.

In 1796, the year after Washington delivered his Farewell Address, Jean Jacques Dufour left his father's vineyard at Vevey (the French spelling) in Switzerland with an ambitious plan to found a Swiss winegrowing colony in America. He organized the Kentucky Vineyard Society in 1798 and planted European and Alexander vines along the Kentucky River twenty-five miles south of Lexington. His Kentucky vineyards were damaged by frost and plant pests and were abandoned by 1809. Dufour meanwhile bought the present site of Vevay and named it for his Swiss home. Here he planted the grape variety which Pierre Legaux of Philadelphia had falsely named "the Cape grape," really a chance Labrusca hybrid, the Alexander. Legaux's mistake turned out to be Dufour's good fortune, for the hardy Alexander flourished at Vevay, where any European grape would have perished. At Vevay, Dufour wrote one of the first American books about winegrowing, *The American Vine Dresser's Guide.* It was published in 1826, a few months before he died.

The next chapter in Indiana's wine history began in 1814, when "Father" George Rapp abandoned his utopian winegrowing colony at Harmony near Pittsburgh and resettled some 400 of his celibate Rappists on a tract along the Wabash, which he named Harmonie. He found winegrowing there "somewhat better here than in Pennsylvania, yet not so good by far as in the old country." As recorded earlier, the Harmonie Society abandoned Indiana and moved back to Pennsylvania in 1825. Another utopian named Robert Owen bought the land and renamed it New Harmony. Since restored by the state for its historical importance, New Harmony now helps attract visitors to the new Golden Rain Tree Winery nearby.

Winegrowing continued at Vevay until Dufour's death, when it went into a gradual decline. Thomas Jefferson and Secretary of State Henry Clay approved of Vevay wine, and Clay once had a dozen bottles sent to him, to be served to some distinguished visitors. When he opened the bottles he found all twelve filled with whiskey, substituted by his son James, who must have liked the wine.

When Nicholas Longworth introduced the Catawba to Ohio, the Indiana winegrowers switched their plantings to that "wonder grape." By 1880 Indiana was producing 100,000 gallons of wine yearly and selling much of it in Cincinnati. But by then the rot which had killed Longworth's vines had spread to such Indiana vineyard centers as Vevay. Grape production in the Hoosier State reached an all-time high in 1911, when its crop totaled 11,000 tons. It declined during and after Prohibition, until by 1954 only 900 tons were produced.

• 17 •

Kentucky has become a winegrowing state again, six years after Indiana. The first estate-bottled commercial wines produced in the Blue Grass State in this century went on sale in November 1977 at the Colcord Winery in Paris, Bourbon County, for which Kentucky whiskey is named.

"Again" is the accurate term because although the Kentucky Vineyard Society's attempt in the early nineteenth century to grow wine south of Lexington ended in failure, wineries prospered in eastern Kentucky sixty years later when Nicholas Longworth was making his Ohio wines famous at Cincinnati.

In my first edition I mentioned a Kentucky winery established in 1848 by Trappist monks from France, who planted vines on the hillsides when they founded the Trappist Abbey of Gethsemani in Nelson County, and I added that most of that vineyard was abandoned in 1940. I omitted a more important historical item, that the 1880 federal census of winegrowing showed 138,173 gallons of wine produced that year in Logan, Boyle, Washington, and twenty-seven other Kentucky counties.

With its past winegrowing history, why wasn't Kentucky's wine industry revived following the repeal of National Prohibition? There were two reasons. For one thing, two thirds of Kentucky counties remained legally dry under local prohibition laws. For another, the state's minimum license fee for wineries was $1,500 per year, far too much for any small winery to pay.

In the late 1960s, when wine-drinking was becoming newly popular in many parts of this country, it occurred to F. Carlton Colcord, a Europe-traveled member of a Kentucky family with coal-mining interests, that winegrowing might offer a way to improve the depressed economy of the state's Appalachian region. Colcord consulted William Schwerin, a veteran wine hobbyist and maker of vine-tying tools, who has been growing wine grapes since 1945 at Alexandria in Campbell County and selling them to home winemakers and Ohio wineries. Schwerin showed him his flourishing fifteen-acre vineyard of French hybrids, Cabernet Sauvignon, Gewürztraminer, and Gamay Beaujolais.

Colcord in 1970 planted twenty acres of hybrids on his farm four miles east of Paris, and his vines produced well. He sold the first crops to the Oliver Winery and others in Indiana and Ohio, and planted a dozen acres more. I tasted there in 1975 a Chelois made by a home winemaker from Colcord's grapes that was as fine as any red wine made commercially in the East.

With other Kentucky grape growers, Colcord sought the assistance of the State Agricultural Commission to get the winery license fee reduced. In 1974, a bill modeled on Indiana's Small Winery Act was introduced in the Kentucky Legislature. It was opposed by the state's liquor dealers. They objected to letting wineries sell to anyone except licensed wholesalers, and the bill was defeated. It was re-introduced in 1976. Th's time the liquor lobby, unable to defeat the bill, got it amended to bar a winery from selling to stores or restaurants except through wholesalers, and to limit retail sale at a winery to one liter per variety per customer. The amended measure was passed, and Colcord established his winery that year in a remodeled brick former blacksmith shop on a street corner in the old section of Paris.

Colcord spends most of each year in London, where he manages the Kuwait National Petroleum Company. In charge of the vineyard and 7,000-gallon winery is winemaker William T. Pease, who studied viticulture at Sonoma State and Napa Colleges, worked for two California wineries, and made wine for four seasons at William Oliver's winery in Indiana. Pease, incidentally, thinks the Kentucky Vineyard Society should be revived as an agency to promote Blue Grass State wines.

The Colcord Winery's first wines offered for sale were Cane Ridge estate-bottled Bourbon County Kentucky 1976 Villard Blanc, aged in new Kentucky oak, and 1977 Chelois *nouveau*. The brand name stands for the Cane Ridge Meeting House near the Colcord farm, where the Disciples of Christ Church was founded in 1804. Since the several distilleries that once made whiskey around Paris have all moved to other parts of Kentucky, "Bourbon County" has become solely an appellation of origin for wine.

Indiana vintner Oliver, who was born in Kentucky, planted five acres with French hybrid vines in 1971 on reclaimed strip-mined coal land at Jackson in Breathitt County for the Falcon Coal Company. Five years later he made good wines and put them on sale, labeled Falcon Aurora, Cascade, and Rosé, with this added inscription: "Grapes harvested on reclaimed land." Oliver says grapes can be grown on ten thousand acres of such Kentucky land that may be unsuitable for other crops.

The prospect of planting vineyards on coal strip-mine land is interesting others in starting Kentucky wineries. Joseph K. Discher, director of the state real property division, has planted an experimental vineyard at his home at the northern edge of Frankfort and has joined with three other officials to start the Kentucky River Products winery there. Now the University of Kentucky is starting a study of vine rootstocks most suitable for vineyards on former coal mines, in charge of Horticulture Professor Carl Chaplin.

• 18 •

Illinois is the third state in the nation in wine production, making seven million gallons per year. But as will be seen in a later chapter on the kosher wine producers, almost all of it is made by the giant Mogen David Wine Corporation in Chicago from grapes grown in Michigan, Missouri, Pennsylvania, and New York. Yet the Prairie State once had many winegrowers, and it has two of the most interesting small wineries in the Midwest.

On the Mississippi River at the far western edge of the state is a winery that has grown its own grapes for more than a century. Few people in Chicago or Springfield know it exists. Fred Baxter's Gem City Vineland vineyard and winery at Nauvoo produces six Labrusca-type wines, ranging from Niagara and Concord to red, white, rosé, burgundy, and sauterne.

The cellars and the 120-acre vineyard date from 1857, eight years after Baxter's English great-grandfather came to Nauvoo with Etienne Cabet's French communistic Icarian sect. Members of the Baxter family are glad to show you the winery with its original steam-operated wine press and century-old casks. Until 1977, the Illinois beverage law would not let them sell you their wine or even offer you a taste. It was modified in 1976 to allow a winery to sell part of its production at retail. The Baxters promptly built a tasting room, where visitors now can sample the wines with Nauvoo blue cheese. But there still are other unreasonable restrictions in the law, which is why there aren't many more vineyards and wineries in Illinois.

Old Nauvoo is especially worth visiting for its strange history, its restored homes of the original Mormons, the caves of its old wineries, and for the annual symbolic Wedding of Wine and Cheese, an ancient French ceremony that is part of the Nauvoo Grape Festival on the weekend before Labor Day. In the wedding pageant, written by the Benedictine Sisters of St. Mary's Academy in Nauvoo, the bride places the wine on a barrel which symbolizes the altar; the groom places the cheese beside it, and the magistrate encircles both articles with a wooden barrel hoop, which symbolizes the wedding ring.

Nauvoo was founded by the first Mormons, led by their founder, Prophet Joseph Smith. They fled here from western Missouri in 1836 and drained malarial swamps to build their temple and the city, "Nauvoo the Beautiful," which then was ten times the size of Chicago. Political quarrels with non-Mormons led to riots, and in 1844 a raging mob in Carthage shot and killed Joseph Smith and his brother Hyrum; and two years later the temple was burned to the ground. To escape further persecution, the Mormons in 1846 abandoned Nauvoo, leaving it a virtual ghost town, and began their epic wagon journey into Utah, led by Brigham Young. To Nauvoo five years later came Cabet and his Icarians, who moved into the empty Mormon homes. The Icarian brand of communism failed to work, and Cabet abandoned his utopia, leaving many of his flock behind. Meanwhile, winegrowing became the leading industry of Nauvoo, John Tanner from Berne in Switzerland having planted the first vineyard in 1847.

The winery Alois Rheinberger from Lichtenstein founded in 1850 now serves as Nauvoo's Historical Museum. Memorabilia on display show that Rheinberger's wines became famous and were known as late as the nineties in such faraway places as St. Paul and New York. In the museum cellar you will see his press and other winemaking implements, and the huge stone he used as a weight on his press is on the lawn nearby. An acre of Rheinberger's vineyard still bears grapes in the Nauvoo State Park. The extent of pre-Prohibition winemaking at Nauvoo can be estimated by counting the dozens of vaulted wine caves that honeycomb the hills along the river shore.

When Prohibition emptied the Nauvoo wineries, it was found that the wine caves had just the proper temperature and degree of moisture for the culture of blue cheese. This was the birth of Nauvoo's cheese industry, now celebrated by the Wedding of Wine and Cheese.

• 19 •

Forty miles southwest of Chicago on Pauling Road near the town of Monee, an ancient Illinois Central railroad station stands in a thirty-acre rolling vineyard of French hybrid, Delaware, and Catawba vines, which are interspersed with rows of White Riesling and Chardonnay. Beneath the quaint old station is a model 18,000-gallon wine cellar that produces bottle-fermented champagne.

This is the Thompson Vineyard and Winery, owned by Dr. John E. Thompson, a nutritionist and former instructor in physiology at the Illinois Institute of Technology, who also owns the adjoining 3,000 acres of Thompson Farms. Dr. Thompson has operated the vineyard and winery as a hobby since he bought it from Bern Ramey and the late Joseph Allen in 1970.

Ramey, a champagne maker from Ohio's Lake Erie Islands, a graduate of the University of California–Davis wine school, and a lecturer and writer on wines in Chicago, planted the vineyard in 1963 because he wanted to prove that wine as fine as any can be grown in Illinois. He proved it by making in 1966 a brut champagne, which I tasted at the winery with Chicago *Tribune* writer Ruth Ellen Church, that was as fine as any produced in the United States.

But inspecting the vineyard one morning in the spring of 1968, Ramey discovered strange streaks on the leaves of the vines. The leaf edges resembled the teeth of a saw—unmistakable symptoms of injury by the weed-killer used on adjoining cornfields, known as 2,4–D. Ramey & Allen Champagne was already on the market and winning connoisseur favor in Illinois, but soon half of the vines were stunted back to year-old size. Part of the vineyard was ploughed under and the model winery was closed. "It cost us a quarter of a million dollars to learn that grapes cannot be grown in corn country," Ramey says.

Dr. Thompson has since restored and expanded the vineyard, neighboring farmers having promised him to spray no more with 2,4–D. His brut white and pink champagnes, named respectively for Père Marquette and Père Hennequin, Jesuit priests who explored the Midwest, can now be bought at the winery and are to be followed by a series of red and white table wines. Thompson teaches classes in wine appreciation at Purdue University and at an Illinois college. Ramey now travels between California and European vineyards as the boss of import sales for Browne Vintners, but visits Monee each year to see how his Illinois vineyard grows.

• 20 •

The 2,4–D weed-killer has also damaged Baxter's vines at Nauvoo, but it has done far more damage in the century-old winegrowing districts of Iowa and Kansas.

Yes, you read correctly: Kansas, the home of Carry Nation, had a well-established wine industry until the state was voted dry in 1880. The Prohibitionists expunged its history from the archives, but the evidence remains in the shells of venerable Kansas wineries, underground cellars walled with stone, which you still can see along the rivers in the eastern part of the state. One of the oldest, three miles northwest of Wathena, was built in 1872 by Emanuel Madinger, who compared the vineyards along the west bank of the Missouri to those of his native Württemberg in the Rhineland. The 1880 census shows that 226,249 gallons of wine were produced in that year by vineyards in Doniphan, Labette, Wyandotte, Leavenworth, and thirty-eight other Kansas counties. When the state went dry, Concords replaced wine grapes in Kansas. This pleased the Dry-dominated State Horticultural Society, which in a 1901 publication referred to grapes as "a fruit too good to be made a chief source of the degradation of the race."

Although the Drys are powerful in Kansas, one of the three states where (as in Tennessee and Utah) you still cannot buy a glass of wine with your meal in a restaurant, wine consumption in the Sunflower State has doubled to three bottles per capita in the past decade. Home winemaking is popular, and several young wine-grape vineyards have been planted in Butler, Chautauqua, Reno, and Sedgwick Counties. Some Kansas grapes have been sold to wineries in Oklahoma and Missouri. Kansas State University is conducting grape-growing research, but wine must not be mentioned publicly, although the grapes are French hybrid wine varieties.

Some grapes still grow in eastern Kansas, but Professor Erwin Abmeyer, superintendent of the state's Northeast Experiment Fields at Wathena, says that even his test plots have been damaged by 2,4–D and that many of the old vineyards have been removed. "I see little hope for their revival," he says, "as long as the use of 2,4–D and 2,3,5–T continues." Damage from the weed-killer is much less, however, in southern Kansas, where the new vineyards are, says Dr. Ronald W. Campbell, head of the KSU Horticulture Department.

· 21 ·

As for Iowa, with 2,4–D killing more vines each year, little is left of the state's once-important wine industry except scattered vineyards around Council Bluffs and near Keokuk, and the ten quaint little wineries of the Amana Colonies.

The Amanas and their wines are something out of another world. The colonies are seven Old World villages on the banks of the Iowa River ten miles north of Interstate 80, eighteen miles southwest of Cedar Rapids. An eighteenth-century German communistic and religious sect called The Community of True Inspiration came here in 1854 from Ebenezer, New York, purchased 25,000 acres of virgin prairie, and built a utopia named Amana, a biblical word meaning "remain true." Three more colonies, Middle, West, and South Amana, were built two miles apart, an hour's travel by ox team. High and Upper South Amana were added in between, and the small town of Homestead was purchased outright.

In the Amana Colonies of Iowa, the principal product is piestengel, a rhubarb wine. Linda and Leslie Ackerman make piestengel in their basement at South Amana.

Communism survived here for almost three generations. Everything was owned by the Amana Society; the members worked without pay in the mills, shops, and fields and had their meals together in communal kitchens. But in 1932 the Depression threatened them with bankruptcy, and communism was forsaken for capitalism. The colonists became stockholders of a corporation which paid them wages, and capitalism worked: one of the colonies' several industries, Amana Refrigeration, has become the biggest maker of home freezers in the world.

Most of the tiny Amana wineries make piestengel and grape wines in the basements of the owners' homes. Piestengel is rhubarb wine; the word means pie stalk in German. It comes dry and sweet, white and pink, and usually doesn't taste of rhubarb; it has a flavor of its own. During the 1970s some of them added dandelion and cherry wines to their assortment, and in some years a few make wines of wild grapes. Nine tenths of Amana wine is sold to tourists, who taste and buy it in the cellars and drink it in the local restaurants. The tourists are happy to pay eight dollars a gallon for the Amana products—more than double the price of many standard wines—because, in the rest of Iowa, wine to take home can only be bought in the state monopoly liquor stores. A special section of the Iowa law, adopted when Prohibition was repealed, allows the native wineries to sell their homemade wines to anyone; but only a few are sold in the state stores. The Amana wineries are so popular with visitors that they have doubled in number; there were only five in 1972. Most Amana wines are labeled "other than standard wine" because to reach their usual 16 percent alcoholic content more sugar must be added than Federal wine regulations allow.

In the old days each Amana colony had its communal winery, which provided each family with a daily allowance of wine. Workers in the fields received an extra portion at three each afternoon. "Our village winery was under our church," the late Friedrich Ackerman, who owned the South Amana Winery, told me when I first visited the Colonies. "But our elders ordered all the barrels emptied when Prohibition became the law in 1920, and the wine ran in the ditches for hours." His grandson Leslie runs the winery now.

The vineyards were abandoned during the 1920s, and when the wineries reopened at Repeal, they got their grapes from a vineyard near Fort Madison on the Mississippi. Then the Fort Madison vineyard was ruined by 2,4–D, and most of the grapes since have come from Council Bluffs or from Fred Baxter's vineyard across the river at Nauvoo. A new Amana vineyard was planted in the 1960s by Ramon Goerler, a Navy veteran and a graduate of the University of Iowa, who with his wife Betty owns the Old Wine Cellar and Colony Wineries; but the deadly weed-killer from nearby cornfields killed his vines, too.

In 1880, when the national census of winegrowing was taken, Iowa produced 334,970 gallons of wine, thirteen times as much as the 26,000 gallons the state produces today.

Some of the best-known Iowa wines came from the hundred-acre White Elk Vineyard of Hiram Barney near Keokuk. An 1879 article in *The American Wine and Grape Grower* said that Barney's wines "have some reputation in the East but are better known in the West and South." White Elk wines bore varietal labels such as Catawba, Ives, Norton's Virginia, Delaware, and Clinton, and were described as "the pure juice of the grapes whose names they bear."

Nebraska, across the Missouri River from Council Bluffs, also had many wineries in the 1880s, principally around Omaha, Plattsmouth, and Nebraska City in Cass, Nemaha, and Sarby Counties. The vineyard of Julius Pitts, who had a winery near Plattsmouth, was still producing grapes in the 1970s.

• 22 •

"Wisconsin is no place to grow grapes," I was told in 1973 by Dr. Malcolm Dana, chairman of that state university's department of horticulture. Yes, he said, there are seven wineries in Wisconsin, but they mostly make cherry wines, although one has also made a wine of wild grapes. Then Dr. Dana told me about a young electrical engineer and home winemaker, employed part time at the university, who was interested in growing grapes at Prairie du Sac, twenty miles away. His name was Robert Wollersheim.

Wollersheim, when I reached him by telephone, told me a surprising story. He had just bought a nineteenth-century stone winery with hillside caves and traces of a vineyard that had once been owned by the Hungarian immigrant "Count" Agoston Haraszthy, who later made winegrowing history in California.

The Haraszthy story was familiar; he had settled in Wisconsin about 1840, founded a town he named Haraszthy, which later became Sauk City; had raised livestock, started a sawmill and hopyard, had run a Mississippi steamboat and the first ferry across the Wisconsin River; had planted European grapevines, most of which froze during the first winter, and had left for California when word came of the discovery of gold there in 1848. Title records of Wollersheim's property showed that

Ruins of long-forgotten nineteenth-century wineries dot many states across America. This cave, across the river from Sauk City, Wisconsin, may have been dug by "Count" Haraszthy before he emigrated to California in 1848.

Haraszthy had owned it in 1847. The later dates in the records don't contradict the story. Carved in stone with a bunch of grapes on Wollersheim's seventeen-room house adjoining the winery was the legend "P. Kehl 1858," and the native limestone winery bore the date of 1867.

Three years after that telephone conversation, I visited the Wollersheim Winery, which is on Highway 188 across the river from Prairie du Sac and Sauk City. Bob Wollersheim, his pretty wife Jo Ann, and Bob's parents had already harvested two vintages from the fourteen acres of French hybrids they had planted since 1973 on the south-facing hillside that the former owners had called "the Kehl Weinberg." Bob had equipped the vaulted cellar with stainless steel tanks, century-old casks from an Ohio winery, and new European and American oak barrels. His estate-bottled 1975 Seyval Blanc and Aurora wines, on sale in the tasting room upstairs, were as well made, fruity and pleasing as any comparable wines grown in the East. There were a half dozen other wines, made of White Riesling, Chardonnay, and hybrid grapes Wollersheim had bought from Pennsylvania, and a wine he makes of Door County cherries. Jo Ann was conducting a bevy of visitors on the one-dollar tour of the vineyard, winery, and the re-opened hillside tunnels. She later sold them sausage, cheese, home-winemaking supplies, foreign wines, wine books, and local art in the tasting room. The Wollersheim children were helping, Steve in the cellar, Julie and Eva elsewhere. The winery, now listed in the National Register of Historic Places, attracted 30,000 visitors during 1976.

Bob was still working half time at the University, teaching engineering and heading a weather project in the space science center. What did he think of growing wine grapes in the corn and dairy country of Wisconsin, where the winters are severe? Bob replied that Peter Kehl from the Rhineland, who bought the place from Haraszthy, grew Riesling as well as native grapes of the Labrusca family, but that Kehl's vineyard was killed by the record winter freeze of 1899 and was never replanted.

Wollersheim's experimental planting of White Riesling and Chardonnay had suffered in winter and produced only skimpy crops; his best yields had come from the hybrids Seyval Blanc and Maréchal Foch. He had thought of covering his vines with earth from fall until spring, but had only hilled up earth around the trunks. "We have a longer growing season, up to 170 days, than many winegrowing districts of the East and Midwest," Wollersheim said. "Wine grapes can grow as well here as in the

The Wine Institute Library

Agoston Haraszthy, the colorful Hungarian "Count" who founded Sauk City in Wisconsin, then emigrated to Sonoma, where he became "the father of modern California viticulture."

Finger Lakes district of New York." Others in Wisconsin share his confidence and have bought vines from the Wollersheim vineyard with the idea of starting wineries along the state's Lake Michigan shore.

• 23 •

Another Wisconsin vineyard, 150 miles northwest of Wollersheim's, created a sensation during the 1970s by growing a grape called "Variety 439." Newspaper headlines called it "the first wine grape with a fur coat" because it was said to withstand six weeks of thirty-below-zero weather without winter covering, which if true would make possible the development of a winegrowing industry in the northern tier of states.

On two acres of his former dairy farm east of Osceola, hobbyist grape breeder Elmer Swenson bred "Variety 439," which resembles Vinifera and French hybrids in appearance and texture, by crossing Minnesota No. 78, a descendant of the wild grape that survives the coldest midwestern winters, with the Seibel hybrid 11803. A virtual teetotaler uninterested in wine, Swenson gave the University of Minnesota his rights to the grape after he was hired to manage the University's fruit farms.

Excitement about Swenson's grape cooled, however, when questions were raised about just how winter-hardy it is, and it was learned that Swenson usually buries his vines in fall to protect them from cold. Although "439" (which Swenson calls "Norvin"; the University calls it "Swenson's Red") makes a pungent, non-foxy, straw-colored wine, it is now thought to be more suitable as a fresh table grape.

• 24 •

Minnesota, where the winter-hardiness of grapes is a first concern, has joined the list of winegrowing states.

In a former creamery at Maple Lake, thirty-five miles northwest of Minneapolis, hobbyist grape grower David Macgregor bonded his Lake Sylvia Vineyard winery in 1976. His first seven-hundred-gallon vintage was made of grapes Macgregor bred himself, blended with Swenson's "Variety 439" and with French hybrids. It was the first commercial wine grown in Minnesota since the turn of the century, when a winery at Stillwater had made wine of grapes grown there. Macgregor, a businessman's son, has been growing grapes and making wine since he was sixteen years old. He studied horticulture at the University of Minnesota, met Elmer Swenson there, and started his own grape-breeding project on his two-acre vineyard beside Lake Sylvia, which is near Maple Lake. He has written a monograph on viticulture in Minnesota, published by the state grape growers' association.

In 1977, the North Star State's second commercial winery opened for business in a brand-new Minnesota log cabin on the Alexis Bailly Vineyard near the town of Hastings, fifteen miles southeast of Minneapolis. Lawyer David Bailly named his ten-acre vineyard and 5,000-gallon winery for his great-great-great-grandfather, who founded Hastings in 1854. David Bailly planted his vineyard on Kirby Avenue in 1973 with French hybrids and a few vines of "Variety 439," which he finds no more winter-hardy than the hybrids. His wines, a white of Seyval Blanc and reds of Maréchal Foch and Léon Millot, were due on the market in 1978. His 1976 Léon Millot has shown particular promise, with deep color and full body and flavor. Bailly also makes a mead of Minnesota honey, an apple wine, and a grape-and-apple blend. Besides his own grapes, he uses some of Swenson's and the crops of other Minnesota vineyards, including engineer Gerald Eisert's two acres near Red Wing, and insuranceman Richard Williams's five acres near Cambridge.

Macgregor's monograph says grapevines in Minnesota should be buried each fall under straw or other mulch and covered with earth. Wild grapevines survive without cover in Minnesota winters as cold as forty below zero. At the Laboratory of Plant Hardiness on the University's St. Paul campus, Professor Cecil Stushnoff is breeding blueberry vines that need no winter protection because their dwarf size keeps them covered with snow. Graduate student Patrick Pierquet ferments Swenson's grapes there, testing them for wine quality, and studies hybrid grapevines in the quest for some that may survive Minnesota winters without cover, as the wild vines do.

• 25 •

Near Caney in southern Oklahoma, ten poor families settled in surplus government house trailers on a 160-acre tract of virgin land during the spring of 1972 and planted thirty acres of French hybrids as the start of a Federal project to make welfare recipients self-sufficient by growing grapes for wine. They were the first of 300 families who were to plant vineyards of twelve acres each, which officials estimated would earn $7,000 a year per family when their crops would be harvested after four years.

This was the plan that Captain Paul Garrett and Harry Hopkins proposed in Georgia forty years earlier, only to be frustrated by the Drys in Congress, and the same that was proposed for West Virginia in 1966 and vetoed by state officials there.

When Oklahoma Office of Economic Opportunity director Rex Sparger planned the project, he first considered starting the welfare families on rabbit or catfish farms. When he announced the decision to have them grow wine grapes instead, several thousand families applied to join. French hybrids from New York State and Canada were chosen for planting, on the advice of Oklahoma State University horticulturists and of Professor John Einset, who came to Oklahoma as a consultant from the Geneva Experiment Station of New York. Two groups of Oklahomans were interested in starting wineries as soon as enough wine grapes could be produced.

But there came a change in the state administration; Sparger was removed, and the planting at Caney stopped. Gradually, nine of the ten families drifted away. When I stopped at Caney in 1976, only Jim Dodd, a former oilfield worker, his wife Leona and their three children were left living in their trailer among fifty acres of flourishing vines. Twenty acres were Dodd's; the rest, including a dozen acres of Vinifera varieties, had been added by Tulsa investor Clare Miller in 1974. Miller's foreman, Arkansas horticulture graduate Stuart Chaney, was also caring for Dodd's vines. Arkansas wineries and home winemakers were buying the grapes. Dodd was using some to make wine for his family.

Two wineries started in Oklahoma in the early 1970s. One at

Keystone began as a hobby of Dr. Robert Rheinfrank, but it became inactive when the doctor's health declined. Peter Schwarz, whose 20,000-gallon winery is at Okarche, buys his grapes from Tontitown in Arkansas, 230 miles away, because he says his land at Okarche is unsuited for grapes. Schwarz makes a sweet and a sweeter Concord wine and also a dandelion wine. He sells all he makes at the winery, which is on a country road a mile east of town.

A winery that operated at Oklahoma City in the 1890s has been designated as a national historic site. Former Mayor George Shirk found records at the state historical society showing that one Edward Fairchild had come to the city about the time of the 1889 land run and soon had begun making wine. Shirk looked up the land records, paced off Fairchild's site, and found the winery half buried in mud.

Professor Herman A. Hinrichs of the University at Stillwater says grapes are a dependable crop in Oklahoma. He has tested many wine varieties and has seen them grown successfully by wine hobbyists in several parts of the state. He believes there is a commercial future for Oklahoma wines.

• 26 •

When I tell my friends in the East and West that good table wines and champagnes are now being made in Arkansas, they are amazed and some are openly skeptical, because few Americans, even former Arkansans, have ever associated Arkansas with the gentle art of appreciating wines. Yet it is true that in this part of the changing South, new vineyards of wine-grape varieties have been spreading through the Ozark backwoods, and that five of the state's eleven wineries are now concentrating on the production of table wines for mealtime use. Two of them are making Arkansas champagnes.

Most of this is taking place around a little town called Altus in the Ozark plateau region in the northwestern part of the state. Near the outskirts of Altus a narrow road that winds up St. Mary's Mountain through the woods has been named Champagne Drive. About a mile up the road, in a wide clearing at the summit, stands a wine cellar that resembles a Swiss chalet. Nearby are clusters of wine tanks of fiberglass and stainless steel. These are the Wiederkehr Wine Cellars, which with its capacity of 1,500,000 gallons is the largest and most modern winery in the Southwest. Adjoining is a two-story Alpine inn with a tasting room, gift shop, and a Swiss Wein Keller

The first Wine Festival at the Wiederkehr Wine Cellars in Arkansas, 1966.

Restaurant which serves such dishes as quiche Lorraine and poulet rôti au vin blanc.

Here, in August of each year, the Altus Grape Festival is celebrated with pageantry, music, vineyard workers wearing *lederhosen,* pretty girls in bright Swiss peasant frocks, and with a King Bacchus crowning the festival queen. At the edge of the clearing the Wiederkehr vineyards begin. Symmetrical rows of grapevines stretch across the sandy plateau that slopes toward the wide Arkansas River Valley—325 acres planted to French hybrids, Delaware, Campbell's Early, Cynthiana, the best red-wine grape of the Ozarks, and a hundred acres of young Johannisberg Riesling, Chardonnay, Gewürztraminer, Cabernet Sauvignon, and other Vinifera vines.

The settlers of Arkansas made wine more than a century ago from the Scuppernong and other Muscadine grapes that grow wild through most of the state, but the frontiersmen generally preferred moonshine whiskey to wine. Between 1879 and 1900, Swiss, German, and Italian immigrants settled in the Ozark plateau country and began cultivating American bunch grapes. They made wine for their own use, then opened small wineries to make it for sale. Prohibition closed the wineries and brought to Arkansas scouts of the Welch Company, looking for new lands to grow more Concords for Welch grape juice and jelly. In

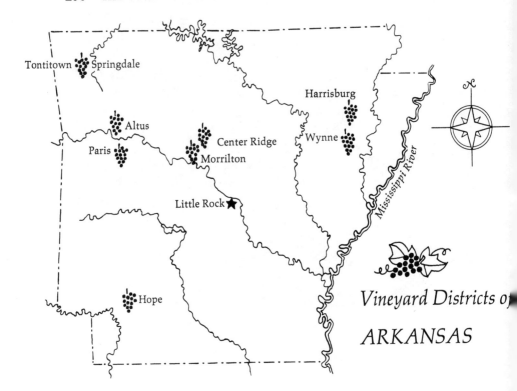

Vineyard Districts of

ARKANSAS

1923, a Welch plant was built at Springdale and a boom in Concord-planting ensued. Vineyard acreage in Arkansas expanded to 9,000 acres by 1925, almost four times the 2,400 acres there now.

During the Depression, Arkansas faced a grape surplus, so at the repeal of Prohibition in 1933 the state legislature voted to revive the wineries. This was done by taxing wines from outside the state seventy-five cents a gallon and letting Arkansas wines pay only a five cent tax. More than a hundred wineries sprang up in Arkansas, but the chief product they turned out was 20 percent "sneaky pete," made from surplus Concords as a cheap intoxicant for hillbillies. This brought a reaction; many Arkansas counties voted themselves dry, closing the wineries. By 1957 only sixteen were left.

Though by then most of the grapes grown were Concords, the Swiss and German growers whose families had settled at Altus about 1880 still grew the native wine grapes. One of these was Herman Wiederkehr, who made table wines, the kinds his father, Johann Andreas Wiederkehr from Weinfeld in Switzer-

land, had always served at home. Herman and Mary Weider-
kehr worried that Franklin County might vote dry at any time
and close their little winery. Seeing no future in wine, they sent
their five sons to college to study for other professions. But their
youngest son, Alcuin, coming home on his vacations from
Notre Dame and the University of Arkansas Law School, kept
saying he wanted to be a winegrower. When a new Arkansas
law was passed to let a winery continue operating even if its
county went dry, Alcuin quit law school, went to the University
of California at Davis to study viticulture and enology, joining
his older brother Leo there. Alcuin had a chance to go to Europe
as an exchange student in 1962. He requested France, and was
sent to Bordeaux. He worked in the vineyards, helped in the
vintage, and after ten months came home filled with new ideas.
He began planting the French hybrid grapes he had seen used
to make French wines, and added an experimental plot of
Vinifera vines from Dr. Konstantin Frank. During the next five
years the two brothers enlarged the Wiederkehr vineyards and
built the family winery to twenty times its original size.

By 1965, Alcuin was campaigning for a bill that would allow
the state's restaurants to sell Arkansas table wine with meals.
The bill wasn't expected to pass, but Alcuin arranged to have
half-bottles of Wiederkehr table wines served at the Governor's
Ball. The ladies present approved of the samples, especially
when cherubic, curly-headed young Alcuin danced with them,
and some took home the bottles as souvenirs. The next
morning the bill passed the Senate, and when the restaurants in
eleven cities began offering wine with dinners, table wine sales
in Arkansas quadrupled in a few months.

Most of the Wiederkehr wines and champagnes have resembled the principal wines of the northeastern states, but the 1973
White (Johannisberg) Riesling, which I have tasted on four
occasions, could have passed for a fine German or California
wine. The assortment at the winery includes such specialties as
Cynthiana, Edelweiss, Vin Blanc Sec, and two different rosés. A
dry cocktail sherry of Villard Blanc was very good, and a muscat
table wine called "Arkansas Mountain Moscato di Tanta Maria" was outstanding. On my first visit to the winery several
years ago I tasted from the cask a dry Cynthiana that had
sufficient tannin and body to develop bouquet with age, but
samples I tasted later were still young. Perhaps such a Cynthiana, if given bottle-age, eventually will win recognition
beyond Arkansas as the state's most distinctive wine. Alcuin
Wiederkehr doesn't agree. He hopes someday to compete

against European and California wines with Arkansas Rieslings and Chardonnays.

• 27 •

At the botton of St. Mary's Mountain, with a Swiss chalet front like Wiederkehr's, is the 400,000-gallon Post Winery. The Wiederkehrs and the Posts, who are cousins, turn out the lion's share of the million gallons now produced in Arkansas, and both now sell some of their wines in neighboring states.

Five-foot-five Mathew J. Post, who is the mayor of Altus, insists that his winery is a year older than the Wiederkehrs' because his great-grandfather, Jacob Post from Bavaria, found-ed it in 1880. Like his uphill neighbors, Post welcomes visitors, inviting them to tour his attractive cellar and to taste his assortment of wines, which include a really admirable dry champagne with the character of the best French hybrid grapes, a reasonably dry burgundy, a medium-sweet Cynthiana, white and red Muscadine wines, various Labrusca table wine types, port, and sherry. Matt Post and his wife Betty have twelve children, ten of whom help at various jobs in the vineyard and winery, including Matt Junior, who is now the general manag-er, and Joe, who became the cellar tour guide at the age of eleven. With the rising demand for dry and semi-dry table wines in Arkansas, the Posts have added twenty-five acres of French hybrids to their 160 acres of vines, and also some of the new North Carolina varieties of Muscadine grapes, which are recommended by horticulturist Dr. Justin Morris of the Univer-sity of Arkansas.

Adjoining Mathew Post's winery is the smaller Mount Bethel Cellar, operated by his brother Eugene. The younger Post has been making table wines since the restaurant bill became law. Henry Sax, with his 5,000-gallon winery at Altus, added French hybrids to his vineyard when his son Charles began studying horticulture at the University. At Paris, south of Altus, Robert and Betty Kay Cowie, who opened their small winery in 1967, make only three products, Cynthiana, Campbell's Early, and Ives red table wines. The two wineries at Center Ridge, the Heckmanns at Harrisburg, and Freyaldenhoven's at Morrilton, make both table and dessert types.

There is one winery, Emmett Neil's, among the Concord vineyards west of Tontitown in the northwestern corner of Arkansas. Italian residents of that community still celebrate their annual grape festival, which honors the memory of Father

Pietro Bandini, who was sent from Italy in 1897 to investigate the condition of Italian immigrants in America. Finding a half-starved, malaria-ridden colony on Lake Chicot in the southeastern Arkansas cotton country, he bought a tract of several hundred acres in Washington County and moved the families there. He started them planting grapes as they had always done in Italy.

• 28 •

Texas produced wine a century before wine grapes were introduced to California. Franciscan priests brought the Mission vine from Mexico to the El Paso Valley when they established Ysleta Mission in 1662 and grew wine there for the Mass. During the next two centuries immigrants from European winegrowing countries brought Old World grapes to the central and northern parts of the state. When their Vinifera vines succumbed to the weather and plant pests, they made wines of native grapes, including the wild Mustang.

Dozens of wineries flourished on vineyards around El Paso, Montague, and Fredericksburg until early in this century, when competition from California and the approach of Prohibition caused their sales of wine to decline. The last ones closed in 1919 when the state legislature voted Texas legally dry.

At the end of the dry era, one pre-Prohibition winery reopened on the Rio Grande across from Mexico, but for three more decades no effort was made to revive the winegrowing industry. Agriculture professors continued their teaching about grapes but were forbidden to do any work connected with wine.

When the boom in table wine comsumption and vineyard-planting spread nationwide in the late 1960s and early 1970s, almost a hundred new vineyards sprang up across the Lone Star State. Influential Texans, accustomed to thinking big, visualized millions of acres being planted with vines and adding wine to the impressive list of products for which Texas is a major source.

With money donated by businessmen, Texas A.& M. University was assigned to make a statewide feasibility study of wine-grape production as a potential new source of agricultural income. The study, by horticulture professors Ronald Perry and Hollis Bowen, was finished in 1974. It showed that almost every part of the state's vast expanse could grow grapes for wines of some kind; table and dessert wines in western Texas, French and American hybrid types in central and north central areas,

Muscadine wines in the south and east. Each area presented hazards of weather and related plant diseases, and some had water supply problems. Texas wines were not pictured as competition for California. But high quality dessert wines could be made in some localities, and in parts of far western Texas with cool summers, better than standard table wines could be grown.

Two years after the study was released, the first new Texas winery built in this century opened on Farm Market Road 1585 three miles south of Lubbock in the northwestern high plains region. It is the 15,000-gallon Llano Estacado or Staked Plain Winery, owned by three Texas Tech University professors, Drs. Clinton McPherson and Roy Mitchell of the chemistry department and horticulturist Dr. Robert Reed. Their seven-acre vineyard a few miles from the winery was planted in 1971 with more than a hundred Vinifera, French hybrid, and Muscadine grape varieties. All of the vines except the Muscadines were flourishing when I was there. They call it Sagmor Vineyard because the trellis holding the vines sags almost to breaking point in the strong West Texas winds. The winery is in a legally wet precinct; the vineyard is in a precinct that is dry. Llano Estacado is Spanish for the Staked Plain region of Texas, named, legend says, for the wooden stakes Francisco Vasquez Coronado drove in the giant buffalo grass to guide him back from his exploring trip to New Mexico in 1542. The first Llano Estacado wines, ready for sale in 1978, are named Cíbola Roja (red), Blanca (white), and Rosé for the fabled seven cities of Cíbola which the Spanish explorers sought in the belief they contained fabulous wealth.

The professors began planting wine grapes on the University campus in 1965 and made their first wines in the basement chemistry lab. That is where I sampled their 1974 vintage because the winery wasn't yet ready. Their best was a Ruby Cabernet, which, though it had not been stored in wood, was a quite acceptable dinner wine. Mrs. Lyndon B. (Lady Bird) Johnson gave their white wine a better testimonial than mine. Visiting the University in 1975, and hearing of the professors' vineyard, she had her limousine drive her there, and she tasted several of the wines in the barn. Mrs. Johnson pronounced one of the whites "a delightful Chenin Blanc like what we used to serve in the White House."

Lubbock is classed by the feasibility study as one of Texas' priority regions for wine grapes. Water is scarce, but the drip irrigation method devised in Israel keeps the vines alive.

Sub-zero winter temperatures, the study says, may injure Vinifera vines at Lubbock in one year out of five. Growing-season temperatures there compare to the parts of California's hot Central Valley classed as Region V (page 224). A problem in west Texas is hailstorms, in which hailstones as big as golfballs can strip a vine of grapes. Despite such drawbacks, Sagmor Vineyard is already being doubled in size.

Three hundred miles south of Lubbock is the Val Verde Winery of the Qualia family, who have made unique Texas wines since 1883, except during the fifteen years the state was legally dry. Their winery, a two-story building of adobe brick, is on palm-lined Hudson Drive halfway between Del Rio, the county seat of Val Verde County, and the bridge across the Rio Grande to the Mexican city of Ciudad Acuña.

Beside the winery is the Qualias' main vineyard, fourteen acres of two South Carolina grapes that so far as I know are grown by no other American winery—the red Herbemont, which has white juice, and the black Lenoir, Jacquez, or Black Spanish, which has red juice. The Qualias grow these grapes because they produce well in this hot, moist climate and are tolerant of Pierce's Disease, which kills most other bunch grapes in the southeastern states and in southern and eastern Texas. They make four kinds of table wine—dry and sweet amber from Herbemont and dry and sweet red from Lenoir. The wines are named Felipe del Rio for the spring that irrigates the vineyard. The Qualias sell all they can make, six thousand gallons per year, to local residents and tourists who come to the winery. The Herbemont has a distinctive varietal aroma and flavor that might interest connoisseurs if the juice were fermented at low temperature—which the Qualias had never done but were preparing to do when I was there. They were re-equipping the winery with a new press, refrigeration machinery, and new steel tanks.

Louis F. Qualia's parents came from Milan in 1880, planted vines and fruit trees, irrigated them by building a canal from the nearby spring, and began making wine for sale. Louis, born there in 1897, built the present winery in 1919 but immediately closed it because that was the year Texas went dry. He reopened it in 1936 when the state repealed its dry law and kept it going as a matter of family pride. It is Del Rio's oldest industry. Louis sent his oldest son, John, to the University of California at Davis and his youngest son Tom to Texas Tech University. When Tom finished college he and his wife Linda joined the Peace Corps and spent three years in Bolivia. When they returned, father Louis planted sixteen more acres of Herbemont and Lenoir in the Quemado Valley, thirty miles south of Del Rio. Tom became proprietor of the winery with Louis his viticulturist.

In central Texas, most of the new vineyards are of French hybrid grapes because winters in these areas are considered too cold for Vinifera. The largest planting thus far is Arlington doctor Bobby G. Smith's eleven-acre Buena Vida Vineyard off Route 199 four miles south of Springtown. He calls it "the Napa Valley of Texas." He is building a winery, even though Parker County is legally dry (as are a sixth of Texas' 254 counties.) Presumably his wines will be sold in nearby counties, which are wet. Other new central Texas vineyards include retired publisher Lyndol Hart's five acres in Parker County, attorney Harold Malloy's three acres at Bastrop, and livestock breeder Peter Gifford's Wolf Run Ranch vineyard of mixed hybrids fifty miles north of Dallas. Dr. George Ray McEachern, the university extension horticulturist who coordinates wine-grape work, thinks the Hill Country around Fredericksburg is an especially good location for small hybrid vineyards and for wineries that could retail Texas specialty wines at their premises.

Although most of the west Texas climates suitable for growing Vinifera grapes are as hot in summer as California's sizzling Central Valley, there also are cool mountain slopes where maximum temperatures correspond to the California coastal valleys that grow premium table wines and champagnes. On such a mountain site, Gretchen Glasscock of San Antonio, who is sometimes called the oil princess of Texas, has undertaken to grow wines finer than California's, which could make her the state's wine princess instead. Gretchen is the daughter of the late William D. Glasscock, who began his career in the four Glasscock Brothers' high-wire circus act for Barnum and Bailey and Ringling Brothers and went on to become one of Texas' oil and cattle kings.

In April 1977, in a mountainside ceremony attended by 250 members of officialdom and San Antonio society, the former oil princess planted the first vines of thirty acres of Cabernet Sauvignon, Merlot, Sauvignon Blanc, and other noble grape varieties. Her vineyard is a mile high on the southeastern slope of Blue Mountain, seven miles south of Fort Davis. Guiding her project are two of America's leading authorities on fine-wine production, enologist Dimitri Tchelistcheff of Ensenada and viticulturist John Moramarco of California's Callaway Vineyard.

The resident vineyard manager is Moramarco's son Jon, on leave from the University of California at Davis.

Gretchen plans to build a winery on the vineyard when her first grape crop matures. If grapes of Region II or III quality (page 224) grow successfully in the Glasscock Vineyard, the former oil princess will have a chance in the 1980s to produce the first truly fine Texas table wines.

At Manhattan in the same Davis Mountain range, Gretchen's friend Roxanna Donnell has a seven-acre Vinifera vineyard planted a year before. Another west Texas Vinifera vineyard was planted still earlier by rancher James Conway, who plans a winery on his 400-acre farm two miles southeast of Clint in El Paso County.

• 29 •

There is a five-acre vineyard at Denison on the Red River in north central Texas that exists for a reason unlike any other in the world. The T.V. Munson Memorial Vineyard was planted in 1975 beside the Denison Airport on the Grayson County College west campus as a monument to America's most famous grape breeder, Dr. Thomas Volney Munson. Munson and Hermann Jaeger of Missouri were awarded the French Legion of Honor cross of Mérite Agricole in 1888 for saving the vineyards of France. Like his friend Jaeger, Munson shipped carloads of American phylloxera-resistant vine roots to France during the 1870s. Onto those roots the Old World wine grapes were grafted, thus saving them from the phylloxera scourge.

But Dr. Munson's greater achievement was the breeding of native American grapes that were resistant to midwestern weather and plant pests. He had developed more than 300 new grape varieties when he died at the age of seventy in 1913. But the prohibition movement was spreading, wineries were closing, vineyards were being uprooted, and most of Munson's collection was lost. The only commercial wines named for Munson's wine grapes now are Missouri vintner James Hofherr's Neva Munson, his neighbor Lucian Dressel's Münch, and Brights winery of Canada's President Port.

In recent years grape enthusiast Wallace E. Dancy of Arkansas has enlisted students of the vine in many states in a movement to restore the Munson collection. The W.B. Munson Foundation of Denison has financed the Memorial Vineyard, to which a museum and library are being added. At Grayson

College, Professor of Agriculture Roy Renfro, in charge of the Munson Vineyard, has started teaching a viticulture course. At this writing 115 of Munson's varieties have been located, some as far away as Japan, and fifty have already been planted in the vineyard at Denison. While the collection is being reassembled, the Munson grapes are being tested for their wine quality and for their ability to grow in various parts of Texas and the Midwest.

11

Wines of Michigan

ALTHOUGH Michigan ranks fourth among the states in grape growing and fifth in wine production, few of our connoisseur writers ever write anything about Michigan wines. Yet I have tasted many Michigan wines and found them all clean and sound, and more than a few lately that I have rated as excellent. The fruit belt of Michigan is as capable, climatically speaking, of producing fine wines as most of the other viticultural districts east of the Rockies, including even the justly famous Finger Lakes region of New York. But until very lately, the Michigan wineries never tried to produce anything fine, for reasons only their history and their peculiar state law can explain. Now, however, with newly planted Old World wine grape varieties, with new modern wineries and modernization of some of the old, they are trying, and the image of their wines has begun to change.

The best way to know Michigan wines is to visit the wineries, which numbered a dozen at last count, with at least three more planned. They are hospitable, offering tasting and tours from spring through fall daily including Sunday afternoons. There is a three-day grape and wine festival at the fairgrounds near Paw Paw in the latter half of September, when you can sniff the grape fragrance as you approach the town. Some of the individual wineries also hold festivals of their own.

• 2 •

Michigan's western counties, behind the towering sand dunes on the Lake Michigan shore, are one of the great fruit-producing sections of the earth. The deep lake waters, which rarely freeze over, yield warmth for the vineyards and orchards in winter, and cool winds from the lake in spring usually retard the buds from opening until danger of killing frosts has passed. This beneficent climatic influence enables fruit to grow all the way from the Indiana border north to Grand Traverse Bay, a stretch of some two hundred miles.

In four southwestern counties—Van Buren, Berrien, Cass, and Allegan—more than 15,000 acres are planted to grapes, mostly picked by the new mechanical harvesting machines since 1968. All but a few hundred acres here are Concords, because four fifths of the state's grape crop is used for juice and jelly or is sold fresh for table use. The other fifth goes into wine.

At the far northern end of the fruit belt, the lake-bordered peninsula that is Leelanau County and the Old Mission Peninsula to the east have climates that are less hospitable to Concords and more hospitable to wine grapes. Until now cherries have been the principal fruit crop on these two peninsulas, which extend north of Traverse City, the sour cherry capital of America. Vineyards of French hybrid and Vinifera wine grapes have been newly planted among the cherry orchards, and the four newest Michigan wineries are here.

Michigan's new interest in winegrowing has also inspired some planting of vines on the eastern side of the state between Lakes Huron and Erie. A new winery there, however, makes mainly wines of fruits other than grapes. I even have heard reports of a vineyard being planned on Michigan's Upper Peninsula, which crosses the forty-sixth parallel, almost as far north as Germany's Rhineland and the Champagne district of France.

What has caused the recent increase in Michigan winegrowing is that wine consumption in the state has more than doubled in this decade. So many new vineyards have been planted that Horticulture Professor Gordon S. Howell of the state university has warned Michigan farmers about creating grape surpluses, of which this state has had its share in the past.

• 3 •

The wineries of Michigan are still young. There were no famous wineries with castlelike cellars in the state before Prohibition, such as those in Ohio, Missouri, and New York. But actually, the growing of fruit, including grapes, began in southern Michigan in the mid-nineteenth century. By 1880, when the national winegrowing census was taken, there were 2,266 acres of vineyards in the state, and Michigan wine production in that year was 62,361 gallons valued at $75,617. At that time more wine was made in southeastern Michigan, along the Lake Erie shore, than on the Lake Michigan side. Philip Wagner, who grew up at Ann Arbor, recalls that before Prohibition there were many small wineries operated by German farmers in Monroe and Muskegon counties.

What started the massive vineyard plantings in southwestern Michigan was the grape juice boom. When the Welch Grape Juice Company, with its newly built plant at Westfield, New York, began about 1900 to buy Concords from neighboring states, the planting of Concords began in Van Buren and Berrien Counties.

The original Michigan wineries were closed by Wartime Prohibition in 1919, but the grape boom continued, for in that year Welch established its own grape juice plant at Lawton, near Paw Paw. Then a huge demand developed throughout the nation for grapes for bootleg and homemade wine, an opportunity in which the Michigan vineyardists shared.

Still another outlet opened for Michigan grapes during the 1920s: four new wineries sprang up in the Canadian town of Windsor, across the river from Detroit. Much of their "exported" wine, consigned to distant countries, traveled only as far as the Michigan and Ohio shores.

Next came the Great Depression, and with it Repeal in 1933—and the market for grapes collapsed. The price of Michigan Concords fell to as low as ten dollars a ton. Fifteen wineries began operating in the Detroit area, including two that were moved, complete with crushers and casks, across the river from Canada. Soon there was a surplus of wine as well as of grapes, because Michigan wines, made of the foxy Concord, could not compete with those coming from other states and from abroad.

Michigan's grape-growing industry was in serious trouble. One of the Canadian vintners from Windsor, the late Major Maurice R. Twomey, proposed a remedy: reserve the Michigan wine market for Michigan wines. Twomey, who had established the La Salle winery at Farmington, designed the peculiar Michigan wine law, which levies a tax of 50 cents a gallon on table wines from outside the state but taxes Michigan wines only 4 cents, provided they are made at least 75 percent of Michigan-grown grapes for which the winery has paid the grower at least $100* a ton. The remaining 25 percent of the grapes is allowed to come from outside the state, and arrives principally in tank cars from California. Principal author of the

---

*Originally $55 a ton in 1937.

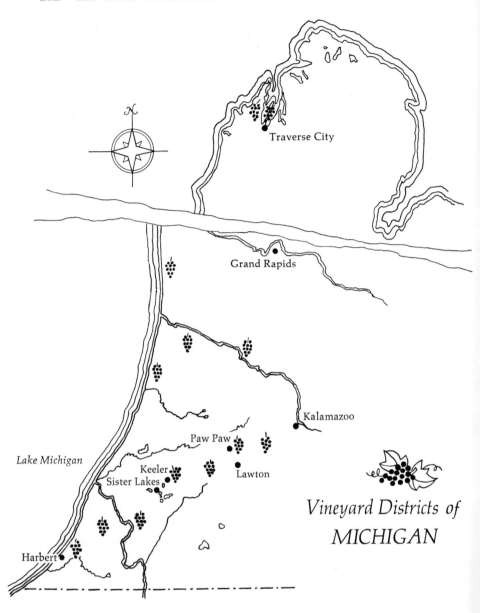

Vineyard Districts of
MICHIGAN

law was William C. Geagley, the chief chemist of the Michigan
Department of Agriculture, a man with rigid ideas of his own
about wine. One of Geagley's ideas was that all wines over 16
percent in alcoholic content should be classified as hard liquor,
and this was written into the Michigan law in 1937. Geagley
thereby created in Michigan an entirely new class of wine

previously unknown in America—16 percent "light" ports and "light" sherries. The sale of standard ports and sherries, which range from 17 to 20 percent, was restricted to the state-operated liquor stores, while the "light" versions were freely sold in Michigan food stores along with the 12 percent table and sparkling wines. Wineries in California, New York, and Ohio were thereby compelled to begin making these 16 percent dessert wine types—which are sold nowhere else—in order to compete with the Michigan wineries.*

For two decades, prospering with their protective state tax, Michigan wineries made no attempt to compete with out-of-state premium wines. But when, after the Second World War, some of their customers discovered they preferred dry table wines to the peculiar local products, the Michigan producers saw their sales beginning to shrink. From the four-fifths share of the Michigan wine market they had enjoyed before the war, their share dropped by 1965 to less than a third. The Michigan vintners began paying new attention to the making of dry table wines and champagnes. Their trade association, the Michigan Wine Institute, started meetings between the winemakers and the scientists of Michigan State University, at which the wines were tasted and criticized. Some of the Michigan vintners then took a leaf from the successful experience of New York State wineries and began calling attention to their better wines by labeling them "Michigan" instead of merely "American." The University's research program since has concentrated on districts' microclimates and soils suitable for particular grape varieties, and there are trial plantings in many sections of the state.

• 4 •

The first Michigan producer to improve the quality of its table wines was the one called Bronte, whose million-gallon winery is on its vineyard five miles south of Hartford on the road to Keeler in Van Buren County. Bronte's Italian-trained winemaker, Angelo Spinazze, was responsible for planting the company's first fifty acres of French hybrids beginning in 1953. When "Bronte Michigan State Baco Dinner Wine" was introduced in 1962 it was the first commercial wine in this country to be labeled with the name of a French hybrid grape. I remember tasting at the winery in the early 1970s a dry red, proudly

---

*But this also taught California vintners a valuable lesson; see the discussion of minimum alcoholic content standards on pages 242 and 577.

labeled "Sister Lakes District Premium Baco Noir," that was superior to most of the burgundies then made in the East. It had enough of the powerful Baco aroma to give the wine character and in addition it had developed, from aging in cask and bottle, the bouquet that distinguishes fine from ordinary red wines. When I returned to Keeler in 1975, Spinazze had replaced the rest of Bronte's Concord vines with hybrids and had introduced two pleasant new wines named Beau Blanc and Beau Rouge.

Bronte was started in May 1933, six months before Repeal, by retired dentist Theodore Wozniak in the old Columbia brewery building on Riopelle Street in Detroit. Its first product was 3.2 percent wine, which had just been legalized together with 3.2 percent beer. To make this curious potion, full-strength wine was diluted to 3.2 percent alcoholic content with water and a fluid extract of the South American beverage herb called *maté* which tastes somewhat like tea. "Bronte," the name of the extract, was chosen as the company's name. At Repeal, Dr. Wozniak made wine out of Concord grapes that were trucked to Detroit from the fruit belt. In 1943, he bought the farm in the Sister Lakes District near Keeler and built the present winery there. Bronte was the first winery in Michigan to make champagne (in 1946) and claims to have been the first in the world (in 1964) to bottle the sparkling wine called "Cold Duck" (a claim which others share).

• 5 •

Biggest vintner in the state is Warner Vineyards, which has three million gallons' capacity in its winery on Kalamazoo Street in Paw Paw and in its fermenting cellar at nearby Lawton. A farmer and banker, the late John Turner, founded the firm, originally named Michigan Wineries, in 1938. His son-in-law and his grandson, James K. and James J. Warner, and members of the Turner family own five hundred acres of vineyards and buy grapes from four hundred other growers. Besides still wines, the company makes champagnes, still and carbonated grape juices, grape concentrate, and grape essence (the methyl anthranilate ester extracted from Concord grapes, which is used to impart the pungent Labrusca flavor to grape drinks).

Warner Vineyards has steadily improved its wines since winemaker Richard Vine came in 1973 from the Pleasant Valley winery in Hammondsport, New York, after an attempt to start his own winery near Niagara Falls. Notable in the assortment

The Warner Vineyard winery at Paw Paw is the largest in Michigan.

now available for tasting in Warner's "Ye Olde Wine Haus" tasting room are bottle- and bulk-fermented champagnes, ports and sherries, Chelois, De Chaunac rosé, Maréchal Foch, estate-bottled Seyval Blanc and Aurora Blanc, and a sweet white wine named Liebestrauben. Vine (who has since left for Mississippi) thinks that Michigan's best red wine in the future will be made of the hybrid named Chancellor. He has urged growers in Michigan and the other lake-district states to adopt "Great Lakes" as the appellation of origin for their wines.

A recent Vine exploit was his answer to a Grosse Pointe woman who wrote in her family's newspaper that "Michigan wines are the worst in the world." Vine challenged her to attend a "blind" tasting in which more than a hundred Grosse Pointe wine buffs compared eight Michigan wines, four from Warner and four from the Tabor Hill vineyard, with an equal number of famous California, French, and German wines. Warner's L'Aurore Superior won first place in the sweet white category, and the other Michigan wines scored two second places and two thirds. The other first places went to samples from California, Germany, and France. When the results were unveiled, they were widely reported in Michigan newspapers and in national wine trade publications, but the woman whose invective started it all remarked: "I still think Michigan wines are bad."

• 6 •

Three more wineries in Paw Paw offer tours and tasting. Next door to Warner on Kalamazoo Street is the million-gallon St. Julian cellar, with a handsome tasting room built since a fire destroyed part of the building in 1972. Mariano Meconi started this company in 1921 at Windsor, Ontario, as the Meconi Wine Cellars, moved it at Repeal to Detroit, and five years later brought most of its equipment to Paw Paw. It is named for the patron saint of his birthplace, the village of Falaria near Rome. Meconi's son-in-law Paul Braganini and Meconi's grandson David run the winery now.

The half-million-gallon Frontenac winery on West Michigan Avenue makes forty different wines and offers them all for tasting, along with a delicious hot spiced wine, in its attractive retail store. Most of the Frontenac table wines have the Labrusca flavor of Concord and the other native grapes principally grown around Paw Paw.

On Highway 51 four miles west of Paw Paw is Ford engineer John Coleman's little Vendramino winery, with sausage and cheese for sale and with picnic tables, slides and swings to occupy children while their parents taste his three French-hybrid wines. Coleman started a home-winemaking supply business in 1970 at Dearborn, near Detroit. Three years later he planted a ten-acre vineyard north of Paw Paw, and in 1977 he opened his 2,500-gallon winery. His specialty product, not for tasting but for use in cooking, is an onion wine.

Four miles farther north on Highway 43, Nathan Stackhouse, a consultant to various Michigan wineries, is starting his own Castle Weinberg winery, where he plans to make mainly champagne of Pinot Noir and Chardonnay.

The southernmost winery in western Michigan is the Lakeside or Molly Pitcher cellar at Harbert, a quarter mile from Lake Michigan. It attracts crowds of tourists because it is on the busy Red Arrow Highway just off I-94. Food faddist William Lett Ruttledge from Ireland started the Molly Pitcher winery in 1934 to make port wine, then found he couldn't sell it, and switched to making Concord wine because it is the only kind California doesn't produce. Cecil Pond bought the winery from Ruttledge in 1975 and makes both French hybrid wines and the Concord kinds that tourists seem to like.

• 7 •

When Len Olson's Tabor Hill Vineyard and Wine Cellar opened for business in July 1972, it was the first new winery to

Leonard Olson found Botrytis, the "noble mold," growing on his Vidal Blanc grapes in Michigan in November 1975.

start in Michigan in a quarter of a century. Three additional "firsts" distinguish this establishment near Baroda in Berrien County: It was the first in Michigan devoted exclusively to growing premium-quality wines; the first to grow such noble Vinifera grapes as White Riesling and Chardonnay, and the first (in 1974) to have its wines served in the White House. President Ford served Tabor Hill Baco Noir and its hybrid white called Trebbiano at a state dinner for the chancellor of Austria.

Olson, a former steel salesman, looks more like a football player than a winegrower, which is understandable; he played left half on the University of Illinois team that defeated Washington in the 1964 Rose Bowl game. He works year-'round with his wife Ellen and their four youngsters in their 60,000-gallon winery and twenty-acre vineyard. He believes Michigan's fine-wine future will be achieved with Vinifera grapes, but his principal wines thus far are hybrid blends labeled Cuvée Blanc, Rouge, and Rosé. The Tabor Hill 1975 Riesling and Chardonnay, which I sampled from European oak, could have won prizes in California. Next best of those I have tasted was his 1974 Maréchal Foch. Olson also made local history in 1975 by producing Michigan's first late-harvest (botrytized) Riesling and Vidal Blanc.

To find Tabor Hill, take the Bridgman exit from I-94 and head east seven miles, keeping a lookout for the series of signs that lead you to the winery. The building above the vineyard that looks like a ski chalet is the tasting room.

• 8 •

The Welsch family's Fenn Valley Vineyard, three miles southeast of Fennville in Allegan County, is Michigan's closest approach to a European winegrowing estate. The romance of wine attracted Chicago lumberman William Welsch and his biology teacher son Douglas, both home winemakers, to Fenn

Valley in 1974. They built homes for their families there and began planting their first forty acres of hybrid and Vinifera vines. A year later they built a château-like winery into the adjoining hillside. While waiting for their vines to produce, they made their first wines of local blueberries and cherries, then brought Riesling and Gewürztraminer grapes from Washington State, and made some excellent table wines. Theirs is a family undertaking. Douglas, with degrees in biology and chemistry, is the winemaker. His wife Lynn, who teaches school, and his father and mother all help in the business. The 60,000-gallon winery is a model of completeness for its size, with a tasting room, a home-winemaking supply shop, and balconies from which visitors can watch how the wines are made. The first estate-bottled Fenn Valley De Chaunac was due in 1978. To reach Fenn Valley Vineyard, take the Fenn exit (M-89) east from I-196 for three miles, then turn right on 72nd Street one mile to 122nd Avenue.

• 9 •

From the Welschs' vineyard at Fennville it is 200 miles due north to Traverse City and six miles still farther on Highway 37 to the Château Grand Travers vineyard and winery. This is a third of the way along Old Mission Peninsula, the spectacular narrow finger of land that extends eighteen miles to the middle of Grand Traverse Bay.

To this spot chunky millionaire entrepreneur and ex-college gymnast Edward O'Keefe, of the Canadian brewing family, brought Geisenheim-trained viticulturist Bernd Philippi from Germany in 1975 to plant the chateau's fifty-acre vineyard of White Riesling and Chardonnay facing the western arm of the bay. The equipping of the 40,000-gallon winery was supervised by Karl Werner, the onetime winemaster of Schloss Vollrads in the Rheingau, who is now the winemaker consultant to the Callaway Vineyard and Winery in California. Until its vineyard comes into bearing, Château Grand Travers is making Montmorency Cherry and Morning Apple wines and is bottling wines from California for sale under its Old Mission label.

O'Keefe was only the first to plant vines and build his winery on the Old Mission Peninsula. Bernard Rink, the librarian of Northwest Michigan College at Traverse City, and Michigan State University emeritus chemistry professor Robert Herbst had pioneered the growing of French hybrid wine grapes on the Leelanau County peninsula for more than a decade, in Rink's case since 1965. Bernie Rink bonded his own 20,000-gallon

Boskydel Vineyard winery on his twenty-acre vineyard in 1976 and offered his first half dozen hybrid wines—the best of which were a white Vignoles and a red De Chaunac—for sale. Rink's winery, a cave in the hillside facing Lake Leelanau, is sixteen miles north of Traverse City on county road 641. The town of Lake Leelanau is three miles farther north.

Rink is able to keep his full-time job as a librarian because, he explains, "I have an indulgent wife and five sons," who help him in the vineyard and winery. Dr. Herbst grows wine as a hobby at his vineyard four miles to the west.

With Lake Michigan on the west and Grand Traverse Bay on the east, the Leelanau and Old Mission peninsulas have the climate-moderating lake influence on both their sides. "If we can find enough good microclimates for wine grapes here," says Bernie Rink, "the Leelanau Peninsula can become the Napa Valley of Michigan."

As though to support Rink's prediction, fruit grower Charles Kalchik in 1975 began planting sixty acres of French hybrids and Vinifera on his nearby Hilltop Farms. He also commissioned Nathan Stackhouse to establish the 30,000-gallon Leelanau Wine Cellars winery with the latest stainless-steel equipment at Omena, twenty-five miles north of Traverse City on Highway 22, with a tasting room five miles south of Traverse City on US 31 and M-37.

The Leelanau wine rush was on. Lawrence and Edward Mawby of Sutton's Bay began planting French hybrids near their cherry and apple orchards in 1975 and opened their own Mawby Vineyards Winery in 1977.

Hearing of this excitement, I paid a flying visit to Traverse City in the spring of 1977 and toured the vineyards with Stackhouse and Professor Howell, visiting the new wineries and tasting Rink's and Dr. Herbst's impressive young wines. Dr. Howell thinks the microclimates and deep, light, well-drained soils of this new northern Michigan grape district may be especially adapted for fine white wines. The "lake effect" is said to account for the district's cool spring, when vines bloom almost three weeks later than in southern Michigan, for its cool summers, long, cool autumns, and warmer winters than in the counties to the south and east. Nate Stackhouse, a graduate in enology from the University of California's wine school at Davis, agrees with Dr. Howell but believes the best red wines will be grown here, too. "Michigan's climate for winegrowing is better than California's," says Stackhouse, "because California weather in some respects is too good for grapes."

Bernard Rink's Boskydel winery
and vineyard at Lake Leelanau,
Michigan.

• 10 •

Michigan's chief contribution to the wine world is Cold Duck,
the bubbly pink wine that exploded from Detroit during the
1960s to revolutionize festive drinking halfway around the
world. Its story is as bizarre as its name.

In Germany early in this century—authorities disagree on
just when—partygoers who saved the contents of open wine
bottles by pouring them together after a celebration, called the
mixtures *kalte ende* (cold end), a German phrase for leftovers.
Because *ende* sounds like *Ente* (duck in German), the term for
leftover wine became *kalte Ente;* it was a German pun. Kalte
Ente became the name of a popular drink in Germany. It is
usually made there of white wine and *Schaumwein* (champagne), flavored with a spiral of lemon rind and sugar, and is
served either in a punch bowl or by the glass.

Back in the 1930s, Detroit restaurateur Harold Borgman, on a
wine-buying trip in Germany, tasted Kalte Ente, and on returning home introduced it as a bar drink in his restaurant, the
Pontchartrain Wine Cellars. He made it by mixing a New York
State champagne and a California burgundy. It was Borgman
who translated the name into English—the duck you don't eat,
but drink. It became locally famous.

Two Detroit vintners, both Pontchartrain patrons, claim to
have originated the idea of putting Cold Duck into bottles. Bob
Wozniak, whose father heads the Bronte winery, says he first
thought of it in 1963. But, at the same time, Detroit importer
William O'Connor gave the Mandia winery of Clintondale,
New York, an order to make and bottle the mixture for him.

The name and taste of the concoction tickled the celebration bone of Americans. Within months, vintners in other states followed with their own versions, inevitably with duck wings on the labels. The Internal Revenue Service officially recognized the product as a blend of champagne and sparkling burgundy, requiring that the label specify bulk process if the champagne is made that way.

Because the first Cold Ducks were made of eastern Labrusca grapes, the big California wineries found it necessary to import vast quantities of Concord juice from the State of Washington to make their versions taste the same. Other California producers found their Cold Ducks sold as well or better without Labrusca grapes, so long as the wines were made new, fresh, foamy, and sweet.

Cold Duck had only begun to fly. In 1970 its production spread to Canada, then to faraway Australia, and finally reached Europe. French vintners began shipping French Cold Duck to this country, followed by Cold Ducks from Italy and from Germany. The bubbly pink drink was also introduced in France, its name translated there to *Canard Froid Froid.* In America, the brewing industry responded with a Malt Duck, while vintners created a Cold Hawk, a Blueberry Duck, a Strawberry Duck, and a carbonated mixture of white wine and cranberry juice called Cold Turkey.

Now I hear that bottled Cold Duck may not have originated in Michigan after all, that German vintners have been selling white Kalte Ente in bottles since before the Korean war, and that they have a red version called Turkenblut. There is also a story that attributes the original *kalte Ente* pun to the famous German diplomat, Franz von Papen, at a dinner given by Kaiser Wilhelm II.

But perhaps this is merely history, for vintners now report that Cold Duck sales in the United States have slumped ominously since the celebration of the New Year in 1972. One of my champagne producer friends, who never got around to producing a Cold Duck of his own, is gleefully predicting it may even become a dead duck erelong.

12

California—Paradise for the Vine

UCH OF what has been written since Repeal about California wines stresses the industry's colorful history, such as the fact that the Spanish mission fathers brought wine grapes here from Mexico two centuries ago, as though that were the reason this state has nine tenths of this country's vineyard acres and produces four fifths of American wine.

The real reason, seldom mentioned and therefore not understood, was best expressed almost a century ago by Professor George Husmann, explaining why he abandoned his post as professor of horticulture at the University of Missouri to become a winegrower in California:

A visit to this shore, in the summer of 1881, convinced me that this was the true home of the grape, and that California . . . was destined to be the vine land of the world . . . We have the finest climate in the world and can always make a good produce even in the most unfavorable seasons. We can raise grapes and make wine cheaper than any other nation or climate. We have the world for a market. We can satisfy every taste.

Husmann, of course, did not dwell on the spring frost disasters that strike California vineyard districts at least once in each decade, nor on the constant hazards of vine diseases, pests, sunburn, or water shortages, which keep vineyardists from enjoying a carefree life in California or anywhere else.

Yet it is true that it is easier to raise Vinifera grapes in the fabulous climates of California than in any other part of the globe. The Old World grape varieties will grow and ripen anywhere there is water and good soil in the Golden State, except at frigid mountain elevations and on the foggiest portions of the northern seacoast. California's long, warm, nor-

Vineyard Districts
of CALIFORNIA

Ukiah

Healdsburg

Sonoma　Napa

Plymouth

Lodi

Modesto

Livermore　Livingston

Gilroy　Madera

Fresno

Greenfield

Tulare

Delano

Paso Robles

Arvin

Santa Maria

Los Olivos

Santa Barbara

Cucamonga

Temecula　Coachella

San Diego

mally rainless growing seasons, its mild winters, and its low humidity which discourages most vine pests make it a paradise for the Vinifera vine. Only one percent of the earth's surface has weather that resembles—but for growing Vinifera grapes scarcely equals—that of the great viticultural districts of California. Yet few of the state's present generation of winegrowers realize how fortunate they are, or how great their wines can be. Few of them are aware that their climates are the secret envy of the winegrowers of Europe.

California has not only one, but so wide an assortment of such climates, that within its borders there are produced, year after year, wines of all the traditional types grown in the leading wine countries of the world—and with no need to add sugar to the juice of the grape, the practice that is common elsewhere in North America and in the famous winelands of Europe.

The ranges of these climates, which are evident when you glance at the state map, help to explain the wide differences you find in the qualities and prices of California wines. The light-yielding, delicate, costly grape varieties which make the finest table wines (such as the Rieslings, the Pinots, and Cabernet Sauvignon) develop their highest flavors when grown in the valleys near the coast, where the sunny days are cooled by ocean breezes and fogs. The University of California classes these premium table wine districts, in the order of the coolness of their climates, as Regions I, II, and III.* The northern San Joaquin Valley, farther inland, is much warmer in summer and is classed as Region IV; vineyards there yield more tons to the acre. This district produces many excellent wine grapes and includes Lodi, where the famous Flame Tokay table grape grows. In the still hotter central and southern San Joaquin

---

*In 1938, Professors Albert Winkler and Maynard Amerine classified the climates of California vineyard districts into five regions by their average daily temperatures during the growing season (April through October) and compared them to the wine districts of Europe. They measured "degree-days," the number of days when temperatures exceed 50° F. For example, when the temperatures for a day averaged 70°, it was expressed as "20 degree-days." Region I means 2500 degree-days or less and includes Geisenheim (1709) and Trier (1730) in Germany, Beaune (2400) in the French Burgundy region, and Sonoma (2360) and Oakville (2300) in the coolest parts of the Sonoma and Napa Valleys. Region II means 2500 to 3000 degree-days and includes Bordeaux (2519), the Italian Piedmont region (2980), and most parts of the Napa and Sonoma Valleys. Region III means 3000 to 3500 degree-days and includes the Livermore Valley in California and Tuscany in Italy. Region IV, 3500 to 4000 degree-days, covers central Spain, areas from Lodi to Ceres in the northern part of the San Joaquin Valley, Davis in Yolo County, and Cucamonga in Southern California. Over 4000 degree-days is Region V and includes the central and southern San Joaquin Valley and the Sacramento Valley.

Valley—Region V—the vineyards are chiefly of table and raisin varieties, especially the Thompson Seedless. They yield tremendous crops, which are used for wine and brandy as well as for sale as fresh and dried fruit. In the past, most of the wines made in Region V were the sweet dessert types, but the production of table wines now greatly exceeds the production of dessert wines. Vast acreages in the hot valley have been planted with grapes for table wines since 1968. The Cucamonga district, east of Los Angeles, has a Region IV climate and produces mainly inexpensive wine grapes for all types of wine. Finally, there is the Coachella Valley near Salton Sea in the southeastern corner of the state, where, in almost furnacelike heat, great irrigated vineyards supply ripe grapes for fresh table use as early as May and June to bring high prices in the eastern markets for fresh fruit.

In sunny California, grapes develop higher sugar content than in the sun-starved northern wine districts of Europe, but their acidity (tartness) is usually not as high. This is why, in "blind" tastings—the popular social game in which you try to distinguish one wine from another by smell and taste—the easiest way to tell California wines and champagnes from those of Europe is to mark those with higher acidity as European; the California samples are likely to be softer, less tart.

Even the cooler California districts may be too warm and sunny for some of the noble Old World wine-grape varieties, in particular Germany's White (Johannisberg) Riesling and Burgundy's Pinot Noir. Though the Riesling and Pinot Noir ripen early with high sugar contents and make consistently fine wines in California, their wines have not yet achieved the greatness they attain in their cloudy Old World homelands, where these grapes barely ripen by the end of the season. Perhaps California's climate is too ideal. Wines, like people, seem to be more interesting, to have greater depth and complexity of character, if they have to struggle to reach maturity.

Another characteristic of California weather—low humidity—prevents in some districts the growth of the "noble mold" *(Botrytis cinerea)* that grows on ripe grapes in Europe and gives unique flavors to French sauternes and to Germany's rare Trockenbeerenauslese wines.

These few differences between the finest European and California table wines are easy to recognize in "blind" sampling. But if the wines you are tasting are red Bordeaux or white burgundy types, and the California and French samples are both made of the same grape varieties, grown in the best climates (and have been stored in the same kind of oak barrels), they will be much more difficult to tell apart. For the grapes that make these latter two wine types develop ideal acidity in balance with their sugar content in the California coastal valleys and make some of the finest wines in the world.

Still another difference between California and European table wines—which you cannot detect by taste—is in alcoholic strength, which is also the result of climate. Because it is the grape sugar that fermentation turns into alcohol, California table wines are usually one to three points higher than their European counterparts in percentage of alcohol by volume. The Riesling in Germany, for example, seldom makes wines of more than 9 or 10 percent; in California its wines usually reach twelve. Perhaps grape-growing locations will yet be found in California with climates in which this grape can develop the zestful yet delicate flavor it attains in the vineyards of the Moselle and Rheingau.

What European growers envy most about California weather is that the grapes ripen sufficiently every year to make sound wine without chaptalization—the addition of sugar to their juice (see Chapter 26). This is why it is often said (and as often challenged) that "every year is a vintage year in California." Of course, the truth of this statement depends on what is meant by "a vintage year."

In the European fine-wine districts, which are subject to cold and rainy weather during their growing seasons, the grapes ripen fully in the occasional years when they receive sufficient sunshine; in their normal years it is necessary to add sugar to the grapes. The purpose of vintage labels on European wines therefore is to enable buyers to choose the wines of the "vintage" (good) years—to avoid buying the mediocre or the bad. In sunny California no such purpose is served by vintage labels. Here, about once in a decade, abnormally early autumn rains result in lower-than-normal grape sugars; but even then, the sugar levels are sufficient to make sound wines. The three worst-weather autumn seasons in California vintners' recent memory, 1948, 1957, and 1972, would have been considered "vintage years" in Europe, for in each of those seasons lovely natural wines were made.

Of course, the wines from individual California vineyards vary in flavor and quality from year to year as the weather and the grapes inevitably vary, and vintage dates on California wines are important guides for connoisseurs. But here again, the point is that sound wines are produced every year from the juice of the grape alone. By European standards, the claim that "every year is a vintage year in California" is therefore literally true.

• 2 •

Some of the highlights of California's wine history were reviewed in Chapter 2, and the colorful stories of individual California districts and vintners are contained in the regional chapters that follow. But the overall story of California wines before, during, and since Prohibition has not yet been clearly told.

While wines were made first at the Franciscan missions, the chain of church settlements established from San Diego to Sonoma between 1769 and 1823, the wines the padres made could not have been very good. The inferior Vinifera grape they introduced—the Mission variety—impeded the development of fine wine in California for almost a century.* Most writers dwell at length on how this grape was grown by the Jesuits in Baja California and was brought north by the great Franciscan friar, Junípero Serra. Yet the Mission grape, also called the Criolla, had been grown throughout the two preceding centuries in mainland Mexico.

The well-annotated histories of early California wines by Herbert B. Leggett, Irving McKee, and Vincent Carosso tell the fantastic story of Agoston Haraszthy, the Hungarian "count" or "colonel" (he was neither), and credit him with introducing the better Vinifera varieties from Europe to California between 1851 and 1862. But Haraszthy was not the first to do this, nor was he the first to introduce the Zinfandel grape to America. As a later chapter on "varietal grapes" will show, the Zinfandel was already here when Haraszthy left Hungary for the United States.

Because the Prohibitionists labored for years in California, as elsewhere, to erase the history of wine in America, its role in building the economy of the Golden State—more important than the mining of gold—is seldom if ever mentioned in the school books. Grapes, mostly used by wineries, are California's most important fruit crop. Many people who now bear the names of great pioneer California families—in agriculture, government, banking, publishing, education, and industry—

---

*Although it is of the Vinifera species, no counterpart of the Mission grape has ever been found in Europe. Ampelographers say it probably grew from a seed brought from Spain via Mexico by the *conquistadores*.

may not know that their forebears were prominent winegrowers, who contributed to the character of the state's wines of today.

Vineyards were flourishing and wine was being made at nearly all of the twenty-one Spanish missions by the second decade of the nineteenth century. The chief exception was Mission Dolores at foggy, chilly San Francisco, where the padres used grapes they obtained from Missions Santa Clara and San Jose.

When commercial viniculture began at Los Angeles in the 1830s, at the time the Mexican government secularized the missions and caused most of them to be abandoned, there were 100,000 vines on the site of the present City of the Angels. An early writer, Alexander Forbes, was already telling America and Europe that California offered "a wide and promising field for the cultivation of the grape in all varieties."

The first commercial winegrower of note in California, Jean Louis Vignes (appropriately named; *vigne* is French for vine), was so successful at his El Aliso Vineyard in Los Angeles that in 1834 he sent to France for eight of his relatives to join him, for he believed that this land was destined to rival "la belle France" in both the quantity and quality of its wines, including champagnes. It was Vignes, not Haraszthy, who was the first to bring European wine-grape cuttings to California, having them sent in the early 1830s to Boston and then brought around Cape Horn to Los Angeles.

How swiftly winegrowing spread through the state is evident from the fact that, before the discovery of gold on the American River in 1848, there already were vineyards as far north as Santa Clara, Alameda, Contra Costa, Sacramento, Yolo, Sonoma, and Napa Counties. The Gold Rush brought the first wine boom in the 1850s; many of the newcomers found winemaking a surer road to riches than the trail to the mines. When the California Legislature in 1859 exempted new vineyards from taxation, grape-planting fever reached epidemic proportions. By 1863 there were twelve million vines in the state, most of them planted in the preceding half-dozen years.

Glowing descriptions of California's marvelous winegrowing climate were published abroad before the Civil War. The French viticultural journal, *Revue Viticole,* reported in a series of articles between 1859 and 1862 what French viticultural experts found in a survey of the state: that California has a climate that makes it capable someday of "becoming a serious competitor" to France in the production of fine wine. This may help to explain why

Drawn by P. Frenzeny from an illustration in *Harper's Weekly*

Vintage scene in California *circa* 1877.

France, to this day, still refuses to admit any regular commercial shipments of California wine, although it imports wine in vast quantities from almost everywhere else. (Praise California wine to a proud Frenchman and see him scowl!)

• 3 •

Leggett brings out another characteristic of the California industry: its periodic wine-price declines, its recurring cycles of boom and bust. The first bust was recorded in 1858 and 1859 at Los Angeles, where wine was so plentiful and some of it so poorly made that the value of vineyard land suddenly dropped by half, and wine was difficult to sell at fifty cents a gallon. "But the bubble wasn't broken," Leggett comments, "it had merely shrunk temporarily."

Much of the early-day California wine was obviously bad, and a great deal of it was sold under counterfeit European labels. However, the wine that Vignes and his nephews made was good enough by 1860 to be sold under their own name in New York; and a San Francisco firm of vintners, Kohler & Frohling, was regularly shipping its bulk wines to England, Germany, Russia, Japan, China, and South America as early as 1856. Some improvement in the quality of California wines was evidenced during the 1860s and 70s. This is generally credited to the spectacular "Count" Haraszthy, to his expedition to Europe in 1861 for vine cuttings, and to his voluminous writings about viniculture. Later chapters will show, however, that there were many other viniculturists, principally from Europe and more experienced than the "Count," who imported their own foreign vines and who were making good wines from superior grapes before he made any from his.

The second wine-market bust came in 1876. Although the world economic depression of the 1870s had begun three years earlier, grape planting in California had continued without a letup, from 30 million vines in 1873 to 43 million by 1876. When the break came, grape prices plunged to two dollars a ton, wine to 10 cents a gallon, and brandy to 37 cents. Barnyard animals were turned into the vineyards to dispose of the grapes. Many vineyardists uprooted their vines and planted fruit trees instead. But those winegrowers who survived the crash planted better grape varieties and improved the quality of their wines. With the help of late spring frosts in 1879, which reduced that year's grape crop by a third, the industry prospered again by 1880.

During the early 1880s, the devastation of European vineyards by the phylloxera vine louse was at its height, and the resulting shortage of French wines helped the California growers to sell theirs at a profit. What they did not know—and had failed to realize even when the destructive vine pest was positively identified on vines at Sonoma in 1873—was that the plague was killing their own vineyards at the same time.

• 4 •

It was the phylloxera—when it spread statewide and threatened to destroy the entire California industry—that influenced the legislature, by the act of 1880, to establish a State Board of Viticultural Commissioners, and also a department for viticultural research and instruction in the University of California. Although there was bitter rivalry between the Commissioners and the University, which led to the abolition of the Viticultural Commission in 1894,* the spread of phylloxera was finally checked. It was controlled by the same means as in France—by grafting the Old World vines onto phylloxera-resistant native American roots. The roots which saved the California vineyards came principally from Missouri, but were actually imported from France. Californians first tried to use the roots of the local wild vine, *Vitis californica,* then learned the French were having

*A Board of Viticultural Commissioners was established again by the legislature in 1913, and it continued until Prohibition.

success with the midwestern roots and began ordering theirs from France.

Two men are credited with eventually stopping the havoc wrought by phylloxera in the state. One was Professor Husmann, the erstwhile Missourian. The other was Eugene Waldemar Hilgard, professor and later dean of agriculture at the University of California. Born at Belleville, Illinois, where his German-born father grew grapes, Hilgard experimented with viticulture in Mississippi and Michigan before coming to California in 1875. Working first on the phylloxera problem, he planted a vineyard on the Berkeley campus, where the Life Sciences Building now stands, and a wine cellar near old South Hall. (The University vineyard was bitterly protested by the Livermore winegrowers, who feared the wind might carry the phylloxera pest over the Berkeley hills to them.)

Hilgard made important contributions to wine improvement in the state. At a time when some of the small vintners were still having their grapes trodden by Chinese coolies and Indians, he called for the building of large, modern wineries that could be operated scientifically. He advocated the slow fermentation of wines at controlled low temperatures. He was the first to point out the sole defect in California's climate, that when grapes are left on the vines until their sugar content is at its peak, their

When frost threatens vines in spring, sprinklers in this California vineyard turn on automatically. Ice forms as temperature drops, releasing heat that keeps the buds from freezing. Sprinkling continues until danger is past.

acidity drops too low—thus challenging the European idea, in which the California growers believed, that every additional day of sunshine is so much gain to the quality of wine. He urged that the grapes be harvested early, when their acid is in balance with their sugar, because "what is true in the cloudy climate of Europe is not necessarily true in California." He also opposed overcropping (letting vines bear too heavy crops), which lowers the quality of the grapes and wines. These are lessons that many California growers have only lately begun to learn.

Abhorring drunkenness, and himself a user of light red wines with his meals, Hilgard also advocated that the alcoholic content of California table wines should be kept low. In this he was opposed by Charles Wetmore of the Cresta Blanca Vineyard, the executive officer of the Viticultural Commission, who favored fermenting them to 15 percent strength. Hilgard's assistant and successor, Professor Frederic T. Bioletti, was the first to divide California into viticultural districts by their climates—the coastal counties for table wines and the interior valleys for dessert types.

• 5 •

The prosperity of the winegrowers lasted until 1886, when a bumper grape crop, the result of still more planting, brought on the third California wine bust. This time bulk-wine prices sank to 6 and 8 cents a gallon. In 1889, Publisher William Randolph Hearst, whose father, Senator George Hearst, owned a vineyard in Sonoma County, published in his San Francisco *Examiner* a call for "all patriotic citizens to do all in their power to assist in placing the business of winemaking, which is of such vast importance to the state, on the best and firmest basis."

Most of the published replies to Hearst urged the planting of fewer grapes, the drying of more raisins, and the distilling of more brandy—remedies for overproduction that were still being attempted seven decades later. But Professor Hilgard's reply to Hearst was that the best remedy would be expert winemaking and longer aging to improve the quality of the wines.

Quality did improve. Although the bulk wines that went begging may not have been very good, there were in California, by 1890, at least a hundred great winegrowing estates owned by some of the wealthiest families of the state, who produced fine wines for pride rather than for profit alone, and who won medals for them in international competitions. Glimpses of the glamour and wealth of these nineteenth-century winegrowers can be had in Frona Eunice Wait's *Wines and Vines of California,* published at San Francisco in 1889, with its descriptions of such opulent estates as Captain Gustav Niebaum's Inglenook Vineyard at Rutherford, "Lucky" Baldwin's Santa Anita Ranch, Senator Hearst's Madrone Vineyard near Agua Caliente, Tiburcio Parrott's "Miravalle" in the Napa Valley, and the Warm Springs Vineyard of Josiah Stanford, brother of the governor and senator, who had his own great vineyard at Vina in the Sacramento Valley.

It is not generally realized that many of these pre-Prohibition wines were great. During the 1920s and 30s, I tasted numerous California wines of the 1914, 1915, and 1916 vintages. The long-lived Cabernets and Zinfandels, in particular, and also some of the dessert wines, were superb. I have a few of these venerable bottles in my cellar, given to me by heirs to the collections of departed connoisseurs, and I find an occasional one still good after half a century.

· 6 ·

The third depression in the California wine industry lasted from 1886 to the mid-90s. In 1892, when Zinfandel grapes were selling at San Francisco for ten dollars a ton and Missions, if they could find buyers, at half that price, a brilliant British accountant named Percy T. Morgan had arrived in that city with two dollars in his pocket. He registered at the Palace Hotel and soon enlisted some prosperous clients, including the old vintner firm of S. Lachman & Company. Within two years, the persuasive Morgan convinced his client and six other big wine firms to form the California Wine Association. The CWA grew to giant size, operating as many as sixty-four California wineries. Another such group, the Winemakers Corporation, was formed at about the same time. The CWA and the Corporation stabilized prices by bringing grape and bulk-wine supplies under their control. Meanwhile, the grape crop was being reduced by the continuing ravages of phylloxera, and still further by the severe spring frost of 1896, which helped to bring the third wine bust to an end.

The San Francisco earthquake and fire of 1906 destroyed 15 million gallons of the CWA's inventory and gutted all but one of its several cellars in the city. Morgan then built, on the shore of San Francisco Bay near Richmond, what was at that time the largest winery in the world, which he named Winehaven. From Winehaven, with its own pier for ocean vessels, the CWA shipped California wines, in bottles under its "Calwa" label and in barrels under its "Big Tree" brand, to most countries of the world.

By 1911 an oversupply of grapes broke the wine market for the fourth time, and Morgan retired to his mansion in the Los Altos Hills. Most of Winehaven's vast wine stores eventually were shipped to Britain and Germany, which could not pay for them during the Great Depression of the early 1930s; also, an entire cargo was lost in a North Sea shipwreck. Winehaven was not finally emptied of its wine until 1937. The huge, fortresslike red brick structure and its small city of workmen's homes still stand as a monument to Percy Morgan; they are now part of a naval fuel depot.

• 7 •

The tragic developments in California at the start of Prohibition were briefly reviewed in Chapter 2: the initial uprooting of vineyards, the short-lived boom in "juice grapes," the unfortunate grafting-over from delicate fine-wine grapes to coarse varieties that shipped well, and the grape market bust in 1925 when too many grapes were shipped east. In 1927, halfway through the Prohibition period, California vineyards covered 635,000 acres, an all-time high and much of it surplus, almost what the state has today.* The California Vineyardists Association, formed the year before, employed a "czar" for the industry, who promised to find new uses for the grape surplus. Herbert Hoover, then Secretary of Commerce, had picked a railroad expert, Donald D. Conn, for the job. Conn's ideas for new products, such as grape candy, grape salad, grape pie, and raisinade, failed to sell any fruit. And fresh California grape juice, made from the bland-tasting Vinifera varieties, could not compete with the more flavorful Concord juice from other states.

A law proposed at that time to prohibit further planting of vines was ruled unconstitutional. Farmers then were offered five dollars per acre to uproot their vines, but only a few of them did. This was when Captain Paul Garrett formed Fruit Industries, with Donald Conn as its head, to salvage the grape surplus by selling it as concentrate for home winemaking—only to have its "Vine-Glo" advertisements suppressed by the Hoo-

*Vineyards in the 1920s produced fewer tons per acre than now. Yields have increased enormously in recent years. The 1927 crop from 635,000 acres totaled 2.2 million tons, compared to almost 4 million tons produced from only 536,000 bearing acres in 1975.

ver Administration in 1931 under pressure from the Drys. In 1930, the Federal Farm Board and California banks lent nearly 25 million dollars to convert surplus grapes into raisins and grape concentrate, and to limit shipments of fresh grapes to eastern markets. Almost half a million tons were thus diverted from the marketing channels in that year. This staved off bankruptcy for the grape growers, and the short crop of 1931 kept them in business until the wineries, anticipating Repeal, bought and crushed extra quantities of grapes in 1932 and 1933.

The California vintners flooded the nation with wine at Repeal in December of 1933, then found they had far too much left. Almost overnight, more than seven hundred wineries had been bonded in the state, many of them by bootleggers to whom the Government granted amnesty, conditioned on their payment of Federal taxes on their stocks. Much of their wine had soured and was later condemned by the State Department of Public Health. The California industry remained in a depressed condition as severe as that during the latter Prohibition years.

At the end of the dry era, wine in California was sold principally in bulk, as was still the custom in the European wine countries at that time. The bulk wines were sold in "barrel houses." The typical "barrel house" was a liquor store with a rack holding from six to a dozen barrels with spigots, from which buyers who weren't too fastidious about vinegar and flies could fill their own gallon jugs or demijohns for a few dimes per gallon. Chain food stores refused to stock any wines at all until the "barrel houses" were outlawed several years later.

Most California wines were shipped in tank cars to bottlers in other states, and, when inexpertly handled before bottling, were of poor quality when sold. The nation's connoisseurs failed to appreciate the few—bottled in California by the handful of premium-quality producers who had survived Prohibition—that were fine.

• 8 •

During the first five post-Repeal years, overly bountiful sunshine presented the California vineyardists with three bumper grape crops and two of moderate size, far more than the struggling wineries, the raisin packers, and the fresh-grape shippers could absorb. Each spring the growers prayed that frost might come to reduce the yield (naturally, of their neighbors' vineyards, not their own), but their prayers were in vain.

The curse of Prohibition was replaced by the curse of plenty, which was more to be feared than frost.

In the fifth Repeal year, the situation was so desperate, with a record grape crop of 2,531,000 tons, half of it surplus, that an "artificial frost"—the Grape Prorate of 1938—was voted under a California farm law. That emergency measure required every vineyardist to convert 45 percent of his harvested grape crop into brandy and to hold it off the market for at least two years.

The grape growers in the coast counties bitterly opposed the Prorate. They maintained that the surplus existed in the hot San Joaquin Valley, not in the cool districts near the coast. Their leaders in the Wine Institute backed an opposite kind of plan, the Wine Advisory Board consumer-education program.* Voted in the same year as the Prorate, the wine-education program was unpopular with some of the larger wineries, several of whom fought for several years in the courts to avoid paying the assessment that supported the Board. They could not believe that wine would ever become popular in the whiskey, beer, and cola drinking United States. Renewals of the Board program were almost defeated twice, but each time the old table-wine producers, who believed that Americans someday would learn to drink table wine with meals, produced enough votes to keep it alive.

The 1938 Prorate was a success as an emergency surplus-control measure. Half a million tons of that season's grapes were converted into brandy under the Prorate—and this later turned out to have been fortunate in another way, as we shall see. But the coast counties winegrowers meanwhile pushed a bill through the legislature specifying that no such program could ever apply to their grapes again.

The year following the Prorate brought still another disastrously heavy crop. The resulting 1939 wine glut forced twenty large San Joaquin Valley wineries into a conglomerate called "Central California Wineries Inc." Intended to keep surplus bulk wine off the market and thereby to bolster grape and wine prices, the CCW merger nearly got the wine industry and cooperating bankers indicted under the Federal antitrust laws.

---

*The Wine Institute was incorporated in 1934 as the successor to the Grape Growers League (1931) and the Wine Producers Association (1933). The Marketing Order for Wine, assented to by two thirds of the California wineries in 1938, created the Wine Advisory Board as an instrumentality of the State Department of Agriculture. The Marketing Order, renewable every three years, levied assessments—of 1 cent and 1½ cents on each gallon of California table and dessert wines shipped to market—which supported the Board's program. The Board contracted with the Wine Institute to perform most of the educational and market-expansion work until the Marketing Order was terminated in 1975.

The refusal by the grand jury at San Francisco to vote that indictment was one of the few defeats in the legal career of a certain bright young lawyer in the antitrust division. He was Joseph Alioto, who three decades later became the mayor of the city.

Then came the Second World War, which suddenly cut off the supplies of European wines and diverted raisin grapes for food. This temporarily ended the surplus. The war years were a period of wine shortages, high prices, and frenzied prosperity for the growers and vintners. But when the conflict ended, the grape surplus was back to haunt them—and the wine market crashed in 1947.

"Artificial frosts" in new forms were tried again. A state marketing order for wine processors kept some of the surplus wine off the market between 1949 and 1952 by limiting the quantity which each winery was allowed to sell in bulk during specified periods. At the same time, a "marketing order for grape stabilization" was adopted to raise millions for the purchase and diversion of surplus grapes from normal marketing channels. Nature, however, obliged with natural frosts that reduced the 1949 and 1950 crops, and the stabilization funds were given back to the wineries. Again, in 1961, a new "artificial frost" was voted, this time under Federal auspices. It diverted almost 40 million gallons of surplus Central Valley dessert wine into industrial alcohol, and functioned for two years, but was defeated by another grower vote in 1963. Attempts during the next several years to hatch new surplus control plans met with failure.

• 9 •

Of what did the surplus consist? Not of wine grapes; California had been woefully short of wine grapes since Repeal. It consisted of the heavy crops of raisin- and table-grape varieties grown in the hot San Joaquin Valley—grapes which could also be used to make low-priced dessert wines and brandy. The chief raisin variety, the Thompson Seedless, was widely planted by the valley vineyardists after Repeal because it had three outlets. It could be sold in July as a fresh table grape, or laid on trays between the vine rows in August to be sun-dried as a raisin, or if market prices for table grapes and raisins proved unattractive during the summer, the Thompson crop could be left on the vines until October and sold to the wineries. Table grapes such as the Flame Tokay, Malaga, and Emperor were widely planted,

Bethlehem Steel Corporation

America's only wine tanker, the SS *Angelo Petri*, carried full cargoes of bulk wines from Stockton, California, through the Golden Gate and the Panama Canal to east coast ports from 1957 to 1971.

too, because they had two outlets: whatever part of their crops the growers could not sell to be eaten fresh did not need to go to waste; the leftover grapes were delivered to the wineries for crushing.

Thus the valley wineries became victims of the viticultural calendar, serving as the salvage receptacle for the leftover three-way Thompsons and two-way table grapes. Some grower-owned wineries in the valley existed solely to salvage the table-grape culls. Better grapes, needed to make better wines, remained scarce. Growers in the valley saw no reason to plant wine-grape varieties, which have only one use—to make wine.

The planting of three-way Thompsons and two-way table grapes, easy to grow and dispose of, doubled in the San Joaquin Valley after the Second World War. By the mid-1960s the acreage of Thompson vines in the valley amounted to almost half of the grape acreage in the state, and the valley's table-grape acreage represented almost a sixth. California's annual grape harvest was averaging more than three million tons, and less than a fifth of it consisted of wine grapes. The valley's wine industry was dominated by leaders of the raisin and table-grape industries, some of whom owned wineries but who seldom drank any wine themselves; they regarded it as a drink for skid row. It was they who dictated the artificial frost programs, which treated wine as a by-product of grapes. They argued that grape growing is a single industry of three segments—fresh, dried, and crushed—and that the wineries, coming last, must salvage the vast surplus tonnage in order to prevent waste. This made economic sense of a sort, and economists, bankers, and government agencies readily agreed. The fact they ignored was that the salvage outlet was using half of the valley's grape crop.

• 10 •

Prosperity had come to the coast-counties vineyards by the mid-60s because Americans since the war had been learning to drink table wines, especially those with the varietal names of coast-counties grapes. Soon there was a shortage of such premium wine grapes as the Rieslings, the Pinots, and Cabernet.

At the same time, urban sprawl was gobbling up old vineyards in the districts close to San Francisco Bay. The California climate that favors vines also attracts people, and the best vineyard land is also the best for housing tracts, the worst destroyers of vines. The state's population had jumped from 6 million at Repeal in 1933 to 15 million by 1960 and rose to 20 million in 1970, a rate of growth that could mean 38 million or even 40 million by the year 2000. To save the coast-counties vineyards, a state law in the 1960s provided for the creation of agricultural preserves—known as "green belts"—in which land is taxed on its value for farming, not at the higher rates charged for homes. The agricultural-preserve law came too late to save some of the vineyards. Fortunately, however, a few of the coast vintners found new climatically favored lands in sparsely settled areas outside the path of population growth and moved their vineyards there—a dramatic development described in the chapters on those areas.

• 11 •

But also since the Second World War, California vintners, including those in the San Joaquin Valley, had gotten around to doing some of the things that Professor Hilgard had advised seven decades earlier. They were modernizing their wineries, outfitting them with refrigeration and new equipment of the latest scientific designs. The new generation of enologists, taught in the University of California's wine school at Davis and at the new Department of Viticulture and Enology at Fresno

State University, brought scientific new cellar treatments to the ancient art of making wine.

In addition to dessert wines—their chief product—the valley wineries had always produced some dry and semisweet table wines, but those had averaged poor in quality and had been used primarily for blending with coast-counties wines. Gradually, the valley table wines began to improve, and became at least reliably palatable and sound. In the 1960s, the valley vintners finally learned to make acceptable table wines out of their raisin and table-grape varieties. They achieved this by adopting early harvesting and low-temperature fermentation, which Hilgard had advocated in vain. For such grapes as Flame Tokay, Thompson Seedless, and Emperor are, after all, members of the Vinifera (wine-bearing) family, and their juices when expertly handled can be made into clean, though bland-flavored table wines and even into champagnes, at remarkably low cost. (This helps to explain some of the extremely low-priced, yet quite palatable California table and sparkling wines found on the market in recent years; there is Tokay or Thompson juice in many of the whites and even in some of the rosés and reds.)

• 12 •

A different vineyard product—brandy—emerged after the Second World War to provide a home for some of the San Joaquin Valley grapes. In a way never expected, it turned out that the bitterly fought 1938 Prorate had been a boon, after all. By forcing the production and aging of vast quantities of brandy in that year, the Prorate had launched the California brandy industry on its way. During the war, emigré experts trained in brandy-blending in Europe had surveyed and tasted the aging Prorate stocks. From the best of them, these experts had blended a new type of beverage brandy, lighter than the cognacs and armagnacs of France and different in bouquet. At the war's end, new-type distilleries were designed to make this distinctive brandy. So popular did it become that brandy consumption in the United States quadrupled between the war and 1970; three-fourths was this new California type. These European experts made still another notable discovery: that the Thompson Seedless, if harvested when its sugar-acid ratio is in balance, is an excellent basic grape for brandy. By 1969, an eighth of the valley grape harvest—320,000 tons, mostly of surplus Thompsons—was distilled to make sixteen million wine gallons of the new type of brandy that Americans have shown they prefer.

· 13 ·

Then came another remarkable development—the introduction of "pop wines." When in 1955 the Government first authorized "special natural wines" to contain natural pure flavors without paying an extra excise tax, the San Joaquin Valley wineries introduced a wide assortment of new flavored wines with exotic coined names. The first of these were mostly of 20 percent alcoholic content, and they sold well, but they mainly succeeded in reducing the wineries' sales of their sherries, ports, tokays, and muscatels. Three years later, the Congress voted to allow "still" grape wines to contain carbon dioxide gas up to seven pounds pressure per square inch— enough to produce a slight "pop" when the bottle is opened— also without paying any additional tax. It then occurred to the makers of flavored wines that there might be some Americans who would like low-alcohol wines with flavors of other fruits besides grapes, also carbonated with seven pounds* of "pop." When these apple, strawberry, and tropical fruit types, mostly 8 to 10 percent in alcoholic content, hit the market in the late 1960s and early 70s, they scored an overnight success.

Suddenly the remainder of the surplus Thompson crop, which had depressed the valley's vineyard industry for two decades, was no more. For there is no better grape than the bland-tasting Thompson to blend with the exotic fruit flavors of the "pop" wines, which by 1971 accounted for almost a tenth of all the wine consumed that year in the United States!

The "pop" wines attracted new consumers, particularly the young. They served as a temporary bridge between the sweet taste of bubbly soda-pop and the traditional non-carbonated dry and semi-dry mealtime wines. Many buyers of the novel new "pop" types soon discovered they preferred the drier traditional wines. Sales of the "pops" slumped by a tenth in 1976 from their peak the year before, and the trend continues down.

· 14 ·

When the consumption of table wines first outstripped dessert wines in 1968 and set off the wine revolution, it caught both the California grape growers and the vintners by surprise. In 1849 the cry was "gold," now the cry was "wine grapes." The planting rush started in the coast counties, regions I, II, and III, but it soon became evident that the coast could not

---

*Increased to fourteen pounds by an act of Congress in 1975.

produce enough, that the hot interior valley henceforth must supply most of the table wines. Soon much of the San Joaquin's agriculture was in ferment, shifting from table grapes, raisins, cotton, peaches, and oranges, to grow "varietal" grapes for table wines instead.

In 1971 came startling news from the University: Dr. Harold Olmo had bred for hot climates a dozen new red-grape hybrids which—planted in the San Joaquin Valley—had made experimental wines described by some tasters as equal to most coast-counties Cabernet Sauvignons. The new vines had yielded eleven tons per acre at Fresno, almost double what the true Cabernet produces in cooler climates. Wines made from these grapes at Fresno State University had traces of Cabernet character and were superior to most reds heretofore grown in the valley. The first of these grapes, a cross of Cabernet Sauvignon with Grenache and Carignane called "Variety 12" or "Carnelian," was introduced for general planting in 1973. An even better red-wine grape named "Centurion" followed in 1975.

Equally sensational, for the Central Valley, were the University's new experiments in hot-climate winegrowing. The scientists showed that by retraining vines on trellises to let the leaves shade the grapes from the scorching valley sun, ripening of the fruit could be slowed, the sugar content increased without lowering the acidity, and the flavor thereby enhanced. This and other advances made it possible to grow appealingly palatable table wines in the Central Valley. It showed that California has enough potential vineyard land—despite the alarming population growth along the coast—to produce literally billions of gallons of good table wines per year, more than the total output of France, Italy, Spain, or Portugal.

Another advance in California, though of a different kind, was the amendment of the state standards for dessert wines in 1971. The amendment allows California sherries to be bottled at 17 percent alcoholic content, which improves their flavor, instead of at the old California minimum standard of $19^{1}/_{2}$ percent, and allows port and other dessert wines to be shipped at 18 percent. Sherries made in the state improved still further when the submerged-culture flor process, invented in Canada, came into general use. Premium wineries' port wines, too, became better with the planting of the better port-grape varieties, such as Tinta Madeira, Tinta Cão, Souzão, and Touriga. This suggested that a way to reverse the recent decline in popularity of the traditional California dessert wine types would be to further improve their quality.

• 15 •

When the explosive national gains in table-wine shipments began in the late 1960s, out-of-state investors suddenly became interested in winegrowing, which they had long ignored as an unstable business. Multimillion-dollar companies, visioning table wine as an American growth industry in its earliest stages, sought to buy out famous California wineries. In 1967, National Distillers, which had owned three California wineries during the Second World War but had sold them after the conflict, returned to winegrowing, buying the Almadén Vineyards and pouring millions into their expansion. In 1969, Heublein, the Connecticut company which two decades earlier had introduced Americans to vodka, bought control of the giant United Vintners group of farmer-owned wineries, and also purchased Beaulieu Vineyard, one of the top-rated Napa Valley producers. By 1970, fully 60 percent of the state's entire wine output was controlled by just two companies—Heublein and the giant of the industry, the Gallo wineries. In 1972, the Joseph Schlitz Brewing Company of Milwaukee bought the Geyser Peak Winery in Sonoma County, and a year later the great Moët-Hennessy champagne and brandy combine of France invaded California, planting seven hundred acres of vineyards and starting to build a huge champagne winery in the Napa Valley. In the same year the Coca-Cola Bottling Company of New York, already owning the Mogen David Wine Corporation of Chicago, bought the Franzia Brothers winery at Ripon, California's fourth largest (followed five years later by the Coca-Cola Company of Atlanta, which bought the Sterling Vineyard and winery at Calistoga and the Monterey Vineyard winery in the Salinas Valley).

In 1973, when wine shipments in the United States had reached 347 million gallons, economists at the Bank of America issued a forecast that the figure would reach 650 million gallons per year by 1980. In the rush to get in on the table wine bonanza, new owners reopened half a dozen old cellars that had been gathering cobwebs for years. New California wineries were being opened during the mid-1970s at the rate of thirty per year; more than a hundred new ones were operating by 1977. Farmers and private investors across the nation, backed by giant insurance companies and banks, financed the planting of 163,000 new acres of wine grapes (four times the total vineyard acreage of New York State) between 1970 and 1973, including 60,000 acres in 1973 alone.

Meanwhile some old-time vineyardists, who remembered the

This wind machine protects vines from frost damage in the Napa Valley. Propellers mix freezing air near the ground with warmer air above.

industry's past boom-and-bust history, were issuing stern warnings against the grape-planting and winery-building spree. Recalling that Americans have never been wine-drinkers, they foresaw the danger of creating a grape and wine surplus again.

· 16 ·

The warnings came true. In 1973, some coast-counties wineries had paid more than a thousand dollars per ton for scarce lots of "varietal" grapes. Word of such record prices helped to stimulate the reckless planting during that year. By 1974, when the new vineyards began bearing their first crops, grape prices plummeted to a third below the previous year. The bubble appeared to have burst. Newspaper headlines announced "the end of the wine boom" and described "rivers of surplus wine." The headlines were wrong, however, because the boom in table-wine sales had not been interrupted. Dessert wine movement was slumping as it had been for a decade. Table-wine shipments were continuing their steady gain, averaging 8 percent per year. It was true that too many vines had been planted too soon. Many speculators in vineyards lost their investments. Big financing agencies found themselves owning vineyards they had never intended to buy. Yet as mentioned in an earlier chapter, the overplanting turned out to have been a fortunate mistake. Wine grapes became scarce in the drought years of 1976 and 1977, and the surplus grapes averted a severe shortage of California wine in those years.

A depressing development in 1975 was the sudden end of the industry's consumer-education program after it had operated successfully for thirty-seven years. Large California wineries, in an auditing dispute with the State Department of Agriculture, killed the wine marketing order and the Wine Advisory Board, which collected the funds that had kept the program alive. Only a vestige of the wine-education and research effort was continued by the Wine Institute, the industry's voluntary-membership trade association.

• 17 •

Some entirely new kinds of California wine appeared during the mid-1970s. The white-wine sales boom was partly responsible; many growers were grafting white-wine grape varieties to their red-grape vines. White wines and rosés were made from such noble red grapes as Pinot Noir and Cabernet Sauvignon. Weeks-old *nouveau* or *primeur* red types competed with the Beaujolais *primeur* wines from France. Botrytized "late-harvest" whites matched the semisweet German *Spätlese* types with exotic aromas and flavors created by the *Edelfäule* or "noble mold." Some California wineries introduced unfiltered and unfined red wines that purported to deliver extra flavor but required decanting before they could be served. An increasingly discriminating wine-buying public, disillusioned of the generations-old myth that fine wines could come only from Europe, besieged wine shops of the nation to buy the new California rarities.

Increasing numbers of California wineries adopted vintage-year labeling, which they long had avoided because they felt such information did not sufficiently interest or inform consumers to warrant the trouble and extra cost. Back-labels appeared on many bottles describing the acidity and sweetness of the grapes, the length and temperature of fermentation, and the kinds of oak casks in which the wines had been aged—details scarcely understood by even the most knowledgeable wine buyers. Labels of some reds even named the future year when the contents of a bottle should mature with optimum flavor and bouquet and be ready to drink. No wines from other countries had ever flooded buyers with such technical details. New names of local vineyard districts, such as those that enhance the market values of French wines under the *appellation contrôlée* system, appeared on estate-bottled California wines. Many wineries even began naming their wines for individual vineyards or patches of vines.

Still lacking in the Golden State, however, were enough wines with sufficient age to compete directly with the rare treasures in great cellars of the world—wines with great bouquet and taste from many years spent mellowing in cask and bottle. This lack was partly corrected by an action of the California Legislature in 1970. The amended law permits a vintner's inventory of wines and brandies to be taxed by county assessors only once, in the month of March following the vintage, and to be aged for as many more years as the vintner might choose, without paying this tax again. A few limited lots of Cabernet Sauvignon were set aside to be aged five years before release. But few vintners had yet seen the opportunity to age their sherries for whole decades in oak, as is done in Spain by the *solera* system of blending young wines with the very old.

• 18 •

Although the overplanting during the 1970s was a costly mistake, the temporary threat of grape surpluses was a cloud with a silver lining because the new grape surplus produced tremendous improvements in the quality of California wines. By the mid-1970s wine-grape varieties represented more than half of the tons used for wine and brandy, compared to less than a fifth used in the mid-1960s.

By 1975, there were eighteen times more acres of Chardonnay in the state than sixteen years before, fifty times more of White Riesling, fifty times more of Pinot Noir, ninety times more of Cabernet Sauvignon, two hundred times more of Barbera, and there were comparable increases in acreages of dozens of other wine-grape varieties that had been lamentably scarce in California since Repeal.

As the young vines gradually came into bearing, enough fine wines were being made to prove to additional millions of buyers the vinous greatness that can be achieved in this paradise for the vine. This is why the former sneers at California wines by visiting writers changed abruptly during the 1970s to increasingly effulgent praise.

• 19 •

The California vineyard and wine scene visible to the tourist is also changing markedly each year. The new mechanical harvesting machines, given their first trials here in 1968, already are picking some of the raisin and wine grapes and are expected to be picking two thirds of the state's entire grape crop by 1980. (European winegrowers, facing labor shortages, are experimenting with the grape-picking robots, too.) Winemakers

Upright, Inc.

Flexible arms shake grapes off the vines onto a conveyor belt as this mechanical harvester straddles a vineyard row in California.

say mechanical harvesting, because it is speedy, will result in better wines, because hand-picking in the vineyards is slow and can be done only by day. The robots can harvest by night, picking the grapes when they are cool and fresh, and precisely when they reach ideal ripeness. Also new in the 1970s is crushing of the grapes in the vineyard to reduce the time the juice is exposed to air. Some mechanical harvesters have crushers mounted on the machines, the juice protected by sulfur dioxide and a blanket of carbon dioxide until it reaches the winery. The prospect is that we may see wineries of the future receiving no whole grapes at all, but only the newly-crushed grapes, called must.

Subterranean wine cellars, usually damp and moldy, became passé years ago, when vintners learned to build insulated, spotlessly clean cellars above the ground. Stainless- and epoxy-lined steel tanks have replaced most of the old redwood and concrete vats for the fermenting and storage of wine. Now you see many wineries with no roofs at all: batteries of steel tanks that stand exposed to the sun while temperature-controlled water circulates inside their shells and keeps the wine as cool as though it were underground.

The Wine Institute

Old-fashioned redwood tanks in a Lodi, California, winery.

Many modern wineries use centrifuges instead of filters to remove yeast cells and other solids from their newly-fermented wines.

Though grape growing and winemaking will become increasingly mechanized and automated in years to come, in California and other states, vineyards will always be beautiful, and there will be increasing use of picturesque small oak casks for the aging of wine. The romance of the vineyards and cellars will always be part of the flavors of their wines.

• 20 •

To the visitor who would explore the California wine country, the puzzle is where to begin, for more than 12,000 vineyards and almost 400 wineries and brandy distilleries dot the countryside in 43 of the state's 48 counties, and they cover 645,000 acres or almost a thousand square miles.

But a tour is well worth undertaking, and it can start almost anywhere, for more than a hundred of the wineries welcome visitors to taste their wines, and an equal number in addition can be visited by appointment made in advance. Some also provide space for scheduled benefit concerts and plays. In fact, wine-touring, with tasting, has become one of California's chief visitor attractions, vying with redwood forests, Spanish missions, and Disneyland for the tourist trade.

There are wineries of every description: charming ivy-clad castles; grape-processing plants with steel storage tanks that resemble oil refinery tank farms; family-sized vineyards that specialize in delivering wine by the jug to their customers' doorsteps; estates of gentlemen farmers who grow wine only as an avocation; Church-owned cellars alongside monasteries; and also, scores of tasting rooms, which, though related to wineries, operate mainly at city and highway locations to sell their wines to the public.

Though representative California wines are now available in all of the fifty states and increasing numbers of foreign countries, the only way to get acquainted with the full assortment is to go where the wines are produced. The rarest vintages still seldom leave the state. Made in small quantities, they usually are snapped up by California connoisseurs. Many of the small wineries sell their entire output at their cellar doors or to their mailing lists of loyal customers throughout the state. Only a few attempt to ship their wines to other states, most of which have burdensome tax and licensing requirements that are relics of Prohibition. And United States postal law on this subject, another such relic, does not allow a winegrower to send you even a single bottle of his wine through the mails; you can only use parcel delivery or express.

Californians themselves drink almost a fifth of the wine produced in their state. Not only because they are Californians;

Temperature-controlled stainless steel tanks. A freezing solution flows between the inner and outer shell of each tank. The winemaker is Michael Robbins, Spring Mountain Vineyards winery.

seven out of ten of them were born somewhere else and discovered wine after they arrived. The main reason for California's high wine consumption, nearly four gallons per capita per year including imports, is that the state's laws recognize wine as food and allow it to be sold freely in all kinds of stores and at the lowest state excise tax rates in the nation—1 cent per gallon on table wine, 2 cents on dessert types, 30 cents on champagnes.

If you wish to cover all of the California wine districts, to meet the vintners in person and sample their products at the cellars, the trip will take at least a month. Since three million tourists each year now visit the wineries, some of which haven't enough of the finest and oldest wines to serve the crowds, you should plan your tour with enough time to search for the best.

13

Sonoma, Mendocino, and Lake

EADING toward the north coast wine country from San Francisco, you cross the Golden Gate Bridge and drive through suburban Marin County. Since the Second World War, housing tracts have replaced the scores of Marin vineyards that flourished before Prohibition. In 1969, oenothusiast Richard Duncan planted eight acres of Cabernet Sauvignon vines instead of trees on the west side of Quail Hill in northern San Rafael when he had the Commerce Clearing House publishing plant built on the crest. A year later, Herbert Rowland planted five more acres at his birthplace, Rancho Pacheco, beside the US 101 freeway opposite the Hamilton Field airbase. The Cuvaison Winery in Napa County bought both their crops and in 1977 released the first Marin County Cabernet bottled since early in this century. It brought ten dollars a bottle. Now Marin also has a winery, college physiology teacher Richard Dye's 5,000-gallon Grand Pacific cellar, which he opened in 1975 near the Northgate Shopping Center in San Rafael. He makes his wine from Merlot grapes he trucks south from Sonoma County.

At Ignacio in northern Marin, you turn inland on the Black Point Cutoff, cross the Petaluma River into southern Sonoma County, then follow Highways 121 and 12 into Sonoma Valley, which Jack London named the Valley of the Moon.

You begin to see more vineyards here because the weather becomes warmer as you travel north. The lower part of the valley, only seven miles from San Pablo Bay, is Region I in the classification of wine districts by climate (page 224). A few miles farther, as the valley narrows between the Sonoma and Mayacamas ridges of the Coast Range, it becomes Region II, and farther on, Region III.

Highway 12 leads to the picturesque Spanish pueblo of Sonoma and to the restored Mission San Francisco Solano de Sonoma (founded 1823), the northernmost of the Franciscan mission chain, and to the valley's several wineries, of which Buena Vista, Sebastiani, and Hanzell are the best known.

Sonoma Mission is where winegrowing north of San Francisco began. When the mission was abandoned by order of the Mexican Government in 1834, the provincial *comandante,* General Mariano Guadalupe Vallejo, took over its vineyard, planted more vines on his own extensive lands, and became Sonoma's first commercial winegrower. At his home, Lachryma Montis, northwest of the town plaza, you can see the awards his vintage 1857 Sonoma Red and Sonoma White wines received at the 1858 California State Fair. Vallejo's example soon was followed by his brother-in-law, Jacob Leese, and by many others, including Jacob Gundlach, an experienced winemaker from Germany.

In 1856 came the spectacular "Count" Agoston Haraszthy, attracted by the success of the Sonoma winegrowers. Haraszthy, a political exile from Hungary, was a promotional genius of many interests, among which was a passion for raising grapes. He had tried and failed to grow them in Wisconsin, where he founded the town of Haraszthy (now Sauk City) before migrating to California in 1848. He imported European vines to San Diego, where he speculated in farming and was elected sheriff. Settling later in San Francisco, he planted European vines near Mission, Dolores, where they failed to ripen because of the summer fogs. He then moved them to a location near the Crystal Springs Lakes in adjoining San Mateo County, where they failed again.

On his 1856 visit to Sonoma, Haraszthy found the vines there thriving, and promptly bought the vineyard originally established by General Vallejo's brother, Salvador. The "Count" transplanted his vines again, this time to Sonoma. He built a palatial Pompeian villa on a knoll, surrounded it with formal gardens and fountains, and named it Buena Vista. He wrote pamphlets extolling California's winegrowing climate and sold cuttings of his imported vines to farmers throughout the state. In 1861, he got himself appointed by Governor John G. Downey to visit Europe to study winegrowing and to import more grape varieties. From this trip he brought back 100,000 vines of some 300 varieties (for which the state failed to pay him) and material for his book *Grape Culture, Wines, and Wine Making.* For these exploits he became known as "the father of modern California viticulture."

Two years after his return from Europe, with financial backing from San Francisco banker William Ralston, Haraszthy organized the Buena Vista Vinicultural Society. Two sandstone wineries were built at Buena Vista, with tunnels extending into the hillside. The "Count" became General Vallejo's rival in the State Fair wine competitions, but Vallejo had employed a French winemaker, a Dr. Faure, and usually won more medals than Haraszthy. The rivalry was friendly; Haraszthy's sons, Arpad and Attila, had married two of the General's daughters.

Haraszthy had sent Arpad to France to learn champagne making in the Moët et Chandon cellars at Épernay, but Arpad's attempts to make champagne at Sonoma were failures. And financially, so was the Buena Vista Society, even when its champagne was finally perfected by a French expert; the San Francisco *Alta California* described it as "the largest winegrowing estate in the world, and also the most unprofitable." At length, banker Ralston refused to supply any more capital. Haraszthy was accused of extravagance and was deposed as head of the Society in 1866. In disgust, the "Count" left for Nicaragua and a new adventure, to establish a sugar cane plantation and make rum for the export trade. In 1869 he disappeared. On his plantation was a stream infested with alligators. It is believed that he tried to cross it on a tree limb, and fell.

During the 1870s, the phylloxera vine louse invaded Buena Vista and neighboring vineyards. By then, Arpad Haraszthy had moved to San Francisco and become a wine merchant, later acquiring the Orleans Vineyard in Yolo County.

The aging tunnels of Buena Vista collapsed during the earthquake of 1906. The vineyards were virtually gone, and the wineries had been closed. During Prohibition the Haraszthy story was forgotten.

• 2 •

At an auction held in Sacramento in 1941, San Francisco newsman Frank Bartholomew bought a 435-acre tract of Sonoma land that he had never seen, intending to build a country home. Coming to inspect his purchase, he found on the property two abandoned stone buildings that might once have been wineries. Nobody in the neighborhood could tell him what they were. Thinking that I might know their history, Bart asked me to come to Sonoma and look them over. When I told him the strange Haraszthy story and that he had bought historic Buena Vista, he was amazed.

Journalist Bartholomew perceived what such a story might be worth in prestige if, as a winery owner, he could bring back Buena Vista wines. That, in the following decade, is what he and his wife Antonia did. They reopened the tunnels, replanted the vineyard, employed expert help to produce premium Buena Vista wines, and by retelling the spectacular Haraszthy story made them nationally known.

Buena Vista, beautifully situated in a grove of majestic eucalyptus trees, welcomes visitors and invites you to taste its wines, of which there now are seventeen "varietal" types. The best, year after year, have been the cask-numbered Cabernet Sauvignon, Pinot Noir, a luscious Sylvaner named Vine Brook, and a Cabernet Sauvignon rosé. Also pleasing to drink is the Green Hungarian, made from a grape that other vintners used only for blending until the Bartholomews, liking the name, popularized it as a "varietal" white wine. A relatively recent addition is Sparkling Sonoma Brut Champagne, given its secondary fermentation in Buena Vista bottles by Hanns Kornell at St. Helena.

The Bartholomews succeeded where Haraszthy had failed; they made Buena Vista pay. Having done so, they sold the old Buena Vista cellars, which by then were too small. The buyer, Vernon Underwood for Young's Market Company of Los Angeles, bought seven hundred acres of former grazing land on Ramal Road in the southeastern corner of Sonoma Valley, planted it with new drip-irrigated vineyards, and built an ultramodern half-million-gallon winery there. Buena Vista's Chilean-born winemaster René Lacasia lives beside the new winery and daily drives the six miles to the old.

Bartholomew retained his home and most of the original Buena Vista vineyard and sold his grapes to the new owner of the cellars for a specified period of years. In 1973, at the age of seventy-five, Bartholomew opened his own Hacienda Wine Cellars in a former hospital beside his home. Hacienda "varietal" wines, made by UC Davis-trained Steven MacRostie, began winning medals at the Los Angeles County Fair, and by 1977 the Hacienda winery was being doubled in size. Buena Vista and Hacienda are only a few hundred yards apart, but Buena Vista is reached by Old Winery Road, while to get to the Hacienda Cellars you take Castle Road and then Vineyard Lane.

• 3 •

The revival of Sonoma's wine industry is celebrated by its annual vintage festival during the last weekend of September with pageants, nostalgic costume parades, and the ceremonial blessing of the grapes. These events are held around such landmarks as the Mission, the historic structures around the Plaza, and the Bear Flag Monument where in 1846 California was proclaimed a republic free of Mexican rule.

Among the more conspicuous Sonoma landmarks are those named Sebastiani, for the founder of the town's principal winery. These include the Sebastiani Theater, Sebastiani Hotel, Sebastiani Dance Hall, Sebastiani Cannery, Sebastiani Bowling Alley, Sebastiani Skating Rink, Sebastiani Motel, and the Sebastiani Bus Depot. In fact, the late Samuele Sebastiani is said to have once offered the city fathers a fabulous sum if they would rename Sonoma for him.

His son August, who now owns the Sebastiani Winery at Spain and Fourth Streets, tells how his father arrived in Sonoma in 1896 from Tuscany, saved enough money while making cobblestones for San Francisco streets to buy the old Milani winery in 1904, outlasted Prohibition by making sacramental and tonic wines, and became Sonoma's leading citizen, building some of its streets and giving it a parochial school.

August Sebastiani wears striped bib overalls around the winery as his father did, though since some visitors began commenting, he now has them tailor-made. Since taking over the winery in 1934, he has transformed it from an anonymous bulk wine operation to one of California's leading producers of varietally labeled table wines.

He entered the premium wine field in the early 1960s by winning prizes with his Barbera, a deep-flavored, well-aged, dry yet fruity red wine. Connoisseurs who admired the Barbera discovered they also liked the other Sebastiani products, which were blends of old and young wines. Many buyers, however, were asking for bottles with vintage dates. At first August answered them by giving bin numbers to his oldest blends, but as demand for them grew, he found it necessary to adopt vintage labels for all his wines except those sold in jugs.

When the wine revolution exploded in the late 60s and early 70s, giant liquor and food companies flooded August with scores of offers to buy him out. He turned them all down, saying "What would we do with ourselves if we sold?"

With his sons Sam and Don, he replanted parts of the onetime Vallejo land with such varieties as Cabernet Sauvignon, Pinot Noir, Gamay Beaujolais, White Riesling, Gewürztraminer, and Chardonnay, replaced old redwood tanks with temperature-controlled stainless steel, and added thousands of oak barrels to age his sherries, Chardonnays, and reds. August Sebastiani's favorite wines are his barrel-aged reds. His winery is one of the few who have Cabernets for sale that are five to fourteen years of age. But he also sells America's youngest red. In 1972, he introduced America's first *vin nouveau,* a six-week-old Gamay, and put it on the market at the same time the equally young Beaujolais *primeurs* arrived from France. Later came another Sebastiani "first," a white wine of Pinot Noir, which August named "Eye of the Swan." By 1977, Sebastiani wines were being sold in all fifty states and in six foreign countries, and the winery capacity had been increased to five million gallons.

The most important function of wine, says August Sebastiani, is to make the food it accompanies more enjoyable to eat. His favorite foods are those cooked by his wife Sylvia, whose cookbook *Mangiamo* (Let's Eat) has been sold at the winery since 1970 at the rate of five thousand copies per year. August's other interests besides wine and food are his collections of Indian artifacts and birds. At home uphill from the winery, he breeds scores of different kinds of birds, from rare plumed doves and crested pigeons to Australian black swans, and supplies them to zoos around the world.

• 4 •

In the Vineburg district two miles southeast of Sonoma, best reached via the Lovall Valley and Thornsberry Roads, is the historic Gundlach-Bundschu Rhinefarm and its winery, reopened in 1973 to produce again its once famous Bacchus wines. Winegrower Jacob Gundlach from Bavaria and architect Emil Dresel from Geisenheim founded the Rhinefarm in 1858. In that year Gundlach returned to Germany and brought back the first Riesling vines to be planted in Sonoma County. With the addition of his son-in-law Charles Bundschu, the firm became Gundlach-Bundschu in 1895 and built great wine vaults in San Francisco, which were destroyed in the earthquake and fire of 1906. Sixty-seven years later, Gundlach's great-grandson Towle Bundschu was still cultivating the 120-acre Rhinefarm, selling the grapes, when his son Jim, trained in farming, and son-in-law John Merritt, a dairy chemist, rebuilt the 15,000-gallon winery around three of its original stone walls. Their first wines were a white named Kleinberger, a Sylvaner called Sonoma Riesling, and Zinfandel. The Rhinefarm grows the only Kleinberger grapes (known as Elbling in Germany) produced commercially in the United States. The winery is open to visitors on weekends.

• 5 •

On a private road up a hillside just north of Sonoma there is a tiny jewel of a winery, a millionaire's plaything that is unique in the world of wine. On twenty acres of beautifully terraced vines stands a partial copy of the Clos de Vougeot château in Burgundy, with a miniature model winery inside. The vineyard is called Hanzell (Zell for the late financier and United States Ambassador to Italy, James D. Zellerbach, who had it planted in 1952, and Han for Hana, his wife). A procession of subsequent owners have preserved the Hanzell name and also the price of its Chardonnay and Pinot Noir, six dollars a bottle, which is precisely what Zellerbach found they cost him to produce. The small output is snapped up each year by buyers who prize Hanzell wines as superb rarities, which they are.

What Zellerbach never knew, as he died in 1963, was that one of his expensive whims would lead to the solution of a century-old winemaking mystery and would cause scores of America's leading vintners to make an important change in the flavor of their wines.

While living in Europe during the 1940s, Zellerbach had developed a liking for the Montrachet and Romanée Conti wines of Burgundy's Côte d'Or. He conceived the idea of attempting to grow identical wines on his 200-acre Sonoma estate. While home on a visit, he invited the viticultural experts of the University of California at Davis to tell him how this might be achieved.

He followed every costly, specific detail of their advice, except one. Instead of American white oak barrels, customarily used to age wines in this country, he insisted on ordering from France the wooden-hooped oak barrels, called *pièces*, that he had seen in the cellars of Burgundy; he liked their primitive look.

When the first Hanzell wine, the 1956 Chardonnay, was ready, he had his winemaker, Ralph Bradford Webb, send him a quantity in Rome. Zellerbach submitted it to European experts to taste. They identified it as a white burgundy, but couldn't decide from which Côte d'Or vineyard it came.

California vintners tasted Hanzell wines and recognized their French flavor. It was the elusive flavor certain French wines possess, often described as their "complexity." American researchers had tried for years to explain it, attributing it to peculiarities of French climate or soil. Now its source was known: the barrels Zellerbach had bought in France. California wineries began buying similar barrels from coopers in Beaune and Bordeaux. Their wines, too, acquired that elusive "complex" taste.

But why should French barrels make a difference? Aren't all oak barrels the same? The explanation was found in forestry libraries: Different species of oak trees grow-on the European and American continents. European oaks, usually referred to by French coopers as Limousin, Nevers, Austrian, or Yugoslavian according to the localities where they grow, have a varietal vanilla-like fragrance markedly different from that of American white oaks*—a fragrance that the wood imparts to the wine.

Now that wineries here have filled whole cellars with European barrels, some have decided they prefer American oak after all. A little Limousin or Nevers oak flavor in a Chardonnay or a Pinot Noir is desirable, they say, but too much hides the aroma of the grape and can even ruin a fine wine. "It gives me splinters in my esophagus," said one of my connoisseur friends recently, describing a Chardonnay that had spent too much time in European oak.

Since 1975, Hanzell has been owned by young Australian-born Countess Barbara de Brye (nee Smith), who was educated in England, studying archaeology at Cambridge, and is so devoted to winegrowing that she once planted an English vineyard. With her Parisian banker husband Jacques, she often comes to stay at her Sonoma estate and to visit their California friends. The Countess prefers clarets to burgundies, so winemaster Robert Sessions has planted four acres of Cabernet Sauvignon on the ridge above the original vineyard. This will increase the number of Hanzell wines to three.

· 6 ·

There were more than a hundred wineries around Sonoma in the last century, when the hills on both sides of the valley were clad with vines. Sonoma Valley wines rivaled those of the Napa Valley, the more famous neighbor to the east. Among the most celebrated vineyards were Captain J. H. Drummond's Dunfillan Vineyard north of Sonoma, the nearby Madrone Vineyard of the United States Senator George Hearst,** Charles Kunde's

---

*Native American white oaks, from which most barrels for wine and liquor aging are made, are chiefly of the species *Quercus alba, Q. Lyrata, Q. prinus,* and *Q. bicolor.* The main oak species grown in Europe for wine or brandy barrels are *Quercus robur* and *Q. sessilis.* Suppliers of cooperage say these species do not grow in this country, except perhaps in some northeastern states.

**The multimillionaire mine owner and newspaper publisher, the father of William Randolph Hearst. The Senator bought the Madrone Vineyard in 1885, planted it with the finest Bordeaux varieties, and was proud to serve his own wines and brandy to his guests in the national capital. At his death in 1891 his widow, Phoebe Apperson Hearst, sold the winery to the California Wine Association.

Wildwood Vineyard near Kenwood, and Kohler & Frohling's Tokay Vineyard at Glen Ellen, which is now part of the Jack London State Park.

During Prohibition, the lower Sonoma Valley became a summer playground for sporting types from San Francisco because it is close to the city. Great vineyards were chopped up into small holdings, while the vineyard estates of wealthy San Franciscans in the Napa Valley remained more or less intact. After Repeal, the several wineries that reopened in Sonoma Valley sold jug wines to passersby or in bulk to the bigger wineries.

Now, since the table wine boom of the 1960s, winegrowing in the valley has come back to life. Besides the new plantings by the Bundschus and Sebastianis, Arthur and Fred Kunde have enlarged and replanted their grandfather's Wildwood Vineyard, which again stretches into the eastern hills.

On Burndale Road in Sonoma, winery systems engineer Gino Zepponi and optics engineer Norman de Leuze equipped an old farm building as a 5,000-gallon model winery and have made fine oak-aged Chardonnays, Rieslings, Gewürztraminers, and Pinot Noirs since 1969. Their grapes come mostly from the Carneros district six miles southeast of Sonoma in Napa County, but their best 1975 Chardonnay was grown on Zepponi's young three-acre vineyard fronting Sonoma's Broadway. There are no visitor facilities at the "ZD" winery. Its wines are offered to interested buyers at periodic invitational tastings.

In 1971, young wine-buff engineers Robert Magnani and Allen Ferrara with three partners bought an inactive eighty-five-year-old bulk winery and thirty-acre Zinfandel vineyard off Highway 12 near Glen Ellen, added a chalet-style superstructure, and adopted Grand Cru Vineyards as its name. Besides the usual table wine types, winemaker Magnani makes champagne, a white Zinfandel, a Gewürztraminer of grapes artificially inoculated with the Botrytis mold, and a red *vin nouveau* by the ancient method called *macération carbonique.* Whole, uncrushed grapes including stems are put into tanks, where their weight releases juice and fermentation occurs spontaneously in the intact grapes without oxygen. Carbon dioxide is released and "macerates" the grapes. (Grand Cru's tasting room is open on weekends.)

In Kenwood on Highway 12 is the Kenwood Winery, built in 1905 by Julius Pagani to make bulk wine, but purchased in 1970 by young John Sheela, Martin and Michael Lee to make premium table wines. They have replanted the pre-Prohibition mixed-variety vineyard with vines of noble lineage, installed stainless steel tanks and new oak barrels in the cellar, and converted the front into a tasting area, which is open daily except on holidays. Research chemist Dr. Robert Kozlowski is the winemaker.

But the closeness of Sonoma Valley to San Francisco and other nearby cities poses a new threat to the vineyards—urban sprawl. The county is threatening to convert winding Highway 12 into a four-lane expressway, which would cut off part of the Kenwood Vineyard and encourage the building of more housing tracts, drive-ins, and hotdog stands. The young Sonoma winegrowers are fighting the project, following a successful example set by their Napa neighbors, of which more later.

• 7 •

Just past Kenwood, beside the road that climbs Adobe Canyon to Sugarloaf State Park in the Mayacamas mountain range, is Chateau St. Jean, one of California's newest and most spectacular winegrowing estates. Three wealthy San Joaquin Valley grape growers visualized and financed this version of what should constitute a modern Sonoma Valley chateau: a French Mediterranean-style mansion, formal gardens, dining rooms for catered gourmet luncheons, picnic grounds and hiking trails for guests, vineyards climbing a mountain, a winery modeled after Château Lafite, and the other essential— high-priced, high-quality wines and champagnes.

Another essential is the dedicated young winemaster, Santa Rosa-born Richard Arrowood, trained at two state colleges and in three older Sonoma County wineries (Korbel, Italian Swiss Colony, and Sonoma Vineyards). Big, cherub-faced Dick Arrowood received his dream assignment in 1974, when he made the first Chateau St. Jean wines in leased space at the Sonoma Vineyards winery. The chateau's 105-acre vineyard was planted in the following year, but the winery wasn't finished until 1977.

Arrowood has already amazed the wine trade by introducing seven different Chardonnays of the same vintage, eight different Rieslings varying in flavor, and four different reds of Cabernet and Zinfandel—all from different vineyards, some of which were identified on the labels. Some of his creations have already begun winning medals. One of his botrytized 1975 Rieslings had the initials "TBA" on its label, signifying that if it had been made in Germany, it would have qualified in the proportion of botrytized grapes to be called a *Trockenbeerenauslese* wine. It was priced at forty dollars a bottle. But in 1978 the Washington bureau that approves wine labels notified Arrowood that "TBA" could no longer be allowed on an American wine label. The German Government had complained to the bureau that the initials could be construed as meaning it was a German wine.

(Note there is no accent over the first "a" in this winery's name. This may remind you to pronounce "Jean" the American, not the French way. No saint is involved; the winery is named for Mrs. Jean Merzoian, one of the investors' wives.)

Chateau St. Jean is open to visitors Wednesdays through weekends. The tasting room is in the mansion, which was built about 1920 by Duluth lumber and mining magnate Ezra Goff as his California home. Bargains sold only at the tasting room are the winery's press-wines, labeled Vin Rouge and Vin Blanc. The first St. Jean champagne, a four-year-old blanc de blancs, was introduced in 1977.

From Kenwood, a side trip south and west on Warm Springs Road will take you over a range of hills to the Bennett Valley, an old Sonoma wine district making a comeback in the 1970s. Off Bennett Valley Road below Bennett Mountain, David and Sandra Steiner are converting their dairy barn into the 10,000-gallon Matanzas Creek Winery to use the grapes from their forty acres of young vineyards nearby. Their manager is Davis-trained Meredith (Merry) Edwards, formerly of the Mt. Eden Vineyard in Santa Clara County. She is one of the first three women winemakers to begin to manage California wineries in this decade.

• 8 •

When you leave the upper Sonoma Valley and travel west and north, you will see few vineyards until you pass Santa Rosa, the bustling county seat. Before Prohibition, there were vineyards on the hills of southwestern Sonoma County between Penngrove and Petaluma, and there was a winery in Petaluma city. On the Petaluma River shore near Lakeville, United States Senator James G. Fair, for whom San Francisco's Fairmont Hotel is named, had a large vineyard, winery, and brandy distillery, which the present owner has converted into a summer home.

Some of the greatest California wines before and after Prohibition came from the famous Fountain Grove Vineyard, which stood on a hillside four miles north of Santa Rosa. It was to Fountain Grove that the mystical prophet, Thomas Lake Harris, moved his Brotherhood of the New Life in 1875 from Brocton, New York. Among the disciples who came with Harris to his new California heaven were the Missouri viticulturist, Dr. John W. Hyde, and the Japanese prince, Baron Kanaye Nagasawa. While the Fountain Grove Press poured forth Harris's pamphlets, sermons, and hymns, Dr. Hyde and his pupil, Nagasawa, planted four hundred acres with Pinot Noir, Cabernet, and Zinfandel. By the early 1880s Harris was shipping Fountain Grove wines, "potentialized with the electro-vinous spirit of joy," across the United States and as far as his old headquarters in England. Involved in new scandals about free love practices at his utopia, Harris departed suddenly for England in 1892. Nagasawa was left in charge and became Fountain Grove's owner when Harris died in 1906. The Baron was noted as a wine judge and for his knowledge of viniculture, acquired from Dr. Hyde and their mutual friend, Luther Burbank, the Santa Rosa botanical wizard. Nagasawa maintained the vineyard and was preparing to reopen the winery at the repeal of Prohibition, when he died. His estate hired an incompetent winemaker, and the first post-Repeal Fountain Grove wines were moldy and sour. Then mining magnate Errol MacBoyle bought the estate, partly to acquire the Baron's collection of samurai swords and Japanese art, and partly to impress his millionaire friends with his own private brand of champagne. MacBoyle hired two winemakers, emigrés from Germany, Kurt Opper and his cousin, Hanns Kornell. During the 1940s Opper restored Fountain Grove to greatness. His 1945 champagne, Johannisberg Riesling, and his Pinot Noir were the finest made that year in the state. But after MacBoyle's death in 1949, his widow Glendolyn remarried and let the vineyard fall into neglect. Opper then quit to join the Paul Masson Vineyard at Saratoga, and in 1951 Fountain Grove was closed for good.

• 9 •

In the Santa Rosa Valley, homes and shopping centers compete with vineyards for space. But to the west, between Forestville and Sebastopol, prune orchards and even some of Sonoma County's famous Gravenstein apple orchards have been displaced by new vineyards since vintners began paying record prices for coast-counties grapes. Thirty new wineries have opened in Sonoma County in the past decade, raising the total to fifty-five. This has created a demand for instruction in grape growing and winemaking. Viticulture instructor Richard Thomas at Santa Rosa Junior College had more than fifty enrolled in his class by 1977. Each student helps cultivate the college's ten-acre vineyard. A wine laboratory is being added, but the college faced a problem in getting state clearance for it to operate, because of California's minimum twenty-one-year drinking age.

From an old cottage at the country crossroads called Trenton, ten miles northwest of Santa Rosa, come two red wines prized by many California connoisseurs, Swan Vineyard Zinfandel and Pinot Noir. Joe Swan, the son of a teetotaler North Dakota schoolteacher, first became interested in wine by reading about it in novels, and made his first vintage of rhubarb at the age of fifteen. When he grew up and became an airline pilot, he continued making wine at home as a hobby, and once planted a Chardonnay vineyard at 5,000 feet elevation in eastern Tulare County just to see what kind of wine that mountain climate could produce. Winemaking fitted into flying, which was mostly on Western Airlines' San Francisco–Los Angeles run. He took short courses in winemaking at the UC Davis wine school, and in 1969 bonded a 2,000-gallon cellar in his house. His Zinfandel made that year, of grapes fermented extra-long on the skins and clarified without filtering, was the first to win him fame. His 1972 Pinot Noir, which he fermented with some of the grape stems as they do in Burgundy, was one of the few I have tasted in California that had the Côte d'Or cachet. Swan retired from flying in 1974 but did not enlarge his winery. Winegrowing for him is still a hobby and he believes that small winegrowers should stay small. He credits the quality of his wines to his unofficial advisor, Napa enologist André Tchelistcheff. The ten-acre Swan vineyard, where his wife June and daughter Sandy help pick the grapes, contains Pinot Noir, Chardonnay, and a patch of Cabernet Sauvignon; he buys his Zinfandels.

On the Gravenstein Highway (Route 116) a mile south of Forestville is the Russian River Vineyard winery, modeled after a hop kiln, with a twenty-five-acre vineyard planted in 1964. This establishment won some fame in the 1970s for the quality of its restaurant, in which its first winemaker Robert Lasdin was the chef. At this writing, the winery's new owner had not decided on his plans.

Southeast of Forestville, near the intersection of Guerneville and Vine Hill Roads, young Thomas Dehlinger and his Berkeley radiologist father Klaus have planted a fourteen-acre vineyard and built the 14,000-gallon Dehlinger Winery especially to produce premium wines. Tom, a UC Davis graduate, was one of Bradford Webb's successors as the winemaker at Hanzell Vineyard. He lives uphill from the winery in an octagonal house that he built for himself.

On Laguna Road a mile east of Dehlinger is the 2-million-gallon Martini & Prati Winery, a group of old wooden and concrete cellars, one of which dates from 1881. Elmo Martini and Edward Prati, descendants of old Sonoma winegrowing families, make mainly bulk table wines for other California wineries. When the Fountain Grove winery closed, they bought its famous label and used it to introduce their own bottled wines, which are sold in their tasting room and in Bay Area stores.

Trenton is at the lower end of the Russian River Valley, so named because Russian fur hunters from Alaska settled on the Sonoma coast in 1812 and remained there for thirty years. The Russian River rises some 200 miles farther north in Mendocino County and flows almost due south between parallel ridges of the Coast Range. In prehistoric times the river emptied into San Francisco Bay until upheavals of the earth forced it to cut a new channel westward through the coastal hills to the sea.

Most Sonoma County wine now comes from the two dozen wineries and some 20,000 acres of vineyards scattered through this valley and its series of tributary valleys with local names.

• 10 •

On the left bank of the Russian River, two miles east of Guerneville and just past the woodsy summer resort colony of Rio Nido, are the Korbel vineyards and champagne cellars with their quaint Norman tower, which once housed a brandy still.

The winery dates from 1886, when the Korbel brothers, natives of Bohemia, gave up lumbering along the Russian River because they had cut down most of the trees. They planted vines where there had been a grove of redwoods, and built the cellar with bricks they baked in a homemade kiln. They made only still wines and brandy until 1896, when they were joined by an expert winemaker named Franz Hazek from Prague. Hazek brought choice vine cuttings from Europe and made a dry sparkling wine called Grand Pacific to compete with Arpad Haraszthy's "Eclipse" and the champagne of Paul Masson. The Korbels renamed the wine Korbel Sec and followed it with a sparkling burgundy named Korbel Rouge. Hazek's successor was another Czech named Jan Hanuska, who so jealously guarded his secret *cuvées* that nobody was allowed to enter the winery in his absence, not even the Korbels.

Korbel is now owned by the Heck family, whose progenitor Adolf from Strasbourg reopened the Cook's Imperial champagne vaults for the American Wine Company in St. Louis at the repeal of Prohibition. He sent his eldest son Adolf L. Heck to the Geisenheim Institute in Germany to learn winemaking, and made him Cook's champagne master when he returned. When the Government seized the American Wine Company in 1944 because of its Nazi ownership, the younger Heck moved to the Sweet Valley winery in Sandusky, and for six years made Ohio champagne.

In 1951, Adolf L. Heck came to California to succeed General John R. Deane as president of the Italian Swiss Colony, and his late brother Paul managed the Colony's Sonoma County winery at Asti. Then came the opportunity the Heck brothers had been waiting for: Anton (Tony) Korbel, less interested in champagne than in judging dog shows, was offering the Korbel vineyards and winery for sale. The brothers bought it, Paul took charge of the vineyards, and the youngest brother Ben became the sales manager. Adolf L., with his champagne-making experience in Germany, Missouri, and Ohio, became the president and winemaker of Korbel.

The Hecks enlarged the vineyards, bought the neighboring Santa Nella winery, and added more champagnes: Korbel Natural, which is bone-dry; Korbel Brut, which is almost dry; Extra Dry, sweeter but not as sweet as the Sec; and a sparkling Korbel Rosé, which is semi-dry. They also added a brandy that is distilled for them in the San Joaquin Valley, and an assortment of table wines. They installed a tasting room in an old railroad depot which Tony Korbel had bought for five dollars from the Northwestern Pacific in 1935.

More changes have taken place in later years. Allan Hemphill, the first enology graduate from Fresno State University, came in 1962 and took charge of production. Jim Huntsinger came six years later from Almadén and became Korbel's winemaker. Adolf L.'s son Gary grew up and joined the company as a vice president. The vineyards were replanted and expanded to 600 acres. A complex of new wine cellars and a brandy-blending plant were built in one of the older vineyards. The original brandy warehouse was converted into a wine shop, with a gay-nineties-style tasting room adjoining.

A machine was invented at Korbel that riddles (shakes) thousands of champagne bottles at once to send the sediment, formed by fermentation, down into the bottle necks; it is fascinating to watch. Another machine, invented in France, disgorges the bottles (removes the sediment) automatically. This enables Korbel to advertise that its champagnes are "fermented in *this* bottle," a slap at bottle-fermenting competitors who use the modern transfer method of disgorging.

Korbel has reduced its production of table wines since 1974. The five it now makes are sold only at the winery and in a few Northern California cities.

• 11 •

Climatically, the Russian River Valley equals the Sonoma and Napa Valleys as a potential premium wine district, with summer temperatures ranging from Region I to Region III. But except at Korbel and the Italian Swiss Colony, this valley until the late 1960s produced mostly ordinary grapes and bulk wines because those were what the winegrowers here knew how to produce and sell.

The wine boom set big and small investors scrambling to start new premium vineyards and wineries, and the valley shows a dramatic contrast between the old and the new.

In the village of Windsor, eight miles north of Santa Rosa, the 750,000-gallon Sonoma County Co-operative Winery still ferments the grapes of its farmer members into bulk wine that is shipped in tank trucks to the Gallo Winery at Modesto. The building is a relic of the past, the last of the statewide chain of wineries established by Kohler & Frohling, the greatest of early California wine firms, established in 1853 at Los Angeles by Charles Kohler and John Frohling, musicians from Germany. The company at one time owned wineries at Glen Ellen and in the Sacramento and San Joaquin Valleys, wine depots in New York, in the Montgomery Block of San Francisco, and the basement of the Los Angeles City Hall, and shipped California bulk wines to Europe, South America, the Orient, and Australia. In 1894, Kohler & Frohling was absorbed by the California Wine Association, which operated the cellar until Prohibition. The Co-op was organized in 1935 to provide a home for its members' crops.

Beside the Highway 101 freeway just north of the Windsor offramp is the Landmark Vineyards winery, an example of what is new. A Spanish-style mansion of the 1920s, reached through an avenue of giant cypresses, has been converted into a tasting room and office for the 14,000-gallon winery newly built in the rear. William Mabry III, a 1974 alumnus of the UC Davis wine school, is the winemaker and lives upstairs with his wife

Michele. Bill's father, a retired Air Force colonel, embarked in winegrowing in 1972, planting a hundred acres of premium grape varieties, some at his Sonoma home and some in the Alexander Valley. Then, from millionaire civic leader William Matson Roth, he bought the Windsor site, which was a prune orchard, and added a ten-acre patch of vines there. The first Landmark wines were Chardonnay, Pinot Noir, and Cabernet Sauvignon. They can be bought at the winery, but appointments are required for tasting and tours.

• 12 •

The main tourist attraction around Windsor is the 3-million-gallon Sonoma Vineyards winery, flanked by its vineyards, on the Old Redwood Highway east of the freeway. The main winery is shaped like a cross with four metal-roofed wings rising from the vineyard level to a high center structure that contains a tasting room, offices, and a rooftop promenade. On the north side is a landscaped amphitheater where benefit concerts, operas, and ballet performances are held.

Another name of this establishment is Windsor Vineyards, which is the label on the dozens of wines and champagnes it sells by mail to some half-million customers across the nation.

Sonoma and Windsor Vineyards is the creation of a retired professional dancer who likes to make wine and an advertising man who saw the first sparks of the table wine explosion. In 1960, when Rodney Duane Strong was thirty-three, he disbanded his Rod Strong Dance Quartet after performing on Broadway and at the Lido in Paris, "because I didn't want to be an old dancer." His grandparents had been winegrowers in Germany and he had caught the wine bug during his terpsichorean tours of Europe. In a century-old railroad men's boarding house on the waterfront of Tiburon, across the bay from San Francisco, Strong began bottling and selling bulk wine under the name of Tiburon Vintners. Four years later he was joined by New Yorker Peter Friedman, who had an idea that Americans would buy wine by mail if a winery would print their names on "personalized labels" on the bottles, with such legends as "Bottled Expressly for Tom and Mary Jones." Friedman's idea proved a sensational salesmaker, so they leased the old Monte Carlo vineyard and winery near the Co-op at Windsor. Strong began making wines there to supplement those they bought. They chose the name Windsor Vineyards for the mail-order wines. Mrs. Strong, the willowy former Charlotte Winson of

Red wine ages in barrels, then in bottles, in Sonoma Vineyards winery.

Guys and Dolls, turned an old farm cottage into their Windsor tasting room.

When the cruciform winery, named Sonoma Vineyards, was built in 1970, the national table-wine boom was reaching its peak. It was a year when to invest in a vineyard or winery seemed a quick way to get rich. The Sonoma-Windsor-Tiburon firm "went public," selling enough stock to plant five thousand more acres of vineyards. From six dollars a share in 1970, the stock rose to forty-one dollars by 1972.

The 1974 grape bust, caused by vineyard overplanting, caught Sonoma Vineyards over-extended, unable to pay its bills, and the price of its shares plummeted to seventy-five cents. Creditors brought in financial wizards, who bought stock in the company. Renfield Importers became a part owner when it took over sale of the Sonoma Vineyards wines.

Windsor Vineyard's mail-order business has continued booming, mainly with purchased wines. Rodney Strong, still the winemaker, makes four estate-bottled Sonoma Vineyards table wines, a fermented-in-bottle brut champagne, and twelve more premium and "mid-varietal"vintage-dated wines mostly bottled in magnum sizes. Two thousand of the company's acres are producing premium grapes. Business at the Tiburon tasting room, where it all started, is thriving, too. Sonoma-Windsor-Tiburon seems to have weathered the storm.

• 13 •

North of Sonoma Vineyards, Limerick Lane leads east across the freeway to the 28,000-gallon Sotoyome Winery, built in 1974 beside an old Zinfandel vineyard by former University of California history instructor William Chaikin and printer John Stampfli, who was trained in enology at the UC Davis wine school. The name refers to the Sotoyome land grant, named for the Indian tribe that once inhabited this part of the Russian River Valley. Dr. Chaikin plans to build a tasting room, but until it is ready will welcome visitors who phone ahead for an appointment to taste the vintage-dated Sotoyome Cabernet Sauvignon, Gamay, Zinfandel, and Chardonnay.

At the end of Grant Avenue two miles southeast of Healdsburg is the Cambiaso Winery, which Giovanni and Maria Cambiaso built on their hillside vineyard in 1934. Their son Joseph and daughters Rita and Theresa took it over in the 1940s and began replacing the Carignane vines with Cabernet Sauvignon. In 1972 they sold out to the Likitprakong family, distillers in Thailand, who quadrupled the winery capacity to 600,000 gallons with stainless steel tanks. The new enologist is Robert Fredson, a fourth-generation member of the Sonoma family that for almost a century has operated the Fredson winery on Dry Creek Road. Robert is a 1973 graduate of the enology course at Fresno State University. The Cambiaso wines range from Cabernet Sauvignon and Sauvignon Blanc in bottles and half gallons to burgundy, chablis, and rosé in gallon jugs. The winery is open to visitors daily except Sundays and holidays.

Between the Old Redwood Highway and the Russian River on the west are the 200-acre Foppiano Vineyard and million-gallon winery, which the descendants of John Foppiano from Genoa have owned since 1896. Louis Joseph Foppiano, the founder's grandson, switched during the 1960s from shipping bulk burgundy and chablis in tank cars to eastern bottlers to begin supplying "varietal" wines to other California wineries. He also opened a tasting room at the winery and discovered that visiting connoisseurs would gladly pay a dollar a bottle more for his Cabernet Sauvignon and Pinot Noir than for his burgundy made of Zinfandel. He sent his son Louis M. to Notre Dame to study business and son Rodney to Fresno State University to study viticulture and enology.

The fourth generation of Foppianos, now in charge, have replanted parts of the vineyard with additional noble grape varieties. Foppiano wines, always full-flavored, have added new delicacy and bouquet. The family still sells burgundy and chablis, but its varietal labels now bear vintage dates, "estate bottled," and the appellation "Russian River Valley."

• 14 •

From the Foppiano Winery it is a quarter mile north to Healdsburg, the wine capital of Sonoma County. Healdsburg has celebrated that fact since 1972 with its annual Russian River Wine Festival. On the festival day, a Saturday in mid-May, some twenty Sonoma wineries set up tables in the town plaza and offer samples to those who buy tickets. The ticket buyers later go on from the plaza to the nearby wineries' tasting rooms, where the sampling is free.

On Healdsburg Avenue a half-mile north of town is the venerable stone half-million-gallon Simi Winery, which has landscaped gardens, a picnic area, and a banquet room that can be reserved for catered luncheons and dinners. The story of Simi epitomizes the dramatic changes that have occurred in the Healdsburg area in less than a decade. The winery dates from 1876, when it was built by San Francisco wine dealers Giuseppe and Pietro Simi. They named it Montepulciano for the town in central Italy where they were born. It produced bulk wine before and following Prohibition, except during the Second World War wine shortage, when British winemaker George Remington took charge and bottled some prize-winning table and dessert wines and made bulk-process champagnes. Montepulciano was too tongue-twisting a name, so the wines were sold under the Hotel Del Monte label, then eventually were renamed Simi.

In 1970 this winery was a picture of neglect and disarray from its leaking roof down to the cobwebbed stacks of bottles, dating from the 1930s, in its cellar. That was the year when Russell Green, a former president of the Signal Oil Company, came seeking a home for the grapes he had begun planting eleven years before at his boyhood summer home in the neighboring

America's first woman college-trained head winemaker, Mary Ann Graf of the Simi Winery at Healdsburg, California, won her enology degree at UC Davis in 1965.

Alexander Valley. Green bought the winery from Giuseppe Simi's octogenarian daughter, Isabelle Simi Haigh. He repaired the roof, discarded the rusty crusher, installed new stainless steel tanks, and ripped out most of the old redwood vats to build a rustic tasting room of their staves. Green hired an outstanding team of winemakers, UC Davis-trained Mary Ann Graf and consulting enologist André Tchelistcheff, who soon began winning medals for the new Simi wines. Mary Ann is one of the few women winemakers in this country and as the first female member of the board of directors of the American Society of Enologists she ranks as the foremost of her sex. In 1973, Green won federal approval to use "Alexander Valley" as the appellation of origin on the labels of Simi wines.

The early 70s were years when emissaries of food and liquor companies roamed California valleys, boosting their multimillion offers to buy out old established wineries. Among them was Michael G. Dacres Dixon, chairman of Scottish & Newcastle Vintners, the American arm of a Scotland-based beer and whiskey empire. In 1974, Dixon bought the Simi winery from Green and contracted for the exclusive use of Green's grape crops for five years.

Another firm then seeking entry to the California wine business was Schieffelin & Company, the nearly two-century-old New York importing firm, which until then had never handled an American product. In 1976, Schieffelin became the third new owner of Simi Winery in six years, continuing Dixon as president. As an importer of prestigious European wines and spirits, Schieffelin ordered the Simi wine assortment slashed to remove lesser "varietals" and such semigeneric labels of European origin as burgundy and chablis. These discontinued wines were sold by the winery at such sacrifice prices that André Tchelistcheff joined the crowds to buy some at a dollar a bottle for himself.

What happened to Simi's stock of thirty- and forty-year-old wines? Russell Green had dumped those that spoiled, but had found some great reds bottled in English winemaker Remington's time. One 1935 Carignane had a bouquet so powerful that Green had Simi continue making wine of Carignane despite its reputation as one of the commonest of red-wine grapes. (But Schieffelin ordered it dropped from the Simi list.) Most of the fine Simi red wines of the 1930s and 1940s have been snapped up by connoisseurs and the few bottles left are not for sale.

The six-year transformation of Simi Winery was complete in all respects except one when I last stopped by in 1977. Eighty-five-year-old Isabelle Simi Haigh was still seated behind the counter in the tasting room, recalling the winery's history, each day from ten in the morning until closing time at five.

· 15 ·

When in 1959 Los Angeles oilman Russell Green planted his first fifty acres of vines in the Alexander Valley, there was only one winery in that ten-mile-long valley east of Healdsburg between the Russian River and Highway 128. Several wineries had operated in the area in the late 1880s and early 1900s, but most of the vineyards had been replaced during Prohibition by prune orchards and livestock farms. Since the wine revolution of the 1960s and 70s, most of the valley has become carpeted with vineyards, and by 1977 the number of wineries had increased to six.

The oldest winery, the Soda Rock cellar, dates from pre-Prohibition days. It made only bulk wines and is no longer active; other Sonoma County wineries use its tanks for storage. Abele Ferrari bought Soda Rock in 1925 and later was joined by his son-in-law, Leo Demostene. In 1973, Demostene's widow Rose and their children David, Edward, Rosalee, and Lucinda converted an old prune dehydrator into the attractive new 100,000-gallon Sausal Winery, named for a nearby creek. They equipped it with stainless steel and new oak casks and within a year had produced their first Zinfandel. David makes the wine, Edward cares for their 150 acres of vines, Rosalee is the chemist, and Lucinda runs the business.

While the Demostenes were starting their Sausal Winery, Harry (Hank) Wetzel III was still a year from winning his degree in enology at the UC Davis wine school. His father Harry Jr. was superintending construction of their 18,000-gallon Alexander Valley Vineyards winery, which was finished in time for the 1975 crush. Two years later the Wetzels released their first estate-bottled wines, White Riesling and Chardonnay. Their 1975 Cabernet Sauvignon, with twelve percent Merlot in the blend, was due in 1978.

Uphill from the Wetzels' winery are the adobe home and family graveyard of Cyrus Alexander, the Rocky Mountains trapper who came to Healdsbu4g in 1840 to manage the Sotoyome land grant for Captain Henry Fitch of San Diego, and for whom the valley is named.

Across the road and north of the Wetzels is the Johnson brothers' Rancho Sotoyome winery, also opened in 1975. Tom, Jay, and county supervisor Will Johnson salvaged equipment from older wineries to begin bottling wine in their rebuilt old barn. Their first "Johnson's Alexander Valley Wines" were fermented in a leased Healdsburg cellar where Tom, a veteran home winemaker, had worked for two years learning to make wine on a commercial scale. They also bought a huge theater pipe organ from a church near Sacramento to adorn their tasting room. There organist Bud Kurz plays for monthly open-house events, at one of which they hold an annual judging of homemade wines. Tom has replanted their forty-five-acre vineyard with additional premium grape varieties.

A quarter-mile southeast of the Wetzels, on former Berkeley mayor Wallace Johnson's 800-acre Redwood Ranch, is his revolutionary 40,000-gallon Field Stone Winery, bonded in 1977. All you can see of his winery is its front stone wall, in which there is an arched redwood door. All the rest, the fermenting and oak aging casks, the centrifuge and the bottling, are hidden inside a sylvan oak-bordered knoll.

What is revolutionary about the winery is not that it is underground—subterranean cellars are still common in Europe—but that it lacks either a crusher or a press. The grapes are both crushed and pressed in Johnson's vineyard. Only the juice reaches the winery minutes after the grapes are picked, "capturing the fresh grape fragrance," Wallace Johnson explains, "that otherwise is quickly lost."

Field Stone's winemaker is William Arbios, Hank Wetzel's classmate at UC Davis and the former assistant winemaker at the Château Souverain winery. He makes only white wines and rosés from Redwood Ranch Riesling, Gewürztraminer, Chenin Blanc, Cabernet Sauvignon, and Petite Sirah. Johnson hasn't yet invented a way to make red wines without fermenting the juice in contact with the grape pulp and skins, but he isn't ready to concede that it can't be done.

Crushing grapes in the vineyard is no longer very new, because Johnson added field-crushing equipment to his Upright mechanical harvester in 1969. The new invention is his traveling press, which applies gentle pressure to the crushed grapes and sends the juice to the winery, protected by a blanket of carbon dioxide, in a tank that follows the harvesting and field-crushing machine.

Born in Iowa to a family of Swedish immigrants, Johnson studied engineering at the California Institute of Technology and started his Upright Company to make portable scaffolds. In 1965 he switched to making harvesters because grapes were the only California crop not yet picked mechanically. Four years later he planted a 150-acre vineyard on his livestock ranch. The winery is still an experiment; he sells other wineries most of his grapes. His Upright harvesters, which straddle the rows of vines while flexible fingers strike the trellis wires causing the grapes to drop onto conveyors, are picking grapes in nine countries in both the northern and southern hemispheres.

From Alexander Valley Road three miles north of Healdsburg, a new two-lane private road winds uphill through oak groves to a champagne-yellow, red-tile-roofed château with red-shuttered windows edged in cut stone. The exterior suggests a Bordeaux château, though neither France nor any other winegrowing country has a winery quite like this. Inside are batteries of shiny temperature-controlled stainless steel fermenting tanks, rows of upright American and European oak casks, and thousands of new oak barrels, bungs at their sides, standing seven tiers high.

This and the 270-acre vineyard (four fifths Cabernet Sauvignon, one fifth Merlot) stretching north from Alexander Valley Road to Lytton Station Road comprise the Jordan Winery and Vineyard, which crushed its first 100,000-gallon vintage in 1976. The winery is built to hold a half-million gallons because four vintages must age here in oak and bottle to full maturity before the 1976 vintage of Jordan estate-bottled Cabernet Sauvignon will be released in 1980. There will be only this one Jordan wine.

Thomas Nicholas Jordan, Jr., Illinois-born Denver geologist, athletic, dark-haired, amiable, cigar-smoking friend of the Rothschilds, a director of the Banque National de Paris, world-traveled owner of the Filon Exploration Company, is an admirer of Bordeaux clarets. In 1970 he had decided to buy a château in Bordeaux when on one of his occasional visits to San Francisco he was discussing Bordeaux vintages with a waiter at Ernie's

Restaurant. The waiter asked whether he had tasted any California Cabernets. Jordan had not.

"When I had my first taste of a twelve-year-old private reserve Beaulieu Cabernet," says Jordan, "I realized I wouldn't have to cross the ocean to visit my château if I could build one in California; so that's what I've done."

Jordan tasted more California Cabernets with bottle age before he made up his mind. He consulted André Tchelistcheff, who had made the great Beaulieu wine, assigned Davis-trained J. Michael Rowan to plant his vineyard where there had been orchards of prunes, and chose as his winemaker another Davis graduate who had apprenticed and been trained at the Robert Mondavi Winery. Tall, charming, blue-eyed former English teacher Sally Jordan discussed with architect Robert Arrigoni and designer Richard Keith how a winery exterior could express the quality of a fine California Cabernet. The design finally chosen includes apartment suites at the north end of the winery to house distinguished visiting buyers of wine. Future plans still under discussion include a French restaurant and an *auberge* or inn.

The Jordans and their three children still live in Denver, but are planning to build a California home.

The decision to release no wine until it has been aged for four years was Jordan's because, he says, "All this will be for nothing unless we grow a great wine."

• 16 •

Westside Road takes you west under the freeway from Mill Street in Healdsburg and heads south along the west bank of the Russian River toward Guerneville. On your right a mile from the freeway is the 50,000-gallon Mill Creek Vineyards winery, a family operation of Charles and Vera Kreck, their sons, and daughters-in-law. They equipped a former cattle barn with stainless steel tanks and oak barrels in time to produce their first estate-bottled "varietal" wines in 1975. Son Bill cultivated the vineyard while son Bob helped consulting enologist Robert Stemmler, formerly of the Simi Winery, make the wine. Because of the white-wine boom, the Krecks tried during their second vintage to make a white wine of their Cabernet Sauvignon grapes, but the white juice unexpectedly picked up a reddish instead of a golden tinge, yet wasn't pink enough to be sold as rosé. California wine writer Jerry Mead happened by, tasted the wine, and at his suggestion they named it Cabernet Blush.

The vineyard a half-mile south belongs to Santa Rosa restaurateur Claus Neumann, who has the Krecks make wine from his grapes and bottle it under his Claus Vineyard label.

Five miles farther south, you will see a picturesque three-towered stone hop barn on your left. Its two lower floors contain Martha and Dr. Loyal Martin Griffin's little Hop Kiln Winery, a delightful stop. Noted physician-conservationist Griffin and his wife, a Missouri congressman's daughter who writes popular books for children, rebuilt the barn to preserve it as a state historical monument to Sonoma County's onetime hopgrowing industry, which died after the Second World War when American brewers cut down the hoppy bitterness of beers to please women buyers' sweet taste.

The Griffins bonded the Hop Kiln Winery in 1975 because their friends wanted to buy some of the homemade wines Dr. Griffin had been producing in the barn since he bought the surrounding sixty-five-acre Sweetwater Springs Vineyard seventeen years before. While awaiting delivery of a crusher-stemmer, the Griffins crushed their first commercial vintage the old-fashioned way with their bare feet. Their subsequent vintages are mostly estate-bottled "varietals," but they have two wines with original names. One is Sweetwater Springs "Marty Griffin's Big Red," made from four unidentified black grape varieties that have grown since the 1880s in one corner of the vineyard. Martha has given the name "One Thousand Flowers" to their White Riesling-Colombard blend. The Griffins live beside their much-photographed hop barn in a century-old Italianate Victorian house that they found in a town across the Russian River, bought and chainsawed into five pieces to be hauled and reassembled here.

Another mile south and uphill from the "River Bend Ranch" sign on your right is a onetime hop kiln that has lost its drying tower. This has been Davis Bynum's Winery since he moved in 1973 from his first one, started in the rear of a store near Berkeley eight years before. Bynum and his son Hampton make medal-winning Chardonnays, Pinot Noirs, and *flor* sherries and also a mead called Camelot. But they are most famous for their Bynum's Barefoot Burgundy, a pleasant young red that Davis originally named as a spoof on big wineries' fluffy advertisements. The name inspired a manufacturer to print millions of sweatshirts bearing the legend "Chateau La Feet." Davis Bynum regards his twenty-acre vineyard and 85,000-gallon winery as his hobbies, for winemaking was his hobby from boyhood until he quit his job on the San Francisco

Chronicle to start his first winery. At his new tasting room on Solano Avenue, north of Berkeley, he sells two-case "futures" of his aging vintage wines for delivery when the wines are ready to drink.

• 17 •

Offramps of the 101 freeway north from Healdsburg past Geyserville lead to many more wineries, both new and old. The Lytton Springs exit takes you west to an old fifty-acre Zinfandel and Petite Sirah vineyard at the intersection of Chiquita Lane. Some of the best Zinfandels sold in the early 1970s by the Ridge Vineyard winery of Cupertino were made of grapes from this Lytton Springs Vineyard. Then a group headed by Dee Sindt, editor of *Wine World* magazine, bought the vineyard and built the Lytton Springs winery across the road. Mississippi-born winemaker Bura Walters made the first vintage there in 1977.

The Independence Lane exit, farther north, leads west and uphill to the architecturally appealing 2.4 million-gallon Souverain Cellar which was designed to resemble a hop kiln, and to its Souverain Restaurant, from which you get an excellent view of the upper Alexander Valley to the east. In summer the fountain in front of the winery becomes a stage and the courtyard serves as an outdoor theater for dramatic and musical events.

Ownership of three separate wineries named Souverain has changed repeatedly since 1970. J. Leland Stewart, whom we shall meet in a later chapter, first gave the Souverain name to a winery east of St. Helena that has now become Burgess Cellars. A group of Napa Valley vineyard owners, who bought that winery from Stewart and sold it to Tom Burgess, built two entirely new Souverain wineries, naming this one Souverain of Alexander Valley and another, in the Napa Valley, Souverain of Rutherford. While this Souverain of Alexander Valley winery was being built during 1972, the Pillsbury flour-milling firm of Minneapolis ventured into the wine business, guided by the late Frank Schoonmaker, and bought both of the new Souverain wineries. Three years later, Pillsbury had lost millions on its wine venture and offered the two Souverains for sale. Owners of St. Helena's Freemark Abbey cellar bought Souverain of Rutherford and renamed it the Rutherford Hill Winery. Souverain of Alexander Valley was purchased in 1976 by North Coast Cellars, a group of 179 grape growers in Sonoma, Napa, and Mendocino Counties.

Souverain's Conegliano-trained winemaker William Bonetti, having made twenty-three vintages at three California wineries (Gallo, Cresta Blanca, Charles Krug) before he came to Souverain in 1972, seems unconcerned by ownership changes. Choosing the best grapes grown in 179 different vineyards, he is making the best wines of his entire career. Souverain wines became available nationally in 1977 through the century-old New York importing firm of Julius Wile & Sons, which had not marketed a California wine since it sold those of the Fountain Grove Vineyard during the Second World War.

Across the freeway from Souverain, Independence Lane leads to the 140-acre Trentadue Vineyard and the 50,000-gallon Trentadue Winery. Leo and Evelyn Trentadue grew grapes in the Santa Clara Valley before they came to Sonoma County and built their winery and tasting room in 1969. Their labels display the number "32," which is trentadue in Italian.

Back on freeway 101, a short drive north takes you to the Canyon Road exit, where you go west and take a right turn on Chianti Road to the 2-million-gallon Geyser Peak Winery on the hill to your left. The Joseph Schlitz Brewing Company of Milwaukee has transformed this old wood and field stone building into a château-like showplace since buying it in 1972. The original structure dates from 1880, when one Augustus Quitzow built it as both a winery and a brandy distillery. There were several later owners until Dante and William Bagnani bought it after Repeal to make wine vinegar, which they sold under their Four Monks brand. For years a pixyish sign facing the road read: "Sorry—no retail sales—we drink it all." The brewers of Schlitz beer spared no expense in making their entry into the wine business architecturally attractive. They built a visitor center with stained-glass windows, a flagstone terrace, and a fountain guarded by high black iron gates. Geyser Peak now hosts popular brown-bag opera performances there in conjunction with summer Sunday winery tours.

Veteran winemaker Alfred Huntsinger and his assistant Armand Bussone came to Geyser Peak from Almadén, where for a decade they had made notable wines and champagnes. Bordeaux-born, UC Davis-trained viticulturist Jean-Marie Martin has planted several hundred acres of additional Geyser Peak vineyards in the Russian River and Sonoma Valleys. Geyser Peak's wine assortment ranges from vintage-dated "varietals" under its Voltaire and Geyser Peak brands to generically-labeled Summit brand table wines in bottles and jugs, and includes "Wine Sellar" plastic bags of table wines with dispensing nozzles projecting from the cartons in which the bags are packed. A trial cuvée of bottle-fermented brut champagne is due for introduction in 1979.

Chianti Road also leads to electrical engineer Keith Nelson's 7,000-gallon hilltop winery named Vina Vista for the view it commands of the Russian River. A short distance farther, beside the onetime Chianti railroad station, is a pre-Prohibition patch of Sangiovese or San Gioveto, the authentic Italian Chianti grape. The station, transplanted from the nearby railroad, serves as the office of the Seghesio family's vineyards and wineries at Healdsburg and Cloverdale. Eugene Seghesio has replanted half of his 300 acres with superior grape varieties and supplies "varietal" wines in tank trucks to well-known premium wineries.

On Canyon Road a mile west of the freeway is the 400,000-gallon Pedroncelli Brothers' Winery. This was one of the first in northern Sonoma County to change from bulk to bottled premium wines. John and James Pedroncelli took over their father's hillside vineyard and small wooden cellar in 1955, when John completed a short course in enology at the University. In the following year, the brothers bottled three of their wines and entered them in the California State Fair wine competition. To their surprise, all three won medals, silvers for their burgundy and rosé and bronze for their Zinfandel. This attracted the notice of Bordeaux-born San Francisco wine merchant and importer Henry Vandervoort, who was looking for a new supply of California bulk table wines good enough to bottle for his restaurant customers under their private labels. The Pedroncelli wines bottled by Vandervoort sold well, so the brothers began bottling some under their own name. When Vandervoort saw them making their rosé entirely out of Zinfandel, he suggested they give it a varietal name. In 1958 it became California's first Zinfandel Rosé to win commercial fame. Five years later, they made a cask of Cabernet Sauvignon so outstanding that Vandervoort had them set it aside for extra aging and bottle it under two-inch corks with his own label as "An Importer's Choice." The Pedroncellis found that finer wines are easier to sell, and have doubled their father's original sixty acres with such classic varieties as Cabernet Sauvignon and Pinot Noir. They have added an extra cellar for aging wines in oak casks, and a tasting room, and they continue winning awards each year at the Pomona fair.

• 18 •

Almost ten miles of vineyards line the Dry Creek Valley from the projected Warm Springs Dam northwest of Geyserville south to Healdsburg, where the creek joins the Russian River. If you enter this valley on Dry Creek Road from the Healdsburg area, you will see a mass of stainless steel tanks on a hill to your right after you pass Lytton Springs Road. They are part of the two-million-gallon Frei Brothers' Winery, which dates from 1880 but which since the 1950s has produced table wines for shipment in tank trucks to the Gallo Winery at Modesto. Gallo bought the winery from the Frei family in 1976.

Across Dry Creek Road from the Frei Brothers' driveway, Lambert Bridge Road leads west to the 45,000-gallon Dry Creek Vineyard winery. A visit to France in 1970 with his wife Gail inspired David Stare, a civil-engineering graduate from the Massachusetts Institute of Technology, with the idea of some-day owning a Médoc-style winegrowing estate. The Stares came to California after a disappointing try at growing French hybrid grapes in Maryland. David took graduate courses in viticulture at UC Davis, bought this Dry Creek Valley site, and planted fifty acres of premium grapes on the former prune orchard. In 1972 he built the first wing of his château, bought grapes for his first few vintages, and within three years was producing medal-winning wines. The Stares welcome visitors to their winery. There is space for tasting in the entrance, where you can buy their premium wines and also some inexpensive blends under their Idlewood brand.

Across the road from the Dry Creek Vineyard, another winery was being built in 1978 by German-born consulting enologist Robert Stemmler beside his home.

Cross Lambert Bridge and drive a short distance south on West Dry Creek Road to another premium winery, built in 1976. Gerard Barnes Lambert, a scion of the St. Louis pharmaceutical firm (Listerine) Lamberts, designed his 40,000-gallon cellar himself especially to produce estate-bottled Cabernet Sauvignon and Chardonnay from his eighty-acre vineyard, planted seven years before. To avoid confusion about which was here first, he named the winery Lambert Bridge instead of for himself. Lambert and his wife Margaret live across the road on a hill in which they plan to construct aging tunnels. Their wines are aged in 135-gallon puncheons of European oak. The Lamberts' winemaker, Ed Samperton, formerly worked at Dr. Mowbray's winery in Maryland, also at a winery in Morocco, and for two years at the Dry Creek Vineyard with David Stare.

A short distance north of Lambert Bridge, you come to the Rafanelli winery at your left. Americo Rafanelli made bulk wine at an old winery in Healdsburg until that winery was torn down to make room for a new school. Realizing that premium wines were replacing the bulk product, Rafanelli added more Cabernet Sauvignon and Gamay Beaujolais to his twenty-five-acre vineyard. Then he converted a two-story storage barn at his home into a 10,000-gallon premium winery, and began producing only estate-bottled, vintage-dated red wines.

Four miles farther north, where West Dry Creek Road dead-ends at Peña Creek, young Stanford business school graduate Louis Preston and his wife Susan installed modern winemaking equipment in a former prune dehydrator and opened the 5,000-gallon Preston Winery in 1975. While managing his family's orchards, Preston had become fascinated with wine. He devoted a year to part-time study of viticulture and enology before embarking on his winegrowing career. He has planted forty acres of premium varieties and is keeping twenty acres of old Zinfandel vines.

• 19 •

The Italian Swiss Colony at Asti, four miles southeast of Cloverdale, is huge, historic, and unique. More people visit this winery—400,000 a year—than any other in the world, because it borders the main tourist route between the Pacific Northwest and California, US 101, and signs for miles beckon them to stop. Costumed guides show crowds daily through its 8-million-gallon forest of redwood and steel tanks, then usher them into the big Swiss chalet tasting hall to sample the vast assortment of wines now sold under the Italian Swiss name.

Its early history is that of a philanthropic farming venture, started by San Francisco grocer-turned-banker Andrea Sbarboro in 1880 to settle penniless Italian and Swiss immigrant farmers on land where they could support themselves by growing grapes. Each worker would be given board, room, and wine for his daily use and would be paid monthly wages of thirty-five dollars, but five dollars would be deducted each month for the purchase of stock in the Colony, which would make him an independent vineyard owner in twenty-five years. Vines were planted, and the place was named Asti for the resemblance of the hills to those around Asti and Canelli in the Italian Piedmont. The colonists, however, refused to allow the deduction from their wages; they preferred dollars in hand to independence in the future. Sbarboro accepted defeat, and the Colony became a private vineyard venture.

A winery was built in 1887, but the first vintage turned to vinegar. Sbarboro then persuaded one of the Colony's original supporters, San Francisco druggist Pietro C. Rossi, to take charge. A graduate in pharmacy of the University of Turin, Rossi knew the principles of winemaking, and under him the Colony prospered for two decades. Before the turn of the century Asti wines were winning medals for excellence in Europe and America and were being shipped in barrels to Europe, South America, China, and Japan. The Colony acquired more vineyards and wineries at nearby Fulton and Sebastopol, at Clayton in Contra Costa County, and at Madera, Kingsburg, and Lemoore in the San Joaquin Valley.

During a price war in 1897, Rossi kept surplus Sonoma wine off the market by building at Asti what was then the world's biggest underground wine tank. Made of concrete, it held 300,000 gallons. Its completion before the vintage was celebrated with dancing inside the tank to the music of a military band. The tank is still in use today.

Sbarboro and Rossi erected elegant villas for their families and entertained famous personages from around the world. In 1907, the Colony built its famous "church shaped like a wine barrel," the El Carmelo Chapel, on land donated by the Archbishop of San Francisco. When Rossi's twin sons, Edmund and Robert, won their science degrees at the University of California, the family celebrated with a trip through Europe. While in France, Pietro Rossi met champagne maker Charles Jadeau of Saumur and persuaded him to come to Asti. Two years later, Jadeau's Golden State Extra Dry Champagne won the grand prix at the Turin international exposition.

Tipo Chianti red and white, bottled in raffia-covered Italian *fiaschi*, were the Colony's most popular wines, but the Italian Government objected to an American wine being called chianti. In 1910 the Colony renamed the wines "Tipo Red" and "Tipo White," not to please Italy, but to stop other wineries from calling their wines "Tipo." This four-letter word in Italian means "type" or "imitation," but in one of the quirks of wine nomenclature, it has become the American name for any wine in a chianti flask. The original Tipo Red was a tannic, long-lived wine unlike Italian chiantis, which are softened by blending white grapes with red. The 1914 Tipo, which was served at a Wine and Food Society banquet in the San Francisco Stock

Exchange Club in 1936, was one of the best pre-Prohibition California wines.

Pietro Rossi was killed in a horse and buggy accident in 1911. Two years later, the Italian Swiss Colony was taken over by the California Wine Association. In 1920 came the next disaster, Prohibition. Sbarboro had fought the Drys to the last. His solution for intemperance was to encourage the drinking of wine instead of hard liquor. Chronic drunkards, he said, should be jailed for thirty days and given dry wine with their meals, and if not cured should be given the same treatment for sixty days more. His disparagement of liquor so annoyed some whiskey distillers that they attempted a boycott of the Colony's wines.

During Prohibition Edmund and Robert Rossi with vineyard superintendent Enrico Prati bought back the Colony from the CWA and supplied grapes, juice, and concentrate to home winemakers until Repeal. The Rossi twins foresaw the failure of Prohibition, and it was they who in 1931 led the old-time California winegrowers in forming the Grape Growers League, which became the Wine Institute three years later.

During the years before the Second World War, the Italian Swiss Colony under the Rossis became the third largest wine company in the nation, with its La Paloma Winery near Fresno using the surplus grapes of Joseph Di Giorgio's vast vineyards in the San Joaquin Valley. When the whiskey distillers invaded the wine industry during the war, National Distillers bought the Colony and added another winery, Shewan-Jones, at Lodi. Thence came the French-sounding name, Lejon, for the Colony's brandy and champagnes; Lejon is a contraction of the name of Lee Jones, the kindly, crusty former revenue inspector who founded Shewan-Jones.

When the Rossi brothers retired, Edmund became the manager of the Wine Advisory Board and guided its national program of wine education until 1960. And the brothers' sons are still concerned with the making of Italian Swiss wines; Edmund, Jr., does research on new products, and Robert, Jr., is in charge of production.

The story of the Colony's purchase by Louis Petri and then by Heublein, and of the appearance of its strange new "pop" wines, which are made at Madera, will be told later. The huge winery at Asti now mainly bottles brandies and makes mostly the Colony's "varietal" table wines. It also again makes Tipo, which has regained some of its old-time flavor, but more for sentimental reasons than for sales, because at today's cost of labor the hand-wrapped Tipo bottle costs more than the wine inside. All Italian Swiss wines except Tipo now come in screw-capped bottles. This is a departure from custom for varietally-named wines. Most wines with grape-name labels come in bottles with straight corks.

• 20 •

The next offramp north of Asti, marked Dutcher Creek Road, leads to the 150,000-gallon Rege winery, where tasting is offered but there is no tour. The Reges make mainly jug wines for restaurants and for the family trade in San Francisco, where they have a retail store.

Hiatt Road, from the frontage road a mile north of the Reges, leads west to San Francisco psychiatrist Douglass Cartwright's 4,000-gallon Jade Mountain Winery and vineyard. The place is named for the mass of unpolished jade Dr. Cartwright once dreamed of finding, but never found, on Mount Alice nearby. The gate to the winery is kept locked except when the doctor, his psychologist wife Lillian, and their four children are there. Their first estate-bottled wine, a 1973 Cabernet Sauvignon aged in European oak, was released in 1977.

Downhill from the Cartwrights, a sign facing Hiatt Road from an eight-acre patch of Chardonnay vines reads "Icaria Vineyard." This sign, and the name of Icaria Creek on the map of northern Sonoma County, are the sole visible reminders that a communistic colony of French winegrowers operating five wineries flourished along this road from the 1880s until the early years of Prohibition. The Icarians who settled in Sonoma County were remnants of the utopian communistic sect that Etienne Cabet led in 1849 from France to Nauvoo, Illinois, where as related in an earlier chapter, they planted vineyards and continued producing wine long after Cabet abandoned the Nauvoo Icarian colony in 1856. San Franciscans Russell and Catherine Clark named their vineyard for the Icarians to preserve this long-forgotten chapter of Sonoma County's winegrowing history.

There were dozens more wineries around Cloverdale before Prohibition, but this northern Sonoma community forgot its winegrowing heritage during the dry years and began to celebrate an annual citrus fair. There again is an active winery in Cloverdale, Bandiera Wines on Cherry Creek Road. Marc Black and Chris Bilbro, the late Emil Bandiera's grandson, have installed stainless steel tanks in the old cellar and have introduced a new assortment of varietally labeled, vintage-dated wines.

• 21 •

Three miles beyond Cloverdale, still following the Russian River, you enter Mendocino, northernmost of the important coastal wine counties, where lumbering is still the principal industry. Formerly Mendocino, like northern Sonoma, produced mainly bulk table wines, but with the accelerated planting of superior grape varieties since the 1960s, it has become one of the premium wine districts of the state.

There were almost nine thousand acres of vines in the county in 1977, a third more than a decade before. Most of the vineyards are in the Ukiah, Redwood, McDowell, and Feliz Creek valleys, where the climate is Region III, but newer plantings have sprouted west of the mountains around Philo and Boonville in the Anderson Valley along the Navarro River, which is classed as Region I. There is a young Johannisberg Riesling vineyard at Hearst on the Eel River east of Willits, and six hundred acres have been planted in Potter Valley, protected by sprinklers from frost.

Mendocino has eight wineries, of which the best known is the million-gallon Parducci Wine Cellars, situated west of the 101 freeway three miles north of Ukiah. Adolph Parducci opened this winery at the repeal of Prohibition, selling most of his wine to the roadside trade and shipping the rest in tank trucks to vintners in the San Joaquin Valley. In 1964 his sons John and George ventured to enter the State Fair competition with a fresh, fruity dry wine of French Colombard, a name that had not appeared on a California label before. It was awarded a silver medal, and mail orders for Parducci wines began coming from Bay Area gourmets. When the sons took over the business, they began planting the family vineyard with premium varieties, planted more in the Talmage district, and embarked on a long-range program of producing premium wines.

In 1973, several thousand California school teachers, investors in the Teachers Management Institute, bought majority ownership of the winery, but wisely kept their partners, the Parducci brothers, in charge of producing the wines. With the new capital thus provided, the Parduccis enlarged the winery and built a Mediterranean-style hospitality building and tasting room with space for exhibits of local art and an adjoining picnic area that visiting groups can book in advance.

An innovator in winemaking, John Parducci is aging some of his best red wines entirely in stainless steel tanks instead of in oak. He thinks aging of wines in wood hides the varietal flavors of grapes and is overdone, especially in France. He concedes that a Cabernet Sauvignon that is not stored in oak barrels lacks complexity, but says "the complexity will come with age in the bottle, when the tannins start breaking down." However, while waiting for time to prove him right or wrong, John continues aging some lots of Cabernet, Pinot Noir, Petite Sirah, and Carignane in American oak barrels for those buyers who appreciate the complexity and aging potential contributed by aging in wood. All Parducci wines are now vintage-dated, including burgundy, chablis, and rosé in 1½-liter jugs.

Across the freeway from Parducci, on Brush Street, there stood until recently a winery that represented the past of Mendocino wines. It was built in 1910 by the French American Wine Company; then during the dry era it produced a famous grape concentrate named Caligrapo for home winemaking. At Repeal it made the California Grape Products Company's Victor Mendocino Zinfandel that was popular in New York City, and in the 1940s it became the property of Garrett of New York State, whose name was still displayed on the building until it was destroyed in the mid-1970s.

On State Street north of Ukiah is the home winery and tasting room of the Cresta Blanca Wine Company, whose name has had varied prominence for a century in the history of premium-priced California wines. This 1½-million-gallon cellar was built by the Mendocino Growers Co-operative in 1946, then became the Mendocino winery of Guild Wineries and Distilleries of Lodi and for a decade produced the best of the Guild's assortment of table wines. When the Guild in 1971 purchased the famous Cresta Blanca name from Schenley Distillers, the original Cresta Blanca winery at Livermore had been closed for several years. Though owned by the Guild, Cresta Blanca then was made a separate entity, and the Ukiah cellar became its named winery, producing some seventeen premium table wines from Mendocino, Sonoma, and Napa County grapes. Two of the wines made here by North Carolina-born, UC Davis-trained enologist Gerald Furman—Zinfandel and Petite Sirah—have won national acclaim as best buys among California premium reds. Displayed in the tasting room is the complete Cresta Blanca assortment of table, dessert wines, bottle-fermented champagnes, and brandy, more than half of which are produced in other parts of the state.

Also on State Street, adjoining the freeway where Highway 20 takes off north of Calpella, is the Mendocino County winery built in 1972 by the Weibel family of Alameda County to process the grapes from their 250 acres of Mendocino and Sonoma vineyards. The wines made here are transported in bulk to the Weibel winery at Mission San Jose for finishing and bottling. Beside this Mendocino winery is an elaborate tasting room shaped like an upturned champagne glass, in which the dozens of Weibel wines and champagnes are displayed.

In a secluded western arm of nearby Redwood Valley, reached by Uva Drive and Bel Arbres Road, is the Fetzer Vineyards winery. Five buildings of a homemade château design stand in a parklike setting of lovely vineyards against the spectacular backdrop of heavily wooded Black Hill. Visitors are welcome, but no sampling is offered here; you can taste the Fetzer wines at their tasting room in Hopland.

Bernard and Kathleen Fetzer bought the property in 1957, a two-mile-long ranch with vines a century old. They moved into the biggest building, an early-day stagecoach stop, with their five daughters and six sons, their future vineyard and winery staff. Taught winegrowing in his youth by his father and German grandfather, who had a Labrusca vineyard in Lancaster County, Nebraska, Fetzer replanted 150 acres with premium varieties, principally Cabernet Sauvignon, Sémillon, and Sauvignon Blanc. He sold his first crops to amateur winemakers, shipping both grapes and juice by air freight as far as the Atlantic Coast. Meanwhile, he built the winery and equipped it with temperature-controlled stainless steel fermenters, bottling equipment from Germany, and 200 Nevers oak casks from Bordeaux. It was finished in time to ferment the 1968 vintage. The first Fetzer Vineyard wines had too much European oak flavor, but this was corrected during the next few years. Each bottle, "100% varietal," is proudly labeled "Mendocino" because, Fetzer says, "this county has the best climate in California and our wines eventually will put Napa County in second place." His best wines thus far are his Zinfandels and Cabernets, which have won top acclaim in some blind tastings against French clarets and other California reds. Nine of the eleven Fetzer offspring still help run the place. John, at the age of thirty, was promoted to head winemaker, and Jim, five years younger, now manages the vineyards.

Mendocino County's newest wine district, the Anderson Valley, is across the hills from Ukiah on the Navarro River, only twelve miles from the Pacific Ocean. In this Region I climate, three small winegrowing estates clustered along Highway 128 three miles beyond the village of Philo are producing some extraordinary table wines.

First to open a winery here were Wilton (Tony) Husch, a former San Francisco city planner, and Gretchen, his talented artist wife. They planted twenty acres of premium varieties in 1968 and three years later made their first Gewürztraminer and Chardonnay. Gretchen welcomes visitors to their rustic tasting room, where she sells their four estate-bottled, vintage-dated wines and also her own watercolor landscape paintings.

The Edmeades Vineyard winery opened a year after the Husches and has been enlarged to 20,000 gallons since UC Davis-trained Jed Steele became the winemaker and Edward (Ted) Bennett became Deron Edmeades' partner in 1975.

Bennett, who sold his stereo business in Berkeley to become a winegrower, has also started his own Navarro River vineyard and 4,000-gallon winery across the road from Edmeades. He has joined with Edmeades in opening a tasting room in the coastal town of Mendocino and in selling their wines jointly under a label that reads "Mendocino Wine Guild."

• 22 •

The wine awakening of America has revived vine-planting in neighboring Lake County, which has a glamorous but long-forgotten winegrowing past. From less than 300 acres in 1965, vineyards in this county multiplied to 2,500 acres by 1977 while groups of farmers laid plans to build wineries and to promote Lake County wines.

Before Prohibition, Lake County had thirty-three wineries and 1,000 acres of vines. Among the county's famous winegrowers were California's first chief justice, Serranus Clinton Hastings, who owned the Carsonia Vineyard and Champagne Cellars at Upper Lake; Colonel Charles Mifflin Hammond, whose Ma Tel Vineyard at Nice on Clear Lake produced wines that won awards at the Paris Exposition in 1900; and the English actress Lily Langtry, who brought a *vigneron* from Bordeaux to tend her vineyard near Middletown and bottled wines with her portrait on the labels, but was prevented from selling them when Prohibition came in 1920.

At Repeal in 1933, only 600 acres of vines, mostly Zinfandels, remained in the county. The grapes were being sold to the leading wineries in neighboring Mendocino, Napa, and Sonoma. John Parducci, who thinks Lake County black grapes are among the best in the nation, has often sold wines labeled Parducci Lake County Cabernet Sauvignon.

The new Lake County vineyards are almost entirely of red wine grapes, principally Cabernet Sauvignon, followed in acreage by Zinfandel, Gamay, Merlot, and Petite Sirah. They are mainly situated in the valleys surrounding nineteen-mile-long Clear Lake and around lofty Mount Konocti. The climate at the average 1,300-foot elevation ranges from Region II to above Region III. Overhead sprinklers protect most of the vines from spring and fall frosts. Some of the oldest and newest plantings extend south beyond Middletown almost to the border of Napa County.

Lake County again has a winery, the first built in the county since the Prohibition era. It is the 3,000-gallon Lower Lake Winery on Highway 29 a mile south of the town of Lower Lake. Alhambra orthopedic surgeon Harry Stuermer and his wife Marjorie financed the redwood building, its stainless steel tanks and oak barrels for their son Daniel, his wife Betty, Dan's sister Harriet and her husband Tom Scavone. Dan, a chemist at the Lawrence Radiation Laboratory in Livermore, is the winemaker. The winery was finished in time to crush the 1977 vintage, twenty tons of local red grapes, to be aged and bottled for sale in 1980.

Humboldt County, north of Mendocino and Lake, thus far has only a few acres of grapes, but has three wineries of a few thousand gallons each around Eureka, the county seat. Dr. J. Roy Wittwer's cellar is in the city; oceanography instructor Robert Hodgson's is at Fieldbrook, and Dean Williams's is at McKinleyville. Hodgson and Williams have an acre or two of vines each, but most wines made in Humboldt County thus far have been made of Napa County grapes.

Professor Albert Winkler, the University of California viticulturist, searching for potential new premium grape districts, has found climates favorable for winegrowing in eastern Humboldt, around Alderport and Blocksburg. Dr. Winkler suggests that "a real adventurer might find it interesting" to plant vines on some of the slopes near the Hoopa Indian Reservation around Weitchpec, the steelhead fishermen's paradise on the upper Klamath River.

Someday the north coast wine district may stretch northward beyond Mendocino and Lake for another hundred miles.

14

Napa, the Winiest County

NAPA COUNTY, separated from Sonoma on the west by a spur of the Mayacamas mountain range, is the winiest county in the United States. It has sixty-six bonded wine cellars and 24,000 acres of vineyards, almost as many acres as Sonoma, which is twice Napa's size.

The Napa Valley, where most of the county's vineyards and wineries are, is only one to five miles in width and thirty-five miles long. Outside the town centers, this valley is an almost unbroken expanse of grapevines, a scene that is idyllic and unique.

Visitors come here from all over the world. Highway 29, which traverses the valley, is known as "The Wine Road," and it merits the name. On one eleven-mile stretch there are ten wineries, almost one per mile, which welcome the public to tour their cellars and taste their wines. Tourists' cars on the road are bumper-to-bumper on an average weekend. The visitors listen to the lectures the winery guides give, sip the samples offered afterward, and make purchases of the wines they like best. Some of the guests make a day of it, moving from one winery to the next and the next, until the tasting rooms close at four in the afternoon. (Eighteen Napa wineries now offer tasting; thirty-five receive visitors by appointment only; the rest are mostly production or storage cellars closed to the public.) Some winery owners say they may someday begin to charge for parking, or even begin closing on weekends, in order to reduce the size of the crowds.

Meanwhile the fame of Napa wines is spreading, in gourmet publications, in travel magazines, in the new wine books, on select wine lists. But except for the motorized crowds, this is really a repetition of their history, for Napa wines first became famous almost a century ago.

• 2 •

The Napa River, Napa County, and Napa city are named for the Napa Indians, one of the so-called Digger tribes who once lived there. "Napa" is said to mean "plenty" or "homeland," but some early records say it was originally the Indians' word for fish, which abounded then in the streams and supplemented their diet of roots, seeds, grasshoppers, and worms.

Some five thousand Indians inhabited the county before white settlers came from Sonoma during the 1830s. Forty years later, smallpox and bloody wars with the newcomers had reduced the Indians' numbers to scarcely a score. The wholesale slaughter of the Indians is commemorated in the grisly name that was given in 1839 to the Rancho Carne Humana land grant south of Calistoga. *Carne humana* is Spanish for human flesh.

From Sonoma, the first settlers brought the Mission grape to Napa. In 1836, George Calvert Yount, the North Carolinian trapper and explorer, built his fortified log blockhouse two miles north of present-day Yountville and two years later planted Mission vines he brought from the Sonoma vineyard of General Mariano Vallejo. Yount's first vintage could have been in 1841. There is additional evidence that wine was being made at several locations in Napa County during the 1840s, but the earliest records available show Yount producing 200 gallons annually by 1844. Planting of the better imported European grape varieties was begun about 1852 by William and Simpson Thompson on their Suscol land grant south of Napa city. In 1859, Samuel Brannan, the ex-Mormon millionaire of San Francisco, purchased three square miles at Calistoga and began planting choice cuttings he had collected on a tour through Europe.

Robert Louis Stevenson, honeymooning in the valley and writing his *Silverado Squatters* in 1880, described the Napa vintners' search for the best vineyard sites: "One corner of land after another is tried with one kind of grape after another," he wrote. "This is a failure; that is better; a third best. So, bit by bit, they grope about for their Clos Vougeot and Lafite . . . and the wine is bottled poetry."

By the late 1800s there were 4,000 acres of vines and 142 wineries in Napa County. In Napa city, the rivershore was lined with wineries, such as the Uncle Sam and Napa Valley cellars, from which wine was barged to San Francisco, much of it for shipment around Cape Horn to Atlantic ports. Connoisseurs in

New York and San Francisco were already serving wines from the To Kalon Vineyard of Hamilton Crabb near Oakville, from the Inglenook Vineyard of Captain Niebaum at Rutherford, and from the vineyards of Charles Krug and Jacob Schram at St. Helena and Calistoga, to mention a few.

Napa vineyards covered 18,000 acres in 1891. Since then, like a magic green carpet, they have shrunk dramatically and spread repeatedly in response to alternating plagues and booms.

The phylloxera plague, which had begun a decade earlier, devastated all but 3,000 acres before 1900, but during the following decade nearly half of the dead vineyards were replanted with vines grafted on resistant roots.

Napa again had almost 10,000 acres in 1920, when an even worse plague—Prohibition—struck. It did not destroy the vineyards, but economics compelled the growers to graft over their Cabernet, Pinot, and Riesling vines to the tough-skinned varieties that were preferred by the buyers of grapes shipped east for homemade and bootleg wines. Repeal in 1933 was a disappointment to the Napa winegrowers, too, because it brought little demand for their dry table wines. There still were only 11,500 acres of vines in the county by 1965.

Then the wine boom reached its height, and vines began to spread throughout the valley again. As vintners raised their offers for "varietal" grapes, growers grafted back their vineyards from shipping varieties to the noble Cabernets, Rieslings, and Pinots. The growers started buying sprinkler systems and $6,000 wind machines to guard their vines from frostbite on chilly spring nights. You now see more of these huge fans in the Napa Valley than in any other vineyard district in the world. When disastrous frosts hit the coast counties in late April of 1970, the wind machines throbbed and smudge pots burned all night—much to the annoyance of those valley residents who do not grow grapes—and saved half of the crop. The least loss, incidentally, was in those vineyards protected by sprinklers, which kept the vines coated with a protective film of ice.

As the planting fever reached a climax in the late '60s, scores of Napa prune orchards were ripped out and replaced with wine grapes. New vineyards also sprang up in the mountains west and east of the valley, on slopes that had been bare of vines since the phylloxera epidemic eighty years before. A dozen pre-Prohibition Napa wineries meanwhile were refurbished and reopened for business. Twenty-three entirely new wineries were built in the county between 1970 and 1977, and at least five more were in the planning stage. Giant conglomerates began buying up the old established Napa wineries, but most of them, enjoying their new-found prosperity and proud of their family histories, turned down multimillion-dollar offers to sell.

Vineyard plantings in Napa County have doubled since the mid-1960s and may soon exceed 25,000 acres. But not by much, for that is all the space left in the county with the soil, drainage, and climatic conditions considered suitable for the commercial cultivation of wine grapes.

A bitter struggle has raged for a decade to protect this open space from urban sprawl, which already has wiped out many fine vineyards in the other counties neighboring San Francisco Bay. When in 1968 the Napa Board of Supervisors blocked the subdividers' bulldozers by enacting a minimum twenty-acre agricultural preserve zoning law,* the land-development interests challenged the law in the courts. The Supervisors also compelled the state highway division to reroute a projected new freeway that would have cut a six-lane swath through the valley's main vineyard areas. While these battles dragged on, alarmed conservationists came up with an idea to save the vineyards if all other measures fail. They hoped to persuade the Federal Government to designate the Bay Area grape-growing districts as a National Vineyard, like the National Parks.

• 3 •

To get acquainted with Napa wines, you should tour the vineyards along the side roads and in the hills as well as those along the highway before you join the crowds in the tasting rooms. You will find that Napa, like Sonoma and Mendocino, has many climatically different winegrowing districts.

A striking example is the Carneros ("sheep" in Spanish) district, through which you pass when driving east from Sonoma on Highway 12-121. You enter the Napa Valley at its lower end. The vineyards here are close to San Pablo Bay. Because the Carneros is cooled in summer by winds and fogs from the salty bay, it is called the burgundy district of Napa County; its climate is rated as "low Region I." Such burgundian grape varieties as Chardonnay and Pinot Noir are said to develop higher flavors here—at least one more point of acidity

---

*Under this Napa County law, no house may now be erected in the main vineyard areas on any parcel of land smaller than twenty acres. Another measure that is helping to protect the vineyards is the state's 1965 Land Conservation Act. Under the state law, landowners who pledge to use their property only for agriculture for at least ten years can have it taxed on its value for farmland instead of at its higher value for business or for subdivisions. This is called "greenbelting the land."

in balance with their sugar content when ripe—than when grown farther up the valley. Vintners whose main vineyards are in those warmer areas have acquired lands in this district to grow these two grape varieties in particular. On the other hand, Cabernet Sauvignon, a Bordeaux variety, fails to ripen fully in some of the Carneros vineyards except in unusually warm years, although when it does reach full ripeness here, it makes a superlative wine.

There is only one producing winery in the Carneros, the new 35,000-gallon Carneros Creek cellar on Dealy Lane, just north of Highway 12-121. Self-taught young winemaker Francis V. Mahoney with partners Balfour and Anita Gibson of Connoisseur Wine Imports built this winery in 1973 primarily to specialize in growing Pinot Noir. They are testing twenty different clones of that classic red burgundy grape in their ten-acre vineyard, planted in the following year. While waiting for the Pinot Noir vineyard to mature, The Carneros Creek Winery has specialized in making full-bodied, oak-aged Zinfandels from Amador and Yolo Counties hillsides.

Before Prohibition there were many more wineries in the Carneros, the greatest of which was Judge John Stanly's La Loma cellar on Stanly Lane. Another famous winery was the stone castle that can be seen from the highway, in the spectacular Winery Lake Vineyard to the left with its lake and modernistic sculptures. It is now the baronial residence of art collector Rene di Rosa, who replanted the century-old vineyard in 1961.

Different climates are also found in the uplands, where temperatures vary with the altitude and with the angle of exposure of each slope to the sun. The upland growers will tell you that certain grape varieties, Riesling in particular, develop higher aromas and more delicate balance in upland vineyards than when grown on the valley floor. Before you continue up the valley, a side trip into the hills to explore this aspect will be worth your while.

· 4 ·

Redwood Road, at the north end of Napa city, takes off in a northwesterly direction through a thickly wooded canyon into the hills. In a six-mile drive of many turns, you climb a thousand feet and reach a lovely, undulating mountain meadow that is carpeted with almost a hundred and fifty acres of vines.

Side by side in this vineyard stand the imposing mission-style

This vineyard on Mount Veeder, Napa County, dates from 1864. It was replanted by Theodore Gier, who built the adjoining winery in 1903. The Christian Brothers bought it and built their Mont La Salle Novitiate beside the winery in 1930.

monastery of the Christian Brothers,* an ivy-clad stone winery, a wooden tasting room with a "Visitors Welcome" sign, and a modest brick office building that faces the road.

The monastery is the Novitiate of Mont La Salle, where young men are trained to join this worldwide Catholic teaching order, founded in France in 1680 by Saint Jean Baptiste de la Salle. The old winery is one of five the Brothers own; it is where they have made their table wines. The brick building is the corporate headquarters of their Mont La Salle Vineyards, which, the Brothers want you to know, is a taxpaying concern like any other commercial vintner.

The Brothers are now the largest producers of Napa grapes and wines, and also of California brandy and premium-priced California dessert wines. Remembering that winemaking monks in the monasteries of Europe advanced the art and science of the vintager through the Middle Ages, it is of historical interest that the Christian Brothers of California are now the largest Church-owned producer of wine in the world. They are also the oldest winery owners in Napa County,

*Officially, Fratres Scholarum Christianarum (the initials F.S.C. follow the members' names) or Brothers of the Christian Schools.

because the other sixty-five Napa wineries have been founded or have changed ownership during the four decades since the Brothers arrived.

Though the Brothers are educators, not priests, they take vows similar to those taken by priests and wear much the same clerical garb, including black ankle-length robes. Members who live at the Napa monastery supervise the vineyards and wineries. Brother U. Gregory, who was Hubert Schiefelbein when he gave up a successful business career to join the order, became the president when his predecessor, Brother John, died in 1963. He was succeeded in 1970 by Brother Frederick, who was born Uvaldo Portillo and had served as principal of two of the order's California high schools when he became Brother Gregory's assistant three years before. The cellarmaster and vice president is courtly Brother Timothy, whose picture you see in the magazine ads. Brother Tim was graduated from the Brothers' high school in Los Angeles as Anthony Diener, then taught chemistry before coming to Mont La Salle in 1936. He is also famous for his collection of some 1,200 corkscrews and as the chief officer of the London-headquartered International Correspondence of Corkscrew Addicts.

In their upland vineyard, its northeasterly slope exposed to the morning sun, the Brothers grow the grapes for their three estate-bottled wines—the fragrant, full-bodied Napa Fumé, the delicate Pineau de la Loire, and the deep-flavored red Pinot St. George.

Including their altar wines, which are sold only to the clergy, the Brothers make some fifty different products, ranging from burgundy and brandy through nearly the entire list of generic and "varietal" table, dessert, and sparkling wine types. Many of them are distinctive, especially the Château La Salle, a sweet but non-cloying light table wine made principally of the Muscat

Brother Timothy (Anthony Diener), the chemistry teacher who became cellarmaster of The Christian Brothers wineries in 1936.

Canelli or Frontignan grape; it is the best-known wine of its type in the world. Newest is their slightly bubbly La Salle Rosé, which many Americans prefer to its Portuguese equivalents, Lancers and Mateus.

For almost a century the Brothers refused to label their wines with vintage dates, preferring to blend different vintages to keep each type uniform in taste. As consumer demand grew in the mid-'70s, they began labeling special blends with lot numbers in which you could read the vintage years the blends contained. In 1977, the Brothers unbent further and introduced their first-ever vintage-dated wine, a special lot of 1976 Gewürz-traminer.

The Brothers began making wine in 1882 at their original novitiate in Martinez, first for their table and altar use, then for sale. The city of Martinez began growing up around the novitiate, so they decided to move, and in 1930 bought the Napa upland site. The vineyard there was originally planted by one H. Hudemann about 1864, later was owned by Rudolf Jordan of the pre-Prohibition wine firm of A. Repsold, then was purchased and replanted by Oakland vintner Theodore Gier, who built the stone cellar in 1903.

When the building of the new novitiate was finished in the depression year of 1932, the western schools of the Christian Brothers were in imminent danger of going bankrupt, their property heavily mortgaged. Their creditors suggested that the Brothers' altar wine business, which had continued during the dry years, should go commercial, now that the repeal of Prohibition appeared imminent. The Brothers agreed, and began to pray for Repeal.

The winemaking job at the Napa winery was given to stalwart young Brother John, who before he joined the order was Stanley (Biff) Hoffman of Oregon gridiron fame. Brother John's first act was to enroll at the University of California in Berkeley for a crash course in enology under Professor William V. Cruess. Returning to the winery, he managed to put some reasonably sound wines on the market in San Francisco by the end of 1934. He next sent his younger brother, John Hoffman, to the Davis campus for more advanced training, and then made John his winemaker, a job John still holds. ("Brother John's brother John is on the phone," my secretary used to say.)

In 1937, the astute Brother John teamed with the Europe-trained wine merchants, Fromm and Sichel, to launch the wines on the national market. The name on the Brothers' wine labels was then changed from Mont La Salle, which is still used on their altar wines, to "The Christian Brothers"—which many buyers still mistake as meaning some brothers named Christian. The Christian Brothers' Wine Museum, which no wine-loving visitor to San Francisco can afford to miss, was opened near Fisherman's Wharf in 1974 as a joint effort with Alfred Fromm to acquaint Americans with the noble cultural history of wine.

In 1940, the Brothers' first brandy blend made its debut. Since then, as their sales grew, they have added several more vineyards in the Napa Valley, making a total of 1,400 acres in the county, and 1,000 more in the San Joaquin Valley. They also added four more wineries, two of them at St. Helena and one each at Reedley and Fresno. By 1977 their wines were known throughout the nation and were being exported commercially to forty countries around the world, and their brandy to seventeen. They now have an additional brandy, named "XO Rare Reserve," which resembles French cognac because it contains 50 percent potsill brandy aged in wood for eight years.

• 5 •

From Mont La Salle, if you have telephoned ahead for appointments, a tortuous drive up Mount Veeder Road to wineries on the slopes of that 2,600-foot extinct volcano is well worthwhile. Two winding miles beyond the Brothers' monastery, a dirt road leads left to the Pickle Canyon Vineyards of John Wright and Moët-Hennessy, of whom more is told on a later page. A short way farther are the 8,500-gallon Mount Veeder Winery and thirteen-acre vineyard of retired lawyer Michael Bernstein and his wife Arlene, who began planting vines around their summer home in 1968.

Still farther, where Lokoya Road takes off to the west, is the Veedercrest Vineyard, on which a winery may be built by 1979. Former college professor and professional mountaineer Alfred Baxter chose this location when he bonded the Veedercrest winery beneath his home in the Berkeley hills in 1972 and made medal-winning wines there from purchased grapes. He later moved the winery to a temporary location in industrial Emeryville and with two dozen partners began planting the mountain vineyard in 1974.

Lokoya Road takes you west to the spectacular Mayacamas Vineyard, the highest in Napa County, and its forty-five acres of terraced vines. At this elevation, far above the valley fogs, the grapes ripen with high acidity a week earlier than on the valley floor. In an average winter the vineyard is blanketed with snow.

In late summer when the ripening grapes become juicy and sweet, birds become a major threat. Then large areas of the mountain vineyards are covered with nets, particularly along the borders where the feathered robbers first attack.

In the volcanic crater stands a three-story cellar of native stone, built by John Henry Fischer from Stuttgart in 1889. This is the kind of place that lures amateurs who dream of owning a winery and growing great wines. In 1941, just such amateurs, British-born chemist J.F.M. (Jack) Taylor and his American wife Mary purchased Mayacamas. The Taylors replanted the abandoned vineyard, fenced it against the deer who ate the first shoots, and then fought off the grape-stealing birds. They reopened the old winery, and a succession of winemakers made them some wines, of which the best, to my taste, was an occasional lot of Cabernet. To help keep the enterprise going, some 500 customers bought stock in Mayacamas at ten dollars a share, which entitled them to buy the wines at a discount. Handsomely labeled, the wines eventually acquired top-level distribution in several states. The Taylors devoted three decades to their labor of love, and then began looking for someone else to carry on.

A young San Francisco investment banker educated at Stanford, Robert Travers, had caught the wine bug about 1963 when he began reading wine literature. He visited wineries, studied viticultural texts, took short courses in enology at Davis, and then spent six months touring the vineyards of Europe and South America before deciding to make the break. In 1967, he shed his Brooks Brothers suit for Levi's and took a job working in the Heitz winery to gain experience, searching meanwhile for a vineyard site. A year later, with six limited partners, Travers purchased Mayacamas. He bought out all the little stockholders, and moved with his wife Elinor and their first child into the old still house beside the winery on the mountain.

Travers has reduced the list of Mayacamas wines from seventeen to three, and is specializing in the vintage-dated "varietals" that he makes himself—Cabernet Sauvignon, Chardonnay, and Zinfandel. In some years he also has made a late-harvest 17 percent Zinfandel essence from Amador County grapes.

• 6 •

Returning to the Wine Road near Napa and heading up the valley, you can experience the change in climate as you drive. It may be noticeably cool until you reach Oakville, because the lower valley is in Region I. From Oakville to St. Helena, the weather becomes warmer, averaging in Region II. When you approach Calistoga, summer days are still warmer, and that part of the valley is classed as Region III.

After leaving Napa you will see a large expanse of vineyards at your right, extending north from Oak Knoll Avenue, and a venerable orange-colored three-story winery in a grove of oaks near the highway. This is the Trefethen Vineyard, which has a checkered past. Napa bankers James and George Goodman built the winery in 1886 and named the place Eshcol for the brook in Biblical Canaan where the Israelites sent by Moses found the enormous grape cluster described in Numbers 13:17-24. Eshcol wines won medals in the late 1890s and achieved considerable fame. Farmer Clark Fawver bought Eshcol from the Goodmans in 1904, but made only bulk wine; Fawver drank nothing except an occasional beer. He closed the winery during Prohibition and reopened it at Repeal. After his death, it served as a storage cellar for the Beringer winery until connoisseur-industrialist Eugene Trefethen bought it from the Fawver estate in 1968. Trefethen's son John, a onetime Navy diver trained for a law career, has modernized the winery and the 500-acre vineyard. From 1973 to 1976 he shared the cellar with the French firm Moët-Hennessy, which produced there the first vintages of its California champagnes while its own winery at nearby Yountville was being built.

In 1977 John and his bride Janet introduced the first estate-grown Trefethen Vineyard wines, 1974 White Riesling and Chardonnay, both of outstanding quality. These were followed a year later by the 1973 Chardonnay and 1974 Cabernet Sauvignon. (Call ahead for an appointment if you wish to visit this great winegrowing estate.)

Across the freeway, north of the Red Hen restaurant, is one of Napa County's newest wineries, the 10,000-gallon Altimira Vineyard cellar of former Lockheed engineer Bruce Newlan and his wife Jonette, bonded in 1977 on their vineyard planted eight years before. It is named for Padre José Altimira, who founded Sonoma Mission in 1823. Two miles farther, past Ragatz Lane, the seventy-acre vineyard on your right is now owned by Walt Disney's widow, Mrs. John Louis Truyens, and her daughters, who may build a winery there.

At Yountville village, three miles north of Trefethen, the big brick Groezinger winery and distillery has been transformed into a tourist shopping complex named "Vintage 1870." That was the year when Gottlieb Groezinger from Württemberg began building the structure and planting his great vineyard nearby. The Groezinger cellar stood idle through Prohibition and until the wine shortage during the Second World War, when for a few seasons wine was made there again. Now the old buildings contain restaurants, a theater, and dozens of shops, including one where most of the wines grown in Napa County are for sale.

• 7 •

Across the freeway from Yountville, beside the old state Veterans' Home, is Moët-Hennessy's Domaine Chandon, a glamorous showplace of vaulted stone champagne cellars and tunnels, complete with a French restaurant featuring *haute cuisine* and a museum of antique implements used in France to produce champagne, opened in 1977. Visitor tours (Wednesdays through Sundays) begin in the museum, then show the bottling, the secondary fermentation, the aging *en tirage,* the riddling, and the disgorging by the traditional *méthode champenoise.* The tours end in a salon where the champagnes can be purchased by the bottle or by the glass.

Moët-Hennessy, the giant French champagne-brandy-Dior perfume firm, made history in 1973 when it became the first important French firm to enter the American winegrowing industry, acquiring 700 acres of Napa County vineyard land through its California subsidiary, Domaine Chandon. Chandon president John Wright purchased 400 acres in the Carneros district, 100 at Yountville, 200 on Mount Veeder, and ten acres on that mountain for a vineyard of his own.

For the first cuvées, blends of 1973 and 1974 wines, grapes were purchased from several Napa vineyards and were vinified at the Trefethen winery. Edmond Maudière, chef de caves of Moët et Chandon at Epernay, shuttled between France and Napa five times each year to make the blends with Chandon's Chilean-born, Davis-trained winemaker Sergio Traverso-Rueda. Introduced in 1976, they were labeled "sparkling wine"—not "champagne," which, the French insist, comes only from 55,000 delimited acres between Epernay and Rheims.

The first Chandon Napa Valley Brut was crisp, almost bone-dry, slightly more tart and thereby more French-tasting than most California champagnes. Maudière used mainly Pinot Noir and Chardonnay wines with a tenth of Pinot Blanc and Ugni Blanc in the blend. The second wine, Blanc de Noirs (100%), was an equally brut but slightly fruitier pink champagne, actually salmon-color, the shade the French call *oeil de perdrix* (partridge's eye). Products to follow included an all-Chardonnay blanc de blanc champagne and a sweet apéritif named Panache. The latter is an unfermented juice of Pinot Noir with added brandy, similar to the Ratafia de Champagne and Pineau des Charentes sold in those regions of France.

Moët-Hennessy's first California wine, however, was not a champagne, but a tart Chardonnay press-wine labeled "Fred's Friends," made at Trefethen two years before Domaine Chandon was built. It was named, with Gallic jocularity, during a visit to Napa by Moët-Hennessy president Count Frédéric Chandon de Briailles from Epernay, and become so popular that it was followed in 1978 by a "Fred's Friends" Pinot Noir Blanc.

California is not the only place outside France where Moët-Hennessy produces champagnes. Subsidiaries make "Graf Chandon Sekt" at Wiesbaden in Germany and "M. Chandon Champaña" at Mendoza in Argentina, and more such operations are planned in Australia and Brazil.

Three miles past Yountville is an abandoned great stone cellar a half mile to the left. Captain John Benson built it during the 1880s; the label on his wines showed a little girl sleeping in a hammock and the slogan "Without a Care." The adjoining vineyard, west of Oakville, was once the famous To Kalon, founded by Hamilton Walker Crabb in 1868 but now divided among several owners.

Nearby, on the Oakville Grade Road, is the state-owned vineyard where the University of California tests new grape varieties for suitability to the Napa climate. Many such experimental vineyards were maintained by the Federal Department of Agriculture in several grape-growing states before Prohibition. All were abandoned during the dry era except the ones at Oakville and Fresno. The former was deeded to the University in 1947.

In Oakville village, there is a stucco-fronted winery on the right that dates from 1877. Originally it was the Nouveau Médoc Vineyard cellar of Brun & Chaix, who were refugees from the troubles in France following the Franco-Prussian war. Jean Adolph Brun knew winemaking, and his partner, Jean Chaix, was experienced in growing grapes. They bought a small vineyard on Howell Mountain, east of St. Helena, and built their cellar on the flat at Oakville, close to the railroad. By 1889 their vineyards covered 115 acres; their Nouveau Médoc sweetish red wine was the favorite in New Orleans, and their whites were popular in California and the East. But Brun died young, and in 1913 Chaix and his widow sold the property. The buyer was the California Wine Association, which in turn sold to the Covick Company, makers of sacramental wines during Prohibition. In 1940 the cellar was sold at auction to the Napa Wine Company of Louis Stralla. He sold it six years later for a quarter-million to the Cella Vineyards of Fresno. Now United Vintners crushes and ferments the grapes there for Inglenook table wines.

Next door is another old cellar, built as the Madonna Winery in 1892. It was used after Repeal to make wine and brandy by the Bartolucci Brothers, who own extensive vineyards nearby, and in 1969 became the winery of Oakville Vineyards, a group of connoisseurs headed by Wilfred E. van Loben Sels, which became defunct in 1977. Then United Vintners bought it to increase the production of Inglenook wines.

• 8 •

On the left just past Oakville is the winery of Robert Mondavi, one of the best-known vintner names in America.

His handsome mission-style winery, with its bell tower, wide lawns, and three pleasant tasting rooms, attracts annually some 200,000 visitors who tour the cellars in groups and buy almost a tenth of his output. Thousands more attend the benefit concerts and art shows, with tasting at the intermissions, scheduled there through the year.

Connoisseurs near and far discuss the relative merits of Mondavi's vintages of Cabernet Sauvignon, Pinot Noir, Petite Sirah, Zinfandel, Napa Gamay, Fumé (Sauvignon) Blanc, Chenin Blanc, Riesling, Chardonnay (unfiltered), Gamay Rosé, and of his moderately-priced everyday red, white, and rosé table wines.

In 1965, at the age of fifty-four, Robert left his family's Charles Krug Winery, of which he is part owner, in a dispute with brother Peter, and built this winery for himself and his sons. His court fight (of which more presently) with Peter over Charles Krug ownership raged through the 1970s. Meanwhile his own winery, in which the Rainier (formerly brewing) Companies first owned a half interest, grew in size from 100,000 to 1.8 million gallons and his vineyard holdings were expanded to six hundred acres.

Bouncy, enthusiastic Robert travels three continents studying developments in winemaking equipment and different varieties of oak for wine-aging casks. Son Michael manages the business while Davis-trained younger son Timothy manages production with enologist Zelma Long, and daughter Marcia handles his east coast sales.

When the business of the neighboring Oakville Vineyards was liquidated in 1977, Robert Mondavi bought its wine stocks and name and began producing a new line of Oakville Vineyards wines.

Mondavi's is now the only winery on the Wine Road with both a tasting room and an Oakville address. Jack and Dolores Cakebread's 5,000-gallon Cakebread Cellars, opened in 1975 on their vineyard across the road from Mondavi, receives visitors by appointment only and gets its mail at Rutherford. The Cakebreads built their winery in time off from their auto repair shop and photography business in Oakland. Their son Bruce will become their winemaker when he graduates from the wine school at Davis.

• 9 •

Next on your route is the hamlet of Rutherford, the home of two famous wineries with similar ownership but contrasting histories and competing managements—Inglenook and Beaulieu.

When the Finnish sea captain, Gustave Ferdinand Niebaum (originally Nybom), had made his fortune in the Alaska fur-sealing trade, he wanted to build a ship. But his wife did not share his love of the sea, so he adopted winegrowing as a hobby instead. In 1879 he bought a young vineyard named Inglenook from one W.C. Watson and retained the name, which suggests a pleasant nook by a fireside. Niebaum replanted the place with vines he imported from the best wine districts of Europe. He then built the three-story Gothic winery of stone, now covered with ivy, at the end of Niebaum Lane. It was finished in 1887, when the captain was forty-five.

Niebaum's aim was to grow wines as fine as any in the world, regardless of expense or financial gain. He often said that the only wines on which he ever made a profit were those he gave to his friends. A perfectionist, he wore white cotton gloves when he inspected his cellars, and woe betide the employees if his gloves became soiled. His sample room was a gustatory chapel with tinted Dutch glass windows and antiquities worthy of a European museum. He also made brandy, but becoming offended one day by the manner in which a revenue agent inspected his distillery, the captain ordered it to be torn down the following morning.

Frona Eunice Wait, writing in 1889, described Inglenook as the California equivalent of Schloss Johannisberg in Germany or of Châteaux Lafite and d'Yquem in France. In that year Niebaum achieved his goal when Inglenook wines won quality awards at the Paris Exposition. They continued to do so until his death in 1908 at the age of sixty-six. Twelve years later came Prohibition, and the winery was closed.

At Repeal in 1933, Niebaum's widow Suzanne entrusted the reopening of Inglenook to Carl Bundschu of the great pre-Prohibition wine firm of Gundlach & Bundschu. Six years later, Mrs. Niebaum's grandnephew, John Daniel, Jr., took charge. Captain Niebaum had never allowed the Inglenook brand to appear on any bottles except his best. Bundschu and Daniel were enjoined by Mrs. Niebaum to conduct the business the same way. They seldom made any profit for Inglenook, but they restored it to the eminence it had reached in the captain's day.

In 1939, the San Francisco Wine & Food Society held a dinner in tribute to Inglenook, at the Palace Hotel. Among the wines served were four relics supplied by Daniel from the family cellar: Inglenook Sauterne 1907, Riesling 1910, Pinot Noir 1892, and Napa Valley Red 1884. Those ancient vintages, though frail and varying from bottle to bottle, gave us proof of the great longevity of Napa Valley wines. The Pinot Noir, which had been recorked in 1912, was exquisitely delicate, rich in bouquet, magnificent. That evening we also drank up the last few bottles of Niebaum's brandy, *circa* 1885.

It was that dinner which caused me to choose the Cabernet of Inglenook to start my own cellar collection of Napa Valley reds, which now includes every vintage bottled since 1938. Two years are missing, because the entire '45 and '47 vintages of Cabernet were sold in bulk; John Daniel didn't consider them fine enough to bear the Inglenook name. The Cabernets of the early 1940s required ten to eleven years of aging in wood and glass to develop great bouquet, and some of them have retained it for over thirty years. I wasn't surprised when a case of the 1941 vintage brought twenty dollars a bottle at the 1969 Heublein auction in Chicago.

Daniel was one of the first premium vintners to adopt (in 1940) varietal instead of generic labels for most of his table wines. The exception was his rosé, first made in 1935, which he named Navalle for the creek that curves through the Niebaum estate.

Under Daniel, Inglenook carried on the Niebaum tradition for twenty-five years. It therefore was a shock to the lovers of

its wines and of antiquity to learn in 1964 that the old winery
had been sold to the giant United Vintners wine firm—even
though John Daniel stayed on. He continued to live in the great
Niebaum house, which is uphill from the cellars. He retained
and enlarged the family vineyards, and he continued as a
member of the Inglenook tasting panel until his death in 1970.
Why did he sell the winery? He never gave his friends a reason,
but Daniel, unlike the Rothschilds of Europe, had no sons to
carry on.

The same dozen estate-bottled, vintage-dated Inglenook "varietals" are still being made, as well as the "cask selection"
vintages of Cabernet Sauvignon, Pinot Noir, and Pinot St.
George. My favorite winemaker, George Deuer, retired when
Inglenook was sold and was succeeded seven years later by
young Davis-trained Thomas Ferrell. No wine has been made
at Inglenook since the crushing and fermentation were moved
to Oakville. Huge barrel-aging and bottling cellars have been
built, the former unhappily placed directly in front of the old
winery, partly obscuring its classic facade. The "estate" represented by the "estate-bottled" label had been enlarged to
include 1,500 more Napa Valley acres owned by Bruno Solari
and other members of the Allied Grape Growers co-operative,
of which United Vintners is the marketing arm. Five generic
and "varietal" coast-counties "district wines" have been added
under an Inglenook Vintage label that is priced a fourth lower
than the estate-bottled line, plus ten still-less-expensive "Navalle" wines that can come from anywhere in California and are
bottled at the Asti Italian Swiss Colony winery. The two San
Joaquin Valley dessert wines that Inglenook used to blend and
age have been increased to six. Inglenook wines, formerly sold
in only seventeen states, have attained national distribution
since Heublein bought control of United Vintners in 1968 and
multiplied its once small volume to some three million gallons.

To those of us who are sentimental about old Inglenook,
there may be some comfort in what Daniel's immediate successor as manager, Lelio N. (Bob) Bianchini, told me the year after
the takeover—that Inglenook operations were showing a profit
for the first time in many years.

The great Victorian Niebaum home uphill from the winery
has changed hands repeatedly since John Daniel's death. At
this writing the resident owner was movie entrepreneur Francis
Ford Coppola of *The Godfather* fame. Visitors who stop to tour
the Inglenook cellars sometimes see helicopters overhead,
bearing Coppola and Hollywood film crews from San Francisco
to shoot new Coppola epics on Napa Valley locations.

• 10 •

In 1883, while Captain Niebaum was building the great Inglenook winery, a stocky little twenty-six-year-old Frenchman, Georges de Latour from Périgord, arrived in San Francisco to seek his fortune. During a try at gold-mining in the Sierra foothills, he lost what little money he had. Then, because his family in France had made wine and he had learned chemistry at the École Centrale in Paris, he took himself to the north coast wine country. He traveled by horse and wagon among the wineries, buying the sediment and crust (argols) from their wine tanks to make cream of tartar, which he sold to be made into baking powder. For sixteen years he built up his cream of tartar business at Healdsburg in Sonoma County, but meanwhile planned to become a winegrower. In 1899, when Inglenook wines were already famed at home and abroad, de Latour bought an orchard and wheatfield immediately north of Inglenook. His wife Fernande named it Beaulieu, "beautiful place." He went to France, brought back vines of the best French varieties to plant on his land, and opened his first small winery. Several years later he acquired additional vineyards at Oakville and on the east side of the valley along the Silverado Trail. In 1923 he bought the Seneca Ewer winery across the road from his home vineyard, enlarged its stone cellar, and made it the main Beaulieu winery.

When Inglenook, its owner long dead, was closed down at the beginning of Prohibition, de Latour kept Beaulieu open, for he held the approbation of San Francisco Archbishop Patrick Riordan as a supplier of altar wines, which were legal, to the Catholic Church. He prospered during the dry years, building a nationwide business in altar wines, which Beaulieu still enjoyed in the 1970s. At Repeal he was one of the few vintners ready to supply fine, fully aged California wines to the connoisseur trade. In the wine judging at the Golden Gate International Exposition in 1939, his Beaulieu Burgundy (which he made of Cabernet Sauvignon grapes) was chosen above a hundred other entries to receive the grand prize for red wines.

At the home vineyard, de Latour and his wife—a stately, gracious *grande dame*—added wings to their rambling country house, planted formal gardens studded with fountains and statuary, and made Beaulieu the most famous estate in the Napa Valley. They dispensed hospitality to San Francisco high society and entertained such illustrious personages as President Herbert Hoover, Sir Winston Churchill, and visiting nobility. They made annual visits to France, which was how it happened that their daughter, Helene, was married in 1924 to the Marquis Galcerand de Pins, himself a winegrower at his ancestral estate, the Château de Monbrun in Gascony.

Georges de Latour was said to be the colorful central character of the best-selling novel of 1942, *The Cup and the Sword,* which fifteen years later became the feature movie *This Earth Is Mine.* I can confirm this because, after his death in 1940, I furnished the background material to the author, Alice Tisdale Hobart; and she rewarded me by making me a recognizable character (Galen Ritter, the ex-newspaperman) in the book. The French winegrower hero of the story, Jean-Philippe Rambeau, portrayed in the movie by Claude Rains, bore only basic resemblance to de Latour because Mrs. Hobart took pains to alter his picture sufficiently—by giving him wineries in both the San Joaquin and Napa Valleys—to avoid the possibility of a lawsuit. (I was disappointed by the novel, however, for the author put all of her dramatic writing into her fictional scenes and none into the single episode that was true—the climax to de Latour's career—the greatest funeral held in San Francisco in that decade, at which four archbishops presided.)

De Latour was a great judge of wine and also of winemakers. When his enologist, Professor Leon Bonnet, retired in 1937, de Latour and the Marquis de Pins traveled to France to find a successor. At the Institut National Agronomique in Paris, they asked Professor Paul Marsais to recommend a man. Marsais had a Russian assistant, a research enologist named André Tchelistcheff, who might be right for the job. Tchelistcheff was hired and arrived at Rutherford in time for the 1938 vintage.

San Francisco *Examiner*

Georges de Latour, the founder of Beaulieu Vineyard.

In bringing Tchelistcheff to California, de Latour did as much for the state's wines in general—and later for the wines of northern Mexico and of the State of Washington—as for the wines of Beaulieu. Tchelistcheff was born in Moscow in 1901, the son of a law professor, and was educated in Czechoslovakia after serving in the czarist and White Russian armies. This intense little man was thirty-seven when he left France. He brought to California the latest findings of French enological and viticultural research.

When Tchelistcheff first tasted Napa wines, he decided that Cabernet Sauvignon grown in this climate was destined to become one of the great wines of the world. He persuaded de Latour to build a separate cellar to age Beaulieu Cabernet in oak barrels for at least two years. When the Cabernet from the new cellar was bottle-ripe, he matured it for another two years in glass. Released the year after the founder's death, it was named "Georges de Latour Private Reserve." It was the 1936 vintage and was priced at a dollar and a half. (At this writing, the ten-year-old Private Reserve brings twenty dollars a bottle in the few stores that have any in stock. The five-year-old can be bought at the Beaulieu tasting room in Rutherford for six dollars, but there is a limit of two bottles per buyer. BV Private Reserve Cabernet has become the single most-praised and most sought-after American wine.)

For years Tchelistcheff urged the Beaulieu owners to concentrate on producing only Cabernet Sauvignon or at most one or two other fine wines—to discontinue selling their dozens of different types. "With thirty wines to take care of," he argued, "I am producing little starlets when I should produce only great stars." But like other medium-sized American wineries which try to sell their brands nationally, Beaulieu had to continue offering "a complete line." BV still sells both generic and "varietal" table wines, five dessert wines purchased in the San Joaquin Valley and aged at Rutherford, and since 1955 has offered an assortment of bottle-fermented, vintage-dated champagnes. Its best buys, in my opinion, are the second-grade Cabernet and the Burgundy, priced about half and about a fifth, respectively, as much as the Private Reserve. BV also produces an excellent chablis, a Grenache Rosé, a sweet Sauvignon Blanc, a Gamay Beaujolais, and one dessert wine of its own, Muscat Frontignan, from this choicest of Muscat grapes, which de Latour planted in his vineyard on the Silverado Trail. Added since 1976 are a Cabernet-Merlot blend named Beau Tour and a new Pinot Noir named Beau Velours.

André Tchelistcheff, "the wine-maker's winemaker," was born in Russia, educated in Czechoslovakia, and trained in France before coming to California in 1938 at age 37.

About 1960, Tchelistcheff tasted a Pinot Noir made by Louis Martini from grapes grown in the cool Carneros district, and found it finer than Beaulieu's. He persuaded Madame de Pins to let him plant a Beaulieu vineyard in the Carneros. It is vineyard number five, 140 acres of Pinot Noir and Chardonnay, planted in 1963. If you compare Tchelistcheff's 1966 (Rutherford) Pinot Noir and Chardonnay with his later (Carneros) wines, you will find that he was right.

Besides managing the BV vineyards and winery, Tchelistcheff for fifteen years maintained his own enological laboratory in St. Helena and served as consultant to other Napa and Sonoma wineries. He tutored several young enologists at those wineries who since have made some of the finest post-Repeal California wines. One of those he trained was his son Dimitri, who later produced some of the best wines thus far made in Mexico. André Tchelistcheff himself has guided the Washington State wine industry in its first concerted effort to produce premium European-type table wines. Since retiring from BV in 1973, he has been consultant for a dozen wineries in California and Oregon as well as in Washington, besides guiding many of his small winegrower friends in their quest for enological greatness.

In 1969 the admirers of Napa wines, still perturbed over the sale of Inglenook four years earlier, got another shock when Beaulieu and four of its five vineyards were sold to the Heublein liquor, wine, and food conglomerate. "Another Winery Swallowed by the Giants!" the newspaper headline read. The sale was not made through Allied Grape Growers and United Vintners as in Inglenook's case, but to Heublein direct.

"It's a terrible wrench," said the Marquise de Pins, who had succeeded her late mother as Beaulieu president, "but circumstances force changes; it's more practical for a big organization to operate in these times." However, the de Pins' and their daughter, Dagmar Sullivan, have kept the Beaulieu estate, which is de Latour's original Cabernet vineyard and the source of the grapes for BV Private Reserve. They are selling the grapes to Heublein, but a small winery stands on the old vineyard, and there is a de Latour grandson, Walter Sullivan III, who someday may be interested in following his ancestor's steps.

Despite the change in ownership, Tchelistcheff, now in his late seventies, still keeps a loving eye on Beaulieu vineyards and wines. His standards are maintained there by his son Dimitri, who since 1973 has been BV's technical director, working with President Legh Knowles, Cellarmaster Theo Rosenbrand, and Davis-trained enologist Thomas Selfridge. At the 1970 meeting of the American Society of Enologists, André Tchelistcheff's pupils and the rest of the nation's wine industry joined to pay him tribute as "the winemaker's winemaker," presenting him with the annual A.S.E. merit award.

Although Inglenook and Beaulieu both are now Heublein companies, they are competitors like Cadillac and Oldsmobile, managed by separate Heublein divisions. Inglenook is the top brand of United Vintners, which also owns Italian Swiss Colony and the numerous Petri brands. Beaulieu wines are sold by the division which sells most of the Heublein imports. People at first wondered which of the two would be featured as Heublein's best California wine. Beaulieu wines, bringing higher prices, seem to be winning the competition, but United Vintners has answered this with full-page magazine ads for Inglenook, saying: "Our only competitor . . . is us."

Beaulieu, with a visitor center built in 1974, including a theater where a film on winegrowing is shown, is one of the most attractive tasting stops on the entire Wine Road.

• 11 •

Across the Wine Road and north from Beaulieu is the new stucco-fronted 40,000-gallon Grgich Hills Cellar of Croatia-born winemaker Miljenko (Mike) Grgich and Austin Hills of San Francisco's Hills Brothers coffee dynasty. Grgich is famous as the producer of the California Chardonnay (Château Montelena 1973) which triumphed over four leading white burgundies of France in the internationally publicized blind tasting by French experts in Paris in 1976. The building of this winery in 1977 realized a dream Grgich had cherished since emigrating from Yugoslavia nineteen years before. A winemaker since boyhood when he trod grapes in his father's winery, he holds degrees in viniculture from Zagreb University and worked in five Napa wineries before leaving Château Montelena to achieve his goal, a winery of his own. His 1973 Chardonnay was a blend from three vineyards, two in Napa Valley and one in the Alexander Valley of Sonoma County. He now can choose from Hills's vineyards but expects to buy grapes elsewhere, too.

A half mile farther north, in the eucalyptus grove at your left, is another new winery, Bernard and Evelyn Skoda's 30,000-gallon red-tile-roofed Rutherford Vintners cellar and tasting room. French-born Skoda has worked in wineries since his youth in Alsace. A Second World War veteran of the French and American armies, he presided for fifteen years at the nearby Martini winery tasting room until with the help of friends he could build his own winery. The Skodas have two vineyards, of White Riesling at the winery and of Cabernet Sauvignon a half mile south.

On your right, with its entrance on Galleron Road, is the redwood-front 360,000-gallon Franciscan Vineyards winery. A billboard south of Napa advertises that the Franciscan tasting room offers "premium wines at affordable prices." This expresses the realistic view of the wine business held by Franciscan winemaker-president Justin Meyer and his financial partner Raymond Duncan. They learned it partly from the failures of two previous owners of Franciscan, which was built in 1971.

On taking over the bankrupt business in 1975, Meyer promptly sold out most of its stock at a dollar a bottle and in bulk. Then he established two grades of premium-priced Franciscan wines—a full range of vintage-dated "varietals" and also two "Friars Table" jug wines simply labeled "Table Wine," red and white. One of the "varietals" was the first (1975) wine made commercially of Carnelian, the light red University of California grape variety developed by crossing Cabernet Sauvignon, Carignane, and Grenache. Meyer bought the first seven-ton commercial crop from the University vineyard.

Meanwhile Meyer and Duncan have acquired a thousand

acres of vineyards in Napa, Sonoma, and Lake Counties. They make Franciscan wines of their best grapes and sell the rest to other wineries. For Lake County neighbors who plan a future winery, Franciscan makes a line of "Konocti Cellars" Lake County wines. Franciscan has also opened a bonded bottling cellar in Denver to sell "Purgatory Cellars" Zinfandel and Chenin Blanc. Duncan, who lives and has an oil company in Colorado, owns the Purgatory Ski Resort.

Separate from the Franciscan winery, Meyer and Duncan age a super-premium Cabernet Sauvignon in their 20,000-gallon Silver Oak Cellar off Oakville Cross Road three miles southeast of Rutherford. Silver Oak, with its 1972 vintage, became the first American winery to offer only a single wine aged five years in cask and bottle before sale. Released in 1977, Silver Oak Cabernet 1972 went on sale at six dollars a bottle in the Franciscan and Denver tasting rooms.

Meyer, a Davis graduate in viticulture and enology, served fifteen years as assistant cellarmaster of the Christian Brothers at Napa. Assistant winemaker at Franciscan is Davis-trained Leonard Berg, a son and nephew of noted enologists.

A mile north of Franciscan, right turns on Zinfandel Lane and Wheeler Way take you to the small new winery on the 90-acre vineyard planted in 1971 by Roy Raymond and sons, the year after Raymond quit as manager of the Beringer winery at its purchase by Nestlé of Switzerland. Roy's wife Martha Jane is a great-granddaughter of Jacob Beringer. The first estate-bottled Raymond Vineyard wine, botrytized, perfectly-balanced 1975 White Riesling, won a gold medal at the Los Angeles Fair in 1977, the year it was released for sale. Roy Jr., the Beringer viticulturist, planted the vineyard. Roy's other son Walter made the wine.

Wineries line both sides of the Wine Road as you approach St. Helena. At White Lane on your right is the white stucco V. Sattui cellar and cheese shop, built in 1975. It offers tasting and sells sausages, patés, cheeses, and breads that you can enjoy in its adjoining picnic ground. Daryl Sattui and his blonde Finnish wife Mirja named it for the winery his great grandfather Vittorio operated on Bryant Street in San Francisco's Mission district from 1894 until 1920, when it was closed by National Prohibition. Daryl makes "natural, unfined and unfiltered" red wines, mostly of grapes trucked down from Amador County.

A little farther on your right, a sign invites you to the Heitz Cellar tasting room, which fronts on a Grignolino vineyard. It is worth a stop, but be sure to save time for a later visit (but phone ahead) to the Heitz family's winery and vineyard two miles to the east.

On the left is the big Napa Valley Co-operative Winery, which makes wine out of Napa grapes for Gallo and sends it all, except what the grower members drink themselves, in tank trucks to Modesto. The Co-op cellar is two wineries in one, for it was built around a much older stone winery that once belonged to Oakland vintner Theodore Gier.

Next door to the Co-op is the Sutter Home winery, a fixture at this Napa location since 1906. But its excellent products are not Napa wines. What it mainly produces are full-bodied, flavorful Zinfandels from grapes trucked down from the Sierra foothills of Amador County, a hundred miles to the east. It also makes a white wine of Zinfandel and delicious light sweet muscat table wines, which with assorted apéritif wines can be sampled in the tasting room. The winery name goes back to 1890, when John Sutter, a cousin of the Captain Sutter of Sutter's Fort fame, founded a winery on Howell Mountain. It was moved to St. Helena in 1906 and after Prohibition made bulk wine. Sutter Home has been owned by the Trinchero family since 1947. Having no vineyards, Louis (Bob) Trinchero began buying Zinfandel grapes from an old Amador vineyard west of Plymouth. So popular has the Zinfandel become that the Trincheros have expanded the winery to 180,000 gallons.

• 12 •

Across the road from Sutter Home, there is a 2½-million-gallon ivy-clad concrete winery with a tasting room and a modest sign facing the highway that says "Louis M. Martini Winery." The name is also the brand on Martini wines, respected everywhere California wines are sold, although the winery's colorful founder died in 1974 at the age of seventy-eight.

Louis Michael Martini was born in 1887 in the seaport of Pietra Ligure on the Italian Riviera, the son of a shoemaker. When Louis was thirteen, he crossed the Atlantic in the steerage to join his father, Agostino, who had emigrated six years before and started a shellfish business in San Francisco. During his teens, Louis dug clams on the bay mudflats, gathered mussels from the piers, and gill-netted striped bass on one of his father's gaff-rigged fishing boats. In the earthquake year of 1906, his father started a back-yard winery near Hunter's Point because the clam population in the south bay was

Louis Michael Martini, who said he
made his famous Moscato Amabile
wine by accident.

dying from pollution. The whole first vintage turned out
spoiled, so Louis, then nineteen, was sent to Italy to learn how
to make wine. After eight months in the Alba enology school,
he came home in time to make the 1907 vintage, which didn't
spoil. Louis peddled the wine, together with mussels and clams,
to the San Francisco fish markets and then sold wine from door
to door in the Italian North Beach district. He later made wine
at a vineyard his father rented between Pleasanton and Suñol in
Alameda County, then in successive seasons was the winemaker at the Bradford Winery in Thornton and the Guasti Vineyard
near Cucamonga. Early in the Prohibition era, as a partner in
the former Italian Swiss Colony winery at Kingsburg, Fresno
County, he made a grape concentrate called "Forbidden Fruit,"
a name which appealed to the nation's home winemakers. At
Repeal he switched to making bulk wine and shipped it across
the country in tank cars to eastern wineries.

I remember my first meeting with Louis Martini because he
would never let me forget it. It was in 1935 at the Hotel Senator
in Sacramento where we were attending a hearing on wine
taxes. The fiery, blue-eyed, square-jawed ex-fisherman always
loved to argue. I have heard him say, in order to heat up a
discussion, "I don't agree with you—and if you agree with me,
I'll change my mind!" That evening in Sacramento he said to
me, "Five years from now, mark my words, I'll be making the
best dry wines in California." I judged him then as either a
boaster or a dreamer, for how could a San Joaquin Valley bulk
wine maker fulfill so absurd a promise?

What I didn't know was that Martini a few years earlier had

bought a St. Helena vineyard, had built a new winery there, and had begun quietly amassing a hoard of fine, aged table and dessert wines, not a drop of which would be released until all were bottled and ready.

In 1940, Martini sold his Kingsburg plant to the Central California Wineries merger, moved with his family to St. Helena, and put his whole line of aged wines on the market at once. At that time when fine California wines were scarce, their quality created a sensation. He became famous overnight as one of the coast counties premium table-wine producers. For decades afterward, Martini reminded me each time we met, "What did I tell you that night at the Hotel Senator in Sacramento?"

One of the wines he introduced in 1940 was his Moscato Amabile. It is still sold, but only at the winery. At 10 percent alcohol it is so delicate that it must be kept refrigerated until served. When I first asked Martini how he made it, he said it was a secret; but years later he said it was an accident. At Kingsburg, in 1928, he found several barrels of Muscat of Alexandria juice that had lain in a corner of the winery all winter because his fermenting tanks were full. In spring, when the juice was tasted, Martini expected it to be spoiled, but instead it sparkled like champagne. He couldn't remember what else had been put in those barrels, but kept experimenting until another batch, fermented for four years in a cold room, turned out the same as the original. Moscato Amabile has yet to be duplicated in this country. However, Cyril Ray describes in his *Wines of Italy* a semi-sparkling 8 percent Muscat wine called Moscatello, made in Liguria and favored there for family picnics.

A handsome stone winery built in 1883 at the west end of Zinfandel Lane is where Martini got his start in the Napa Valley. This was where he amassed his secret stock of fine wines during the 1930s, and beside it he built his home. In 1937, he bought the 300-acre Mount Pisgah Vineyard on the Sonoma County side of the Mayacamas range, a thousand feet above Agua Caliente, and renamed it Monte Rosso for its red volcanic soil. With half of his grapes coming from Sonoma, he could not call his wines "Napa" so he used the appellation "mountain" instead. He kept adding vineyards: a part of the Stanly Carneros property in 1942, 200 acres on the Russian River below Healdsburg in 1962, more Carneros acreage two years later, and in 1970 he planted 15 acres in 900-foot-high Chiles Valley, five miles east of St. Helena, making almost 900 acres in all.

Nothing much has changed at the Martini winery since the founder's death except the successive vintage dates on its some thirty varietally and generically labeled table wines. Six-foot-four Louis Peter Martini, Louis Michael's son, who studied enology and viticulture at the University's Berkeley and Davis campuses, has headed the winery since 1960. Louis Peter's son Michael, trained at Fresno State University and UC Davis, is now the enologist. Michael's sister Carolyn manages the office and sister Patricia is learning wine sales by working at a nearby store. Louis Peter lives with his wife Elizabeth and their daughters on the old Edge Hill Vineyard, founded in 1870 by the pioneer Indian fighter, General E.D. Keyes. Their home has two-foot-thick walls, for it was once the Edge Hill winery. Martini vineyards have been enlarged with new plantings at Carneros and Chiles Valley, and there are new stainless steel tanks in the winery, although some of the old redwood and concrete tanks remain. You still can buy half-gallon jugs of non-vintage, ready-to-drink Martini Mountain Red, White, and Rosé in half-gallon jugs at everyday prices. The "varietals" cost more, and still more is charged for the old "Special Selection" and "Private Reserve" Cabernets, Pinot Noirs, and Zinfandels, which are sold only at the winery. The Gewürztraminer is outstanding, drier and spicier than most on the market. Martini Pale Dry Sherry is the best of its type in California, a blend of wines as old as fifteen years with younger submerged-culture *flor* sherries. Martini is still the only winery that makes a "varietal" wine of Folle Blanche, a white grape grown in the Monte Rosso Vineyard. I once congratulated old Louis on having planted Folle Blanche, a grape the University doesn't recommend for California, but which makes a lovely dry, crisp wine resembling chablis. "I didn't plant it," he replied; "it was growing there when I bought the vineyard."

Louis Peter adheres to the word "mountain" as the label designation for Martini table wines despite its adoption by wineries in other districts for their least expensive wines. He declines to use local appellations for the wines from the various Martini vineyards because he prefers to blend the wines from different districts. "The most important thing on a label is the brand name, the name of the winery," he says. That he is right is evidenced by the fabulous offers he constantly receives and rejects from big distillers and conglomerates who would like to buy the Martini name as an entry into the expanding wine industry.

• 13 •

Next door to Martini is the impressive South St. Helena Cellar of the Christian Brothers. Built in 1965 to store bottled wines, it has been enlarged as the beginning of a winery complex more immense than anything the valley has ever seen. New crushers and presses have been installed, and the Brothers now make their Napa table wines and eventually will bottle them here. In the next several years they plan a circular complex of new champagne cellars, warehouses, offices, tasting rooms, catering kitchens, and a tourist facility to accommodate millions of visitors.

The old town of St. Helena has eleven bonded wineries within the city limits and also a considerable acreage of vineyards, which unfortunately are not protected by the county zoning law. Although most of the city's 4,000 population are concerned in some way with winegrowing, there are many who oppose the drinking of wine. They are the Seventh Day Adventists, whose big St. Helena Sanitarium frowns down on the vineyards from the hill east of town; they also oppose the consumption of tea, coffee, and meat.

The St. Helena Library contains the only public wine library in the United States. It is supported by the Napa Valley Wine Library Association, which anyone may join for five dollars a year, and which conducts periodic wine tastings and wine appreciation courses, the latter taught by the local winemakers.

On the main street is the Sunny St. Helena Winery, a co-operative of twenty-five growers headed by Charles Forni, which produces bulk wine for the Charles Krug Winery. Many venerable stone buildings on the side streets are pre-Prohibition wineries, since remodeled to house small business ventures. Several historic wine cellars in the neighborhood have been converted into attractive homes.

• 14 •

From St. Helena, a half-hour climb of Spring Mountain Road affords glimpses of some once-famous mountain vineyards, replanted during the 1970s in response to the soaring demand for fine table wines.

The elegant estate with the steepled century-old mansion at the left, where the hill begins, was Tiburcio Parrott's Miravalle, named for its view of the valley. Parrott, a gentleman farmer and friend of the Beringer Brothers, grew here a claret he called Margaux, which the late Almond R. Morrow told me, was the greatest California wine produced before Prohibition.

Miravalle is coming back. In 1974 the estate was purchased by Shirley and Michael Robbins, who already owned a winery called Spring Mountain Vineyards. They restored the Parrott mansion, moved in with their two sons, built a new 60,000-gallon Spring Mountain Vineyards winery on the site of the original Miravalle cellar, and began replanting the hillside where Parrott had grown grapes until his death in 1896.

Nine years earlier Mike Robbins, an Annapolis graduate engineer and property manager, visiting St. Helena from Iowa, saw a neglected Victorian house on the Wine Road north of St. Helena, bought and rebuilt it, and began making wine downstairs. "Coming from Iowa, we discovered a new world of wine here," he explains. He planted an acre of vines in front of the house, took winemaking lessons from neighbors and from consultant Brad Webb, equipped the basement as a miniature model winery, and named it for Spring Mountain. He bought more vineyards near Rutherford and Napa, leased space in other wineries, and gradually won a connoisseur following for his flavorful wines. As his winemaker he hired Charles Ortman, a commercial artist who began winemaking as an amateur and then apprenticed at the Heitz Cellar, where some of Robbins's wines were made.

When Robbins bought the Parrott estate, he sold his first Spring Mountain winery, retired from property management to become a full-time winegrower, and set about restoring Miravalle to its greatness of a century ago. His new winery, its Victorian front designed to match the mansion, includes a ninety-foot tunnel in the hillside where Parrott aged his wines. It was built in time to crush the 1976 vintage.

A half mile further, a narrow private road through forests of oaks and redwoods leads to the great La Perla Vineyard, which is one of the most spectacular in the world. Literally miles of valleys and hills, rising to 1,500 feet elevation, are contoured or terraced and carpeted with vines, most of them replanted during the past decade. Charles Lemme from Germany built the stone La Perla winery in the 1870s. His successor was Claus Schilling of the San Francisco family of dealers in wine, spice, coffee, and tea. Now La Perla is owned by realtor-vineyardist Jerome Draper, whose son Jerome Jr. plans someday to rebuild and reopen the winery.

A mile beyond the La Perla entrance, also on a private road, is Château Chevalier. With its Victorian exterior, twin steeples and stained-glass windows, this is one of the loveliest old stone cellars in the United States. Gregory Bissonette, once a jet-fighter pilot, was a San Francisco stockbroker when he began making wine at home and took some enology short courses at the University of California. In 1969 with a partner he bought the abandoned château that wine merchant George Chevalier had built in 1891. Bissonette quit his job and moved with his wife Kathy and their six children into the top two floors of the winery. He cleared the steep hillside of trees and brush and replanted sixty acres with Cabernet and Chardonnay, doing most of the back-breaking work himself. He purchased grapes to make his first wines in 1972 and chose the name "Mountainside Vineyards" to sell them, reserving "Château Chevalier" for wines of his own grapes. In 1976 the first estate-grown wines were released, a deep-colored, deep-flavored 1974 Cabernet Sauvignon and a 1975 late-harvest Chardonnay. Bissonette says he still owes a million dollars, but with the whole family living in the winery and working in the vineyard or cellar or delivering the wines to stores and restaurants, and with son Doug now studying viticulture and enology at Davis, Greg thinks the future of Château Chevalier looks secure.

On Langtry Lane, above the La Perla Vineyard, Fritz Maytag of the Newton, Iowa, family owns the hundred-acre York Creek Vineyard, which once was part of La Perla. But Maytag, who is busy running the Anchor Steam Beer Brewery in San Francisco, sells his choice grapes to premium-producing wineries, makes wine at home for his own use, and although he has no plan to enter the wine business, says "I may have a winery someday."

Uphill from Langtry Lane, a gravel road winds a mile northward to the Robert Keenan vineyard. The stone winery, built by Peter Conradi in 1904, had lain idle since 1937. Keenan, the owner of a San Francisco insurance firm, bought and remodeled the cellar, replanted the surrounding vineyard with thirty-two acres of Cabernet Sauvignon and Chardonnay, and with former Chappellet Vineyard winemaker Joseph Cafaro in charge, made wine there again in 1977.

Still higher on the mountain, at almost two thousand feet elevation, Fred Aves and his son Russell have built the handsome stone Yverdon winery, which has quatrefoil stained-glass windows, Tudor arches, and the first hillside tunnels dug in Napa County during this century. Aves, a Los Angeles manufacturer of auto supplies, began making wine in his bathtub in 1962, planted vines around his home in Beverly Glen, then sold his factory because he was bored and wanted to become a winegrower. Father and son have cut and laid every stone of the winery by hand and have assembled their casks and barrels from staves imported from Italy. They have planted vines on

The Château Chevalier winery, built in 1891 on Spring Mountain in Napa County, was abandoned during Prohibition and reopened eighty years later during the wine revolution.

the mountain beside the stone castle where the father lives, but their wines since 1970 came mainly from a vineyard they own on Tubbs Lane near Calistoga. Yverdon is the name of the village in Switzerland where Aves's grandparents were wine-growers.

At the mountain crest an unpaved road at the right leads to an area where old vine stumps and abandoned tunnels are traces of vineyards and wineries, their names long forgotten, which flourished here from the 1880s until Prohibition. New pioneers have cleared and replanted vines in patches of brush and forest and have opened two small wineries.

One is Dr. Peter Minor, who was practicing dentistry and home winemaking in Berkeley when in 1967 he began planting his four-acre Ritchie Creek Vineyard on the mountain. He built a home of field stones and in 1974 dug his 3,000-gallon winery into the hill below to make his first Cabernet Sauvignon, for which his wife Margaret designed the label. He since has moved his dental practice to Sonoma.

The road branches right from Minor's place to the other winery, the 15,000-gallon Smith-Madrone Vineyards cellar of Stuart and Charles Smith. Stuart was an enology teaching assistant at UC Davis and Charles was teaching grammar school in San Leandro when they began clearing and planting their forty acres in 1971. They built the concrete, sod-roofed winery themselves, and Stuart moved into the upper story. Their first crush in 1977 was from their own young vines of White Riesling, Chardonnay, Cabernet Sauvignon, and Pinot Noir.

• 15 •

Just beyond the business district of St. Helena is the Beringer Brothers winery, with its picturesque Rhine House, gardens, and maze of wine-aging tunnels dug a thousand feet into the limestone hillside almost a century ago—a tourist attraction that brings hordes of visitors throughout the year.

The title of "oldest Napa winegrower" belongs to this winery because it has never closed since it was built in 1876 and has produced wine in every vintage since 1879, including the Prohibition years when it made sacramental wines.

Jacob and Frederick Beringer came to the United States from Mainz on the Rhine, where Jacob began his winemaking career. From 1872 to 1878, Jacob worked at the nearby Charles Krug winery while the Beringer cellars and vineyards were being established. Frederick then joined him and built the Rhine House, the elegant seventeen-room mansion with carved oak panels and slate roof, which stands beside the winery. A counterpart of the Rhine House was built by their uphill neighbor Tiburcio Parrott, who also grew grapes for the Beringers on his Miravalle estate.

After the Beringer brothers died, the descendants of Jacob bought the shares held by the widow and children of "Uncle Fritz" who sold the Rhine House and moved away. Jacob's son, Charles Tiburcio Beringer, let the quality of the wines decline, but was succeeded by his nephew Otto, who improved them and bought back the Rhine House from absentee owners, transforming it into a colorful visitor center and tasting hall. Otto also rediscovered an old Beringer wine called Barenblut ("bear's blood"), a pleasing blend of Grignolino and Pinot Noir.

In 1970, President Gerard J. Gogniat of Nestlé, the multinational Swiss maker of chocolate, Nescafé, and a hundred other food products, decided to enter the fast-growing wine business in the United States. He bought Beringer and its 700 acres of vineyards at St. Helena, Yountville, Knights Valley, and in the Carneros district, where Beringer stores wine in the old Garetto winery on Buchli Road.

Myron Nightingale, the famed creator of Cresta Blanca Premier Sémillon, became the winemaster of Beringer and set new goals of excellence for its wine. A new winery with stainless steel crushers and batteries of temperature-controlled fermenting tanks was built across the Wine Road, while the old winery and its tunnels became exclusively an oak cellar for the aging of wines. More land was acquired and planted throughout the valley, increasing Beringer vineyards to 2,800 acres. In 1976 Beringer's centennial was celebrated with centennial bottlings of Cabernet Sauvignon 1973 and Chardonnay 1974. Nightingale has produced a new Beringer proprietary wine named Trauben-gold, "gold of the grape," from White Riesling grown in the Tepusquet vineyards of Santa Barbara County. Other Beringer table wines made from purchased grapes are sold under the winery's original Los Hermanos name in magnums and jugs and in the company's patented airline package containing a single bottle and a glass.

Although Nestlé owns the winery and vineyards, Beringer is operated by the Labruyere family of Macon in France. This is explained by Nestlé's ownership of the Stauffer Corporation, which has restaurants selling wine in the United States. The winery is also the headquarters for the related international importing firm, Wine World, which markets the Crosse & Blackwell line of French and German wines.

• 16 •

Next door to Beringer is the most prodigious structure in this part of the valley, the Greystone cellar of the Christian Brothers. Millions have toured its cavernous tunnels, which hold two and a half million gallons of aging wine, have watched in fascination how the Brothers' champagnes are made upstairs, have exclaimed over Brother Tim's corkscrew collection on display, and have sampled the Brothers' wines on the main floor. Also fascinating is the history of the colossal building, which when it was built in 1889, was the largest stone winery in the world. During the 1880s, the small Napa winegrowers could not afford to age their wines and had to sell them in bulk to San Francisco wine merchants at ruinously low prices, for no bank would accept wine as collateral for loans. William Bourn, the wealthy young owner of two Napa vineyards, of San Francisco's Spring Valley Water Company, and of sundry mines, conceived of an altruistic scheme. He offered to build this winery to make wine of the growers' grapes, to age the wine, and to lend them ten cents a gallon until it could be sold. When Greystone was opened, however, the phylloxera vine plague had caused a shortage of wine, and the building became a white elephant. It had a procession of owners during the next half century: Charles Carpy, the California Wine Association, Bisceglia Brothers, Central California Wineries, Roma, and Cresta Blanca. The low point in its history was in the Depression year of 1931, when Bisceglia bought it at auction for ten thousand dollars. By 1945, the Christian Brothers needed extra space in which to age their growing stocks of table wines, and rented part of Greystone from Roma. Five years later they bought it, and when Brother John decided in 1955 to begin making champagnes, that department was installed on the third floor. In the cornerstone of the building, according to an early issue of the St. Helena *Star,* there repose, among other historic objects, bottles of Charles Krug and Bourn & Wise wines of the 1884 to 1877 vintages, and a bottle of 1883 Beringer Brandy.

• 17 •

In the competition to be called "the oldest," the Charles Krug winery, across the road from Greystone, cites the date of 1861 when the Prussian emigré for whom it is named built his first winery there. However, only one stone wall of that winery remains, and credit for the many good and fine wines now made there belongs not to Krug, but to the Italian family named Mondavi, who have owned the site since 1943.

Krug was one of the pioneer winegrowers in the valley, but he was not the first. George Yount and several others preceded him by as much as twenty years. Charles (née Karl) Krug came to the United States in 1847, taught for a year in a free-thinkers' school in Philadelphia, returned to Germany and was imprisoned for participating in a revolt against the reactionary parliament, then came back to the United States and became editor of the first German newspaper on the Pacific Coast, published in Oakland. In 1854 he tried farming for several months near "Count" Haraszthy's failing vineyard in San Mateo County, next worked briefly in the San Francisco Mint, then followed Haraszthy to Sonoma, learned winemaking from the "Count" and General Vallejo, and planted a vineyard there. In 1860, the year Abraham Lincoln was elected President, Krug sold his Sonoma vineyard, moved to St. Helena, and married Vallejo's grandniece, Caroline, the daughter of Dr. Edward T. Bale. Her dowry was the land on which he planted vines and erected the original winery in the following year.

During the next two decades, Krug became "the wine king of

Napa Valley" and a prominent member of the first State Viticultural Commission. His wines and brandy were sold in the East, in Mexico, Germany, and England. Then phylloxera destroyed most of his vineyard, and Krug's estate was in debt when he died in 1892. A nephew ran the winery until Prohibition, when the then owners, the Moffitt family of bankers and paper merchants, closed it down.

At Repeal, the cellar was leased to Louis Stralla's Napa Wine Company until Stralla moved to the old Brun & Chaix place at Oakville in 1940. The Moffitts meanwhile declined to sell the estate, hoping to find a buyer who could reestablish the earlier prestige of its wines.

In Lodi, one day in 1935, when Robert and Peter Mondavi were home from their studies at Stanford, their father asked them what kind of careers, if any, they had in mind after college. Cesare Mondavi, who had come to America from Italy twenty-seven years before, had a grape shipping business in Lodi and Fresno and had begun making bulk wine at the Acampo Winery at Repeal. When the boys replied that they would like to get into the wine business, Cesare advised them that the future lay in table wines and that the Napa Valley was the place to go.

After graduation, both sons were taught enology by University of California scientists. To start them off, Cesare bought the Sunny St. Helena Winery in 1937. When the chance came six years later to buy the Krug estate for $75,000, the Sunny St. Helena and Acampo wineries were sold.

When C. Mondavi & Sons took over at Krug, bulk wine shipped in tank cars to regional bottlers was the mainstay of their business. To rehabilitate the hundred-acre vineyard, to develop a stock of fine wines, and to introduce a new generation to the name of the long-dead Charles Krug should have taken many years. But the Mondavis wisely kept their bulk wine business and bottled only their finest wines under the Krug name. Within five years they were winning medals at the State Fair. They opened a tasting room, invited visitors to hold picnics and tastings (by reservation) on the estate, published a newsletter named *Bottles and Bins* which has been circulating more than twenty years, and started holding August Moon Concerts on the winery lawn.

In 1965 policy disagreements between the two Mondavi brothers, brewing since their father's death six years earlier, exploded into a family schism. Their mother and sisters joined Peter, the younger brother and winemaker, in opposition to

Robert, who was in charge of sales, telling him his son Michael could not be employed by the winery. Robert responded by building his own winery six miles down the road, but he remained on the Krug board of directors and continued living on the Krug estate. At a directors' meeting in 1972, a $32 million offer by the Schlitz brewery to buy the winery was turned down, Bob and sister Helen voting to sell but Peter, their mother, and sister Mary voting no. Then Bob sued to force a sale, and a bitter four-year court fight ensued. It ended, after the mother's death in 1976, in victory for Robert. The court ordered the winery sold. Trustees banished Peter from the winery. Finally Peter and Helen bought Bob's interest, ending the family feud. Charles Krug is now again run by Peter, assisted by his UC Davis-trained son Marc and in summer by Peter, Jr., who will join them when he finishes college.

The Charles Krug (or C. Mondavi & Sons) winery has a capacity of some four million gallons, but this does not count the contract-production at the Sunny St. Helena Winery or the wines the firm owns but has in storage at wineries outside of Napa County. Only the company's best wines, thirteen under varietal labels and ten generically labeled, plus a "vintage select" Cabernet Sauvignon, are sold under the Charles Krug label. The rest are jug-quality "CK" Mondavi wines, available in sizes up to gallons, which include some from the San Joaquin Valley.

With vineyards in various Napa Valley microclimates from St. Helena to the Carneros district, the firm and members of Peter's family have some twelve hundred acres in vines.

• 18 •

Continuing north on the Wine Road past Krug, the winery on the right, with the steel tanks in front, is the former St. Helena Co-operative, now one of the chain of United Vintners-Heublein wine-processing plants.

Beyond the old co-op, the century-old Victorian house at the left, with the acre of vines in front, is where Mike and Shirley Robbins started their miniature basement Spring Mountain Vineyards winery, selling it after they moved to the Tiburcio Parrott estate. The buyers were San Francisco ophthalmologist William J. Casey and his wife Alexandra, wine enthusiasts who had planned for years to own a winery. They renamed it St. Clement Vineyard for the doctor's ancestral home, St. Clement's Manor in Maryland, a seventh-century grant from the

English crown, where the doctor had helped plant a vineyard. By 1976 they made their first Cabernet Sauvignon and Chardonnay, the doctor working weekends and commuting to his practice in the city.

On Lodi Lane, the next road to the right, is a pre-Prohibition stone cellar renamed by owner Charles Abela in 1977 as the Round Hill Vineyards winery. It bottles coast-counties wines named for the round hill west of St. Helena where Ernest Van Asperen, of Ernie's Wine Stores, lives and grows grapes, some of which reach the market in Round Hill wines. Ernie owns four Napa Valley vineyards but produces no wine commercially. He is a talented home winemaker, and some of the best wines in California are those he makes for his own table.

Next on the right is Freemark Abbey, the moss-covered stone cellar with the gourmet shops and Abbey Restaurant upstairs, around the corner from Wine Country Inn on Lodi Lane. The "Abbey" dates from 1895 and was never a monastery; it was named by a group of former owners who combined syllables from their names. The basement was reactivated as a modern winery in 1967; six years later the bottling cellar was added in the rear. No tasting is offered, but there are cellar tours twice a day. Seven partners, three of them grape growers, own the winery, which has first choice of grapes from the grower-partners' six hundred acres of vineyards. Grapes are bought from other vineyards to make special-name wines, such as John Bosché's Cabernet Sauvignon. Consulting enologist Bradford Webb, who made the Hanzell Vineyard wines that introduced European oak to California, is one of the grower partners. The chief partner is Charles Carpy, whose Bordeaux-born grandfather owned the Uncle Sam Cellars in Napa city in 1887 and was the largest shareholder in the California Wine Association when it was formed in 1894. In 1976 the Freemark group and additional investors acquired the Rutherford Hill winery, which will be described on a later page. Some Freemark wines have set new high standards for California. The first wine grown in the state that I might have mistaken for a good vintage of Château Margaux was Freemark Abbey 1968 Cabernet Sauvignon. The 1973 Edelwein, a botrytized White Riesling, might have been labeled Beerenauslese if it had been grown in the Rheingau.

On Ehlers Lane, a mile north of Freemark Abbey, is a venerable stone cellar with arched windows and a carving above the door that reads: "B. Ehlers, 1886." It is named in Frona Eunice Wait's 1889 book of California wines, and though idle during the Prohibition era, again produced wine for two decades after Repeal. During the 1970s, the young vineyards of William and Kathleen Collins west of St. Helena were ready to bear their first crops. They planned to build a winery, but found this empty cellar, leased it, installed modern equipment, and named it the Conn Creek Winery for their vineyards a few miles southwest, through which Conn Creek flows. With experienced winemaker John Henderson, they produced their 1976 vintage here. Collins, an Annapolis graduate who served on missile submarines in the Second World War, has a partner, Stanford Professor William Beaver.

• 19 •

A short distance farther there is an unmarked private road on the left. If you have made an appointment, you may climb almost two miles up the dirt road and visit Stony Hill Vineyard. The vines rise almost a thousand feet above the valley and cover some thirty-eight acres of rocky soil, which explains the name. The four wines made here—Chardonnay, Gewürztraminer, White Riesling, and in some years a Sémillon de Soleil (sweet, made from sun-dried grapes) are so prized by connoisseurs that most of the supply is sold before it is ready to be shipped.

The story of Fred and Eleanor McCrea has inspired many others to embark on winegrowing careers. Eleanor has carried on the business since Fred, a San Francisco advertising executive, died in 1977. Looking for a place on which to build a summer house, the McCreas bought their Napa hillside in 1943, then wondered what to do with the extra space. Neighbors said it would be good for only goats or grapes, so they chose grapes. Knowing nothing about winegrowing, they asked University experts what to plant, and were advised to try Chardonnay. Waiting for their vines to mature, the McCreas practiced winemaking in their home, and threw their first batch away. Then, guided by friendly Napa vintners, they had their winery built and equipped by 1951. Nine years later, their Chardonnay was awarded the highest prize in the state, a gold medal at the State Fair. Orders for the wine came in floods, but the McCreas kept their winery small—several dozen oak barrels holding five thousand gallons when full—and sold most of their grapes to neighboring wineries.

Each September, when Stony Hill wines have a year or two of bottle age, a letter goes to a small mailing list stating which wines are ready for sale. If you place your order promptly it is likely to be filled, but it is wiser to order a year ahead.

On Larkmead Lane, a quarter mile off the Wine Road, are the champagne cellars of Hanns Kornell, where he makes his excellent "Third Generation" sparkling wines and also the champagnes that some other wineries sell as their own.

The Larkmead Vineyard has been famous since the 1880s, when it was owned by Mrs. Lillie Hitchcock Coit. She was known then as a sort of mascot to the San Francisco Fire Department because of her passion for running to fires, but she is remembered now as the donor of Coit Tower on that city's Telegraph Hill. Another owner before Prohibition was the Felix Salmina family from Switzerland, who after Repeal made a great wine from the true Petite Sirah or Shiraz grape. A succession of proprietors followed, including National Distillers, Bruno Solari, and the Larkmead Co-operative, until Kornell took over in 1958.

Kornell is a stocky little man of incredible stamina and energy. He is more of a legend than his winery. In 1915, at the age of four, he was picking grapes in his grandfather's vineyard at Lublinitz in Germany. At five, he was already cleaning bottles in the cellar. During his school years his father taught him the art of tasting. At graduation he was sent to the Geisenheim enological institute, then worked in wineries in France, Italy, and England. When he was ready in 1939 to take over the family vineyard, the gathering war clouds warned him to go to America. With two dollars in his wallet, he started hitchhiking from New York to California. He worked first as a laborer, then briefly at the old Los Amigos Winery, and next at the Fountain Grove Vineyard, where he was succeeded by his cousin Kurt Opper. In 1942, Kornell went to Covington, Kentucky, to work for the Gibson Wine Company. There he made the first Kentucky champagne (out of California wine) in 1942. Three years later, on a visit to the American Wine Company cellars in St. Louis, whom should I find three stories underground making Cook's Imperial Champagne, but Hanns Kornell? After the American Wine Company was sold to Schenley, Kornell returned to California in 1952, leased the rundown former Tribuno winery at Sonoma, and made his own champagne. Bottling and riddling by night and selling by day, he saved enough in six years to buy Larkmead, and moved to St. Helena. In that same year, he married Marielouise Rossini, whose grandfather planted the first Souverain Vineyard seventy-two years before.

At the Kornell Champagne Cellars you are shown every step in the making of bottle-fermented champagne. Your amiable guide may be the indefatigable owner himself, for he still works fourteen hours a day, or perhaps a member of the Fourth Generation, daughter Paula or son Peter Hanns, who help in the cellar and taste wine regularly with their parents. There are seven Kornell champagnes, brut, sec, extra dry, demi-sec, rouge, Muscat of Alexandria, and Sehr Trocken (extremely dry). The latter is aged five years or more on the yeast before it is disgorged. Kornell champagnes are unlike the French product because Hanns prefers Riesling, with its flowery aroma, to the traditional champagne grape, Chardonnay. That many others agree with his taste is evident from his steadily increasing business, including his exports to other countries, especially to Switzerland and Germany.

• 21 •

Five miles north of St. Helena, a small sign at the left of the highway reads "Schramsberg Champagne Cellars—Founded 1862." A narrow road from there winds nearly a mile up the southern slope of Mount Diamond through a thicket of redwoods, buckeyes, and madrones. In a wide clearing at the end is the scene that Robert Louis Stevenson described in *Silverado Squatters,* the same house with its broad verandas where RLS and his bride were entertained in 1880 by Jacob and Annie Schram, and the five underground cellars "dug deep in the hillside like a bandit's cave."

Schram (originally Schramm) arrived in America from the Rhineland in 1842, became an itinerant barber, and stopped in San Francisco long enough to get married. When he reached Napa in 1862, Charles Krug had begun building his winery on the valley floor two years before. Schram had saved enough money to buy a mountainside of his own. While Annie supervised the planting of their vines, Schram continued tramping from farm to farm with his razor and shears. Eighteen years later, Stevenson found Schramsberg "the picture of prosperity." Schramsberger Hock, Golden Chasselas, and Burgundy of Refosco had already won a place on such wine lists as the Palace Hotel's in San Francisco and the Carlton Club's in London.

When Schram died in 1904, his son Herman took over and made wine until Prohibition, when he sold the estate for a summer home. Following Repeal there were two brief revivals, the first by Joseph Gargano's California Champagne Company in 1940, the second in 1951 by the Douglas Pringles. Pringle, a flamboyant interior decorator, revived the Schramsberg label and made rather poor champagnes for a few years. The winery was closed again, and Pringle killed himself in 1960.

Meanwhile, a Stanford and Harvard Business School graduate named Jack L. Davies had joined the San Francisco Wine and Food Society and had developed a taste for fine wines. In 1961 he invested in a Cabernet-planting venture with Martin Ray in Santa Clara County, then sold his interest after a dispute with that controversial vintner; but Davies's fascination with winegrowing increased. In 1965, he formed a corporation with fourteen fellow wine lovers and bought Schramsberg from Pringle's former wife, Mrs. Louis de Laveaga Cebrian. He quit his job as a management consultant, moved with his wife, Jamie Louise, and their three children into the ninety-year-old Schram house on the mountain, and set out to make the world's finest champagne.

The next seven years were difficult at Schramsberg. The cobwebbed, long-neglected tunnels were cleared and the earth floors paved; the old vineyard was torn out and replanted with Chardonnay and Pinot Noir. Grapes were purchased from nearby hillsides in 1966, but the new crusher broke down on the first day; and with a ton of Chardonnays left, Jamie took off her shoes and finished the crushing the age-old way. The first two-year-old Blanc de Blancs champagne was released in 1968, followed by a sparkling pink Cuvée de Gamay. A Blanc de Noir champagne made in 1967 from Pinot Noir and Chardonnay was offered in 1971. Davies succeeded in getting the wines stocked by a limited number of prestige wine shops around the country, including one in Washington, D.C. He then told his partners they might hope for sufficient sales to turn the corner financially in another year or two.

In February 1972, Schramsberg Champagne became world-famous overnight. President Richard M. Nixon had flown an American champagne to Peking to serve at his historic, globally-televised banquet for Red Chinese Premier Chou Enlai. On the day of the banquet a Washington newspaper columnist identified the shipment as thirteen cases of Schramsberg, Nixon's favorite champagne. Press, TV, and radio spread the name, Davies's story, and the fame of Napa Valley wine.

Schramsberg and its vineyard have been gradually enlarged in subsequent years in efforts to keep up with the growing demand for its champagnes. A semi-sparkling, demisec Crémant champagne has been added to the list. Two buildings have been erected in front of the main aging tunnels, and visitors who make appointments in advance are taken on cellar tours.

• 22 •

Diamond Mountain, like Mt. Veeder and Spring Mountain also on the west side of Napa Valley, is regarded as a viticultural district separate from the rest of Napa County. If the Federal plan to delimit American vineyard areas goes ahead, wines from all three of these mountainsides may someday bear label designations of their own.

Diamond Mountain Road, a mile north of the entrance to Schramsberg, climbs from Highway 29 to several new vineyards and to a pre-Prohibition stone winery whose name nobody in the vicinity remembers, on the face of which the initials "RS" are carved with the date of 1888. This cellar, with tunnels carved into the mountain, is where Albert Brounstein ages his three distinctly different Diamond Creek Vineyards Cabernet Sauvignon wines.

A wine-appreciation course taught by Los Angeles *Times* writer Nathan Chroman in 1965 and a subsequent wine tour of France inspired Brounstein to give up his wholesale drug business and to plant twenty acres of Cabernet and Merlot on Mount Diamond three years later. Finding three different soil types on his vineyard, he kept the grapes from each patch of vines separate and named their wines Red Rock Terrace, Gravelly Meadow, and Volcanic Hill. Brounstein invites selected visitors to picnic and taste his wines at a lake beside the vineyard, and takes their advance orders for the next Cabernet vintages he will release for sale.

• 23 •

As you approach the valley's upper end, a white monastery-like structure comes into view atop the range of hills to the east. It is the Sterling Vineyards winery, the most spectacular in America and quite possibly in the world.

To reach the winery, you turn right on Dunaweal Lane, pass a smaller winery (of which more in a moment) and board an aerial tramway like those you find at the costlier mountain ski resorts. For a $2.50 fare, a yellow four-person gondola lifts you 250 feet to the winery, which commands a dramatic view of the valley winescape and of towering Mount St. Helena.

On disembarking, you take an instructive self-tour of the

crushing and fermenting areas, then pass through stained-glass-illuminated cellars where some 400,000 gallons of wine age in oak barrels and casks. You then arrive in an area of mosaic-lined patios, fountains, and flowers overlooked by a carillon of European church bells that chime the hours. Here selected wines are offered for tasting and for purchase to take home.

Sterling had its inception in 1964 when Yale-educated former Navy fighter pilot Michael P.W. Stone and former London journalist Peter Newton, among the owners of a San Francisco paper products firm called Sterling International, invested in planting the 400-acre vineyard on the valley floor. When the vineyard bore its first full crop in 1968, they built a temporary winery and chose as Sterling's winemaster Richard R. (Ric) Forman, who was just winning his master's degree in enology at UC Davis at the age of twenty-four. By the time the hilltop winery was built in 1973, Sterling Vineyard wines were already winning awards at the Los Angeles County Fair. Its most consistent gold medal winners at this writing were its Chardonnays and its Merlots, which closely resemble the leading Pomerols of Bordeaux.

In 1977, the Coca-Cola Company of Atlanta, which had entered the wine field by purchasing the Taylor and Great Western wineries of New York State, bought the Sterling Vineyards and winery. Stone and Newton, continuing in charge for the new owner, announced that Sterling would discontinue the use of purchased grapes, was acquiring two more Napa vineyards, and henceforth would be the largest exclusively estate-bottling winery in the United States.

Returning from Sterling to the Wine Road, you will find it interesting to stop for a visit to the small (40,000-gallon) Stonegate Winery, which you passed on Dunaweal Lane. The owners of Stonegate are University of California journalism instructor James Spaulding and his wife Barbara. Their son David, trained in enology at Santa Rosa Junior College and in short courses at UC Davis, is the winemaker. The Spauldings came to California from Wisconsin in 1969 after a disappointing attempt to grow wine grapes at Mequon, a suburb of Milwaukee. They produce estate-bottled Pinot Noir, Cabernet Sauvignon, Chardonnay, and Sauvignon Blanc wines from thirty acres of vineyard, half of which is at the winery and half on the upper slopes of Diamond Mountain. Stonegate wines, aged mostly in European oak, have already won a connoisseur following.

• 24 •

A mile and a half farther north is Calistoga, the city that
began in 1859 as the personal empire and obsession of the
fabulous Sam Brannan. He is said to have named Calistoga by a
slip of his tongue, saying: "I'll make this place the Calistoga of
Sarafornia."

So spectacular were Brannan's other exploits that his role as a
major Napa winegrower of the 1860s appears to have been
forgotten. Little of his story can be learned in Calistoga, which
is a sleepy tourist town with numerous bathhouses situated
around the founder's hot mineral springs. To recall his memory
there are only a side street named Brannan, a plaque, and two
small, faded wooden buildings.

One must dig into libraries elsewhere to read the fantastic
story of that wandering printer from the Ohio vineyard center
of Painesville, who joined the original Mormons, brought two
hundred of them to San Francisco by sea, founded that city's
first newspaper, led the Vigilantes, quarreled with Brigham
Young, and then abandoned the Mormon faith.

California's first millionaire, Brannan bought 2,000 acres to
found Calistoga around its natural mudpots and geysers, spent
millions planting the 125,000 vines that he personally brought
from Europe, and built a winery, brandy distillery, hotels,
racetrack, and luxury baths. Brannan's Calistoga empire collapsed after his divorce in 1870. He soon lost his fortune, and in
1889 died penniless near Escondido in the arms of an Indian
squaw.

Two miles north of Calistoga, hidden in a grove a few
hundred yards from Tubbs Lane, is an historic winery named
Château Montelena. Its facade of many arches, pilasters,
parapets, and towers is an architectural curio, reminiscent of
some nineteenth-century Italian palace. It was built of native
stone in 1882 by cordage manufacturer Alfred L. Tubbs, the
patriarch of a noted San Francisco family, and has often been
compared to Château Lafite. Tubbs, with Charles Krug and
other winery owners, organized the Napa Valley Wine Company in 1883 to sell their wines and those of independent
vineyardists to the retail trade. Eleven years later, the company
was absorbed by the California Wine Association. A grandson,
Chapin Tubbs, made wine sporadically here for a few years
following the repeal of Prohibition. In 1947, a Chinese engineer
bought the property, made the upper story of the empty winery

his home, and built the Oriental Water Gardens, a five-acre lake with four islands, arched bridges, and an authentic five-ton Chinese junk in the center.

The winery had lain idle for some thirty years when in 1968 it was purchased by Lee and Helen Paschich, dedicated home winemakers who found it pleasant to live upstairs.

Then the wine revolution exploded, and many investors became interested in old Napa Valley wineries that might be revived to capitalize on the boom. Among those who saw the possibilities in Château Montelena were Southern California attorney James L. Barrett and Chicago supermarket developer Ernest Hahn. They became Paschich's partners, replanted much of the hundred-acre vineyard, installed modern equipment to hold some 40,000 gallons, and in 1972 brought in the great winemaker Miljenko (Mike) Grgich, whom we met a few pages ago. Grgich made Château Montelena nationally famous with one of the wines in his second vintage—the 1973 Chardonnay—for this was the California white wine that those nine French experts, at that blind-tasting in Paris, chose as finer than four of the top white burgundies of France and five other California Chardonnays.

When Grgich left in 1977 to start his own winery, Montelena was fortunate again in choosing its new winemaker. He was young Jerry Luper, an enology graduate of Fresno State University, who had made many fine wines during six years at Freemark Abbey, including the 1973 "Edelwein," Freemark's botrytized late-harvest Riesling that has won nationwide praise.

Château Montelena's vineyard is planted entirely to red varieties, mostly Cabernet Sauvignon and Zinfandel. Its white wines are made of purchased grapes. The winery has a second label, Silverado Cellars, for any vintages that do not meet the standard for its Château wines.

• 25 •

Beyond Tubbs Lane, Highway 29 climbs the foothills of Mount St. Helena and heads for Lake County. It is time to turn back down the Napa Valley, this time taking the east-side highway, the Silverado Trail.

The first winery to be seen is the handsome new 60,000-gallon Cuvaison cellar, built in 1974 just south of Dunaweal Lane. Mission style with stained-glass windows and a red tile roof, it replaces a rustic earlier structure opened four years earlier by the first owner, Dr. Thomas Parkhill, who contributed the name: a French word for the fermenting of red wines on the skins of grapes.

When noted French-trained winemaker Philip Togni took charge at Cuvaison in 1975, he announced that the winery thenceforth would specialize in producing only three wines, Chardonnay, Cabernet Sauvignon, and Zinfandel. One of the Cabernets was the first produced in this century from Marin County grapes.

At press time the present owners, affiliated with the Commerce Clearing House publishing firm, were reported negotiating to sell the winery to a group of grape growers. Tasting was still being offered Thursdays through Mondays in the attractive hospitality room.

• 26 •

A left turn on Deer Park Road takes you uphill some two and a half miles to a small sign at your left that points to Burgess Cellars. Former Air Force pilot Tom Burgess and his wife Linda bought this 37,000-gallon winery and its twenty-acre vineyard in 1972. Originally it was the Rossini vineyard, planted by Marielouise Kornell's grandfather in 1880. J. Leland Stewart built the winery in 1943 and called it Souverain Cellars, a name later applied, after Stewart retired in 1970 (he is still active elsewhere), to two newer wineries in Napa and Sonoma Counties. The Burgesses operate their winery as Stewart did, welcoming visitors daily except on holidays but offering no tasting. They make a few wines from their own grapes, but buy most of their needs from other vineyards, some of whose names appear on Burgess labels. Their wines are highly praised, which they credit to their enologist Bill Sorenson, a Fresno State University graduate who once operated the experimental winery at that institution.

From Burgess Cellars you may wish to drive several miles farther east on Howell Mountain Road across the hills to Napa County's northernmost winery in Pope Valley. There are several vineyards in this valley, which has a warmer climate than the rest of Napa County. The Pope Valley winery dates from 1909. It had been closed for several years after its founder Sam Haus retired, when James and Arlene Devitt, dealers in home-winemaking supplies, came from Thousand Oaks to reopen the old wooden buildings in 1972. Their sons Bob and

Steve were making wine there from purchased Napa, Sonoma, and Lake Counties grapes when I last paid them a visit.

• 27 •

Returning to Silverado Trail and continuing three miles south, you reach Taplin Road, which extends to your left. A short drive past a green wooden schoolhouse takes you to a curiously constructed gateway constructed of recycled lumber from century-old California railroad bridges. This is the entrance to Joseph Phelps Vineyards. Joseph Phelps is a builder, headquartered at Greeley, Colorado. In 1972, while building the Souverain wineries in California, he bought land on Taplin Road to establish his own winegrowing estate. The old Spring Valley Schoolhouse became his vineyard headquarters. As his winemaster Phelps chose German-born, Geisenheim-trained Walter Schug, who had had experience with two California wineries since coming to this country in 1961. Schug planted 120 acres of noble varieties for Phelps beginning in 1973, including twenty acres of Syrah, the red Rhone wine variety of Hermitage, which differs from California's Petite Sirah. The 50,000-gallon Phelps winery, whose facade resembles the vineyard gate, was built in time to ferment the 1974 vintage. Phelps Vineyards wines have received lyric praises since the introduction of the 1975 vintage, made from neighbors' grapes. The highest accolades have been for the delicate yet luscious late-harvest Johannisberg Riesling.

Touring and tasting are not offered at the Phelps winery, but you can buy wines by the case there on most weekdays. An invitational tasting is held on the first Saturday of each month, when you may meet Walter Schug, Phelps's charming daughter Leslie, and if he isn't away on some building project, perhaps Phelps himself.

• 28 •

Taplin Road continues past Phelps Vineyard to the winery and vineyard of Joseph and Alice Heitz. An appointment is worth making in advance, for their wines are among the finest in Napa County.

In 1944, after two years in a midwestern college, Airman Joe Heitz was chief of a night-fighter ground crew at the field near the Italian Swiss Colony winery outside Fresno. Dale Mills, the winemaker there, put Joe to work in the cellar by day, and discovered that he had an exceptionally keen palate. Mills advised him, on his discharge from the Air Force, to enroll at Davis and study enology. Heitz did so and won his master's degree in 1949. For ten years he worked at Beaulieu and other wineries, then taught enology at Fresno State College for four years. In 1961, married and with three children, Heitz decided to start his own wine business.

He bought Leon Brendel's "Only One" Grignolino vineyard on The Wine Road south of St. Helena, the site of the Heitz tasting room today. The orange-pink Grignolino wine he made there could not support his family, but Heitz has the rare ability to select lots from other wineries that will improve with blending and aging. The quality of these Heitz selections, of his Grignolino and of wines he made from purchased grapes, attracted connoisseurs to the little old winery. Five-foot-tall Alice Heitz developed a mailing list and sent periodic letters to their customers, announcing each new Heitz selection.

Soon a larger winery was needed, and in 1965 Heitz found the place in a small valley at the end of Taplin Road. On the property was an empty seventy-year-old winery building and an old house. He equipped the cellar with a new crusher, stainless steel fermenters, and racks of French oak casks, some of them from the Hanzell Vineyard, while Alice made the ancient house livable. In the next few years he planted twenty more acres of Grignolino, Chardonnay, and Pinot Noir. In 1972, when son David graduated from Fresno State and went to work with his parents, an additional winery was built, raising their capacity to 160,000 gallons. Most grapes for Heitz wines are produced by others, some of whose names appear on the labels. Most famous vineyard-labeled Heitz wine is the Cabernet Sauvignon grown on Martha May's vineyard near Oakville.

Although the wines are sold mostly to those on Alice's mailing list and at the highway tasting room, restaurants and wine merchants feature some of the rarities. Recent offerings to the mailing list, which will give you an idea, ranged from Chablis at $2.55 a bottle and Grignolino at $3.25, to 1972 Chardonnay Lot Z-21 at $10 and the 1969 Martha's Vineyard Cabernet at $35 each.

• 29 •

A mile or so south of Taplin Road, a private road leads a half-mile uphill to the handsome Rutherford Hill winery. This was named Souverain of Rutherford when it was built in 1972 while the Souverain of Alexander Valley cellar, visited in the preceding chapter, was being built near Geyserville in Sonoma County. In 1976, when Pillsbury Mills of Minneapolis sold both Souverain wineries, a group formed by vineyardist William Jaeger and other owners of Freemark Abbey bought this one and renamed it Rutherford Hill. Philip Baxter is the winemaker. Cellar tours and use of the picnic area are by appointment.

Just south of the road to Rutherford Hill, Highway 128 leads east to two more Napa wineries and a future third. Opposite Lake Hennessy, Sage Canyon Road climbs steep Pritchard Hill to the vineyard of Robert Long and his wife Zelma, the enologist at Robert Mondavi winery. The Longs are planning a winery of their own. The road continues farther to the hundred-acre hilltop vineyard and spectacular winery of Donn Chappellet, who left the food-vending business in Los Angeles to found this winery in 1967. The cellar, a triangular pyramid designed by Santa Rosa structural engineer Richard Keith, has rust-colored metal roofs. Chappellet's past enologists have been Philip Togni, more recently at Cuvaison, and Joseph Cafaro, who later joined the Robert Keenan Vineyard on Spring Mountain. Six wines have been made at Chappellet: Cabernet, Merlot, Chardonnay, Riesling, Chenin Blanc, and a Pritchard Hill White.

Four miles farther east on Highway 128 is the hilltop winery of Jim Nichelini. It is an old-fashioned roadside cellar, built in 1890 by Jim's grandfather, Anton Nichelini from Switzerland. Open to the public on weekends, it is a cheery place. Visitors are invited to sample the wines on the terrace, which Jim calls "the only outdoor tasting room in California." Sometimes Jim plays his accordion for the visitors. Several red and white wines are made, but the Nichelini specialties are Chenin Blanc and Sauvignon Vert. The wines are inexpensive and are stocked in a few Bay Area restaurants and stores, although a good part is sold to people passing the winery en route to and from Lake Berryessa nearby. The fifty-acre Nichelini vineyard is a mile beyond the winery in Chiles Valley, where the Kentucky trapper, Colonel Joseph Chiles, was the first winegrower during the 1860s.

The climate of Chiles Valley, nine hundred feet high, has attracted the interest of vintners who are looking for more Napa land suitable for vines. The first to plant extensively there was Louis P. Martini, whose land is three miles north of Nichelini's. For many years, Chiles Valley was considered too warm for the premium wine grapes, because the hills there turn brown in summer; the locality "looks warm." But Martini took thermo-graph readings for four years before he began planting and discovered that the temperatures are those of "low Region II." Cool, fresh afternoon winds are apparently the cause. There also are some premium grape plantings in Wooden Valley, ten miles to the southeast, as well as those in Pope Valley to the north.

• 30 •

There are five more Napa Valley wineries still to be seen off the Silverado Trail, and two more in Napa City.

On Conn Creek Road, which takes off from Route 128 toward Rutherford, veteran vineyardist Charles Wagner has built the 30,000-gallon Caymus Vineyard winery (named for the Caymus land grant) to produce estate-bottled wines of the best grape varieties grown on his seventy-acre vineyard. His wife Lorna and their son Charles J. (Chuck) work with him. Besides their Cabernet Sauvignon, Pinot Noir, and Riesling, they make Zinfandel from purchased grapes and sell it under a separate "Liberty School" label that pictures the one-room school Charles attended nearby in his youth.

A mile farther south on Oakville Cross Road, a sign on a stone pillar reads "Mount Eden Ranch." A private road from the pillar leads to Villa Mt. Eden, the winegrowing estate of San Francisco financier James McWilliams and his wife Anne, the granddaughter of Bank of America founder A.P. Giannini. Since making this their country home in 1970, they have replanted half of the eighty-acre vineyard, which dates from 1881, and have re-equipped and air-conditioned the winery. Their winemaster Nils Venge, a 1967 graduate of UC Davis, came here in 1973 after working with the Charles Krug and Sterling wineries. The first estate-bottled Villa Mt. Eden wines released were the 1975 Gewürztraminer, Chenin Blanc, and Napa Gamay. At this writing, their estate-bottled 1974 Char-donnay and Cabernet Sauvignon were still aging in bottles.

• 31 •

A mile south of Yountville Cross Road, you come to two Stag's Leap wineries, a few hundred yards apart, whose owners have fought in the courts since 1972 over which is entitled to use the name.

Stag's Leap is a rocky promontory overlooking a vineyard valley east of Silverado Trail. Chicago financier Horace Chase is said to have named it for a legendary stag when in 1888 he built the residence that later became the Stag's Leap Hotel. Warren and Barbara Winiarski left teaching jobs at the University of Chicago in 1964 to become winegrowers in the Napa Valley. They bought part of the Stag's Leap valley, planted vines, and in 1972 built the 70,000-gallon "Stag's Leap Wine Cellars." Two years earlier, while the Winiarskis were still planning their winery, Carl and Joanne Doumani, wine buffs from Los Angeles, bought the old Stag's Leap Hotel, part of the original vineyard, and the ruins of Chase's winery. They tore off the third story of the hotel to make their home in the two lower floors. The Doumanis had Rutherford Hill Winery make wine for them, stored it in a cave bonded behind the ruined winery, and sold the wine labeled "Stag's Leap Vineyards." Lawsuits ensued, the Winiarskis won, and the Doumanis appealed.

Meanwhile, the Winiarskis' "Stag's Leap Wine Cellars" suddenly became world famous. Their 1973 Cabernet Sauvignon outscored four world-famous château red wines of Bordeaux at that blind-tasting by French experts in Paris in 1976.

At this writing, both the Winiarskis and Doumanis were selling wines with pictures of stags on their labels. The Doumanis were building new walls and a roof on the ruins of Chase's winery. The Winiarskis were sold out of their 1973 Cabernet and of some of their 1975 Cabernet and Merlot. (Neither winery offers any tasting or cellar tours.)

• 32 •

Next on your left, almost surrounded by the Chimney Rock Golf Course, is the Clos du Val vineyard and winery, the second investment by wine interests of France in Napa Valley winegrowing. At the same time when Moët-Hennessy was buying land to begin producing its Domaine Chandon champagne at Yountville, three miles across the valley from here, a different group of French investors was establishing this vineyard to grow Bordeaux-style red wines. Owner of the 120-acre vineyard and 75,000-gallon winery is the Areti Corporation of California, headed by John Goelet, a wealthy American who lives in France and whose group has vineyard properties there, in Australia, and South America.

Clos du Val's winemaker-manager is Bernard Portet, a 1968 graduate of the French national wine school at Montpellier. He worked in South Africa and at a château near Toulouse before coming here. His father, André Portet, was the long-time manager of world-famed Château Lafite.

Only two wines are produced, a Cabernet Sauvignon blended fifteen percent with Merlot, and a Zinfandel. The Cabernet is dark, intense, and austere like a Médoc. Portet says his Zinfandel, equally dark, may outlast his Cabernet, but that Bordeaux wine merchants would consider it "too big." He hopes someday to see his wines sold in France. The first three Clos du Val vintages were made of grapes purchased from neighboring vineyards; the 1975s were Clos du Val's first estate-bottled wines.

A short distance north of Clos du Val is the much bigger Occidental Winery, built in 1878 by T.L. Grigsby, who helped to raise the Bear Flag over Sonoma Plaza when California declared its independence of Mexico in 1846. Portet leases the century-old cellar to store his aging wines. No tasting is offered at Clos du Val, but the wines can be purchased at the winery in case lots.

• 33 •

I have not yet described all the wineries in Napa County. This chapter had already been written when I found the Tulocay Winery on a hilltop above Coombsville Road east of Napa. Former stockbroker Charles Cadman and his wife Barbara had assembled some stainless-steel former dairy tanks and several dozen new oak barrels in an airconditioned former ranch building. They were finishing their second 6,000-gallon vintage of Pinot Noir. Now I hear that Bechtel Corporation President Jerome Komes is preparing to reopen the century-old Brockhoff winery, once owned by the late Louis M. Martini, at the end of Zinfandel Lane. Back in 1885 Napa County had 105 wineries. The sixty-three now bonded appear only to be a start.

15

Alameda, Contra Costa, and Solano

CALIFORNIA's new "green belt" laws, enacted to preserve farmlands from urbanization, have given a new lease on life to the few vineyards that remain in Alameda, Contra Costa, and Solano Counties, east of San Francisco Bay. Although forecasts of population growth envision the East Bay cities soon expanding into a virtual megalopolis, some of the historic vineyards in their environs have been replanted in response to today's unprecedented table wine boom.

One can see this happening by visiting the Livermore Valley, which is reached by the MacArthur Freeway (Interstate 580) from the San Francisco-Oakland Bay Bridge, less than an hour's drive. It doesn't look like a valley, for it is an almost flat basin, fourteen miles long, between the low grassy foothills of the Diablo and Hamilton mountain ranges. Beyond the Altamont Hills, only seventeen miles farther east, lies the hot San Joaquin Valley. But the climate of Livermore is Region III, like the upper Napa Valley and northern Sonoma County, because sunny days in Livermore are followed by evening breezes from the Bay.

Most California wine literature describes Livermore as a white wine district. Some writers state flatly that its climate and gravelly soil are unsuited for the growing of red wine grapes. Though the only Livermore wines that have attained national fame are white, the reason is neither climate nor soil, as we'll see presently, and you will find the red wines grown here quite as good as the whites.

Once primarily a vineyard and livestock center, the City of Livermore has multiplied nine times in size since the University of California built the Lawrence Radiation Laboratory in 1952.

Nuclear and electronic industries have followed the mile-square "Rad lab," and subdivisions to house new residents have crowded out many farms. One of the biggest vineyards has become a housing tract of 5,000 people and five schools.

During the 1960s mounting real estate values were threatening to tax out of existence Livermore's two principal vineyards—Wente and Concannon—which are two miles southeast of the city on Tesla Road. Members of the third generations of these two old winegrowing families, each with growing sons, pondered whether to sell out and move. In 1968 they decided to stay. By signing ten-year contracts with the county under the new legislation they dedicated their vineyards as "green belts" or agricultural preserves, which are taxable only on their highest value as farms. Both families have since turned down scores of seven-figure offers from giant corporations that want to buy their names.

• 2 •

The Concannon Vineyard of 250 acres, on the left of Livermore Avenue, has a brick-fronted, old-fashioned winery that is filled to the rafters with oak and redwood wine-aging casks of miscellaneous sizes. It has no separate tasting room. Visitors are invited into the cellar to taste the Concannon wines. The present generation of owners, Joseph Concannon, Jr., and his winemaker brother Jim, like it that way. Their only concessions to recent advances in wine technology are their twenty new temperature-controlled stainless steel tanks, a new French press, and a new bottling line that uses inert gas to keep oxygen from getting into their bottles while they are being corked.

Founder of the winery was their grandfather, James Concannon, who emigrated from Ireland in 1865 at the age of eighteen. He landed in Maine and worked his way up from bellhop to management of a hotel, going to night school meanwhile. Ten years later he was traveling the west coast from San Francisco selling a new invention—rubber stamps—which were quite the rage before typewriters came into general use. His travels took him as far as Mexico City. There the resourceful Concannon got a franchise from Dictator Porfirio Díaz to set up the capital's first street-cleaning system, promptly selling it at a profit to a French syndicate. Back in San Francisco, he learned from Archbishop Joseph Alemany that money could also be made by producing altar wines for the Catholic Church. In 1883 Concannon bought a farm in the Livermore Valley and planted vines imported from France, which others were beginning to plant there at that time. With his vineyard started, he needed capital to develop his winery. He returned to Mexico and got another concession from President Díaz—to introduce French wine grapes to that country, where only the inferior Criolla or Mission grape had been grown until then. Between 1889 and 1904, Concannon shipped several million vine cuttings from Livermore to haciendas throughout the southern republic. For what happened to the Mexican vineyards, see page 521 in my chapter on Mexico. Concannon returned to Livermore and died there in 1911.

Altar wines were the Concannon winery's main products. Altar wines also kept the winery going through the thirteen years of Prohibition, when the founder's son, Captain Joseph Concannon, was in charge. Every five years for the rest of his life, "Captain Joe" expressed his appreciation by sending a gift barrel of his finest Muscat de Frontignan to the Pope in Rome.

Altar wines, sold mostly to the Catholic clergy, are still a fourth of the Concannon Vineyard's business today. This helps explain why most of its wines are white. A red wine would stain the purificator napkin with which the priest wipes the chalice during Mass.

Even so, the best wine that Captain Concannon made was not white. His St. Julien, a wonderfully smooth, flavorful claret blend, was my favorite California dinner wine during the first few years after Repeal. But in 1936, the new Federal labeling regulations issued from Washington contained a provision specifically prohibiting use of the St. Julien name except on wines from that Bordeaux commune. This so angered "Captain Joe" that he withdrew his St. Julien from the market, and he never made that blend again.

Today another red is the best-seller among the fifteen Concannon table and dessert wines, which are sold in some thirty-two states. It is a dry, medium-bodied "varietal" of the Petite Sirah grape that grows beside the winery. Equally fine are the vintage-dated, limited estate-bottlings of Concannon Cabernet Sauvignon, Muscat Blanc, Château Concannon, and Rkatsiteli. The latter is a Russian white wine grape of which the Concannons have planted several acres since 1969.

• 3 •

The Wente Brothers winery is at the right a half mile beyond Concannon and is more than four times as big, because Wente table wines (the only types it makes) are sold in all fifty states. The winery and its separate tasting room are new and ultra-modern, having been built in the late 1960s when the old facilities proved too small.

Carl Heinrich Wente came from Hanover to this country in 1880, learned winemaking from Charles Krug in the Napa Valley, then moved to Livermore and in 1883 acquired an interest in the fifty-acre vineyard planted four years earlier by Dr. George Bernard. Wente expanded his holdings and soon was cultivating a total of 300 acres.

He had three sons. The oldest, Carl F. Wente, was advised by his father to study bookkeeping, got a job as a bank messenger, and forty-five years later became president of the worldwide Bank of America. The second son, Ernest, preferred farming, was sent to the College of Agriculture at Davis, and on graduation took charge of the vineyards. The youngest son, Herman, studied enology at the University in Berkeley and became a winemaker, one of the greatest California has yet known.

Like the Concannons, the Wentes specialized in white wines, though for a different reason: In the old days bulk red wines, sold inter-winery, brought producers as little as ten cents a gallon, while bulk whites seldom sold for less than fifty cents. The Wentes see no reason to change their specialties now.

Before Prohibition, the Wentes sold their entire output in bulk, much of it to the Napa & Sonoma Wine Company of San Francisco, of which they were part owners, and some to Oakland vintner Theodore Gier. During the dry era they made altar wine in bulk for Georges de Latour of Beaulieu, but sold most of their grapes fresh.

In 1934, the year following Repeal, they bottled some wines for the first time, calling them "Valle de Oro"; the name of Wente wasn't yet known outside of Livermore. Then in 1939, Valle de Oro Sauvignon Blanc won the grand prize for white wines at San Francisco's Golden Gate International Exposition. This brought importer Frank Schoonmaker from New York, looking for California wines to introduce nationally with his import line. The first he chose were the Wentes' Sauvignon Blanc, Sémillon, Grey Reisling, Pinot Blanc, Ugni Blanc, and a light-bodied red named Mourastel. Though the labels called them "Schoonmaker Selections," the name of the Wentes was shown as the producer and became known in the East and Midwest.

By 1963, when there was no space for the Wentes to expand

at Livermore, a new 300-acre Wente vineyard of white and red grapes was planted in the Arroyo Seco section of the Salinas Valley near Greenfield in Monterey County. Their Arroyo Seco Vineyard has since spread to 800 acres, more than twice the Wente acreage at Livermore. "Monterey" became the appellation of origin for Wente Brothers Johannisberg Riesling.

The Wentes always had made a red wine for their family use, and had sold a burgundy after Repeal. During the 1960s they introduced annual vintages of Pinot Noir, Gamay Beaujolais, Petite Sirah, and Zinfandel. (The Mourastel was discontinued during the Second World War.) Ugni Blanc was never popular because of its hard-to-pronounce name and was withdrawn from the market, but reappeared in 1967 in a blend with Chenin Blanc under a new name: Wente Bros. Blanc de Blancs. But the best-selling Wente wine is their Grey Riesling, which may also be the single most popular "varietal" white wine sold under a single brand in the United States.

Wente wines come in bottle and half-bottle sizes and in magnums for some varieties, but also available at the winery tasting room are two Valle de Oro wines in half-gallon jugs. Priced a third to a sixth as much as Wente wines, these are best buys. The jug white is so popular that people drive to the winery from the Bay Area to load their cars with it in case lots.

At Herman Wente's death in 1961, Ernest's son Karl became head of the firm. When Karl died in 1977 at the age of 49, his sons Eric and Philip, with degrees lately earned at the UC Davis wine school, were beginning to take charge of the winery, Eric as winemaker, Philip as the viticulturist. The name "Wente Bros." on Wente labels again was becoming literally true.

• 4 •

The most historic vineyard in the valley is Cresta Blanca. To get there from Livermore Avenue, take Wente Street (there is also a Concannon Boulevard), Marina Boulevard, and Arroyo Road. The million-gallon Cresta Blanca winery, with its great tunnels bored into the hillside, is used only for wine storage now, but even to see it from the exterior is worth the extra drive.

Cresta Blanca was founded by journalist Charles Wetmore. A reporter for San Francisco newspapers, he became interested in wine and went to France in 1879 to report on the Paris Exposition for the California Vinicultural Society. He then wrote a series of sensational articles, declaring that 95 percent of French wine imported to the United States was adulterated *vin ordinaire.* He denounced San Francisco restaurateurs for featuring European wines while selling the best California wines under counterfeit French labels or as their "house" wines with no labels at all. Wetmore's articles helped to get the State Board of Viticultural Commissioners established by an act of the Legislature in 1880. Wetmore became the Board's executive officer and then decided to become a winegrower himself. He bought 480 acres of Livermore pasture land for $200 in gold coin, set out his vineyard, and named it Cresta Blanca for the white-crested cliff above. Wetmore then learned that the wife of Louis Mel, the French-born owner of the El Mocho Vineyard, was a friend of the Marquis de Lur-Saluces, the proprietor of world-famed Château d'Yquem near Bordeaux. Armed with a letter from Madame Mel, Wetmore went again to France and obtained from the Marquis cuttings of the three grape varieties that make the Yquem blend—Sémillon, Sauvignon Blanc, and Muscadelle Bordelais.

Wetmore divided the Yquem cuttings between his vineyard and that of Louis Mel, who later sold El Mocho to the Wentes. In Wetmore's vineyard, the vines from France produced wines that won two gold medals for Cresta Blanca in the Paris Exposition of 1889.

During the 1840s, a successor to the Marquis de Lur-Saluces visited Livermore "to see how my children are doing." On tasting a sample of Herman Wente's Sauvignon Blanc, the Marquis told Herman that no Bordeaux vintner had ever made a wine of such quality from that grape alone—that it was impossible in the Bordeaux climate.

Perhaps the direct importation of vines from Yquem explains why, through the years, I have found Livermore Sauvignon Blancs richer and spicier in flavor than those made from this grape grown elsewhere in California. The Livermore producers, however, insist the reason is their climate and in particular their gravelly soil, which holds the heat after the summer sun goes down. I recall tasting a Sauvignon Blanc made by Herman Wente that was magnificent at the age of twenty years.

Cresta Blanca wines with such names as Sauterne Souvenir and Médoc Souvenir were nationally famous before Prohibition. They again were at the top rank of California wines after Repeal, when the vineyard was owned by Wetmore's younger brother, Clarence, and later by his chief salesman, Lucien B. Johnson.

In 1941, during the wartime liquor shortage, Schenley whiskey king Lewis Rosenstiel bought Cresta Blanca from Johnson.

Beringer Brothers, St. Helena CA

Myron Nightingale, who made "Premier Sémillon," California's first botrytized wine, by spraying botrytis spores on grapes at Cresta Blanca in 1956.

This enabled Rosenstiel to advertise on radio, from which his liquor brands were barred by the broadcasting industry code. In 1942 he produced the first advertising program for a wine brand to be aired on a national network. It introduced the first singing commercial for a California wine: "C-R-E-S-T-A" in rising notes and "B-L-A-N-C-A" going down the scale, then the two words repeated in the same notes and followed by the pop of a cork. Rosenstiel introduced the first California sherries to be priced higher than Spanish imports, Cresta Blanca Dry Watch and Triple Cream. But when wines came under wartime price controls, he used the Cresta Blanca label to sell enormous quantities of other wines—something wine merchants remembered when the war ended; his competitors wouldn't let them forget.

History was again made at Cresta Blanca in 1956, when winemaker Myron Nightingale and University enologists produced there the first French-style sauterne ever made commercially outside of Bordeaux. They did it by spraying Sémillon and Sauvignon Blanc grapes in the winery with spores of *Botrytis cinerea,* the "noble mold" which grows naturally on late-harvested grapes in the Sauternes district of Bordeaux. Rosenstiel named the wine Premier Sémillon, priced it six dollars a bottle, and in 1961 unveiled it at a nationally publicized San Francisco tasting. In a speech later inserted in the *Congressional Record,* Senator Tom Kuchel hailed Premier Sémillon as "this product that has broken a European monopoly in one of the gourmet treasures of the world."

What made Premier Sémillon seem a historic breakthrough was a belief long expressed in textbooks, that not enough botrytis grows in California's dry climates to botrytize grapes naturally. In 1969 the Wentes found so much of the mold growing on Riesling grapes in their Monterey vineyard that they left the grapes to ripen for three extra weeks and produced California's first natural Spätlese Riesling. In 1973 they produced both a Spätlese and an Auslese, in both of which the botrytis flavor was unmistakable. Now so many botrytized "late harvest"* Rieslings, Chenin Blancs, and Sauvignon Blancs are produced almost every year in the California coast counties that the 1961 publicity about the artificially-botrytized Livermore wine seems ludicrous in retrospect.

Premier Sémillon wasn't enough to restore Cresta Blanca to its prewar prestige. In 1965 the winery was closed to the public and winemaker Nightingale and his wines were shipped to Schenley's big Roma winery at Fresno. When, six years later, Schenley sold the Cresta Blanca name to the Guild Wine Company of Lodi, Nightingale quit to join the Beringer winery in the Napa Valley. No more Premier Sémillon was made after the 1966 vintage. I have one bottle left in my cellar.

Cresta Blanca wines have now come back on the market from a winery in Mendocino County, and the famous Cresta commercial has returned to the air.

• 5 •

North of the Cresta Blanca vineyard, the name "Olivina" appears on the arch over an imposing stone gate at the intersection of Arroyo and Wetmore roads. Julius Paul Smith of "20-Mule-Team Borax" fame founded Olivina and planted vines there in 1881. The Olivina Vineyard was killed by phylloxera long ago, and except for the crumbling shell of the winery, the fields are bare. No trace remains of such other early Livermore winegrowing estates as Alexander Duval's Château Bellevue on Vallecitos Road, nor of the Chauché & Bon winery on Stanley Boulevard, nor of the vineyard Theodore Gier named Giersburg, four miles south of town.

But if you drive west along Vineyard Avenue toward Pleasanton, you still may see old vineyards, such as the Oakdale or Hagemann tract of 200 acres, which is under lease to Almadén. Next is the equally large Ruby Hill Vineyard, planted by John Crellin in 1883 and named for the red knoll on which its handsome brick and stone winery stands. Ernest Ferrario bought the Crellin estate early in the Prohibition era, reopened

---

*Federal rulings now prohibit American wines from being labeled with the German terms Spätlese, Auslese, Beerenauslese, and Trockenbeerenauslese. But many "late harvest" California wines are described on back labels as meeting the German standards for wines to bear these terms, in degrees of sugar content produced by Botrytis.

the winery at Repeal, and produced excellent wines for three decades, including the best Malvasia Bianca then made in the state. With no sons to carry on his business, Ferarrio quit making wine during the mid-1960s and stored wines made by other wineries until his death in 1974, when the land was sold to the Southern Pacific. A year later, eight amateur winemakers headed by Harry Rosingana leased Ruby Hill, renamed it Stony Ridge, and produced several creditable estate-bottled table wines. Then the SP moved to replace the vineyard with a housing development. The City of Pleasanton and county "no-growth" forces blocked the housing project, and at last reports Rosingana's group was still making wine and hoping to buy Ruby Hill.

In Pleasanton city, a half block north of Main Street, is the million-gallon Villa Armando Winery, which has changed with the times. It was built in 1902 by Frank Garatti and except during Prohibition when it was closed, made mostly bulk wine until 1962. Then Brooklyn wine merchant Anthony Scotto bought it to produce the wines his Italian customers along the eastern seaboard preferred, the kinds they had made themselves during Prohibition. One was a 16 percent earthy, semidry red called Vino Rustico. Another, made of Muscat grapes from Delano, was called Orobianco. By the 1970s, Scotto found that people's tastes were changing, and began adding such California wines as dry Sémillon and Zinfandel with vintage labels. He built a tasting room in front of the winery, bought a vineyard in Lodi, and planted another in the Suñol Valley. Some of his wines began winning medals at the Los Angeles County Fair.

• 6 •

Six miles south of Pleasanton (via Suñol Boulevard and Interstate Highway 680) there is an old Alameda County winegrowing district that is being replanted with premium wine grapes. This is the Suñol Valley, which can never become urbanized because it is part of San Francisco's municipal water system. In 1969 the city granted Almadén Vineyards a forty-year lease on almost a thousand acres there and in the nearby San Antonio Valley. Almadén later chose to plant instead in Monterey County. Other vintners began negotiating for the land. Anthony Scotto was the first to obtain a lease. In 1974 he planted there two hundred acres of such vines as Chardonnay, Pinot Blanc, Cabernet Sauvignon, and Merlot to supply his Villa Armando winery at Pleasanton.

The vineyards of Alameda County declined from 7,000 acres in 1900 to less than 2,000 acres in 1972, but will be increased by more than half when the area around Suñol is fully planted with vines. At least 3,000 more acres of this San Francisco-owned watershed are considered suitable for vineyards. If all are planted, Alameda County will produce more fine wine in the future than it ever did in the past.

• 7 •

Many other parts of the county, including Niles and the present cities of San Lorenzo, Hayward, and Alameda, were winegrowing districts a century ago. But the Mission San José district is older still.

Four miles south of Suñol, the Mission Boulevard exit from the freeway leads to the Mission San José de Guadalupe, founded in 1797. There the Franciscan Fathers planted the first vineyards in Alameda County, a quarter century before those at Sonoma. From the mission the padres at Mission Dolores in San Francisco obtained the grapes to make their wines for the Mass. And from there the English seaman Robert Livermore obtained the vines that he was the first to plant, during the 1840s, in the valley that bears his name. Among early-day wineries near the mission were Joseph Palmer's Peak Vineyard, planted in 1852 with vines imported from Europe; the Los Amigos Vineyard of Grau & Werner, Conrad Weller's Willow Glen Vineyard, and Linda Vista, the vineyard and wine cellars of Charles McIver. Bigger than any of the Livermore vineyards was the 1,000-acre tract which Juan Gallegos, a former Costa Rican coffee planter, owned around the Mission in the 1880s. The million-gallon Gallegos winery and distillery, two miles west at Irvington, was damaged by the earthquake of 1906 and had to be destroyed.

• 8 •

Four miles south of the mission, a spring of hot water gushing from a hillside was visited by early Spanish California ladies who found it a convenient place to wash their linens. The place was named Rancho Agua Caliente, the Warm Springs Ranch. Clement Colombet from France built a stone winery there about 1850 and later built the Warm Springs Hotel around the springs. It was the most fashionable suburban spa around San Francisco until it was wrecked by the earthquake of 1868.

In the following year came Leland Stanford, the railroad

builder, California governor, and United States senator, who bought a square mile around the springs. He cultivated a hundred acres of vines and made 50,000 gallons of wine per year. He later gave the place to his brother Josiah, who tripled its size and added a brandy distillery. Had the property not been occupied by his brother's prospering wine business, the Senator might have built Stanford University there rather than at his Palo Alto horse farm. Josiah Stanford's son inherited the property and made 250,000 gallons of wine per year until phylloxera destroyed the Warm Springs vineyard during the 1890s. Meanwhile another earthquake shut off the springs.

In 1945, half a century later, Rudolf Weibel, the proprietor of the Weibel Champagne Cellar in San Francisco, went looking around the Bay Area for land on which to plant a vineyard of his own. Weibel had arrived nine years earlier from Switzerland with his son Fred and had prospered making champagne under other vintners' brands. He bought the abandoned vineyard at Warm Springs, patched the old buildings, and replanted the vines. Weibel had never heard of Stanford or of the winery's history. He didn't learn it until a year later, when he came to consult me about his new labels, and I happened to tell him the Stanford story.

At Warm Springs, the Weibels continued making champagnes for other vintners, using the Charmat process, but fermented their best in bottles under their own name. They added table and dessert wines and a citrus-and-herb-flavored apéritif wine Rudolf had made in Switzerland, named Tangor.

When Rudolf Weibel died in 1971, a new city named Fremont had grown up around Warm Springs, embracing the mission and several surrounding towns. Fred Weibel then bought vineyards in Mendocino and Sonoma Counties and built a new Weibel winery at Ukiah. He plans to stay at Warm Springs, keeping his Chardonnay vineyard and making his champagnes there.

The Weibel winery on Stanford Avenue, four miles south of the mission, gets thousands of visitors per month because it is near both the 680 and 17 freeways. The visitors are received in an adobe-style "hacienda" tasting room, where champagne is now dispensed on tap by a new patented invention. On weekdays, a girl from the winery office takes them on a tour of the old brick buildings, then around the sherry *soleras* and stainless steel tanks the Weibels and another vintner have added. Between the cellars and the vineyard is a pergola for picnics and a bandstand for concerts.

Among the three dozen wines labeled "Weibel," I have tasted some that were outstanding, but have found the Chardonnay Brut Champagne and the Dry Bin Sherry to be the best.

The winery still makes champagnes for other vintners and uses so many hundreds of different labels that it has its own printing plant. To tell whether a champagne comes from Weibel, look for the address on the bottom of the label, which may read either Warm Springs, Fremont, or Mission San José.

• 9 •

One winery inside another is Llords & Elwood, which has its main bonded winery in a corner of Weibel's property.

For two decades after Repeal, the late Julius Hugh (Mike) Elwood owned the Llords & Elwood chain of prestigious liquor stores in Los Angeles. He stocked the private wine cellars of such Hollywood luminaries as Charlie Chaplin, Ronald Reagan, and Gloria Swanson almost exclusively with European wines. American wines lacked age and glamour and were not expensive enough. Then in 1953 Elwood and his wife took their first trip through the vineyards of Europe. He came back convinced that California wines could excel imports if someone would just give them enough aging and care. He decided that he was the one to do it, sold his stores, and became a vintner.

With his own ideas of how wines should taste, Elwood created his own blends. He bought grapes and wines and leased space in three wineries, two in San Jose for crushing and barrel-aging and part of Weibel for bottling. He also gave his wines beguiling names, such as Castle Magic Riesling, Velvet Hill Pinot Noir, Ancient Proverb Port, and Dry Wit Sherry; and retained the name of a liquor store once named Llord's "because it sounds better than Elwood alone." His wines, introduced in 1961, have won regularly over costly imports in blind tastings because he chose and finished them well. Elwood's widow Irene and son Richard have carried on the business since Mike's death in 1974.

• 10 •

Alameda County also has three wineries in its cities. One that many Bay Area residents enjoy visiting is Wine and the People on University Avenue in Berkeley, west of the University of California campus. It began in 1970 when home winemaker Peter Brehm opened a store to sell supplies to fellow amateurs. As his business grew, he offered winemaking lessons, then added fresh grapes from northern California vineyards to his stock of merchandise. In 1977 he moved to a larger store across the street, added a crusher, press, tanks, and barrels, and sold his own vintage-dated wines in bottles and also in bulk to customers who bring their own barrels and jugs to be filled.

In a former bakery on Park Avenue in industrial Emeryville, young wine lecturer James Lee Olsen makes medal-winning vintage port wines from coast-counties grapes to prove his contention that fruit grown in cool climates makes ports superior to those from grapes grown in the hot Central Valley. His small winery is named the J.W. Morris Port Works for the father of his wife Teri.

In a nondescript concrete laboratory building in Emeryville, Alfred Baxter makes Veedercrest wines, which have commanded high prices across the United States since 1975. Veedercrest is the 300-acre vineyard Baxter and his associates planted in that year on Mount Veeder in Napa County. They plan to build a winery on that mountain when their vines begin producing grapes in 1979.

• 11 •

Contra Costa County, despite its rapid housing and industrial growth since the Second World War, still has almost a thousand acres of vineyards. Few of its residents today are aware that this county had 6,000 acres of vines and twenty-seven wineries and was one of California's finest winegrowing districts before Prohibition. Dr. John Marsh, the first physician in the county and its first winegrower, was producing wine as early as 1846 on his great ranch south of Brentwood. Another physician, Dr. John Strentzel from Poland, planted vines in the Alhambra Valley during the 1850s. He was succeeded by his son-in-law, the great naturalist John Muir. The Muir House, beside Highway 4 two miles south of Martinez, is now a national historic site, and includes a half acre of Muir's Vineyard, replanted in 1969.

Another Contra Costa winegrower was the educator John Swett. The wines from his Hill Girt Vineyard, which he planted during the 1880s, regularly won prizes at the State Fair. His son Frank continued making wine there until Prohibition. Grapes still grow on the Hill Girt Farm on Alhambra Avenue, mainly Concords planted during Prohibition, but lately supplemented by Cabernet Sauvignon.

In 1891, such major vintners as the Italian Swiss Colony and

Theodore Gier had wineries in the Clayton Valley, and the Brookside Winery in the Ygnacio Valley was operated by the California Wine Association. In Martinez were the original novitiate and vineyard of the Christian Brothers, where they began making wine in 1882.

At Repeal, Joseph E. (Joe) Digardi reopened the winery in the Vine Hill district south of Martinez which his father had founded half a century before. Digardi sent two of his sons to Davis and by the 1940s the wines they helped him make were winning awards at the State Fair. When his Diablo Valley Gamay won a gold medal in 1948, he sold most of it to Frank Schoonmaker for six dollars a case. Later, at the Mayflower Hotel in Washington, Digardi ordered a bottle of his Gamay. It cost him three dollars. The Digardi vineyard is gone, ruined by smog from the oil refineries, but son Francis Digardi continues operating the winery with grapes from other coast counties.

Hidden beyond a hill a half mile west of Digardi is the small Conrad Viano Winery on Morello Avenue, off the Highway 4 freeway, still making wine from its own grapes. Connoisseurs who know its location buy its wines by the case, especially the Zinfandel and Cabernet Sauvignon. All of the reds are aged in oak for three to six years and binned for at least six months. Viano's son Clement is a 1958 graduate of the enology school at Davis and wants to stay in the wine business. The Vianos have dedicated their vineyard as an agricultural preserve and have expanded it to 125 acres. There are more vineyards in the far eastern corner of the county, where the climate is Region IV. Their grapes are usually shipped fresh to eastern markets.

• 12 •

In Solano County, the "green belt" or agricultural-preserve laws have saved some old vineyards from urban sprawl and also have encouraged the planting of more than 1,000 new acres of vines.

Before Prohibition there were 2,000 acres growing grapes and a dozen wineries in Green Valley, Suisun Valley, and around Rockville, Cordelia, Fairfield, and Vacaville. By 1972, only 700 acres and two wineries were left.

But the almost century-old Mangels Vineyard on Highway 80 at Cordelia, although its million-gallon Solano Winery has been closed since the Second World War and the vines are in the path of encroaching subdivisions, is still producing grapes. Fifty acres of new vineyards have been planted near Mankas Corner around the Wooden Valley Winery of Mario Lanza (no relative of the late singer, whose real name was Cocozza). The winery, established in 1932, is busier than ever, patronized by families from the huge Travis Air Force Base a few miles away.

There also is new activity at Frank Cadenasso's vineyard and winery, just east of the Interstate 80 freeway at Fairfield. Frank's father planted his first vineyard in Green Valley in 1906, moved to Fairfield and planted another, sold it to the county as a hospital site, then planted the present vineyard, his third, across the road from the hospital, in 1926. Since then Fairfield has more than quadrupled in population. Now that his Davis-trained son-in-law Shayne Cunningham has joined the winery, and Frank's son John is studying viniculture at Fresno State University, Cadenasso is starting to expand. He has planted new vineyards on former prune and pear orchards in Green and Suisun Valleys, dedicating the land as an agricultural preserve. He now has 265 acres of vines, double what he had in 1973. He plans to move his winery to one of his other vineyards across the freeway.

Cadenasso's wines, especially his estate-grown Pinot Noir and Zinfandel, have long been excellent and so reasonably priced that some of my friends have traveled from San Francisco to buy them by the case. "After starving for years when people wouldn't buy good wine at a decent price, I'm finally making a living and the future looks good for my family," says Cadenasso, adding: "Don't write off Solano County as a wine district yet."

This chapter was already in type when, returning from Europe, I learned of the death in May 1978 of Joseph S. Concannon at the age of fifty. The winery at Livermore continues, with his winemaker brother Jim in charge.

16

Santa Clara and Other
Central Coast Counties

HE COUNTIES north and east of the Gold-
en Gate, described in the three preceding
chapters, are publicized nowadays as "California's fine wine
country." Yet there is fully as much to interest the visitor—
famous wineries, great vineyards, and fine wines—in the coast
counties situated south of the Bay. In fact, the visitor who
travels south instead of north from San Francisco may get a
clearer concept of the past, present, and future of premium
California wines.

Viticulture is changing more dramatically in this central coast
region than anywhere else in America. Because of exploding
population around the Bay, the old vineyards in the upper Santa
Clara Valley are fast being paved over for housing tracts and
shopping centers. The historic showplace wineries remain, but
the grape is retreating southward to less-populated areas,
including some where vines were not grown commercially
before. For example, a single new district, the Salinas Valley of
Monterey County, already is larger than either Napa or Sonoma County in vineyard acreage and someday may even surpass
both in "fine wine country" importance.

Climatically, as the California map shows, the same ocean
breezes and fogs which cool the sunny valleys of the northern
Coast Range Mountains perform the same beneficent function
for the valleys of these mountain ranges extending south from
San Francisco through San Mateo, Santa Clara, Santa Cruz,
San Benito, and San Luis Obispo Counties—a distance of more
than two hundred miles. Summer temperatures in most of this
area range from Region I to Region III, the best for growing
grapes for superior table wines and champagnes. The new
central coast vineyards are therefore equal in climate to the old
ones they replace, and they are already greater in size.

• 2 •

The best route south from San Francisco is the scenic Interstate 280 freeway. It passes first through what was once a high-quality winegrowing area in now-urbanized San Mateo County. At the south end of San Andreas Lake is the site where "Count" Haraszthy planted his ill-fated San Mateo County vineyard in 1854. The hills farther south, beyond the Crystal Springs Reservoirs, have warmer weather, and were dotted with vineyards before Prohibition. Emmett Rixford's La Questa Vineyard at Woodside, planted in 1883, grew some of the most prized of all California Cabernets. His elegant winery was closed by the dry law, was operated again by his sons for a few years after Repeal, and has since been converted into a residence. Another handsome cellar, at Menlo Park, once belonged to Governor Leland Stanford. It now houses a bank in the Stanford Shopping Center.

San Mateo land is too costly now for commercial vineyards, but the county has many avocational winegrowers. Two of them in the wealthy town of Woodside have bonded their hobby wineries. When home winemakers Robert and Polly Mullen built their new house on Kings Mountain Road in 1961, they did so primarily to provide a 4,000-gallon winery downstairs. They have two acres of Pinot Noir and Chardonnay vines beside their house. They also care for and use the Cabernet grapes produced on the three remaining acres of La Questa Vineyard. The Mullens produce enough wines to supply themselves, the friends and neighbors who attend their spring wine tastings, and the Village Church, which uses their Woodside Vineyard wines for communion. Occasionally a few bottles are available for sale to callers (by appointment on weekends only).

The other Woodside winery is in the cellar of the Woodside Post Office. Electronics engineer Nathaniel Sherrill and his wife Jan, a Stanford University education counselor, rented and bonded the 3,600-gallon Sherrill Cellar in 1973 and four years later won two gold medals for red wines at the Los Angeles County Fair. They are partners in a two-acre Riesling vineyard in nearby Portola Valley. Roberts General Store in Woodside usually stocks both Sherrill and Woodside Vineyard wines.

• 3 •

Santa Clara is the oldest of the northern California wine districts and was one of the best. The Franciscan Fathers planted grapes at Mission Santa Clara de Asis soon after its

founding in 1777. This was almost half a century before
Sonoma Mission (1823), from which winegrowing spread north
of the Bay. Mission records show the Santa Clara padres
producing twenty barrels of wine annually by 1827 and supplying some of it thereafter to Mission Dolores at San Francisco.
They also gave vine cuttings to neighboring rancheros, who
made their own wine. By mid-century there were half a dozen
commercial winegrowers around Santa Clara and its satellite
pueblo of San José. Many of them were French, and the Gallic
influence was evident in the character of the top Santa Clara
wines. By 1854 one of the French *vignerons*, Antoine Delmas,
was already importing superior wine-grape varieties from his
homeland and replacing his Mission vines.

After the Civil War, winegrowing spread south through the
Santa Clara Valley, then east and west into the foothills of the
Diablo and Santa Cruz mountain ranges, and became the
county's main industry. Names on San Jose maps recall such
early vineyardists as Captain Elisha Stevens, Isaac Branham,
and James Lick (the millionaire donor of Lick Observatory),
whose winery was on the Santa Clara–Alviso Road. Another
was retired Union Army General Henry M. Naglee (Naglee
Street was named for him), who made fine wines but became
most famous for his prize-winning brandy. Phylloxera attacked
the Santa Clara vineyards during the 1890s, but they were saved
by grafting to resistant American roots brought back from
France. By the turn of the century, Santa Clara County had
more than a hundred wineries and 8,500 acres of vines, more
than in Napa County and almost as many as in Sonoma.

Prohibition failed to kill the vineyards. Grapes brought high
prices when shipped east for basement winemaking, and a few
local wineries continued making sacramental and tonic wines,
so the farmers planted still more grapes. Prune growing meanwhile had become a rival industry, but there were still nearly
8,000 acres of vines in 1933. When the dry law was repealed in
that year, sixty-four Santa Clara wineries reopened for business.

Then came the great westward migration, sparked by the
Second World War. Millions of new California residents had to
be housed. Chambers of commerce advertised the climatic
advantages of the area south of the Bay, and subdivisions began
invading the prime farmland on the valley floor. When land
values soared, the vineyards were taxed more as real estate than
their crops were worth, and one by one the grape growers were
forced to sell. Of the 8,000 acres that were producing grapes in

this county in 1948, three-fourths had disappeared by 1970. In two decades of wild urban growth, the upper part of the valley, the onetime "garden of the world," was transformed into a sprawling Los Angeles of the North, and then came the smog. Why didn't Santa Clara preserve its vineyards, fresh air, and open space, as Napa has thus far? The chambers of commerce did their work too well.

Although urbanization destroyed most of the vineyards in the northern Santa Clara Valley, several new wineries opened and a few planted small vineyards when the wine revolution reached its height in the 1970s. Santa Clara County still had 2,000 acres of vines and twenty-five wineries, six of them new, in 1977. On Page Mill Road in the Lupine Valley across Interstate 280 from residential Los Altos Hills, electronics expert Richard Stark and his wife Alison have planted an acre of Chardonnay, Merlot, and Zinfandel, excavated a wine cellar beneath their home, named it the Page Mill Winery, and made their first two vintages of grapes from the Napa Valley. On busy El Camino Real (Highway 82) south of San Antonio Road in the city of Mountain View, Mario Gemello continues making some of California's finest vintage-dated Cabernet Sauvignons in the 66,000-gallon winery his father established behind his wine shop in 1934. Also in Mountain View, chemical engineer Richard Keezer and his wife Melanie, long-time home winemakers, have equipped a building on Wyandotte Street with stainless steel tanks and oak casks as the Sommelier Winery and made their first vintage of red wines from coast-counties grapes in 1976. Two more avocational winemakers have started similar small wineries in the nearby city of Sunnyvale since 1975.

• 4 •

There still are some lovely vineyards tucked away in the foothills of Santa Cruz Mountains above and west of residential Saratoga. The loveliest is Paul Masson's renowned 2,000-foot-high "vineyard in the sky." On steep slopes the venerable Pinot, Cabernet, and Riesling vines are still mostly cultivated by hand. The sparse crops of grapes they yield are no longer crushed in the venerable three-story stone Mountain Winery, which is State Historical Landmark No. 733. The fine old oak casks inside mainly store ports and sherries, made elsewhere and sent here for long aging. The main Paul Masson vineyards and two producing wineries are now in the Salinas Valley of Monterey County and near Madera in the San Joaquin Valley.

The vine-clad hillsides form a natural amphitheater in front of the stately Mountain Winery, with its twelfth-century Romanesque portal, brought around Cape Horn from Spain. In this dramatic setting the famous, often-televised Music at the Vineyards concerts have been held on summer weekends since 1958. Noted artists perform melodic masterworks, chilled Paul Masson Brut Champagne is usually served at the intermissions, and Bay Area music lovers reserve months ahead for the concert tickets, which benefit various charitable funds. The vineyard terrace, with its magnificent view of the valley below, is often loaned to connoisseur groups for catered luncheons and dinners. Otherwise the gates to the precipitous road up the mountain are kept closed.

On the valley floor in Saratoga are the Paul Masson Champagne Cellars, built in 1959, one of the most spectacular winery structures in the world. On a spiral ramp leading from the rotunda, a 153-foot-long mosaic mural depicts the history of wine from ancient times. Almost 200,000 visitors climb the ramp each year. At the top, they see a brief sound film and walk on an elevated gallery through the cellars, where each step in champagne making, wine aging and bottling is viewed and is explained by a recorded voice. The circuit ends in the tasting hall, where the guests sample their choices among the company's more than forty different wines and five champagnes.

Four of the wines here are Paul Masson originals with proprietary names. An international favorite is Emerald Dry, which I can best describe as the kind of wine the growers on the Moselle strive to produce but can't in Germany's rigorous climate (though I love their failures!). Emerald Dry is named for the Emerald Riesling grape, the principal variety used in its uniquely flavorful, fresh-tasting blend. An original Paul Masson red called Rubion has an aged-claret flavor and bouquet, yet is soft and light and is even pleasant served chilled. Baroque is a richer red, resembling some of the Rhone wines, with a bouquet from the old cask-aged red wines in its blend. Among Masson's other specialties are its new Pinnacles Selection of higher-priced "varietal" table wines and its old dessert wine rarities, which come in heart-shaped, numbered bottles.

The colorful story of Paul Masson Vineyards parallels that of Santa Clara wines. In 1852, two years after California became a state, Etienne Thée, a *vigneron* from Bordeaux, planted vines along Guadalupe Creek, five miles east of present-day Los Gatos. Thée was succeeded by his son-in-law, Charles Lefranc,

Paul Masson, who brought the Gamay Beaujolais grapevine from Burgundy to California during the nineteenth century.

and the latter by his son-in-law, Paul Masson. Since these and subsequent owners have produced wine continuously since Thée's vineyard first bore grapes, the present Paul Masson Vineyards is California's oldest winegrower.

Born in 1859 near Beaune in Burgundy, Paul Masson came to California at the age of nineteen. The phylloxera vine plague had devastated the vineyard on the Côte d'Or where his family had made wine for three centuries, and glowing descriptions of California's fabulous climate had already drawn many French winegrowers here. Young Masson first enrolled to study science at the University of the Pacific, which then was located in Santa Clara. While there he became acquainted with his compatriot Charles Lefranc, and soon became Lefranc's employee. In 1884 Masson went to France, brought back champagne-making equipment and French experts to install it, and began making champagne for Lefranc. Four years later, he married his employer's daughter, Louise, and the firm became Lefranc & Masson. In 1892 he bought the interest of Lefranc's son Henry and founded his own Paul Masson Champagne Company. His champagnes won numerous awards, including the grand prize at the Louisiana Purchase Exposition of 1904. But Masson was always proudest of the honorable mention an international jury gave them at the Paris Exposition of 1900.

In 1896, Masson began planting the mountain vineyard, which he called La Cresta, and nine years later started building the Mountain Winery. When the 1906 earthquake destroyed St. Patrick's Church in San Jose, he bought its ancient portal and erected it as part of the winery facade.

Masson, the broad-shouldered, jovial Burgundian, was both a noted epicure and a flamboyant host. His lavish entertainments of San Francisco society and of such theatrical luminaries as singer Anna Held and Charlie Chaplin are legend, but local historians disagree on where they took place. The chief controversy concerns which bathtub he used to give Miss Held her famous champagne bath in 1917—the tub in his château at the mountain vineyard or the one in his Los Gatos villa.* Robert Balzer, his latest biographer, says it must have been at La Cresta because at Los Gatos Mrs. Masson wouldn't have permitted such goings-on.

During the early Prohibition years Masson continued to prosper because he held the first government permit to make medicinal champagne, sold by druggists on doctors' prescriptions. But one night in 1929, an armed hijacking gang, posing as Federal prohibition agents, raided his mountain winery, and in four truckloads emptied it of wine. At the approach of Repeal in 1933, Masson sold the Los Gatos winery, but continued making champagne in a San Jose cellar for three more years. By then he was seventy-seven years old, a widower with an unmarried daughter. He sold out and retired, and four years later he died.

A stockbroker turned realtor named Martin Ray bought Masson's mountain domain in 1936. In that year the expert winemaker at the Jesuit Fathers' Novitiate of Los Gatos winery, Brother Oliver Goulet, had quit his job and the priestly order to get married. Goulet went to work for Ray, and the Paul Masson wines that Goulet made continued winning medals as before.

In the war year of 1942, when the big liquor distillers were buying up California wineries, the House of Seagram bought Paul Masson from Ray. After the war, the late Seagram whiskey king, Samuel Bronfman, foresaw the enormous potential growth of winegrowing in America, and while his competitors in the liquor business got rid of their wineries, Bronfman

---

*A more likely version, attributed to an old vineyard worker on the mountain, is that no bathtub was used, that Masson merely shook up a magnum of unchilled champagne, held his thumb over the mouth, and sprayed the lady with the foam.

kept a silent (majority) interest in Masson. When the present wine boom exploded and the other distillers rushed back into the wine business, Seagram (which also owns many European and Latin American wineries) took over Paul Masson marketing in 1971 and combined it with Browne Vintners, its worldwide wine-importing firm.

Seagram's partners in Paul Masson Vineyards were Alfred Fromm, the late Franz Sichel, and Otto E. Meyer, emigrés from Germany, where their families had owned wine firms for generations. Fromm, a graduate of the great Geisenheim wine school, also heads Fromm and Sichel, the worldwide marketer of the Christian Brothers' wines and brandy. Otto Meyer, trained from boyhood in his grandfather's winery on the Rhine, took charge of Masson's production in 1945. Endowed with a phenomenally keen sense of smell, Meyer was the creator of the unique California brandy blend that in this country far outsells the cognacs of France. A Masson magazine ad in 1971 pictured him in close-up profile with the caption, "The secret of our brandy is Otto Meyer's nose." In 1960, Masson became the first American winegrower to establish an export department and to pioneer foreign markets for bottled California wines. "We decided," Meyer explained, "that our wines, like our opera stars, must go abroad to enhance their reputation in order to become fully appreciated at home." Within a decade, Masson wines had established commercial distribution in some fifty countries around the world, including England, Germany, Italy, Belgium, Switzerland, Australia, the Philippines, and Japan. Meyer headed a Masson tasting team that once included the great Kurt Opper and Hans Hyba from Germany and which now stars California-trained Leo Berti, Guy Baldwin, James Vahl, E. J. Lowe, and Joseph Stillman.

In 1971, Seagram bought the interests of Fromm and Meyer in Masson and began a program of expansion. Masson's vineyards in Santa Clara, Monterey, and Madera Counties now exceed 5,000 acres. The 28 million gallons total capacity of its wineries at Saratoga, Soledad, and Madera make Masson the seventh largest wine company in the United States.

Until 1977, Paul Masson and the Christian Brothers were the only California premium producers who refused to use any vintage labels, preferring to blend young wines for freshness with old wines for bouquet and to keep the blends uniform, each wine ready to drink. In 1977, the year the Christian Brothers introduced their first two vintage-dated wines, Masson introduced seven dated Pinnacles Selections—a 1974 Johannisberg Riesling Champagne, 1975 Riesling and Chardonnay, and 1976 Gewürztraminer as well as Riesling and Chardonnay.

• 5 •

Several vineyards and four more wineries are scattered through the rugged hills west and north of Saratoga. A mile uphill on Congress Springs Road (Highway 9) from the Masson Mountain Winery entrance, a steep dirt road on your left climbs a knoll to the three-acre Congress Springs Vineyard and what is left of the pre-Prohibition winery of Pierre Pourroy. Former Masson tour guide Daniel Gehrs and his wife Robin moved into Pourroy's house in 1976, established their winery in its cellar, and made their first vintage.

From Mount Eden Road northwest of Saratoga, a bumpy road winds up Table Mountain to five vineyards and two small wineries that controversial vintner Martin Ray established during three decades after he sold Masson to Seagram in 1942. Ray preached that his were the only fine American wines, priced them astronomically, and sold patches of land to investors, who waged court battles with him for years. When he died in 1976, a group of those investors owned his hilltop winery and the main Mount Eden Vineyard, and Ray had five acres left near his downhill home with his winery in the basement. Mount Eden wines, made by UC Davis graduate Meredith (Merry) Edwards and her successor, Davis-trained William Anderson, are rarities much admired by connoisseurs. Ray's adopted stepson, Stanford plant physiology professor Peter Martin Ray, again is producing some excellent Martin Ray wines.

Montebello Road, which starts at Stevens Creek Reservoir, climbs a ridge of towering Black Mountain and reaches an elevation of 2,600 feet. There is the Ridge Vineyard, a 100,000-gallon winegrowing enterprise owned by eight families of wine enthusiasts. It began in 1960 when a talented home winemaker named David Bennion interested three of his fellow scientists at Stanford Research Institute in renovating an old vineyard and a ramshackle wooden cellar on the mountain to make wine for themselves and for sale to their friends. With their wives and children, the partners climbed the mountain on weekends to tend the vineyard, to which a previous owner had added several acres of Cabernet and Chardonnay. Each autumn the families had great fun picking and crushing the grapes, and later everyone helped to bottle the wines.

Bennion soon found wine more exciting than electronics research, and quit his Stanford job in 1968. A year later came wine-lover Paul Draper, who had made wine in Chile and had traveled in France, and joined the partners, relieving Bennion as the winemaker. They then moved their equipment and wines uphill to a better cellar, the old stone Montebello Winery, which Dr. Osea Perrone had closed thirty years before.* Then original partners Bennion, Hewitt Crane, and Charles Rosen were joined by four more, Stanford Professor Carl Djerassi, Los Angeles industrialist Richard Foster, and pharmaceutical manufacturers Alejandro Zaffaroni and George Rosenkramz.

Ridge Vineyard has fifty acres of vines; most of its wines, nearly all red and predominantly Zinfandel, are made of grapes purchased from Sonoma, Napa, San Joaquin, and Amador Counties' vineyards, whose locations are named on the Ridge labels. Some, named Monte Bello Ridge, come from opera singer James Schwabacher's nearby Jimsomare Vineyard. Ridge Vineyard wines are intense in flavor, from mostly old vines and extra days of fermentation on the skins and from aging in small oak casks. They seldom are fined or filtered; it usually is advisable to decant the reds.

• 6 •

Los Gatos, on Highway 17, is the home of a historic winery. High above that city, against a spectacular backdrop of hilltop vineyard, stands the Sacred Heart Novitiate, established in 1888 to train young men, enrolled as novices, for membership in the Jesuit Order as priests or as brothers. Beside the imposing building is the Novitiate of Los Gatos Winery, which during all those years has produced wines in accordance with the canon law of the Catholic Church, the sale of wine helping to support the Order's educational work.

Father Louis Franklin manages the winery and Father James Ransford and Brother Lee Williams supervise the winemaking, helped by eight brothers and six lay employees. The previous winemaker was Father Thomas Dutton Terry, who became president of the University of Santa Clara; he is the only winemaker-college president in this country, if not in the world. Father Henri Charvet manages the Novitiate's six hundred

---

*The Montebello name then was acquired by a St. Helena winery, which since has changed hands twice. "Montebello" wines now come from a winery in northern Sonoma County.

acres of vineyards in Santa Clara, San Benito, and Stanislaus Counties.

The training of novices was moved in 1967 to a new seminary at Montecito in Southern California, and the old Novitiate was turned into a Jesuit residence. Each autumn, however, the novices return to help harvest the grapes. The oldest vineyard, the one behind the winery, has shrunk in recent years, and a larger one near Almadén has been sold and chopped up into housing tracts. But the Novitiate still grows grapes around the old Jesuit Alma College on Bear Creek Road, and its new vineyards north of San Juan Bautista and near Modesto supply more grapes than the winery used before.

Until recent years, four fifths of the Novitiate output consisted of altar wines with such names as L'Admirable, Villa Joseph, Guadalupe, and Vin Doré. The rest was sold commercially, labeled "Novitiate Jesuit Wines," and included Cabernet, Pinot Blanc, Château Novitiate, Flor Sherry, Angelica, and Black Muscat. Best known to connoisseurs was the Black Muscat, one of the few fine red muscatels in the world.

Unlike the Christian Brothers, who have built their well-advertised wine and brandy business nationwide, the Jesuit Fathers long de-emphasized their commercial wines. Until recently they could only be bought in Los Gatos and in the few cities where there were distributors of Novitiate altar wines. Now this is changing. The capacity of the Novitiate winery, now 650,000 gallons, is soon to be doubled. More wines (Chenin Blanc, Pinot Noir) have been added, and the Fathers are making their wines available across the United States. A public tasting room has been opened in one of the moss-covered cellar tunnels, is now kept open daily except Sunday, and wine tours with Brother Norbert Korte are offered Monday through Friday and on Saturday mornings.

In the past, several Church-owned wineries carried on the monastic tradition of winegrowing in the United States. Another Jesuit winery, the Villa Maria Vineyard on Stevens Creek Road southwest of Cupertino, was operated by the University of Santa Clara until 1938. The only ones left are the Novitiate, the Christian Brothers, and the O-Neh-Da Vineyard and winery in upstate New York.

• 7 •

Bear Creek Road, where the Novitiate has its vineyards around Alma College, extends into Santa Cruz County and reaches an altitude of 2,000 feet. At that height, two miles past the county line, Dr. David Bruce, whose dermatology practice is in San Jose, pursues his three-day-a-week avocation of growing fine wines. When he bought this hilltop in 1961, there was a century-old farmhouse on the property and traces of a former vineyard. The doctor terraced the land and began planting his present twenty-five acres of Chardonnay, White Riesling, Pinot Noir, and Cabernet. He studied texts on viticulture and enology, practiced making wine in small quantities, then bonded a temporary winery in 1964, and three years later put David Bruce wines on sale in a few San Jose stores. He later built a two-story concrete-block cellar with modern equipment, some of it his own design, and has won a reputation with several unique table wines, which he sells at five to twelve dollars a bottle, mostly to California connoisseurs who order them by mail. The best I have tasted are his Chardonnays and Zinfandels, but the most unusual is a wine he had not planned to make. During the first vintage in his temporary winery, he discovered he had more red grapes than his aging-casks could hold, so he fermented the white juice of his Zinfandel grapes without the skins, bottled the wine young, and named it Zinfandel Blanc de Noir. It developed with a full Zinfandel aroma, but it has an orange tinge. He since has also made a white wine of Pinot Noir. Although Dr. Bruce specializes in vintage wines of the high-priced noble varieties, he hopes also someday to "bring the mountain-grown Zinfandel to the place it deserves in the world of fine wines." He now holds tastings at the winery on Saturdays, but it is advisable to 'phone ahead if you plan to attend.

• 8 •

Santa Cruz was a famous wine county before Prohibition, when thirty-nine wineries cultivated 1,600 acres of vineyards between Ben Lomond, Boulder Creek, Corralitos, Felton, Glenwood, and Soquel. At this writing less than 100 acres were left; many old vineyards had been replanted with Christmas trees, which in this mountainous region are easier to cultivate than vines. But the wine-revolution demand during the 1970s for rare, superfine wines, combined with the romantic lure of hobby winegrowing in this Region I climate, have begun to revive Santa Cruz County viniculture. Seven new wineries opened during this decade and an old one was reopened, increasing the number in the county to twelve. Because open space here is threatened by an influx of commuters from urbanized San Jose, county officials have encouraged vine-planting. Farms of ten acres or more now can be "greenbelted" (taxed for agricultural rather than residential use) under the Williamson Act.

After Repeal, the best-known Santa Cruz wines came from lawyer Chaffee Hall's Hallcrest Vineyard on Empire Road at Felton. He closed the winery before he died in 1969, and his choice Riesling and Cabernet grapes went to the Concannon winery at Livermore. In 1976, Hall's daughter leased Hallcrest to Ridge Vineyard biochemist Leo McCloskey, Bonny Doon grape grower Jim Beauregard, and Western Airlines pilot John Pollard. They renamed it Felton-Empire Vineyard, installed new modern winery equipment, and within a year were producing finer wines than those that made Hallcrest wines famous in the past. Their best was a Riesling with the full botrytized character of German *Auslese* wines.

In 1977, Richard Smothers of Smothers Brothers TV program fame opened the small but modern Vine Hill winery that he had just built on the pre-Prohibition Schermerhorn Vineyard, which extends east from Vine Hill Road to Highway 17. Smothers' enologist and viticulturist are McCloskey and Beauregard, mentioned above. The other Smothers Brother, Tom, was also thinking about planting wine grapes in the Sonoma Valley, where he lives.

Vine Hill Road leads south and east toward four more small wineries, all but one opened during the 1970s. On Jarvis Road, Orange County contractor and restaurateur Kenneth Burnap and his wife Rae grow only a single wine, estate-bottled Pinot Noir, on their twelve-acre Santa Cruz Mountain Vineyard, planted in 1970. Their first vintage, unfined and unfiltered, was the 1975. Off nearby Mountain View Road, two engineer-emigrants from Los Angeles have operated their Roudon-Smith Vineyards winery on the site of a pre-Prohibition vineyard since 1972. Robert Roudon and his wife Annamaria live at the winery; Jim and June Smith come to help on weekends. After making their first five vintages from purchased grapes, they produced their first estate-bottled Riesling in 1976. A hand-hewn cave in the mountains above Nicasio Way near St. Clare's Retreat is electronic engineer Dan Wheeler's 5,000-gallon Nicasio Vineyard winery, his hobby since 1952. He makes champagnes and table wines for sale to his mailing list of customers. Equally tiny is Sunnyvale periodontist Dr. Michael T. Parsons' winery and one-acre vineyard on Hidden Valley Road to the south.

Still more wineries are scattered west of Highway 17. On Bonny Doon Road only three miles from the Pacific, former Los Angeles paper firm executive William Frick and his wife Judith, a professional weaver and artist, have converted a garage into the Frick winery and since 1976 have planted five acres of Gewürztraminer and Pinot Noir on Smith Grade. Perched on a cliff at the top of Hopkins Gulch Road, four miles northeast of Boulder Creek, is the six-acre vineyard of San Jose State University art professor Paul Staiger and his wife Marjorie. They bonded their little P. & M. Staiger winery in 1973 and four years later their Zinfandels were winning gold and silver medals at the Los Angeles Fair. At the northern end of Empire Grade Road, adjoining the Lockheed missile plant, biochemist Keith Hohlfeldt and health-planner Eugene Lokey have leased former county supervisor Vincent Locatelli's old winery and still older vineyard planted in 1902, have renamed it the Los Gatos Vineyards Winery, and with new equipment have made wines since 1976 from grapes mostly grown around Los Gatos and Morgan Hill. Off Highway 9 near the intersection of Highway 236 is Dexter and Valerie Ahlgren's winery on their newly-planted Chardonnay vineyard. They made their first wine of purchased grapes in 1976. Ahlgren is a consulting civil engineer at Boulder Creek.

Oldest and biggest winery in the county is Martinelli at Watsonville. It dates from 1868, but it makes only hard apple cider, light apple wines, and nonalcoholic sparkling cider and apple juice from local fruit.

The 125,000-gallon Bargetto Winery in Soquel is the only one in the county with a public tasting room and daily cellar tours. Lawrence and Ralph Bargetto took over the winery from their father in 1964 and converted it into a premium-wine operation. They have bought grapes from various Santa Cruz vineyards, including one near Glenwood owned by Alfred Hitchcock of movie-thriller fame. The Bargettos have also begun making mead and fruit wines from local honey, apricots, peaches, and plums.

• 9 •

Returning to Santa Clara County, only one winery is left in the Guadalupe Creek district east of Los Gatos, where there were a dozen a few decades ago. Hedged in by the new housing tracts along Blossom Hill Road is the huge, sprawling home winery of Almadén Vineyards. This is where Almadén gets its founding date of 1852, which it shares with Paul Masson; for it was there in that year that Etienne Thée planted his vineyard, where he was succeeded by son-in-law Charles Lefranc and by Lefranc's son-in-law, Masson.

Only eighteen acres of the once-great vineyard remain, serving mainly to separate the winery from the surrounding homes. The original small adobe-and-brick cellar and the lovely Lefranc-Masson French gardens have been preserved. They are surrounded now by a new office building and by bustling modern cellars, in which Almadén wines are finished and bottled and where the company's champagnes are made. Its producing wineries are now two in San Benito County and a third in Fresno County. There are seven thousand acres of Almadén Vineyards in San Benito, Monterey, and Alameda Counties.

Almadén invites visitors to tour its Los Gatos cellars, but offers tastings only at its attractive tasting room on Pacheco Pass Road, Highway 152. To taste them all would be an undertaking, for at last count there were more than fifty, ranging from moderately-priced table wines in jugs for everyday mealtime use to top-quality vintage-dated wines and champagnes. (Tasting will be offered at the winery by 1979.)

The first wines named Almadén* were introduced by Henry Lefranc before the turn of the century. The name again appeared on labels at Repeal in 1933, when Charles Jones and his associates reopened the old winery and for a few years sold wines they called "Almadén Maison Blanc" and "Almadén Maison Rouge."

In 1941, the late San Francisco socialite Louis Benoist, then president of the Lawrence Warehouse Company, bought the property as a place to entertain his weekend guests. He persuaded a great chef, Madame Louise Savin, to close her nearby restaurant and take charge of the kitchen at Almadén.

Benoist started looking for someone to tell him what to do with his winery. Learning that the importer and wine-writer Frank Schoonmaker was having success selling premiun California wines in New York, Benoist placed a call for him there. That day Schoonmaker happened to be in San Francisco, where

*For the old quicksilver mine in the hills. Almadén means "mine" in Spanish.

he had a wine shop on Maiden Lane. He became the wine advisor to Benoist, originated the distinctive style of Almadén labels, and wrote the company's "News from the Vineyards" until 1973. Schoonmaker also found a winemaker for Benoist; he knew that Oliver Goulet was having a disagreement with Martin Ray. Goulet went to work for Almadén and made fine wines there until his death in 1962.

One day soon after the purchase, inspecting the old vineyard with Benoist and Goulet, Schoonmaker noticed some Grenache grapes, which Goulet said were being used to make port wine. Schoonmaker asked him why they weren't used to make rosé, as in France's Rhone district of Tavel. Goulet's puzzled answer was: "What's rosé?" Six months later, Almadén started the pink-wine vogue in the United States by launching its first Grenache Rosé. And with its fresh varietal aroma and intriguing puckery taste, Grenache Rosé is still one of the company's best-selling wines.

Benoist bought and planted more vineyards in the Santa Clara Valley and in the Santa Cruz Mountains. During the Second World War Almadén Champagne and Rosé became nationally known. But when the wine market crashed following the war, the firm began to lose money. Benoist then worked out a merger with the Madrone Vineyards of Eugene Selvage, boss of the Lucky Lager Brewery. They couldn't agree on what to name the merged firm, so it became "Almadén-Madrone." The merger lasted until 1950, when Selvage's Canadian backers suddenly ordered Madrone closed down. Almadén again became independent, with a new manager, Hans Peter Jurgens, who had headed Madrone.

Then suburban subdivisionitis began to bite chunks out of Almadén's 900 Santa Clara and Santa Cruz acres, and Benoist saw his vineyards there were doomed. In 1954 the company began acquiring land in San Benito County and started planting there four years later. When the new vines came into bearing, all but a few dozen acres of the historic vineyard near Los Gatos gave way to a housing tract named "Almadén Estates."

In 1967, when Louis and Kay Benoist owned seven houses, two airplanes, and a 110-foot yacht named *Le Voyageur,* something went wrong between Benoist and his Lawrence Warehouse Company. The Benoists suddenly sold their yacht and their Aptos beach house, and Almadén was offered for sale. The wineries and vineyards were snapped up for $14 million by National Distillers, which had owned three California wineries during the Second World War but had sold them all when the conflict ended.

Under the new ownership, with William Dieppe as chairman and John McClelland as president, Almadén has enlarged its vineyards and wineries and also become an importer of European wines. With its total storage capacity of 27 million gallons, it is now the eighth largest wine company in the nation. It covers the entire spectrum of wine prices, quality, sizes, colors, and labels. On the one hand, it leads the industry in supplying table wines to restaurants for by-the-glass-and-carafe service, using the three- and five-gallon plastic container called "bag in the box." At the same time, it courts the buyers of luxury wines with new vintage "varietals," including a spicy Gewürztraminer and a botrytized late-harvest Johannisberg Riesling that compares to the Auslesen of Germany. These are the creations of German-born and trained Klaus Mathes, who succeeded Alfred Huntsinger, Oliver Goulet's former assistant, as Almadén's winemaster in 1974. To Almadén's assortment of bottle-fermented champagnes, which includes both the inexpensive "Le Domaine" group and the top-rated "Blanc de Blancs" cuvée, Mathes has added a bone-dry vintage "Chardonnay Nature" and "Eye of the Partridge" bronze sparkling wine produced from Pinot Noir, Pinot Blanc, and Chardonnay.

• 10 •

There is one winery in the center of San Jose that ferments its own grapes there and offers daily tasting and cellar tours. The 300,000-gallon Turgeon & Lohr Winery was built in 1974 on Lenzen Avenue, around the corner from the city's historic main artery, The Alameda, which is State Highway 82. Homebuilders Bernard Turgeon and Jerome Lohr of Saratoga had planted their 280-acre vineyard three years earlier in the Salinas Valley of Monterey County and decided to build a winery in San Jose instead of eighty miles away. As a partner in the winery they enlisted young UC Davis-trained winemaker Peter Stern. Turgeon & Lohr was too much of a mouthful, so they chose "J. Lohr" as the name for their first wines, each of which bears a back label reproducing Peter Stern's handwritten description of the grape variety from which it was produced and the oak casks in which it was aged. All are estate-grown, vintage-dated varietals except their proprietary semi-dry Johannisberg Riesling blend named Jade. Lohr manages the vineyard while Turgeon works in the winery with Stern.

• 11 •

Across the Santa Clara Valley, in the Evergreen district on the slope of Mount Hamilton, Mirassou Vineyards invites visitors to tour its winery and to sample the wines in its hospitality room. Since five generations of their family have grown grapes for wine continuously since 1854, the Mirassous are the oldest winegrowing family in North America. Although their wines are among the best produced in California, their name is still one of the newest on labels in restaurants and retail stores.

The Mirassous' ancestor, Pierre Pellier from La Rochelle in France, came to San Jose in 1853, bringing wine-grape cuttings ordered by his brother Louis, who had founded the Pellier Gardens nursery there three years before. When the vines were planted, Pierre went back to France for more cuttings, returning in 1858. On the sailing ship he carefully placed each twig in a sliced potato to protect it from drying out during the six-month trip around Cape Horn. In 1859 Pierre planted the present vineyard in the Evergreen district and built a cellar to age his wines. Pellier's son-in-law Pierre Mirassou succeeded him, followed by his son Peter, and then by Peter's sons Edmund and Norbert, the fourth generation since Pellier.

Edmund and Norbert, who own the winery, made only bulk wines for sale mainly to champagne producers until 1942, when they had a few labels printed in order to sell a few bottles to their neighbors. Then they entered a few wines in the State Fair judgings, and when they received gold and silver medals, connoisseurs began coming to the winery to buy.

Meanwhile, boys of the family's fifth generation were growing up, getting experience in the vineyards and winery, and beginning to rear a sixth generation of Mirassous. In 1966, the fifth generation started taking over. Edmund's son Peter was already in charge of the Mirassou vineyards, which had spread to the Salinas Valley of Monterey County. His brother Dan took over marketing with brother James and Norbert's son Steve. Norbert's son-in-law Don Alexander became the winemaker, trained by Max Huebner, who had been with the Mirassous since 1941.

At this writing, Mirassou vineyards and wineries totaled 1,125 acres and 2.3 million gallons, including the Wehner vineyard and winery two miles to the southeast, established in the 1880s and taken over from the Cribari family in 1964. Mirassou wines were already sold in forty-six states and in five foreign countries.

The wines at this writing totaled twenty, all vintage-dated and except for the champagnes, all labeled with the counties where the grapes were grown, whether in Santa Clara or in Monterey County, or in both. There were six reds, a Petite Sirah rosé whose name the fifth generation abbreviated to Petite Rosé, six whites, including a proprietary blend of Gewürztraminer, White Riesling, and Pinot Blanc, named Fleuri Blanc, and four bottle-fermented champagnes—a bone-dry "au Naturel," a brut, a late-disgorged brut called "LD" (aged four years before disgorging), and a Sparkling Gamay Beaujolais. The champagnes were automatically riddled by the method introduced at the Korbel winery in Sonoma County. Six of the "varietal" table wines came in numbered bottles called "Limited Harvest Selection," priced a fourth to a fifth above the regular line. The sixth red was the month-old Gamay Beaujolais *primeur*, bottled and introduced November 7, 1977.

· 12 ·

South of the Evergreen district, there are no more wineries until Morgan Hill, fifteen miles from San Jose. There were scores of vineyards and wineries before Prohibition from Morgan Hill south to beyond Gilroy. Now the vineyards are being invaded by housing tracts. A movement has begun, backed by the Friends of the Winemakers, to preserve the Joseph Malaguera winery, built in 1869 off Burnett Avenue in Morgan Hill, as a Santa Clara County Wine Museum. Before Prohibition, most of the small wineries here sold their product in bulk to the California Wine Association, which operated wineries at Evergreen, Los Gatos, and Gilroy. At Repeal, these winegrowers again sold in bulk to big wineries, but some of them developed a business of delivering wine in jugs each week to Italian stores and to the doorsteps of wine-drinking families, much as the dairies deliver milk.

One of the latter is the Emilio Guglielmo Winery with its 150-acre vineyard on Main Avenue two miles east of Morgan Hill. Before the Second World War, Emilio's Cavalcade Burgundy delivered to homes in gallon jugs at $1.50 was one of the best wine buys in San Francisco. His son George took over after the war, expanded the winery with stainless steel tanks to 400,000 gallons, opened a tasting room next door to his home, and since has been joined by his sons George E. and Eugene. Cavalcade and Emile's burgundy, chablis, and Grignolino Rosé, sold at the winery in inexpensive jugs, are still the Guglielmos' main wines, but they now sell costlier bottle-numbered claret and vintage-dated "varietals," too.

Another that once specialized in doorstep delivery of jugs was John Pedrizetti's winery at his vineyard on San Pedro Avenue, a mile southeast of Guglielmo. Since John's son Edward and daughter-in-law Phyllis took over the winery in 1968, changes have been made. Phyllis has converted the old Burnett School on Monterey Avenue into a Pedrizetti Tasting Room and has introduced a line of premium wines, including estate-bottled, vintage-dated Petite Sirah and Zinfandel. Edward has installed stainless steel tanks and has doubled the winery capacity to 350,000 gallons. In 1977 he was joined by son Dan, an ordained Baptist minister who had been operating a farm for boys in Arkansas. The Pedrizettis have begun selling some of their wines in three-gallon plastic bags together with attractive cabinets with spouts, from which restaurants dispense burgundy and chilled rosé and chablis to patrons by the glass or carafe.

On Edmundson Avenue, east of Morgan Hill, is a 20,000-gallon winery that produces some of the best sherries and ports in California. When Walter Richert, a veteran enologist who once was editor of the *Wine Review*, started his winery in 1953, he planned that his sons would carry it on someday. So, although his boys were still of preschool age, Richert optimistically named his business "Richert & Sons." His hopes were fulfilled when Robert and Scott finished college and joined him in his enological specialties, blending and long-aging of choice sherries and ports and producing apricot and berry wines.

• 13 •

For decades, billboards along Highway 101 have invited tourists to stop at a winery tasting room on Monterey Road in San Martin, four miles south of Morgan Hill. It is across the railroad tracks from the venerable 2-million-gallon brick San Martin winery, built in 1892 by Bruno Filice from Cosenza in southern Italy, the only big winery in southern Santa Clara County. During the 1960s, Filice family descendants were making almost every conceivable kind of wine there, ranging from Pinot Noir to apricot and strawberry champagnes. San Martin was selling a tenth of its output through its chain of tasting rooms.

In 1973, the wine revolution reached San Martin. It was purchased by the Houston, Texas conglomerate named Southdown, which had just planted vast vineyards in Monterey

County. Four years later, Southdown sold the winery to billion-dollar Norton Simon, Inc. A five-fold program of winery expansion and national distribution of San Martin table wines and champagnes then was launched through Somerset Importers of New York, another Norton Simon subsidiary like Hunt-Wesson Foods, Max Factor, and Canada Dry.

Newly modernized with refrigerated stainless steel and new oak casks and with a new winemaster, Edmund Friedrich, San Martin within those four years became one of California's premium wine producers. Friedrich, trained in the viticultural institute at Trier on the Moselle where he was born, came to San Martin in 1973 after fourteen years at Paul Masson's Pinnacles Vineyard winery and a season at the Wiederkehr cellars in Arkansas.

On a study trip to Germany in 1975, it occurred to Friedrich that the softness of Germany's best white wines might be due to the low alcoholic content they reach in the cool German growing-season, often 9 percent or even less, compared to the 11 and 12 percent usually reached in sunny California. He reasoned that the alcohol which preserves the wine also reduces the taste buds' ability to enjoy the softness and fruitiness of fresh grape flavor. Back at San Martin, Friedrich cold-fermented his 1975 Monterey Chenin Blanc juice to only 9.3 percent alcohol, then centrifuged it to remove the yeast, and introduced America's first "Soft Chenin Blanc." Sensationally delicious, it soon was followed by a "Soft Johannisberg Riesling" and a red "Soft Gamay Beaujolais"—but at 10 percent because a twenty-year-old state regulation sets a 10 percent minimum for California white wines. At last reports, legal machinery was being prepared to modernize that outdated regulation to conform to the Federal minimum of 7 percent.

San Martin no longer owns vineyards, but contracts for the Filice family's grapes grown in southern Santa Clara County and for others grown in Monterey and Santa Barbara Counties.

· 14 ·

Gilroy is known as the nation's garlic capital, and the pungent aroma from the dehydrators east of the city is sometimes quite pronounced. But traveling west of town on Highway 152, the road to Hecker Pass, you breathe a different aroma in autumn—the heady smell of fermenting wine. Clustered in two neighboring verdant, scenic valleys are eight wineries surrounded by vineyards of their own. In past years, mostly bulk wines were grown here by the Italian-born Gilroy vintners for sale to larger wineries or in jugs, demijohns or barrels delivered to family homes, or sold to the roadside trade. Now, enthusiastic new arrivals have taken over some of the cellars, and since Americans discovered wine in the 1960s and 1970s, have begun replanting the vineyards with the grape varieties that make premium wines. People from San Jose and the bay cities come here looking for wine bargains, in such numbers that five of the Gilroy vintners have opened public tasting rooms. Peter Scagliotti was the first to post billboards on Highway 152 to attract tourists to his Live Oaks Winery. This inspired Angelo Bertero and his sons, whose winery is directly across the road, to do the same. Then Mario and Ernest Fortino, who come from Calabria, took over the old Cassa vineyard and winery, and operated it as the Fortino Winery with such success that Mario has started his own Hecker Pass Winery, also complete with tasting, next door.

In 1971, young ex-salesman Thomas Kruse from Chicago, having learned home winemaking from Gilroy vineyardist John Roffinella, bought an old vineyard on Day Road, bonded an old building near the Fortinos as a winery, and started making a Grignolino rosé. Meanwhile, Tom started teaching a course in winemaking in a neighborhood auditorium and was recruited to teach another on wine appreciation, at a San Francisco beverage store. Later, as an experiment, he bought some grapes near Fresno and made the only wine I have ever seen labeled "Thompson Seedless"; it was neutral in flavor but quite drinkable, and Kruse has made and sold it every year since. His latest interest is in making bottle-fermented champagnes, and he has produced what may be the state's first Cuvée de Grignolino and Cuvée de Zinfandel. When I last stopped at the Kruse winery, customers were flocking to buy his interesting wines.

Across the hill in the well-named Uvas Valley (*uvas* is Spanish for grapes), a transformation has occurred at the former Louis Bonesio Winery since it was purchased in 1976 by the family of Nikola Kirigin-Chargin, an enologist from Yugoslavia, and renamed the Kirigin Cellars. Stainless steel tanks have been installed, and Malvasia Bianca, Cabernet Sauvignon, and Pinot Noir are now the featured wines, phasing out such old Gilroy favorite grapes as Mataro and Malvasia Nera. Chargin, a graduate of the University of Zagreb in Croatia, came to the United States in 1960 and served as an enologist at such wineries as Almadén and Perelli-Minetti & Sons before deciding to buy a winery of his own. Forty-eight acres of the former 140-acre Bonesio vineyard are now Chargin's. House-holders to whom the Bonesios once delivered jug wines no longer enjoy that convenience, but gallons of some types are available at the winery and in stores. Kirigin Cellars offers tasting, and there is a picnic area with tables under the trees.

On Uvas Road a mile northwest of Kirigin, schoolteachers Walter and Mary Kaye Parks have modernized the old Marchetti winery and renamed it Sycamore Creek Vineyards for the stream that runs through their sixteen acres of vines. In 1977 they introduced a White Riesling and estate-bottled Carignane and Zinfandel Rosé, which can be sampled in the tasting room they have opened in their barn. They also have begun replacing some of the old Carignane vines with Cabernet Sauvignon and Chardonnay.

Two of the oldest Gilroy wineries, Conrotto and Giretti, have taken down their "wine for sale" signs, but still supply their old customers with country-style wine by the barrel, demijohn or jug.

Other vineyards are located three miles east of Gilroy on Highway 152. Near where the highway joins Ferguson Road are some recent plantings of the Filice family and Paul Masson's 300-acre San Ysidro Vineyard, planted under direction of University viticulturists. It contains, among other varieties, the first commercial plantings of Dr. Harold Olmo's original wine-grape creations, Emerald Riesling and Ruby Cabernet.

• 15 •

From San Juan Bautista, a half hour's drive south of Gilroy, the San Benito Valley extends southeastward between the Diablo and Gavilán (Hawk) mountain ranges for some sixty miles. To this sparsely populated valley, outside the path of urban sprawl, came Louis Benoist of Almadén in 1954, seeking land to replace his doomed vineyards in the Santa Clara Valley. The northern part of San Benito County is one of the oldest winegrowing districts in the state. The Franciscan friars who founded Mission San Juan Bautista in 1797 planted vines in the mission garden to make wine for the Mass. A half century later, Théophile Vaché established the first commercial vineyard in the Cienega Valley, eight miles southeast of the mission, and hauled his wine to market in a puncheon on wheels drawn by oxen. By the 1880s, there were 400 acres of vines in San Benito County, and wines made at Cienega by William Palmtag, the mayor of Hollister, were winning medals in Europe. Palmtag's successor was Dr. Harold Ohrwall of San Francisco, who was joined in 1908 by Professor Frederic Bioletti of viticultural fame. During Prohibition, the San Benito wineries closed, but more vineyards were planted to supply grapes to the home-winemaking trade. There were 2,000 acres of vines and eight bonded wineries in the county at Repeal in 1933. Edwin Valliant then owned the Palmtag winery, and during the late 1930s he made some of the best Rieslings in the state. He sold out to a subsidiary of the Hiram Walker distillers during the Second World War.

When Benoist came to San Benito County, he first leased and later purchased the Cienega winery and vineyard. In 1958 he began planting lands near Paicines, thirteen miles farther south, and soon afterward built a brandy distillery and a second winery there. By 1967, when he sold Almadén to National Distillers, his San Benito vineyards covered almost 4,500 acres, which then was the largest planting of premium-variety grapes under a single ownership in the world.

It is worth a trip through the valley to see these spectacular vineyards, five square miles of rolling hills carpeted with vines. They are watered by permanent overhead sprinklers, fed through hundreds of miles of underground plastic pipe. The sprinklers also protect the vines from frost; when temperatures drop to freezing, they switch on automatically to insulate the vines with a protective coating of ice. Fifty electronic scare-crows, loudspeakers on towers, frighten off grape-eating birds by broadcasting their tape-recorded calls of distress.

Almadén's Cienega Valley cellar is world-famous as "the walking winery." Palmtag unwittingly built the old cellar precisely astride the San Andreas earthquake fault, the most active earthquake belt in the United States; the halves of the winery move a half inch farther apart each year. Seismologists come from many countries to observe the deep cleft in the cement floor because it keeps widening with each tremor of the earth. Although the winery is not open to visitors, you can stop and see the cleft in a concrete drain outside the building. In 1960, a comparatively mild temblor jolted a redwood tank off balance, and eight thousand gallons of wine were lost through its loosened staves.

There is another amazing sight across the road: a single roof covers four acres of barrels and tanks of aging wines. Almadén makes only red wines at Cienega; the whites are made at the Paicines winery; the company's sherry *soleras* are also there.

Almadén brandy is distilled in the San Joaquin Valley and is blended and bottled by National Distillers at Cincinnati, Ohio.

• 16 •

Across the Gavilán Mountains from the San Benito Valley, the Salinas Valley stretches southeastward through Monterey County for some eighty miles. To the west are the rugged Santa Lucia Mountains, which rise abruptly from the Pacific shore twenty-five miles away. The valley is mostly a level plain ten to twenty miles wide, from which side valleys climb into the foothills on both sides.

A viticultural revolution has taken place in the area since 1962. Long known as the "Salad Bowl of the World" for its vast plantings of iceberg lettuce and celery, the Salinas Valley has become, in less than two decades, the "wine bowl" instead— the newest and potentially the most important premium wine-growing district in North America.

During the century when pioneer vintners were establishing the vineyards around San Francisco Bay, the Salinas Valley was considered a poor place to grow grapes. Of four hundred acres of vines in Monterey County during Prohibition, more than half were abandoned after Repeal. The chief reason was scant rainfall, only ten inches annually, half of the minimum required for adequate vineyard yields. And the strong wind that sweeps unimpeded up the valley from Monterey Bay each afternoon from May to November was regarded as injurious to vines.

Consequently, when Professors Winkler and Amerine at the University published their analyses of California climates, begun in 1935, their findings about the Salinas Valley went unnoticed. One of their findings was that growing-season temperatures in the north-central part of this valley are the same as in the most-favored north coast districts, Region I and Region II.

Twenty-five years later, as cities began closing in on the Santa Clara vineyards, the Mirassou brothers and their Paul Masson neighbors began an urgent search for other areas in which to plant vines. They first surveyed Sonoma County, and the Sierra foothills next, but neither offered sufficient flat open space. Then they noticed the old Winkler-Amerine figures on summer temperatures in the Salinas Valley, and decided to investigate there for themselves. They discovered that the sparse Salinas rainfall was actually no problem, for through this remarkable valley flows the Salinas River, the greatest under-ground stream in America. Plentiful water, pumped from only a hundred feet below the parched surface, already supplied artificial rain for the lettuce crops; it could do the same for grapevines. They saw that the afternoon gales could not damage the grapes if the vine rows were simply planted parallel to the wind. In fact, the wind is the key to the Salinas climate; it keeps the valley cool. They found still another advantage: vines planted on fertile benchlands above the valley floor would be virtually immune from damage by frost. And of perhaps greatest importance, this area, situated far from the fast-growing cities to the north and south, seemed safe for many years from urban sprawl.

In a multimillion-dollar gamble, these two vintners in 1957 bought 1,300 acres in the valley between Soledad and Greenfield, and in 1962 began planting vines in what for grapes was virgin soil. The Mirassous set out 300 acres on the west side near the now-restored Mission Nuestra Señora de la Soledad. On the east side along Metz Road, Masson planted 1,000 acres and named it the Pinnacles Vineyard for the Pinnacles National Monument, the area of lofty crags and weird caves in the Gavilán range nearby. A year later, the Wente Brothers of Livermore followed, choosing 300 acres near the Arroyo Seco, southwest of the Mirassous. Normally, four years would have elapsed before the results of the gamble could be known. By the third year, however, the grapes showed such promise that Masson began building a winery on its Pinnacles Vineyard and started sending its grapes there from Santa Clara to be crushed.

The 1966 vintage proved that Winkler and Amerine were right. The Mirassou and Masson vineyards in that year harvested Gewürztraminers that made wines richer in spicy Gewürz fragrance, better balanced, and more delicious than any Traminers from Alsace. Masson in 1966 made a Johannisberg Riesling from its Pinnacles Vineyard grapes that excelled any in the Santa Clara Valley. Had I still been judging wines at the California State Fair, I would have voted gold medals for the Mirassous' 1966 "First Monterey Harvest" Pinot Noir and Cabernet Sauvignon and for the Spätlese Riesling the Wente Brothers grew in their Monterey vineyard in 1969.

A historic luncheon was held among the casks in Masson's new Pinnacles winery at Soledad in October of 1966. It was a gathering of wine industry and Monterey County civic leaders to honor Professors Winkler and Amerine. Toasts were drunk to their health and to their achievement, "the world's first fine wine district established as the direct result of scientific temperature research."

In the next few years, vineyard planting in the Salinas Valley multiplied no less than twelve times. Mirassou planted 600 more acres on its San Vicente Ranch. Masson added 4,000 acres around Greenfield and Soledad and expanded its Pinnacles winery to 11 million gallons. Almadén followed in 1970, buying 2,500 acres of grazing and vegetable land below King City and San Lucas, and started planting there. The Texas conglomerate named Southdown planted the 6,000-acre Viña Monterey below King City, a vineyard so immense that special machines were built to pick the grapes from four rows of its vines at a time. International Vineyards, related to the Gold Seal winery of New York State, planted 900 acres between Chualar and Greenfield. Myron and Gerald McFarland, of the Kern County family for whom the town of McFarland is named, formed twenty-eight investor partnerships for whom they planted 9,600 acres, mostly around Gonzales. By then Monterey County, with 34,000 acres of vines, led all other counties in the state in its acreage of Gewürztraminer, Chardonnay, White Riesling, Sauvignon Blanc, and a half-dozen other premium wine grapes. But this was only the beginning, said Edmund Mirassou. "If the demand for coast-counties table wine and champagne continues growing at its present rate, vineyards in the Salinas Valley can reach a hundred thousand acres by the end of this century—more than all the vineyards of Napa, Sonoma, Mendocino, and the other coast counties combined."

During the late 1960s the Mirassous and Wentes, with their new Monterey vineyards almost a hundred miles distant from their wineries, faced a problem of keeping their grapes perfectly fresh during the long trip north. Peter Mirassou solved it in 1969 by adding to one of his family's new mechanical-harvesting machines a grape-crusher-stemmer and a tank of carbon dioxide gas. The crushed grapes, protected from air by a blanket of CO_2, then traveled in a cooled and pressurized tank truck to the Mirassou winery at San Jose. The resulting wine was later compared in blind tastings—and found superior—to wine made from the same grapes picked that day by hand.

• 17 •

The second large Salinas Valley winery, after Masson's Pinnacles cellar at Soledad, is the 2.2-million-gallon Monterey Vineyard cellar beside Highway 101 just south of Gonzales. It was built in time to process the 1974 crop from the vineyards planted by the McFarland partners. The large, modern winery is attractive, with stained-glass windows and an observation tower and deck that offers a dramatic view across the valley to the Gavilán mountain range. As the first winery in Monterey County to offer daily tasting and cellar tours, it has been visited and admired by travelers from throughout the world.

Winemaker at the Monterey Vineyard winery is Dr. Richard Peterson, one of America's leading enologists. After winning his Ph.D. at UC Berkeley in 1958, he served ten years as research director of the Gallo winery at Modesto, then five years as enologist at Beaulieu Vineyard with the great André Tchelistcheff, whom he succeeded when the latter retired to consult for other wineries. What attracted Dr. Peterson to the Salinas Valley was the challenge of pioneering fine wine production in that as yet new viticultural district. Monterey County became his home. The stained-glass windows in the winery are the work of his wife Diane. Their daughter Heidi enrolled at UC-Davis and spent her summers working in the cellars.

In 1976, the Monterey Vineyard winery severed its connection with the McFarland partnerships. For two seasons it produced more wine under contracts for other vintners than for sale under its own name. Then in 1977, it was purchased by the Coca-Cola Company of Atlanta. Earlier that year, giant "Coke" had invaded the wine business by buying the Taylor and Pleasant Valley wineries of New York State and the Sterling Vineyard and winery of Calistoga. What "Coke" might have in mind for this third of its winery acquisitions was evident from the fact that the 2.2-million-gallon size of the Monterey cellar was only a third of the capacity for which it was originally designed.

• 18 •

Dr. Peterson, who continued in charge of the winery, says Monterey wines have some unique flavor characteristics. He considers the northern part of the Salinas Valley, from Chualar south to Soledad, the coolest winegrowing region in the United States, comparable to the Burgundy and Champagne districts of France. By the UC method of measuring growing-season temperatures, the northern part is Region I and Region II; the southern part is Region III. In some years Zinfandel grown around Gonzales may not reach balanced ripeness until November or even December, a month to two months later than in the Napa Valley. An example is the "December Harvest Zinfandel" that Dr. Peterson produced for the Monterey Vineyard winery in 1974. He adds that botrytis, the "noble mold," grows on the grapes in the valley's northern vineyards every year. This led him that season to produce the first California approach to the sweet sauternes of Bordeaux, which are made from botrytized Sémillon and Sauvignon Blanc. His Monterey classic sauternes type, produced mainly from the latter variety, is named "Botrytis Sauvignon Blanc."

In the mid-1970s, some connoisseurs reported tasting a "vegetative" or "bed-pepper" flavor in some Salinas Valley red wines. I have judged wines with these tasters without perceiving any such flavor. What they may be describing, says Dr. Peterson, is the intense varietal flavors of Monterey grapes, which he ascribes to the cool climate and to the fact that vines in the valley are planted on their own roots instead of being grafted on phylloxera-resistant rootstocks. (Phylloxera has not been found in the valley.) In Monterey vintages of the late 1970s, some of the intense varietal flavors were muted by leaving some grape varieties longer on the vines. Since then I have heard less talk about "bell-pepper" tastes.

• 19 •

One Monterey County vineyard, nine steep miles and 2,000 feet above the Salinas Valley, is a vinicultural oddity. It is the 125-acre Chalone Vineyard on the Chalone bench of the Gavilán Mountains. Moisture is so scarce at that elevation that water must be hauled up the mountain in tank trucks to water the vines. The grapes it yields are of such quality that during the 1940s and 50s, long before "varietals" became scarce, Wente and Almadén were paying the then-owner, William Silvear, some of the highest prices in the state for his crops.

In 1965, Richard Graff, a Harvard music graduate who had studied for a year at the UC Davis wine school, bought Chalone from a group of hobbyists. They had converted a small farm building into a winery but had given up after a single season. Graff experimented making champagne and also sold some of the Chalone grapes in bulk. He unveiled his first Chalone bottled table wines in 1969 and they immediately became popular with connoisseurs. Since then Graff has been joined by his younger brothers, John with a Ph.D. in chemistry from the University of Chicago, and Peter, a 1970 Davis graduate. The winery has been expanded to 25,000 gallons and the vineyard to more than twice its original size. Even at such prices as ten dollars a bottle for Pinot Noir, there still are not enough Chalone wines to supply the demand.

• 20 •

In western Monterey County, across a ridge of the Santa Lucia Mountains from the Salinas, is the lovely Carmel River Valley, famed nowadays as a tennis player's paradise. On a hilltop above the river is the Carmel Valley's first winery, which crushed its first grapes in 1977. It stands on the sixty-acre "dream vineyard" of Los Angeles businessman and wine lover William W. Durney. His 1,200-acre estate, where he raises rare Belted Galloway cattle, is named El Rancho del Sueño, Spanish for dreamland.

Uphill from the new 25,000-gallon adobe brown winery is Durney's architectural gem of a summer house. Beside the house is his Ste. Genevieve Chapel, which is topped with a bell from Portugal, adorned inside with rare paintings and carvings, and complete with an organ and nave for a choir. A series of baptisms and weddings have taken place there. His private wine cellar is in a nearby hillside cave.

Durney, a member of the Confrérie des Chevaliers du Tastevin, planted his first twenty acres of vines in 1966 when expert viticulturists advised him that fine wines could be produced in his area's climate, which borders Region I and Region II. The first wines of Durney's grapes were made by Mario Gemello at Mountain View. His 1974 Chenin Blanc and Gamay Beaujolais won gold medals at the Los Angeles County Fair. In 1975, his son-in-law Ken Roberts won his degree at the UC Davis wine school and moved with his wife Christine to Rancho del Sueño to begin building the winery.

A forest fire in August 1977 threatened to destroy Durney's dream. For twenty-four hours Durney was on the fire line until the blaze was controlled. He now plans to build a heliport between his house and the nearby satellite tracking station.

• 21 •

Winemaking has also spread west toward the Monterey Peninsula, the locale of John Steinbeck's "Cannery Row." In 1974, local dentists Deryck Nuckton and Roy Thomas converted the former Cademartori's Restaurant, a mile east of Monterey Airport at the intersection of Highways 68 and 218, into the Monterey Peninsula Winery and tasting room. Both veteran home winemakers, they bought premium grapes and in the old restaurant's cellar, which has stone walls four feet thick, they made wines that won medals at the Los Angeles Fair. Their tasting room is open daily until dark and attracts crowds, especially in vintage season when their benefit wine stomp is held.

Another duo of amateur winemakers, Fredrick Crummey and G. Robert Eyerman, opened the 2,500-gallon Carmel Bay Winery in 1977 in a former navy air force hangar across the road from the Monterey Airport. Without a tasting room, they planned to sell their wines by mail.

The third winery in the Salinas Valley was built that year to start production in 1978. Former navy jet pilot J. Douglas Meador and his wife Shirley planted their 300-acre Ventana Vineyard in 1973 on Los Coches Road, six miles south of Soledad. While equipping the winery, they were converting a former barn to serve as a tasting room for the sale of their future estate-bottled wines.

In less than two decades Monterey, although still with only seven wineries, has become one of the most important wine counties of the state. This is celebrated each September at Soledad Mission, established by the Franciscan padres in 1791 and reconstructed since the 1960s. Since 1976, a wine festival has also been held during the first week of December by the Monterey Peninsula hotels.

• 22 •

San Luis Obispo County, where the Salinas River begins, is an old winegrowing district that is becoming important again. Since the 1960s, when Americans developed a taste for table wines, vineyard acreage in this county has jumped from seven hundred to 4,000 acres. "This is only the beginning," says County Farm Advisor John Foott. "We have at least thirty thousand acres suitable for wine grapes, in districts with climates ranging from Region I to Region IV." Wines made of grapes from some of the youngest vineyards in the county are already becoming recognized as equal to the nation's best.

Paso Robles, an hour's drive south of San Lucas, is the mailing address of two new premium wineries, soon to be followed by a third. On Adelaida Road in the rugged Santa Lucia Mountain foothills six miles west of town, the new Hoffman Mountain Ranch winery is producing estate-grown Chardonnays, Pinot Noirs, and Cabernets that are destined to rank among the California greats.

A dream of growing fine wines inspired Dr. Stanley Hoffman, a noted Beverly Hills cardiologist and amateur winemaker, to plant a sixty-acre vineyard in 1964 on his 1,200-acre San Luis Obispo County walnut orchard. Part of his dream was to leave the rigors of Southern California medical practice and his university professorship and to become a country doctor. When he moved with his wife Teressa to Paso Robles in 1973, he turned out to be the only cardiologist for miles around, and he soon became as busy as before.

His sons David and Michael, then in their mid-twenties, stepped in and took charge. In 1976, guided by the great winemaster André Tchelistcheff, they built a rustic though completely modern 70,000-gallon winery beside the temporary cellar where David and his father had made four prize-winning vintages of "HMR" wines. Michael, after a study trip to European vineyards with Tchelistcheff, became the Hoffmans' enologist while David prepared to plant another fifty acres of Pinot Noir.

Although Tchelistcheff thinks Pinot Noir and Chardonnay may be the best varieties in the steep vineyards and gravelly lime soil here, the Hoffmans also produce excellent White Riesling, Franken Riesling (Sylvaner), Chenin Blanc, Grenache Rosé, and Zinfandel, which are sold together with "HMR" walnuts in their tasting room at the Black Oak corner in downtown Paso Robles. The Zinfandel is of special interest because the Hoffman vineyard borders the San Ignacio Ranch where world-renowned musician-statesman Ignace Paderewski grew Zinfandels that made medal-winning wines before Prohibition. Paderewski, incapacitated by an arthritis attack during a concert tour in 1913, was advised to go to Paso Robles for the mud baths there and found the baths relieved his pain. He returned often for treatments, fell in love with the district, planted an orchard and vineyard on his ranch, and once considered starting a winery of his own. His vines were still producing grapes when he died in 1941, but they later became neglected and were removed.

• 23 •

Six miles east of Paso Robles and a mile east of the airport, one of the most spectacular wineries in California stands atop a hill facing Highway 46. With its observation towers it is visible for miles. The 300,000-gallon Estrella Vineyards winery crushed its first vintage in 1977 from the square mile of vineyards planted five years earlier between the Estrella River and the highway.

Viticulturist and winemaster of Estrella Vineyards is Pittsburgh-born cellular geneticist W. Gary Eberle. He was working for his Ph.D. at Louisiana State University, with ambitions of teaching micro-anatomy in medical school, when his half-brother, Los Angeles businessman Clifford Giacobine, persuaded him to take a year of graduate work in viniculture at UC Davis and become a winegrower. Eberle studied this area's Region II and III climates and chose to plant the true French Syrah variety, Cabernet Sauvignon, Barbera, Zinfandel, Muscat Blanc, Chardonnay, Chenin Blanc, and Sauvignon Blanc. The vineyard is protected from frost by overhead sprinklers.

Tastings in an adjoining building, still to be built, and winery tours on an elevated walkway through the cellar of stainless steel tanks and oak aging casks are likely to make Estrella Vineyards one of the county's leading tourist attractions.

Another winery as spectacular as the Estrella cellar may be built by 1979 on the 500-acre Tierra Rejada vineyard five miles farther east. A quartet of film and television luminaries headed by Wayne Rogers, formerly of the M-A-S-H TV series, are behind this project, named Star Crest Vineyards and Continental Vintners. The others are Jack Webb, Peter Falk, and James Caan. Tierra Rejada, Spanish for "furrowed earth," is 2,000 acres of grain and cattle-grazing land, on which the vineyard was planted in 1972. The group's first wines, Zinfandels made from 1976 and 1977 grapes by an unnamed winery, are now appearing on the California market under the "Star Crest" brand. Merlot later will be the featured type because the vineyard has California's largest single planting of that variety. Manager of Continental/Star Crest is former TV producer Herman Schwartz, who lives at the vineyard.

Eight miles southeast of Tierra Rejada, south of the town of Shandon, is one of three new San Luis Obispo winegrowing districts planted since the 1960s. The largest single planting in the Shandon area is the 400-acre San Juan Vineyard planted in the 1970s by Louis A. Lucas, Jr., for Tepusquet Vineyards, a group that includes his family of table grape growers at Delano in Kern County. A graduate of Notre Dame and of the Fresno State University vinicultural courses, Louis Lucas brought the expertise of table-grape growing, taught him by his father, to wine-grape culture in the coast counties. Some of the other new vineyards he has planted will be visited later in this chapter.

• 24 •

A much older wine district in the county is around Templeton, six miles south of Paso Robles. Old vineyards there line both sides of Highway 101. The Templeton area has long been noted for its Zinfandel grapes, which north coast wineries bought for use in their blends. There are three small wineries near Templeton, and two of them are among the oldest in the state. Because of their location, about halfway between San Francisco and Los Angeles, their wines were sold mostly to the local and tourist trade. Until the Hoffman Mountain Ranch eight miles to the northwest introduced its vintaged "varietals," few wines labeled with San Luis Obispo County as their origin had ever been tasted by connoisseurs.

The Rotta Winery on Vineyard Road dates from 1856, when a French farmer named Adolph Siot planted the first grapes in this locality. The Rotta vineyard was showing signs of advanced age when the place was bought from Mervin Rotta in 1976 by John and Della Mertens of San Jose. The Pesenti Winery, the Rotta winery's neighbor, has only been in business since Repeal. The York Mountain Winery, eight miles west on the road to Cambria, was built in 1882, and became briefly famous sixty years later by making medal-winning wine from Ignace Paderewski's Zinfandel grapes. Since 1970, the York Mountain Winery has had a new owner, veteran enologist Max Goldman, who after forty years of winemaking in California and New York, bought the place from the founder's grandson, Wilfred York. Goldman and his son Steve have built a tasting room onto the old cellar and have replanted some of the rundown vineyard with premium varieties, including some Zinfandel with which to recapture York Mountain's onetime fame.

• 25 •

Another new winegrowing area in the county is the Edna Valley, twenty-five miles south of Templeton, below the city of San Luis Obispo, and only six miles from the Pacific Ocean, nearly on a direct line from Pismo Beach. Six hundred acres of drip-irrigated vineyards were planted here in 1973 by Louis Lucas, who considers the climate Region II, ideal for premium grape varieties. A 200,000-gallon winery, to be named Edna Valley Cellars, has been designed for building in 1979 on a Chardonnay block of the vineyard facing Biddle Ranch Road off Highway 227. An observation tower and visitors' tasting center are among the plans. The winery is intended to process grapes from four nearby districts, including Los Angeles "Stuft Shirt" restaurateur Norman Goss's Chamisal Vineyard on Orcutt Road near San Luis Obispo, the San Juan Vineyard near Shandon, the Tepusquet Mesa Vineyard near Santa Maria, and the Sisquoc River Vineyard east of Santa Maria. The Edna Valley label may appear meanwhile on wines made by other wineries from the participants' grapes.

The president of Edna Valley Cellars is J. Leland Stewart, one of California's great winemakers. In 1943, at the age of thirty-nine, Stewart retired from business in San Francisco and founded the first Souverain Cellars in the hills east of St. Helena, where he produced an impressive list of medal-winning vintages. He was the first vintner (in 1945) to make a "varietal" Green Hungarian wine. After selling the original Souverain in 1970 (it later became the Burgess Cellars), he continued working as consultant to the two new Souverains at Rutherford and Geyserville. Now in his fourth career in a new California area, he hopes to produce some of the state's best Rieslings, Chardonnays, and Pinot Noirs.

• 26 •

In my first edition, this chapter on the central coast counties ended at the southern border of San Luis Obispo County, the Santa Maria River. However, the new vinicultural pioneers who have planted 6,000 acres of new vineyards and built five new wineries in the northern two thirds of Santa Barbara County since the mid-1960s consider themselves part of the same "central coast" area as their San Luis Obispo neighbors. I am not the one to dispute them.

Santa Barbara County, and also nearby Ventura, were important wine producers in the past century, as evidenced by the various "Vineyard Roads" you still see on their maps. Vineyards flourished in the Santa Ynez Valley and east of the Sisquoc River long before Prohibition. What is now downtown Santa Barbara was dotted with vineyards a century ago. Santa Cruz Island, thirty miles off the coast, was renowned before the dry era for the prize-winning wines grown there by the late San Francisco importer and hardware merchant Justinian Caire. His heirs made wine there for a short time following Repeal, but the island winery was destroyed by fire and the vineyard was torn out. The city of Santa Barbara again has a producing winery, established on Anacapa Street in 1962 by wine-buff architect

Pierre Lafond. He uses Santa Barbara and San Luis Obispo grapes and berries to make several creditable wines.

The current revival is most extensive in a sparsely populated twenty-mile-long belt of foothill land inland from Santa Maria, on the slopes of the Sierra and San Rafael mountain ranges. What is significant is the district's climate, cooled by ocean fog and by the Santa Maria wind. Its growing-season temperatures are Region I, said by the University to be the best for the top-rated table wine and champagne grapes. Beginning in 1964 a hundred acres of such premium varieties as White Riesling, Cabernet Sauvignon, and Chardonnay were planted under sprinklers by San Joaquin Valley table grape grower Uriel Nielsen near the juncture of Tepusquet Creek and the Sisquoc River. His first Rieslings were made into wine three years later at the Christian Brothers winery near Napa. Justin Meyer, the former Brother Justin, found the wine of superior quality. Between 1969 and 1973, more than a dozen additional vineyards spread across Santa Maria's former broccoli and bean fields. The grapes were bought by North Coast premium wineries and markedly improved some of their wines. I know of an instance in which Santa Maria Riesling made so fragrant a wine at a Napa winery that to sell it in jugs under its second label, the winery blended it down with a neutral grape variety and kept the jug wine from excelling the Riesling under its top brand.

The Tepusquet and Santa Maria Vineyards, 1,400 acres managed by Louis Lucas, are the largest in the new district. There are young vineyards on part of the 36,000-acre Rancho Sisquoc, owned by descendants of early California mining tycoon James Flood, and on the Newhall Land Company's even larger Suey Ranch. The Floods have bonded a small experimental winery, and their ranch foreman Harold Pfeiffer has made an excellent Rancho Sisquoc Cabernet Sauvignon. I am told that the Santa Maria district has sufficient land and enough water to provide 10,000 vineyard acres, almost "another Napa Valley."

Across the Solomon Hills to the west is still another new vineyard district in the Los Alamos Valley, with several hundred acres of vines planted since 1972. Los Angeles attorney and avocational winemaker Samuel D. Hale has equipped a pilot 5,000-gallon winery on his 350-acre Los Alamos Vineyards. Most of his grapes have been vinified by a Monterey winery for sale under the Los Alamos Vineyards label together with the wines he has made.

A dozen vineyards have been planted since 1972 in the rich residential, agricultural, and tourist-oriented Santa Ynez Valley, some twenty miles south of Santa Maria. Most of them are along Zaca Station and Foxen Canyon Roads north of Los Olivos, an area where they may help to hold off the current threat of urbanization. A showplace winery was built in 1974 on the Firestone Vineyard, and another of 40,000 gallons capacity is scheduled for construction on the 160-acre Zaca Mesa Vineyard of former Atlantic-Richfield executive Louis M. Ream. His winery site is on Foxen Canyon Road two miles east of Aliso Canyon Road. Zaca Mesa wines of the 1975 to 1977 vintages were produced at the Monterey Winery for sale beginning in 1978.

Between the charming Danish village of Solvang and the town of Santa Ynez is the Santa Ynez Winery, in a former dairy building on North Refugio Road. Lee Bettencourt and UC Davis-trained winemaker C. Frederic Brander operate the 15,000-gallon cellar. One of their first wines was a 1976 dry Blanc de Sauvignon.

Nine miles west of Buellton, among the flower-seed farms and cattle ranches along the Santa Ynez River, is the 110-acre Sanford & Benedict Vineyard and 24,000-gallon winery in a converted barn. Former television executive J. Richard Sanford and UC-Santa Barbara island-biology instructor Michael Benedict began planting the vineyard of Pinot Noir and other noble varieties in 1972. They became full-time winegrowers five years later when their first wine, an estate-bottled dry White Riesling, was ready for sale.

• 27 •

Anthony Brooks Firestone had ended his twelfth year working in his family's tire and rubber business when in 1972 his father, the then United States Ambassador to Belgium Leonard K. Firestone, asked him to come and look at a piece of prospective vineyard property in the Santa Ynez Valley. "Grapes and wine immediately caught my interest," Brooks now muses in retrospect, "because until then I'd been selling something black and round that people didn't want to buy." The visit was the beginning of Brooks Firestone's winegrowing career, in which he now manages the 300-acre and 200,000-gallon Firestone Vineyard and winery five miles north of Los Olivos on Zaca Station Road.

The vineyards were planted on oak-dotted cow pastures in 1973, on the advice of great enologist André Tchelistcheff, with

Pinot Noir, Cabernet Sauvignon, Merlot, Gewürztraminer, White Riesling, and Chardonnay. The winery is one of the most modern in the nation and it fits the Santa Ynez Valley landscape. Its masonry front resembles handmade adobe blocks, its overhanging roof is sheathed with reddish brown steel, and its wings enclose a courtyard of olive trees reminiscent of the haciendas of early California. It includes a visitor tasting area that is open daily except Sunday from 10 to 4.

Firestone Vineyard is a joint venture of the Firestones and Suntory Limited, which produces its own wines as well as its famous barley malt whiskey in Japan. Suntory, with a 31 percent interest, receives a third of the Firestone wine production.

Enologist at the winery is UC Davis graduate Anthony Austin, who came here after two years of training at the Simi Winery under Tchelistcheff. His assistant is Alison Green, the daughter of Sonoma County vineyardist Russell Green. Winery visitors often meet Brooks's charming wife Kate, the former ballerina with the London Royal Ballet, because with the title of bonded weighmaster, she helps in vintage season to weigh the grapes, and also sometimes serves as a winery tour guide. The Firestones are extremely busy people, with their three children and their nearby 2,300-acre cattle ranch.

The first Firestone Vineyard wines released were the 1975 vintage rosés of Cabernet Sauvignon and Pinot Noir, followed by Johannisberg Riesling and Chardonnay. Best of the list thus far is the 1976 Johannisberg Riesling, flowery with the scent of botrytis, the noble mold, which grows on the grapes each year in this climate that ranges from Region II to Region I.

A new concept in American wine labeling has been introduced on Firestone wines. Because the winery was still unfinished when the 1975 wines were released, their labels contained a drawing by Napa artist Sebastian Titus of the building, then lacking half its roof. A second wine reproduced a Titus drawing of a harvest scene, and others to follow are picture stages of winegrowing all the way to the bottling line.

This chapter has covered 246 air miles through seven coast counties, 50,000 acres of vineyards, and sixty producing wineries, all south of the Golden Gate. As stated at the beginning, this area encompasses a great deal of the future, as well as the past and present, of California wines.

17

Southern California

A T THIS writing, the winegrowing scene in Southern California, where the state's great vineyard industry was born two centuries ago, is in a process of dramatic change.

A half dozen venerable wineries are still turning out the unique wines which the region has produced for generations, but their vineyards are being decimated by smog and urban sprawl from nearby cities, where population is growing faster than anywhere else in the United States. Yet at the same time, entirely new Southern California vineyards have sprung up on virgin lands outside the path of population growth, where the air is still clean. Wines from one of these new vineyards are already being compared to the best in the state, even to the best in the world.

• 2 •

The Franciscan Fathers brought Vinifera vines to their Southern California missions from Mexico after the founding of San Diego Mission in 1769. Vineyards were set out at each of the missions. The padres made wine mainly for the Mass and for their own table use, but they also sold some of their wine and their *aguardiente* (brandy) to the early Spanish and American settlers. Their biggest wineries were at the San Gabriel and San Fernando Missions in present-day Los Angeles County. By 1821, San Gabriel, with three wine presses, was producing 400 barrels of wine and half that many of brandy each year. You can still see, behind that restored mission, the adobe building with its stone floor and sump where the Indians once crushed the grapes with their feet.

Within a few decades, vineyards were thriving where some of today's great southern cities stand. Vignes Street in downtown Los Angeles commemorates California's first professional winegrower, Jean Louis Vignes from Bordeaux. Aliso Street is where, by 1833, Vignes had imported European vines to his El Aliso Vineyard, which was entered through a grape arbor a quarter-mile long. Boyle Heights recalls Andrew Boyle from County Galway, whose thirty-acre vineyard flourished in 1860 below the cliff on which his brick home stood. The first mayor of Los Angeles, Benjamin Davis Wilson, for whom Mount Wilson is named, won fame for the white wines from his Lake Vineyard, established near San Gabriel in 1852. Thirty-five years later, Wilson's son-in-law, J. de Barth Shorb, was boasting that his San Gabriel Winery, with a capacity of 15 million gallons, was the largest in the world. At Santa Anita Race Track in nearby Arcadia the fabulous Elias (Lucky) Baldwin produced medal-winning wines and brandies on his 1,200-acre vineyard, which was described in the 1880s as "a second Garden of Eden, bewildering in its beauty." Baldwin's gingerbread mansion still stands as a historical monument. Anaheim in neighboring Orange County, the home today of Disneyland and the baseball Angels, began in 1857 as a utopian winegrowing colony of German immigrants. Anaheim was one of the leading wine districts of the state until 1884, when the vines suddenly died of a mysterious disease (the Anaheim or Pierce's Disease, whose bacterial cause has only lately been found). Other parts of Orange County had wineries and 600 acres of vineyards as late as 1910. In that year Los Angeles, San Bernardino, San Diego, and Ventura Counties still had scores of wineries and 37,000 acres of vines.

There still were 5,000 acres of vineyards and forty-nine wineries in Los Angeles County alone at the beginning of the Second World War. Then came the flood of new population to the Los Angeles basin, and the vines soon were virtually gone. The last big vineyard, at John McClure's Burbank Winery above San Fernando Boulevard, was bulldozed in 1947 to make room for a subdivision.

One Los Angeles winery survives because the city has saved it from razing for a development, by naming it Cultural Historical Monument No. 42. The 80,000-gallon San Antonio Winery, with cellar tour, tasting, picnic garden, café and delicatessen, is an oasis at the dead end of Lamar Street, two miles from downtown. No other American city has anything quite like it. Four members of the Riboli family make some forty different

Anaheim Public Library

Anaheim Colony vineyards and wineries thrived from 1857 to 1884 on the present site of Disneyland in California. A mysterious disease (later called the Anaheim or Pierce's Disease) killed the vines.

wines from Cucamonga, Lodi, and Sonoma grapes. Steve, Maddalena, Santo, and Cathy Riboli took over the winery from Steve's uncle, Italian-born Santo Cambianica, who founded it in 1917.

• 3 •

The Cucamonga Valley, forty-five miles east of Los Angeles, has grown the bulk of Southern California wine during the present century. The vineyard area extends from Ontario east to Fontana and from the base of the San Gabriel Mountains southward to the Jurupa Hills in Riverside County. The climate, though tempered by winds from the ocean, is as warm as the northern San Joaquin Valley and is classed as Region IV.

Tiburcio Tapia planted the first vines in San Bernardino County on his Cucamonga Rancho in 1838. When the railroad arrived forty years later, others began growing grapes along the streams in the rich foothills north of Cucamonga and between Redlands and Banning in southern San Bernardino and northwestern Riverside County.

But nobody thought of planting vines or anything else in the vast flat, sandy waste in between—the Cucamonga desert—until Secondo Guasti came. Guasti arrived in Los Angeles in 1878 from the Italian Piedmont via Mexico, an unschooled, penniless youth. He shoveled coal in the freight yards, cooked in a restaurant, married the owner's daughter, and saved enough to start a small Los Angeles winery and to buy a vineyard in West Glendale. On occasional visits to the Cucamonga Valley, he noticed that the winter floods from the mountains flowed only as far as the desert and there disappeared. It occurred to Guasti that there might be water beneath the desert sand. One day he found a scraggly vine growing in the parched waste. Borrowing a shovel, he dug to find its root. Legend says that he discovered moisture after digging down twenty-four feet. Back in Los Angeles in 1900, Guasti organized the Italian Vineyard Company, selling shares to his countrymen. He bought eight square miles of the Cucamonga desert, built fences against rabbits, and planted a hundred varieties of grapes. He brought whole families from Italy to till the land and built an Italian town—which he named Guasti—with its own school, inn, general store, fire house, post office, and a church as lovely as those in the Italian countryside. Others planted in the desert, and more wineries were built. In 1911, Captain Paul Garrett acquired his 2,000 acres at Cucamonga to grow grapes for Virginia Dare wine. By 1917, Guasti was advertising the IVC vineyard as "four thousand acres, the largest in the world." San Bernardino County had 20,000 acres of vineyards, more than in Sonoma and twice as many as in Napa County—when Prohibition came in 1920.

During the early dry years, instead of pulling out their vines, the Cucamonga growers reaped a bonanza by shipping their grapes fresh across the country to the eastern bootleg and home-winemaking trade. The Guasti winery switched to making the legal sacramental and kosher wines. Then Captain Garrett, at his Mission Vineyard and Winery in Cucamonga, created Virginia Dare Wine Tonic by adding beef extract, pepsin, and iron to port and sherry, which made the concoction salable under the dry law. Guasti and the big Padre winery followed with their own wine tonic brands. When in 1929 Captain Garrett formed the Fruit Industries merger of old wineries to produce "Vine-Glo" grape concentrate, the Italian Vineyard Company was one of the first to join. By then Secondo Guasti had died. Much of the nation's supply of "Vine-Glo" was made at Guasti during the latter Prohibition years.

At Repeal in 1933, the Cucamonga district wineries had an opportunity to interest the connoisseur trade in at least three distinctive local wines. The late great wine judge, Almond R. Morrow, rated Cucamonga port the finest in the state. Cucamonga Zinfandel and Grignolino, grown in the district's unique climate and soil, are unusually soft to the palate, yet possess pronounced flavors and aromas unlike any other red table wines. Home winemakers in the East long paid premium prices for Cucamonga Zinfandel grapes because of their distinctive, almost cheesy taste. Because of it, some Northern California winemakers refuse to use Cucamonga wine in their blends. But the Cucamonga vintners, instead of capitalizing on the unique character of their grapes, ignored the connoisseur trade and tried to compete with the San Joaquin Valley wineries for the Los Angeles mass market in cheap wines. There was one brief attempt before the Second World War to sell Cucamonga wines as something different. Nicola Giulii, Guasti's brother-in-law, took the Italian Vineyard Company out of Fruit Industries in 1940 and advertised IVC wines as "better because they are made from non-irrigated grapes." Few people were impressed, however, because the IVC wines were low in price. Whatever the reason, Cucamonga wines have been sold at bargain prices during most of the years since Repeal. The reds some of the wineries were still selling at 69 to 80 cents at bottle in 1972 were the best wine bargains in the United States.

When Henry Kaiser built his huge steel plant among the vines at Fontana in 1942, an industrial and housing boom began spreading eastward from Los Angeles. When the military flying field adjoining Guasti was expanded after the war to become Ontario International Airport, it displaced hundreds of acres of vineyards. Still more acres were bulldozed during the 1960s to make room for the adjoining Holiday Inn and for the mammoth new Ontario Motor Speedway.

Meanwhile smog, already withering the leaves of southern citrus groves and even threatening to kill the Ponderosa pines in the San Gabriel Mountains, began to affect the Cucamonga vineyards, too. What smog does to grapevines was strikingly shown by University experimenters who in 1968 built plastic greenhouses around patches of vines at Cucamonga and filtered the air inside. The vines left exposed to smog yielded only half as many grapes, with only four fifths of the sugar content, as the grapes grown in filtered air.

In 1966, the Crop Reporting Service listed San Bernardino County as having 19,460 acres of vineyards. This was almost a seventh of the state's total acreage of wine grapes. By 1977, barely half, only 9,658 acres, were left. During the very peak of the nationwide boom in table wine use, when vineyards expanded at a record rate elsewhere in the state, the Cucamonga district experienced the exact reverse. This was the toll taken by befouled air and urban sprawl.

• 4 •

Yet, on my most recent trip to Southern California, old Guasti, the wine town in the desert, appeared little changed by the passage of years. The massive stone winery buildings, the workers' dwellings, the Louisa Guasti School, the post office, the store, and the lovely San Secondo d'Asti Church seemed much the same as I remembered them from earlier times. Secondo Guasti's baronial residence, with its luxuriant tropical gardens, was empty now, as were the old distillery and the fermenting room.

But there was bustling new activity around two of the buildings. The main aging cellar, with its three-foot-thick walls, had been occupied since 1957 by the Brookside Vineyard Company, organized by the French family Biane, who are Philo, his sons Michael and Pierre, and Philo's nephew, René. The adjoining cooper shop, converted into a Brookside tasting room, was crowded with visitors, who overflowed onto a picnic

The San Secondo d'Asti Church in the winery village at Guasti, California.

Brookside Vineyard Co.

area under the trees. There until 1976 a ceremonial blessing of
the grapes had been held annually following High Mass in the
church, with folk dancing afterward on the winery grounds, but
unruly crowds caused the event to be canceled in the following
year. Since moving to Guasti, the Bianes had added thirty
Brookside and Brookside-Mills winery branches to sell, in their
unique winery-to-consumer operation, their eighty different
Assumption Abbey, Brookside, Vaché, and Vins de Biane
Frères wines. The newest branches are in Nevada, Arizona, and
two in Illinois, one at Elgin and the other in Arlington Heights.
Illinois entered the picture after Brookside in 1973 became a
subsidiary of Chicago's Beatrice Foods conglomerate, which
owns hundreds of companies that sell us every kind of products,
ranging from milk, ice cream, and Chinese food to trailers,
yachts, and mobile homes.

In a corner of the aging cellar, the Bianes had opened a
Brookside wine museum. Some of the exhibits told how things
had changed at Guasti since the founder's time. During the
wartime wine shortage, Horace Lanza of Delano bought the
Italian Vineyard Company to get control of the huge Guasti
grape crop. In 1945 the heirs of Captain Garrett bought Guasti
from Lanza, transferred the Garrett winemaking operation
there from New York, and changed Virginia Dare into a
California wine. When the Garrett company was liquidated in
1961, its business was sold to Alta Vineyards of Fresno, but the
Guasti vineyards were sold to Los Angeles oilman and real
estate developer Edwin Pauley, who leased them back to the
Alta interests. Then Alta was merged with Guild wines of Lodi,
which licensed Canandaigua Industries of New York to revive
Garrett's Virginia Dare as an eastern wine.

Other exhibits in the Brookside wine museum traced Califor-
nia wine history made by the forebears of the Bianes. Théophile
Vaché from France started a wine business at Monterey in 1832
and pioneered winegrowing in the Cienega Valley of San Benito
County about 1849. His nephews, Adolphe, Emile, and
Théophile, moved to Southern California and established the
Brookside winery near Redlands in 1883. The late Marius Biane
came from Gascony in 1892, served the Vachés as their wine-
maker, and married Adolphe's daughter, Marcelline. Marius
Biane moved to Cucamonga in 1916 to make wine for Captain
Garrett and acquired his own vineyards there. His sons, Philo
and the late François, succeeded him, making wine for Fruit
Industries, Secondo Guasti, Captain Garrett, and the Cucamon-
ga Growers Co–op Winery. In 1952, Philo Biane took the

Cucamonga Co–op out of Fruit Industries and reestablished the Brookside Vineyard Company near Cucamonga. Five years later he bought the Guasti cellar and moved Brookside head-quarters there. Winemaking at Guasti had ceased after Guild took over the Garrett cellar and converted it into a warehouse for Guild wines. Brookside wines were made at the old Cuca-monga Pioneer Winery until Brookside bought the 4-million-gallon Gallo bulk winery on Arrow Boulevard in 1972.

Brookside-Mills Cellar table wines could still be bought for $1.25 a bottle in 1977, but the "varietal" Assumption Abbey table wines, frequent medal winners at the Pomona Fair, were priced as high as $3.60. Brookside's oldest and best red table wine, Dido Noir, was priced almost as high as the varietal reds. Full-bodied, fruity in flavor, and with an impressive bouquet, Dido was a blend of Cucamonga Ruby Cabernet with Carignane grapes grown on one of the few vineyards left in the old Escondido district of San Diego; Escondido inspired its name. (The Assumption Abbey brand is used on Brookside altar and commercial wines by an arrangement made in 1956 with the Benedictine monks at that abbey in Richardton, North Dakota.)

• 5 •

Other Cucamonga district vineyards and wineries still showed some signs of continuing life. Philo Biane, though still a director of big Brookside, has opened a charming new 14,000-gallon winery of his own, named Rancho de Philo, on the fourteen remaining acres of vines around his home on Wilson Avenue, east of Archibald. It is the first new winery built in San Bernardino County since Repeal. He produces only cream sherry in a solera (fractional blending) system using small oak casks, one of his lifetime hobbies. Rancho de Philo is well worth a visit because visitors are permitted to taste, although Philo's sherry may only be purchased in case lots.

Bonded Winery No. 1, the $2^{1}/_{2}$-million-gallon former Vai Brothers or Padre Winery on Eighth Street in Cucamonga, has been doing a brisk business with its Cuvée d'Or table wines and champagnes and with custom production for other producers since the winery was purchased in 1976 by Philo Biane's son Pierre. This was the leading Southern California winery before the Second World War, when colorful James L. "Padre Jim" Vai was making, from Cucamonga Burger grapes, one of the better champagnes in the state. His nephew, Cesare, operated the winery as the Cucamonga Vineyard Company following Padre Jim's death in 1961. The great Padre vineyards are no more, and the Padre and Vai Brothers names have been sold. But Primo Scorsatto, who made the first Padre champagne for the Vais in 1935, is still the winemaster after forty-four years. At last reports, Pierre Biane was planning to reopen the "old crusher" tasting and retail sales room.

Liveliest winery in the area is Joseph A. Filippi's 800,000-gallon cellar on his family's vineyard at Jurupa and Etiwanda Avenues in Mira Loma (which originally was named Wineville when the big Charles Stern vineyard was established there). Joseph's wife Elena operates a gift shop at the winery inside a 600,000-gallon former wine tank. Joseph's grandfather Giovanni and his father Joseph Sr. established the winery in 1934, the year after Repeal, and sent Joseph A. to UC Davis to be trained in modern winemaking. He now makes some three dozen wines and sells them in half a dozen Château Filippi tasting rooms around Southern California. His biggest branch is the former Thomas cellar in the center of Cucamonga, which some say is the oldest winery building in the state.

Bernard and Mary Galleano still make wines for sale at the cellar among their vineyards on Wineville Avenue. One of their wines, Green Valley Mission Rosé, is one of the state's few remaining "varietal" table wines of the Mission grape.

Near the Freeway in Fontana, Eugene Cherpin still cultivates the family vineyards and sells wines at retail and to Los Angeles restaurants. The late John Ellena's 2-million-gallon Regina Winery at Etiwanda has been stripped of its champagne-making equipment and closed to the public. Heublein now owns the Regina Winery and makes only wine for vinegar there.

But while winegrowing in the Cucamonga district continues to decline, there now is a new winery in another part of San Bernardino County, thirty-five miles to the east. In the Oak Glen hills that rise to 5,000 feet beyond Yucaipa, former newspaper publisher and one-time Napa Valley winery proprietor Charles B. Colby established the Oak Glen Winery in 1977. His first wines are made of apples and pears, but he plans to plant noble wine grape varieties among the apple orchards and develop a new vineyard district there.

• 6 •

New Southern California vineyards and wineries have sprung up since the late 1960s in districts closer to the Pacific Coast.

The Escondido district in northwestern San Diego County had 5,000 acres of vines in the 1930s, and eight wineries opened there when Prohibition was repealed. Two of the old Escondido wineries are left, the Ferrara family's 45,000-gallon cellar on their two remaining acres west of the city, and Ross Rizzo's somewhat larger Bernardo Winery, reached by Pomerado Road from Interstate 15. In 1973, Judge Charles Froelich and San Diego attorney Milton Fredman leased some San Diego city property along Highland Valley Road south of Escondido, planted a hundred acres of premium wine grape varieties, and four years later built the 40,000-gallon San Pasqual Vineyards winery on San Pasqual Road. Their UC Davis-trained winemaker David Allen said the first San Pasqual Sauvignon Blanc, Chenin Blanc, and Gamay would be ready for release in 1978. San Diego County now has 500 acres of vines.

In Orange County, an eight-acre drip-irrigated vineyard of White Riesling, Chenin Blanc, Cabernet Sauvignon, and Petite Sirah was planted in 1973 on the O'Neill family's 42,000-acre Rancho Mission Viejo, twelve miles north of Mission San Juan Capistrano. When I last visited the vineyard, additional plantings and construction of a winery were being planned.

The most extensive new Southern California vineyards cover some 2,000 acres in the southwestern corner of Riverside County, a smog-free area twenty-three miles from the Pacific Ocean. Most of them are within Rancho California, the unique planned community of ranches built since 1965 by the mammoth Kaiser-Aetna land development combine. On sixty square miles of rolling land east of Temecula, there are country homes, a man-made lake, livestock farms, avocado and citrus groves, with another seventy square miles of Temecula held in reserve.

Rancho California was formerly range land, too arid for grape growing, but 500-foot-deep wells now provide sufficient water for the farms. On a mesa designated for tree crops and vines, Rancho California during the late 1960s offered ready-made forty-acre and larger vineyards with viticultural care provided—a novel phase of the early winegrowing boom. The vineyards planted are mostly such premium varieties as Cabernet Sauvignon, Gamay Beaujolais, White Riesling, and Chenin Blanc, in contrast to those grown at Cucamonga, which have been primarily Mission, Zinfandel, Grenache, Palomino, and Mataro.

By the University system of measuring degree-days, Temecula is Region III; Cucamonga is Region IV. Largest vineyard in Rancho California is 450 acres that supply the Brookside

Vineyard Company winery at Guasti. There now are two Temecula wineries, both of which welcome visitors and sell their wines at retail. On Rancho California Road five miles east of Interstate 15 (US 395) is the 100,000-gallon Callaway Vineyard and Winery, built beginning in 1974 by Ely R. Callaway, Jr., the former president of Burlington Industries. A mile farther east is former Los Angeles radio station owner John Poole's 12,000-gallon Mount Palomar Winery, opened two years later. Grapes from most other vineyards in the area supply Northern California premium wineries.

• 7 •

Ely Callaway, of the Georgia family best known for their public gift of Callaway Gardens south of Atlanta, retired from the presidency of the world's largest textile firm in 1973 at the age of fifty-four. Four years earlier, planning for retirement to farming and golfing, he had planted 134 acres of premium wine grape varieties on a hill in Rancho California. On annual visits there from New York, he had studied the effect of climates on the qualities of grapes and wines. His findings convinced him that breezes flowing from the Pacific through Rainbow Gap and across his vineyard gave it a microclimate comparable to that of the north coastal counties and that his vineyard's granitic soil should produce fine wines. He decided to build a winery.

Visiting his vineyard in the autumn of 1973, I found Callaway ruefully surveying a gray mold that had formed on his first crop of Chenin Blanc grapes. The whole Chenin Blanc crop was about to be discarded. Curious, I examined the grapes and suggested that the mold might be botrytis. "What's botrytis?" Callaway asked. I explained that botrytis is the prized noble rot, rare in dry California climates, that in Europe makes it possible to produce the greatest German Rieslings and French sauternes. The mold on his Chenin Blanc was indeed botrytis. Callaway sent the grapes to a Napa winery and had them made into California's first-ever botrytized Chenin Blanc. He named the wine "Sweet Nancy" for his wife and sold the 1973 vintage for fifteen dollars a bottle.

Callaway hired Karl Werner, the former winemaster of Germany's famed Schloss Vollrads, and in the following year built his winery, which Werner equipped with winemaking apparatus of all the most advanced designs.

The first Callaway wines were released in late 1975 and received rave reviews from connoisseurs. His 1974 White Ries-

Ely Callaway, Jr.

Botrytis, the "noble mold," is starting to grow on these Chenin Blanc grapes in the Callaway Vineyard at Temecula, California.

ling was chosen by the Pilgrims Club for serving to England's Queen Elizabeth and Prince Philip at their bicentennial luncheon in New York. Virtually overnight Callaway wines became the first from Southern California to win a place beside the world's great vintages featured on wine lists and in stores. Many call it "the Callaway miracle."

Callaway wines bring premium prices that compare with the top "varietals" from the Northern California wineries with which they compete. But the 1975 "Sweet Nancy" is priced at sixteen dollars a bottle and the 1975 "TBA" White Riesling brings twenty-five. "TBA" means the proportion of botrytized grapes that meets the German standard for *Trockenbeerenauslese* wines. Botrytis forms every year on grapes at Temecula unless it is controlled by sprays. Morning mists are part of the local climate, which explains the town's Indian name, Temeku, which means "land where the sun shines through the white mist." The other Callaway wines include Cabernet Sauvignon, Petite Sirah, Zinfandel, the dry White Riesling, and two different Sauvignon Blancs, dry and Fumé. Callaway attributes their quality as much to especially meticulous vineyard-to-winery care as to climate and soil. John Moramarco, his tenth-generation viticulturist, personally finish-prunes and later cluster-thins each grapevine following these operations by the vineyard crew. In the cellar, where Fresno State University-trained Stephen O'Donnell is the winemaster with Karl Werner as consulting enologist, Callaway wines receive their final aging in barrels custom-made under Werner's supervision in Germany from oak grown on Spessart Mountain between Frankfurt and Würzburg.

As to climate, Callaway believes the time has come for those who study the temperatures of California winegrowing areas to recognize the western portion of Southern California as a separate "South Coastal Mountains" region.

18

Lodi, Sacramento,
the Foothills, and Davis

WHEN PEOPLE say "Lodi" (pronounced *low-dye*), they mean the fifty-square-mile expanse of flat, extremely fertile vineyards which completely encircle that city at the edge of the Sacramento-San Joaquin River Delta in northern San Joaquin County, California.

Along a six-mile stretch of Highway 50–99, which bisects the town of Lodi, are twelve bonded wineries which store some 40 million gallons of wine. Three of them have public tasting rooms and highway billboards inviting travelers to stop and sample their wines. The leading industry of Lodi is the production of grapes, wine, and brandy distilled from wine. The most elaborate vintage celebration in the United States is the Lodi Grape Festival and National Wine Show, held in mid-September with grape exhibits, tastings, and a spectacular Sunday parade.

The Lodi district is viticulturally unique. Grapevines grow to enormous size in its deep sandy-loam soil, washed down from the mountains for centuries. Many vines around Lodi are eight feet tall and have trunks as large around as trees. Summer days in San Joaquin County are less torrid than in the main Central Valley; the county's climate is Region IV. At Lodi, however, the vines are further cooled at night by moist westerly winds from the nearby Delta with its thousand miles of tidewater rivers, bays, and sloughs. This is why the Flame Tokay table grape develops its flaming red color, which attracts buyers in the fresh fruit markets, only in the Lodi district. Lodi produces 98 percent of the Flame Tokays in the nation. Nineteen thousand acres are planted to Tokays and 14,000 to wine grapes. Most of the latter are Zinfandels and Carignanes, two wine varieties of which Lodi grows more than any other district in the state.

A tenth of California's wine output is made in Lodi. But you seldom can tell from labels which wines are Lodi-grown, because fleets of tank trucks bring millions of gallons from elsewhere to be bottled there, and other trucks take Lodi grapes and wines to wineries in other districts, which use them in their blends. In the past, the Lodi wineries produced mostly sherry and port. The chamber of commerce once sought to publicize Lodi as "America's Sherryland," and even got Federal recognition of Lodi as a delimited district for wine labeling purposes. The wine revolution since the late '60s has compelled the wineries to switch to making mostly table wines.

• 2 •

Grape growing in San Joaquin County began in 1850 at Stockton, twelve miles south of Lodi, when Captain Charles Weber founded that city and planted Mission vines in his garden. Eight years later, a gold miner from Massachusetts, George West, planted vines he got from Captain Weber and began building his El Pinal Winery on West Lane, two miles north of Stockton. By the end of the Civil War, West had one of the greatest vineyards in California. In later years he and his son Frank owned vineyards and wineries in Fresno, Madera, and Kings Counties and shipped wines and brandy to their own sales depot in New York.

Lodi was watermelon and grain country during that time. Vineyards were already established in the Sierra foothills and the rest of the Central Valley, but there were only scattered grape plantings at Lodi until Tokays were planted at the turn of the century. Then the eastern fruit auctions, supplied by trains of new refrigerator cars, made cross-country shipping of fresh grapes profitable. In two decades Lodi, with its brilliant red Tokays, became the most prosperous grape district in the United States. At Stockton, where Tokays ripened as elsewhere with only a dull buckskin color, the vineyards were attacked by phylloxera and died.

The first few wineries around Lodi were built after 1900, using the local wine grapes and providing a home for leftover Tokays. When Prohibition came in 1920, some of the wine grapes were shipped east for home winemaking and the rest were used to make grape juice, concentrate, and sacramental and tonic wines. Huge tonnages of surplus Tokays were left to rot on the vines.

In 1933, as Repeal approached, the growers expected the new

demand for wine to make them rich. But in that vintage season, only five Lodi wineries were ready to crush any grapes. When the wineries, flooded with grapes, offered the growers only twelve dollars a ton, then seven dollars, and in a subsequent rainy season only five dollars, the angry growers decided to build wineries of their own. Twelve farmer-co-operative cellars were opened around Lodi during the next few years, and growers' groups built a dozen more co-op wineries in other parts of the state. The co-op wineries banded together in two Lodi-based marketing organizations to sell their wines.

One was Fruit Industries, the combine that had made "Vine-Glo" concentrate for home winemaking during Prohibition. The other, started in 1937 by the late Lawrence K. Marshall with a nucleus of two new Lodi co-ops, was California Wine Sales, which later became the Wine Growers Guild and the Guild Wineries & Distilleries of today.

Fruit Industries, managed by Walter E. Taylor of Lodi, became the post-Repeal giant of the wine industry, bigger than the California Wine Association of pre-Prohibition days. In 1950, Fruit Industries, with eleven wineries throughout the state, changed its name to California Wine Association and adopted "Eleven Cellars" as its chief brand name. The choice of that name soon proved embarrassing, because one by one the member wineries began dropping out of the group. CWA's "Eleven Cellars" have now dwindled to one at Delano.

The Guild in 1962 combined with a Fresno merger of old commercial wine firms (Alta Vineyards, A. Mattei, Cameo Vineyards, B. Cribari & Sons, Garrett). It then bought the wineries of its co-op members and became a single co-op owned by its grower members throughout the state. In 1970, the Guild bought Schenley's Roma and Cresta Blanca wineries at Fresno, Kingsburg, and Delano and increased its membership to more than 1,000 growers. Already owning six wineries—three at Lodi, one at Ukiah, two at Fresno—the Guild thereby increased its total to nine. With its total capacity of 57 million gallons, the Guild is now the third largest vintner in the nation. As the nation's largest winegrowers' co-op, the Guild in 1974 added to its "Winemasters" line of California wines thirty more produced by co-op-owned wineries in France, Italy, Germany, and Spain.

Most of the wine labeled with Lodi as the bottling address comes from the Guild's blending, bottling, and champagne-making winery at the northeast edge of town. There, too, is the Guild's big Winemaster Hospitality House and restaurant, where hundreds of tourists stop daily to taste the wines and to be conducted on cellar tours, and where summer lawn concerts are held accompanied by complimentary wines.

Of the Guild's 118 different wines, brandies, and Charmat-process champagnes (not counting the assortment from its Cresta Blanca subsidiary), the most interesting and one of its best-sellers is a red table wine called Vino da Tavola, with a label that resembles a red-and-white-checkered tablecloth.

One night in 1949, three sales executives of the Guild, dining in an Italian restaurant in Chicago, were discussing the main problem of the wine industry—why most native Americans were rejecting dry red wines as "sour." Then they noticed that most of the people at tables around them were drinking dry red wine with Italian food. This gave them an idea: why not sweeten dry red wine with a little port and sell it with a label like the restaurant's tablecloth and with an Italian name? Then and there they designed the label and chose the name, Vino da Tavola, which in Italian means "wine for the table." Back in Lodi, they challenged the Guild's then Winemaster Lawrence Quaccia to blend a wine to fit the name. He did it with Lodi Zinfandel, a touch of port, and a wood-aged Mendocino Carignane, a coast-counties wine "to give it life," he said. Other wineries had made sweetened "vinos" before, but lively red Tavola with its tablecloth label quickly outstripped them all in sales. In the years since, it has taught millions of Americans to enjoy red wine with their meals. "What wine is served in the French Embassy in Washington, D.C.?" read a Guild magazine advertisement in 1969. It pictured General Charles de Gaulle hiding a jug with a checkered label and saying, "I'll never tell." The French Government protested indignantly to our State Department, but to no avail, for the Frenchmen at the Embassy had indeed been consuming Tavola by the case.

Best of the Guild's many brandies is one distilled at its Bear Creek Winery near Lodi, entirely from Flame Tokay grapes. The first American brandy ever to bear a vintage date (1966), it is sold under the Cresta Blanca brand, which the Guild now owns.

A half-mile south of the Guild is the 5-million-gallon East-Side Winery, so named because it is on the east side of town. This is the only local co-op that bottles most of its wine. Eighty Lodi families, led by Jacob Kurtz and his neighbors, the Mettlers, Preszlers, and Handels, joined in East-Side in 1934. Most of its members, and many in other Lodi co-ops, are descendants of German families who migrated to Russia in the time of Catherine the Great, then three generations later to the

Dakotas, and finally to Lodi around the turn of this century. In front of the winery office stands "Das Weinhaus," a 50,000-gallon redwood wine tank converted into an attractive tasting room. On display inside are some of the hundreds of medals awarded to East-Side's Royal Host wines while Herman Ehlers was the winemaker, a job from which he retired in 1970 after thirty-seven years.

Ehlers and a few other East-Side members were among the first to plant in Lodi, during the 1950s, small acreages of superior grape varieties for table wines. Though East-Side still makes its popular Royal Host wines, it now offers ten "select premium" varietally labeled table wines under its Conti Royale brand. The best I have tasted was a Grey Riesling that equaled most coast counties wines made of that grape. Also of premium quality were the Ruby Cabernet, Emerald Riesling, Chenin Blanc, Dry Sémillon, and a semidry white made of the University's new grape variety named Gold. In recent years East-Side has installed stainless steel tanks, small oak casks for aging, and the special cooling equipment needed—and until now lacking in most Lodi wineries—to protect delicate table wines. East-Side's other specialties include its Conti Royale and Royal Host brandies, and "Mission 1773," a classic Angelica Antigua made of Mission grapes and aged eight years in small oak casks.

Across the road from East-Side is the old Roma winery, a relic of Lodi wines of the past. The massive brick building is now a warehouse for surplus cans, but wine is still stored there for various vintners who rent the use of its great concrete tanks. It was here, when Prohibition ended, that the Cella brothers, Battista and Lorenzo, began expanding their Roma Wine Company into the biggest commercial producer of California wines of the early post-Repeal years. On the roof of the winery, Roma wines were once "solarized"—an advertising gimmick that consisted of pumping them through glass tubing exposed to the sun—which did the wines harm instead of good. Roma's radio slogan was "Don't drink it, sip it," first broadcast by Art Linkletter from the Wine Temple at the San Francisco 1939 world's fair. When the co-op wineries were built during the 1930s to crush most of the local grapes, the Cellas moved from Lodi to the Roma (now Cribari) winery in Fresno.

On Turner Road, across the highway from Roma, is a warehouse that once was the Shewan-Jones winery, which made the best Lodi table wines at the time of Repeal. There a great winemaker named Elbert McSherry Brown and his then assistant, Herman Ehlers, made Tokay and Burger juice into a sweet sauterne which Shewan-Jones sold as "Château Yquem." When the Federal Government in 1936 outlawed "Château Yquem" labels on American wines, owner Lee Jones created a French-sounding word out of his own Welsh name, and made the wine nationally famous as "Château Lejon."

In the village of Acampo, about two miles north of Lodi, is the 1.7-million-gallon Barengo Winery, an example of how the local wineries have changed through the years. The main brick cellar was originally a granary. At Repeal a group of grape growers headed by Cesare Mondavi bought it and named it the Acampo Winery. As their winemaker they hired Dino Barengo, who like Herman Ehlers had been trained in winemaking by Elbert Brown at Shewan-Jones. Barengo became the winery's owner when the Mondavis sold it to buy the Charles Krug cellar in the Napa Valley. Barengo in 1949 became the first Lodi vintner to make a wine of Ruby Cabernet. Nineteen years later, Sacramento importer Darrell Corti happened to taste Barengo's Ruby Cabernet, and persuaded him to age some of it in European oak barrels. In a few months the wine tasted like an unusually fine red Bordeaux. Corti bought the entire bottling and sold it at a higher price than most of his Bordeaux imports.

Barengo continued making bulk wine for the Mondavis, but developed specialties of his own, including the principal May wine (woodruff-flavored, white) produced in the United States. In connoisseur circles, however, Barengo became best known for his flavorful wine vinegar, which he aged in a *solera* of barrels like those in the sherry *bodegas* of Spain. In 1973, he sold the winery to a group named Winkler-Scheid, who had planted 3,000 acres of premium wine grapes in Monterey County. Three years later, Winkler-Scheid sold it to Santa Clara County developer-builder Ira Kerkorian, who needed a home for the 640 acres of wine grapes he had planted in Fresno County. Kerkorian enlarged and modernized the old cellar and bought top "varietal" grapes from the coast counties to produce a complete line of wines, ranging from premium vintages to those usually sold in jugs, and increased the production of Barengo vinegar. Half of the winery's output is sold in six Barengo tasting rooms.

Beside the Coloma tasting room at the north end of Lodi is the former Da Roza Winery, which still crushes grapes but doesn't ferment any into wine. Instead, it extracts the water by a vacuum process and turns out "Wine-Art" and "Homewine" grape concentrates for the American and Canadian home winemaker trade. Strange to say, there are some vineyardists around Lodi who are Prohibitionists and refuse to sell their grapes to wineries. They are glad, however, to sell them to the California Concentrate Company, even though they know the product eventually will be made into wine. Founder of this operation was veteran Lodi winemaker Wallace Pohle, who went to Canada in 1961 to build two wineries in British Columbia. There he met Stanley Anderson, who had started a home winemaking supply business called "Wine-Art," selling concentrates from Spain and Greece. Pohle convinced Anderson he could make better concentrate from California grapes, returned to Lodi, and founded Wine-Art of America here in 1968.

The 6-million-gallon former Cherokee winery on Woodbridge Road has had six different names since it was built by the Cherokee growers' co-op, a member of Fruit Industries, in 1936. In recent years it has made wines under such names as Montcalm Vintners and Filice, but when I last checked, it was producing bulk wines for C. Mondavi & Sons.

Other wineries in the Lodi district include Bear Creek and Del Rio, the two original members of the Guild; the old Community co-op, which was the first of the CWA's "Eleven Cellars" but is now owned by Heublein's United Vintners; Kenneth Knapp's Rio Vista Winery, once operated by the Sebastianis of Sonoma; the Woodbridge and Lodi Vintners independent co-ops; and the Liberty Winery, which has produced wine for Gallo in recent years. The former Lockeford co-op, in the northeastern corner of the district, has lately been an independent producer of Charmat champagnes, assorted wines, and brandy.

• 3 •

The Flame Tokay is an oval, thick-skinned, fleshy grape with three seeds. It was introduced to this country a century ago from Algeria, where it is known as the Ahmeur bou Ahmeur. It has nothing to do with the medium-sweet, pinkish-red California dessert wine type called Tokay, which can be made from any grape. It is usually a blend of sherry and port. Neither the grape nor the wine is in any way related to the Tokay or Tokai wines of Hungary, which are traditionally made of a grape called Furmint that is grown only experimentally in the United States. I know of only one "varietal" Tokay wine; the East-Side Winery makes it entirely of that grape and labels it Flame Tokay. J. Walter Fleming, the first manager of the Lockeford

Winery, once named a brandy "Lodi Tokay" and sold Tokay table wine to producers of sparkling wines, who made it into champagne.

When Jim Kissler, a graduate of the University's wine school at Davis, became San Joaquin County's farm advisor in 1957, he began trying to persuade Lodi growers to change from Tokays to the "varietal" grapes for table wines, such as Grey Riesling and Ruby Cabernet. Carl Mettler, an East-Side director, donated two acres for test plantings. The tests showed that several of the "varietals" are well suited to the Lodi climate and soil. Kissler's efforts have had some success. By 1976, San Joaquin County had almost 4,000 acres of French Colombard, Chenin Blanc, Cabernet Sauvignon, and Gamay, most of it planted during the five preceding years. But these include plantings outside the Lodi district. Of Ruby Cabernet—the variety that has made the best Lodi table wine—the entire county still had only six hundred acres. The farmers are reluctant to plant more Ruby Cabernet because the stem of its cluster is especially tough; vineyard workers have to be paid extra to pick the grapes.

Despite the rising costs of growing grapes to be eaten fresh—which can't be harvested by machine—and the declining sale of fresh fruit in general, Lodi growers have kept replanting Tokays. "Why should we change?" one of them recently asked, "when our wineries have won all those medals at the fairs with wines made of Tokay?" What they ignore is that much of the Tokay crop is now made into white table wines and that neither these nor the medal-winning wines were made of ordinary Tokays. To make good table wine, this grape must be harvested when its acidity is high, when its sugar content tests only 17 to 19 on the Balling or Brix scale, instead of the customary 22. The wineries have only recently recognized this, by agreeing to pay growers the same price per ton for 19-Balling Tokays as for those fully ripe at 22. (And a similar change has occurred in the case of the Thompson Seedless; the wineries now pay the same price for "early Tokays" and "early Thompsons" as for fully ripe grapes.

Kissler has been more successful in getting "varietal" grapes planted outside the Tokay district. Some 1,500 acres of recent plantings are on Mandeville, McDonald, and Bacon Islands, fifteen miles west of Lodi in the vast San Joaquin-Sacramento River Delta region. The islands are below sea level, protected by levees from flooding; they are the Netherlands of the West. Their soil is mostly inflammable peat; there used to be signs along the levee roads warning motorists that "This land will burn!" But the soils at higher elevations on the islands are not peat and have lately been proved suitable for vines. Kissler finds the islands' climate cooler and the grapes grown there of such quality that he foresees an entirely new table wine district of 3,000 acres developing in the Delta in future years.

• 4 •

The Sacramento Valley, which stretches northwest from Lodi and the Delta region for almost 200 miles, is older in winegrowing than the San Joaquin. Before Prohibition there were scores of wineries and nearly 40,000 acres of vineyards in the nine Sacramento Valley counties. By 1970 only four wineries and less than 500 acres were left. But 6,000 acres of new vineyards planted in the valley since the wine revolution reached its peak in the early '70s have made it important in winegrowing again.

In 1842, Captain John Augustus Sutter, the Swiss adventurer turned empire builder, began distilling brandy out of wild grapes in his fort at Sacramento, which he named New Helvetia. Ruined instead of enriched by the discovery of gold in 1848 at his Coloma sawmill, Sutter gave up his fort and moved to his 600-acre Hock Farm on the Feather River in Sutter County eight miles south of Yuba City. There he planted a vineyard with cuttings he imported from Europe. Sutter's vineyard helped support him until he left California in 1866 for Washington, D.C., where he died fourteen years later.

Sutter County is also where farmer William Thompson of Yuba City in 1872 introduced the English hothouse grape he named Thompson's Seedless, which became the most widely planted variety in California.

Neighboring Butte County's wine industry was founded in 1847 by Captain Sutter's aide-de-camp, General John Bidwell, on his ranch at Chico. Twenty-one years later Bidwell married a fanatical Prohibitionist. Before the wedding he emptied his winery, uprooted his wine grapes, planted table and raisin grapes instead, and in 1892 he became the Prohibition Party's candidate for President of the United States. At the turn of the century, Butte County still had five wineries and 1,000 acres in grapes. In 1970 it had about fifty acres, mostly scattered among fruit orchards and olive groves, and only one winery, the retail wine cellar of the Ghianda family on their old hilltop vineyard at Thermalito, a suburb of Oroville. By 1976, Butte County again had 1,000 acres of grapes, mainly Cabernet Sauvignon and

Zinfandel. The first Butte County Chardonnay, of grapes from the Jeanelle Vineyard south of Vina, was made in 1977 by the Mirassou winery at San Jose.

In Yuba County, which borders Sutter and Butte, winegrowing was begun in 1855 by Charles Covillaud from Cognac, who planted grapes at Simpson's Crossing, a mile north of Marysville, the city Covillaud named for his wife, the former Mary Murphy. Within five years the county had four more wineries and 800 acres of vines, which expanded by 1930 to a thousand acres, but then were gradually replaced by orchards of peaches and prunes. Since the grape-planting boom of the early 1970s, Yuba County again has 700 acres of vines. One of the new Yuba vineyards is a project of the Fellowship of Friends, a hundred-member independent church colony in the northern foothills gold country near Oregon House, where the members tend orchards and operate a nonprofit printing shop and book bindery. The member leading the winegrowing project is the noted German-born consulting enologist Karl Werner, whose clients include the Callaway Vineyard and Winery at Temecula and the Château Grand Travers winegrowing estate in Michigan. Planting of the Fellowship of Friends colony's Renaissance Vineyard began in 1976 and a winery is planned by 1979.

In Tehama County, Peter Lassen, the Danish pioneer for whom volcanic Mount Lassen is named, planted the upper Sacramento Valley's first acre of Mission vines in 1846. This was at Vina, on the east bank of the river twenty miles north of Chico. At Lassen's death seven years later, Henry Gerke from Germany enlarged the vineyard and built a 100,000-gallon winery. Gerke made brandy as well as wine and is said to have shipped some to Europe.

Then came wealthy California ex-Governor Leland Stanford, who bought the Vina property from Gerke in 1881. Stanford expanded the vineyard to 5,000 acres, making it then the largest in the world. He built there the costliest winery in the state to hold 2 million gallons of wine, and brought expert winemakers from France.

Stanford had two altruistic objectives in winegrowing: to prove that California could produce finer wines than those of Europe, and to combat drunkenness in America by mass-producing good table wines and promoting their temperate mealtime use. But though successful in his other careers as lawyer, merchant, railroad builder, and breeder of champion racehorses, Stanford made a series of grievous winegrowing mistakes.

His first error was in turning over his original vineyard in Alameda County to his brother Josiah, because that coastal district would have been ideal for his purposes. His second was in choosing Vina and in planting there such varieties as Zinfandel, which in the hot Sacramento Valley in the days before refrigeration could make only poor table wines. When Stanford's first Vina vintage was ready in 1886, he saw his mistake; the wines had an objectionable earthy taste. He then switched to making only dessert wines and brandy and Stanford became the largest distiller of brandy in the world. Barges brought his product in barrels down the then-navigable Sacramento River from Red Bluff to be loaded on ships for New York. His brandy was excellent, if the one I tasted at a Wine and Food Society dinner at the time of Repeal was a fair example. Having learned his lesson about climate, Stanford succeeded in growing some fine table wines in a third vineyard, which he purchased in 1888 at Menlo Park in San Mateo County. But he did not live to taste them; he died in 1893. All that remains of his third winegrowing venture is the winery building, which stands in the Stanford Shopping Center and has been converted into a bank.

At his death, the great Vina estate with its winery and distillery were bequeathed to Stanford University at Palo Alto, which he had founded eight years earlier in memory of his only son, who had died in Italy at the age of fifteen. The sale of wine and brandy helped support the University for a time. But Palo Alto was a wineless community, for Stanford had made still another mistake: The deed to land he had bought to expand the campus contained a proviso that no alcoholic beverage could ever be sold there. (Downtown Palo Alto remained dry until 1970, when a court declared the eighty-year-old proviso void.) Also, Stanford's wife Jane was a teetotaler, violently opposed to wine except for medicinal use. She disrupted the University's management of its beverage business until she was mysteriously murdered by poisoning in 1905. Drys attacked the Stanford trustees for letting alcoholic drinks support the University. When a fire damaged the winery in 1915, the trustees ordered the vineyards uprooted and sold the land in parcels for farms. The winery land and buildings were purchased in 1955 by Trappist monks from Kentucky as the site for their monastery, Our Lady of New Clairvaux.

In Stanford's time, Tehama County had two dozen wineries and 10,000 acres in grapes. After half a century, Stanford's Vina Vineyard is again growing grapes for wine. Tehama County's new vineyards, planted since 1965, are mainly of high-acid varieties such as French Colombard, which if harvested early and properly handled can make good table wines. The grapes are trucked to wineries in cooler districts, such as the coastal counties and the northern San Joaquin Valley.

In Stanford's time there were vineyards as far up the valley as Redding in Shasta County, which counted 400 acres of grapes in 1890. Shasta County again had forty acres of vines by 1977.

But the most extensive pre-Prohibition vineyards in the valley were in Sacramento County. Sacramento Sheriff Benjamin Bugbey grew wines at Folsom that won medals at the 1863 State Fair. In 1889 there were twenty-four wineries between Sacramento, Mormon Island on the American River, Folsom, and Galt. The old Mormon Island wineries are now inundated by Folsom Lake. The Natoma Vineyard south of Folsom covered nearly 2,000 acres. The California Winery on R Street in Sacramento was four decades old when Prohibition in 1920 forced it to close. The vineyards then were concentrated around Florin, Galt, and Elk Grove. There still were 12,000 acres of vines in Sacramento County in 1933, and eight wineries reopened for business at Repeal in that year. Then came urbanization, particularly after the Second World War, and the old vineyards were swallowed up by towns. Without grapes to crush, five of the wineries closed. The Frasinetti Winery, south of Florin, and the Mills Winery on Folsom Boulevard became retail outlets, the latter with numerous branches. The 3-million-gallon Gibson Winery near Elk Grove continues producing, but it makes mostly berry and other fruit wines, which can be sampled at the winery's tasting room on Highway 99 nearby. Gibson is now owned by the former Sanger growers' co-op of Fresno County and bottles the grape wines shipped from Sanger. Among the numerous Gibson products are retsina and kokinelli, the resin-flavored wines favored by consumers born in Greece; a "wassail" honey wine; Akadama burgundy, rosé, and chablis, and the grape-wine base of the Akadama plum wine that Suntory originally shipped unblended from Japan.

The only Sacramento County winery that produces only grape wines is City College English instructor Charles Myers's 5,000-gallon Harbor Winery near the Port of Sacramento. Myers has been making prize-winning wines there since 1972, but exclusively from Napa Valley and Amador County grapes.

Grape-growing in Sacramento County virtually disappeared by 1960, when only 220 acres were left. Then came the table wine boom of the early 1970s, and Sacramento vineyards multiplied to 3,147 acres by 1977. But the revival was not where vineyards had flourished in the past. The vineyards are in new areas. Some are along the Cosumnes River not far from Interstate 5. The rest are mostly in the Sacramento River Delta between Clarksburg and Courtland, an area where the climate resembles Lodi and the San Joaquin County delta islands. A few of the young Delta vineyards are across the river in Yolo County, which again had 510 acres of vines in 1977.

A historical question that puzzled me for many years was: Why did 40,000 acres of vines disappear from the Sacramento Valley, while almost 300,000 acres were being planted in the southern San Joaquin Valley counties of Fresno, Tulare, and Kern—since both of these districts have mainly Region V climates? The answer is related to autumn rainfall. When Prohibition shut down the wineries in the upper Sacramento Valley, the grapes that remained were mainly sun-dried for raisins, which can be ruined by early autumn rains. The raisin-growing industry then became concentrated around arid Fresno, where in most years the grapes can be dried before the rain comes.

• 5 •

Scores of new vineyards and seven new wineries have sprung up in the historic Sierra foothills gold-mining country in response to the table wine boom. Acreage planted to grapes in Amador, Calaveras, El Dorado, and Placer Counties increased by more than half between 1965 and 1977.

The foothills counties, popularly known as the Mother Lode, have a winegrowing history as old as the state. In Gold Rush days many miners, when the precious metal supply petered out, planted vines around their diggings and turned to making wine. El Dorado County alone had more vineyards in 1860 than either Sonoma or Napa. By 1890, more than a hundred wineries were operating at such locations as Nevada City, Colfax, Lincoln, Penryn, Auburn, Placerville, Coloma, Shingle Springs, Ione, Fiddletown, Volcano, Jackson, San Adreas, Sonora, Columbia, and Jamestown. When Prohibition closed the foothills wineries, grape growing gradually moved to the hot valley regions, where irrigated vineyards yield heavier crops.

In the mid-1960s, when urban sprawl compelled the coast-counties vintners to seek new places to plant vines, the foothill counties did not interest them because the available tracts in the rolling hills are too small for mass cultivation, and only those foothill locations with air drainage are safe from crop injury by frosts. There are enough such locations, however, with sufficient space for small winegrowing estates.

Test plots of premium wine grapes were planted about 1965 in foothill counties from Siskiyou to Mariposa, a stretch of 300 miles. Wine samples made at UC Davis of grapes from the test plots showed that wines of coast-counties quality could be grown in the Mother Lode.

At the same time, wine connoisseurs in the lowlands made a discovery about a grape grown in the foothills to which nobody had called their attention before. They discovered that Zinfandel grown in the Shenandoah Valley and around Fiddletown in Amador County makes a wine of more intense flavor and higher alcoholic content than wine from Zinfandel grown elsewhere in the state. The discovery is credited to Harbor Winery proprietor Charles Myers of Sacramento. While still a home winemaker in the 1960s, Myers vinified some Zinfandel from Ken Deaver's vineyard in the Shenandoah Valley. Sacramento importer Darrell Corti tasted Myers's Zinfandel and was so impressed that he arranged for the Sutter Home Winery at St. Helena to make Deaver Vineyard Zinfandel for Corti to sell. The fame of Sutter Home Amador Zinfandel quickly spread. Within a few years, seven premium Napa, Santa Clara, and Alameda County wineries were producing Zinfandels labeled "Amador" and selling them for as much as five dollars a bottle.

There already was an old winery in the Shenandoah Valley that had been making Amador Zinfandel for at least three decades but labeling it burgundy and selling it for sixty-seven cents a bottle. The D'Agostini family's 185,000-gallon cellar, on Shenandoah Road eight miles northeast of Plymouth, dates from 1856, when Adam Uhlinger from Switzerland quarried rock from the hillside to build the cellar walls. Enrico D'Agostini bought the place from Uhlinger in 1911 and made wine until Prohibition. He was succeeded by his four sons, who enlarged the vineyard to 125 acres. After Repeal they made mostly old-fashioned sauterne, burgundy, and dry Muscat and sold it at the cellar door. But now that Amador Zinfandel has become recognized as something special, the D'Agostinis label theirs "estate bottled" and are selling all they can make at four times the old price.

More wineries have opened in the Shenandoah Valley. In 1973, Cary Gott, a winemaker's son trained at UC Davis and at two Napa Valley wineries, built the 30,000-gallon Monteviña winery three miles from Plymouth on Shenandoah School Road. His partners are his wife Vicki and her father, Gilroy banker Walker Field. Gott credits the quality of Amador Zinfandel to the local climate of warm days and cool summer nights and equally to the area's red volcanic soil. He says the Zinfandels grown here differ perceptibly from coast-counties Zinfandels; they grow in looser bunches and have higher acidity and sugar content. Gott's Zinfandels grow on two old vineyards that he bought in 1972, but he has planted eighty more acres to other grape varieties, including Cabernet Sauvignon, the Nebbiolo grape of the Italian Piedmont, and Sauvignon Blanc.

Another Shenandoah Valley winery is Sacramento veterinarian Eugene Story's 30,000-gallon brick Cosumnes River Vineyard cellar on Bell Road, where the road crosses the river into El Dorado County. Dr. Story, a long-time home winemaker, bought his forty-year-old vineyard in 1969, built his winery four years later, and now flies there on weekends in his own plane. On Steiner Road, between the Monteviña and D'Agostini wineries, is the 8,000-gallon Shenandoah Vineyards winery, opened by ceramic engineer Leon Sobon and his wife Shirley in 1977. Former home winemakers, they made their first vintage of local purchased Zinfandels and began planting their own ten-acre vineyard of Zinfandel and Sauvignon Blanc.

Other parts of Amador County have new wineries, too. Near the famous gold-mining town of Sutter Creek is Gary Porteous's Stoneridge cellar on Ridge Road two miles east of town. Porteous, another veteran home winemaker, crushed his first vintage in 1975 of Ruby Cabernet from his three-acre vineyard planted four years before, supplemented by the crops of pre-Prohibition Zinfandel vineyards that he cultivates nearby. Porteous works six days a week as a utility lineman and at carving gravestone monuments, and in his spare time has built a brick home. He was preparing to add a tasting room when I was last there.

Between Ione and Plymouth is the 5,000-gallon Argonaut Winery, opened in time for Lodi winemaker Neal Overboe to crush the 1976 vintage of Shenandoah Valley grapes. The winery is off Willow Creek Road four miles north of Ione. Beside it are a vineyard of Barbera that was planted in 1972 and the home of one of the five owners, Sacramento engineer James R. Payne.

"But Amador is not the only foothill county with the ideal climate and volcanic red soil for Zinfandel," says Edio Delfino, the agricultural commissioner of El Dorado County, which borders Amador on the north. "We have the same climate and soils, and moreover the ideal conditions to grow at least a dozen other fine wine varieties, and so has our neighbor, Placer County, too. I may be prejudiced, but we don't lack anything that Amador has."

The 177 acres of vineyards in El Dorado County at this writing are almost all new and of premium varieties, planted since 1975. In that year Delfino and Farm Advisor Richard Bethell planted test vineyards on their farms, and it was not until wines were made at UC Davis from their grapes that the revival of winegrowing here began. There already are three new wineries around Placerville, the county seat.

Gregory and Susan Boeger opened their 6,000-gallon Boeger Winery in the Apple Hill district two miles east of Placerville in 1973. It is on the site of the Lombardo Fossati vineyard and winery, established in 1860. The Boegers, in partnership with Dr. George Babbin, a Sacramento surgeon, planted fourteen acres of Zinfandel, Cabernet Sauvignon, Merlot, Chardonnay, Sauvignon Blanc, and Sémillon on the hillside where a pear orchard had replaced the original Fossati vineyard when the winery was closed in 1919. They have built a new concrete-block cellar and are using the original winery as their tasting room. The Boegers' first vintages were made of grapes from Amador and Placer Counties and from the former Hempt Vineyard near Coloma. Their own vineyard bore its first full crop in 1977. The best seller among the Boegers' seven Sierra foothills wines is a blend they call Hangtown Red. It is named for Placerville, which was called Hangtown when scores of bad men were strung up there during the lawless Gold Rush days. Boeger, a UC Davis graduate and former grape statistician, thinks he was destined to become a winegrower because he is a grandson of Anton Nichelini, who founded the Nichelini winery in Napa County in 1890. The Boeger winery is on Carson Road, reached from Highway 50 via Apple Hill Drive.

Four miles east of the Boegers, civil engineer Earl McGuire and his wife Jo Anne began replacing the pear trees in their Apple Hill orchard with wine grapes in 1975. A year later they converted the apple shed beside their house into the Eldorado Vineyard Winery. McGuire is a civil engineer and the former city manager of Placerville. The winery faces Carson Road at the Camino exit from US 50.

The newest El Dorado County winery, bonded in 1977, is the 5,000-gallon Sierra Vista Vineyard cellar of former Sacramento electrical engineer John MacCready and his wife Barbara. A

long-time home winemaker, MacCready in 1975 bought eighty
acres of virgin land twelve miles southeast of Placerville and two
miles west of Pleasant Valley, and began planting it to Cabernet
Sauvignon. Other young vineyards around Placerville supplied
the grapes for the MacCreadys' first vintage. Owners of some
twenty such young vineyards have formed the El Dorado
Winegrowers Association.

• 6 •

In pre-Prohibition times Yolo County, situated between
Sacramento and Napa, had 2,000 acres of vineyards and more
than fifty wineries, scattered from Woodland to Winters, Madison, and Capay. The largest was the Orleans Vineyard of Arpad
Haraszthy & Company, three miles west of Esparto, with its
winery four stories high. Another was on a farm at Davisville,
where Jerome Davis, a member of the Bear Flag rebellion, had
settled about 1852. Yolo vineyards increased to 4,000 acres
during Prohibition, then dwindled after Repeal, when grape
growing in the Sacramento Valley declined.

Davisville, fourteen miles west of Sacramento, was renamed
Davis when the University of California bought the Davis ranch
in 1906 and opened a practical farming school with a beginning
class of forty, including Ernest Wente of Livermore. Since then,
the farm has become a university of 18,000 students in forty-five
departments, including a complete medical school. It now
covers six square miles on both sides of Freeway 80, is by far the
largest of the nine UC campuses, and even has its own airport,
from which Davis experts fly to the University's experiment
stations and the other campuses where agricultural courses are
taught.

Davis still has a winery and 140 acres of vineyard. They are
parts of the University's Department of Viticulture and Enology. More than 100 men and women full-time students, a sixth
of them from foreign countries, are enrolled in the dozen grape,
wine, and brandy courses and in many research projects. More
than 600 students in other fields take the introductory enology
course. Short courses and seminars are also offered periodically
for those professionally or avocationally engaged in growing
grapes or making wine. The demand for Davis graduates to
man wineries in the United States and abroad is more than the
school can fill.

In the two-semester general viticulture course, each student
plants vines in a practice vineyard, cultivates, fertilizes, prunes,

and thins them, and harvests the fruit for fresh use, for raisins, and for wine. Each three-term enology student makes red, white, pink, and sparkling wines, performing each step from crushing through fermentation, racking, aging, finishing, stabilization, and bottling to the analysis and tasting of the final product. Many also take the brandy-distilling course. What they make, however, cannot be drunk or taken from the department buildings. More than 100,000 research samples made since 1935 are stored in the temperature-controlled cellars under the Enology Building, where the winery and distillery are. The rest goes down the drain.

The University is still doing the same job the legislature assigned it in 1880, when Professor Hilgard began his work at Berkeley.

Hilgard in 1889 hired as his cellar foreman Frederic Bioletti, an Englishman with an Italian name, who had worked in California and South African wineries, and who eventually succeeded Hilgard in charge of the work on wine. Among those trained by Bioletti were William Vere Cruess, who became the world's most renowned food scientist of his time, and Texas-born Albert Julius Winkler, who attained equal viticultural fame. Cruess in turn taught winemaking to several of his graduate students, especially one named Maynard Alexander Joslyn. At the repeal of Prohibition, this group around Bioletti, with French-born Professor Edmund H. Twight, trained most of the winemakers who since have rebuilt the quality of the state's wines.

In 1933, Bioletti chose from among his graduates a tall, blond, green-thumbed young geneticist named Harold Paul Olmo and gave him a lifetime project—to breed better grapes for the unique climates of California. Olmo became the Burbank of the grape. He planted seedlings of old varieties to develop new ones and crossed old varieties to combine their best characteristics in new hybrid grapes. Then from tens of thousands of vines, he chose the best producers, made wines from their grapes, aged and evaluated the wines. The few dozen best vines were replanted in different climates and soils, repeating the whole process until from among the dozens, a promising new variety was chosen. In 1946, Olmo introduced his first successful wine varieties. Ruby Cabernet and Emerald Riesling*, and four new

*Ruby Cabernet—Cabernet Sauvignon x Carignane—combines the quality of the noble Cabernet with the productivity and vigor of Carignane. Emerald Riesling is White Riesling x Muscadelle, an old French variety. Both crosses are high in acidity and flavor. They make excellent wines in Regions III and IV and acceptable wines in Region V.

table grapes. Twelve years later, he brought out five more new wine grapes and five more table varieties. To create and complete the testing of a single new wine grape takes him fifteen to eighteen years. And that is only the beginning, for the rest depends on the vineyardist, then on the vintner, and finally on the people who will buy the wine.

Olmo also found time to travel to other grape-growing countries. He traced the routes through which the wine-bearing *Vitis vinifera* grape has been carried through the centuries, evolving its thousands of varieties in different soils and climates. He hoped someday to discover Vinifera's birthplace and the vine in its primitive state. In 1948, on a 7,000-mile trek by plane, train, muleback and on foot, his quest came to an end. In mud-walled villages at the border of ancient Persia and Afghanistan Olmo found the original Vinifera vine growing wild. He brought seeds back to Davis, made them part of his breeding program, and began the ages-old evolution of the wine grape over again.

More than 100,000 different grape varieties grow in the Davis vineyard. About 1,000 are the principal named varieties that are cultivated around the world. The rest are Olmo's crosses and seedlings, which he is testing for planting in the future. They cannot all be tested at Davis, where the climate is Region IV. Varieties for cooler regions are tested at the Oakville Vineyard; those for hot regions at four San Joaquin Valley locations.

Olmo has bred a dozen new varieties of Cabernet parentage especially to make improved red table wines in the hot Central Valley. They are new crosses involving other crosses of Carignane, Cabernet Sauvignon, and Grenache. The first two such varieties, Carnelian and Centurion, were released beginning in 1973. If the valley wineries make wines from them as flavorful as the samples I have thus far tasted, they may eventually replace such old valley mass-production standbys as Mission, Alicante, and even Zinfandel. In 1976, Olmo introduced Carmine, a Cabernet-Grenache-Merlot cross for the cool coast counties, which has more Cabernet flavor than its principal parent, ripens earlier, and is more resistant to disease. Some of his other creations not yet released include white Cabernets and an improved Muscat for aromatic dry table wines.

Beginning back in 1935, much of the University's wine research work was shifted gradually from Berkeley to the Davis campus, where the vineyards are.

In that year Dr. Winkler, Bioletti's successor as chairman of viticulture, hired as his junior enologist at Davis a young graduate student named Maynard Andrew Amerine, who then was studying for his Ph.D. The only son of a California farming family, Amerine had grown up at Modesto, where his father raised grapes and other fruits. He had attended junior college there with Ernest and Julio Gallo, who lived a mile away. While the Gallo boys at their graduation went into the grape industry, Amerine continued his studies at Berkeley, where he received his plant-science degree.

Amerine's first task under Winkler at Davis was to make experimental wines from grapes grown in each viticultural district of the state. The several thousand wines he made became the basis of the 1938 Winkler-Amerine classification of California climates that has had such a profound effect on the Salinas Valley. Amerine later initiated scores of other research programs, ranging from studies of grape sugar-acid ratios at ripening to improved methods of analysis and sensory testing of wines. By 1957, when he succeeded Winkler as department chairman, his bibliography totaled 122 separate publications. Four years later, bachelor Amerine gave up the department chairmanship to gain time for travel and more research. Interested in vinicultural progress in the Soviet Union, he spent two years learning the Russian language before going to that country in 1962. Since then he has been virtually commuting to the European and Iron Curtain wine countries and has visited all the other winelands of the world. Wherever he goes, he is consulted on winegrowing problems, and other nations have invited several of his colleagues to come and advise them on the results of UC research. When Clark Kerr was president of the University, he, too, traveled abroad a good deal. "In every wine country," Dr. Kerr reported, "as soon as I mentioned that I came from California, people would ask me, 'Do you know Professor Maynard Amerine?' "

The first texts on winemaking after Repeal were published by Drs. Cruess, Joslyn, and their Berkeley colleagues in 1934. Six years later, Amerine teamed with Joslyn in writing a series of University bulletins and circulars on the commercial production of wines and brandies, Amerine presenting the viticultural aspects and Joslyn the enological side. The first Amerine-Joslyn bulletin on table wine summarized their scientific knowledge of that subject in 143 pages. By 1951 they had published a new 397-page text covering the same ground more fully. The same book appeared in 1970 in a second edition of 997 pages—a good index to how much has been learned by California investigators about this ancient art and science of table wine production in a span of only thirty years.

At present the Department of Viticulture and Enology staff at Davis numbers fifty-two, including such noted research workers and professors as Chairman A. Dinsmoor Webb, Curtis J. Alley, Roger Boulton, James A. Cook, Mark M. Kliewer, Ralph E. Kunkee, Lloyd A. Lider, W. Robert Logan, Klayton E. Nelson, Ann C. Noble, Cornelius Ough, Vernon L. Singleton, and Robert J. Weaver. Drs. Olmo, Winkler, and James F. Guymon and former Chairman Harold Berg are still actively engaged in research and consulting, although they are officially retired. Also at Davis are Dr. Austin Goheen, the Federal Government expert on grape virus diseases; professors in four other UC departments dealing with grapes or wine, and UC's extension viticulturists, George M. Cooke and Amand N. Kasimatis. The Davis wine school is now larger than such famous European stations as those at Geisenheim, Montpellier, and Conegliano, but the Russian vinicultural station at Yalta is twice as large.

• 7 •

The 1,000-gallon Sequoia Cellar in Woodland, the Yolo County seat twelve miles from Davis, is the avocational undertaking of two housewives and mothers, Carol Gehrmann and Patricia Riley. It is the first winery in the nation owned and operated exclusively by women. They say "we use our husbands as cheap labor." Carol, a former New York high school English teacher, is married to Dr. John Gehrmann, who does pharmacological research at UC Davis. Patricia, a Sacramento social worker, gets expert help from her husband James, who formerly worked at the Guild winery in Lodi. Carol has two children, Patricia one. Sequoia Cellar's first vintage consisted of 1977 Yolo County Carnelian Rosé and Deaver Ranch Amador Zinfandel.

19

The Main San Joaquin Valley

ALL OF THE vineyard districts covered in the last six chapters comprise only the top third of the California wine iceberg, so to speak. The other two thirds of the state's wine production comes from the main San Joaquin Valley, a fabulous agricultural empire in which grapes are the chief income crop and the chief wineries are the biggest in the world.

From the Delta region west of Lodi, the valley of the San Joaquin River extends southeastward more than two hundred miles. It is a trough, thirty to fifty miles wide and almost as flat as a table, between the snowcapped Sierra Nevada mountains on the east, and the Coast Range on the west. A twentieth of its total surface is covered by vineyards—some 450,000 acres, more than seven hundred square miles.

The summer climate is hot, mainly Region IV toward the northern end, and becomes still hotter—Region V—in the south. No rain falls there until autumn, and what falls thereafter is sparse, averaging only fourteen inches at Stockton and less than six inches at Bakersfield. Much of the land was a dry, barren waste until a century ago, when men began building dams in the Sierra to trap the melting snows and started to dig the irrigation canals that now crisscross most of the valley. Mountain water has transformed once-parched wasteland into lush farms more fabulously productive than the delta of the Nile.

In the sizzling heat and the rich valley soil, washed down from the mountains for eons, irrigated vines yield enormous grape crops, double the average in the coast counties. Here, eight to twelve tons per acre is considered a normal harvest of the common wine-grape varieties, and seventeen tons is not

430

unusual from an acre of overcropped Thompson Seedless vines. From this valley come all of the raisins produced in the United States, two thirds of the California table grapes that are eaten fresh, nearly all of the port, sherry, muscatel, and brandy produced in the state, and more than half—a figure steadily rising—of California table wines and champagnes.

Much of the San Joaquin's agriculture is conducted by corporate farmers on a gigantic scale of mechanized "agribusiness," a term coined here. Airplanes are commonly used to spray the larger vineyards. Some of the big table-grape growers employ helicopters to dry their grapes on the vines after early rains. Vineyard foremen and grape buyers travel such vast distances daily that, to keep in touch with their offices, most of them have radio-telephones in their air-conditioned cars.

Fleets of wine-tank trucks, like those used to transport milk, ply the highways night and day through the year, exchanging their vinous cargoes between wineries in the different parts of the state. Who owns or makes what in the California wine industry is increasingly difficult to figure out nowadays, but some of the answers may be found here. Don't expect to find romantic, vine-draped little château wineries with aging-tunnels, such as are seen in the coast counties; the average valley winery is merely a processing plant among the farms.

• 2 •

The main valley is reached via Highway 99 from Stockton to the Manteca-Escalon district in the southeastern corner of San Joaquin County. (We explored Lodi, with its Tokays that color red on cool nights, in the preceding chapter because Lodi differs climatically from the rest of the valley; it is a distinct viticultural district by itself.)

In the Manteca-Escalon area, chiefly wine-grape varieties are grown, especially the red Grenache, which retains some of its pronounced aroma when grown in Region IV. This district has supplied most of the Grenache grapes used by wineries in other parts of the state to make their Grenache rosés.

First on the route from Stockton is the attractive ten-million-gallon Delicato winery and tasting room, built in 1976, four miles above Manteca on the west frontage road beside Highway 99. The original small cellar was called the Sam-Jasper Winery when Gaspare (Jasper) Indelicato and his brother-in-law Sebastiano (Sam) Luppino built it in 1935. Jasper's three sons and his daughter Dorothy Indelicato operate the winery now, but they call it Delicato Vineyards, a considerable improvement over the family name. They sell fourteen wines in bottles, jugs, and in three-gallon plastic pouches, but most of their production is in bulk for wineries in other parts of the state.

On Austin Road, off the freeway south of Manteca, is the 40,000-gallon Bella Napoli Winery, founded in 1934 by Tony R. Hat, who was born Anthony Cappello near Naples but translated his name to its English equivalent when he came to the United States in 1899. His four sons cultivate 500 acres of vineyards, which once grew mainly Carignane and Grenache, but to which they lately have added Chenin Blanc, French Colombard, and Chardonnay. The eldest son, Lucas Hat, operates the winery, which has new stainless steel tanks. Its table wines are sold to local restaurants and at the cellar door. A third local winery, operated by Raymond and Theodore Cadlolo in the town of Escalon, has a tasting room, but most of its quarter-million-gallon capacity is used to produce bulk wine for other wineries. On Highway 99 just north of Salida in neighboring Stanislaus County, Alfred Pirrone owns the winery his father built in 1936. He has increased its capacity to a million gallons, has built a tasting room, and has replanted the 400-acre vineyard with "varietal" grapes for table wines, which he produces mainly for Gallo of Modesto.

The winery that is especially interesting to see in this district is Franzia, on Highway 120 six miles east of Manteca and five miles north of Ripon. It is an exemplar of mass wine production. On one of the company's 4,200 acres of vineyards, rows of shining stainless and epoxy-lined steel tanks stand outdoors and hold 28 million gallons of wine. The narrower ones are pressurized; they hold Charmat-process champagnes. The tanks are partially hidden from the highway by the brick and concrete cellars, where the wine is processed and most of it is bottled for shipment throughout California and to forty-four other states. Franzia makes thirty-three different wines and champagnes, as well as brandy and grape concentrate. The wines are bottled under several different brands, such as Franzia, Yosemite Road, FB, Mountain Castle, Louis the Fifth, Old Château, and Grand Maison. You usually can recognize Franzia wines under other brands by the name of Ripon in small type at the bottom of the labels, because this is the only winery that uses Ripon as a post office address.

Franzia wines are among the lowest-priced in California, selling for 69¢ under some brands to $1.49 for cork-stoppered "varietals" in 1977. They are usually young, made for immediate consumption, but are reliable in taste. You can sample them yourself in the attractive tasting room that faces the highway. You also can tour the winery if you make an appointment in advance and bring a group of friends. The competence of Franzia winemakers Louis Quaccia and James Walls is evident from the medals their wines regularly won during the years they were entered in the Los Angeles County Fair.

Five Franzia brothers and six of their sons formerly operated the vineyards and winery, with Joe, the youngest, as president of the firm. At the height of the table-wine sales explosion in 1971, three of the brothers sold their interest to eastern investors. Two years later the company was bought by the Coca-Cola Bottling Company of New York, which by already owning Mogen David of Illinois and Tribuno Vermouth of New Jersey, became the sixth largest vintner in the nation. Joe Franzia Sr. still runs the Franzia winery for the new owners because he enjoys his old job, and he works at it ten hours a day. His brother John is a company consultant. Their sons left the winery when the company was sold. What the sons did is told on a later page.

The father of the family, Giuseppe, came to California from Genoa in 1892, worked for fifty cents an hour in truck gardens around San Francisco, saved enough by 1906 to establish the family vineyard, and started his winery nine years later. It was closed during Prohibition, but his sons kept up the vineyard and reopened the winery at Repeal. They sold their wine mainly in tank cars to eastern bottlers until the Second World War, then began concentrating on bottled wines, adopting the mass-production techniques introduced by the Gallos. Incidentally, Franzia's toughest competitors are the Gallos, although Ernest Gallo is Joe's and John's brother-in-law.

• 3 •

Three miles toward Escalon from the Franzias is a winery almost as large. It was once the main Petri winery, from which in the 1950s grew the Petri-United Vintners complex of nine wineries with a tank ship, all of which in 1968 became part of the Heublein wine and liquor empire. The sign in front read "United Vintners Inc." and "Petri Wine Co." until a few years ago, but the "Petri" portion has been painted out. Since the table-wine boom, the winery now makes only table wine and ships it to the United Vintners plant at Madera for bottling.

Back in 1887, when California bulk wine was eight cents a gallon, an immigrant from Tuscany named Raffaello Petri, who owned a hotel in the North Beach district of San Francisco, began selling wine as a sideline. When his son Angelo grew up, he joined his Uncle Amadeo's cigar factory, rolling fermented tobacco leaves into the twisted, double-ended, strong-tasting black Italian cheroots called Toscani. During the First World War, Marca Petri wine and Marca Petri cigars both became so popular among Italians across the country that Raffaello and a partner named Dante Foresti acquired their own vineyards and winery at Escalon.

During Prohibition, Foresti managed the vineyard and sold the grapes for home winemaking while the Petris concentrated on their cigar factory in San Francisco and later on a boot-making venture in Tennessee. At Repeal, Angelo Petri returned the family to the wine business, leasing wineries in Napa and Sonoma Counties, and then reopening the Alba winery at Escalon, all this in conjunction with the cigar company.

In 1933, Angelo's younger son, Louis, had enrolled to study medicine at St. Louis University; his parents wanted him to become a physician. But Louis was in love with Flori, the younger daughter of Roma Winery president Battista Cella, and Flori's love letters from Lodi told him about exciting happenings in the reviving wine business. In his sophomore year Louis abruptly quit medical school, came to San Francisco, married Flori, and went to work washing barrels at seventy-five dollars a month in the cellar of the Petri cigar factory on Battery Street. In 1944, at the age of thirty-two, he became president of the Petri Wine Company.

Louis Petri, a restless young man who stuttered when excited, set out to dominate the wine industry. During the next eight years he bought the Tulare and Mission Bell wineries, and in a major coup, bought from National Distillers the Italian Swiss Colony wineries at Asti and Fresno, the Shewan-Jones winery at Lodi, and the Gambarelli & Davitto cellars at New York. Meanwhile, seeing more profit in selling wine than in making it, Petri organized the Allied Grape Growers co-operative, then sold his wineries to the co-op for $24 million, retaining their operation and the wine-marketing rights in United Vintners, which he headed as president. In 1957, he built the first wine tank ship ever to serve under the American flag, naming it the *Angelo Petri* for his father. He almost lost it one day three years later, when the ship became disabled outside the Golden Gate and drifted, rudderless, toward the beach. An SOS brought three tugs in time to tow the vessel back to port for repairs. Delivering two-and-a-half-million-gallon cargoes of bulk wine from the Port of Stockton to Atlantic Coast ports through the Panama Canal seven times a year, and bottling the two dozen United Vintners wine brands in cellars in Newark, Chicago, and California, he was selling nearly a fourth of all the wine consumed in the United States. At forty-four Louis Petri was the wine king of America.

Meanwhile, at Modesto in Stanislaus County, twelve miles south of Petri's Escalon winery, a rival—the E. & J. Gallo Winery—was beginning to challenge him for leadership in wine sales. The Gallo Brothers had bid in 1953 to buy the Italian Swiss Colony before Petri bought it for $16 million. The duel of Gallo versus Petri for dominance in the wine industry—billed in the trade press as "the battle of the giants"—lasted for more than a decade.

When, in 1957, Petri built the first American wine tanker for $7 million, his saving in freight costs enabled him to sell his wines for ten cents less per bottle in eastern market centers than wines that were shipped east by rail. The Gallos parried by building at Modesto for $6 million the first glass factory ever owned by a winery. By making their own lightweight bottles, the Gallos could sell their wines in the East at the same price as Petri's and advertise that their wines were bottled in California.

Nine years later, Petri added the prestigious Inglenook Vineyard to his kingdom, but the Gallos stuck to their policy of making and selling only inexpensive wines.

Gallo's sales crept up on Petri's during the sixties. By 1968, Gallo was well ahead. Bruno (Larry) Solari had replaced Petri as board chairman, and in that year Heublein bought control of United Vintners for $33 million in Heublein stock. Three years later, the wine tanker *Angelo Petri* was sold. Meanwhile, Heublein joined a glass company in building a $16 million bottle factory, like Gallo's, beside its Mission Bell winery at Madera. Since then, all of its enormous volume of California wines has been bottled in California.

Louis Petri continued in the wine business as the largest single member of the Allied Growers co-op, supplying grapes from his vineyards in Napa County to the complex of wineries he once controlled. He sold his last vineyard to Heublein in 1971 and, now a multimillionaire, he concentrates on his realty and hotel investments in Hawaii and San Francisco.

• 4 •

In the Repeal year of 1933, young Ernest and Julio Gallo rented an old warehouse in Modesto, bought some new redwood tanks and a grape crusher on credit, and made their first wine. Ernest was twenty-four, Julio a year younger. While at Modesto Junior College, they had planned to start a winery whenever Prohibition ended.

During boyhood they had worked in their father's vineyard west of Modesto, and they remembered the small winery their grandfather, from Italy's Piedmont, had operated at Hanford before Prohibition. But all that the boys knew about winemaking was how their father had made wine in their basement for his own use. In the Modesto public library they luckily found two of the University's pre-Prohibition pamphlets on winemaking, and the red wine they made in 1933 turned out sound. When it was ready, Ernest boarded a plane for New York with samples, called on the wine bottlers there, and sold them the 1933 vintage in bulk. Two years later, the brothers built a small concrete winery in the southern outskirts of Modesto on the bank of Dry Creek.

I remember stopping there one day in the late 1930s. In a cramped office in front of the cellar I found young Ernest Gallo. He told me that he and his brother were only making bulk wine to get started, but that someday the Gallo name with their family crest (the rooster, for which *gallo* is the Italian word) would appear on bottles that would be sold throughout the United States. His confidence impressed me, though his chances didn't.

Today at that same location the Gallos are bottling more than a fourth of the wine consumed in the United States. Their 60-million-gallon Modesto winery is almost a city by itself, with its hundreds of giant steel tanks, the biggest of which holds a million gallons; enormous bottling cellars, bottle and cap factories, research laboratories, and vast warehouses from which Gallo wines are shipped by the trainload to all fifty states. There is also, surrounded by parkland, an elegant new "contemporary-classical" administration building (pictured on some Gallo labels), where the brothers, their sons, and a son-in-law have their offices. Gallo wineries are not open to the public, though there is talk of someday building a visitor center at Modesto with a tasting hall and a wine museum. There are more Gallo wineries at Livingston, Fresno, and Healdsburg, which bring the total capacity to 226 million gallons. The

100-million-gallon one at Livingston is the biggest in the world. A dozen other wineries around the state, some operating on long-term contracts, make all or most of their wines for Gallo. Altogether, more than a hundred thousand acres of California vineyards, including five thousand owned by the family, produce the grapes for the company's wines.

When the Gallo name first appeared on bottles in 1940, the brothers' goal was to become the Campbell Soup Company of the wine industry, to supply the nation with reliable mass-produced wines under a single name, priced for everyday use. But their wines were not yet reliably palatable; troublesome vineyard and winery problems had to be solved. During the early 1940s, many California table wines, especially those grown in the San Joaquin Valley, were heavy, coarse, harsh, puckery with excessive tannin, usually oxidized, and often unpleasant to drink. In the next fifteen years the Gallos eliminated those defects. They brought wines from Napa and Sonoma wineries to improve the taste of their valley table-wine blends. They planted better grape varieties in their vineyards, induced other growers to plant them by offering fifteen-year contracts at guaranteed minimum prices, and established a field staff to guide the growers in planting, cultivating, and harvesting their grapes. The Gallos also were the first vintners to launch their own research program. Their staff of research enologists at Modesto is now the biggest at any winery anywhere.

To get rid of unpleasant wine flavors, the Gallos did some revolutionary things. They eliminated woody and musty-wood taste by ripping out all of the wooden cooperage in their winery and replacing it with tanks of epoxy-lined and stainless steel. Some of the discarded redwood tank staves were salvaged in 1957 by their younger brother, Joe Gallo, who built a new house with them; for years afterward, the rooms of his house smelled of wine. To get rid of the mouth-puckering tannin in their press wines (red wines pressed from the pomace after fermentation), they began making Gallo wines entirely from the free-run (unpressed) juice. This inspired their radio-advertising jingle, nationally broadcast in the late 1950s: "Only the first/ squeezing of the grapes/ goes into Gallo wine." But Gallo Burgundy, when made from only free-run juice, lacked flavor; its taste was too bland. To remedy this, the Gallos then added some press wine—abandoning their "first squeezing" jingle—and in 1964 introduced the new blend as their "Hearty Burgundy," which since has been praised by wine authorities as one of the better

© 1978 by Ted Streshinsky

The Gallo winery, warehouses, and Gallo bottle factories at Modesto.

California reds. To prevent the oxidized or sherrylike taste caused when wine is exposed to sunlight, the Gallo bottle factory introduced an amber-green "flavorguard" glass, which filters out the damaging ultraviolet rays.

Connoisseurs of the Wine & Food Society rarely discussed or even mentioned Gallo wines because they were all mass-produced, screw-capped rather than corked, and moderate in price. The Gallos were irritated and amused when they heard their connoisseur friends rhapsodize over high-priced imports, in which the Gallos usually could taste flavor defects. They once expressed these feelings rather snidely in a television commercial that said: "Gallo—for the man who doesn't care *what* it costs." Ernest Gallo has his own original method of judging the quality of wine. He serves many bottles of different wines to a group of consumers, lets them pour for themselves, and keeps watch while the contents of the bottles disappear. He reasons that the wines in the bottles that are emptied soonest (and Gallo products have scored high by this test) must be the best. As for the screw caps on their bottles versus the corks that premium and foreign wineries use, the Gallos claimed that the screw caps protected their wines better; that corks don't "breathe" as is generally believed, but only leak.

But as the "wine revolution" approached its height in the 70s, the Gallos saw millions of newly wine-educated Americans buying corked, varietally labeled wines at considerably higher prices than theirs. So in 1974 they introduced seven corked "varietals" of their own with an advertising campaign comparing them to the world's best. Their "varietals," however, included no oak-aged wines, and in particular no Cabernet Sauvignon. In 1977, the Gallos went the rest of the way. They contracted for the crops of big new Cabernet vineyards in Monterey County. They dug an enormous cave in the park beside their office building and bought enough oak tanks to age 2.6 million gallons of wine; their oak-aging cellar would be the biggest in the United States. The tanks, 4,000 gallons each of Yugoslavian oak, were being fabricated in Italy, so the first "super-premium" Gallo wines were not due to reach the market until 1980. But meanwhile the Gallos, who had never participated in any competitive wine judging, won eight awards for their current "varietals" in the first national wine competition, held at Washington in 1977.

While their oak-aged premium wines will put them into the highest-priced field, the Gallos still compete in the market for low-priced table wines with their "Red Mountain" brand line, which sells at a fifth less than their regular burgundy. The "Red Mountain" label says the wine is bottled by the "Carlo Rossi Vineyards, Modesto." But Modesto means Gallo, and Carlo (Charles) Rossi is a Gallo cousin and sales executive. Another Gallo item with an in-house brand name is the company's grappa (colorless, neutral-flavored brandy), introduced in 1977. It is called "Spirito Ballatore" for a long-time member of the Gallo production staff, whose photograph and signature are reproduced on the label.

A family-owned corporation, Gallo is firmly ruled by Ernest as chairman and brother Julio as president. The other directors are Ernest's sons, David and Joey, Julio's son, Bob, and his son-in-law, Jim Coleman. Ernest concentrates on marketing, Julio on the vineyards and wineries, but important company decisions are made only by both brothers, and they taste their wines daily together. Ernest, poker-faced behind his horn-rimmed glasses, is formidable in any business dealing, and he is cagy; those who seek interviews with him soon discover that he is interviewing them. For three decades he traveled each year through each market where his wines were on sale, calling on fifty stores a day, watching how his bottles were displayed. Though now a multimillionaire, he still makes store calls wherever he goes. Julio, a farmer and hobbyist organic gardener, resembles Ernest but is more easygoing, yet doesn't tell you what he is thinking, either.

The Gallos long ago achieved their original objectives and then invaded wider fields. Theirs was the first American winery to introduce the new flavored wines, beginning with Thunderbird in 1957, and then the lightly-carbonated "pop" wines, starting with Ripple in 1960. They brought out their first Charmat-process champagnes in 1966 and started selling a Gallo brandy named "E. & J." in 1968. When they entered the glamorous champagne field, the Gallos departed from their single-brand-name idea. Their first champagne was called "Eden Roc," for the fashionable beach club at Cap D'Antibes, but it soon was replaced by another called simply "Gallo Champagne." A lower-priced champagne named André followed, and became the largest-selling sparkling wine in the United States.

In the mid-'70s Michigan and New York wineries came out with "Cold Duck" sparkling wines made of Concord grapes, which do not grow well in California. The Gallos went to the State of Washington for a supply and contracted for the entire output of the grape growers' co-ooperative at Grandview in the Yakima Valley, which ships them Concord juice in refrigerated tank cars.

But the Gallos' most radical departure from old-fashioned wines is their pioneering with the low-alcohol, slightly gassy "pop" wines made not only of grapes, but also of apples, strawberries, and pears. Their popular Spañada is an eleven percent grape wine, flavored to resemble the Spanish wine-and-fruit punch called *sangría* (a word that relates to blood). Their Boone's Farm apple wine, labeled 11 percent, in 1970 became the largest-selling single wine of any kind in the United States. It was followed a year later by 9 percent Boone's Farm Strawberry Hill, a carbonated apple wine with strawberry flavor, and then by Wild Mountain, a 9 percent wine that tastes mainly of Concord grapes. By lowering the alcoholic content of some of their "special natural" wines to 9 percent (when the California legal minimum for standard white table wines is 10 and most table wines made in the state are labeled 12), the Gallos have invaded the enormous national market for beers. Their Ripple, originally 11 percent, now comes in three versions—Pear Ripple (white) at 10, Red at 11, and Pagan Pink (flavored with passion fruit) at 10. And when the Gallos popularized apple wines nationally in the 1970s, they created a stir in the world market for that ancient fruit. They imported apple concentrate from several foreign countries, and in 1972 planted their own 2,000-acre apple orchard near Hopeton in Merced County.

When department stores across the nation began soliciting youngsters to buy new T-shirts that reproduce the labels of Boone's Farm Apple, Pagan Pink Ripple, and Thunderbird, Gallo wines had achieved a kind of folk fame never equaled by Campbell Soups.

• 5 •

Winegrowing in Stanislaus County dates from 1854, when George H. Krause from the Rhineland laid out his Red Mountain Vineyard near Knight's Ferry in the foothills some twenty miles east of Modesto. Krause and his successors made good wines before Prohibition, including a sherry in my cellar that is still in fair condition. Their cellar, a tunnel cut into the stone hillside, was again operated briefly after Repeal by Modesto restaurateur Emanuel Galas, who called it the Oakdale Winery. More than a century later, the original name, "Red Mountain," was adopted by the Gallos and combined with "Carlo Rossi" as the brand for their bargain-priced wines.

As in the neighboring Manteca-Escalon district of San Joaquin County, wine grapes predominate in the vineyards around Modesto, the Stanislaus County seat. Modesto, incidentally, means "modest." When the site of its railroad station was chosen in 1870, rail magnate Timothy Hopkins offered to name it for his associate, William Ralston, but Ralston declined the honor. Hearing this, a Mexican companion exclaimed *"El señor es muy modesto!"* The sound of the Spanish word pleased Hopkins, who promptly marked it on the map.

But vineyardists around Modesto are not modest about the quality of their wine grapes, having planted some 6,000 new acres of Chenin Blanc, French Colombard, Barbera, Ruby Cabernet, Cabernet Sauvignon, Sauvignon Blanc, and Chardonnay since the prices for these table wine "varietals" skyrocketed in the late 1960s. Led by Stanislaus County Farm Advisor Paul La Vine, the growers have organized a Grape Improvement Association and are trying to convince the wineries that their grapes are as good as those grown in adjoining San Joaquin County. The argument, however, is more about climate than grapes.

The growers' problem is that the University's classification in 1938 of California wine-district climates placed only three

Stanislaus districts (Ceres, Hughson, and Vernalis) in Region IV. This seemed to leave Modesto, Salida, and the rest of the county in the hotter Region V. In consequence, they complain, wineries have paid growers ten dollars a ton less for grapes grown at Salida or Modesto than for those across the Stanislaus River in San Joaquin County, where the Escalon-Manteca district is recognized as in Region IV. "You could throw a rock across the river from a ninety-dollar vineyard to a hundred-dollar vineyard of the same grape variety," says La Vine. He claims that a cooling wind from the Delta blows through this part of the valley each afternoon and brings down the temperature by four or five degrees. La Vine hopes to persuade the University to reclassify Stanislaus County as Region IV, hopefully even as Region III.

Growers in northern Merced County, Stanislaus' southern neighbor, claim that they, too, get that afternoon wind, and they have joined enthusiastically in La Vine's campaign. This raises the puzzling question of where Region IV really ends and Region V begins. La Vine now suggests that the Merced River is the proper boundary, which would include about half of that county's vineyards.

University bioclimatologists reply that the valley's climate needs further study before any such boundary can be redefined. They concede that parts of Stanislaus and Merced may belong in Region IV, but add that some parts of the present Region IV may yet be found to belong in Region III, or even, unhappily, in Region V.

In France and Italy, with their hundreds of district appellations of origin for wines, controversies have raged for generations over which vineyards are or are not entitled to label their wines with famous district names, which determine how much each bottle of wine is worth. Now that grape-district boundaries have become an issue in California, such questions have begun to be hotly argued there, too.

• 6 •

What did the sons of Joe and John Franzia do when the Franzia Winery was sold in 1973? Within a year they built their own JFJ Bronco Winery at Bystrum and Keyes Roads, three miles southwest of Ceres in Stanislaus County, six miles south of Modesto. The two Js stand for cousins John Junior and Joseph S. and the F. stands for Fred T., Joe's older brother, the president of their firm. Although "Bronco" in Italian means a trunk, stem, bough, or stump, they explain that it is also a colloquial Italian expression for "brothers and cousins," which these Franzias are.

Their Bronco winery held two million gallons in its stainless-steel tanks when I was last there, but was designed for eventual expansion to sixty million gallons. It crushes no grapes; it only receives, blends, finishes and bottles bulk wines from other wineries and also makes three kinds of Charmat-process champagnes.

A second Bronco Winery was built in 1977 ninety miles southeast in Fresno County, but that one produces only bulk wine in a joint venture with the $3 billion Getty Oil Company, on whose 3000-acre vineyard it stands. Production of the second Bronco winery is sold to other vintners, including Bronco at Ceres.

Bronco specializes in young, inexpensive "easy-to-drink" generically and varietally-labeled table wines. It sells them under three brands, CC Vineyard, JFJ Winery, and Three Mountains, in bottles, carafes, and jugs. During 1977 the lowest-priced Bronco wines in California were 99¢ per quart carafe.

• 7 •

Merced County, with 15,000 acres of vines, is in the upper half of the San Joaquin Valley. Although four fifths of its vineyards are now planted to wine grapes, this county had no wineries for almost two decades, its few small ones having closed following the Second World War. But in 1970, when the Gallos' Modesto plant reached its limit of expansion, they built a new 15-million-gallon winery on their vineyard along the south bank of the Merced River west of Livingston. In the next few years it was expanded to 100 million gallons, and all the grapes that formerly went to Modesto now go to Livingston to be crushed. The Gallos' Livingston vineyard covers 3,500 acres, and they are expected to plant more near their apple orchard in northern Merced County, fifteen miles up the river near Hopeton.

Next to Merced is Madera County, and then Fresno, which marks the center of the valley vineyard area. Winegrowing began in this part of the valley about 1873, when Francis Eisen from Sweden planted the first commercial vineyard at Fresno and built his winery two years later. Half a dozen more wineries soon sprang up in the neighborhood, including the Eggers,

Barton, Margherita, Mattei, and Henrietta estates. In 1880, George West & Son came south from Stockton to Minturn in Madera County and became partners with Thomas Minturn in the big Sierra Vista vineyard and winery there. Before the turn of the century, the Wests were operating additional wineries at Fresno, Selma, and at Hanford. By 1900 the Italian Swiss Colony of Asti owned a winery at Madera and had built new wineries at Kingsburg and Lemoore.

The most colorful of the pioneer valley vintners was George H. Malter, whose St. George Winery was five miles east of Fresno on Fancher Creek. Malter, born in Germany, had already made a fortune as a mining engineer when he became a winegrower in 1879. He named his vineyard Maltermoro, issued his own scrip or currency, and advertised his wines and brandy as the best in the world. One of his products was a "bathing brandy," which he recommended as a feminine beauty aid.

The early wineries in this region made mostly sweet dessert wines and brandy; their table wines were poor. For this reason, Malter's St. George Winery bought the grapes for its table wines in the cooler coastal districts and fermented them in a northern St. George cellar at Antioch in Contra Costa County.

When Eisen laid out his vineyard at Fresno, one of the grapes he planted was the Muscat of Alexandria, which makes both wine and raisins. When the Thompson Seedless was introduced from Sutter County in the 1890s, Fresno became both the sweet wine and raisin capital of the nation. In 1900, with almost 70,000 acres of vineyards producing wine, raisins, and table grapes, Fresno was the leading vineyard county in the United States, the rank it still holds.

As dry agitation reached its height in the early 1900s and Prohibition became a threat, the Fresno community preferred to publicize itself as the raisin capital. Its wine and brandy industry, under increasing attack, was not the basis of community pride. When the wineries, idle during the dry era, reopened at Repeal in 1933, and the coast-counties wine towns revived their wine festivals, Fresno continued to celebrate its annual Raisin Day. This may explain why histories of Fresno County tell only of Eisen's part in founding the raisin industry, and omit mention of his winegrowing career. And descriptions of the county's Kearney Park, seven miles west of Fresno, refer to Kearney as a leader of the raisin industry, but ignore his role as a wine industry pioneer. (M. Theo. Kearney was an eccentric man of mystery; his Fresno neighbors never learned his full name. He willed his five-thousand-acre estate, which he called Château Fresno, to the University of California, which exchanged it after his death for county land near Parlier and built its Kearney Horticultural Field Station there. At Kearney Park, which comprises the remaining 350 acres of Château Fresno, there is nothing to mark the site of the Kearney Winery, which stood near the eastern corner of the estate.)

Such bits of local history also help explain why, during three decades following Repeal, wine in the valley was treated as the salvage by-product of the raisin and table-grape industries, even when the by-product was using most of the valley grapes. Related facts were the flat, earthy taste of table wines then made in the valley, and that its people, including the vintners, seldom drank wine of any kind.

It was considered impossible to produce acceptable dry table wine in the hot valley climate, and with the coast counties producing more wine following Repeal than they could sell, there was no reason to try. Considerable quantities of "sauterne" and "burgundy" were nevertheless made in the valley, but were blended with table wines from the coast to make them palatable and were sold as "north coast and valley blends." Yet Almond R. Morrow, the great wine taster of the old California Wine Association, told me at the time of Repeal that "excellent dry wines can be made in the valley if you know how." Professor Hilgard, too, had known how, but had failed to convince the vintners that in sunny California, unlike Europe, grapes for good table wines must be harvested early, before their sugar content becomes too high and their acidity too low.

For thirty years after Repeal, the valley wineries continued paying the grape growers a premium for each extra degree of sugar content in their fruit. Grape prices per ton were based on "22 Balling, plus or minus $1 for each sugar point above or below 22." Moreover, the big wineries delayed buying grapes until after September 20, the last day it is considered safe for growers to lay their Thompsons on trays to make raisins without risking damage from early rains. The purpose was to keep the huge annual Thompson surplus out of the wineries by forcing them onto the trays. Table wines made in the valley from grapes harvested in late October or November, sometimes as late as December, did more than Prohibition to make Americans refuse to drink wine and turn to liquor or beer.

The abrupt, complete flip-flop that occurred in the San Joaquin Valley grape industry in less than a decade was partially described in Chapter 12. But not until the mid-1960s, when national consumption of table wines was about to exceed that of dessert wines, and the coast counties no longer could produce enough to supply the mounting demand, did the big vintners in the lower valley begin to realize that they were doing everything wrong. The demand for better table wines compelled them to learn the lesson of early harvesting that Hilgard had tried to teach eighty years before. Now, September instead of October has become the start of harvest season for wine in the valley, and some grapes for table wine are picked as early as the beginning of August. Now, farmers who previously grew only raisin and table grapes have planted the table-wine "varietals" that are newly in demand. For the first time in this century, people in the valley are beginning to realize that the main product of their vineyards is neither raisins nor table grapes, but wine and brandy, which now utilize almost two thirds of the entire California grape crop.

Equally important is the revolution taking place in winemaking, for the valley wineries have adopted radically new production methods and installed refrigeration and other equipment needed to produce acceptable dry table wines. "Since I began making really good dry wine," the winemaker at one of the major valley wineries confided to me recently, "I've begun drinking it with my dinner every night."

• 8 •

The first fine table wines to be grown, bottled, and labeled as local products in Region V came in 1962 from the little Ficklin Vineyard winery, on Avenue 7½, seven miles south of Madera.* Fourteen years earlier, the late Walter Ficklin, a wealthy farmer and wine buff, with his Davis-trained sons, Walter, Jr., and David, had built his 40,000-gallon cellar with the idea of making one superior wine. Believing that the only fine wine that could be grown in Region V would have to be either a port or a sherry, they chose port. They obtained cuttings of Tinta Madeira, Tinta Cão Souzão, and other superior port varieties from the University, and made some of the finest ports thus far produced in the United States. But, needing some table wine for their own use, the Ficklins also planted an acre of Professor Harold Olmo's then-new hybrid Vinifera grapes for hot climates, Emerald Riesling and Ruby Cabernet. They picked these

*From 1956 to 1968, Horace Lanza's Cal-Grape winery near Delano produced and bottled small quantities of a creditable dry red table wine from the Italian Nebbiolo grape, but the Nebbiolo label gave the company's San Francisco address.

grapes in mid-August and fermented them at low temperatures. Soon their neighbors and visiting connoisseurs, who came to buy their port, were also buying all the table wine the Ficklins could produce. Introduced to San Franciscans at a gourmet banquet in the Hotel St. Francis in 1965, Ficklin Emerald Riesling 1962 was chosen by many of those present in preference to a château-bottled white Bordeaux. Their Ruby Cabernet has since proved even better than their white. The Ficklins still make only enough table wine to sell at the winery, because they are too busy supplying the mounting demand for their ports, of which there are two kinds. Their Tinta Port is a *solera* of all the vintages since 1948; the others are limited bottlings of vintage ports, obtainable only direct from the winery. Both kinds in my cellar have developed greater bouquet with each passing year.

At the Avenue 9 exit from Highway 9 six miles south of Madera, there is a new 3-million-gallon winery that has shown even more impressively than the Ficklins that Almond Morrow was right when he said "excellent dry wines can be made in the valley if you know how." Angelo Papagni has astonished the wine world and contradicted the opinions of experts about Region V grapes with the fine table wines he has produced in his Papagni Vineyards winery since it was built in 1973.

In his temperature-controlled showcase cellar with the latest equipment provided by modern technology, Papagni has made sixteen estate-bottled, vintage-dated but medium-priced wines that are winning praises from many connoisseurs. Some writers withhold their praise because the wines come from Region V. His Chenin Blancs, dry and medium-dry, his Zinfandels and Barbera are being compared favorably to coast-counties wines, and his Madera Rosé has won a gold medal at the Los Angeles County Fair. But Papagni's most surprising wine is a full-bodied, flavorful "varietal" of Alicante Bouschet, a grape hitherto scorned by everyone except those home winemakers who prize it only for its red juice. His three Charmat-process champagnes include a delicious equivalent of Italy's Asti Spumante that he calls Spumante d'Angelo, and its Muscat flavor is equally delicate in his non-sparkling Moscato d'Angelo and in a drier version named Muscat Alexandria.

Papagni credits the quality of his wines to the way his father, from Bari in southeastern Italy, taught him from boyhood to grow table and wine grapes for shipment across the United States. "As growers of 3,000 acres of grapes mainly for sale fresh, we have to know how to manage the vines," he says. "We do it by the way and the times we irrigate; we balance nature with added moisture. We neither overcrop nor under-crop, and we don't rush the grapes; we know just when to pick." But there is still another explanation for the smooth tastes of his red wines: his winery is one of the few in the valley that age all their reds in 50-gallon oak barrels.

The Papagni winery offers tours by appointment, but at this writing had not yet added a tasting room. The winemaker is John Daddino, a veteran trained at three of the older valley wineries. Papagni's wife Blanche and their daughter Rosemary help in the office. The winery also produces a white wine named Fu Jin for Chinese restaurants and several table wines sold in plastic bags, both of the latter for the California House Wine Company.

Another ultramodern new Madera winery is the 10-million-gallon Paul Masson sherry cellar near Berenda, fifteen miles northwest of Papagni. Masson, headquartered at Saratoga in Santa Clara County, produces more table wine than sherry in this winery, built in 1974. It is designed to be doubled in capacity when required by the growing sales of Masson wines.

• 9 •

On Avenue 13 four miles southwest of Madera is the Heublein-United Vintners' 40-million-gallon Madera winery, once known as Mission Bell. Its 120-foot-high distillery tower dominates the landscape for miles around. With its lately-added champagne cellar and bottle factory, this winery now is almost as big as Gallo's Modesto plant. It is not open to visitors, either, but is worth the side trip from Madera to see it from the outside.

This winery has had many owners. Before Prohibition it belonged to the Italian Swiss Colony of Asti, which later was absorbed by the California Wine Association. During the dry years, it was purchased and named Mission Bell by Krikor Arakelian, the one-time melon king of California, who had become one of the biggest grape growers in the state. Arakeli-an, who came to America in 1895 from Armenia with five dollars in his pocket, made Mission Bell after Repeal the second-largest independent winery in the nation, then sold it in 1949 for $3¼ million to Louis Petri, who in turn sold it two years later to the Allied Grape Growers co-operative. Then came Heublein, the Hartford, Connecticut, firm that John Martin had built from a small manufacturer of "A-1" meat sauce into one of the world's largest marketers of vodka, premixed cocktails, rum, tequila, cordials, beer, and European wines.

Since buying control of United Vintners from Allied in 1968,

Heublein has made this its biggest California winery. Most of Heublein's American wines and champagnes (except Beaulieu, Inglenook, and Tipo table wines) are now bottled at Madera. The labels on many bottles, however, give the address as "Italian Swiss Colony, California." That is the name of a post office United Vintners established for labeling purposes at the Madera winery in 1964. (Some of the other labels that go on bottles at Madera read "San Francisco," where United Vintners has its office.) The wines that come from Madera include Petri, Lejon, Jacques Bonet, and such flavored and "pop" wines as Bali Hai, Arriba, Silver Satin, and the new Italian Swiss Colony "pop" wines named Annie Green Springs, Swiss Up, Sangrole, and T. J. Swann. United Vintners also owns many older names, such as G & D, Padre, Margo, Sante Fe, Greystone, and Parma, which are used to supply distributors in local markets where these brands have a consumer following.

Allied Grape Growers, supplying Heublein-United Vintners with grapes, meanwhile has become the world's biggest co-operative of vineyardists, with some 1,600 members, including a growers' co-op in the Yakima Valley of Washington that ships refrigerated Concord juice to Madera for use in making the United Vintners' brands of Cold Duck.

Two miles east of United Vintners is the 4-million-gallon Bisceglia Brothers winery, since 1974 a subsidiary of the Sands family's group of wineries at Canandaigua and Hammondsport, New York; Petersburg, Virginia; and Patrick, South Carolina. It is managed by Bruno Bisceglia, whose family began producing wine at San Jose in 1888 and operated wineries at St. Helena and Fresno before taking over the former Yosemite Co-operative cellar, which they now occupy. Besides supplying blending wines to the Sandses, it markets bottled California wines under such brands as Alfonse F. Bisceglia, Richards, Paradise, Old Rose, and La Croix.

The sixth, newest, and smallest Madera winery uses no Madera grapes. Andrew Quady, a UC Davis-trained former Lodi winemaker who works as a process engineer at the United Vintners winery, built this 30,000-gallon cellar in 1977 behind his home a half-mile away to pursue his spare-time hobby of producing vintage port wine from Zinfandel grapes he brings from Amador County. To arrest fermentation, he uses an aromatic brandy especially distilled for him at Lodi.

Vineyards in Madera County increased from 35,000 to 60,000 acres during the 1970s rush to plant table wine "varietals" in the San Joaquin Valley.

• 10 •

Fresno County has twenty-three wineries. They are a surprising assortment of sizes and kinds. Only a few bottle what they produce, and still fewer invite the public to visit their cellars.

Passengers on airliners approaching Fresno Airport can see three of the principal wineries strung along Clovis Avenue, north and south of the field. The clump of enormous wine tanks a mile south is Gallo's Fresno winery, which now holds 66 million gallons, five million more than the Modesto plant. On its site in 1890, Benjamin Woodworth established his Las Palmas Vineyard, which he named for the line of palms that led to his estate. At Repeal the Cribari family of San Jose bought the old wooden cellar and continued making wine there until 1954, when Gallo bought and replaced it with tanks of steel. Each season now, this single winery crushes more than 300,000 tons of grapes.

Directly across McKinley Avenue from the airfield is the 4-million-gallon Cameo winery, built by Harry Hitzl and associates in 1938. After the Second World War it became part of the Alta Vineyards Company, which sued the city for damages when the airport was built next door, claiming that the vibrations of plane motors disturbed the aging wines (the suit was lost). When Alta merged with the Guild of Lodi in 1962, this winery became the principal Fresno cellar of the Guild.

Two miles north of the airfield is the La Paloma Winery with its handsome ivy-clad tower, built by vineyardist M. F. Tarpey in 1895. During the Second World War, National Distillers bought La Paloma and added its output to that of the Italian Swiss Colony, then sold it, with the winery at Asti, to Petri's United Vintners. All that remains to recall the Tarpey family is the adjoining Tarpey Village housing tract.

To the wine tourist, the most interesting of the big Fresno cellars is the old Roma winery—newly renamed B. Cribari & Sons—at Church and East Avenues in the city's industrial district. The huge casks in its great air-conditioned oak cellar are among the most spectacular in the state. When the Guild company of Lodi bought Roma from Schenley Distillers in 1971, it moved the bottling of Roma wines to the Guild cellars at Lodi, where it bottles the Cribari, Winemasters Guild, and Vino da Tavola brands. Since 1976 the big tasting room of the Fresno cellar, open daily, has featured only the twenty-eight Cribari table, dessert, and sparkling wines.

Albert Cribari, the eldest grandson of Cribari founder Benjamin, is the Guild's vice president and winemaster, working with UC Berkeley-trained vice president-production Elie Skofis, whose career with the Italian Swiss Colony, Schenley, Roma, and Guild dates from 1946. Before the Second World War the House of Cribari, founded in 1904, owned thousands of acres in the Santa Clara Valley and operated wineries at Madrone, Fresno, and New York City.

Next door to the former-Roma-now-Cribari winery is the Schenley whiskey, gin, and vodka distillery, which was not included in the sale to the Guild. This is the source of this country's supply of Dubonnet apéritif wines, American rights to which are Schenley-owned.

The story of the Cella family, who once owned Roma, parallels that of the Petris. John Battista Cella and his brother Lorenzo came to the United States in 1898 from Bardi in northern Italy. They worked as waiters in a New York restaurant, then went into the wholesale grocery business. They bought their cigars and wine from Raffaello Petri and Dante Foresti, whom Battista visited on trips to California. Three years before National Prohibition began, Battista bought the old Scatena wineries at Lodi, Manteca, and Healdsburg from Foresti, and made Roma sacramental wine there through the dry era, while Lorenzo stayed in New York to handle the sales. Then, when Lodi vineyardists began building their co-op wineries, he moved from Lodi to the Santa Lucia winery at Fresno, renamed it Roma, and made his headquarters there. In 1942, the king of Schenley Distillers, Lewis Rosenstiel, bought Roma and Cresta Blanca (events I especially remember because Rosenstiel then summoned me to his summer home at Tucson to give him a complete education in wine in three days. Rosenstiel thereupon tried unsuccessfully to convert the state's vintners to his pet liquor-selling ideas). Cella soon resigned from Roma and in 1944 bought the Rusconi vineyard and winery near Wahtoke, north of Reedley, which he renamed the Cella Vineyards and expanded to 12 million gallons. Following the deaths of Battista and Lorenzo Cella, the latter's son, John B. Cella II, became the president of Cella Vineyards. In 1955 the vineyard firm joined Allied Grape Growers and sold the Wahtoke winery to United Vintners; and John II, still the president of Cella Vineyards, is now United Vintners' vice chairman.

The oldest winery in Fresno County is probably the one at Lacjac, between Reedley and Parlier. Since 1945 it has been the Mount Tivy or Reedley winery of the Christian Brothers of Napa; the Brothers produce and bottle their dessert wines and brandy there. Originally this was the Sanford winery, but nobody seems to know when it was built. In 1899 Lachman & Jacobi, the San Francisco wine merchants who then were fighting the California Wine Association's attempt to monopolize the state's wine supply, bought and enlarged the Sanford cellar to a million gallons and began to make their own wine. They later were absorbed by the CWA. At Repeal, Fresno Assemblyman Lucius Powers and associates reopened the old winery and changed its name from Lacjac to Mount Tivy, for a mountain named for an early settler of the county. During the Second World War, Seagram bought it from an intermediate owner and at the end of the conflict sold it to the Christian Brothers. Today the great cellars and the clusters of new outdoor stainless steel tanks hold four million gallons of aging dessert wines, and the big distillery, with its continuous and pot stills, makes the Brothers' brandies, which outsell all others in the United States. The Brothers own a thousand acres of vineyards in the vicinity, in which they grow three dozen wine-grape varieties. Included are Tinta Madeira for their port wines and Muscat Canelli or Frontignan, which accounts in part for the delicacy of their Château La Salle sweet white table wine.

Two wineries in Fresno County are owned by groups of grape growers. The 5-million-gallon Gibson winery in the center of Sanger is owned by a co-op of 140 members formed in 1945 as the Sanger Winery Association. It also owns the Gibson winery at Elk Grove and ships the wines from Sanger for bottling there. The 2-million-gallon Del Rey winery, on Central Avenue near Malaga, was organized in 1945 as a co-op, but in 1971 was changed to a grower-owned corporation. Built to make bulk dessert wine, Del Rey now also makes table wine, bottles some of its output, and offers it for sampling and sale in a Pullman club car converted into a tasting room.

At Monmouth, a crossroads on the county map between Caruthers and Selma, are several acres of stainless steel tanks and warehouses that resemble an army depot. This is the unique Vie-Del Company, headed by Massud Nury. It makes more than a dozen different winy products, but sells only two under the Vie-Del name. One is its trio of "Wine Chef" dealcoholized concentrated wine flavors (Burgundy, Sauterne, and Sherry) for gourmet cookery. The other is "Winecraft" grape concentrate for home winemaking. It comes in various-sized cans and also in a home winemaking kit, complete with fermentation lock, siphon hose, yeast, yeast-nutrient, bottle caps, and instructions for making four gallons of "select Burgundy wine." Another interesting item is blending-sherry, of which Vie-Del, partly owned by Seagram, is the nation's chief supplier. This is the heavy-bodied sherry that is blended with fine whiskeys, brandies, and rums, and accounts for their smooth taste. But the main product at Vie-Del is brandy. Its heady aroma can be breathed in the air at Monmouth, for almost fifteen million gallons of it—the biggest concentration of brandy in the world—is aging in barrels in the warehouses for other producers, who have their brandy made or aged there.

On Central Avenue between Cornelia and Chateau Fresno Avenues is the second Bronco Winery of the Franzia sons and cousins, mentioned on an earlier page. It was built in 1977 on the 3,000-acre vineyard planted five years earlier by the Getty Oil Company, mainly with wine-grape varieties and including the new red Carnelian and Centurion. Harvesting is done by machines that pick the grapes from two rows of vines at a time.

There are two wineries in the Kerman area of western Fresno County. The million-gallon former Morello cellar on Modoc Avenue in Kerman is now the Villa Bianchi winery. Joseph Bianchi has modernized it to make six types of table wines which he sells in bottles and jugs. Southeast of Kerman, adjoining the late William H. Noble's 25,000-acre cattle ranch, is a new kind of winery, built in 1971. The 2.4-million-gallon Noble Vineyards winery consists of a stemmer-crusher and refrigerated tanks of stainless steel which stand on a concrete pad in a 3,000-acre vineyard of "varietal" grapes. It converts the grapes, minutes after picking, into bulk table wines for shipment to a dozen wineries in other parts of the state. In 1977 the Noble Vineyards and winery were acquired by Chilean-born Augustin Huneeus (hue-*nay*-us), the former president of Paul Masson, who also once headed the worldwide wine operations of Seagram. Huneeus heads a group which has vineyard investments in this country, Europe, and Latin America.

In contrast to the giant valley wineries is the old-fashioned 75,000-gallon cellar of the Nonini family on their 200-acre vineyard in the Rolinda district, eight miles northwest of Fresno. When Antonio Nonini began making table wine in 1936, his principal customers were Basque sheepherders who came down from the mountains each year to have their barrels filled with his burgundy, made from his Barbera grapes. Antonio's sons, Reno, Gildo, and Geno, still make their burgundy to the sheepmen's taste. It is 14 percent in alcohol content because the Noninis wait until October to pick these grapes. Their

Zinfandel and their rosé, made from Mission grapes, are somewhat easier to drink. The Noninis have built a small tasting room, where their wines are sold mostly by the bottle and jug. But now that table wine is becoming a popular mealtime drink in the valley, numerous Fresno householders have begun emulating the Basque sheepherders, buying their table wines from the Noninis in small barrels and bringing them back to be refilled at the bargain barrel price.

Also unique is the small cellar of the Nicholas Verry family, opposite the railroad tracks in the town of Parlier. The Verrys make retsina, the resin-flavored wine that is popular among the Greeks. Their other specialty is a light white wine they call Philery, which means "quick love" in Greek.

There are three old wineries between Selma and Kingsburg, raisin-growing centers along Highway 99. On Huntsman Avenue is the Selma Winery, a producer of bulk wine. Next, on Sierra Street in Kingsburg, is the one-time Italian Swiss Colony Kingsburg cellar, which became Schenley's after Louis Martini moved to the Napa Valley; it is now owned by Almadén of Los Gatos. The one-time Muscat Co-operative Winery, a mile north of there, is now operated by Vie-Del.

The Sun-Maid Growers raisin-processing plant, on Bethel Avenue two miles northwest of Kingsburg, is the biggest of its kind in the world and is worth a visit to take the 25-minute plant tour (offered on weekdays) showing how the co-op stems, washes and packages the sun-dried Thompson, Muscat, Sultana, and Zante currant grapes of its 2,000 members. Sun-Maid was organized in 1912 and during the First World War promoted its five-cent package of raisins at candy counters with the slogan "Have you had your iron today?"—until it was stopped by the discovery that raisins contain very little iron.

For many years, any mention that grapes also make wine was taboo in promoting the sale of raisins. At Sun-Maid you are told a legend of how the Fresno raisin industry began. In 1873, the story goes, an unprecedented hot spell dried Francis Eisen's grapes on his vines before he could pick them. What is omitted from the story is that Eisen's purpose in growing grapes was to make them into wine. According to the legend, Eisen salvaged the heat-shriveled fruit by shipping it to a San Francisco grocer who, inspired by the arrival that morning of a ship from Peru, put them on sale as "Peruvian delicacies." Soon the grocer was regularly sending Eisen orders for more.

The taboo against mentioning wine was finally lifted in 1970. In that year raisin industry leaders, seeking a way to reverse the declining sale of their product, hit on the idea of taking advantage of the nationwide home-winemaking craze. The Raisin Advisory Board organized an "American Raisin Vintners Guild" and began selling, for two dollars and a boxtop from any brand of California raisins, a home-winemaking kit with equipment and instructions for fermenting raisins into "balanced, mellow, aromatic, beautiful wines." Although raisins normally make only white wine with a somewhat raisiny taste, an extra recipe in the kit explains that adding beets will change it to rosé.

· 11 ·

The Fresno area ranks next to Davis as a center of vinicultural teaching and research. There are two Federal Government experimental vineyards, one at Clovis, the other on Peach Avenue in the southeastern outskirts of Fresno. On Manning Avenue near Parlier is the University of California's big Kearney Horticultural Field Station, where all kinds of vineyard problems are explored, and where Dr. Harold Olmo tests his new wine-grape hybrids for Region V. There is still another UC fruit-tasting station at Five Points on the west side of the valley.

Research is combined with the teaching of grape growing, winemaking, and raisin production at Fresno State University. Almost a third of the 600-acre campus on Shaw Avenue in northeastern Fresno is occupied by the University vineyard. Adjoining it is a 5,000-gallon model winery, built in 1958 despite vehement protests by local Drys. More than 150 students major in viticultural subjects, half of them in enology. Twenty are graduate students, who participate in research. Many Fresno State graduates now manage vineyards and wineries throughout California and in two dozen foreign countries; the demand for them is greater than the school can fill.

Vincent Petrucci, an Escalon farm boy and one-time high school football coach, has headed the Fresno State viticulture program since 1947, when he got his master's degree at UC under Drs. Winkler and Olmo. Although Fresno lacks the scientific staff UC has at Davis, Petrucci has pioneered many research projects that are contributing to the improvement of valley wines. He was the first, in 1966, to attempt vineyard climate-control. Petrucci believes wine use in the U.S. will treble within the next decade, and predicts that the wine grapes now being planted in the San Joaquin Valley will eventually supply most of the nation's "better than average" table wines.

The enology-food science course at Fresno State is taught by

UC Berkeley-trained Dr. Fred S. Nury with the help of wine-maker Kenneth Fugelsang. Each student is taught wine tasting and analysis and learns to make all of the principal types of still and sparkling wines. What troubles Dr. Nury is having to destroy the wines his students make, a requirement of the Federal law that governs colleges' experimental wine cellars. "We at least ought to be allowed to sell our wines to the wineries instead of pouring it all down the drain," Dr. Nury says.

The University does sell the grapes that students produce as part of their viticulture course. Each student is assigned about five acres to farm, and he shares in the profit when the fruit is sold. Some earn as much as several hundred dollars in a season.

In 1966, this enabled one of Petrucci's students, twenty-year-old Dale Landis, to start the first new winery built in Fresno County in more than twenty years. Dale started by buying the best wine grapes grown by his classmates, making them into wine in the tool shed behind his father's home in the Oleander district of Fresno. Then he persuaded his father, a semiretired dentist, to help him build an 8,000-gallon cellar adjoining the house and to equip it with oak cooperage and refrigeration. He makes Ruby Cabernet and Zinfandel, and also a pair of sherries, which he buys from the Vie-Del winery and ages in small oak barrels. His Landis winery label uses "San Joaquin Valley" instead of "California" as the appellation of origin for his wines. No other Fresno vintner has done anything like this since the 1930s, when the old Mattei winery sold a wine labeled "Mattevista Fresno Port."

Fresno County counted 198,000 acres of vineyards in 1977, three tenths of the state total in that year. More than a fifth, 41,000 acres, were wine varieties; the rest were raisin and table grapes.

• 12 •

Tulare County is second to Fresno in the extent of its vineyards, with 72,847 acres in 1977, of which more than a fifth were wine grapes.

At Calgro, beside the tiny Armenian village of Yettem (Armenian for Garden of Paradise) on Highway 201 four miles south of Cutler, is the California Growers Winery, lately enlarged from four to twelve million gallons. Of the four wineries in Tulare County, it is the only one that invites visitors and offers tasting (Monday through Friday afternoons).

Established in 1936 by raisin industry leader Arpaxat (Sox)

Setrakian, the Calgro winery was primarily a producer of bulk dessert wines and brandy until 1972. Since then, son Robert Setrakian has transformed it into what he believes some of the other San Joaquin Valley wineries will become in the future, an efficient mass-producer of moderate-priced bottled table wines and champagnes for sale under their own brand names. With its new stainless-steel crushers, refrigerated storage and Charmat champagne tanks, and five automatic bottling lines, his winery produces a complete assortment of still and sparkling wines under the Robert Setrakian, L. Le Blanc, and Bounty Vineyards brands as well as under the original "Growers" name and customers' private brands. The table wines, except for the Robert Setrakian and Bounty premium "varietals," are sold in sizes ranging from bottles to gallon jugs, priced as low in California as 99¢ for the Growers brand in 1977.

Stanford-educated Robert Setrakian has several interests. One is music; he sang at a Palo Alto night club during his college days. Another is flying a replica of the 1911-vintage biplane named "Vin Fiz," the first plane ever to cross the continent, a flight he aims to duplicate someday. He gives his winery visitors envelopes labeled "grow a grape and step on it"; the envelopes contain grape seeds. Setrakian thinks the white-wine boom of the 1970s is really a cold-wine boom and he predicts that table wine will become the national mealtime beverage when people start serving the lighter red wines chilled. He also believes that coast-counties-quality "varietals" such as White Riesling can be grown successfully in Region V climates. His Fresno State- and UC Davis-trained winemaster Sam Balakian produced a White Riesling in 1975 with more Riesling flavor than many then on the market, by picking the grapes early and fermenting them cold.

Setrakian farms were among the first to plant large blocks of wine grapes in the valley in 1965 at the first signs of the table wine boom. The firm now has more than 2,000 acres of "valley varietals" in Tulare and Kern Counties.

The Sierra winery, a bulk producer on Highway 43 northeast of Tulare, also exemplifies the striking changes taking place in the valley wine industry. Since 1972 it has expanded from six million to twenty-nine million gallons and has added a second winery near Delano. Back in 1904, Frank Giannini, from the island of Elba, owned a vineyard here and made wine for himself and his friends. His favorite was a dry wine of Aleatico, the red Muscat grape of Elba; only one California winery (Filippi of Mira Loma) makes it anymore. Giannini had so many thirsty friends that he built a winery and began selling them his wines. After his death in 1944, his winery had various owners until a group of vineyardists headed by Ross Bagdasarian and Berge Kirkorian bought and enlarged the old cellar in 1963 to provide a home for their grapes.

Nine tenths of Sierra's output during the sixties was port and sherry, shipped in tank cars to eastern bottlers. The table wine boom has reversed this; almost all of its production now is table wine, produced for other California wineries. An exception is one specialty of Sierra winemaster Philip Posson. In 1975, Sierra began bottling "Philip Posson Dry Flor Sherry" for sale on the California market at four dollars a bottle. When Posson came to Tulare in 1964, he began making sherry by the submerged-culture *flor* process. Sierra became the first American winery to produce sherry on a commercial scale by this speedy method, invented in Canada. Posson ages it in fifty-gallon barrels outdoors, where he says sherry flavor improves because it cools at night and warms during the day. He supplies it by tank truck to other California producers, who have begun using it in their dry sherry blends.

• 13 •

Kern County, where the San Joaquin Valley ends in the foothills of the Tehachapi Mountains, had 73,375 acres of vineyards in 1977, centered between Delano and Wheeler Ridge, over half of it wine grapes planted since 1972. This is John Steinbeck country, the setting of his Pulitzer Prize-winning novel of 1940, *The Grapes of Wrath.* Thompsons and table grapes once comprised most of the county's grape acreage, but those varieties now represent less than half of the total. There are five big wineries in the county, and two more across the Tulare County line at Trocha are regarded as within the Delano district, making a total of seven in the area.

At Trocha, five miles northeast of Delano, are the Delano Growers co-op, the former Cal-Grape winery, which is now owned by Sierra, and the one-time Del Vista cellar, which is now the L.K. Marshall Winery of the Guild. South of Delano, at Pond Road, is the winery of A. Perelli-Minetti & Sons. At Highway 99 and Whistler Road south of McFarland is the 9.4-million-gallon California Mission winery, built for rancher Hollis B. Roberts in 1974. At Edison, six miles east of Bakersfield, is the 10-million-gallon Giumarra Vineyards winery. Eight miles farther south, at Di Giorgio, is the 36-million-gallon Bear Mountain co-op. Perelli-Minetti, Giumarra, and Bear

Mountain offer tastings and invite visitors to tour their plants.

Grape growing at this end of the valley began in 1888, when the waters of the Kern River were diverted for irrigation. To Kern County in 1919 came the fabulous Giuseppe (Joseph) Di Giorgio, the Sicilian immigrant who rose from an eight-dollar-a-week clerk for a New York fruit jobber at the age of fourteen to become, at thirty-seven, the biggest grower and marketer of fresh fruits in the world.

Di Giorgio began planting grapes around Delano, where predecessors were already cultivating 7,000 acres of vines. Then he went exploring farther south in a virtual desert near Arvin, then known as "the weed patch." He found underground water, which eventually covered 5,600 acres. That is the vineyard district which is now Di Giorgio on state maps.

When Prohibition began in 1920 and the market for grapes boomed, bootleggers and home winemakers swarmed at the fruit auctions, which Di Giorgio controlled, for hundreds of thousands were making their own wines. Then Di Giorgio heard of a winemaker at Ukiah in Mendocino County, who was making a grape syrup called Caligrapo, which bore an inviting label: "When diluted, do not store in a warm place because it will ferment, which is against the law." Di Giorgio saw that, for home winemaking, concentrated grape juice was an improvement over fresh grapes. He went to Ukiah, brought the winemaker to Kern County in 1922, had his surplus grapes made into concentrate during the remaining Prohibition years, and at Repeal established his own wineries at Delano, at Kerman in Fresno County, and at Di Giorgio.

• 14 •

That one-time Ukiah winemaker, Antonio Perelli-Minetti, stayed in Kern County and built his own winery three miles south of Delano at the Pond Road exit from Highway 99. At his death in 1976 at the age of ninety-five, he was the oldest pre-Prohibition vintner still active in the state. His career was as colorful as Di Giorgio's.

He was born in 1882 at Barletta on the Adriatic coast of southern Italy, where his father owned two wineries. At nineteen, Tony was completing his studies at the Conegliano Viticultural Institute when Dr. Ollino of the Italian Swiss Colony, recruiting winemakers in Italy, persuaded the young man's father to send him to California. Perelli traveled to the Colony at Asti in 1902, made wine there, then at Livermore for

Antonio Perelli-Minetti, who was the oldest pre-Prohibition wine-grower when he died in 1976 at the age of 95.

the California Wine Association, and later at two Healdsburg wineries. Eight years later, Perelli went broke attempting in a partnership wine-selling venture at San Francisco to compete with the giant CWA.

Told by a visiting Mexican vintner that he could recoup his fortunes quickly in Mexico, Perelli went there in 1910 and was hired to plant a vineyard near Torreón. In his sixth year below the border, the chaos of the Mexican Revolution compelled Perelli to return to California. He later returned many times to Mexico and helped to build and equip some of that country's leading wineries.

Back in California, Perelli settled at Ukiah, where Di Giorgio found him making Caligrapo in 1922. When Di Giorgio brought him to Kern County, Perelli began planting his own Delano vineyard, but kept his home at Ukiah for a dozen more years. During that time he built two more Delano wineries, moving to his third, the present one, in 1936. Today the Perelli-Minetti family's vineyards spread over 1,500 acres on both sides of the freeway and their plant holds 20 million gallons of wine, brandy, and champagne. Visitors can sample the wines in CWA's attractive new tasting room.

In 1971 the winery acquired an additional name, that of the California Wine Association. Remember that the CWA, formed in 1894, swallowed up sixty-four California wineries and controlled most of the state's wine supply until Prohibition, and that in 1929 the CWA and other old wine firms combined as Fruit Industries—the days of the "Vine-Glo" concentrate. At the height of its power in 1950, Fruit Industries resumed the name of the old California Wine Association, and counting eleven wineries among its members, introduced its Eleven Cellars brand. But then, one by one, the members dropped out, until in 1971 the Cherokee co-op winery of Lodi finally withdrew, which left Perelli-Minetti as the last of the Eleven Cellars.

This unravels several who-owns-which-wine puzzles, such as why the Perelli-Minettis at Delano now bottle and sell wines bearing such old-time names as L & J (Lachman & Jacobi), Greystone (for the Christian Brothers' showplace cellar at St. Helena), F.I., Guasti, Calwa, Ambassador, and Eleven Cellars, and brandies called Aristocrat and A.R. Morrow. As the last CWA member, the Perelli winery now owns all of these names, and more than 200 additional famous wine and brandy brands of the past.

CWA's varietally-labeled Fino Eleven Cellars table wines are produced by north coast-counties wineries and are labeled "Napa" or "Sonoma." In 1975 the Perellis introduced lines of "valley varietals" made at Delano from grapes grown in the valley, under their Ambassador and Guasti brands. Their leading brandy is called Aristocrat. Under the A.R. Morrow name, they sell one of the few bottled-in-bond (100 proof) brandies made in the United States.

The vineyards, the winery with its new bottling and champagne cellars, and CWA sales were managed until recently by three of Perelli's sons, William, Fred, and Mario, respectively. In 1977, CWA employed Jerry Stanners as its new president, and a new production manager, Yugoslavia-born, French-trained George Kolarovich, who had spent the fifteen preceding years as winemaker and as general manager of the Barossa Valley Co-op winery in Australia.

Because Tony Perelli-Minetti preferred coast-counties table wines for their higher acidity than valley wines, his hobby after moving to Delano was to plant seedlings of those grapes he found in his vineyard that matured with high acidity late in the season. By doing this for almost thirty years, Perelli developed a half dozen new red-wine grapes and patented the first, which he called "Perelli 101." It develops 1.12 acidity at 22 Balling and doesn't ripen until mid-November, sometimes not until early December. I have tasted its wine, which is full-bodied and fresh and could easily be mistaken for a north-coast wine. Perelli planted 350 acres with his "101" vine. CWA has included "101" wine in some of its blends and plans to introduce it under its own name, tentatively as "Perelli Noir." Other vintners have scored sensational sales successes by introducing new "varietal" wines, only to face competition as soon as other vintners could introduce wines bearing the same varietal names. Perelli, by breeding and patenting his own new grapes, found a way to sell wines with varietal names no other vintner could copy, that would be exclusively his own.

• 15 •

The vast Di Giorgio vineyards and the big winery near the Di Giorgio post office have new names now.

When the founder died in 1951, he owned almost fourteen square miles of vineyards, more than anyone else in the world. His nephews became the heads of the Di Giorgio Fruit Corporation; Joe had no sons. Until then, the entire output of the Di Giorgio wineries had been sold in bulk to bottlers and to other wineries. The nephews decided to try selling it in bottles. They bought the old Santa Fe, Padre, and Vai Brothers brand names, acquired bottling cellars in Los Angeles, and introduced "the Di Giorgio family of fine wines." After six years they gave that up, sold the brands to Petri's United Vintners, and returned to selling the wines in bulk. Then, because irrigation water reaching their part of the valley in Federal projects from the north was denied to single owners of more than 160 acres, they began disposing of the Di Giorgio vineyards. They sold the winery in 1966 to a new Bear Mountain grape growers' cooperative, organized by their winery manager, Keith Nylander, and erased "fruit" from their corporation's name.

The Bear Mountain Winery, ex-Di Giorgio, is named for a nearby peak in the Greenhorn Mountains, which rise east of Bakersfield. Many of the co-op's more than a hundred growers planted "varietal" grapes on large blocks of their vineyards during the 1970s. The winery's size was quadrupled from eight to thirty-six million gallons and most of the new capacity was shifted to making table wines. In 1969, Bear Mountain became the first Kern County winery to bottle its own line of wines and the first to open a tasting room. Much of its production is sold in bulk or is bottled under the brands of distributors in many states, but the bottle labels seldom mention the Di Giorgio address. Some give it as Arvin, which is four miles south. Bear Mountain's line of cork-stopped premium wines is labeled "M. Lamont" and the address is Lamont, which is four miles west of the winery. There also are M. Lamont wines in carafes and jugs. Noted enologist Leonard Berg, retired at age sixty-five from the Christian Brothers winery at Napa, became Bear Mountain's winemaster in 1975. Two years later, the winery introduced under its M. Lamont brand the first bottled Chardonnay and Gewürztraminer made of Kern County grapes. Berg's chief assistant is UC Davis-trained Paula Weight, the winery's director of quality control.

In 1978, Bear Mountain's grower members offered the winery for sale. The Labatt breweries of Canada were the leading bidder at press time.

• 16 •

Six miles east of Bakersfield, facing Edison Highway at Edison Road, is the Giumarra Vineyards winery, which was built in 1946 to make bulk dessert wines, but which became a producer of bottled premium "valley varietals" in 1973. Giuseppe (Joe) Giumarra came to America from Sicily, sold bananas from a pushcart in Toronto, brought his family to Bakersfield, bought a ranch, and by the 1960s became the biggest shipper of fresh grapes in the United States. Joe still rises at six each weekday morning to spend his day in the 8,000-acre vineyard behind the family's winery.

His younger brother, John Giumarra, Sr., put the family into the bottled "varietal" wine business, building a three-million-gallon air-conditioned addition to the winery, and adding a tasting room that now is open Wednesdays through Sundays. Two years later he began marketing the first vintage-dated Kern County wines. The Zinfandel, made of Lodi and Cucamonga grapes, promptly won a gold medal at the Los Angeles County Fair.

The Giumarras now grow a thousand "varietal" acres of their own in their vineyards, bordered by Breckenridge Road. Their new assortment of twenty "GV" wines, introduced in 1978, includes premium "Varietals" and generics and also "mountain" wines in cork-stoppered bottles, decanters, various-sized jugs, and two sizes of plastic pouches especially for the restaurant trade.

Giumarra's winemaker Dale Anderson and winemaster Jim Lawrence, a 1966 enology graduate from Fresno State University, have made wines from grapes that are not supposed to grow in Region V, including Chardonnay, Johannisberg Riesling, Cabernet Sauvignon, Pinot Noir, and Gamay Beaujolais. Sampling some of them recently, I found each uniformly good; I could easily have mistaken them for coast-counties wines. Equally satisfactory were their "mountain" types, burgundy, chablis, two rosés, French Colombard, Zinfandel, and Ruby Cabernet.

• 17 •

The most important aspect of the wine revolution of the 1970s was the rush to plant "varietal" grapes for table wines in the San Joaquin Valley.

On the east side of the valley, where most of the wineries are, new vineyards are scattered all the way from Manteca to the Tehachapi, vines even sprouting among the oil wells. East of Arvin, on the lower slope of Bear Mountain, is a 2,400-acre vineyard, planted under set sprinklers in 1971, in which the vine rows are four and half miles long. Its grapes are machine-harvested beginning at midnight and delivered to the Bear Mountain winery at six in the morning, thus missing the severe heat of the day.

Seven thousand acres of certified vines were planted beginning in 1971 on part of the 450-square-mile Tejon Ranch in southeastern Kern County. Partly owned by the Los Angeles Times-Mirror Company, Tejon Ranch is the largest private landholding in California. Its 1976 crop, field-crushed at night into thirty-ton tank trucks, went to the Bear Mountain and Sierra wineries. In the following year, the grapes were sold. When the Tejon Vineyard reaches full production by 1980, it will produce 70,000 tons of grapes per year.

Also important are recent plantings on the west side of the valley. Much of the west side still is virtually desert, not badlands in the usual sense, but contaminated with boron and other minerals. In prehistoric times this was ocean floor. To this arid wasteland in the early 1970s, the man-made river called the California Aqueduct began delivering northern water, which in the next few decades is expected to leach out the minerals and create a quarter-million to a half-million new acres of fertile farms. The west side is an area of immense landhold-ings of farming corporations, oil companies, and European-owned conglomerates. Some of them are eligible to receive water from the California Aqueduct. The 160-acre limitation on water to single owners does not apply there because the new aqueduct is primarily a state, not wholly a Federal, project. To these big landholders, a hundred acres of new vineyard is merely a test plot. If they decide to go ahead with wine-grape planting, a test plot can expand to a thousand or even to ten thousand acres.

In 1976, the Blackwell Land Company, with 1,500 acres coming into production between Lost Hills and Blackwells Corner, began marketing "Lost Hills" wines in California. The wines were produced and bottled for Blackwell by wineries in Sonoma and Tulare Counties under supervision of Blackwell's own enologist, Fresno State-trained Curt Meyer. He says Blackwell intends eventually to have a winery of its own.

While the potential of future west-side acreage causes concern among vineyardists who remember the disastrous California grape and wine gluts of the past, it is reassuring to consumers to know that there is no danger of permanent shortages or of sky-high wine prices while hundreds of thousands of acres are still available for planting of wine grapes in this part of the state.

The valley plantings of "varietals" thus far are mainly of those recommended by the University as producing good table wines and champagnes in Region IV and Region V climates, such as French Colombard, Emerald Riesling, Chenin Blanc, Barbera, Ruby Cabernet, and the new Carnelian and Centurion. The University has strongly advised the valley growers not to plant the "noble" varieties such as the Pinots, Chardonnay, White Riesling, and Cabernet Sauvignon, which produce fine wines in the cool coast counties, Regions I, II, and III. Some valley vineyardists, tempted by the high prices per ton paid for the noble grapes by coast-counties vintners during the seventies, have nevertheless planted these in some Region IV and Region V localities. University viticulturists have denounced this, saying that those varietal names should not be thus "debased."

That the San Joaquin Valley can produce better than everyday-quality table wines and champagnes is already evident in the contents of the bottles and jugs available at moderate prices in stores throughout the nation. The valley whites thus far have averaged much better than the valley reds. Some valley wines I have tasted lately at wineries and at Fresno State University, which makes wines from the newest Olmo grape varieties, have been superior, as well as merely good.

Reading the results of some of the recent wine-quality competitions, it occurred to me to count the awards won by valley wines. Of the 138 medal and honorable-mention awards for table and sparkling wines in the 1977 Los Angeles County Fair "open division," I found that forty-three, or almost a third of the total, went to wineries situated in San Joaquin, Madera, Fresno, Tulare, and Kern Counties. Included were twelve silver medals, and one gold (for Angelo Pagagni's rosé).

20

Wines of Other Western States

WHEN Dr. Konstantin Frank introduced his New York State Johannisberg Riesling and Chardonnay wines in 1965, writers of articles in national magazines heralded the news as a sensation because to them this meant that California no longer was the only state that could grow the true Vinifera wine grapes of Europe.

What none of them seemed to notice was that Vinifera grapes, unheralded, had been grown for much of this century in Washington, Oregon, Arizona, Idaho, and Utah. The reason these other western states were ignored was that in all of those years they had never produced any fine wines of European types.

Since 1970, premium quality Vinifera "varietal" wines grown in Washington and Oregon have appeared on the wine market in California, and some are already rivaling California's finest wines. More than 3,000 new acres of the best Vinifera grape varieties have been planted lately in eastern Washington and western Oregon. Twenty-four new wineries have been opened in the Northwest to specialize in making Vinifera wines and there are plans to build more. There is a new winery in Idaho and more wine grapes are being planted there.

What has caused this is the nationwide table wine boom, with the increased prices of wine grapes in California and the stampede during the early 1970s to plant new vineyards there.

• 2 •

The State of Washington ranks third in the nation in grape production, though its record harvest of 111,000 tons in 1975 was exceeded by New York's 185,000 tons and was dwarfed by California's nearly 4-million-ton crop. Washington is only sixth, however, after Virginia, in the quantity of wine it produces. Only about 1.3 million gallons have been produced annually because only a tenth of Washington grapes in recent years have been used to make Washington wine. Almost nine tenths of the state's 22,500 acres of vineyards grow Concords that are mechanically harvested and either go into fresh grape juice or are shipped as juice to California wineries to make their Cold Ducks and "pop" wines. Most of the 12,000 acres of new vineyards planted since 1968 are Concords for the California wineries. University economists predict that Washington before many years will displace New York as the nation's second largest grape-producing state. Before the new plantings began,

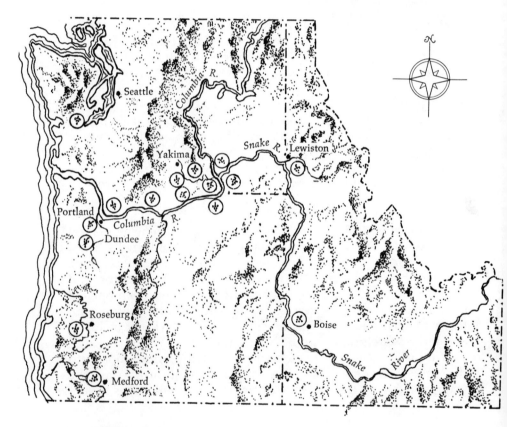

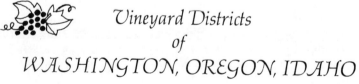

Vineyard Districts
of
WASHINGTON, OREGON, IDAHO

there were only about 500 acres of Vinifera, mainly of common varieties. But by 1977 Vinifera acreage in Washington exceeded 2,000 acres, including mostly such premium grapes as Cabernet Sauvignon, White Riesling, Chardonnay, Chenin Blanc, Gewürztraminer, and Merlot.

The first grapevines in Washington were planted in 1872 by a Confederate Civil War veteran named Lambert B. Evans on Stretch Island in the southern part of Puget Sound. To the island about 1890 came Adam Eckert from the Chautauqua Grape Belt of New York. Eckert sent to New York for more vines and later bred a black Labrusca grape variety he called the Island Belle. Plantings spread to neighboring islands and to the mainland, where a village was founded and named Grapeview.

Around 1906, irrigation water from the Cascade watershed began transforming the Yakima Valley in eastern Washington from an almost rainless desert into a lush fruit-growing region. The Island Belle grape was then brought there from the western part of the state. Grape juice plants were built at Yakima, Grandview, and Prosser, and the Island Belle soon was largely displaced by the Concord grape of the East.

There are no records of any wineries operating in Washington before 1933. The only reports of early wine production were of occasional seizures of bootleg wine during the 1920s.

At Repeal, realtor Charles Somers started on Stretch Island the St. Charles Winery, the first in the state. Almost overnight, everyone in Washington with so much as a berry patch wanted to build a winery; there were forty-two in operation, including three on Stretch Island, by 1937. Others started along the Columbia River, but the largest ones were at Seattle and in the Yakima Valley.

At Sunnyside, twenty miles down the valley from Yakima, lived a farmer, lawyer, and ex-school teacher named William B. Bridgman. Born on a farm beside Jordan Creek on the Niagara Peninsula of Ontario, where his father grew Labrusca grapes, Bridgman came to Sunnyside in 1902 aboard a horse-drawn stage when the valley's principal crop still was sagebrush. He promoted the local irrigation system, was elected mayor of Sunnyside, and became one of the area's principal grape growers. At Repeal, Bridgman built a winery, but he also took time to make a study of California and European vineyards. He concluded that the Yakima Valley climate is better for wine-growing than that of central France, having more days of sunshine, and noted that its latitude (46 degrees north) is midway between the latitudes of Burgundy and Bordeaux. This

convinced Bridgman that Washington could grow finer European grapes than California could. He imported many Vinifera
varieties and supplied neighboring growers with cuttings from
his vines. He hired a German winemaker and produced such
wines as Johannisberg Riesling and Cabernet. Unfortunately,
however—and I recall this because I tasted an assortment that
the late Herman Wente brought from Washington during the
1940s—Bridgman's wines were poorly made, and they soon
were withdrawn from sale.

Another unfortunate development was the Washington liquor control law, adopted at Repeal, which established state
monopoly liquor stores, thus discouraging most people from
buying table wines. Washington wineries were allowed to sell
directly to taverns, which gave them an advantage over the
out-of-state wineries. Prospering under their legal umbrella, the
Washington vintners were content to make ordinary dessert
wines such as port and sherry, mainly out of Labrusca grapes.
In 1965, however, the Washington wineries saw that their
protective law was about to be changed, and they persuaded the
State University to start a wine research program at its Prosser
Station. (The law was amended four years later to allow wine
sales by privately-owned stores.)

In 1966, I visited the Yakima Valley and saw several vineyards
of such pedigreed varieties as Cabernet Sauvignon and Pinot
Noir. I was amazed to find the wineries were wasting these
costly grapes, mixing them with Concord in nondescript port
and burgundy blends. The only fine Vinifera wine I tasted on
that trip was a Grenache rosé made by a home winemaker in
Seattle. I remarked to Victor Allison, then the manager of the
American Wine Growers wineries, that perhaps Washington
vintners might make some good Vinifera wines if they would
bring someone from California to show them how. Allison
asked me: "Such as who?" I mentioned a few good wine
makers, including André Tchelistcheff, the great enologist of
Beaulieu.

Allison persuaded Tchelistcheff to come to Washington in
1967 to discuss the state's winemaking potential. Tchelistcheff
tasted most of the Washington table wines and rejected them
all. But then a friend of the Seattle home winemaker whom I've
mentioned let him sample a Gewürztraminer made from grapes
grown in the Yakima Valley. Tchelistcheff was astounded; he
pronounced it the finest Gewürztraminer yet produced in the
United States. He accepted the challenge to show Washington
vintners how to make fine wines.

Tchelistcheff first directed that the Vinifera vines in the American Wine Growers' vineyards be immediately pruned to reduce the crop and to achieve proper sugar-acid balance in the grapes. He returned to Washington that September, selected perfect batches of Cabernet Sauvignon, Pinot Noir, Sémillon, and Grenache, and had them fermented at controlled temperatures. He had the Cabernet stored in American white oak barrels and the Pinot Noir in new Limousin oak from France.

In 1969, I accompanied Tchelistcheff to Seattle to sample his one-and two-year-old Washington wines. We tasted separately, scoring them as unfinished wines, and then compared our notes. Tchelistcheff gave the 1967 Cabernet seventeen out of a possible twenty points, sixteen to the 1968 Sémillon, and fifteen and sixteen to the two Grenache rosés. The Pinot Noir wasn't yet ready to be tasted. I scored each Cabernet a point higher and my other scores were close to Tchelistcheff's.

A year later bottled samples of these wines, under the American Wine Growers' Ste. Michelle label, were sent to California. The San Francisco Sampling Club rated them as "challenging the quality supremacy of California varietal wines." The new Washington wines were then introduced in a few eastern markets and were enthusiastically praised by connoisseurs.

American Wine Growers was purchased in 1973 by a group of Seattle investors and was renamed Ste. Michelle. A year later it was re-sold to the United States Tobacco Company of Connecticut. Five hundred new acres of Vinifera vineyards were planted that year thirty miles east of Yakima. An elegant new 2-million-gallon Ste. Michelle winery was built in 1975 fifteen miles east of Seattle. It is a Bordeaux-style château on an eighty-seven-acre park with trout ponds, footpaths, and picnic tables, off state route 202 outside Woodinville. Opened in 1976, it offered cellar tours and tasting and received two thousand visitors a day.

Grapes are trucked overnight to the winery at Woodinville from the vineyards across the Cascades in eastern Washington, 190 miles away. Ste. Michelle still produces Labrusca-flavored wines in its winery at Grandview, for sale under the American Wine Growers, old Pommerelle, Nawico, and Hadassim brands.

Tchelistcheff flies from California four times a year to work with UC Davis-trained Ste. Michelle enologist Joel Klein at Woodinville and to visit the vineyards in eastern Washington with the company's viticulturist, Lester Fleming.

Ste. Michelle wines thus far released are vintaged-dated Johannisberg Riesling, Sémillon, Gewürztraminer, Chablis, Cabernet Sauvignon, Grenache Rosé, and two Chenin Blancs, one dry and the other botrytized. Production of three bottle-fermented Ste. Michelle champagnes began in 1977.

• 3 •

The home winemaker in Seattle who made the Grenache rosé that I tasted in 1966 is Dr. Lloyd Woodburne, professor of psychology at the University of Washington in Seattle. In 1951, while at home recovering from a cold, Professor Woodburne happened to pick up a copy of Philip Wagner's first book on home winemaking. Intrigued, Woodburne telephoned his famous wine-buff colleague, Angelo Pellegrini, a professor of English, and asked, "Pelly, how difficult is this winemaking thing?" "Easy as boiling an egg," replied Pellegrini, who makes red wine from the Cabernet grapes he gets from his friends at the Louis Martini vineyards in California.

Woodburne bought grapes and a barrel and made a batch of Zinfandel. He and his wife managed to drink it, liberally diluted with soda water. Three years later, he bought Delaware grapes in the Yakima Valley, made white wine, and invited some of his fellow professors over to sample it. They too, began buying grapes and became home winemakers. Soon a total of eighteen families around the campus were doing the same. Someone thought of buying a power crusher, which was installed in the Woodburnes' garage. But a lawyer member, Professor of Law Cornelius Peck, warned them not to ferment their grapes together because the Federal law permits only individual house-holders to make wine in their homes.

Another member, Professor Philip Church, made a study of Washington's climates and found that heat units in the lower Yakima Valley are the same as in Beaune, the center of Burgundy's Côte d'Or. In 1961, ten of the group formed a corporation, Professor Peck supplying the knowhow, and bought five acres adjoining Bridgman's vineyard at Sunnyside. They planted seven Vinifera varieties from UC Davis and added Pinot Noir vines from the American Wine Growers' vineyard. Each member was entitled to a tenth share of the grapes.

When I tasted Woodburne's rosé in 1966 and found it outstanding, I suggested that his group ought to start their own winery. A year later, with Tchelistcheff's praise of their Gewürztraminer (which came from Dr. Church's cellar), the professors took the plunge. They built a small cellar in the Seattle suburb of Kirkland and moved the crusher from the Woodburnes' garage in time for the 1967 vintage. In the following May, as the "Associated Vintners," they introduced the 1967 Riesling and Gewürztraminer in three Seattle gourmet food shops and in the new Mirabeau Restaurant. Connoisseurs heard about it and came from a hundred miles away to buy the wines. By August, all their wines were sold; there were advance orders for the reds, still aging, and for the '68 and '69 vintages as well. Four years later, with the demand for their wines still increasing, they planted twenty more acres at Sunnyside with Cabernet, Pinot Noir, Riesling, Gewürztraminer, Sémillon, and Chardonnay.

Despite their name that suggests a sizeable enterprise, the "Associated Vintners" have preferred to remain small, but their 4,000-gallon winery at Kirkland became too small when their enlarged vineyard began to produce grapes. They moved in 1976 to a 20,000-gallon new cellar at Redmond, another Seattle suburb. There Dr. Woodburne still presides, helped by the other members in vintage season and at bottling times. "Associated Vintners" Gewürztraminer, Chardonnay, and Cabernet Sauvignon shared gold and silver medals with Ste. Michelle and with entries from new Oregon vintners in the judging held by the Enological Society of the Pacific Northwest at Seattle in 1977.

• 4 •

Six new wineries have opened in Washington since 1975, and still more are preparing to start.

Michael Wallace, with a master's degree in enology from UC Davis, teamed with his home-winemaker father Jerrell in 1972 to plant the Hinzerling Vineyard of Riesling, Chardonnay, and Cabernet on Hinzerling Road near Prosser in the Yakima Valley. That winter most of their vines were killed by a freeze. They replanted in the following year and added a second vineyard on a hillside where there is air-drainage. By 1976, with seventeen acres producing grapes, they bonded the 8500-gallon Hinzerling Vineyard winery in a former garage on Highway 12 in Prosser. Their first commercial wines were a *nouveau* red of Cabernet and two Gewürztraminers, one dry and spicy, the other botrytized and sweet, named *der sonne* (of the sun). All three wines were sold out as soon as they were released. In his spare time Mike teaches home winemaking at Columbia Basin College in Pasco.

In 1974, cherry growers Charles and Della Henderson bought

a refrigerated fruit storage building on Highway 14 in the town of Bingen on the Columbia River across the river from Hood River, Oregon. They installed tanks to hold 6,000 gallons, named it the Bingen Wine Cellars, and opened a tasting room. Their first vintage in 1975 included Chenin Blanc, Gewürztraminer, a red Grenache, and Pinot Noir. Grapes from their seventeen-acre vineyard near White Salmon were supplemented from the vineyard of partner Don Graves, fifteen miles upriver at Dallesport. Bingen is named for the wine city in Germany's Rheingau, but local residents call it *bin-jen.* Since the town became a sister city of its namesake, a campaign has begun to adopt the German pronunciation to help develop tourism.

The Preston Wine Cellar on US 395 five miles north of Pasco crushed the first grapes from its fifty-acre vineyard in 1976 and celebrated the event with a grape-stomping. Farmer-tractor-dealer S.W. (Bill) Preston and his wife Joann were already preparing to enlarge the cellar and to build a tasting room. Their first wines, made by UC Davis 1975 graduate Robert Griffin, included Johannisberg Riesling, Chardonnay, Gewürztraminer, and Gamay Beaujolais Rosé, soon to be followed by Chenin Blanc, Sauvignon Blanc, Cabernet Sauvignon, and Merlot.

Northwest of Pasco, on the Columbia River shore, a winery may eventually be built on the spectacular Sagemoor, Bacchus, and Dionysus Vineyards, 500 acres planted since 1972 for groups of Seattle investors headed by attorney Alec Bayless. Grapes from these vineyards have already been shipped to wineries in nine states and Canadian provinces.

In Walla Walla, forty miles southeast of Pasco, machinist Gary Figgins and his wife Nancy bonded their 1,000-gallon Leonetti Wine Cellar on School Avenue in 1977. It was named for their uncle George Leonetti, on whose vineyard their Riesling and Cabernet Sauvignon grapes were grown.

Another winery near Walla Walla was under construction that year. Banker Baker Ferguson had bought the old two-story Lowden School and was installing a winery on the ground floor. He was building a third story on the schoolhouse, where he intends to live and run his winery when he retires from the Baker-Boyer National Bank.

Western Washington has two new wineries and a third is in the planning stage. Rhubarb and berry wines are the main products of Everett Braden's Puyallup Valley winery, opened in 1974 on Twenty-third Street in Puyallup, southeast of Tacoma. Two years later, former restaurateur Manfred Vierthaler, who once studied winemaking at the Geisenheim Institute in Germany, opened an Alpine chalet with a tasting room on Highway 410 a mile east of Sumner and started making wines from eastern Washington and California grapes.

At La Center, twenty miles north of Portland, Seattle computer expert Lincoln Wolverton and his wife Joan have planned a winery ever since they planted their eleven-acre Salishan Vineyard with noble Vinifera varieties in 1971. Their first commercial wine, Salishan Vineyard White Riesling, was made for them in 1977 by Mike Wallace at the Hinzerling Vineyard winery.

Of the forty-two Washington wineries that sprang up following Repeal in the 1930s, only three are left. Two belong to Ste. Michelle, which was a merger of the Pommerelle, National, and Italian wineries. The third is the 600,000-gallon Alhambra Winery at Selah, north of Yakima. Its vineyard, forty miles down the valley at Grandview, consists of Concord, White Diamond, Island Belle, some French hybrids, and Pinot Noir. The company was founded by banker Otis Harlan at Seattle in 1935, was moved to Selah two years later, and the vineyard was purchased after the Second World War. When the St. Charles Winery closed down in 1965, Harlan bought its trademark and has kept Washington supplied with its specialties—17 percent dessert wines made without adding brandy but by the syruped fermentation method used in Ontario. Most interesting of the St. Charles wines is a red appetizer type called Caliante. It tastes like a dry port, and though made from Labrusca grape varieties, it has no foxy flavor.

The original St. Charles vineyard on Stretch Island is still maintained by Charles Somer's son, Bill, but he now sells the Island Belle crop on a "U-pick" basis to people who drive up from Tacoma, thirty miles away. He has transformed the winery into a maritime museum, displaying his hobby collection of old steamboat days, an exhibit well worth crossing the bridge from Grapeview on the mainland to see.

• 5 •

The Columbia Basin and the Yakima Valley, beyond the lofty Cascades in southeastern Washington, are semi-arid; rainfall ranges from six to seven and a half inches per year, but there is plenty of water for irrigation. William Bridgman was right about the area's sunshine, which provides 160 to 210 frost-free days per year. Moreover, days are longer in this northern latitude,

You can't see the vines in this December vineyard scene near Grandview in the Yakima Valley of eastern Washington. The cold-tender Muscat of Alexandria vines were buried with earth after Thanksgiving to protect them from injury during the freezing winter. They were uncovered and tied to the trellis wires in March, when the soil became warm again.

and sunlight is least intense at the beginning and end of the growing season. By the California system of classifying climates, the Prosser Station in the lower Yakima Valley, averaging 2,437 degree-days of heat units, is either Region I or low Region II. Horticulturist Walter J. Clore, retired from the station, says "Washington is better suited for grape growing than New York State; we have milder winters, better soil, ample water, and more sun."

Eastern Washington's defect is low winter temperatures, which drop to seven degrees below zero in one year out of three and to twelve to twenty below in one year out of six. Cold-tender Vinifera vines such as Muscat formerly were buried with earth after each Thanksgiving to protect them during the winter, then were uncovered in March when the soil became warm again. This is no longer done except for the youngest vines. The top Vinifera varieties at the Prosser Station have survived minus-eleven-degree temperatures without covering and have borne either partial or full crops. Vinifera vines are grown on their own roots instead of grafting them to phylloxera-resistant rootstocks as is done in most of California and in Europe. Some of the yields at Prosser are impressive, ranging from 3.8 tons per acre for Chardonnay to 12.5 tons for Melon and 20 tons for the Foch hybrid, yet with acidity and sugar content that requires no amelioration with sugar and water.

Dr. Charles Nagel, the UC Davis-trained enologist at Washington State University, thinks the Columbia Basin eventually will rival Germany with premium white wines and that Washington State Cabernet Sauvignons and Merlots will rival the reds of Bordeaux. "We have only begun to test wine grape varieties to determine which are the best for this area," he adds. Dr. Clore has found that the red Limberger variety, grown in Germany but not in California, does exceptionally well in Washington. The Limberger wine I tasted there was rich in color and had a fruity, almost spicy flavor. Some Limberger vineyards have been planted, but Washington vintners are reluctant to label a wine with the name of this variety because although differently spelled, Limberger may remind consumers of that highly aromatic cheese.

There are at least 50,000 more acres that could grow wine grapes in the Columbia Basin, such as the Wahluke Slope, to which the Grand Coulee Dam brought irrigation water in 1968. Some say eastern Washington has space for as much as 250,000 more acres of vines. In the lower Snake River Valley near Pasco, the largest single Concord vineyard anywhere was planted in the early 1970s. But in the Puget Sound area, where the Washington grape industry began in 1872, less than 100 acres are left. Farmers along the Sound have mostly given up growing the Island Belle grape because heavy rainfall there results in erratic crops.

• 6 •

In Oregon, as in Washington, Vinifera and Labrusca grapes have long flourished side by side. Also, as in Washington, the planting of Vinifera grapes and the number of wineries have multiplied since the late 1960s, though on a different scale. Oregon still has only 1,200 acres of vineyards but already has two dozen wineries and still more on new vineyardists' drawing boards.

Oregon has a longer history of winegrowing than Washington. Among the settlers who came to the territory in wagon trains over the Oregon Trail in the middle of the last century were some who brought vine cuttings and began producing wine in the Willamette Valley south of Portland. Farmers at Ashland in southwestern Oregon grew Vinifera table grapes and were shipping Flame Tokays to market before the Tokay industry developed at Lodi in California. In 1880, when the special national census of winegrowing was taken, Jackson County was listed as producing 15,000 gallons of wine and two Willamette Valley counties, Clackamas and Marion, reported producing 1,900 gallons. Concord grapes were grown as far northeast as Umatilla County in the Columbia Basin.

Around the turn of the century Professor Frederic T. Bioletti, the California expert on viticulture, suggested that several Oregon localities seemed climatically suited for Vinifera grape varieties. But Oregon agricultural authorities were not impressed with the idea of developing the state's wine industry. With the Prohibitionist crusade then at fever pitch, they recommended grape growing for home gardens, not as a commercial enterprise. In fact, as late as 1965, when a new vineyard in Oregon's Umpqua River Valley had already produced its second crop of White Riesling, a circular published by Oregon State University concluded that "the American grapes, *Vitis labrusca*, are more suited (than Vinifera) to Oregon climates."

There were dozens of old farmer wineries in Oregon when Prohibition began in 1920, and the dry law did not put them completely out of business. At Repeal in 1933, the legislature made them legal by establishing a farmer's winery license of $25 per year for anyone making only light wine from fruit of his own production. From twenty-eight such small producers, selling their wines at retail, in 1937, the number dwindled, because few of their sons were interested in winemaking, until only two were left in 1972, still making Labrusca wines.

The wine revolution in Oregon started at that Vinifera vineyard near Roseburg, mentioned two paragraphs earlier. The man who planted it is the father of today's Oregon fine wine industry. When Richard Sommer was studying agronomy at UC Davis in the 1950s, he took an introductory course in viticulture taught by Professor Maynard Amerine. For six years after leaving college, Sommer worked at odd jobs, served a hitch in the army in Korea, then spent another year at the University, uncertain of what he wanted to do. Finally he made up his mind to grow grapes. Remembering what Dr. Amerine had taught, that the finest wine grapes in California are grown in the cooler vineyard districts, Sommer went where it is still cooler, to Oregon. An uncle of his lived in the Rogue River Valley and grew Vinifera table grapes, but Sommer found that locality still too warm. He went farther north, testing the grapes in each locality. At Roseburg in the Umpqua Valley he found some Zinfandels in the eighty-year-old Doerner's Winery vineyard that tested right. In 1961 he bought a hillside farm on Elgarose Road ten miles west of Roseburg, planted vines from the Napa Valley, and bonded his winery two years later. His wines at first were not very good because his methods and cellar equipment were faulty, but one of his White Rieslings was sound and well balanced with the true Riesling aroma, evidence that the Umpqua Valley can produce fine white wine. In a few years his wines improved enough to become featured in gourmet shops and restaurants in Portland, and they even began winning customers in California. In 1975, Sommer built a new 10,000-gallon Hillcrest Vineyard winery with stainless-steel tanks and with oak barrels for aging. He added a tasting room, and he now also produces Chardonnay, Gewürztraminer, Sémillon, Sauvignon Blanc, Zinfandel, and Pinot Noir.

In the same year that Sommer bonded his winery, another Californian named Charles Coury, a climatology graduate of UC at Los Angeles, quit his job selling European wines and enrolled at Davis to learn scientific winegrowing. On winning his master's degree, Coury spent a year in France studying how wine is grown in cool climates. Then, unaware that Sommer had preceded him, Coury, too, chose Oregon as the place to grow great wines. "Roseburg is fine, but too warm for the very greatest whites, which I wanted to grow," Coury says. The locality he chose was the Tualatin Valley, an offshoot of the Willamette thirty miles west of Portland. In 1966 he moved with his wife Shirley and two teen-age sons into a century-old farmhouse on David Hill Road, three miles northwest of Forest Grove, began planting his vineyard and building his winery. In 1972 he began selling the first Charles Coury Vineyards Riesling, Gewürztraminer, and Pinot Noir. The knoll on which Coury planted his vineyard is known to his neighbors as Wine Hill because it was the site of a pre-Prohibition winery. Ernst Reuter, who came from Germany in the 1880s, made a wine there he called Klevner, one of the German names for Chardonnay. Reuter's daughter told Coury that her father's wine was awarded a silver medal at the 1904 St. Louis Exposition. Old residents recall how people would drive to Wine Hill in their buggies from Forest Grove on Sunday afternoons. When they got tipsy, their horses would find the way home, one of the advantages of the era before automobiles. Coury's son Charles joined the winery in 1977 following a year of study at enological institutes in France and Germany. The vineyard has been expanded to fifty-seven acres. A tasting room has been added, and the Coury wines now include Pinot Noir, Chardonnay,

Sylvaner Fumé, a botrytized Riesling, Gewürztraminer, and Muscat Ottonel.

On a rainy January day in 1962, David Lett, a new graduate of the University of Utah, was in San Francisco waiting to start training for a career in dentistry. Having nothing else to do, he visited wineries in the Napa Valley and discovered that wine-growing appealed to him more than dentistry. He enrolled for a two-year viticulture course at UC Davis, earned the bachelor of science degree, then spent nine months visiting the wine countries of Europe, and decided to grow Pinot Noir in Oregon. The locality he chose was the red hills of Dundee in Yamhill County, overlooking the Willamette Valley. In 1965 he planted the valley's first Vinifera vineyard started in five decades. His bride Diana saw a red-tailed hawk soaring to its nest in a nearby tree and named the vineyard The Eyrie. In 1970 the Letts bonded the Eyrie Vineyard winery in a refrigerated former poultry processing plant in nearby McMinnville and a year later introduced their first "Oregon Spring Wine." The Letts specialize in Limousin-oak-aged Pinot Noir and Chardonnay, but also produce Pinot Gris, Pinot Meunier, White Riesling, and Muscat Ottonel. Their wines are sold mostly to restaurants and to customers on their mailing lists, whom they invite to periodic tastings.

The fourth pioneer in Oregon's winegrowing revival is Richard Erath, another emigré from California. On a vacation trip through Oregon in 1967, he bought some of Richard Sommer's grapes, took them home, and made them into wine. Erath, an electronic engineer, then moved with his wife Kina and their children to Beaverton, Oregon, and bought fifty acres in the foothills of the Chehalem Mountains. In 1972, when the vineyard was three years old, he bonded the Erath Vineyards Winery two miles west of Dundee beside Crabtree Park on Worden Hill Road. A year later, a wine-buff Seattle lumber executive named Calvert Knudsen dropped by, tasted Erath's first vintage, and employed him to plant a Knudsen vineyard. Knudsen became a partner in the winery. In 1976, with the two vineyards totaling eighty-six acres, a new 40,000-gallon winery was built and a bottle-fermented Chardonnay champagne was added to the half-dozen Knudsen and Erath wines. Some are labeled Erath, some Knudsen, and still others Knudsen-Erath, depending on which vineyard produced the grapes. There also are two Erath wines with proprietary names, a red blend named Webfooter and a white of Pinot Noir called Turkey wine.

A dozen newer wineries are now scattered through the

Willamette and Tualatin Valleys between Banks, west of Portland, and the state capital at Salem. Wine-touring has become a diversion for Portlanders, who head west and south on weekends to the Oregon wine country served by Highways 8, 47, and 99.

Northwest of Forest Grove, on Seavy Road across a hill from Coury's winery, is the 22,000-gallon Tualatin Vineyard cellar. In 1972 William Lee Fuller, a UC Davis classmate of Coury and Lett, left his job as winemaker at the Louis Martini winery and moved from the Napa Valley with his wife Virginia and their four children to the 160 acres they had bought in Oregon's Tualatin Valley with San Francisco investment banker William Malkmus the year before. They began planting a vineyard on a south-facing slope, equipped a former strawberry shed as a temporary winery, and made their first wines of grapes from Washington's Yakima Valley. Five years later they had completed their modern winery with a tasting room that is open weekends. Their vineyard was bearing grapes, and they were shipping excellent White Riesling, Gewürztraminer, Pinot Noir Rosé, and Dry Muscat of Alexandria to Malkmus for sale in California.

The third winery west of Portland is the 7,000-gallon Côtes de Colombe cellar on Graham Road two miles west of Banks. It is on a six-acre vineyard planted in 1969 by Joseph and his wife Betty. Joe Coulombe sold home-winemaking supplies and taught home winemaking for several years at Portland Community College before starting to make his own for sale. Another winery in Washington County is the 5,000-gallon Elk Cove cellar, bonded by Dr. Joe Campbell and his wife Patricia in 1977 on the twenty-acre vineyard they had begun planting five years before. A herd of elk in the neighborhood inspired the winery's name. It is on Olson Road three miles southwest of Gaston.

Four miles south of Hillsboro, on Burkhalter Road off Highway 219, is the 50,000-gallon Oak Knoll Winery, a former dairy barn. Electronic engineer Ronald Vuylsteke and his wife Marjorie began making rhubarb and berry wines there in 1970. Marjorie taught home-winemaking classes and kept the winery going until Ron left his job to give their business his full time. They later planted a vineyard and now also make grape wines with the help of their daughter and five sons. Their tasting room is open Thursday, Saturday, and Sunday afternoons.

On Vandermost Road five miles south of Beaverton via Highway 210 is the 6,000-gallon Ponzi Vineyard winery, bonded in 1974 on the ten-acre vineyard Richard and Nancy Ponzi, emigrés from California's Santa Clara Valley, began planting four years before. Richard taught mechanical engineering at Portland Community College while waiting for the vineyard to bear grapes. He organized and headed the Winegrowers Council of Oregon in 1972. The Ponzi Vineyard wines are Chardonnay, White Riesling, Pinot Noir, a Chardonnay-Pinot Blanc blend called Oregon Harvest Wine, and the first white wine of Pinot Noir produced in the Northwest. They can be tasted at the winery by appointment on weekends.

Five miles from Newberg, in the foothills of the Chehalem Mountains, is a nineteen-acre Pinot Noir and Chardonnay vineyard, planted by David and Ginny Adelsheim in 1972 when David was the sommelier at L'Omelette Restaurant in Portland. Five years later they began building the 6,000-gallon Adelsheim Vineyard winery, with their first vintage due in 1978.

The Sokol Blosser Winery, bonded in 1977, is two miles south of Dundee on Blanchard Lane. Portland land-use planner William Blosser and his wife, the former Susan Sokol, had planted their forty-acre vineyard, mainly of Pinot Noir, Gewürztraminer, and White Riesling, six years before. They planned to build a tasting room when their first vintage would be ready for sale.

Off Rice Lane two miles northeast of Amity is the 5,000-gallon Amity Vineyards winery, opened in 1976 by population researcher Myron Redford, his mother Ione, and partner Janis Checchia. Their first wine was a Pinot Noir Nouveau, followed by a dry White Riesling, a Sémillon, and an oak-aged Pinot Noir.

Twelve miles northwest of the state capitol in Salem is an eighteen-acre vineyard planted in 1976 by former Seattle naval architect Eric Winquist and his son Victor with Chardonnay and Pinot Noir, especially to make Oregon champagne, but at this writing they had not yet built a winery.

On Fourteenth Street in Salem, a mile east of the capitol, is Oregon's biggest winery, the 160,000-gallon Honeywood cellar, built in 1934 to make wine from Oregon berries and currants. Former California winery sales executive William Miller added a tasting room when he became Honeywood's manager in 1970.

More young vineyards can be seen on south-facing hillsides in the lower Willamette Valley as far south as Eugene in Lane County. The first winery there is the 10,000-gallon cellar bonded in 1977 on the seventeen-acre Forgeron Vineyard on Sheffler Road, a mile northwest of Elmira. George Leland Smith and his wife Linda planted the vineyard in 1970 with Pinot Noir, Chardonnay, Gewürztraminer, and Pinot Gris. Its name, Forgeron, is the word for Smith in French, a language George learned while spending four years in the diplomatic service in France.

The Umpqua Valley around Roseburg, where Richard Sommer's Hillcrest Vineyard is, now has a total of three wineries and soon may have a fourth. Twelve miles southwest of Sommer's winery are the vineyard and 10,000-gallon winery of Paul and Mary Bjelland, established in 1969 on the Reston-Tenmile Road. Bjelland, a former California school teacher, organized the Oregon Winegrowers Association and in 1970 founded the first Oregon Wine Festival.

The third Umpqua Valley winery is a 2,400-gallon cellar on the four-acre Jonicole Vineyard off Highway 42 five miles south of Roseburg, a half mile from the Winston exit from Interstate 5. The name "Jonicole" consists of the first names of its owners, young viticulturist Jon Marker and Tucson and Napa college biology instructors Nic Busch and Cole Cornelius. The three friends once dreamed of becoming winegrowers in Napa County, where Cornelius and Marker lived, but land there proved too expensive. Traveling north in 1973, they found this four-year-old Cabernet and Chardonnay vineyard for sale, bought it, built the winery and its tasting room, and in 1977 put their first three wines on sale. Jon Marker and his wife Laurie live at the winery; Cornelius drives north periodically from Napa, and Busch comes from Arizona in summer to help.

The Umpqua Valley should soon have a fourth winery. Calvin Scott Henry III, whose family have lived at Umpqua for a century, has a thirteen-acre test vineyard of Gewürztraminer, Pinot Noir, and Chardonnay, planted in 1972, on his 5,000-acre livestock, prune, and wheat farm. Henry and his wife Sylvia have plans for a 20,000-gallon winery to be built in 1979 a mile west of Umpqua on the Sutherlin-Umpqua Road. If all goes as planned, the vineyard may be expanded to 500 acres, the largest in Oregon.

Winegrowing is also returning to Oregon's Rogue River Valley, where vineyards and wineries prospered more than a century ago. In 1977, in the Applegate Valley, a tributary of the Rogue, Medford engineer-contractor Frank Wisnovsky and his wife Ann installed equipment for the 10,000-gallon Valley View winery in a farm building on their twenty-three-acre vineyard, planted eight years before. They named it for the Valley View Vineyard winery Peter Britt from Switzerland had established nearby in 1854. The winery is on Applegate Road a mile west of the village of Ruch, eight miles west of Jacksonville and thirty miles southeast of Grants Pass. The first two vintages of Valley View wines were made by William Fuller at the Tualatin Vineyards winery from the Wisnovskys' grapes and those of three other Applegate Valley growers whose vineyards total forty acres. They are former California farm advisor Don Ferrell, who is Valley View's winemaker; David Overacker, and Dick Troon, Applegate Valley's famous carver of carousel animals and birds. Troon, a former Los Angeles engineer, retired in 1967 to his sixty-acre farm and carving shop on Kubli Road, where his wife Jinx paints his animals and birds. A second winery in the area is planned for construction on the thirteen-acre vineyard of Barrie and Roger Layne, neighbors of the Troons. More than sixty Vinifera vineyards have been planted in Jackson and Josephine Counties since 1969.

Oregon still has two of its pre-Prohibition farm wineries. One is the 20,000-gallon Henry's Winery overlooking the Clackamas River at Oregon City, fourteen miles south of Portland. Henry is Henry Endres, Jr., whose father bonded the place in 1936. In addition to a light red Labrusca wine, he makes others of apples, berries, and rhubarb, and a loganberry type he calls "Henry's Lowball." Endres's vineyard is four acres of Concord, Worden, and Campbell's Early, all Labrusca varieties. He thinks this part of the Willamette Valley is better for berries and apples than for grapes. In the Portland suburb of Oak Grove, pixyish spinster Dora Broetje still presides over the little Redwoods Winery, which dates from 1883, but she no longer makes any wine. Her grandfather brought Concord cuttings there from Belleville, Illinois, where there were many vineyards at that time.

• 7 •

How successfully can Oregon and Washington compete with California in Vinifera table wines? The answer will depend on quality and price. The theory that attracted Sommer, Coury, and Lett to Oregon is that the noble grape varieties achieve their highest flavors when they have to struggle to get ripe, which purports to explain the classic wines grown in the miserable climates of the top European districts. A study by UC Davis viticulturists supports the theory. Professors Mark Kliewer and Lloyd Lider found that temperatures lower than those prevailing in most California wine districts produce higher acidity and better color in grapes, but still enough sugar content to make good wines. Another finding in their work, which relates to the cloudy and often rainy weather in western Oregon and in some of California's coastal counties, is that low daylight intensity slows the ripening of grapes. This confirms what Professor Albert Winkler at Davis has taught for many years and stated in his textbook, *General Viticulture:* "Moderately cool weather, under which ripening proceeds slowly, is favorable for the production of dry table wines of quality."

The winegrowers in rainy western Oregon thus far have aimed only to produce premium-priced wines. To establish a high-quality image, they persuaded their state liquor commission in 1977 to adopt the strictest wine-labeling regulation in the nation for Oregon Vinifera table wines. The regulation sets 90 percent as the minimum content of any grape variety used as a wine name, except 75 percent for Cabernet Sauvignon if blended with other red Bordeaux varieties. It prohibits Oregon Vinifera wines from being labeled with such "generic" names as chablis, rhine, sauterne, claret, chianti, or burgundy. The labels must bear appellations of origin, such as Oregon, American, county names, or Willamette, Umpqua, or Rogue Valley, and each wine must be made entirely of grapes grown in the appellation area. The regulation also sets a 2 percent limit on the addition of sugar to the wines, effective in 1981, but the limit can be exceeded if the liquor commission permits.

Vinicultural research is being pursued actively by Oregon State University. A table wine research advisory board, to be financed by a $10 per ton assessment on grapes crushed for wine, was created by the Oregon Legislature in 1977. In the same year, partly with federal funds from the Northwest Regional Commission, test plantings were made in Oregon, Washington, and Idaho of early-maturing German and French clones of Riesling, Pinot Noir, and Chardonnay.

• 8 •

Idaho, like Oregon, had vineyards and wineries long before Prohibition. At the 1898 Chicago World's Fair a prize was awarded to the wine of Robert Schleisler, whose vineyard was in the Clearwater River Valley near Lewiston. J.E. Moore operated the Shaeffer Vineyards winery near Ahsahka in the early 1900s. After Repeal, Gregory Eaves had his winery near Juliaetta for several years.

Grape-planting fever spread from neighboring Washington and Oregon into Idaho in 1969, when it appeared that table wine might soon be freed from the Idaho state monopoly liquor stores and allowed to be sold in food outlets. The legislature voted the change in 1971, and wine use in the state immediately rose, jumping 600 percent in six years. That was when grape planting began in earnest. Much of it was of Concords in the Boise Valley because a grape-juice plant was set up at Meridian. Farmers elsewhere in Idaho planted Vinifera and French hybrids.

In 1971, several University of Idaho faculty members, enthusiastic about a winegrowing feasibility study they had made, opened a winery in the village of Troy, seven miles east of the Moscow campus. Their wine of French hybrids was drinkable, but the winery proved a losing proposition and was closed after three years. Then the Meridian grape-juice plant also closed, and soon more than 200 acres of Idaho's new vineyards were uprooted. In 1976, University geography professors Nancy and John Hultquist, though still hopeful for Idaho winegrowing in the future, gave a lecture entitled "The Rise and Fall of the Idaho Grape Industry."

Their lecture was premature. A second Idaho winery was opened in 1976 by apple grower William Broich, with television cameras recording the event, at his young vineyard on highway 16 at Emmett, twenty-five miles northwest of Boise. His wife Penny named it Sainte Chapelle for a church she had admired on a trip to France. Their enologist, Professor Bruce Schatz, chairman of chemistry at the College of Idaho, chose perfect Riesling grapes for the inaugural vintage from the Symmes Vineyard at Marsing, near the Snake River, thirty miles from the winery. Sainte Chapelle 1976 Idaho State White Riesling equaled most premium California Rieslings. It won a bronze medal at the Enological Society 1977 northwest wine competition in Seattle, and soon sold out at ten dollars a bottle.

There again is grape fever in Idaho, although there are two obstacles to extensive plantings. One is Idaho wheat growers' widespread use of the 2,4-D herbicide, to which grapevines are especially sensitive. The other is Idaho winter temperatures, which occasionally drop to twenty below zero. But University extension horticulturist Anton Horn, testing Vinifera plantings since 1972, has found they produce high quality reliably in the Sunny Slope district below Caldwell and Wilder, and in the Salmon River Valley between Whitebird and Riggins. In the Clearwater River Valley, meteorologist Robert Wing has grown Vinifera successfully since 1972 at his home east of the Lewiston

Airport, producing wines that I have admired and that have scored highly in competitive blind tastings.

Idaho still had 300 acres of producing vineyards in 1977, and there were reports that grape planting might begin again.

• 9 •

Arizona, too, grows Vinifera, and may someday become a wine-producing state. The Grand Canyon State is already eighth among the states in grape production, but its usual 12,000-ton crop consists of table-grape varieties such as Thompson, Cardinal, and Perlette, grown in irrigated desert areas west of Phoenix, in the Salt River Valley to the east, and in Yuma County, which borders California and Mexico. In blazing desert heat, the grapes ripen early and reach the eastern fresh fruit markets ahead of grapes from California's Arvin and Delano districts. Arizona once had a winery at Glendale, but only to distill leftover grapes into wine spirits, and it did not operate after 1966.

If a team of scientists at the University of Arizona in Tucson are right, Arizona can also produce table wines of high enough quality to compete with California. It can be done, they believe, by planting "varietal" grapes in the mountains of eastern Arizona, where at high elevations there are climates as cool as the California coastal valleys, Regions I, II, and III.

Nine test vineyards of such varieties as Barbera, Cabernet Sauvignon, Gamay, Pinot Noir, Ruby Cabernet, and Sauvignon Blanc were planted in 1972 by Dr. Gordon Dutt, a soil specialist, and Dr. Eugene Mielke, a horticulturist. In 1976, Dr. Dutt flew a rented plane to the vineyards and brought the grapes to an experimental winery at the University. There Dr. Wade Wolfe, who earned his doctorate at the University of California with Dr. Harold Olmo, made them into wines. The musts were in balance with grape sugar, acidity, and color, and a tasting panel pronounced the wines of commercial quality.

Before the scientists recommend planting of wine grape vineyards in Arizona, however, solutions must be found for such problems as soil fungi, mineral content, and water storage.

The research is financed by the Four Corners Regional Commission, created by Congress in 1968 to stimulate the economy of Arizona, New Mexico, Colorado, and Utah. It includes similar test plantings in the other three states and the production and evaluation of the resulting wines.

• 10 •

New Mexico, where winegrowing began long before wine grapes reached California, has two new modern wineries and is likely soon to have more.

When the Rio Grande Valley and neighboring west Texas were colonized by Spaniards early in the seventeenth century, grapes were cultivated at the first Franciscan missions to make wines for the Mass. The grapes apparently were the same Mission variety that the Franciscans brought to California from Mexico more than a century later. General Stephen Kearny reported finding viniculture well established in the Rio Grande Valley when he took possession of New Mexico in 1846 to proclaim it a territory of the United States. W.H. Davis in his book, *El Gringo,* published in 1857, described the claret of Bernalillo as "better than that imported from France" and added that "if there was a convenient market to induce an extensive cultivation of the grape . . . wine would become one of the staples of the country, which would be able to supply a large part of the demand in the United States instead of importing it from Europe."

Scores of vineyards and wineries thrived in the Rio Grande and Pecos valleys during the nineteenth century and in the early twentieth until Prohibition in 1920 forced the wineries to close. A dozen of them reopened at Repeal along the roadsides at Algodones, Bernalillo, Corrales, Albuquerque, Belen, Sandoval, Dōna Ana, Mesilla, and Las Cruces. Then, faced with competition from bulk shipments of California wineries, the wineries dwindled in number until by 1977 only the three at Corrales, Albuquerque, and Mesilla remained. Some of them were making their wines of California grapes.

Just when New Mexico's last wineries were closing their doors, the nationwide wine boom created new interest in winegrowing in the state. A move to revive the two-centuries-old industry got under way. Physicists John Lilley of Los Alamos and Baron Brumley of Albuquerque, both hobbyist winegrowers, organized the New Mexico Vine and Wine Society in 1974. One of their members, Italian-trained professional horticulturist Louis Gattoni, made a survey that showed vines growing successfully in seven different regions of the mountainous state. The Four Corners Regional Commission financed the planting of test vineyards and the making of wines at Tucson.

The first new wineries built in New Mexico in at least four

decades were constructed in 1977 and others, including Lilley and Brumley, were planning to build their own. One is the 5,000-gallon La Viña winery off Farm Road 28 six miles west of Anthony in Doña Ana County. Dr. Clarence Cooper, a professor of physics at the University of Texas campus in El Paso, built it of adobe on his flourishing seven-acre Vinifera vineyard. The other is the 40,000-gallon Viña Madre, scheduled to open in 1978 on the Dexter Highway (state route 2), thirteen miles south of Roswell in the Pecos River Valley. Its owners are James and John Hinkle, grandsons of a former New Mexico governor, and James's wife Elaine. It is a two-story brick structure in the style of a Spanish hacienda. The Hinkles' forty-acre vineyard, of all the "noble" Vinifera varieties, was planted in 1972.

In 1976 young Anthony Claiborne, trained in enology at U C Davis and in three California wineries, took over and partly modernized the old Rico's Winery in Albuquerque, which was about to close. On a six thousand-foot-high mountainside near Placitas, Claiborne found a flourishing three-acre Vinifera vineyard. From its black grapes he made a *blanc de noir* wine that he named Ojo de Perdiz (eye of partridge). It was as fine as most premium California wines. Claiborne calls his premium wines Las Animas (the spirits). They include New Mexico Zinfandel, Zinfandel Rosé, El Viejo red table wine, and the Ojo de Perdiz. In addition he continues making the "Rico's Pure Grape Wine" that the old winery sold in jugs until the founder, Enrico Gradi, died in 1974.

Claiborne also serves as vineyard project leader for New Mexico State University under the Four Corners program. He says the intensity of solar radiation at the altitudes of some New Mexico vineyards (6,900 feet above Placitas, 4,000 feet at Las Cruces, 3,500 at Roswell) gives these regions climates that by the University of California system would be classified as Regions I, II, and III.

In arid New Mexico, with annual rainfall ranging from eight inches at Albuquerque to ten inches at Roswell, most of the vineyards have been irrigated by ditches from the rivers. Exposed on river bottom land to below-zero winter temperatures, vines in the northern Rio Grande Valley have been covered with earth each autumn in order to survive. But in southern New Mexico and at high elevations with air drainage as at Placitas, vines require no winter cover and are irrigated from wells or from mountain springs.

Besides Claiborne's excellent Las Animas wines, I have tasted several others equally fine that were made by Dr. Wolfe at Tucson from New Mexico grapes. The time may not be far distant when Land of Enchantment wines (New Mexico's official nickname) will be admired by the nation's connoisseurs.

• 11 •

Utah, land of the Prohibitionist Mormons, grows wine grapes as well as Labrusca varieties and has a winegrowing history that is unknown to most members of that Church. Many farmers in northern Utah grow Concords for home use and for sale. But in the Virgin River Valley of southwestern Utah, called "Dixie" for its warm summers and mild winters, there are many small vineyards of Vinifera varieties, such as Missions and Thompson Seedless, and an old three-story stone winery at Toquerville in Washington County in which the Mormons once produced wine.

J. Walter Fleming of Lodi found the winery by chance while touring the valley some years ago. Inside he found casks and an ancient wine press that showed evidence of generations of use. Local residents told him that wine for Communion had been made there from the 1860s until about 1910. On a later visit, Fleming found the building converted to a granary; all the traces of winemaking were gone.

Knowing that devout Latter-day Saints are teetotalers and are forbidden even coffee and tea, I wrote to the Mormon church historian in Salt Lake City for further information. By return mail came explanatory excerpts from *The Doctrine and Covenants,* which contains the revelations given to Prophet Joseph Smith, the founder of Mormonism; and a mass of historical details about past winemaking in southern Utah. The Saints there made wine not only for the Holy Sacrament, but for medicine, celebrations, and for sale to the Gentiles.

The original Mormons regularly used wine—"yea, pure wine of the grape"—at their services when the Church was organized in 1830 at Fayette, New York, for the Book of Mormon is winier than the Bible. The Saints then became persecuted for their polygamous ways, and were driven from New York to Ohio, then to Missouri and Illinois. One day in Pennsylvania, Prophet Smith was on his way to buy some wine for a religious service, when he was met by a heavenly messenger. "It mattereth not what ye shall eat or what ye shall drink when ye partake of the Sacrament," the messenger told him, according to *The Doctrine and Covenants.* On this revelation, the Mormons now base their use of water instead of wine for Communion. But in so doing, they ignore the rest of the revelation, for the heavenly messenger continued: "A commandment I give unto you, that you shall not purchase wine neither strong drink of your enemies; wherefore, you shall partake of none except it is made new among you." This clearly permits Mormons to use homemade wine, provided it is new. Their Church, however, construes "new" as permitting only unfermented juice.

This was not the view of President Brigham Young, the genius who led the Mormons to Utah in 1847 following the murder of Smith and his brother Hyrum in Missouri. Brigham Young during the 1850s sent Mormon colonists from Salt Lake to southern Utah expressly to plant cotton fields, sugar-cane plantations, and vineyards. He directed them to build wine cellars and to make as much wine as they could. He named an experienced winemaker from Germany, John Naegle, to take charge of the wine industry. Mission grape cuttings, a wine press, and a brandy distillery were brought from California. Brigham Young gave specific instructions for winemaking: "First, by lightly pressing, make white wine. Then give a heavier pressing and make colored wine." He ordered that the wine be "properly graded in quality . . . then stored in oak barrels as far as possible."

He permitted the wine to be drunk for Communion, but he guarded the Saints' sobriety. This he did by ordering special drinking vessels to be made for the Sacrament—"tumblers that will hold a swallow and no more."

"If my counsel is taken," Brigham Young added, "this wine will not be drunk here but will be exported." His counsel wasn't taken. The Dixie Mormons drank the wine at their social functions and used it as an article of trade. They also paid their tithes to the Church in wine, though not of their best, which they reserved for themselves. The Tithing Office at St. George finally decreed that tithes must be paid in other produce or in cash.

Winegrowing in southern Utah reached its peak at the turn of the century, then declined because by then the Church frowned on the Mormons' drinking and because their wines couldn't compete with the better article coming from California.

Not only do wine grapes still grow in "Dixie," but an effort recently was made to revive the local winegrowing industry, apparently inspired by the national boom in table wine consumption and by the promise of irrigation from the Virgin River. Beginning in 1963, Utah State University made test plantings of thirty Vinifera varieties—including such premium wine grapes as White Riesling, Gewürztraminer, Chenin Blanc, and Pinot Noir—on the Clifford Reusch farm in Washington County. University Extension Agent Don Huber, stationed there, says the results were so promising that three farmers have planted new commercial vineyards of Thompsons which they sell to teetotaling Mormons to make grape juice. There has been talk of building a winery there, but the project has not progressed.

• 12 •

In Colorado, a group of hobbyists in 1973 planted about twenty acres of Chardonnay, White Riesling, Cabernet Sauvignon, and other "noble" grape varieties in a fruit-growing area around Palisade, east of Grand Junction, where winters are relatively mild. They hoped to sell their grapes to a winery in Denver, but it was closed in 1974. With their vines already bearing grapes, they planned to start their own Colorado or Rocky Mountain Vineyards winery in Denver. To make it economically feasible, the Colorado Legislature in 1977 passed a farm-winery law modeled after Pennsylvania's. Meanwhile, the grapes were sold to home winemakers. Leaders of the winery group are retired naval officer George Zimmerman of Palisade, writer-artist Menso Boissevain, and James Sewald, proprietor of the Wine-Art winemaking-supply firm in Denver.

There also is a wine-grape vineyard in Montana. Dr. M.J. "Jay" Winship, an internist trained in California, has harvested three crops from an acre near the city limits of Missoula, and is already thinking of starting a winery.

• 13 •

The westernmost American vineyard of wine grapes is 2,000 feet high near Ulupalakua on Maui, second largest of the Hawaiian Islands, 2,000 miles across the Pacific from California. The 4,000-gallon Tedeschi Vineyard winery was bonded in 1977 when the six-acre vineyard was three years old. Its first vintage was of a dry pineapple wine, but Chardonnay, Chenin Blanc, and Carnelian wines were due in the following year.

Winegrowing is not new to the Hawaiian Islands, where in the semi-tropical climate grapevines yield two crops per year. King Kamehameha the Great, who united all the islands under his rule, granted land near Honolulu to Spanish horticulturist Francisco de Paula Marín in 1814 to grow wine for the royal household. Portuguese immigrants from Madeira later had vineyards and wineries on the islands of Hawaii and Maui.

Emil Tedeschi, who had worked in wineries near his home in the Napa Valley, on a vacation trip to the islands became acquainted with C. Pardee Erdman, who raises cattle at Ulupalakua on the least rainy lee side of Mt. Haleakala, a dormant volcano, and arranged with Erdman to plant a vineyard there. When experience shows him which grape varieties do best, Tedeschi plans to expand the vineyard to 100 acres, but to harvest only one crop per year.

21

The Kosher Winemakers

T HE single best-known North American wine, sold halfway around the world and never duplicated elsewhere, is the syrupy-sweet red Concord grape type with the Hebrew word kosher on its label.

Nine tenths of its consumers have no clear idea of what kosher means, not being members of the Jewish faith, but they happen to like the wine's taste. To them, kosher—the Hebrew religious word for proper, fit, or clean—suggests that a wine or food has a pronounced flavor, as in pickles, sausages, and in the "especially sweetened" purplish-red wine with the piquant, grapy Concord taste. Though nowadays there are dozens of wines of different flavors and colors labeled kosher, the one you will find in stores throughout the United States and in hotels as distant as Japan and Australia is Manischewitz Concord Grape in the square bottle with the six-pointed Star of David on its label. It is the one that made kosher a part of the flavor-language of wine.

Dozens of wineries in this country and Canada now produce the kosher Concord type, but to call it kosher they must make it under the strict supervision of an orthodox rabbi, from the picking of the grapes to the bottling of the wine. Each such winery must use separate crushers, tanks, and bottling machinery for the wine in order for the label to bear the rabbi's *hechsher* seal.

Oddly enough, the sweet red Concord kosher type became the best-known American wine purely by happenstance. At Repeal, young Leo Star, the son of a cantor from Russian Poland, bought a few wine tanks, rented a store with a double cellar on Wooster Street in New York City, ambitiously named it the Monarch Wine Company, and began bottling bulk port and sherry from California. Leo Star had bottled kosher port and sherry during the dry years, when anybody could buy it legally by merely joining a Hebrew congregation; but that business had died together with the Eighteenth Amendment.

As a sideline after Repeal, Star also bottled a small quantity of a kosher New York State extra-sweet Concord wine called Mount Zebo, which he also had sold during Prohibition. Its only buyers, when the dry era ended, were New York orthodox Jewish families who were accustomed to using it once a year as an essential part of their Passover feast, or *Seder,* in spring.

When the Passover season of 1934 came to an end, those New York store proprietors who had stocked Mount Zebo for their customers found they had quantities of it left unsold. They told Star to take it all back because they could not sell it again until the following spring. Star took it back, and most of it spoiled. Before the 1935 Passover season, Star notified the store owners that they should order only as much Mount Zebo as they could sell—that he would accept no more returns. Again after Passover, they had leftover stock and wanted Star to take it back. He refused and waited for complaints.

To Star's amazement, instead of complaints, the stores sent him rush reorders. Their non-Jewish customers were trying the kosher wine, finding they liked the sweet Concord taste, and were coming back for more.

Star had launched the kosher wine industry, but he did not know it yet. When more reorders came, he thought the wine sold because it was kosher, so he contracted with the old firm of Manischewitz, famed for its kosher food products such as matzos, to let him use the Manischewitz name on his wine. When his "Man Oh Manischewitz What a Wine" radio commercials went on the air in 1945, he knew that the kosher wine type ("that Massachusetts wine" to many of its buyers) was here to stay.

It was also a happenstance that gave Star's biggest competitor its start. In Chicago on September 23, 1947, at 5:17 P.M., Max Cohen and Henry Marcus, owners of the Wine Corporation of America, sadly opened the drain cocks of their wine tanks and let all 40,000 gallons of their Barloma California port and sherry flow down the drain because something had gone wrong with the wine. The only stock they had left was a small quantity of their kosher sweet red Concord wine called Mogen David (Shield of David), leftover from the preceding Passover season. Until more port and sherry could arrive from California, they began promoting the sale of Mogen David to the nonJewish trade as "the wine like Grandma used to make." It soon so far outsold their Barloma wines that the company became the Mogen David Wine Corporation.

Other vintners saw the sensational sales successes of Manischewitz and Mogen David and rushed into production with their own sweet Concord wines. Gallo in California introduced one called Galloette, backed by a huge billboard advertising campaign. The big Welch Company jumped into the market with its Concord Refreshment Wine. But Gallo and Welch both had ignored a key element in the semantics of thirst, that a wine's label influences its taste. Without Hebrew names and characters and the word kosher, their sweet Concord wines didn't taste the same, and they failed to sell. Other wineries in California, New York, New Jersey, Michigan, the State of Washington, and in Canada saw the light, employed local orthodox rabbis to make their Concord wines kosher, and designed labels liberally adorned with Hebrew characters and stars. Kosher wines with such names as Mazel Tov, Sholom, Mizpah, Maccabee, and Hadassim became a permanent part of their trade.

However, there seems to be a limit on how much specially sweetened red kosher Concord wine people can drink. Sales in the United States rose to ten million gallons in the 1960s but have grown relatively little since. Manischewitz and Mogen David realized that their customers' tastes were turning from sweet toward dry. They began turning out semidry and dry white and pink kosher wines, and started making kosher burgundies, sauternes, rosés, and champagnes. Manischewitz then expanded with a line of nonkosher Colonial Heritage New York State wines, began importing a line of European wines named Tytell, and in 1977 introduced a trio of semi-dry, bubbly, very drinkable Labrusca-flavored kosher wines named Light Concordia White, Pink, and Red. The Mogen David Corporation, purchased in 1970 by the Coca-Cola Bottling Company of New York, has moved into nonkosher semi-dry light table wines and into the "pop wine" market with products called Cold Bear and Black Bear.

Both big kosher wine companies also grow increasing proportions of their own grapes. Mogen David now claims to be the fifth largest American vintner, with 5 million gallons in its two wineries in Chicago and its three in Westfield, New York. Monarch (Manischewitz) has grown to 3 million gallons at the Bush Terminal in Brooklyn, where it has been located since 1938.

Because kosher wines are the only sacramental wines normally sold to the public in this country, they are often used in Christian churches. I once asked the rector of the Episcopal Church in Sausalito which wine he was using for Communion. He couldn't remember the name, except that it was a sacramental wine, but he soon found the bottle for me. It was Manischewitz kosher Concord Grape.

The State of Israel, which displays the Mogen David shield on its flag, now ships kosher wines to the United States. Some of them are even labeled as Concord, though they lack the flavor of the American grape.

22

Wines of Canada

ANADA produces many good wines, including some that are excellent by other
countries' standards, and also makes some unorthodox wines
that are not found anywhere else. The best Canadian wines are
still little known outside the Dominion, however, because their
growing popularity in Canada is something new. For Canada,
too, had Prohibition during most of the years when the United
States were legally dry, and its provincial monopoly liquor store
system, set up afterward, has long discouraged the use of wine.

But Canadians returned from the Second World War and
from travel abroad with a taste for table wine, and the postwar
flood of immigration has brought millions of people from the
wine countries of Europe, starting a swing to mealtime wines.
In less than two decades the country's wine consumption
jumped from 10 million gallons, less than five pints per capita,
to 38 million gallons, more than 1.63 gallons per capita, in
1977*. Almost half the total is Canadian-made, and almost
three-fourths is of low-alcohol types. In the five years ending in
1977, light-wine consumption grew twice as rapidly in Canada
as in the United States.

• 2 •

The wine revolution in Canada parallels that below the border
and has brought revolutionary changes in Canadian vineyards
and wineries. In 1977, the wineries in the Dominion's two
grape-growing provinces were allowed for the first time to open
tasting rooms, to offer the public cellar tours, and to sell their
wines to visitors as wineries do elsewhere. Three new farm

*U.S. gallons, not British imperial gallons, which are approximately a fifth larger.

498

wineries, like those in some of the neighboring American states, have opened in Ontario, and an equal number of grape growers have applied for government permission to open farm wineries in British Columbia. Ontario has abolished its fifty-year-old limit on the number of wineries' retail stores, and new winery outlets have opened in conjunction with department stores. Equally important is that the predominantly Labrusca vineyards in both grape-growing provinces are gradually being replanted with French-hybrid and Vinifera grape varieties, and that Canadian wineries have introduced dozens of wines finer than those they had produced in the past. Spurring the improvement is the fact that wines imported from other countries outsold Canadian wines in 1977 for the first time in many years. The Canadian producers are determined to make their wines better than the imports in order to regain their former lead.

• 3 •

The eastern Canadian wine district—the western district is 2,000 miles away beyond the Rocky Mountains—is centered on the slender arm of the Niagara Peninsula that connects southwestern Ontario to Niagara County, New York. This proximity explains why Ontario wines have basically resembled those of New York State. Almost nine tenths of the vineyards of Canada, some 23,000 acres, are concentrated on that narrow strip, which extends westward from Niagara-on-the-Lake some thirty-five miles toward the city of Hamilton. Farmers call it "the Banana Belt of Canada" because the waters of Lakes Ontario and Erie, on its northern and southern shores, moderate the climate and protect the vines from winter damage and frost.

Most of the vineyards are situated below the Niagara escarpment, the 350-foot-high cliff that crosses the Peninsula north of Niagara Falls. Subdivisions and industries are now competing with farms for the most desirable land, and lately some of the vineyards have retreated up the escarpment. At first the growers were fearful that the higher elevation would expose their vines to cold north winds, but they since have found there is better protective air drainage atop the escarpment than below.

Eight of the nation's twenty-five large commercial wineries are located on the Niagara Peninsula and produce nearly three fourths of all Canadian wine.

On Martindale Road outside St. Catharines, near the original Welland Canal built to carry ocean ships around the Falls, is the

1,500,000-gallon Barnes winery, the oldest in Canada. In 1973, its hundredth year, the winery was sold to Reckitt & Colman (French's mustard, Widmer's New York State wines) by the grandsons and great-grandsons of George and Thomas Barnes, who founded it in 1873. The modern winery is built around the original stone-walled underground vaults. The 100-acre vineyard, called Barnesdale, is planted principally with such Labrusca grapes as Agawam, Catawba, Concord, and Diana, but French hybrids have been added lately to make table wines without the Labrusca taste.

Facing Dorchester Road just outside the city of Niagara Falls is Canada's biggest and second oldest winery, by a year, T. G. Bright & Company, with 11 million gallons and 1,200 acres of vineyards. Lumberman Thomas Bright started the company at Toronto in 1874. He moved it sixteen years later and changed its name to Niagara Falls Wine Company, but after his death his family changed it back to Brights. In 1933, Harry Hatch, boss of the Hiram Walker distillery, purchased Brights and hired Dr. John Eoff from Fruit Industries in California to modernize the winery. Eoff had as his assistant a talented young French chemist named Adhemar de Chaunac.

When de Chaunac started work, Brights was producing only ports and sherries. The young Frenchman searched the company's vineyards, which then consisted mainly of Concords, found some Delaware and Catawba grapes, filled two boxes with them, and took them home. He fermented them into a dry table wine and took it to the winery for Eoff and Hatch to taste. Hatch was so impressed that he started Brights making its first table wines.

With the end of the war in Europe, de Chaunac in 1946 brought several dozen French hybrid varieties to Brights from France, and with them a hundred Vinifera vines, including Chardonnay and Pinot Noir. (This, the company's chief viticulturist, George W. B. Hostetter, points out, was before Dr. Konstantin Frank, who introduced Vinifera to the eastern United States, had left Germany for New York.)

Brights' first champagne, de Chaunac's blend of hybrids and Labrusca varieties, was introduced in 1949 and in the following year it won a bronze medal at the California State Fair. A decade later, Brights brought out Canada's first Chardonnay and a Pinot champagne made entirely from Chardonnay and Pinot Noir. The Chardonnay, which I tasted at the winery a few years ago, could have won a medal, too. There was also a Gewürztraminer, not yet on the market, that might have come from

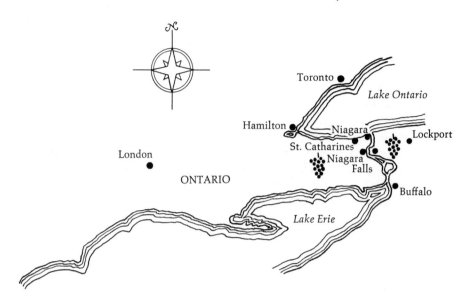

Vineyard Districts of EASTERN CANADA and Niagara County, N.Y.

Alsace. Brights now produces some forty-three different wines. Evidence of their quality is that a tenth of the medals awarded at the Wineries Unlimited eastern wine competition held in Pennsylvania went to Brights' Baco Noir, Du Barry Rosé, and President Port. "President," incidentally, is the name of a rare Munson grape variety from Texas, from which the port is principally made.

De Chaunac retired in 1966 and was fittingly honored by Ontario winegrowers in 1972 when they gave his name to one of the best French hybrid red grapes, Seibel 9549. Brights president, W. Douglas Hatch, recalls when his father, who preferred fine wines to whiskeys, asked de Chaunac to teach Douglas how to make wine: "De Chaunac started me on a ladder taking samples of wine out of the tanks and wouldn't even let me handle a saccharometer at first."

Douglas, whose brother Clifford heads Hiram Walker, is noted for his stable of thoroughbred horses and has given some of them names like Cresta Roja and Cresta Blanca, which are among Brights' many Canadian wine brands.

Also on the outskirts of Niagara Falls is the 5-million-gallon

Château-Gai winery, which dates from 1890. It is now owned by the John Labatt breweries. Château-Gai has two historic distinctions. In 1928 it was the first in North America to make champagne by the Charmat or bulk process, which was perfected in 1907 by Eugene Charmat in France. It also introduced the process to the United States when it opened the Château Gay winery (since closed) across the river at Lewiston, New York. Its other historic contribution was in becoming the first Canadian winery to export some of its wines regularly to Great Britain, starting in 1965. The English connoisseurs who first sampled them at a tasting in London's Ontario House were astonished at their quality, and even more so to learn that any wines are grown in Canada at all. Château-Gai's Algerian-born, French-trained enologist Paul Bosc, in his ninth year with the company, made three of the best Canadian red wines I have thus far tasted, the 1972 Pinot Noir, Cabernet-Merlot, and Gamay Beaujolais.

Off Niagara Parkway a mile north of Queenston is Ontario's first farm or "cottage" winery. It is named Inniskillin for the two-century-old farm on which young nurseryman Donald Ziraldo has planted a twenty-five-acre vineyard of White Riesling, Chardonnay, Gamay Noir, and Gamay Teinturier. Ziraldo started his nursery when he graduated in horticultural science from the University of Guelph in 1971. Karl Kaiser, an economics teacher and home winemaker from Austria, bought some vines from Ziraldo, became his partner and winemaker, and then took advanced studies in biochemistry and bacteriology at Brock University. Ziraldo and Kaiser made the first Inniskillin vintage in 1974 in a converted fruit-packing shed. A year later they were granted the first new Ontario winery license issued since 1929. Their wines thus far include estate-bottled, vintage-dated Gamay Blanc, Gamay Geaujolais and Nouveau, Seyval Blanc, and White Reisling. They also have a Gewürztraminer and a Couderc Muscat, made from purchased grapes. Inniskillin wines have been so well received in Ontario that the partners are preparing to build a new 100,000-gallon winery, treble the cellar's original size.

Ontario's second "cottage winery" is Karl Podamer's champagne cellar on Ontario Street in Beamsville. Podamer's family in Hungary twice had their champagne cellars taken over by the Communist regimes. He emigrated to Toronto in 1956 and earned enough in the meat business to start this cellar with fourteen partners in 1975. His Canadian champagnes are made of French hybrids and Dutchess, the best of the white Labrusca varieties. They are bottle-fermented by the French *méthode champenoise.*

At St. Catharines and Jordan are the Jordan and Ste. Michelle Cellars, totaling 10 million gallons in capacity, owned by the Carling O'Keefe breweries since 1974. Adjoining the Jordan winery, which dates from 1921, is the Jordan Historical Museum of the Twenty. It preserves the life style and relics of the Empire Loyalists who fought on the British side during the American Revolution and who migrated to Canada after the war. The museum's name comes from Twenty Mile Creek, named by the early settlers for the creek mouth's distance from the Niagara frontier.

West of Jordan, via roads lined with vineyards, is the 3-million-gallon Andrés winery at Winona. The stacks of sherry-aging barrels in front of the cellar are a landmark on Queen Elizabeth Way. The first Andrés winery was started in British Columbia in 1961 by Andrew Peller, a Hungarian brewmaster who had sold his brewery at Hamilton, Ontario, several years before. His son, Dr. Joseph Peller, took over Andrés management in 1971 and bought the Winona winery, which was called Beau Chatel when the Imperial Tobacco Company built it in 1967. Andrés and Jordan-Ste. Michelle, each now operating six wineries in as many Canadian provinces, are the Dominion's largest producers of wine.

At Grimsby, east of Winona, is the Rieder Distillery, which since 1973 has been distilling Concord grapes into a Canadian brandy called Bordulac. Ninety miles farther west is the London Winery, still operating in an area where there no longer are vineyards, but where there were many when it was founded in 1925.

During the past century there were wineries as far west as Essex County, opposite Detroit, with their vineyards along the Lake Erie shore. One of the greatest was the Vin Villa Vineyard winery on little Pelee Island, across the international boundary from the Lake Erie Islands of Ohio. Old residents tell how, when the Pelee Island winery was moved to the mainland, its huge casks—too unwieldy to be brought to the mainland on lake boats—were emptied, floated in the lake, hitched to a tugboat, and towed ashore. During Canadian Prohibition, the vineyards in Essex and Kent Counties were replaced by more profitable plantings of vegetables and tobacco. In the late 1960s, when urbanization began to threaten the Niagara Peninsula vineyards, some experimental plantings of grapes were made in the western counties along Lake Erie. Grape yields and quality turned out better than in most of the vineyards farther east.

In 1968, when Allan Eastman was twenty-three, he experimented by planting three acres of vines, including an acre of Vinifera, beside his farm and fruit and vegetable store on Highway 3 west of Blenheim in Kent County. The vineyard did so well that he expanded it to sixty acres, including eight of Riesling and Chardonnay. In 1975, Allan Eastman and his wife Charlotte won government permission to open Ontario's third "cottage winery," which they named Charal, for themselves. Two years later, judges in the eastern wine competition held in Pennsylvania awarded a gold medal to their Charal Chardonnay.

• 4 •

If your interests are in grapes or in wine research, the place to visit in Ontario is the Horticultural Experiment Station at Vineland, off the highway a mile east of Jordan village. There Ralph Crowther can show you the leading wine research laboratory in eastern America, and can introduce you to grape-breeder Oliver (Ollie) Bradt, whose Canadian hybrids are changing the character of many Canadian wines and of some New York and midwestern wines as well.

Crowther, the scientist engaged in wine research, is most noted for his invention of the Crowther-Truscott submerged-culture *flor* sherry-making process, which is revolutionizing the production of dry sherries in Canada and the United States and is even being studied by enologists in the sherry country of Spain. Others have claimed to have invented the process, including a Spanish researcher who even got a patent on it in Spain in 1968. I can testify, however, that Crowther was making his *flor* (Spanish fino-type) sherry at Vineland as far back as 1955, because I was there in July of that year and tasted his then-as-yet-unrevealed "seven-day wonder," the simple, quick way to give sherry the pungent *flor* character which old-time winemakers describe as "the bedbug taste." It takes years to develop by the method used for centuries in Spain. There, the *flor* yeast (*Saccharomyces beticus*) grows naturally as a film on the surface of the wine, but it often fails to do its job, which is how a Spanish sherry becomes an amontillado instead of a fino. Crowther started his work with *flor* yeast in 1952 when the Canadian Wine Institute asked him to try growing it on the surface of wines made from Ontario grapes. At first, Crowther used the Spanish film-yeast method, but the yeast failed to grow on some of his wines. Then he discovered that by agitation—by circulating the *S. beticus* culture through the wine—he could make the yeast work harder and produce the *flor* taste reliably in days instead of years. The Ontario wineries were the first to use his process, and I since have tasted some excellent fino-style sherries in their cellars. Now wineries in the United States have begun adding *flor* wines, made Crowther's way, to many of their sherry blends. The flavor is improved so markedly over that of madeirized (baked) sherries that in years to come sherry with the *flor* character may become the favorite apéritif in Canada and the United States, as it is in the British Isles.

More important than sherry is Vineland's grape-breeding program, because Canadians are learning to appreciate wines without the foxy Labrusca taste. Hundreds of new, nonfoxy wine-grape varieties have been bred at the Vineland station since Ollie Bradt went to work there in 1938. When a new variety, at first designated by a number, has proved itself by several years of testing in the vineyards and wineries, the station releases it to the industry and gives it a name, which in each case begins with the letter *V.* Vineland's first outstanding success was the blue grape named Veeport, released in 1961. At the laboratory I tasted experimental ports made of Veeport, ranging from one to eight years of age. California wineries should be jealous of the lovely bouquets these wines had developed. Veeport and two more Vineland varieties—Vincent for burgundy and Vinered for rosé—have now been widely planted in Canadian vineyards, and Veeport and Vincent have been introduced in some United States vineyards as well.

Vineyard improvement has become the theme of the Niagara Grape and Wine Festival, which is held at St. Catharines during the third week of each September. The festival was started in 1952 to aid tourism with its parade and other events, but its main event now is the crowning of the Grape King, who is chosen from among Ontario growers for the quality of his grape crop. When the king is selected, his vineyard gets an official visit from the premier of the province.

French and Canadian hybrids have replaced many of the Concord vines that once predominated in Ontario. Concords are reported down to 40 percent of the total acreage, compared to 70 percent in New York State. Mechanical grape harvesters, first used in Ontario in 1970, now pick more than half of the crop.

The Ontario wineries have proposed to their provincial government a new set of wine quality standards, stricter than those now in force. It would create a new classification called "Ontario Superior" for table wines made of the Vinifera and French hybrid grapes that have been planted in the province in recent years.

• 5 •

Winemaking began earlier in eastern Canada than in most of the United States. In the year 1636, Jesuit missionaries at Québec were making sacramental wine from the wild grapes that thrive along the St. Lawrence River.

The first commercial winery in Canada was Clair House, established in 1811 by a German ex-soldier, Corporal Johann Schiller, near the shore of Lake Ontario at Cooksville, now a suburb of Toronto. The Toronto *Leader* for July 8, 1867, records that Clair House wines were shipped to France for judging at the Paris Exposition and that the wine jury found them "pure and of excellent quality," comparing them to French *vin ordinaire.*

By the 1890s, there were 5,000 acres of vines and thirteen flourishing wineries in Ontario, but meanwhile the dry crusade in the United States had spread northward into Canada, and towns were voting themselves dry.

Then in 1916 and 1917, while Canadian soldiers were away fighting in Europe, all but one of the Canadian provinces adopted Prohibition laws. Québec, with its French heritage, held out until 1919 and then forbade the sale of liquor, but allowed its people to continue buying wine and beer.

Ontario, then Canada's only wine-producing province, prohibited liquor and beer, but to protect its grape growers, permitted its wineries to continue making wine for local sale. Buyers had to go to the wineries to make a purchase, and by law they could buy no less than a five-gallon keg or a case at a time. The export of wine to foreign countries was also permitted, and when the United States went dry in 1920, several new Ontario wineries opened for business. Canadian wine "exports" rose to levels never reached before or since. Shipments destined ostensibly for faraway countries found their way into the United States despite the American border, lake, and river patrols.

Sailormen along the Canadian shore of Lake Erie still chuckle over recollections of "those one-hour trips to Cuba." When United States Prohibition was repealed, the "exports" of Canadian wines abruptly ceased.

By 1927, Ontario and the neighboring provinces had had enough of Prohibition, and they legalized the sale of liquor. Prohibition had come earlier and had ended sooner in Canada than in the United States. But it left the country's wine industry more handicapped than the industry in the United States was at Repeal, because in place of Prohibition all of the Canadian provinces established government monopoly liquor stores. Until the 1960s, each individual had to buy a two-dollar annual permit in order to purchase any alcoholic beverage. Ontario, however, allowed its wineries to continue selling their wines to consumers. It became easier to buy wine in Ontario than anywhere else in Canada, for besides the government liquor stores, there were fifty-one attractive special wine stores owned by the Ontario wineries. That was the number of wineries in Ontario during Prohibition. The big wineries promptly bought out the small ones and closed them down, because all they wanted was the store licenses. Since 1976, the wineries have been allowed to open as many stores as they wish. The store assortments are limited, however, because a winery may sell only wines of its own production.

Another relic of Prohibition is that Canadian restaurants can buy wine only from the provincial monopoly store systems and must pay the full retail price, plus a service charge. In order to make a profit, the purveyors of course mark up the price. This is why wines in Canadian hotels and restaurants cost more than in such establishments in the United States.

• 6 •

Canada's other winegrowing district is beyond the Rocky Mountains in the far western province of British Columbia. The story of its wines is a curious one, as the following incident will illustrate.

In March 1967, the San Francisco Wine and Food Society and the Medical Friends of Wine were planning to hold a champagne tasting. Having just returned from a research trip to the eastern states and Canada, I suggested that we invite champagne producers outside of California to participate. The committee agreed, and the invitations went out. Acceptances came from nine California wineries, from three located in Canada, three in New York State, and from one each in New Jersey, Ohio, Michigan, and Illinois. When our several hundred members and guests gathered for the event in the Rose Room of San Francisco's Palace Hotel, we faced an array of sixty-seven white, pink, and red sparkling wines—thirty-four from California and thirty-three from outside the state.

As is usual among such tasting audiences in winy San Francisco, those accustomed to California champagnes preferred them to those from the eastern states and Canada, most of which had in varying degrees the Labrusca taste of native American grapes.

But of particular interest to the members of our group were the Canadian champagnes. Typical of the tasters' responses was what "Winemaster" Henry Rubin wrote in his wine column in the San Francisco *Chronicle:* "I was pleased to note some acceptable Canadian wine." He noted that some had "strange" Labrusca flavors, and ended with: "The best one seemed to me the Richelieu De Luxe Champagne Brut of British Columbia."

Because I had visited the British Columbia wineries a few weeks before, I was able to explain to Henry Rubin why he had preferred that particular champagne. It had been made, I told him, entirely from California grapes.

In fact, British Columbia wines have been made partly, and in some years wholly, from California grapes since 1934. The labels say "Canadian champagne," "Canadian sherry," "Canadian burgundy," etc., but some of the grapes have come in refrigerated trucks from California or from the new vineyards in Washington State.

• 7 •

The grape-growing district of British Columbia is the Okanagan Valley, a 120-mile-long, narrow, steep-walled stretch of farmland, lakes, and resorts between the Trepanier Plateau and the Monashee Mountains. It extends from the head of Okanagan Lake, above Vernon on Highway 97, southward across the United States border. When speaking of the Okanagan, you usually include the lower Similkameen River Valley from Keremeos and Cawston to the Washington State line near Osoyoos.

That part of British Columbia was inhabited only by Indians, fur traders, and missionaries until the introduction of placer mining brought gold prospectors after 1860. The Oblate Fathers

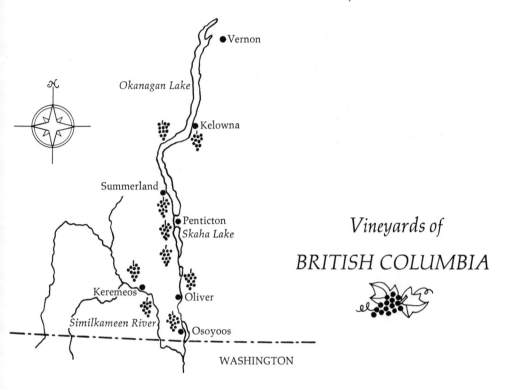

●Vernon

Okanagan Lake

●Kelowna

Summerland ●

●Penticton
Skaha Lake

Keremeos ●
●Oliver

Similkameen River

●Osoyoos

WASHINGTON

Vineyards of

BRITISH COLUMBIA

built a mission about 1864 at a point seven miles south of the present city of Kelowna. The Fathers planted a few vines, but when farmers settled in the valley during the next few decades, they grew apples, peaches, and apricots; nobody thought of planting vineyards.

During the 1920s, the first two British Columbia wineries started operating on Vancouver Island, more than 200 miles west of the Okanagan. The wine they made was not from grapes, but from the loganberries grown north of Victoria on the island's Saanich Peninsula.

About that time a Hungarian winemaker, Dr. Eugene Rittich, visited the Okanagan Valley and thought its climate might be suitable for wine grapes. Most of the valley lies between the 49th and 50th parallels of latitude, which are regarded as the northernmost limits of viticulture; Germany's Rheingau is at 50 latitude and the Champagne district of France is at 49. But the deep waters of Okanagan, Skaha, and the other lakes, dug out by prehistoric glaciers, prevent the temperature from going to extremes and give parts of the Okanagan a growing season as long as 185 days. Farming is on the bench lands above the lake level, and this normally protects the plants from frost. Rainfall is only 8 to 12 inches per year, but water for irrigation is plentiful in the lakes and upland streams.

Dr. Rittich made some experimental plantings that proved him right, and he interested farmer Jesse Willard Hughes in planting a vineyard near the old Oblate Fathers Mission in 1926. Four years later, the first commercial grape wine in British Columbia was made from Hughes's grapes in the Growers' Winery at Victoria.

In 1932, the depth of the Great Depression, Okanagan Valley apples were unsalable at a cent a pound and were rotting on the ground. A Kelowna hardware-store owner named William Andrew Cecil Bennett talked about it with the Italian grocer next door, Pasquale "Cap" Capozzi, and they decided the way to salvage the apples was to turn them into wine. Though both are teetotalers, they became partners and started a winery, Calona Wines Limited, with Bennett as its president. Their apple wine couldn't compete with the Growers' Winery's genuine wine made of Hughes's grapes, so in 1934 Calona started buying grapes from California. The wineries on Vancouver Island began doing the same.

For the next twenty-six years, the British Columbia wineries prospered by making "Canadian wines" almost entirely from California grapes. As wine consumption in the province grew, more B.C. wineries were built.

This was the situation when Bennett, Capozzi's former partner in the Calona winery, became Premier of British Columbia in 1952. He had sold his shares in the winery eleven years earlier when he was first elected to the B.C. parliament.

As premier, teetotaler Bennett turned his attention to the wineries. He decided that if they were to continue selling their wine in the British Columbia government stores, they ought to be required to make it out of B.C. grapes. In 1960, he ordered his Liquor Board to establish quotas, minimum percentages of B.C. grapes which wines made in the province must contain in order to be sold. There then were only 585 acres of vineyards in the Okanagan Valley, so the quota for 1961 was set at 25 percent; but the Board announced it would go up to 50 percent in another year and to 65 percent by 1965.

A stampede to plant more vineyards began. Vines were put into the ground without waiting for grape stakes. In four years the Okanagan Valley vineyards were quadrupled to 2,400 acres. But in December of 1964 a spell of sixteen-below-zero temperatures and forty-mile winds hit the Okanagan, freezing most of

This vineyard facing Okanagan Lake in British Columbia has been thriving since the 1920s, when it was planted by farmer Jesse Willard Hughes.

the vines to the ground. Only 334 tons of grapes were picked in the following autumn, and the Liquor Board rescinded the quota for that vintage. This explains the all-California flavor of the B.C. champagne we tasted at San Francisco in 1967. A decade later, the Okanagan vineyards totaled more than 3,000 acres, and the quota on the proportion of local grapes that B.C. wines must contain had risen to 80 percent.

• 8 •

The Calona Winery was sold by the Capozzi family in 1971 to Standard Brands of Montreal, a subsidiary of Standard Brands in the United States, and its capacity was quadrupled to 4 million gallons. You still could find rotund, cheery "Cap" Capozzi there on occasion because the winery was still headed by his second son, Tom. "Cap" always enjoyed telling how he arrived nearly penniless from Naples in 1905 and worked his way up from a railroad section hand to become the owner of Kelowna's biggest businesses. Calona produces a complete assortment of table, dessert, and sparkling wines. Those which bear its Sommet Blanc, Sommet Rouge, and Okanagan Cellars brands are made almost entirely of French-hybrid grapes.

South of Kelowna, on a knoll overlooking Okanagan Lake, stands one of the most attractive winery buildings in Canada, a mission-style structure with a bell tower. It was named the Mission Hill winery when orchardist R.P. (Tiny) Walrod formed a company to build it in the 1960s, but Walrod died before construction began. In 1969, "Uncle Ben" Ginter, who owned breweries across Canada, bought and renamed it Uncle Ben Ginter's Gourmet Winery. The best-selling wine made by winemaker Joseph Raffeiner was a red called Fuddle Duck. During the 1970s, financial troubles beset Uncle Ben, and the winery was offered for sale. Then came the new regulation allowing B.C. wineries to have tasting rooms and cellar tours and to sell visitors their wines. Other wineries began bidding to buy Mission Hill. At press time, Brights of Ontario had made the highest bid.

At Penticton, between Okanagan and Skaha Lakes thirty-nine miles south of Kelowna, is the million-gallon Casabello winery, built in 1966 by a group of local businessmen headed by former hotel-owner Evans Lougheed. They made the building architecturally attractive, anticipating that B.C. wineries might someday be permitted to receive visitors. When the permission came in 1976, Casabello was the first to open a tasting room. The winery features an "estate selection" of seven Vinifera varieties made by its German-trained winemaker, Tom Hoenisch, in addition to wines with such proprietary names as Fleur de Blanc and Burgon Rouge. It also sells table wines in the plastic "bag in the box" that has become popular for restaurant service in the United States. Lougheed's son-in-law Walter Davidson has a twenty-acre vineyard near Osoyoos, planted in 1972 with French hybrids and such Vinifera varieties as White Riesling, Chardonnay, Chenin Blanc, Gewürztraminer, and Pinot Noir. It supplies the grapes for Casabello's "estate selection" line. The winery was purchased by the Labatt breweries in 1978.

The other two B.C. wineries are in the Vancouver area, 200 miles west of the Okanagan. In Surrey, twenty-five miles southeast of Vancouver, is the 4-million-gallon Ste. Michelle winery, built in 1977 with a partially underground aging cellar and a visitors' reception area. Ste. Michelle is the new name of the Growers' winery, which operated at Victoria on Vancouver Island for fifty-two years until it was purchased by the Carling O'Keefe breweries and moved to this mainland site. It is just off Highway 10 at Johnson and Colebrook Roads. Dieter Güttler, trained at the Geisenheim Institute in Germany, is the winemaster of the three Ste. Michelle and Jordan wineries in Ontario and B.C. Josef Zimmerman, also from Geisenheim, is the assistant winemaster here. The Ste. Michelle B.C. wines include Chardonnay, Grey Riesling, Ruby Cabernet, and proprietary types with such names as Château Blanc, Château Rouge, and Rougelais.

On Vintner Street at Port Moody, ten miles east of Vancouver, is the original Andrés winery. It has grown to 3 million gallons since Andrew Peller had it built in 1961. Visitors are now invited to tour its cellars and taste its B.C. wines, which number more than three dozen, including a pleasant white of Verdelet and an excellent red of B.C.-grown de Chaunac named Similkameen Superior Rouge, of which winemaker Ron Taylor is especially proud. It also produces a nationally popular but very different wine, described on a later page.

• 9 •

The first Andrés winemaker, Wallace Pohle from California, disliked the Labrusca grapes then grown almost exclusively in the Okanagan Valley. Pohle talked Peller into planting French hybrids and a few Vinifera on forty acres near Cawston in the Similkameen. His successor was another Californian, Davis-trained Guy Baldwin (now director of enology for Paul Masson in California and for Seagram-owned wineries on three continents.) It was Baldwin who made the champagne that was praised at our San Francisco tasting.

For three decades, scientists at the Summerland Research Station in the Okanagan had advised the B.C. farmers to plant hybrids and Labrusca grapes, not Vinifera, because Okanagan winters were too cold. Californians Pohle and Baldwin disagreed with the Summerland scientists. Cold-resistant Vinifera varieties should suffer no worse in Okanagan winters than the hybrids, they said, pointing out that Vinifera had long been grown successfully in eastern Washington, only 200 miles south. "If the Okanagan growers would produce three tons per acre instead of six to sixteen tons," said Baldwin, "this part of British Columbia could grow some of the best Vinifera wines in the world."

In 1977, the Inkameep Indian Band planted a hundred acres of Vinifera on their reservation in the Okanagan, the first large-scale test of whether the Californians might be right. The Inkameep tribe are the first North American Indian growers of grapes. "If this test succeeds," commented *Vancouver Maga-*

zine writer Malcolm Parry," we shall see one of the niftiest role reversals ever between immigrant settler and aboriginal population; the Indian will have brought good wine to the white man."

French-hybrid wine grapes were planted first in 1968 on the tribe's 250-acre Inkameep Vineyard at the end of Osoyoos Lake, paid for by a government grant of funds and with an agreement by the Andrés winery to buy the grapes. In their fourth year, half of the hybrids suffered severe winter damage, and meanwhile the government funds for further financing of the vineyard were running out.

Dr. Helmut Becker, director of the Geisenheim Institute in Germany, visited the Okanagan in 1976 and ventured that cold-resistant German clones of Vinifera might do better than the California clones already growing in Walter Davidson's vineyard near Osoyoos. A tribal powwow was held, and the tribe's new chief Sam Baptiste authorized Inkameep's Dutch-born manager Ted Brouwer to buy the German grapes. Seventy-two thousand vines were flown from Germany and planted on the Inkameep Vineyard, a third each of Riesling clone 239 and of two Riesling-Sylvaner crosses named Ehrenfelser and Scheurebe. German clones of forty-four more varieties were planted at Kelowna and Oliver in the spring of 1977 by a B.C. research team guided by Ministry of Agriculture grape specialist John Vielvoye and pomologist Lyall Denby of the Summerland Station. The hope that superfine B.C. wines will be grown in the future may depend on the outcome of these Vinifera tests.

• 10 •

Not to be confused with the Ontario and B.C. wineries are a dozen others, all big, in such places as Truro in Nova Scotia, Moncton in New Brunswick, Moose Jaw in Saskatchewan, Calgary in Alberta, Selkirk, Morris, and Winnipeg in Manitoba, and Dorval, St-Hyacinthe, Lachine, and Laval in Québec. It may seem strange that wine is made in these provinces because no grapes are grown commercially in any of them.

These wineries without vineyards make and sell wines and champagnes of all types, but rarely from Canadian grapes. Their raw materials are mostly either California fresh grapes or juice or grape concentrate (condensed juice) imported from California and from such European countries as France, Spain, Cyprus, and Greece. A few also make wines from locally grown

apples and berries; hard cider is widely sold in Québec. One of
the concentrate wineries has advertised its products as "produced from the finest European grapes, fermented and bottled
in Canada." Some say they expect to sell their concentrate
wines in the United States.

Concentrate wine fits the legal definition of wine in most
countries, including the United States, but in grape-growing
countries concentrate is used only to sweeten wines or to
increase the sugar content of juice. Concentrate has also been
one of the materials for homemade wines since Prohibition
days. There are concentrate wineries in some tropical Latin
American countries, such as Guatemala, that correspond to the
strange new establishments in Canada.

The original reason such wineries were built in Canada
during the 1960s was that by operating a plant in a given
province and by employing local people to ferment and bottle
their wines, the owners automatically got all their products
listed in the province's monopoly liquor stores. Incidentally,
some of these wineries are architecturally handsome, and at
least one province allows them to offer tasting and cellar tours.
Concentrate wines usually have a slightly raisiny taste, but
those of the Maison Secrestat winery at Dorval near Montreal
are blended with wines from France or South America and are
difficult to distinguish from wines of fresh grapes.

As wine consumption continues setting all-time records in
Canada, there is a question of whether the Dominion has
enough land with suitable climates in which to grow grapes to
meet the future demand. Test plantings of grapes have been
made in the area between Lillooet and Lytton in the Fraser River
Valley of British Columbia. Ontario wineries long were required
by the provincial liquor board to make their wines exclusively
from materials grown in Ontario, but this has been modified
since 1977. Actually, several thousand tons of Ontario grapes
are exported each year to the United States, where they are
used by processors, including wineries. But Canada annually
imports many times as much from the U.S. and from countries
south of the Equator for table use or to be made into wine.

• 11 •

Half of Canadian wine is not made in its wineries, but is
fermented in the basements and kitchens of Canadian homes.
Rather than buy from the government liquor stores, which
among other things charge too much for wine, many people

prefer to ferment their own from locally grown or from California grapes or from concentrate. While this is especially true of consumers of European-immigrant backgrounds, large numbers of other Canadians who are not particularly interested in saving money have taken up winemaking as a fascinating hobby. Stanley Anderson of Vancouver, who started the business called Wine-Art, estimates that one of every five families in B.C. makes its own wine. There is a B.C. Amateur Winemakers Association, which outdoes such avocational groups in the United States. Eight of its members even have their own vineyard, six acres on Highway 3A in the Similkameen Valley between Keremeos and Osoyoos.

• 12 •

Canadian wine laws differ from those of the United States, which explains some of the unorthodox Canadian wines. Crackling (semi-sparkling) wines are nationally popular in Canada because they are much less expensive than crackling wines in the United States. The Canadian types mostly get their sparkle from artificial carbonation like American "pop" wines, and pay the same tax rate as still wines if they contain no more than an extra atmosphere of carbon dioxide. In the United States and much of Europe, wines labeled crackling (or *pétillant* or *frizzante*) are costly because they must be fermented in closed containers like champagne and pay the same tax rate as champagne.

More important is a group of Canadian carbonated wines fully as effervescent as champagne, with such names as Baby Duck, Canada Duck, Fuddle Duck, Daddy Duck, Cold Duckling, Baby Deer, Cold Turkey, Lonesome Charlie, and Golden Goose. They usually have Labrusca flavors and are sweet. These are less expensive than the crackling type because they contain no more than 7 percent alcohol and therefore are taxed only half as much as wines over 7 percent. They are permitted under a section of the Canadian law originally intended to encourage the sale of sparkling apple cider. Brights was selling such a wine called Winette in beer bottles in 1953. Fourteen years later, Andrés in B.C. used champagne bottles for one it called Chanté. Sales of the type exploded in 1971 when Andrés named the wine Baby Duck. The company claims it now outsells all other wines in Canada, regardless of source.

The French Government in 1964 sued the Château-Gai winery to stop it from calling its sparkling wines "champagne," and the French won the suit in 1967. But the verdict was handed down in the fiercely French province of Québec by a judge of French descent, and the Canadian wineries appealed it to English-speaking Ottawa, where they expect it eventually to be reversed. Incidentally, bulk-process champagnes in Canada are not required to state that fact, which is mandatory in the United States.

The Canadian monopoly liquor store system does one thing of which many visiting Americans approve. It answers without being asked, one of the questions most frequently posed by shoppers for wines: Is this wine dry or sweet, and if it is sweet, just how sweet? The Canadians have devised a numbering system that ignores such deliciously confusing label terms as dry, semidry, medium dry, extra dry, sec, and brut. Each wine for sale in the Canadian stores has now been given a number between "0" for very dry and "25" for very sweet. The system works very well, although an American kosher wine and an English ginger wine have already broken through the top of the scale with sugar contents of "26."

Canadian wines are seldom given more than passing mention in most wine books, and British author Hugh Johnson omitted them entirely from his *World Atlas of Wine*. When asked to explain, Johnson replied that the one Canadian wine he had tried was the worst he had ever tasted.

The Canadian growers' indignant replies to this slur received nationwide publicity and brought many patriotic drinkers to the defense of their country's wines. In 1976, Toronto wine writer Michael Vaughan carried an assortment of fourteen "Ontario Superior" wines to Britain and invited a dozen London connoisseurs, including Johnson, to sample them in a "blind" tasting at the Ontario House. The British author and the others were all favorably impressed. Johnson gave high praise to three of the samples, and conceded that none of the assortment resembled the Canadian wine he had tasted before.

23

Wines of Mexico

G UIDEBOOKS to Mexico list, among the attractions that lure millions of us across our southern border each year, its archaeological wonders, its colorful native customs, its fabulous scenery, resorts, and excellent fishing—but usually omit any mention of Mexican wines. Partly because of this, few Americans are aware that the land of the conquistadores has extensive vineyards and imposing wineries, some of them centuries older than ours, and that many Mexican wines are good and are getting steadily better.

The chief reason the wines of Mexico are little known is that the nation's wine industry, despite its ancient beginnings, is really new. Its oldest winegrowing estates have just lately been revived, replanted, and rebuilt. Most of the approximately fifty wineries in the Republic have only started operating since the 1950s. A new generation of enologists, technically trained in European and California wine schools, has taken charge of the modern cellars and is producing wines of types and qualities not made in Mexico before. A few are even being exported to the United States.

Why is this happening only now in an industry that began more than four hundred and fifty years ago? The answers are in Mexico's turbulent history and in its relatively recent emergence as a nation of the modern world.

• 2 •

Wine was first made in Mexico in the time of the conqueror, Hernando Cortez. As the governor of New Spain from 1521 to 1527, Cortez established mines and farms. He insisted that all ships coming from Spain to Vera Cruz should bring with them

518

Principal Vineyard Districts of MEXICO

supplies of plants and seeds. In 1524, Cortez made it a rule that every Spaniard holding a *repartimiento* (a grant of land and of Indians to till the soil) must plant, annually for five years, a thousand grapevines for each hundred Indians. Wine was an essential part of the Spaniards' diet and was indispensable for their priests to celebrate the Mass. Ships brought the wine in casks from Spain and the Canary Islands, but space in the ships was limited. The conquistadores first made their wine from wild grapes, then from cultivated grapes when their vineyards bore fruit. By 1554 winegrowing was well established at haciendas as far west as the present state of Michoacán. The first two commercial wineries or *bodegas vinícolas* in Mexico were established in 1593 and 1626 at Parras in Coahuila, 500 miles north of Mexico City. Both again are producing wines today.

But Spain was jealous of the New World's blossoming viniculture. The vintners of Cadiz were complaining as their shipments shrank. Philip II acted in 1595 to keep the wine trade as a Spanish monopoly; he issued an edict forbidding new plantings or replacements of vineyards in New Spain. The viceroys repeated Philip's edict during the next two centuries, and some went so far as to order that all existing vineyards be uprooted. But winemaking continued despite the edict, though without any records of the quantities made. It was from Mexico—not from Europe—that winegrowing spread during the sixteenth century to Peru, Chile, and Argentina, and during the seventeenth and eighteenth centuries to what is now the western United States.

Padre Miguel Hidalgo, the revered Father of Mexican Independence, was the only one who dared openly to defy the Spanish law. At his village of Dolores, the rebel priest taught the natives to raise grapes, which he himself pressed into wine, and the civil authorities came repeatedly to Dolores to tear up his vines. One of Father Hidalgo's aims in launching the revolution against Spain in 1810 was to end the Spanish prohibition against winegrowing in Mexico. Although the revolution finally succeeded eleven years later, Hidalgo meanwhile had been captured and shot.

Viniculture languished during the half-century of disorder that followed. Only two new wineries of any importance were established during the first seven decades of Mexican independence—the Bodegas Ferriño at Cuatro Ciénegas in Coahuila in 1860 and the Bodegas de Santo Tomás in Baja California in 1888. Most of the country's vineyards still grew the same grape variety originally introduced by the conquistadores. It was the Criolla or Mission, which is a member of the Vinifera wine-grape family, but not a very good one, because it is deficient in acidity and color. It is now thought to have grown from a seed brought from Spain in the time of Cortez.

The first step toward better Mexican wines came during the dictatorship of President Porfirio Díaz, who came to power in 1876. Díaz, the *mestizo* "strong man of Mexico," surrounded himself with young men called *científicos* and welcomed foreign capital and modern industry. In 1889, the Irish-American winegrower from Livermore, James Concannon, seeking more capital to develop his own vineyard in California, went to Mexico and convinced Díaz that viticulture in the Republic could be developed on a commercial quality basis and that he, Concannon, was the man to do it. The dictator granted him a concession to introduce better wine grapes to the country, and even assigned him a cavalry escort to impress the *hacendados* whom he would visit. From Livermore, where the better French varieties were just then being planted, Concannon shipped several million cuttings to haciendas throughout Mexico, with pamphlets in Spanish on grape cultural methods, and sent his brother Thomas along to superintend the deliveries. The biggest plantings were made at Hacienda Roque near Celaya, which was owned by the father of Díaz's daughter-in-law. By 1904 the project was completed and Concannon returned to Livermore. Díaz meanwhile assigned a young Hungarian viticulturist, the son of the Hungarian ambassador, to see to it that every state in the Republic would have at least one vineyard. With the better grape varieties from California, the Mexican wine industry started to boom.

In 1910 the boom attracted to Mexico the Italian-American winemaker Antonio Perelli-Minetti from California, seeking an opportunity to recoup the fortune he had lost in a wine venture at San Francisco. On his arrival in Mexico, Perelli was taken to Chapultepec Palace to meet the dictator, who told him about the grape plantings. Díaz encouraged Perelli to join the Mexican industry—"The sky is the limit here"—but warned him to stay out of politics, saying, "Don't let the fever of commanding get hold of you." Perelli went to work for Felipe Cárdenas of Ocampo, a brother of the former governor of Coahuila. His assignment was to plant vines on Cárdenas' Rancho El Fresno near Torreón. Perelli brought from California cuttings of Zinfandel, Petite Sirah, Malaga, and Flame Tokay and planted almost 900 acres, the largest vineyard in Mexico at that time.

Then came the Revolution of 1910, led by Francisco I. Madero, and the bloody civil war that lasted for ten years and cost a million lives. During the chaos, most of the vineyards fell into neglect and many were destroyed. Perelli stayed on at the Cárdenas rancho, guarding his young vines. To Torreón in 1913, the year President Madero was murdered, came Pancho Villa, the former bandit chieftain who had become a general of the Revolution. Perelli promptly presented Villa with a basket of grapes and pleaded for protection for the vineyard. Villa consented and assigned him a guard of three soldiers. But a year later Villa left Torreón to join General Alvaro Obregón in Sonora. Conditions then became so chaotic that Perelli quit his job in 1916 and returned to California, where he went on to make his fortune in the San Joaquin Valley.

Perelli often returned to Mexico after the Revolution, and later it was he who helped to establish some of the new wineries that are making good Mexican wines today.

After the years of conflict, the tragic remnants of Mexico's vineyards continued to shrink. Wineries that started in Baja California imported grapes from San Diego and Cucamonga to make some of their wines.* This was a period when grapes were scarce and sugar cheaper. Mexican wines were often "baptized" (watered), and they earned a poor reputation, something the present industry would prefer to end and forget. The vintners' trade association, the Asociación Nacional de Vitivinicultores, takes the position that though their industry is actually the oldest in the Americas, it is also the youngest. Its director, Alberto Jardi Porres, says "It was not until 1939 that the Mexican wine industry began its true development with characteristics that augur its future."

• 3 •

One summer morning in 1929, a thirty-six-year-old grocery merchant of Saltillo, the capital of Coahuila, went for a drive through the nearby countryside. It was election day, and because Nazario Ortiz Garza was a candidate for governor, he had decided to spend it outside the city. Passing an old hacienda, he noticed a few abandoned grapevines that had grown to enormous size and saw that they bore a crop of luscious-looking grapes. It occurred to him that it might be worthwhile to buy the hacienda, plant more vines, and make the place his country home—which he proceeded to do after winning the election. That day's drive in the country started don Nazario's second career, which made him Mexico's *capitan de la vitivinicultura,* the largest producer of wine and brandy in the Republic.

The vineyard that he planted grew well. When he began making wine, he sent his second son, Mario, to the University of California at Davis to study viticulture and enology. A few years later he won another election which made him a member of the Mexican Senate. Then in 1946 President Miguel Alemán appointed him Mexico's secretary of agriculture. In that post— already owning wineries at both Saltillo and Mexico City—don Nazario traveled on government business throughout the Republic for the next six years. Wherever he went, he distributed grapevine cuttings to everyone who would agree to start a vineyard. He also bought, for his own account, 700 acres of wasteland in the State of Aguascalientes, planted most of it in vines, and there built his third winery in 1952. He went on establishing new vineyards in Coahuila, Durango, and Chihuahua, and at Torreón built his fourth winery in 1966. By then he

*The Mexican Government is reported to have stopped this after the 1965 vintage.

was using, in his four plants, a fourth of the grapes grown in the nation.

• 4 •

Following the Second World War, the Mexican Government stimulated the planting of vineyards by quadrupling the tariffs on European wines and by putting quota restrictions on wine imports. The result was that French, Spanish, and American wines cost two to ten times as much as Mexican wines. When the supply of grapes increased, European and American companies began establishing their own plants in Mexico—such firms as Pedro Domecq, Martell Cognac, Seagram, and Osborne—though primarily to make brandy rather than wine. In three decades the area planted to vineyards in Mexico multiplied twenty-five times, from 4,000 acres in 1939 to almost 100,000 acres in 1977.

Don Nazario says that is only the beginning, that Mexico has enough unused land to multiply its grape crop five hundred times. The country's wine consumption is only about 2 million gallons a year, less than a fourth of a pint per capita, a fiftieth of the rate in the United States. If the Mexican Government would help to remove obstacles to wine use, don Nazario declares, it could be increased ten times within a few years.

One of the obstacles is that wine is still a new product to most of the Mexican people, though such table wines as rosé should go well with the highly seasoned native cuisine. Wine has three formidable competitiors in Mexico: pulque, beer, and soft drinks. Pulque, the ancient Aztec drink fermented from the sap of the maguey cactus or century plant, is a whitish, cloudy liquid of about 4 to 6 percent alcohol. Millions of gallons are sold annually at farms and in the pulquerías in the cities. From special types of pulque the Mexican liquors called tequila and mezcal are distilled.

Another obstacle to wine use is that, selling so little, restaurateurs and storekeepers have not yet learned to store it properly. Consequently much of the table wine becomes partially spoiled before it is used. On my last five visits to Mexico I tasted—at the wineries—some 1,200 wines, and all but five ranged from at least drinkable to very good. But of the table wines served to me in restaurants and hotels, almost a fourth had the objectionable oxidized or sherrylike taste that comes from storage in warm rooms or sunlight or with corked bottles standing upright instead of horizontal. This kind of partial spoilage occurs in other countries, too, especially in South America and in the midwestern United States, but more often in Mexico than anywhere else I have visited. The place to judge Mexican wines therefore is at the wineries, where they have not yet had an opportunity to spoil.

A greater barrier to wine is that the Mexican Government misunderstands the role of table wine as the temperate meal-time beverage, lumps it with distilled spirits, and favors beer as *"la bebida de moderación."* Licenses to sell wine are costly and difficult to obtain, and table wine is taxed beyond the reach of Mexican households, at an average of 19 cents per liter, more than seventy cents per gallon. A law prohibits wineries from owning vineyards, an obstacle the winegrowers circumvent, however, by dividing vineyard ownership among members of their families.

The final obstacle to Mexican wines is the lack of an appreciative audience. What little wine is used is bought mostly by wealthy and upper-middle-class people to serve on special occasions, for which they choose the expensive brands import-ed from Spain and France. Mexican wines thus suffer from snobbery—but of a kind more deeply rooted than that which still hinders American wines in the United States. The Mexican kind even has a name—*malinchismo.** It is the attitude preva-lent among the wealthy in Mexico for four and a half centuries, that no native product or custom can equal its counterpart in Europe, from which civilization came to the New World.

A blow against *malinchismo* was struck by the Mexican Congress in 1965 with a law that requires all restaurants and night clubs in the Republic to offer Mexican-made wines and Mexican cheese on their menus. Since the restriction on imports, some of the Spanish and French wine shippers have licensed Mexican wineries to bottle their best wines under the old European brand names the *malinchistas* have favored in the past. These Mexican wines bring higher prices than the rest and cope with snobbery to some extent.

• 5 •

Mexico has nine main vineyard districts: northern Baja California, the Laguna district at the border of Coahuila and

---

*From Malinche, the Indian girl who, as the interpreter, mistress, and slave of Cortez, guided him up from Vera Cruz to his conquest of Montezuma's Aztec empire between 1519 and 1521. For betraying her race, according to legend, she was condemned to wander forever in tears and agony beneath the waters of Lake Texcoco by day and through the surrounding country by night. *Malinchista* became the term applied to people who show a preference for customs other than Mexican, and their snobbery became *malinchismo.*

Durango, Parras and Saltillo in Coahuila, Aguascalientes, the San Juan del Río region in Querétaro, the area around Fresnillo in Zacatecas, Delicias in Chihuahua, and the Hermosillo-Caborca district in Sonora. Some grapes also are grown in San Luis Potosí, Tlaxcala, Puebla, Guanajuato, and Hidalgo. There are wineries around Mexico City that are supplied with grapes or wines grown farther north.

Some viticultural authorities consider Mexican climates too warm for grapes because almost half of the country lies south of the Tropic of Cancer. But the central vineyards are situated on Mexico's mile-high Central Plateau, where elevation is as important as latitude. For each thousand feet of elevation the average annual temperature decreases about three degrees, and there is a further factor: summer days are shorter than in the higher latitudes. A trouble in the high plateau region is the extreme fluctuation of day and night temperatures. On warm days in the fall the vines continue to grow under cloudless skies, making them vulnerable to freezes that sometimes follow during the nights. This sometimes causes the trunks of the vines to split, which some of the growers try to avert by wrapping newspapers around the trunks. But the main flaw is too little moisture or too much. Dry districts depend on severely limited supplies of water for irrigation. Others have too much rain during the grape-growing season.

• 6 •

One of the water-deficient regions is Baja California. That 750-mile-long, narrow peninsula of Lower California is for the most part a forbidding, moonlike country of rugged mountains and grim deserts. Some sections receive no rain at all over a period of years, while the tropical southern tip, noted for its luxury fishing resorts, gets torrential downpours.

At San Xavier Mission near Loreto on the peninsula, the Jesuit missionary Padre Juan Ugarte introduced the Mission grape from mainland Mexico about 1697 to make altar wine. It was from Loreto that the Franciscan, Padre Junípero Serra, set out in 1769 to colonize Alta California, traveling on foot and horseback and reputedly carrying the Mission grape to San Diego.

In contrast to the rest of the barren peninsula are several temperate fertile valleys in its far northwestern corner. The vineyards of Baja California are in six of these valleys—Santo Tomás, thirty miles south of Ensenada; Santa Isabel, twenty-five miles farther south past San Vicente; Guadalupe, thirty miles below the California border, and the Valle Redondo, Tanama, and Rancho Viejo districts around Tecate, across the border from San Diego County. Rainfall there ranges from only five to eighteen inches per year, and vineyard planting is limited to the supply of underground water for irrigation. Like the coastal counties of Alta California, these valleys are cooled by ocean breezes and fogs from the Pacific, twelve to thirty miles to the west.

The growers call their area "the Napa Valley of Mexico" because of the climate, but also because Baja California has produced the best table wines made in Mexico in recent years. Moreover, with two Ensenada wineries now offering cellar tours and tasting (five days per week), "Baja" has become a popular attraction for wine-interested visitors, who drive down in a little over two hours from San Diego via the new Tijuana-Ensenada toll freeway. A 1978 amendment to California law allows them to take home a bottle of wine or liquor when they cross the border.

Oldest and for many years biggest of the Baja California wineries is the Bodegas de Santo Tomás whose cellars, with 1,700,000 gallons capacity, span Avenida Miramar in Ensenada. It was founded in 1888 by Francisco Andonegui, an Italian gold miner who built an adobe winery near the ruins of Santo Tomás Mission. When Andonegui was dying in the late 1920s, he sold his property to the then governor, General Abelardo Lujan Rodríguez, who owned it for forty years. Rodríguez, the revolutionary general who later became President of Mexico, was prodigiously wealthy, owning fleets of tuna and shrimp boats, canneries, factories, and some eighty other businesses, including the Caliente racetrack, which he sold in 1932. After his term as President ended in 1934, General Rodríguez moved the winery from the Santo Tomás Valley to its present location on Avenida Miramar in the port city of Ensenada. He later planted more vineyards at Rancho Guadalupe to supplement those near the Mission.

In 1962, General Rodríguez hired Dimitri Tchelistcheff, son of the famous André, as the technical director of Santo Tomás. Dimitri, born in Paris in 1930, learned winemaking from his father at Beaulieu, earned his degree in viticulture and enology at UC Davis, and had worked at Napa's Schramsberg Vineyard and at the Gallo Winery in Modesto. Dimitri replanted some of the General's vineyards with Cabernet Sauvignon, Pinot Noir, White Riesling, Chenin Blanc, and Chardonnay, and installed new equipment in the winery for the cold fermentation of white wines. He produced the first two Baja California *vinos espumosos* (champagnes)*, a Charmat-process extra-dry called Cordon Azul and a bottle-fermented brut named Calviñe. An ammunition tunnel dug uphill from the winery during the Second World War became the champagne cellar of Santo Tomás. One of the best wines Dimitri produced was his Barbera, aged two years in oak barrels and two years in bottles. It has been imported to the United States since 1969. Even better than the Barbera were his 1972 Pinot Noir and 1973 Cabernet Sauvignon. After fifteen years, Dimitri left Santo Tomás in 1977 to become a freelance vineyard and winery consultant (though he still makes his home in Ensenada). His successor is his former assistant, Octavio Jiménez, a chemical engineering graduate from the University of Mexico.

General Rodríguez died at his Ensenada home in 1967 at the age of seventy-eight. The vineyards and winery passed to his widow, the former Aida Sullivan of San Diego, and to his three sons, but were sold a year later to the Elias Pando wine-importing firm of Mexico City.

The other Ensenada winery, which also has visiting days, is the 500,000-gallon Vinícola de Ensenada or Padre Kino cellar on Avenida Cipres, the road toward Estero Beach. It was built by Esteban Ferro, who once managed the Santo Tomás winery for General Rodríguez. The winemaker is his son Dr. Enrico Ferro, trained in agricultural sciences at the University of Torino and in enology at Asti. The brand name of their dozen wines is Padre Kino, for the priest who established the missions in Sonora.

The Guadalupe Valley, twenty miles northeast of Ensenada via Highway 3, has some three thousand acres of vineyards and one of the largest olive groves in the world. It was settled early in this century by a religious colony of immigrants from Russia. They are said to have lived in poverty, even robbing beehives for food, until General Rodríguez advised them to plant vineyards and sell him their grapes. There now are three wineries in the valley. The Formex-Ybarra winery, built in 1957, sends its Terrasola wines and brandy to its plant in Mexico City. The wines I have tasted at both places were clean and sound. Three miles farther north, bordered by new trellised vineyards of premium wine grape varieties, is the first ultramodern winery in Baja California, named Vides de Guadalupe, an impressive

---

*During the 1960s, the Government of France persuaded Mexico to prohibit its vintners from calling their sparkling wines champagne.

two-million-gallon cellar facing the highway. Built in 1972 for Pedro Domecq of Mexico especially to make table wines, it is equipped with stainless steel crushers and tanks, a centrifuge, and wooden tanks for the aging of red types. Luis Angel Cetto, who owns three Baja California wineries, manages this one for Domecq and has one of his own across the road. Cetto also manages the Fería de la Uva, sponsored by Domecq, held with much dancing at Colonia de Guadalupe following the vintage in early October.

The original Cetto winery is the Productos de Uva cellar in Tijuana. Angelo Cetto came from Italy to Guadalupe in 1923, worked as a laborer, then went north to Tijuana and began making bulk wine. He sent his sons to college in Mexico City, and when his eldest, Luis Angel, joined his business, it began to grow. The Tijuana cellar began bottling wine under the F. Chauvenet brand of France. Luis now owns vineyards at both Guadalupe and Valle Redondo, and also the winery at Tecate established during the 1950s by José Vasquez. His brother Ferruccio Cetto owns the independent Productos de Uva winery at Aguascalientes.

In Valle Redondo, between Tecate and Tijuana, the principal vineyard is the 125 acres owned by Humberto Pérez. In 1940, when his father Conrado began making El Mirador wines and Casa Blanca brandy in his Vinícola Regional winery in Tijuana, it was "out in the country," but booming Tijuana now surrounds the site. Humberto was trained in viticulture and enology at UC Davis, where one of his classmates was Dimitri Tchelistcheff. It was Humberto who told Tchelistcheff that General Rodríguez wanted to hire a California-trained enologist, and suggest that Dimitri apply for the job. Humberto now teaches biochemistry at the University of Baja California besides running his vineyards and winery.

The remaining Baja California district, Rancho Viejo, is a small valley between brush-covered hills eight miles off the Ensenada-Tecate highway. The vineyard and Rancho Viejo winery there were established about 1940, but production has been limited by the scarcity of water for irrigation.

• 7 •

Hacienda Alamo at Saltillo, where Nazario Ortiz Garza planted his first vines, is now the headquarters of all his *viñedos* (vineyards) in four Mexican states. Though situated directly on Federal Highway 54, only three miles from the modern city, the hacienda cannot have changed much since colonial times. It is a self-contained village with its own ancient adobe church and primary school, with the homes of vineyard workers clustered around the baronial residence of Mario, don Nazario's son. Its vineyard, however, has shrunk lately to half of its original 450-acre size. Lack of water is the reason; the fast-growing city of Saltillo has first call on the supply that is pumped from local wells, which now range in depth from 600 feet to half a mile.

On Xicotencatl Street in Saltillo, near the railway station, is don Nazario's oldest winery, where he now makes only brandies. His own brandies are called Club 45, Señorial, and Saviñón, and he also makes the Mexican brandy of Gonzalez Byass of Spain. French wine and brandy expert Remy H. Remy, a graduate of Montpellier and the University of Caen, is in charge of the Saltillo cellars and of Nazario's largest brandy distillery at La Union near Torreón.

In the State of Aguascalientes, nine miles north of Aguascalientes city, is don Nazario's third winery. If you travel on the Carretera Internacional (CN 45) between El Paso and Mexico City, you cannot miss it, because his property spans the highway. On one side, a mammoth wine bottle perched atop his winery dominates the valley skyline and can be seen for miles. Across the road a rococo portal announces the entrance to his Viñedos San Marcos, which now cover some 800 acres; San Marcos and Alamo are the brands of his principal table and dessert wines. Behind the winery is a hacienda even greater than that of Alamo, again with its own church and primary school. Fifty families live there, and the hacienda has its own school bus that takes the children to the Aguascalientes high school. The residence is also huge. In its central court in 1954, notables from throughout the Republic gathered to celebrate the first annual Fería de la Uva, which marked the emergence of Aguascalientes as a viticultural district. During the five grape-festival days in mid-August, there are parades and dances in the city plaza, a queen is crowned, and Aguascalientes restaurants include wine in their guests' meals.

What is most striking in Aguascalientes, when one views the flourishing vineyards, the big new wineries and brandy distilleries that line the highway and byroads, is to realize that none of them existed before the Second World War. Until then, this area was largely a wasteland of nopal, maguey, and mesquite. Now it leads all the other Mexican states in vineyards of wine grapes with some 18,000 acres.

Aguascalientes table wines achieved premium quality in 1970, when don Nazario employed as his enologist José Romagosa from Chile, who was born in Spain and trained at the Vilafranca del Panadés enological station and the Codorniu champagne cellars nearby. Since Romagosa began to modernize the winery equipment, San Marcos has produced two Cabernet Sauvignons of Bordeaux character and a bottle-fermented champagne of Chardonnay and Pinot Noir, called Champ d'Or 400, that could equal many California champagnes. Mario Ortiz now plans to build a San Marcos visitor facility with an underground railway to transport tourists between the cellars. Another product of the San Marcos winery is a brandy called Fontenac, distilled for Hennessy of Mexico.

The oldest Aguascalientes winery is Bodegas Brandevin, established in an old woolen mill in 1948. Francisco Hill now operates it, making grape concentrate and sangría. The Bodegas de Monte Casino, built in 1955, is now called Vides Domecq. It makes brandy in fourteen pot stills and ships it in tank trucks to Domecq near Mexico City.

· 8 ·

At Paila on the Saltillo-Torreón highway (CN 40) through southern Coahuila, you turn off on state Route 35 through a valley of pecan groves and vineyards to reach Parras de la Fuente, sixteen miles to the south. Most guidebooks neglect Parras, merely mentioning it as the birthplace of the martyred president of Mexico, Francisco I. Madero. It is a lovely, unspoiled colonial town that still has horse cabs, but no tourist guides. For the wine tourist, a visit to the valley is particularly interesting, for the two oldest wineries in Mexico are there.

One is the Vinícola del Marqués de Aguayo, founded in 1593 by a Spanish captain, Francisco de Urdiñola. *Parra* is the Spanish word for grapevine. Urdiñola found wild grapes growing in the valley, and named it Santa María de las Parras, which was changed after the French invasion of 1862-67 to honor Antonio de la Fuente, a hero of that conflict. If local historians are correct, the Parras valley was the cradle of viniculture in the Americas. They say that from here, Urdiñola sent his wines and vines to Peru, Chile, and Argentina before any vineyards existed in South America, and that he continued doing so until the Spanish authorities enforced the royal order that wine in the New World must come only from Spain. Urdiñola's great-granddaughter married a Spaniard, who through the captain's influence was given a title, and when the Marqués inherited the property, he gave it his new name.

Although this is the oldest winery on the American continent, all that remains of the original structure is a single adobe wall, and under its present owners, the Almacénes Guajuardo merchants of Monterrey, its main product is brandy, distilled for another firm.

Second oldest, and with its 10-million-gallon capacity one of the most important in all Mexico, is the Bodegas de San Lorenzo of Casa Madero. Founded in 1626 by Lorenzo Garcia, it is now owned by members of the Madero family, cousins of the late President. There are five more wineries at Parras and the ruins of many more, because despite the Spanish law, every early hacienda had its own vineyard and made wine.

The Maderos have owned the bodegas since 1870. In that year, Evaristo Madero Elizondo, a young merchant from northern Coahuila across the border from the United States, bought Hacienda San Lorenzo and Captain Urdiñola's original property, Hacienda Rosario. Don Evaristo traveled to Europe and brought back superior grape varieties from Italy, Switzerland, Spain, Portugal, and France. In Cognac he bought a brandy still, and brought French experts to install it at Parras. By the turn of the century, don Evaristo's wines and brandies were winning medals at the Paris, Buffalo, and St. Louis expositions. After his death in 1911, the property passed to his sons by his second wife, although he had the foresight to incorporate his Parras holdings. To his sons and grandsons by his first wife he willed lands in the Laguna district. One of these grandsons was Francisco, the idealistic cotton planter and intellectual who started the Revolution of 1910 and became President Madero of Mexico.

In don Evaristo's time, vineyards covered 3,000 acres in the Parras Valley, but most of them were destroyed by the phylloxera and the rest by neglect during the Revolution. The 2,400 acres replanted since, of which the Madero descendants own 500 acres, all are on phylloxera-resistant roots.

Rebuilt since 1962, with its beautiful church beside the cellars, Casa Madero is one of Mexico's handsomest wineries. It is also hospitable; signs on the road from Paila invite you to visit the bodegas. After you tour the cellars and the distillery with its quaint French-type pot stills, you are served wines beside the three-century-old Casa Grande, now turned into a motel. But one time *not* to visit Parras, unless you have reserved accommodations months in advance, is during its Fiesta de Uva in mid-August, the annual grape festival which the Madero family revived in 1946 to celebrate Bodegas San Lorenzo's three hundred and twentieth anniversary.

Casa Madero's main products are pot-still brandies; wines have been less than a fiftieth of its output in recent years. When José Milmo became the manager in 1973, a small modern winery was built within the big winery especially to make table wines with Angel Morales, a graduate of the Technical Institute of Monterrey, in charge. Milmo, trained in enology at Montpellier in France, views wine as the drink of the future in Mexico. The improvement in Casa Madero wines was evident between my last two visits. The best new wines were San Lorenzo Vino Blanco, made of French Colombard, and a red called Mataro but made of Ruby Cabernet. Morales also makes a *mistela*, unfermented juice plus brandy, resembling the Pineau des Charentes of Cognac.

Eduardo Madero, who manages the vineyards, has his son Joaquin studying plant propagation in France. Eduardo's brother Benjamín, who was educated in Michigan and played guitar in the university orchestra there, says Mexican wines will continue to improve as better grape varieties are planted. He has kept temperature records at Parras since 1953 and concludes that Parras, 5,000 feet above sea level, has a Region IV climate, comparable to Lodi in California and Florence in Italy. (Dimitri Tchelistcheff says the climates of Santo Tomás and Guadalupe are between Region II and Region III, but he bases his opinion on his tests of wines, not on temperature records.)

• 9 •

Two hours' drive west of Parras, clustered at the border of Durango and Coahuila, are the charming old triplet cities of Gómez Palacio, Lerdo, and Torreón, only minutes apart. Torreón, the largest, is on the Coahuila side. Around the cities, in the reclaimed Laguna district, hundreds of former cotton fields have been replanted with vineyards since Mexico's grape industry came back to life in the early 1940s. At Torreón in 1966, the Mexican Government established its first mother vineyard with stocks from Davis to propagate and supply the grape growers with virus-free vines.

The two newest wineries in La Laguna, those of Nazario Ortiz Garza and Pedro Domecq near Torreón, were designed to make brandy, into which go more than nine tenths of the grapes grown in Mexico.* Eight times more brandy is now made than wine.

Oldest winery in the district, the Vinícola del Vergel near Gómez Palacio, also makes brandy, but devotes a fourth of its production to wines. It invites visitors to tour its cellars and to taste its assortment of table and dessert wine types.

Vergel (Spanish for flower garden) was built in 1943 by one of the district's leading cotton planters, the late Luis Garza (not related to don Nazario), with equipment supplied by Antonio Perelli-Minetti. The founder's son, Santiago A. Garza, is now in charge. With its outdoor batteries of temperature-controlled tanks of Mexican-made stainless steel, Vergel resembles the modern new wineries of California. But beneath the main building is one of the most spectacular Old World underground cellars in North America. Its vaulted roof and supporting pillars are made entirely of rough marble quarried from the nearby mountains. Each of the large wine casks in the cellar bears the name of a saint.

Santiago Garza says Mexico's vintners have been too busy in recent years trying to keep up with their soaring brandy business to pay enough attention to wine, but that he is now creating a new division in Vergel to specialize in producing only table wines. New vineyards of premium wine-grape varieties have been planted at high elevations in Zacatecas, where the climates are cooler than La Laguna's Region V. Vergel plans to build a winery there especially to make table wine. Five other Vergel bodegas in such districts as Sonora and Aguascalientes make wine for distillation into brandy.

The vineyards around Gómez Palacio still contain many table grape varieties, but Garza has added such wine varieties as Ugni Blanc, Ruby Cabernet, and French Colombard. He has sent his winemaker, Valente Arellano, a graduate of Monterrey, to take the short courses in enology at Davis. Viticulturist Ramon Avila studied at Davis for two years. Vergel manager Fernando Menéndez also was trained at Monterrey and has worked at the Perelli-Minetti winery in California. Of the Vergel table wines I have sampled, the best was an oak-aged red of Ruby

*This came about partly through a quirk in the semantics of drink. The Spanish word for spirits is *aguardiente,* literally burning water. New, water-white grape brandy is *aguardiente de uva,* and aged beverage brandy is *coñac* in Spanish. But after World War II the Mexican government prohibited all *coñac* labels except on those from the Cognac district of France. The Mexican *coñac* distillers, suddenly left without a label for their product, adopted its English name, though there is no such word as brandy in the Spanish language. It turned out to have such snob appeal to Mexicans that brandy has since passed rum and tequila as the chief distilled liquor drunk in Mexico.

Cabernet and Carignane called Viña Santiago. Vergel's regular red is named Noblejo; Verdizo is its most popular Vergel white.

• 10 •

At Hermosillo in the semitropical west coast state of Sonora, vineyards were planted among the orchards and cotton fields beginning about 1961. The grapes, however, were mostly the early-ripening table varieties, intended for shipment to the United States in competition with the early Coachella Valley crop from California. A winery was built at Hermosillo in 1965, but its principal product was brandy, not wine. In the early 1970s, the plantings spread 150 miles north to Caborca, only fifty miles below the Arizona border, again with such grapes as Thompson Seedless and Perlettes. Some growers at Caborca have also planted wine varieties because of the heavy yields. There now are three wineries crushing grapes for brandy at Hermosillo, and a Fiesta Vendímia is held there five days after the first grapes are picked in mid-July. Sonora has become Mexico's chief grape-growing state with 24,000 acres, almost a fourth of the vineyards in the nation.

Table grapes and brandy are also the chief products of the vineyards in Chihuahua. Farmers there found it more profitable to raise grapes than cotton after the Second World War. There are two wineries at Ciudad Delícias, one making brandy, the other table wine.

• 11 •

The southernmost vineyard district of Mexico is the valley of the Río de San Juan, 100 miles north of Mexico City in the state of Querétaro. It is also one of the highest, 6,100 feet above sea level. Though situated two degrees within the Torrid Zone, the valley successfully grows the delicate grape varieties that make superior table wines.

A mile east of the old colonial town of San Juan del Río is a handsome stone winery named Cavas de San Juan, which produces Hidalgo wines. Francisco Domenech, born in Catalonia, where his family produced vermouth, built the winery in 1958 to make both wine and brandy, but primarily table wines. As his enologist he employed Carlos Reulet, a graduate of the vinicultural school of Onde near Bordeaux and a former pilot in the Free French Air Force. Meanwhile, Domenech sent his son, Francisco Domenech T., to the wine school at UC Davis to be trained.

When young Francisco came home, he began replanting the vineyard with such varieties as Cabernet Sauvignon, Pinot Noir, Gamay, Pinot Gris, Chenin Blanc, and Chardonnay. The winery then supplemented its Blanco Seco, Blanco Amabile, Rosado Seco, Clarete, and Tinto with a vintage-dated (as many Mexican wines are now) Cepa Cabernet Sauvignon, a Cepa Pinot Noir, and a Blanc de Blancs of Chenin and Ugni Blanc, and an assortment of Charmat-process *vinos espumosos* (champagnes). Reulet is now assisted by Miguel Angel de Santiago, who was trained in the Rioja district of Spain.

At Calle 9 on the road toward Tequisquiapan is the Cruz Blanca (white cross) winery, established in 1968 by Eugenio Nicolau and his son Eugenio Jr. Cruz Blanca is their very acceptable standard table wine, sold in liters and jugs. They have older wines for sale in restaurants under their Montebello brand. Eugenio Jr. was trained in enology at the Agrario Institute in Trento, Italy. The Nicolaus have a hundred acres of vines, but most of their grapes come from the vineyards of José Fernando Muñoz Castillo, young Nicolau's brother-in-law.

Down the road from Cruz Blanca is the Madrileña winery, which resembles a fort. It was built in 1969 for the Belasco Brothers, Mexico City wine merchants whose father Pedro came from Castile in 1908. Madrileña's enologist, Edgardo Ruggeri, is from Argentina, where he was trained in the Mendoza wine school. He makes a pleasant red wine called "Viñalta Malbec & Cabernet" and a "Tipo Jerez" sherry. Half of the sherry is aged two years in oak barrels in the sun, then is blended with the other half in stainless steel.

Twelve miles north of San Juan del Río, near the picturesque village of Tequisquiapan, are a vineyard, winery, and distillery that produce table wines and brandy for Martell of Mexico, an affiliate of Martell Cognac of France. I was amazed on my last trip to Mexico when I tasted its first red wine, called Clos San José Tinto, for although it was only six months old and came from a stainless steel tank, it was pleasant to drink and had the balance of body, acid, and tannin of a young Bordeaux. The enologist, Georges Mondié from Montpellier via North Africa, said it was Cabernet Sauvignon with a blend of Merlot. Miguel d'Orcasberro makes Martell's Mexican brandy, which is called Cheverny. The 400 acres of vineyards planted since 1965 are principally of Ugni Blanc for the brandy and of Cabernet, Merlot, Sauvignon Blanc, and Grenache for the Clos San José wines.

Wine grapes also grow in the neighboring state of Guanajuato, but only one small winery operates there. It is Hugo Gamba's Bodegas San Luis Rey on Plaza Morelos in the small town of San Luis de la Paz. Founded in 1870, it is worth a visit to see the maze of wine-aging tunnels beneath the cellar, dug centuries ago by Jesuit priests as places to hide from warring native tribes. The tunnels store wines and brandies dating from the Revolution, including a sacramental Muscat of 1912 vintage that is still good to drink.

Not far away, on the road toward Dolores Hidalgo, is the original vineyard of Padre Hidalgo. It recently was restored to honor the martyred Padre's contribution to winegrowing, as well as to liberty, in Mexico.

• 12 •

At altitudes of nearly 7,000 feet, even higher than San Juan del Río, are the vineyards of Mexico's newest wine district, in the state of Zacatecas. More than 3,500 acres have been planted under drip irrigation there since 1970 because land is plentiful, the climate is mainly Region III, and there is minimal damage from summer rains. The first Zacatecas winery, at Daniel Carrera Salcedo's Rancho el Saucito south of Fresnillo, produces mainly wine for brandy, but Vinícola del Vergel has completed plans for a winery at Fresnillo to produce only table wines. Another winery for a group named Sierra Vieja is in the planning stage.

• 13 •

Around Mexico City there are many wine and brandy establishments, and some of them can be visited by appointment, but be sure to telephone for a specific time and to get driving directions before you start out.

In the suburb of Los Reyes, an eleven-mile drive on the road toward Puebla, is the impressive brandy and wine blending, aging, and bottling plant of Pedro Domecq of Mexico. In personal charge there is Pedro F. Domecq, a member of the world-famous sherry-making family of Spain. It is worth the trip to see Domecq's great brandy *soleras*, the lovely "La Sacristía" with its display of glass-fronted barrels showing the year-by-year benefits of aging brandy in oak, the murals depicting the history of Mexican beverages starting with pulque in pre-Columbian times, and also the dozen ornamental but genuine *tinajas*, the giant earthenware vessels in which wines in Spain were aged for centuries before the eras of wooden, then concrete, and now stainless-steel tanks.

Pedro F. Domecq of the Domecq sherry family of Spain heads Domecq wine and brandy production throughout Mexico from his headquarters at Los Reyes, near Mexico City.

Domecq produces several Mexican table wines, but no sherries, because Domecq sherries come only from Spain. Its Los Reyes Tinto, Blanco, and Rosado are among the best table wines in Mexico. Like Domecq's Presidente brandy, the Los Reyes wines are now exported to the United States. The Tinto, when I was last there, was a two-year-old red and had a perceptible flavor of aging in oak. A five-year-old red is called Château Domecq. Marcial Ibarra, who learned enology from Professor Cruess at the University of California and later taught it at the University of Mexico, is the technical director, supervising the seven bodegas and vinicolas that produce Domecq brandies and wines.

At ancient Tlalnepantla, several miles north of the capital, off the road to Querétaro, are the old Bodegas Santa María. Ricardo Fernandez, whose father once owned the winery, now makes brandy and wine there for Bobadilla, the producer of sherries at Jerez. Around Mexico City, too, are the modern plants of such world-famous companies as Seagram, Cinzano, and Martini & Rossi. The latter two make their vermouths from Mexican wines.

There are two wineries in the city. On Calle Nicolás San Juan are the Cavas Bach cellars, opened in 1972 by the owners of the

Bach vineyards and winery at Vilafranca del Panadés near Barcelona. Its chief products are brandy and a pleasant champagne called Champbrule, but it also has table wines from Baja California and Aguascalientes with such varietal labels as Nebbiolo and French Colombard. Cavas Bach also makes a sparkling red wine labeled Cold Duck, whose name printed in English, though translated from a German pun, may be difficult to explain to the Mexican customers of Cavas Bach.

The busiest winery in the area is the Mexico City winery of Nazario Ortiz Garza on Avenida Mixcoac. There he bottles a six-year-old red under the brand name of Federico Paternina of Haro in the Rioja district of Spain, and also a medium-sweet brown sherry, sun-baked in the rear of the Mexico City cellar, called Jerez Solera Alamo.

• 14 •

To visit all of the Mexican vineyard districts in a single trip is impractical except by car, or preferably by private plane. Torreón, Aguascalientes, and Chihuahua are served by scheduled airlines, but at this writing Ensenada, San Juan del Río, and Saltillo are not. For private planes, arrangements can be made to use the airstrip at Parras adjoining the Casa Madero vineyards.

Wine-touring in Mexico will become increasingly interesting in the future, as the better grape varieties lately planted come into bearing and as the quality of Mexican wines, vastly better than they were a decade ago, continues to improve.

24

Hobbyists and Small Wineries

WHILE big wineries are getting bigger in order to slake America's growing thirst for wine, little winemakers are increasing in numbers at an accelerating pace.

Small wineries that sell their own products have more than doubled in numbers since 1965, and, as more states reduce their exorbitant minimum license fees for wineries, will continue to multiply in the next several years. Yet equally important, in terms of millions of gallons, is the fast-growing trend toward winemaking in American homes. Both kinds of small-scale winemaking are doing as much as the commercial wineries to change the face of the nation's viniculture.

• 2 •

Home winemakers, who ferment juice only for their own use, fall into several categories, which sometimes overlap. During Prohibition, more than 30 million gallons were made annually in home basements in this country, especially by immigrant European families to whom wine was a mealtime necessity. Most of their immediate descendants, however, have given up the fermenting of grapes as too much trouble. Today's noncommercial winemakers are a new breed.

They usually start with the simple kitchen experiment of adding yeast to a crock of crushed grapes, juice, or reconstituted concentrate. Some try it once and give it up when they find they have made inferior vinegar instead. But many go on to spend hundreds and even thousands of dollars on crushers, presses, chemicals, and testing instruments, and many even to make their own champagnes.

While some who make wine regularly are merely saving money, another and more numerous category are primarily hobbyists, motivated not by economy but by their fascination with the mystique and romance of wine. They are mostly talented white collar people bitten by the wine bug, who have found in this scientific kind of handicraft a hobby of continuing interest, more esthetically satisfying than collecting coins, stamps or books. Wine, because it keeps changing and takes months and years to mature, gives the winemaker a sense of the future that no other hobby does. The oenothusiast knows that better wine than he makes can usually be bought for little more or even less at the store.

Most devoted of the avocational winemakers are professional people, particularly physicians, engineers, chemists, college professors, accountants, artists, and writers. The doctors are the most avid of them all. Far more MDs than people of any other occupation are counted among the customers of the wine-making supply firms. Why wine especially fascinates physicians was explained in a recent book called *Vine and Scalpel* by Dr. Max Lake, who owns a vineyard in Australia. "The doctor," he wrote, "has a comfortable amount of winemaking science as part of his medical training. He must also learn to evaluate sensory impressions and cultivate mental discipline, two attributes that tend to make him a wine connoisseur."

Hundreds of home winemakers' societies have been formed across the United States because amateur enologists want others to taste and compare their wines. Their national organization, the American Wine Society, lists 1,300 members and seventy-three chapters in three dozen states and publishes its own quarterly journal.

Since a new Federal ruling permits home winemakers to hold competitions with prizes for their best vintages, the lure of possibly winning championship awards is added as a motive for making one's own wine. Amateur winemakers are as proud of their achievements as flower growers, dog breeders, artists, and others who hold quality contests, perhaps even prouder, for winemaking is both an art and a science. (The first public judging of homemade wines in this country was held in August 1972, at Mason City, Iowa, as part of the North Iowa Fair. The first national judging was held in San Francisco in February 1973).

Federal law permits the home production of up to 200 gallons of wine each year without paying a tax on the product, but restricts the privilege to heads of households. It thereby prohibits winemaking by an individual living without his spouse or without dependents in the household under his control. Bachelors of both sexes have long protested this discrimination, and bills to eliminate the head-of-household restriction have been pending in Congress since 1971. A Federal regulation further classifies home winemaking as illegal unless the householder first files Form 1541 with the nearest office of the Internal Revenue Service. Though the form is free, it merely constitutes a registration or a declaration of intent to make wine—not a license or permit—and consequently not many people bother to file it. The Federal Government is not really interested in home winemaking, anyway, but only in seeing that if wine is to be sold, the requirements for permits, bonds, tax stamps, and for payment of the Federal gallonage tax are obeyed.

Another part of the regulation prohibits the amateur from transporting his homemade wine from his dwelling without Federal permission. I haven't heard of any attempt in recent years to enforce either the filing regulation or the transportation taboo. It was the prohibition on transportation that led to the Federal ruling that now permits wine to be taken to places where quality competitions are to be held. Amateur enologists' organizations complained that such contests, with judges awarding prizes for the best wines, have been held for years in England and should be permitted in the United States. (Under the ruling, special permission must be obtained for each competition the home winemaker enters.)

A conservative estimate, based on average annual interstate carlot shipments of fresh grapes from California, is that at least 7 million gallons of wine are now being made noncommercially in the United States each year. But if wines made from grape concentrate are counted, the quantity is probably closer to 10 million gallons, enough to supply a half-million amateurs with forty gallons each. And this does not include the production of those householders who ferment only dandelions, rhubarb, elderberries, blueberries, or honey (to make mead), as their grandmothers and great-grandmothers did.

A multimillion-dollar accessory industry has come into existence to supply amateur enologists with home-winemaking materials, equipment, corks, and even with labels printed with their names, such as "Château Smith Vin Blanc" or "Maison Jones Private Stock." Some firms offer free classes in winemaking and distribute bumper strips with such messages as MAKE WINE NOT WAR.

Purists, of course, prefer to make their wines out of fresh

grapes or juice, which can only be bought at vintage time. Grape concentrate, available year round, is more convenient for winemaking at home. The reviving use of concentrate recalls the Prohibition era a half century ago, when millions of gallons of "Vine-Glo," "Caligrapo," and "Forbidden Fruit" concentrates were fermented to wine in American homes.

Well-made concentrate wines are difficult to distinguish from everyday commercial types, but they generally lack aroma; they are not Sunday wines. Experiments in progress are attempting to extract the aromatic essences of wine grapes before the juice is concentrated. The idea is to supply home winemakers with the bottled essence to be added after the wine is made.

A beginner's winemaking kit, which can be bought nowadays for only a few dollars, contains a quart of concentrate, small envelopes of yeast and chemicals, fermentation locks, siphon hose, a collapsible plastic jug, and a recipe to make a single gallon (five bottles) of table wine. Bigger kits, at twelve to twenty dollars, have become such fast-selling items that department stores have jumped into the homemade-wine-supply business and have sold millions of dollars' worth of such materials and equipment. Their sales are especially big in areas where commercial wines are expensive because of high state wine taxes or where wines can be bought only in state monopoly stores.

Oldest of the firms that sell home-winemaking supplies, the Aetna Bottle Company of Seattle, has customers in every state in the Union, in Canada, India, Thailand, and even in Saudi Arabia. Scores of books are published for home winemakers, and for home brewers of beer. (Home brewing is technically illegal, however, under a change made in the Federal law in 1959; the brewing industry considers it unfair competition. But most commercial wineries favor home winemaking because amateurs help to popularize the drinking of wine, and most of them buy as much wine as they produce.)

• 3 •

The truest of all wine lovers are those who grow their own wine grapes. Their appreciation of the final product is multiplied by the years of back-breaking labor, suffering the depredations of weather and of grape-eating birds, and waiting for their first crops. How patient they must be is evident from the three to five years it takes from the planting of a vine until it bears a usable crop. If you add at least four years for a fine red wine to mature, you see that the new winegrower is investing a decade of his life. Yet there are many who consider the rewards infinitely greater than those from the raising of other crops that one cannot drink.

Philip Wagner, whose books have encouraged thousands of amateurs to plant wine grapes, spells out the attractions. A hundred healthy vines in the lower end of a back yard, he says, will yield a vintage of sixty gallons, which supplies the grower with three hundred bottles, or almost a bottle of table wine per day through the year. (Dr. Albert Winkler calculates that a hundred vines in sunny California can produce three times as much as Wagner's figure.)

An amateur who plants more than a hundred vines can use only a little over a ton of his crop to make wine, because more would exceed the 200-gallon limit. If he makes more, he must bond his cellar and consider selling some of his wine.

• 4 •

Most of the small winegrowers who have bonded their cellars hope to make a profit by selling their wines. Whether they profit or lose depends on many factors, including their talent, industrious habits, business sense, and particularly on whether the law of the state where the small winery is situated favors farm wineries with a reasonable license fee, such as twenty dollars a year. The law must permit the winegrower to offer complimentary tasting, to sell his product at both retail and wholesale, and to stay open on Sunday because that is the day most people like to go on wine tours.

Winegrowing is like most other industries in that it costs multiple millions to start out in competition with the leaders. Yet wine is also one of the few industries in which an individual can start with a small acreage and make something in his home basement that he can sell. Better yet, of course, is to start out wealthy, with no thought of early profits, as many have done. For some there is sufficient reward in merely achieving the admired status of gentleman winegrower.

Decades ago, Herman Wente gave me some advice to pass on to the many would-be winegrowers who have come to me for guidance before entering the wine industry. The small wine-grower can succeed, Herman said, only if he remains small and sells his wine at retail. Thereby he makes not only the profits (if any) of the grape grower and of the wine producer, but the profits of the wholesaler and of the retailer in addition. To my knowledge, those who have followed Herman's advice have prospered thus far.

Small winegrowers also have an advantage that Herman didn't mention. Because their output is limited, their wines become rarities, which lends them extra charm. Connoisseurs nowadays gladly pay extra prices for good wines if they are especially scarce and hard to find. Some small wineries sell all they can make, at prices considerably above those of the nationally known premium brands, by merely sending announcements to the customers on their mailing lists that their latest vintages are ready to be shipped.

A quandary facing small winegrowers is to decide how they would like themselves to be described. Some resent being called "boutique wineries," a term that came into use in the 1970s, because they consider it a slur. Yet "boutique" does suggest to many a small place where things of quality can be found. Some consider "small winery" a sufficient descriptive term. Canada calls its new small winegrowers "cottage wineries" or "craft wineries." In France, small wineries call themselves châteaux, though few of them resemble castles. I prefer to call them "farm wineries" because the term and their very existence helps to educate the public about what wine is. Seeing a small winery on a vineyard teaches people the key fact that distinguishes wine from manufactured beverages, that wine is a natural product grown on a farm like other foods. It tells the story of wine better than any book can.

There is no truth, of course, in the belief held by many wine snobs, that fine wines can only be made in small quantities. The American wines that are now winning high praise around the world come mainly from sizable wineries that have modern equipment and staffs of expert enologists.

Commercial wines need to be filtered, fined, made brilliantly clear and sufficiently stable to survive cross-country transportation and storage in excessive heat and cold while awaiting sale. The small winegrower can let his wines clarify themselves, can bottle them while they still contain grape solids that will precipitate in the bottles, and can explain this to his customers.

In particular, commercial grape growers have found it economically necessary to abandon their old hillside vineyards, which once produced their finest wines. Their tractors and mechanical harvesters cannot operate on steep terrain, and labor costs have made hand-cultivation prohibitively expensive.

(This is also happening in Europe.) Only the avocational winegrower can afford to till the hillsides.

The small winegrower may not make wines that are finer than others, but what he makes will at least be excitingly different. Only he can afford to experiment in localities where grapes have not been grown before, planting new grape varieties and developing wines with new regional characteristics.

I was discussing the future of fine American wines recently with André Tchelistcheff. He pointed out that as the production of the leading vintners in Europe and America continues to grow in volume, their wines become more uniform; they have less opportunity to engage in pioneering experiments. "The apostolic mission of the future," said Tchelistcheff, "belongs to the small winegrower."

25

Some "Varietal Grapes" and Their Wines

WHEN American vintners, during three decades following Repeal, introduced almost a hundred wines newly named for grape varieties, they multiplied the delicious confusion that surrounds the subject of wine. Most of the varietal names on bottle labels and restaurant wine lists present a viticultural puzzle to most buyers of wine.

But in adopting varietal labeling, the vintners also contributed vastly to the improved quality of American wines. For by renaming their best and costliest vintages for the grapes from which they are made, the wineries gave vineyardists a profit motive to plant superior wine-grape varieties in place of the more prolific fresh-juice, raisin, and table grapes that have mainly been grown in this country until very recent years.

If, for example, the vintners had not taught wine merchants that Chardonnay, White (Johannisberg) Riesling, Cabernet Sauvignon, and Pinot Noir make the world's finest table wines, the grape growers would not have planted the more than fifty thousand acres of these four noble varieties that have been added to American vineyards since the mid-1960s. Buyers who have learned to recognize these varietal labels now gladly pay a dollar to three dollars more per bottle for these wines than for their old generically named equivalents—chablis, rhine wine, claret, and burgundy. And once a status-conscious American masters the pronunciation of such tongue-twisting names as Cabernet Sauvignon and Pinot Noir, he proudly orders them in stores and restaurants to display his knowledge of fine wines.

How this motivates vineyard planting is evident from the all-time-record prices some California coast-counties wineries paid growers in 1971 for some "varietal grapes": $625 per ton for Chardonnay, White Riesling, Cabernet Sauvignon, and

Pinot Noir, and $325 for Sauvignon Blanc, Chenin Blanc, and Barbera, compared to the San Joaquin Valley prices of $54 per ton paid that year for Thompson Seedless and $60 for Flame Tokay.* This is why more than two-thirds of the new vineyards planted in California during that year consisted of grape varieties with whose names premium wines are most frequently labeled.

Grapes whose names appear on wine labels are commonly called "varietal grapes," although this is a redundancy, because every grape, including those that make the poorest wines, is a member of some variety, no matter how obscure its botanical parentage may be. Another foggy popular term is "varietal wines," which doesn't describe the wines, but only means that their labels tell you the grape varieties from which they are principally made.

Wines sold under grape names are usually better than those labeled with the old generic names of European geographic origin. Not always, however, because a wine's quality depends also on where the vine grew, whether it was pruned to keep the crop small, when the grapes were picked, and how the vintner processed, blended, and aged the wine.

Adding to the confusion is that most grapes have many different names, by any of which the wines made from them can be called; some examples will follow a few pages hence. Many grapes are misnamed, and European vintners, now imitating the American varietal labels, are adding to the tangle with their own contradictory versions of some variety names. The result is that one needs an ampelography, which can't be found in the average library, to be guided through the wine-nomenclature maze. Moreover, additional new varieties are constantly being bred in the United States and in other countries, so that no ampelography can possibly be kept up to date.

• 2 •

The jumble of varietal names is now being at least partially unraveled, however, for the principal grapes grown for wine-making in the United States. Through a grape-certification program founded by the University of California in 1952, Vinifera vines certified as correctly named, and also as free of virus diseases, are now being supplied to growers and co-

*Grape prices of course vary from year to year, but it was the skyrocketing 1971 prices which set off the overplanting of "varietals" that broke the California grape market three years later.

operating nurseries. Confusion is also being lessened among the many-numbered French hybrid grapes grown east of the Rockies.

The purpose of the California certification program was not to untangle grape nomenclature, but to supply the wine industry with disease-free vines. It was prompted by advances after the Second World War in plant pathology and vine research, which showed that most of the world's vineyards are hosts to a previously unidentified disease called the leafroll virus, which reduces vine vigor and productivity without killing the plants. Were it not for this virus, plant pathologists say, the vineyards of Europe would have more frequent vintage years than they do. One of their surprising discoveries was that the much-admired autumn coloring of vineyards is mostly caused by the leafroll virus—that the leaves of healthy vines seldom develop those spectacularly lovely shades of red!

Unfortunately, when the mad vineyard-planting spree of the late 1960s began, the supply of certified healthy, variety-true vines was not sufficient to meet the demand. Thousands of acres were recklessly planted with cuttings from diseased vines, purchased from infected vineyards and from nurseries with uncertified stocks. When this was realized in 1970, quarantines against virus-infected vines were hurriedly established in the states of Washington and Oregon.

The shortage of certified vines continued until 1971, when two new discoveries shortened the time it had been taking the California program to provide supplies of healthy vines. The first discovery was that by exposing vines to controlled heat for a period of several weeks, cuttings can be taken from them that are completely free of disease. The second was an assembly-line method of growing vines in moisture-controlled greenhouses, called "mist propagation," which makes it possible to produce a million cuttings within a single year from a single parent vine.

• 3 •

In California for almost a century, except during Prohibition, University viticulturists have been testing wine grapes, growing more than a hundred different varieties in various parts of the state, making experimental wines of each variety and evaluating the wines. As the main result of this research, the University has listed some twoscore varieties as "acceptable" or "recommended" for planting in specific climatic regions to make wines of high quality and to earn the growers a profit.

The University strongly recommended that the four *cépages nobles* (Chardonnay, White Riesling, Cabernet Sauvignon, Pinot Noir) be grown only in the cool coast counties, Regions I, II, and III. For Regions IV and V, the varieties mainly recommended were Ruby Cabernet and Barbera for red table wines and French Colombard and Chenin Blanc (for Region IV) for whites. New table-wine varieties have been added since. For port wines in warm climates the University has favored such Portuguese grapes as Tinta Madeira, Touriga, and Souzão.

Most of the University's planting recommendations are being followed, but not all. We have seen how, by the early 1970s, the record high prices vintners were paying for the four noble varieties in the coast counties were tempting farmers in the hot San Joaquin Valley to begin planting them in their Region IV and V climates, where they yield grapes of lower quality but more tons per acre. This alarmed the University savants because there was nothing to prevent wines from the valley being sold to the public under the four most prestigious varietal names. "It would seem wise," warned Professor Maynard Amerine in a 1971 article in *Wines & Vines,* "that these labels not be debased by using wines of varieties grown in regions that do not meet present expectations of quality." If the top varietal names were thus "debased" by the valley growers, he added, the coast-counties vintners might be compelled to start labeling all their products as "Coast Wines."

• 4 •

The Federal regulations adopted in 1936 have allowed any wine to bear a varietal label if it contained as little as 51 percent of the grape named. This said nothing about the other 49 percent, which might have had an entirely different taste.

Now, over forty years later, the Government has set legal machinery in motion to raise the varietal minimum to seventy-five percent. Vintners generally agree with the 75 percent figure. The questions remaining are whether the change should be made in steps, beginning at 65 percent, and whether it should be delayed until 1981 to allow time for more planting of the rarer "varietal" grapes. (European countries had never required any minimum varietal percentage until 1970, when the new German wine law became effective with a minimum of 75 percent.)

Since any minimum over 51 percent will be an improvement, why not make it 100 percent? That would be a mistake, because most wines need blending with wines of different grapes to be at their best. No single grape variety can be relied on, year after year, to produce wines of ideal balance in every respect.

Moreover, complexity of wine flavor, an elusive quality that many American wines still lack, may sometimes be attained with a blend of different grapes. The fine wines of the Champagne region of France are traditionally blends of Pinot Noir and Chardonnay, and the French appellation control permits French champagnes to contain as many as four additional grapes (Pinot Blanc, Pinot Gris, Arbanne, Petit Meslier). The finest clarets of the Médoc district of Bordeaux are always blends: Cabernet Sauvignon there is normally blended with such relatives as Merlot, Cabernet Franc, and Petit Verdot. French sauternes are always blends of Sémillon and Sauvignon Blanc, sometimes with the addition of Muscadelle. While the famous Côte d'Or red burgundies owe their greatness to Pinot Noir and the famous whites to Chardonnay, the Côte d'Or vineyards also contain appreciable acreages of Aligoté, Gamay Noir, Pinot Blanc, Pinot Gris, and Melon (which in the Loire Valley is called Muscadet). And the French appellation control permits as many as fifteen different grapes to be blended in Châteauneuf-du-Pape, the most renowned of Rhone Valley reds.

Although most wine books call Cabernet Sauvignon the chief French claret grape, that variety represents only a fraction of the red-grape acreage of Bordeaux. In the great châteaux of Saint-Émilion, for example, if you ask a *maître du chai* what percentage of Cabernet Sauvignon his wine contains, he is likely to reply, *"Pas du Sauvignon."* Jacquelin and Poulain, in their *Wines and Vineyards of France* (Paul Hamlyn, London, 1965), state that nine tenths of the Château Margaux vineyard is planted to Cabernet Sauvignon but that Château Lafite-Rothschild is five eighths Cabernet Sauvignon and three eighths Cabernet Franc and Merlot. On my several visits to the Médoc, few of the château proprietors of whom I inquired on this point claimed that their wines contained more than a third of Cabernet Sauvignon. In fact, if you wish a wine made 100 percent of that noblest of Bordeaux grapes, you are likely to find it only in California. (In years past, more Cabernet Sauvignon was grown in the Médoc than now. But because its wine required many years to mature, it gradually was replaced by Cabernet Franc and Merlot. However, now that Bordeaux winegrowers have learned—as California winemakers have, too—to speed the aging of their red wines by removing them from the skins before fermentation is complete, they are reported to be planting Cabernet Sauvignon again.)

There is at least one "varietal" wine—Concord—to which the future 75 percent varietal minimum will not apply. The taste of that grape is so powerful that a wine made 75 percent of ripe Concords might be too flavorful to drink. The government is expected to rule that for Concord, other Labrusca varieties, and also for Muscadines, the varietal minimum should remain at 51 percent. Also, California wineries have asked that the minimum for Cabernet Sauvignon be set at 65 percent in order to permit blending of their Cabernet with Merlot.

Some vintners are saying that the trend toward varietal labeling in the United States may have gone too far because many consumers insist on wines made 100 percent of the variety on the label. This discourages vintners from blending for maximum palatability, one of the highest of their arts.

• 5 •

How do you describe the varietal taste of a wine? The grapy or foxy flavor of Labrusca wines is familiar to anyone who has ever tasted grape jelly or Welch's grape juice. Also recognizable, with some practice, are wines made from the scented, aromatic, or "spicy" grapes—the Muscats, Sauvignon Blanc, and Gewürztraminer. The characteristic aromas of Grenache and Gamay Noir, which also make wines that are somewhat "spicy," are readily recognized by at least some connoisseurs. Zinfandel wines are sometimes recognizable, too, because they have an aroma subtly reminiscent of raspberry, which, however, is not often perceptible when the wines are old.

Cabernet Sauvignon wine has a powerful, astringent flavor, as distinctive, when the wine is new, as that of a stale cigar. Professor Amerine says that even when Cabernet Sauvignon is blended down to 51 percent, unless with Zinfandel or another grape of high flavor, the Cabernet will still dominate the blend. Its great virtue is that when its wine is properly aged in cask and in bottle, it gradually loses its astringent taste and develops a fine bouquet. California vintners used to say that Cabernet Sauvignon was undrinkable until it had been aged at least four years in wood and had undergone a malolactic fermentation. Lately, however, I have tasted some Cabernet Sauvignon samples, fermented only briefly on the skins, that were recognizable, fruity, and delicious after only two years in wood.

Most other Vinifera wines have only winy or vinous tastes, developed during vinification and aging, that are not readily identifiable when the wines are new. Chardonnay is the best example. The juice of this tiny, thin-skinned, translucent grape, which makes the greatest white burgundies and champagnes, ferments to a young wine that has no outstanding flavor. But Chardonnay is one of the few white wines that are capable of improving greatly after a year in wood and further aging in glass. Because of its ideal combination of body, delicacy, acidity, and unusually high alcoholic strength, it develops an enchanting winy bouquet. The new winegrowers who are planting Vinifera vines in the East and Midwest choose Chardonnay above other varieties because of its high quality and the high prices its wine commands, and also because it excels most other Old World grapes in its ability to survive their freezing winters. (Other whites besides Chardonnay that are likely to improve with age, but only after bottling, include White Riesling and Sauvignon Blanc.)

Dr. Amerine and Dr. Vernon Singleton, in *Wine—An Introduction for Americans* (University of California Press, 1965), offer some terms descriptive of the principal varietal flavors in Vinifera wines. They describe the taste and aroma of Cabernet Sauvignon as "green olive, herbaceous," Ruby Cabernet as "green olive, weedy, tannic," and Malbec (Cot) as "krautish, soft." They say Pinot Noir is "pepperminty" and that Gamay Beaujolais is "fruity, tart." Nebbiolo they describe as "fruity, licorice," and Tinta Madeira as "prunish, cheddar, rich." Their descriptions of Vinifera white wines mainly use such terms as "fruity," "tart," "spicy," and sometimes "floral," but the character of Chardonnay is described as "applish" and that of Sémillon as "figs, faintly cigar-like." Omitted from their descriptions is the flavor of European oak barrels, which is perceptible in most French clarets and white burgundies and nowadays in many California Chardonnays. The University at Davis does not encourage the use of European cooperage because the oak obscures the delicate flavors contributed by superior grapes.

• 6 •

Muscat grapes, of which there are scores of different varieties, all of them "spicy," are a study by themselves. The one commonly grown in California is Muscat of Alexandria, which is primarily a raisin and table grape but nevertheless makes most of this country's muscatel. Its wines lack the delicacy of the smaller Muscat Blanc, which is called Moscato Canelli in Italy and Muscat Frontignan in France. Canadian and New

York wineries have made superior muscatels from the Canada Muscat, a hybrid developed at the Geneva station in upstate New York.

The name of Muscat seems to lack appeal, however, to most buyers of wine. For example, when the Christian Brothers in the 1940s introduced a delectable table wine called Light Sweet Muscat, few people would buy it; but when they changed its name to Château La Salle, it became one of their best-selling wines. Muscat wines are most delicious when they are made sweet and low in alcohol, as are Louis Martini's Moscato Amabile at ten percent and the Muscat champagne of Italy called Asti Spumante, at nine. Muscat wines are usually harsh or bitter when fermented completely dry.

There also are dark-colored Muscats, such as Aleatico, which makes wines that are popular in Italy, and Black Hamburgh, from which the Novitiate of Los Gatos makes its famous Black Muscat dessert wine. A French ampelography tells an intriguing story about the Black Hamburgh grape. It once was widely grown in France, but when the phylloxera vine louse devastated the French vineyards, the Black Hamburgh disappeared. Many years later, a Frenchman visiting a hothouse in England noticed a beautiful black grape named Venn's Seedling and brought it to France, where it was identified as the long-lost grape. The only thing wrong with the story is that the Black Hamburgh was never lost; it has been grown continuously under its own name for more than a century in graperies in the eastern United States.

• 7 •

A somewhat similar story is told of the plump, oval-shaped Thompson Seedless, the most widely planted grape in California.

Its origin is something of a mystery. Some say it is the Sultanina or Sultanieh of Persia. Others identify it with the Oval Kishmish or Chekirdeksiz of Turkey, the Ak-Kishmish of Russia, or the Sultana of Australia. Sultana in California, however, is a different grape, also seedless, but smaller than the Thompson.

Back in 1872, an Englishman named William Thompson brought to his farm at Yuba City in California's Sacramento Valley a hothouse grape named Lady de Coverly. Some say he had known it in England, but that he bought it from a grapery in Connecticut; others say he found it at Rochester, New York.

Who Lady de Coverly was remains a mystery, too. The Yuba City farmer became known as Seedless Thompson, although he fathered seventeen children. When the raisin industry became important around Fresno in the 1890s, vineyardists there began planting Thompson's seedless grape. It became the three-way grape of the valley, salable for fresh use or dried as a raisin, and after Repeal to make neutral-flavored dessert wines and brandy. When the table-wine revolution came in the 1960s, the valley wineries learned that if harvested early the Thompson makes a clean though bland-tasting table wine, called by some cynics "Fresno Chardonnay." It also is useful in making inexpensive champagnes, and because of its neutral flavor has become the vintners' favorite grape to make both brandy and the sweet-flavored and newly popular "pop" grape wines.

• 8 •

The other famous mystery grape is Zinfandel, the second most widely planted red variety of California, where it is exceeded in acreage only by Carignane. Except for scattered transplants from California to Oregon and Mexico, Zinfandel is said to be found nowhere else in the world.

Zinfandel is a round, thin-skinned, very sweet and juicy grape, and if eaten fresh in any quantity it has a cathartic effect. Depending on where and how it is grown and vinified, it makes many different wines. In the cool coast-counties climates, Regions I to III, it usually makes a fresh, bright-ruby wine with the famous raspberrylike or "bramble" aroma, that is especially delicious when drunk young, like Beaujolais. Grown in Region IV climates, Zinfandel also makes fruity table wines if harvested early, and is useful, blended with other grapes, in making rosés and red ports. In Region V, however, Zinfandel is subject to bunch rot (unless sprayed with the giberellin plant hormone, which makes the berries larger and loosens the bunch), and if harvested late, makes only ordinary port or an alcoholic, flat-tasting table wine. If a well-made coast-counties Zinfandel is aged in wood and in bottle for several years, it develops a bouquet as fine as the noble Cabernet. But few vintners age their Zinfandels more than a year or two, because long aging is costly and unprofitable except for Cabernet and Pinot Noir, the prices of which rise steeply as their wines increase in age. Many California wineries now make delicious Zinfandel rosés, and a few use the colorless juice to make white Zinfandels, which some call Zinfandel Blanc. I also have tasted recently some 17 percent Zinfandel wines made from late-harvested grapes. The best was a Zinfandel Essence, a very sweet red wine made by the Ridge Winery from Lodi grapes.

Hundreds of articles have been written about the mystery of Zinfandel. Who brought it from Europe, when, from where, and what was its original name? Most wine writers credit "Count" Agoston Haraszthy with introducing the grape to California from his native Hungary between 1851 and 1862. But Zinfandel was never listed among his importations, and no such red grape has been found in Hungary—only a white grape named Zierfahndler or Zierfandel (which are among the many names of Sylvaner). Howevet, a red European grape named Zinfandel was grown under glass by William Robert Prince on Long Island, New York, as early as 1830, ten years before Haraszthy emigrated to the United States. Prince wrote in his *Treatise on the Vine,* published in that year, that the Zinfandel came from Hungary. During the 1840s the noted hybridizer, John Fisk Allen, also grew a grape he called "Zinfindal" at Salem, Massachusetts, and his description of it, published in 1848, exactly matches California's adopted foundling Zinfandel.

Since many of the Vinifera grapes brought to California during the nineteenth century came from eastern nurseries rather than directly from Europe—and it was William Prince who first mistakenly called Zinfandel a Hungarian variety—it may well have come from a hothouse in his nursery at Flushing, New York.

If Dr. Austin Goheen, who doesn't claim to be an ampelographer, knows Zinfandel when he sees it on the vine, the mystery of its origin may already have been solved. In the autumn of 1967, Dr. Goheen, the United States Department of Agriculture plant pathologist who originated "mist-propagation," was returning from a meeting in Germany and stopped at Bari in the southeastern Italian province of Puglia to visit his colleague Giovanni Martelli. At dinner on his arrival in Bari, Goheen was served a red wine that tasted to him like Zinfandel. "When did you start importing wine from California?" he asked. Martelli replied that of course the wine was local, of a grape widely grown in Puglia. The next day Goheen visited the vineyards between Bari, Gioia del Colle, and Taranto, and saw grapes and vines that looked exactly like Zinfandel. Farmers called the grapes "Primitivo di Gioia." Goheen arranged with Martelli to send him cuttings of Primitivo, which after a quarantine period were planted at Davis in 1971 beside a row of Zinfandel. Nobody has yet been able to tell the Primitivo vines or their grapes, seeds, juice, or wine from those of Zinfandel. In 1976, Dr. Wade Wolfe at UC Davis made electronic comparisons of the enzyme patterns of Zinfandel and Primitivo and found them identical. Goheen since has learned that a grape resembling Primitivo grows across the Adriatic on the Dalmatian coast of Yugoslavia and on the island of Vis, where it is called "Plavac Mali." At Davis, he has found another clue in wine literature that the Primitivo in Italy has also been called "Zingarello." (Cyril Ray, in his *Wines of Italy,* discusses the Primitivo and mentions that its wine can improve with age—a characteristic of California's Zinfandel.)

Dr. Goheen hasn't yet published his findings, but he is willing to bet that when Harold Olmo makes enough additional trips to Europe to visit the vineyards of Puglia, he will confirm that Goheen has discovered the origin of Zinfandel.

• 9 •

The many French hybrid wines I have tasted in the eastern, midcontinent, and Canadian wineries have been mostly winy, not grapy, in flavor. Many of the whites and some of the reds could easily be mistaken for fine Vinifera wines. The reds generally have tended to be soft and especially pleasant to drink young. Only one red has had an outstanding varietal character, easily recognized when tasted "blind." The name of the grape is Baco Noir; the flavor of its wine is more powerful than that of Cabernet Sauvignon.

Great as has been the impact of the French hybrids on the American wine industry outside California, the change these varieties have made in the vineyards and wines of France is far greater. A fact never mentioned in French wine publicity, and therefore not yet realized in the wine trade, is that fully one fifth of French wine production now comes from the hybrids. Every French vineyard district, including Bordeaux, Burgundy, and Champagne, now grows them extensively, and although the hybrids legally are not permitted to be used in making any of the *appellation contrôlée* wines, many hybrid grapes are specifically recommended by the French Government to be grown for *vins du pays.* (The French, by the way, call them "the American hybrids.")

How and when did this revolutionary change in French viniculture come about? It will be remembered that the phylloxera aphid, accidentally introduced to France on botanical specimens brought from America, spread like a plague and that between 1860 and 1910 it devastated the vineyards of Europe.

About 1869, French viticulturists discovered (as was already known in this country) that the tough roots of native American vines resist the deadly phylloxera. The French then sent to America for rootstocks and replanted their vineyards with American vines, onto which they grafted their Vinifera. It was thus that American roots saved the vineyards of Europe. But the French winegrowers were not satisfied. They wanted *producteurs directs* (direct producers)—phylloxera-resistant vines that would produce grapes without the painstaking labor and expense of grafting. This started their viticulturists in hybridizing (crossing) the robust American wild varieties with the delicate Vinifera. The first resulting hybrid vines did resist the phylloxera, but the grapes they produced tasted like their wild American parents. Hybridizers in the United States had already made such crosses, with the same disappointing results. The French, however, kept trying, because their motive was more compelling; winegrowing is their nation's chief agricultural industry and supports much of the French population. By 1900 they had succeeded in producing a number of hybrids which made wines resembling Vinifera types. These first nonfoxy hybrids were widely planted in France. But much better hybrids were developed in the few following decades, and still better ones have kept coming from France—and also from grape breeders in the United States and Canada—during the past several years.

The vines Philip Wagner first imported to Baltimore during the 1930s were the early creations of two of the first French hybridizers, Maurice Baco and Albert Seibel. The Baco No. 1 variety was the most successful of the early reds. Most of the French hybrid grapes were named for their originators, such as Georges Couderc, Seibel, Baco, Galibert, Landot, Ravat, Seyve-Villard, and Vidal, and were distinguished by the hybridizers' seedling numbers. Lately, however, those that make the best wines have been given names, which have now begun to appear on varietal labels of the wines. For example, Baco No. 1 became Baco Noir; Seyve-Villard 5276 is now Seyval Blanc, and the black Seibel 10878 became Chelois.*

*Other red-wine hybrids include Bellandais (Seibel 14596), Cascade (S.13053), Chambourcin (Joannes-Seyve 26205), Chancellor (S. 7053), Colobel (S. 8357), Couderc (Couderc 7120), De Chaunac (S. 9549), Florental (Burdin 7705), Garonnet (S-V 18283), Landal (Landot 244), Léon Millot (Kuhlmann 194-2), Maréchal Foch (Kuhlmann 188-2), Plantet (S. 5455), Ravat Noir (Ravat 262), Rosette (S. 1000), Rougeon (S. 5898), and Villard Noir (Seyve-Villard 18315). Among white-wine hybrids with new names are Ambros (Seibel 10713), Aurore or Aurora (S. 5279), Baco Blanc (Baco 22A), Rayon d'Or (S. 4986), Ravat Blanc (Ravat 6), Roucaneuf (S-V 12309), Verdelet (S. 9110), Vignoles (Ravat 51), and Villard Blanc (S-V 12375).

Bitter controversy surrounds the French hybrids in Europe. Some countries have restricted them or even have prohibited them from being planted, lest they replace the Vinifera varieties that made their wines famous in the past. Germany prohibits them by law; Italy permits some varieties in the cool Alpine foothill regions. Some small plantings made in southern Germany before the restrictions became effective were allowed to remain. In this country, Dr. Konstantin Frank of course has opposed the planting of hybrids, claiming that Vinifera can survive eastern climates as well as the hybrids can. Philip Wagner recommends the hybrids over Vinifera for the East as more likely to produce annual crops. He says the care of Vinifera vines in eastern climates requires a high order of expertise. Many eastern and midwestern farmers have developed such expertise. They warn, however, that Vinifera succeed in such climates only when planted on ideal sites and when given twice the care the hybrids require. One especially knowledgeable vineyardist comments: "Perhaps they first should grow the hybrids in order to learn how to grow the Vinifera."

It is unfortunate that the demeaning word "hybrid" was attached to the French-American varieties when they were first introduced in the United States. Were it not for this term, the wines made from these grapes would be judged impartially for whatever qualities they possess. After all, many commercially-grown Vinifera wine grapes are also hybrids—crosses made with other varieties either artificially or by chance.

• 10 •

The classic Vinifera varieties are known by many different names in viticultural regions around the world. Moreover, like other plants and animals, including people, each Old World variety has changed through the centuries, by cross-breeding and by natural selection to fit particular environments—into different strains or *clones.* The only grapes that have not yet changed and developed clones are the new hybrids, which when planted as cuttings, produce grapes with the same flavors as the original vines.

There are at least 200 clones of Pinot Noir. Consequently, wines made from different Pinot Noir clones, even when grown in the same vineyard, may differ markedly in aroma and taste. There are dozens of strains of Cabernet Sauvignon in California and many more in France. Clones of both old and new varieties are now being chosen for ease of picking by the new harvesting machines. (Nurserymen who sell the new heat-treated, virus-free Vinifera vines now call them "super-clones.")

Chardonnay is called Weisser Klevner in Germany, Beaunois in the region of Chablis, Auxerrois in the Jura, Pinot Blanc in South America, White Pinot in Australia, and Pinot Chardonnay in the United States. Yet it is not a member of the Pinot family, as are Pinot Noir, Pinot Meunier, and the true Pinot Blanc, another variety that makes fine white burgundies and champagnes.

White Riesling is usually called Johannisberg Riesling because it makes the wines of world-famous Schloss Johannisberg in the Rheingau. It also has many relatives, including such crosses as California's Emerald Riesling and Germany's Müller-Thurgau. Most California wines labeled simply as "Riesling" are not made from White Riesling, but from Sylvaner or Franken Riesling, the variety responsible for the Franconian Steinweins. Sylvaner wines are most fragrant and delectable when young, but the best White Rieslings retain their zestful, fruity, tart-sweet character and gain in velvety texture for several years. Grey Riesling, which makes a delicious, mouth-filling young white wine, is not a Riesling, and is thought by some to be the Chauché Gris of France; nor is Missouri Riesling. Multiple names occur among native American grapes, too; the grape called Norton in Virginia is known as Virginia Seedling in Missouri but is called Cynthiana in Arkansas.

Since varietal labeling reached its present height of popularity, vineyardists have discovered that some of the grapes they have been growing for generations are misnamed. Australian winegrowers have recently learned that the grape they have been calling "Riesling" is really the Sémillon of Bordeaux.

The identification of grapes is a science by itself. When varieties closely resemble one another, only an expert can tell them apart. He studies the canes, shoots, leaves, and the sizes and shapes of the clusters, as well as the single berries, which he must select from the center, not the outside of the bunch, or else he may be fooled. Many vineyardists are not certain of which varieties they grow. (They soon may be supplied with a means of identifying the grapes in their vineyards. Lucie Morton has translated into English the condensed French practical ampelography by Dr. Pierre Galet of the École Nationale Supérieure Agronomique de Montpellier, and it is to be published by the Cornell University Press.)

Each year from 1949 to 1953, wine juries at the California State Fair awarded the gold medal for Traminer to the Charles

The Traminer grape. One of its clones makes the spicy Gewürz-traminer wine.

Krug Winery of St. Helena, until the vineyard was inspected and it turned out the grapes were not Traminer, but Veltliner, an Austrian variety. In a similar case, the Inglenook Vineyard was winning medals regularly for its Barbera wine until Dr. Albert Winkler studied the vines and identified them as a similar variety called Charbono or Charbonneau. For Inglenook the mistake turned out lucky, for its owners enjoyed a monopoly on the hearty red wine labeled Charbono until other vintners began growing the same vine.

Krug meanwhile is back on the market with a wine of the true Gewürztraminer grape. There are several Traminers, but the one called Gewürztraminer has a distinctly "spicy" flavor; Gewürz means "spicy" in German. Incidentally, Gewürztraminer now has a California relative named Flora. UC viticulturist Dr. Harold Olmo developed the Flora by crossing the Gewürz variety with Sémillon. Flora has some Gewürz aroma, yields more tons per acre than its flavorful parent, and shows promise of becoming a popular California "varietal" in years to come.

The viticulturists at Davis say the grape called Petit or Petite Sirah, which makes flavorful, sometimes "peppery" red wines (as well as rosés and ports) in California, is probably misnamed. It differs from the Syrah (Sirah or Shiraz) grape of Persia, which contributes a piquant flavor to the best red wines of Tain-l'Hermitage in the Rhone Valley of France, but more closely resembles another Rhone variety the French call Durif. Dr. Wade Wolfe has found that the enzyme patterns of California's Petite Sirah closely resemble those of Durif and differ from those of Syrah and Shiraz. Dr. Olmo has imported the French Syrah and it has been planted in some California vineyards. Folle Blanche, which means "crazy white" and which makes tart wines that somewhat resemble chablis, is called Picpoule or Piquepoul Blanc in France. Dr. Olmo has identified the Bastardo grape of Portugal as the French variety called Trousseau. The red-wine variety named Refosco in Italy and California is also the Mondeuse of France. The red grape called Early Burgundy in California may be the variety the French call Portugais Bleu. Some authorities are questioning whether the "true" (*vrai*) Pinot Blanc is actually a separate variety. A report from Australia suggests that the French variety Valdiguié may be growing in California under another name; and so it goes. Enough questions about the correct names of popular wine-grape varieties are being raised to make any vineyardist's head swim.

A particularly knotty example is the story of the Gamays, the principal grapes of southern Burgundy. There are both red and white Gamays in France, and some red Gamays whose juice is red instead of white. The French call the latter Gamays *teinturiers,* literally "dyers," and use them to darken their burgundies, which often lack color.

The late Paul Masson, on visits to his native France, brought home to his California vineyards many Burgundian grape varieties, including a red grape named Gamay Beaujolais. His successors labeled its rich, flavorful red wine with the name of the grape.

They believed it to be the variety from which the famous red wines of the Beaujolais region south of Mâcon are made, attributing its richer flavor to the differences in climate and soil.

In 1946, when I still was secretary of the Wine Institute, France formally demanded of the United States Government that the Masson Vineyard be stopped from selling its red wine as Gamay Beaujolais, on the ground that only a French wine should be allowed to use the name of Beaujolais. I prepared the reply for our Government, pointing out that the varietal label was true because ampelographies had long recognized Gamay Beaujolais as the name of the grape. The French, on consulting their own ampelographies, were astounded when they found I was right.

Meanwhile, a more productive red grape named Gamay had been planted extensively by California growers, mainly in Napa and Sonoma Counties. Its wine, when young, has a distinct "spicy" flavor quite different from Gamay Beaujolais. The grape became known as "Napa Gamay" and was regarded as an inferior relative of Gamay Beaujolais.

Because Masson's wine brought higher prices than "Napa Gamay," other California vintners obtained cuttings and began planting additional acres of his Gamay Beaujolais. By the mid-1960s, there were almost two dozen California wineries selling their own brands of Gamay Beaujolais wine.

Then Professor Olmo, on one of his periodic trips to Europe, inspected the vineyards in the French Beaujolais district and found that the principal grape grown there was not Masson's variety, but another called Gamay Noir *à jus blanc,* "black Gamay with white juice." Further research soon convinced Olmo that Masson's Gamay Beaujolais is actually one of the hundreds of clones of Pinot Noir and that "Napa Gamay" was the French Gamay Noir. After announcing his discoveries, Dr. Olmo tried to persuade California vintners to change their Gamay Beaujolais wine labels to "Pinot Noir." Most of them refused, saying that this clone makes wines distinctly different from those of other Pinot Noirs. Besides, their wines were selling too well as Gamay Beaujolais.

If you find this confusing, you are not alone. Most wine merchants and even most grape growers do not understand it yet. Nor do the French, who use "Gamay Beaujolais" as one of their synonyms for Gamay Noir. Meanwhile, some California vintners, amid all the confusion, are labeling their wines of Napa Gamay as "Gamay Beaujolais," which brings a higher price.

· 11 ·

Because the Old World wine grapes have many interchangeable names, vintners naturally choose those which best sell their wines. Before Prohibition, California vineyardists grew a luscious white grape they called "White Zinfandel." After Repeal, when varietal labels were first becoming popular, they learned that one of the names of the grape in France is Pineau Blanc de la Loire, so they began selling its dry wine as "White Pinot." In 1955, the Mondavi brothers of the Charles Krug winery made a semi-dry version of the wine and introduced it under the grape's other French name, Chenin Blanc. Though their customers couldn't spell or pronounce it, they liked both the name and the wine, which is fresh and delicious when drunk young, like the wines this grape makes in the Vouvray district of the Loire. Other wineries soon emulated Krug, and semidry Chenin Blanc (although some wines under this name are dry) has since become the most plentiful of all California "varietal" white wines. The Christian Brothers make two different wines of the same grape: the younger one is called Chenin Blanc, the finer one is their Pineau de la Loire. Krug still sells its dry version as White Pinot.

How much difference a name makes is exemplified by another of the Brothers' wines. For many years, in the vineyard beside their monastery in the hills above Napa, they grew a red grape of uncertain ancestry and sold its tart, chewy wine as Red Pinot. During the 1960s their Red Pinot suddenly began winning medals at the State Fair, whereupon the Brothers learned from Dr. Olmo that the grape's true name is Pinot Saint-George. They reprinted the label, and their estate-bottled Pinot Saint-George became their most famous red table wine.

Wente Brothers of Livermore during the 1940s sold a dry white wine named for their Ugni Blanc grape, but withdrew it from the market when their customers insisted on calling it "Ugly Blank." The Wentes knew Ugni Blanc is called Trebbiano in Italy, where it is one of the four varieties used to make the classic red chianti. Actually, the grape has a third and more salable name, St. Emilion, by which it is called in the Cognac region of France. The Bianes, of the Brookside Vineyard at Guasti, later learned this from a knowledgeable nurseryman, and the Bianes are doing a thriving business with their dry white wine called St. Emilion. The Wentes now identify their Ugni Blanc as part of the blend with Chenin Blanc that they call their "Blanc de Blancs."

Sauvignon Blanc, the grape that contributes the spicy taste to fine French sauternes, makes spicy white wines in California, but its varietal name on wines has never appealed to very many American buyers. Robert Mondavi remembered that Sauvignon Blanc is also the grape that produces the Loire Valley wine named Pouilly-Fumé, and that its name there is Blanc Fumé.* He conceived of the bright idea of renaming his dry Sauvignon Blanc "Fumé Blanc." His wine became so popular that other wineries began also using the name, with some reversing it to "Blanc Fumé."

• 12 •

Because varietal names project glamour and attract buyers who search for new flavors in wines, some vintners sell

---

*The French say the Sauvignon Blanc grown around Pouilly-sur-Loire has both a smoky and a spicy taste; hence *fumé* (smoked).

"varietals" that don't deserve varietal names. Green Hungarian, for example, is a flavorless grape that is valuable only to
make white blending-wines, but its name has an intriguing
winy sound. Semidry wines called Green Hungarian, pleasant
but with no outstanding flavor, first appeared in 1945 and are
now popular throughout the United States. Royalty, Rubired,
and Salvador are grapes with red juice, extensively grown in the
San Joaquin Valley because they are useful to darken wines that
lack color. You can write a letter with their juice in your fountain
pen. There now are dry red table wines named Royalty,
although that grape has a harsh, unpleasant taste. Palomino, a
hardy, tough-skinned grape, is the principal variety grown in
the sherry-producing districts of Spain. Its only virtue for
making sherry is that its juice rapidly becomes oxidized, a grave
fault in making any other type of wine. In California, Palomino
is sometimes miscalled Golden Chasselas, and a few wineries
unfortunately use it to make a white table wine under that
name. It is not related to the true Chasselas grapes, from which
the Germans make their excellent Gutedel and the Swiss make
their Fendant.

A century ago, West & Sons of Stockton brought to their El
Pinal Vineyard from France a vigorous-growing white grape
and named it "West's White Prolific." The late L.K. Marshall of
Lodi rediscovered the variety after Repeal and named it Winkler
for the famous viticulturist. Dr. Winkler, however, declined the
honor. Meanwhile, Dr. Olmo identified the grape as the French
Colombard. Because it is prolific, and its high-acid juice is useful
in making white wines and champagnes, it has become the
principal white-wine variety grown in California, chiefly planted now in Regions IV and V. Although its wine has little
varietal personality, more than a dozen California wineries sell
wines labeled French Colombard.

Carignane, the principal red-wine grape grown in California,
is not noted for any quality except the vigor and high productivity of the vine. However, when Carignane is grown on coast-
counties hillsides without irrigation, it sometimes produces an
excellent, highly flavorful table wine. On the other hand, the
historic Mission grape usually makes poor red table wines, yet
is useful in making some good dessert wine types.

• 13 •

"Blanc de Blancs" and "Blanc de Noir" are terms with varietal
meanings but which don't name any grapes. "Blanc de Blancs"

means "white of whites" and is meant to tell you that champagnes so labeled are *not* made of the principal grape of the French Champagne region—Pinot Noir—but entirely of white grapes, particularly Chardonnay. Most American champagnes are made of white grapes, but were never called "Blanc de Blancs" until Almadén and Schramsberg adopted the term for their special champagnes made mostly of Chardonnay. "Blanc de Blancs" on labels of still white wines, however, merely refers to blends of white grapes and has nothing to do with Chardonnay.

American winemakers used to wonder why the French use Pinot Noir, the black grape with white juice, to make most of their fine champagnes. The answer is in Amerine and Joslyn's 1970 edition of *Table Wines:* "The cool climate [of the French Champagne region]," they say, "necessitates growing the early-ripening Pinot Noir in order to have adequate sugar for a balanced wine." In California climates, white grapes ripen with plenty of sugar every year and black grapes are not needed to make champagne. Nevertheless, four wineries in California now make premium champagnes containing Pinot Noir. They are Schramsberg's Blanc de Noir, Masson's Blanc de Pinot, and Domaine Chandon's Napa Valley Brut and its faintly salmon-tinted "Blanc de Noirs."

• 14 •

In the eastern and mid-continent states, there are many varietally named table-wine types made not of the French hybrids, but of native American grapes. Although the principal variety grown in these states is the Concord, the best "varietal" native wines are Delaware, Dutchess, Catawba, and the Norton or Cynthiana of Virginia, Arkansas, and Missouri. All are less foxy than Concord, and Cynthiana has no foxy flavor at all.

American grapes are tame descendants of the many species of wild grapes that abound in North America. (There are almost no wild grapes south of the Equator.) They are called "slip-skin" grapes because their skins, which are inedible, do not adhere to the pulp. Another term for them is "American hybrids." It is now generally accepted that most of those with Labrusca flavor are chance hybrids with the Vinifera grapes that were brought to this country from Europe during the eighteenth century. Others are artificial crosses made by early grape breeders between various native species, such as *Vitis riparia* and *Vitis labrusca,* and in many cases with Vinifera varieties.

These native "varietal" wines are usually consumed young, while their grapy fragrance is at its height. The foxy aroma is said to disappear as the wines age.

Nicoholas Longworth, the early Ohio winegrower, always maintained that Catawba improved with age. He had trouble convincing his contemporaries, the Dufour brothers, of this. The Dufours preferred the Alexander grape, with which they pioneered winegrowing in Indiana. To win his point, Longworth gave one of the Dufour brothers three bottles of Catawba. Dufour drank one after six months, another at the end of a year, and buried the third in his vineyard. Many years later, when Dufour lay on his deathbed, he made a last request to his doctor, that the bottle be dug up and brought to him for a final taste. Dufour was propped up in his bed, the cork was drawn, a glass was held up to the light, and he tasted the wine. "Ah, doctor," he said, "Longworth was right. Catawba improves with age."

Labrusca-type grapes, such as Concord, are said to be unsuited to the warm climates of California, and California wineries rely on the states of Washington and Oregon to supply them with the Concord juice used in their Labrusca-flavored wines. However, there are some Concord vineyards in the cooler parts of California, and three other Labrusca varieties have been grown experimentally in the Gallo vineyard at Livingston in Merced County. One is Golden Muscat, the "secret magical grape" which the Gallos once advertised as the mysterious ingredient in their Eden Roc Champagne. The others are Iona and Ives.

In Chapter 3, you read that the southeastern states have their own distinctive "varietal" wine called Scuppernong. Scuppernong and its many relatives of the Muscadine (*Vitis rotundifolia*) family are the only usable grapes that grow in the humid lowland areas of these states. American and Vinifera bunch grapes have often been planted in Scuppernong country lowlands, but the vines have always died after producing fruit for a short time. Phylloxera, which does not attack the Muscadines, was long blamed. During the 1950s, however, plant pathologists discovered that what killed the northern bunch grapes was not phylloxera, but the deadly plant pathogen called Pierce's Disease, which thrives in humid climates, and to which the Muscadines and other indigenous grapes of the Southeast are resistant or tolerant. Pierce's Disease (lately identified as bacterial) clogs the tissue channels through which the nonresistant vine gets its moisture and nutrition from the roots.

Scuppernong and other Muscadine vines have been planted experimentally in the vineyard at UC Davis, and Professor Olmo, after twenty years of failures, has succeeded in making fertile crosses of them with several Vinifera grapes, including relatives of Cabernet, Palomino, and Grenache. Olmo has made wines from his Muscadine hybrid grapes, and a panel of tasters has scored them as high as six (good) on a scale of ten. A question this raises is whether—if Olmo's Scuppernong hybrids, with the resistance of their Muscadine parents, were now to be transplanted from Davis to Scuppernong country and were to thrive there—they might develop a wine industry based on bunch grapes in the South. Such plantings have been made, and at least one of the Olmo hybrids has survived in Florida for six years.

There was a time, before the Prohibitionists came into control of agricultural research in this country, when grape breeders in the southern states thought they could tame their wild Mustang, Post-Oak, and River-bank grapes and develop winegrowing industries in such states as Texas, Louisiana, Mississippi, Tennessee, Georgia, Alabama, and Florida. The late Thomas Volney Munson of Denison, Texas, bred a number of promising hybrid bunch grapes there in the early 1900s, and some of Munson's varieties are now being tested for winemaking.

Since 1945, Professors Loren Stover and John Mortensen of the University of Florida experiment station at Leesburg have developed five new bunch grape varieties that are resistant to Pierce's Disease. Some of their hybrids are already being grown in Florida and Alabama for table use and for wine. Another breeding project is at Alachua, Florida, where Dr. Robert Dunstan, who supplied Philip Wagner with some of his first hybrids, has crossed Vinifera and other bunch grapes with Muscadines in an effort to develop additional resistant varieties.

Now that dry influence on the southern agricultural colleges is declining, perhaps horticulturists in these states—who until now have been expressly prohibited from experimenting with grapes for wine—will soon be permitted to engage in this kind of research.

• 15 •

Since wines can be only as fine as the grapes from which they are made, the truly dedicated student of wines must also become a student of grapes.

The only sources of precise data on individual grape varieties

are the colorfully illustrated books about vines, called ampelographies. Hundreds of ampelographies have been published in
Europe. The greatest is the seven-volume *Traité General de
Viticulture* by Professors Pierre Viala and Victor Vermorel, the
French viticulturists who with some sixty collaborators labored
from 1890 to 1910 compiling 24,000 names and synonyms of
grapes and gathering paintings of the principal varieties. The
first American ampelography to picture grapes in full colors was
published by the California Vinicultural Association in 1877,
with water-color paintings, made in the vineyards, of ten
varieties. In 1908, the Geneva, New York, experiment station
published *Grapes of New York,* the monumental work of
Professor Ulysses Prentiss Hedrick, in which he described
almost 1,500 native American grapes.

Dr. Olmo has been compiling a new California ampelography
since 1936. After thirty-five years of research, half a lifetime, he
published in 1971 his work on a single variety, Chardonnay. It
is a four-page folio containing a color photograph of Chardonnay and its foliage, a diagram of its leaf, a history and
description of the variety and its many clones and mutations,
and a bibliography. Olmo plans to follow with similar folios on
forty-nine more varieties, the next ones on Palomino, Pinot
Noir, and Cabernet Sauvignon. The Chardonnay folio is priced
at five dollars. If the rest cost that much, Olmo's complete
ampelography of fifty varieties would cost two hundred and fifty
dollars, which would make it the most expensive new wine
book in the world.

But there can never be a complete book of grapes, for there
are almost ten thousand different grape varieties from which
wines of some sort can be made, including many not yet tried in
the United States; and new varieties are continually being
created by breeders in France, other European countries, Canada, and the United States.

As still more wines appear on the market named for their
grapes, the mystery of wine becomes increasingly fascinating,
because we can never know the full story of any grape.

26

Meanings of Some Wine Terms

Among the reasons American wines far outsell imports in this country, apart from their intrinsic value, is that American wine nomenclature is simpler than that of Europe. Old World labels are a maze of unfamiliar European geographic names, of vintage years that mean little to a buyer who hasn't studied a vintage chart, and of mostly unrecognizable names of châteaux, shippers, and importers. American labels, less cluttered with names and dates, are easier to buy.

But American labeling, though simple by comparison, has become increasingly complex in recent years, and some terms have acquired obscure meanings that need explaining.

Why do Finger Lakes District wineries label some of their wines "Finger Lakes," others "New York State," and still others "American"? The same question applies to wineries elsewhere, including California vintners who label some of their wines with such district names as "Napa" and "Sonoma" but call the rest "California." The reason is that as more and more Americans become winewise, the names of viticultural districts that have become known as producing superior wines increase the prices that buyers readily pay for bottles labeled with these names. "Finger Lakes" and "New York State" wines are usually priced higher than New York wines called "American."

The Federal labeling regulation requires that if an appellation of origin is used, 75 percent* of the wine in the bottle must be derived from fruit grown in the place stated. If more than 25 percent comes from somewhere else, a broader appellation is used.

---

*But 95 percent for wines labeled with a vintage year.

European winegrowers have argued for generations over the precise meanings of their famous district names. Disputes over what American district names mean have only begun. Multimillion-dollar decisions on where to plant vineyards and build wineries are already influenced by which geographic appellation can legally appear on the labels of the wines to be produced.

One of the reasons the French hybrid grapes have been so widely planted by the big New York and Ohio wineries is to protect their labels of origin. In order to reduce the strong flavors of their Labrusca wines, they need neutral blending wines, readily available from California. But when their blends contain more than 25 percent of California wine, the labels change to "American." Now, with their locally grown hybrid grapes available to make neutral blending wines, they can use unlimited quantities and keep their local appellations of origin.

The Federal regulation originally required not only that fruit be grown where labels state, but that it be fermented and that the wine be finished there, too. An amendment in 1972 eliminated the requirement that the fermentation take place where the fruit is grown. One reason for the change was that wineries in some lately urbanized California valleys have planted new vineyards elsewhere while the wineries remained where they were. They now can use the appellation of the new vineyard district so long as the fermentation and finishing of the wine take place in the same state. But now, some Napa wineries are seeking a way to prevent wineries elsewhere from using "Napa" on labels of wines they might make from Napa grapes.

California's state regulation is stricter than the Federal in that it requires any wine labeled with a California name to be made 100 percent from California grapes. When some California wineries began bringing grapes and juice from the State of Washington to blend with their own, they changed "California" on some of their labels to "American." There is nothing in the California regulation, however, to prevent coast-counties vintners from stretching their locally labeled (nonvintage) wines with up to 25 percent of lesser wines from the hot Central Valley.

The United States regulations are much less strict than the *appellation contrôlée* system in France, which has now been copied by Italy. But the American regulations were written to protect the consumer and are strictly enforced. European wine regulations aim primarily to protect the honest grower against competitors. European authorities are also better at writing strict regulations than at enforcing them.

Does "mountain" on a wine label mean that the grapes were mountain-grown? It once did, but it doesn't anymore. In ancient times it was already known that the finest wines are those grown in mountainous regions. Virgil wrote that "Bacchus loves the hillsides." In the United States, Frank Schoonmaker first used "mountain" in 1939 on labels of two wines from the Paul Masson Mountain Vineyard, when he also used "lake" to designate his "varietal" selections from the Widmer Cellars of New York State. Later, "mountain" having never been defined in terms of how high or steep a vineyard should be, the word began to appear on labels of wines made from grapes grown in any of the hilly California coast counties. Then, through the years, "mountain" gradually became the designation of wines sold by coast-counties wineries at much lower prices and of lesser quality than their best.

Are wines whose labels read "Produced and bottled by," preceding the vintner's name, more reliable than others using the words "Made" or "Vinted" or "Cellared" or "Perfected" rather than "Produced"? The Federal regulation defines "produced" as meaning that the vintner fermented and finished at least 75 percent of the wine in the bottle. To the buyer, it signifies that the vintner did not just buy the wine or have it made for him by someone else. "Made" once meant that the winery "produced" at least 10 percent of the wine, but this detail has been eroded by time. It now means only that the vintner produces some of his wine and at least blended or changed this particular wine in some way. Some wineries, however, prefer to say "Made" on all their labels, rather than try to keep separate those they actually produce and those they buy or have other wineries make for them. "Produced" formerly meant also that the named vintner actually crushed the grapes, but this provision was eliminated by an amendment to the regulation in 1972. Advanced technology now makes it possible to crush the grapes at the vineyard and deliver the unfermented must in perfect condition to the winery, protected as described on page 384. (Some of these percentages or definitions may soon be changed in the outcome of proposed amendments debated at public hearings during 1976 and 1977.)

What does "Estate Bottled" on wine labels mean? Originally this was the rare designation permitted only for use by the small winegrowing estates. It was equivalent to the French *mise en bouteille au château,* meaning that 100 percent of the grapes were grown in the owner's vineyard and that every drop of the wine was made and bottled in his adjoining cellar. Some wineries still adhere strictly to this meaning and consequently don't have many "Estate Bottled" wines. But recent Federal rulings in individual cases have allowed certain vintners to label whole assortments of wines as "Estate Bottled" when the grapes came from vineyards they do not own, some of them located many miles away from their cellars. The rulings only limit "Estate Bottled" to mean that the vineyards are in the same county as the winery and that the grapes are grown under the winery's control. But neither is *mise en bouteille au château* any longer a complete assurance of genuine château-bottling in France. Trucks with portable bottling equipment now call each year at some small French wineries, making their bulk wines eligible to be labeled as château-bottled.

Why do most American wine labels omit the year of the vintage, which is commonly stated on labels of European wines? Vintage labels on California wines do not serve the purpose for which they are needed on certain European wines, to differentiate the bad-weather years from the good. Vintage labeling on American wines is useful mainly in identifying batches or casks that vary from others in character, and especially in telling you the age of a wine that you lay down for aging in your cellar. Some wineries refuse to use vintage labels because with large reserve stocks, they can blend together wines of different ages, adding the freshness and aroma of the young to the mellowness and bouquet of the old. Such blending also enables them to maintain year-to-year uniformity in the flavor of each type of wine they sell. A further objection to vintage labeling was that the original Federal regulation required 100 percent of the wine in the bottle to be of the year stated. But some wine evaporates while stored in barrels before bottling, and the barrels need to be "topped" (replenished) frequently to keep the wine from being injured by exposure to air. Vintners seldom had enough additional wine of the same age and type with which to do the topping. In 1972, the United States regulation was amended to permit wines to be topped with up to 5 percent of wines of other ages without losing the right to be labeled with the year of vintage. No European government has such a strict regulation. Germany only requires 75 percent of a vintage-labeled wine to be of the year stated.

Why are some champagnes labeled "bulk process," others "fermented in the bottle," and still others "fermented in this bottle"? For two centuries after champagnization was discovered in France, reputedly by the monk Dom Pérignon, all champagnes were given their secondary fermentation in the bottles in which they were sold. In 1907, Eugene Charmat in France developed his method of fermenting them in large tanks, virtually giant bottles, and bottling them under pressure. Because this is a less costly procedure, the Federal regulation requires such wines to be labeled with such words as "bulk process" to show the method used. If the original wines are of identical quality and are given no additional aging, the Charmat process should produce champagne equally good as that fermented in the bottle. However, leading producers who use the bottle-fermentation method also age their best champagnes in the bottles before disgorging (removing the sediment caused by fermentation). Prolonged contact with the sediment gives these champagnes a flavor and bouquet different from those not so aged.

Since the 1950s, many producers of bottle-fermented champagnes have adopted the "transfer method," developed in Germany, of removing the sediment without the laborious process of disgorging each bottle. Instead, the bottles are emptied under pressure, the champagne is filtered to remove the sediment, and then is rebottled. Producers who use the old disgorging process label their champagnes "fermented in *this* bottle" and sometimes add still other terms, such as *méthode champenoise.* In the Champagne district of France, however, only the disgorging process may be used for wines labeled champagne. French wines champagnized by the Charmat process may only be labeled *vin mousseux,* which means "sparkling wine."

What are crackling wines? Until 1972, the Federal regulation defined crackling, *pétillant,* or *frizzante* wines as those made naturally effervescent—but less so than champagne—by a secondary fermentation in the bottle like champagne. An amendment in 1972 permits crackling wines also to be made by the Charmat process, but if so their labels must say "bulk process."

Since many of the new "pop" wines with such names as Spañada and Strawberry Hill are made effervescent by artificial carbonation, why don't their labels say so? "Pop" wines first appeared in the United States when the Federal law was amended in 1958 to allow table wines to contain up to half an atmosphere (about 7 pounds of pressure per square inch) of added carbon dioxide without paying the higher ($2.40 per gallon)* Federal tax rate on carbonated wines. The law has since been amended, doubling the permissible pressure to a whole atmosphere, about 14.7 pounds, compared to 60 to 90 pounds in champagnes. These wines may not be labeled or represented as effervescent, because if they were so represented, the higher tax rate would apply. At such low carbonation, they give a slight "pop" when opened, but you seldom see any bubbles; they only cause a prickly sensation on the tongue.

Are there any legal definitions of "dry," "brut," "extra dry," "medium dry," and "sweet"? "Dry," which simply means the opposite of sweet, is the most abused single term in the language of alcoholic beverages. Vintners long ago learned that most American and British buyers prefer wines that are labeled "dry" but that taste at least slightly sweet. Champagnes labeled "brut" are almost dry, but "extra dry" means semisweet, and only "natural" means really dry. There are only two legal regulations of dryness or sweetness in North America. One is the definition of "dry" in Ontario, Canada, as meaning sugar content not over one percent. The other is a California regulation that defines the permissible range of sweetness in sherry, dry sherry, sweet or cream sherry, California tokay, and other dessert wine types. Dryness is not a measure of quality, because all musts (unfermented wines) are sweet until their sugar is fermented to the degree of dryness the vintner desires.

What does "solera" on wine labels mean? Solera is the Spanish name of the fractional-blending system used in the sherry bodegas of Spain. Traditionally, a *solera* consists of tiers of barrels containing sherries of different ages. Wine for sale is taken from the oldest barrel at the bottom, which is left at least half full. The quantity withdrawn is replaced from the next oldest, and so on. New wine goes always into the top tier, thus gradually blending the new with the old. This is why sherries rarely are labeled with the year of vintage. Many American wineries maintain fractional-blending systems for both sherries and ports, equivalent to the Spanish *soleras*.

What do the different bottle shapes and colors used by Ameri-

---

*The rate is $3.40 on *naturally* sparkling wines such as champagnes and crackling wines.

can wineries mean? Because buyers of European wines are accustomed to finding particular types of wine in the bottles traditionally used in Old World vineyard districts, most American vintners use the same kinds of bottles for their wines of corresponding types. Wines of burgundy types, or made from Burgundian or similar grapes, usually come in the slope-sided green bottles used in Burgundy. The high-shouldered bottle that represents Bordeaux is used for clarets, sauternes, for such Bordeaux "varietals" as Sémillon, Sauvignon Blanc, and Cabernet, and also for Zinfandel, which is considered a claret type in the United States. Rhine types, including Rieslings and Gewürztraminer, come in the tall, slender, so-called "hock bottle," which in Europe is brown for rhine wines and green for moselles. Colored bottles help to protect wines from injury by ultraviolet light, but some vintners, both European and American, use clear glass bottles (called "flint" in the trade) to display the attractive colors of their wines. Many American vintners have given up trying to follow European traditions and have created their own distinctive bottle shapes.

What do such terms as "Private Stock," "De Luxe," and "Special Selection" on wine labels mean? They usually are an individual vintner's way of distinguishing his higher-priced from his lower-priced wines of the same types. But if a winery sells only one price class of wine, such terms have no meaning.

It is understandable, in our free enterprise system, that every vintner would like to have his winery considered a château and sell his wine at the highest price obtainable. Yet the most important wines that any nation produces are those simply called "red wine," "pink wine," or "white wine," sold young, at low alcoholic content in jugs or returnable bottles, at no higher prices than milk, for consumption with everyday meals.

What do wine-bottle size names such as "fifths" and "magnums" mean? By federal edict in the cause of metrication, effective January 1, 1980, the old "fifth" (25.6 fluid ounces) bottle disappears except for wines bottled before that date, and is replaced by the 3/4 liter (750 milliliter) bottle, which is a quarter-ounce smaller (25.36 ounces). The double-fifth magnum is replaced by the 1.5 liter magnum (50.72 ounces).

Why is the use of sugar prohibited in making California standard wines while it is permitted within legal limits in other states and in most other countries? The addition of cane or beet sugar to the juice of grapes before fermentation is called chaptalization, named for its originator, Jean Chaptal, the French minister of agriculture in Napoleon's time. It is needed when in cool seasons or districts the grapes lack sufficient natural sugar of their own to produce wine of standard alcoholic content. The use of nongrape sugar is prohibited in producing standard still-wine types in California because there it is almost never needed; grapes ripen every year in the California climates. But sugar may be used in California for sweetening champagnes or flavored wines. Some winemakers say California wines could be improved if use of sugar were permitted there.

*What do alcoholic content statements mean on wine labels in this country?** Table (light) wines sold in the United States, if labeled with a specific statement of alcoholic content, may vary within a three-degree range. If the label says "alcohol 12% by volume," it means the alcoholic strength is between $10^{1}/_{2}$ and $13^{1}/_{2}$ percent. Appetizer and dessert wines are permitted a two-degree range; a label that reads "18%" means 17 to 19 percent. The strength of the "light" dessert wines sold in Michigan is usually stated as 16 and may be as low as 15, but in that state it does not exceed 16 percent.

Wines up to 14 percent, the maximum normally reached by fermentation, pay a Federal excise tax of 17 cents per gallon. Between 14 and 21 percent, levels usually reached by adding brandy, the Federal tax is 67 cents.

Labels may omit the alcoholic content if they read "table wine" or "light wine," which means they are not over 14 percent.

The original purpose of requiring alcoholic-content statements on labels was to deal with the ancient practice, still common in some countries, of watering the wine before sale. It also serves some other purposes. In Europe, alcoholic strength is regarded as a measure of wine quality. The French legal minimum standard for Beaujolais wine, for example, is 9 percent; if it reaches 10 it becomes Beaujolais *supérieur. Vin ordinaire* in France is sold in three quality grades, 9, 10, and 11 percent; the higher the alcohol, the higher the price. European families value the stronger wines because they can dilute them

---

*Alcoholic strength of wines is stated as percentage by volume, not by weight as it is for beers, and not as "proof" as it is for distilled spirits. ("Proof" is simply double the percentage of alcohol by volume.)

with water at the table for drinking with meals. For example, the Charles Krug Winery sells a special 14 percent wine named "Fortissimo" under its "CK" brand especially for the Italian trade.

One reason Europeans associate alcohol content with quality is that grapes develop more natural sugar—which ferments to more alcohol—in their years of good weather, the so-called vintage years. By this measure, hot countries should make the best wines, but the opposite is true. Another reason is that in the past, wines laid down for long aging were least likely to spoil when their alcohol content was high.

But advanced technology, such as the use of pure yeast cultures, sterile filtration, and aseptic bottling, now makes it possible to produce wines that keep sound at much lower alcohol levels than in the past. It is unfortunate that the old association of alcoholic content with quality still prevails among Europeans, because many of the most delicious and most healthful wines are as low as 8, 9, and 10 percent.

The Federal minimum standard permits wines as low as 7 percent, and a bill is pending in Congress that would reduce it to one half of 1 percent. But California still sets a 10 percent minimum, higher than necessary, for its standard whites and rosés. As mentioned earlier, this does not apply to flavored wines, and some of the new "pop" types are as low as 8 percent.

California for many years required its dessert wines to be at least 19^1/2 percent in order to prevent spoilage when sweet wines, such as ports, were shipped across the country in bulk. Later the California vintners discovered that the 16 percent "light" sherries and ports they were compelled to produce for sale in Michigan did not spoil and that some were more palatable than those they were selling at 20 percent. During the decades when California had ruinous annual surpluses of grapes, the grape growers strongly resisted proposals to lower the California 19^1/2 percent minimum, because the extra brandy required "burned up more grapes." In 1971, when the grape surplus was no longer a threat, California adopted the lower Federal minimums of 17 percent for sherries and 18 percent for other dessert wines.

27

A Brief Chronology of Wine in North America

1524   Cortez, conqueror of Mexico, ordered vineyards planted in the New World with grapes brought from Spain.

c. 1564   French Huguenots in Florida made wine from native Scuppernong grapes.

1595   Philip II, to suppress competition with Spanish wine exports, prohibited further planting of vines in New Spain.

1609–1716   Franciscans brought the Mission (Criolla) grape from Mexico to their missions in New Mexico and made wine for the Mass.

1619–1773   Unsuccessful attempts to grow European grapes by Lord Delaware in Virginia, Lord Baltimore in Maryland, William Penn near Philadelphia, Thomas Jefferson at Monticello, and by others in Alabama, Georgia, Massachusetts, New Hampshire, New York, Rhode Island, South Carolina.

1636   Jesuit missionaries at Québec in Canada made sacramental wine from wild grapes.

c. 1732–1741   The first domesticated native (Labrusca) grape was planted by James Alexander in Pennsylvania. The Alexander grape was introduced throughout the East and wine was made from it with varying success.

1769   Father Junípero Serra founded Mission San Diego, then brought Mission grapes from Baja California. Wine was being grown at most of the 21 Alta California missions by 1824.

1793   The first commercial winegrowing venture in the United States, the Pennsylvania Vine Company, was formed. It established a vineyard and winery at Spring Mill on the Susquehanna River northwest of Philadelphia.

1801   Jean Jacques Dufour organized the Kentucky Vineyard Society, failed to grow Swiss grapes in Kentucky, then planted the Alexander grape at Vevay, Indiana, in 1804, and a wine industry continued there for many years.

1810   Scuppernong wine was being made and sold at many North Carolina farms.

1811   The first commercial vineyard and winery in Canada was established by Johann Schiller at Cooksville, Ontario.

1818   Deacon Elijah Fay cultivated wild grapes at Brocton in the Chautauqua Grape Belt of New York.

1823   Nicholas Longworth planted his first vineyard at Cincinnati, Ohio. In 1842 he made the first American champagne.

1823   Major John Adlum introduced the Catawba grape at Washington, D.C.

1823   The Florissant vineyard was established near St. Louis, Missouri.

1824   The Harmonists established vineyards and wine vaults at Economy on the Ohio River near Pittsburgh, Pennsylvania. Wine was produced in the Pittsburgh area until 1900.

1824   Joseph Chapman founded California's first commercial vineyard at Los Angeles.

1827   Dr. Richard Underhill planted the first large vineyard in the Hudson River Valley; he later established a winery and sold "Croton Point Wines."

1829   Reverend William Bostwick began cultivating grapes at Hammondsport in the Finger Lakes District of New York, but no wine was made there commercially until after 1860.

1833   Jean Louis Vignes imported French vines to California and planted them in his El Aliso Vineyard at Los Angeles.

1840   German immigrants planted vineyards on the Lake Erie Islands and around Sandusky in northern Ohio.

1850–1860   Grape planting boomed in California during and after the Gold Rush.

1854   The Concord grape was introduced by Ephraim Wales Bull of Massachusetts.

1856   Kohler & Frohling, the San Francisco vintners, began exporting California wines to England, Germany, Russia, China, and Australia.

1859   Southern Ohio vineyards were attacked by black rot and mildew. Winegrowing then expanded in northern Ohio, Arkansas, the Carolinas, Illinois, Indiana, Missouri, and Tennessee.

c. 1860   The phylloxera vine pest attacked vines in France and during the next half century destroyed most of the vineyards of Europe. Phylloxera was controlled, beginning about 1880, by grafting Vinifera vines to American wild-grape roots.

1861   Mrs. Abraham Lincoln began serving American wines in the White House.

1861   "Count" Agoston Haraszthy, assigned to study wine-growing in Europe, sent 100,000 vines of 300 varieties to California.

1862   French viticultural experts, sent to survey American vineyards, reported they found California "capable of entering serious competition with the wines of Europe."

1867   Overplanting of vineyards created a grape surplus in California. Cycles of boom and bust occurred repeatedly in California during the next hundred years.

1869   On completion of the transcontinental railroad, California wines invaded eastern and midwestern markets, competing with Ohio, Missouri, and New York wines.

1870   California became the leading winegrowing state, surpassing Missouri and Ohio.

1870   Drs. Thomas and Charles Welch founded the fresh grape juice industry, introducing "Dr. Welch's Unfermented Wine" at Vineland, New Jersey. The Welch Company moved in 1896 to New York State and later established plants in Pennsylvania, Michigan, Arkansas, and Washington.

1872   William Thompson planted an English hothouse grape on his farm at Yuba City, California, and named it "Thompson's Seedless."

1873   Phylloxera attacked vines at Sonoma. Before it was controlled about 1900, it destroyed many vineyards in the Napa, Sonoma, and Sacramento Valleys.

1876   American wines won two awards at the Paris Exposition.

1880   The University of California began research and instruction in viticulture and winemaking by order of the state legislature.

1880   Wineries were reported thriving in Alabama, Arkansas, California, Georgia, Illinois, Indiana, Iowa, Kansas, Kentucky, Mississippi, New Jersey, New Mexico, New York, North Carolina, western Oregon, Pennsylvania, Tennessee, southern Utah, and Virginia.

1880   Kansas became the first state to adopt statewide Prohibition. By the First World War, 33 of the 48 states were legally dry.

1887   A California law prohibited the use of sugar in winemaking within the state, but an act of Congress in 1894 allowed its limited use in other states.

1900   American wines won three dozen medals at the Paris Exposition.

1904   The first grapes were planted at Outlook in the Yakima Valley of Washington.

1910   During the Mexican revolution, most of the vineyards of Mexico were abandoned or destroyed. They were revived beginning in the early 1940s.

1916   Eight Canadian provinces adopted Prohibition laws, but Ontario wineries prospered, being permitted to make wine for local sale. Seven of the provinces repealed their Prohibition laws in 1927.

1920   National Prohibition began in the United States. More than 100 wineries continued limited production under government permits, making sacramental, medicinal, and salted cooking wines.

1921–1931   Grape growers prospered by supplying home wine-makers and bootleggers during the early Prohibition years, but the grape market crashed in 1925. The Federal Government loaned millions to convert surplus grapes into "Vine-Glo" concentrate for home wine-making, but called a halt when the Drys objected.

c. 1930   The first commercial grape wine in British Columbia was made at Victoria from Okanagan Valley grapes.

1932   Congress legalized 3.2 percent beer and 3.2 percent "McAdoo wine."

1933   National Prohibition ended in the United States, but many states and localities remained legally dry. Oklahoma finally repealed its dry law in 1959, Mississippi in 1966.

1934   Wine consumption in the U.S. was less than 29 million gallons in the first Repeal year.

1934   The Wine Institute was incorporated and California adopted state wine quality standards. Federal wine quality and labeling standards became effective in 1936.

1935   Philip Wagner of Baltimore began importing French hybrid wine grapes, which later spread through the East and Midwest.

1939   Varietally labeled American wines introduced by Frank Schoonmaker began their rise to popularity.

1940   Wine consumption in the U.S. reached 86 million gallons, but less than a third was table wine.

1941–1946   War caused a wine shortage. Whiskey distillers bought many wineries, but sold most of them after the war.

1945   The kosher wine type was first advertised to the general public at New York and soon became the best-known North American wine.

1946   The University of California released the first new wine grape varieties bred at Davis—Emerald Riesling and Ruby Cabernet.

1950   "The wine awakening of America" began after the Second World War, and the consumption of table wine began a steady rise.

1950   The American Society of Enologists was organized in California.

1950   Research begun after the war produced greater advances in the sciences of viticulture and enology than had been made in the preceding 2,000 years.

1951   A Federal move to tax wine on its alcoholic content was defeated, and Congress voted the present tax rates of 17¢ on table wines, 67¢ on dessert wines.

1956   James Zellerbach brought Burgundian barrels to his hobbyist winery at Sonoma, and California vintners discovered the "complex" bouquet of wines aged in European instead of American oak.

1956   California premium producers began nationwide "blind" tastings to prove their wines equal to Europe's best.

1957   After three centuries of repeated failures to grow Vinifera grapes in the East, the first New York State Johannisberg Riesling and Chardonnay grapes were produced by Dr. Konstantin Frank in the Gold Seal Vineyard at Hammondsport.

1959   Congress authorized wines to contain seven pounds (later raised to fourteen pounds) of carbon dioxide pressure without paying an additional Federal tax. Low-alcohol flavored "pop" wines became nationally popular a decade later, competing with beer.

1965   Mechanical harvesting machines began picking grapes in New York State, and later in Pennsylvania, Ohio, Washington, California, and Ontario, Canada.

1968   For the first time since before Prohibition, consumption of table wine exceeded dessert wine in the U.S. The wine revolution followed.

1960–1977   Table-wine consumption more than trebled during these years, causing a nationwide upsurge in winegrowing. Giant corporations in other fields entered the wine industry, buying vineyards and wineries and establishing their own. Americans drank more than 400 million gallons of wine at a rate exceeding 1.851 gallon per capita in 1977, a record expected to double within twenty more years.

Acknowledgments and Notes

IN DOING the research for this book, I have had generous help from hundreds of individuals and institutions, only a small number of whom are named in the text. In expressing my appreciation, I should make it clear that none of them is responsible for the errors and omissions that are unavoidable when one volume attempts to encompass the whole moot subject of North American wines. I also should mention, because the sections on individual wineries often differ from the romantic versions in their advertising, that no vintner has read what I have written about him or his wines before it appeared.

My most valuable single American sources of historical material have been the writings of the great professors of viticulture, George Husmann and Ulysses Prentiss Hedrick; of San Francisco's wine-loving journalist of the 1880s, Frona Eunice Wait Colburn; of Herbert B. Leggett, who in 1941 was the first to attempt a history of the early California wine industry; and of Vincent P. Carosso, who in 1951 published the most complete study of the industry's formative years. Dr. Carosso in turn gives well-deserved credit to the research of Dr. Irving McKee, whom I persuaded in 1943 to undertake his dozen research papers on the histories of California wine counties and their pioneer winegrowers.

Recent painstaking research by Dr. John R. McGrew, the plant pathologist and grape breeder at the U.S. Department of Agriculture Fruit Laboratory in Beltsville, Maryland, has required revisions of my first-edition versions of early winegrowing in Maryland and of the origin of the Alexander or Cape grape. Dr. McGrew's research papers have been published in the *American Wine Society Journal.* Another revision, thanks to avocational winegrower J. Edward Schmidt of Schwenksville, Pennsylvania, credits the Pennsylvania Vine Company, formed in 1793 at Spring Mill near Philadelphia, as this country's first commercial winegrowing venture, rather than the *circa* 1818 winery of Thomas Eichelberger at York.

Early viticultural and wine journals, such as *The Grape Culturist, Cozzens' Wine Press,* and the *American Wine Press and Mineral Water News,* have provided details of many pioneer winegrowers' histories. For California, I have found the best sources to be the three books privately published since 1954 by Ernest Peninou and Sidney Greenleaf. Ernest Peninou still has an unpublished treasure trove of early California wineries' histories, which he has compiled during three decades of travel and persevering research at their sites. Some of the key portions of Chapter 12 on California are based on Professor Maynard Amerine's scholarly study, published in 1962, of Professor Eugene Hilgard's life and contributions to California viticulture.

The winegrowing histories of several states and localities have been amplified since the first edition through contributions by J. Herman Barnett, Jr., and S. McPheeters Glasgow of the Tennessee Viticultural and Oenological Society; by Leland Stanford Barton of Kingman, Arizona, and Frank Wright of Monterey on the historic Barton Estate winery of Fresno; by veteran wine editor Roy Brady of Northridge on early California wineries; by Towle Bundschu's records of Julius Dresel's pre-1850 unsuccessful plantings of Vinifera at San Antonio, Texas; by University of Indiana Professor Ledford C. Carter's research on Jean Jacques Dufour's vineyards in Kentucky and Indiana; by Dr. Arthur Channing Downs, Jr., of Newtown Square, Pennsylvania, on early nineteenth-century grape growing in the Hudson Valley; by Professor R.R. Furgason of the University of Idaho on pre-Prohibition vineyards in that state; by Glen Ellen wine historian William Heintz on the beginnings of several famous California wineries; by William J. Gallagher of the Guadalupe Valley winery at New Braunfels on some nineteenth-century Texas vineyards; by Dr. Ralph B. Hutchinson of Pomona State University on the Anaheim Colony vineyards and wineries; by Robert Hutton of Shooters Hill Vineyard at Alexandria, Virginia, on the precise location of Major John Adlum's vineyard in Rock Creek Park; by Mrs. Mabel Lewelling Johnson of St. Helena on Hamilton Walker Crabb, the founder of the To Kalon Vineyard; by Father Thomas A. Marshall of the Society of Jesus California Province on the Jesuit wineries of Santa Clara County; by Wine Museum of San Francisco director Ernest Mittelberger and assistant curator Melinda Frye on Thomas Jefferson's wine writings and experiments at Monticello; by the late Dr. James M. Merritt of Forestville, New York, on the pioneer vineyards of that state and South Carolina; by historian Henry Kappner Mauldin and Marion Curry Geoble of Lake County, California, on early winegrowing there; by Professor Roy E. Renfro, Jr., of Grayson Community College, Denison, Texas, on the vineyards there in T.V. Munson's time; by Charles L. Sullivan of Los Gatos on the plantings of Zinfandel in California during the 1850s; by Ruth Teiser, project director of the Bancroft Library Wine Industry Oral History Project, on various developments in the California wine industry; by Warren Vaché of Rahway, New Jersey, on the history of his ancestor Théophile Vaché; by Essex County agricultural representative Lee Weber for his history of winegrowing in that Ontario county; and by Professor John L. Williams at the University of Georgia on the Vina Vista Fruit and Winery Association vineyards in Coweta County *circa* 1896.

For the many references to "Count" Agoston Haraszthy I have relied mainly on the Haraszthy research project that Paul Fredericksen undertook in the 1940s at the Wine Institute, and on the study in 1969 by Sister Joan Marie Donohoe, chairman of the Department of History at the College of Notre Dame at Belmont, California. Haraszthy's contributions to the development of California viniculture have been exaggerated, but his fabulous adventures could provide rich material for a historical novel.

The tremendous influence of Captain Paul Garrett (1863–1940) on the American wine scene before and following Prohibition became most apparent when my field and library research were virtually complete. After much correspondence with those associated in his many enterprises, I finally obtained from his daughter, Mrs. Emily Barden, the loan of the Captain's own story, dictated on his deathbed, which cleared up remaining questions about his career.

It would have been impossible to cover all of the interesting small vineyards and wineries of the United States without the excellent annual directory of the wine industry published by the industry's trade publication, *Wines & Vines,* ably edited by my fellow vineyard explorers and tasters Philip and Philip E. Hiaring. Nor can anyone keep up to date on significant developments in the industry without studying every issue of this monthly magazine, which has been published at San Francisco (originally as *The California Grape Grower*) continuously since 1920. Also helpful have been such publications as Phyllis Van Kriedt's *California Wineletter,* J. William Moffett's and Hope Merletti's *Eastern Grape Grower,* Bob Morrisey's *The Wine Spectator,* Hudson Cattell's and H. Lee Stauffer's *Pennsylvania Grape Letter and Wine News,* and Marvin Shanken's *Impact;* also the *Wine Investor, Vintage,* and *Wine World,* and such regional books as the illustrated *California Wineries* series written by Michael Topolos and Betty Dopson, Patricia Latimer, and Richard Paul Hinkle; Marshall C. Harold's *The Ohio Winemakers,* and Tom Stockley's *Winery Trails of the Pacific Northwest.*

For their invaluable help I wish particularly to thank:

The University of California Departments of Viticulture and Enology and Food Science, and especially Drs. Albert J. Winkler, Maynard A. Amerine, Curtis J. Alley, Maynard A. Joslyn, Harold P. Olmo, Lloyd Lider, Vernon Singleton, James Cook, Dinsmoor Webb, Mark Kliewer, Ralph Kunkee, Ann Noble, James Guymon, Professor Harold Berg, and Extension Specialist Amand Kasimatis. Also the great plant pathologist Dr. William B. Hewitt, and Dr. Kirby Moulton, the agricultural economist at UC Berkeley, and his predecessor, Dr. Sherwood W. Shear. Equally generous with assistance have been Dr. Austin C. Goheen, the U.S. Department of Agriculture plant pathologist stationed at UC Davis, and Professor Vincent Petrucci and Dr. Fred Nury, the respective heads of viticulture and enology at Fresno State University; and the dedicated county farm advisors, especially Pete Christiansen, Fresno; Bruce Bearden, Mendocino; Keith Bowers, Napa, and his predecessor James Lider; James Kissler, San Joaquin; Edio Delfino, El Dorado; Donald Luvisi, Kern; Paul La Vine, Stanislaus; Rudy Neja, Monterey-Santa Clara; John H. Foott, San Luis Obispo, and Robert Sisson, Sonoma.

The Wine Institute staff, and especially Legal Consultant Jefferson E. Peyser, Roy Camozzi, James Seff, John R. Peirce, Arthur Silverman, and Henry Gage; the Institute's economic research director Werner Allmendinger and his former assistant Dorothy Huff; Librarians Joan Ingalls and Kay Chadwick; Technical Director Hugh Cook, publicists Harvey Posert and Brian St. Pierre; my former co-workers Doris Brown Paulsen, Roy Taylor, wine consultant Louis R. Gomberg, who was the first head of the Institute's research department; the Institute's president, Dr. John A. De Luca, and its past presidents Don W. McColly and Harry G. Serlis.

University and government horticulturists, food scientists, agricultural economists and statisticans, who have supplied much essential data, including Dr. Wade Wolfe, Richard Pratt,and agricultural agent Lowell F. True at the University of Arizona, Tucson; Dr. John F. Bowen of the Summerland, British Columbia, research station and John Vielvoye, the Ministry of Agriculture grape specialist at Kelowna; Dr. N. Horace Loomis, retired from the USDA research vineyard at Fresno, California; Vernon Cornforth of the Colorado State University Cooperative Extension Service and associate horticulturist James K. Stacey at the Austin experiment station; Joseph Phelps for describing his winegrowing experiments at Greeley, Colorado; Loren H. Stover and Dr. John A. Mortensen of the University of Florida Research Center at Leesburg, and Dr. Robert P. Bates of the Food Science laboratory at Gainesville; Dr. Robert T. Dunstan of Alachua; Byard O. Fry, the retired grape breeder of the University of Georgia; Dr. Ron Lane at the Athens campus, and Bill Ison and M. Aubrey Owen at their respective Georgia nurseries; Extension agent Anton S. Horn of Boise, his collaborator Robert Wing of Lewiston, and Dr. Richard Dailey and R. Bruce Higgins at the University of Idaho at Moscow; Dr. H.C. Barrett of the University of Illinois; Professor A.E. Cott of Iowa State University; Drs. Ronald W. Campbell and Frank Morrison, horticulturists of Kansas State University, and Erwin Abmeyer of the Northeast Kansas Experiment Fields; Michigan State Universtiy pomologist Dr. Gordon S. Howell; Dr. Cecil Stushnoff and Patrick Pierquet of the University of Minnesota in St. Paul and Neil W. Miles of the Agricultural Extension Service; Drs. Burton Wise, Walter Porter, Boris Stojanovic, and Jean Overcash of Mississippi State University; Senator William G. Burgin of Columbus, Dr. Alex P. Mathers of Matherville, and William G. Bodker of Jackson, Mississippi; Professor Delbert D. Hemphill of the University of Missouri; New Jersey Secretary of Agriculture Philip Alampi; Drs. Darrell T. Sullivan and Richard Gomez and Colonel John Carroll of New Mexico State University; John Lilley, Dr. Louis Gattoni, F. Baron Brumley, and Anthony Claiborne of the New Mexico Wine and Vine Society; Drs. John Einset, Robert Pool, Willard Robinson, and Nelson Shaulis, and Professor Elmer S. Phillips of Cornell University; extension agents Trenholm D. Jordan for the Chautauqua Grape Belt, William Sanock at Riverhead, and Tom Jabadal; Carol and James Doolittle of the Bureau of Markets at Albany; William L. Bair of the New York Crop Reporting Service; Drs. Joe F. Brooks, William B. Nesbitt, Dan Carroll, and John Earp of North Carolina State University; Drs. J.N. Beattie, Garth Cahoon, and James Gallander of Ohio's Agricultural Research and Development Center at Wooster; Professor Herman Hinrichs of Oklahoma State University; Dr. Ralph Crowther and Oliver Bradt of the Ontario Research Station at Vineland; Drs. Ralph Garren, Jr. and Hoya K. Yang, Professor Porter Lombard, David E. Passon, and Lloyd W. Martin of Oregon State University; Drs. H.K. Fleming, Carl W. Haeseler, and G.L. Jubb of Pennsylvania State University; Harold C. Abney of the Maison Secrestat winery at Dorval, Québec, and Dennis O'Dowd of Les Vins Andrés de Québec; horticulturist Dr. Harold Sefick, now retired from Clemson University, South Carolina; Drs. George Ray McEachern and Hollis H. Bowen and Professors Ronald Perry and Norman P. Maxwell of Texas A. & M. University; Dr. Dan Hanna and Professor William Lipe at the El Paso and Lubbock Research Stations, and extension food technologist Al B. Wagner; Ryan St. Clair of the University of Texas vineyard at Evergreen Farms; Dr. J. LaMar Anderson of Utah State University, extension specialist Don A. Huber, and W. Grant Lee of the Utah statistical reporting service; Dr. George D. Oberle and Charles R. O'Dell of Virginia Polytechnic Institute; Drs. Raymond J. Folwell and Charles Nagel, Professor Vere Brummund, and Dr. Walter Clore, the retired horticulturist, of Washington State University; John K. Couillard of the Ontario Liquor Control Board; Nancy Plumridge of the Canadian Wine Institute; Dr. Jesus Moncada of the Centro de Investigaciones at Torreón, Mexico, and Ing. Agustin Viesca Cardenas, viticultural coordinator for the Asociación Nacional de Vitivinicultores of Mexico.

Historians, librarians, and others who performed special research on historical questions include Franklin (Busty) Aulls of Hammondsport, N.Y.; John L. Bree of Modesto, California; Aycock Brown of Manteo, N.C.; Irvin Brucker of St. Louis, the late historian of Missouri wines; Julia L. Crawford of the Philadelphia Library; Winifred Cress of Sausalito; Elizabeth L. Crocker, historian of Chautauqua County, New York; Christopher B. Devan, director of the New Castle Library at Wilmington, Delaware; Thomas E. Harman of the Distilled Spirits Institute at Washington, D.C.; Mrs. Renno J. Hawkins, North Carolina Department of Conservation; Grace Hodge of Camp Hill, Pennsylvania, for her investigation of early winegrowing at York;

Mrs. Cornelia K. Lane of Grapevine Cottage, Concord, Massachusetts; Mrs. Maurine Madinger of Wathena, Kansas; Carl Oehl of Amana, Iowa; Eleanora M. Lynn, head of the Maryland Department of the Enoch Pratt Library, Baltimore; John Matthews, assistant historian of Ulster County, New York; Allan R. Ottley, California Section, California State Library; the late J. Allen Mays, Taylor Wine Company; Dr. L. Rosser Littleton of Stateville, North Carolina; Research Supervisor Lauritz G. Petersen of the Church of Jesus Christ of the Latter-day Saints; Marie C. Preston, historian of Livingston County, New York; Reverend Arthur D. Spearman, archivist of the University of Santa Clara's Orradre Library; Sam A. Suhler, Local History Librarian of the Fresno County Library; Mrs. C.A. Stoughton of Fredonia, Kansas; Mrs. Helen Schowengerdt of Independence, Missouri; Edwin S. Underhill III, publisher of the Corning (New York) *Leader;* Wilson B. Tillery of Stevensville, Maryland; Margot Timson of the Boston Library; Roy Wilder, Jr., of the North Carolina Seashore Commission; Rosalie F. Wilson of the Westchester County (New York) Parks Department, and Mrs. Prudence H. Work, editor of the Brocton (New York) *Beacon.*

Additional historical facts of importance were contributed by Allen A. Arthur of Los Angeles, Abraham Buchman of New York, the late Burke H. Critchfield, Andrew G. Frericks, and Louis Stralla of St. Helena; Robert Eaton, Henry Bugatto, and the late Edmund A. Rossi of San Francisco; Rexford G. Tugwell of Santa Barbara; the late Peter Valaer of Washington, D.C.; Douglas Moorhead, Sr., of North East, Pennsylvania; Nicholas H. Paul of Widmer's Wine Cellars, Julius H. Fessler of Berkeley, Guy Baldwin of Los Gatos, Evins Naman of Fresno, Wallace H. Pohle of Stockton, and Dick Sherer of Hammondsport, New York.

I am deeply indebted to the following friends who traveled great distances to investigate particular facets of winegrowing for the book: Dr. Paul Scholten, who explored the vineyards of New Mexico; Dr. Thomas N. Poore, who took the trouble to find grapevines in Hawaii, verifying the point that grapes grow in all fifty states; J. Walter Fleming, who found and revisited the old Mormon winery in Utah; film maker Cheyne Weston, who re-visited the vineyards of Idaho for my second edition; Irwin Phillips of San Francisco City College, who continually explores California and Missouri wine districts and reports the changes he finds between my own trips, and Martha and Dr. Keith Witte of Monroe, who explored the wineries of Wisconsin in my behalf.

Warm personal thanks are due those who so kindly guided me through their respective wine districts, especially viticulturist Lucie T. Morton of Virginia; George W.B. Hostetter and Philip Torno of the Canadian Wine Institute; Mario Ortiz Rodriguez of Saltillo, Coah., Mexico; Dimitri Tchelistcheff and Octavio Jiménez of Ensenada, Baja California; William R. Clayton of the South Carolina Development Board; Eustaquio and Marcial Ibarra of Pedro Domecq, Mexico; Grace and Allen Furman of Raleigh, North Carolina; Bill Konnerth of North East, Pennsylvania; Melvin S. Gordon of Philadelphia; Joel Arrington of the North Carolina Travel Division; Walter S. Taylor and Charles Fournier of Hammondsport, New York; Herman J.B. Wiederkehr of Altus, Arkansas, and Frank Koval of the Michigan Wine Institute. I am further indebted, for advance information on new wineries, to Leon and Pete Peters and Leo Detwiler of Fresno's Valley Foundry; to winery designer Richard Keith of Santa Rosa, and to Robert Ellsworth of The Compleat Winemaker shop in St. Helena.

Professionals and oenothusiasts who supplied invaluable help in many areas include Ann Bailey, curator of the Greyton Taylor Wine Museum at Hammondsport, New York; Raymond F. Baldwin, vice president of Seagram Vintners International, who since 1956 has pioneered the postwar export of American wines to international markets; Judge William O. Beach, Norman Gailar, and their colleagues of the Tennessee Viticultural and Oenological Society; Dr. Helmut Becker, leader of the Grape Breeding and Propagation Institute at the Geisenheim Institute in West Germany, who recently has brought German vinicultural wisdom and planting stocks to the eastern United States and Canada; Andrew Beckstoffer, whose Vinifera Vineyards are among the most important in Napa, Sonoma, and Mendocino Counties; John Berezansky, Jr., of Fairport, New York; Dick Beeler of the *California Farmer,* San Francisco; vineyardist Tom Blackstock at Gainesville, Georgia; nurseryman and avocational winemaker Alfonso Boffa of Clairsville, Ohio; Dick Break, who planted the first vineyards at Rancho California in 1966; Brad Burris, the Minneapolis connoisseur; Eugene Charles, avocational winegrower at Seneca, South Carolina; Jane and Elwood Clapp of Birchrunville, Pennsylvania; Julian Cornell of Central Valley, New York; Thomas R. Clarke of New Canaan, Connecticut; Diana Comini, who teaches about wine and wineries at Yakima, Washington; Professor Gary and Trisha Cox, amateur winegrowers at Piffard, New York, and their partners Howard and Betty Smith of Geneseo in their commerical vineyard of wine grapes at the south end of Conesus Lake; Bryan and Helen Doble, who grow fine Vinifera wines on their Oak Knoll Vineyard in Tryon, North Carolina; Carl Damoth, the talented Detroit amateur winemaker who edits the *American Wine Society Journal;* Dr. Wilfred W. Enders, who grows wine grapes near Moline, Illinois; Philip Faight of the Groezinger Wine Company at Yountville, California; Charles O. Foerster, Jr., of Elsa, Texas; Dr. August W. Denninger of Santa Fe, New Mexico; Fred Galle, the director of horticulture at Callaway Gardens in Georgia; Tom and Cindy Hampton, who grow excellent Foch wines on their Tucquan Vineyard near Holtwood, Pennsylvania; Edward Gogel, the Chicago enologist who has made major contributions to vinicultural progress in the eastern, midwestern, and southern states; Dr. Gerhard Hauser of Sky Ranch at Newport, Tennessee; veteran enologist Ed R. Haynes, who has produced some of the best wines of Ontario and upstate New York; Dr. Gerry P. Haines, who teaches wine-appreciation classes at Freeport, Illinois; avocational champagne maker Dr. Arvin T. Henderson of Palo Alto, California; Mildred Howie of Geyserville, who guides the Sonoma County Winegrowers Association and invites visitors to travel the Russian River Wine Road; Eustaquio and Marcial Ibarra of Pedro Domecq Mexico; wine consultant Dr. Philip Jackisch of Royal Oak, Michigan, and his wife Margo, the guiding light of the American Wine Society; Margie Keith of Nashville, Tennessee; John F. Kistner of Stillwater, Minnesota; my old vintner friend Rudy Kopf of Kobrand, New York City; talented vineyardist Louis Lucas, who planted the principal vineyards of the Santa Maria and Shandon districts in California, and his collaborator Dale Hampton of Coastal Farming; Dr. Wilbur P. McDonald of St. Joseph, Missouri; Galo Maclean, the veteran Ohio winegrower who now propagates Vinifera vines at St. Helena, California, for planting in other states; soil expert Dr. David A. Mays of the Tennessee Valley Authority at Muscle Shoals, who is responsible for the test vineyards on reclaimed strip-mined coal land in Alabama and Tennessee; Cindy and John Moorhead, who grow sensational Cabernets at North East, Pennsylvania; retired journalist John T. Moutoux, who grows grapes among other fruits near Vienna in Virginia; Chicago wine buff George O'Brien, who explores wine grape vineyards of the Midwest; winegrower Humberto Pérez of Tijuana, who keeps me informed of vineyard developments in Mexico; George Riseling of Suitland, Maryland, my correspondent on winegrowing there and in nearby states; retired vintner Brian Roberts, who now guides the Association of British Columbia Wineries; William T. Ryan of Beringer and Crosse & Blackwell Cellars, who keeps me informed of vineyards in Rhode Island, his mother's home state; avocational winegrower Richard Schwerin and his wife Bertha, of Alexandria, Kentucky; enologist-wine consultant Howard Somers, who supplied much of the history of post-Repeal Washington wineries and who now lives at San Anselmo, California; Pennsylvania avocational winegrower Jouko Savolainen, who plans a winery on his Chanceford Vineyard at Brogue; Ben and Leora Sparks of the Possum Trot vineyard and winery in Indiana, who are also the leaders of Indiana's Winegrowers Guild; James E. Spooner of Rolla, Missouri; Dr. David S. Stewart of Rochester, New York; Sergio Traverso-Rueda, the consulting enologist who is an expert on both California and Mexican wines and brandies; my former midwesterern co-worker Otto H. Devinney, who now studies the wine scene from San Diego; Michael Vaughan of Toronto, the best-informed writer on eastern Canadian wines; Howard Weinstein, who manages Georgia's only winery, and his winemaker Eberhard Veit; Warren Taft of Phoenix, Arizona, for his boyhood recollections of the pre-1900 wine caves and terraced vineyards at Stillwater, Minnesota; Marian (Mrs. Carl) Werner of Milwaukee, Oregon, who keeps me informed of developments in the Webfoot State; John and Anne Wickham, who in the 1960s were the first to demonstrate, at their Fruit Farm in Cutchogue, that Vinifera grapes grow well on Long Island, New York; Dennis T. Willis of Tucumcari, New Mexico; Robert and Martha Woodbury, who grow on the Woodbury Fruit Farm at Dunkirk the finest New York State Chardonnay it has yet been my pleasure to taste; Dr. Robert Adamson, his wife Dorothy, and Dr. Bernard Rhodes and his wife Belle, whose vineyards are in the Napa Valley; Gino Zepponi, who now manages production at Domaine Chandon in California; and especially Dr. Ben Fisher of North Chicago, who for many years has kept me informed of the changing wine scene throughout the East.

Finally, I wish to express thanks to my wine-knowledgeable friends who have read some of the chapters for accuracy and clarity and who have made many valuable suggestions: Henry (Winemaster) Rubin, the wine editor of the San Francisco *Chronicle* and *Bon Appétit* magazine; Eleanor Adams, Mabel Bolton, Lee and Jack Pollexfen, and James Field.

Index

Under the more comprehensive subjects, the page numbers of the principal references are in *italics*.

A

C